LATIN AMERICAN GOVERNMENT AND POLITICS

THE DORSEY SERIES IN POLITICAL SCIENCE

EDITOR NORTON E. LONG *Brandeis University*

MACRIDIS & BROWN *The De Gaulle Republic*

MACRIDIS & BROWN (eds.) *Comparative Politics: Notes and Readings* rev. ed.

DRAGNICH *Major European Governments*

ROBINSON *Congress and Foreign Policy-Making: A Study in Legislative Influence and Initiative*

JACOBINI *International Law: A Text*

MANGONE *The Elements of International Law: A Casebook*

GRIPP *Patterns of Soviet Politics*

MINAR *Ideas and Politics: The American Experience*

MEEHAN *The Theory and Method of Political Analysis*

EDELMANN *Latin American Government and Politics: The Dynamics of a Revolutionary Society*

POLITICAL
MAP
of
LATIN
AMERICA

LATIN AMERICAN

GOVERNMENT AND POLITICS

The Dynamics of a Revolutionary Society

BY ALEXANDER T. EDELMANN

Associate Professor of Political Science
University of Nebraska

1965

THE DORSEY PRESS

HOMEWOOD, ILLINOIS

First Printing, July, 1965

Library of Congress Catalog Card No. 65–22417

PRINTED IN THE UNITED STATES OF AMERICA

To Dot—*Mi Esposa, Querida, y Colaboradora*

PREFACE

Anyone who has the temerity to write a basic text about Latin American Government and Politics is immediately confronted with a dilemma. Should he adopt the plan of treating each country individually, or should he deal with the region as a whole? The first approach has some obvious advantages. A picture of each country can be drawn clearly and distinctly, and the pitfalls of questionable generalization avoided. On the other hand, the overall approach has its advantages too. The nations in many respects have common cultural backgrounds, values, and social institutions, including a similarity in the organization and operation of government. As a result, the overall approach obviates a duplication of treatment, and enables a good view of the forest as a whole without the necessity of climbing every tree.

While either one of the two approaches is quite valid for studying the government and politics of the region, I have chosen to follow the second, in the belief that the overall, institutional approach affords a broad, interdisciplinary understanding of the subject.

In presenting this text, I am deeply indebted to a host of scholars—political scientists, historians, sociologists, economists, anthropologists, and others for their labors and dedicated scholarship, whether boldly treating the institutions and problems of the entire region, a whole state, or a minuscule but significant community high in the Andes or deep in Brazil's imposing vastness. I have generously availed myself of their works, as is shown by the many quotations, citations, and suggested readings. I am also grateful to friends in Latin America who have made our trips there so delightful, and whose assistance has been as fervent as their *abrazos*.

I want to express my gratitude too to the Research Council of the University of Nebraska which has awarded me grants for travel, research assistants, and a leave of absence during the academic year 1964–1965 to continue my research on land reform, a project which has broadened my perspective and served generally to enrich this textbook.

ALEXANDER T. EDELMANN

LINCOLN, NEBRASKA
June, 1965

TABLE OF CONTENTS

PAGE

LIST OF TABLES AND FIGURES XV

CHAPTER

PART I. BASES OF NATIONAL POWER

1. THE LAND AND RESOURCES: CHALLENGES TO INGENUITY   3
GEOGRAPHICAL ASPECTS: Area. Location. Topography. CLIMATE. NATURAL
RESOURCES. TRANSPORTATION AND COMMUNICATION: Railroads. River
Steamers. Ocean Liners. Roads. Airplanes. EFFECTS OF TOPOGRAPHY.

2. THE PEOPLE: DEMOGRAPHIC POTPOURRI OF A SOCIETY IN FERMENT . 32
THE WHITES. THE INDIANS. THE NEGROES. DISTRIBUTION OF POPULATION.
POPULATION TRENDS—GROWTH AND CHANGES IN COMPOSITION.

PART II. SOCIAL FOUNTAINHEADS OF POLITICAL ACTION

3. THE CLASS STRUCTURE: THE HIGH HURDLE ON THE WAY UP . . . 55 ✓
CLASSES IN THE COLONIAL ERA: Whites. Indians. Negroes. Mestizos, Mulattos,
and Zambos. SOCIAL CLASSES TODAY: Determinants of Social Status. The
Several Social Classes. Effects of Class Structure on Political Democracy.

4. THE FAMILY: A LOYALTY STILL STRONG BUT WANING 85
THE TYPES OF MARITAL UNIONS. THE PATRIARCHAL UPPER AND MIDDLE CLASS
FAMILY: Role of the Husband. Status and Role of the Wife. Care and
Training of Children. THE CONVENTIONAL FAMILY IN THE LOWER CLASS. THE
MATRIFOCAL OR MATRILINEAL FAMILY IN THE LOWER CLASS. THE EXTENDED
FAMILY AND THE COMPADRE RELATIONSHIP. THE DECLINING INFLUENCE OF
THE FAMILY. ECONOMIC, POLITICAL, AND SOCIAL IMPLICATIONS.

5. EDUCATION: THE OPEN SESAME TO INDIVIDUAL ADVANCEMENT . . . 110
ELEMENTARY AND SECONDARY EDUCATION: Constitutional and Legal Provisions. Lack of Progress and Reasons for This. The Influence of Educa-
tion-minded Leaders. The Desire of Most Citizens for an Education.
Financial Support of Public Education. Construction of Schools. Training
of Teachers. The Curriculum Taught. Increase in Enrollment and Segregation of Sexes. Methods of Instruction. Centralized Control. Adult Education
and Literacy Campaigns. HIGHER EDUCATION: Number of Institutions and
Students. Curriculum and Courses of Study Selected. Methods of In-

CHAPTER   PAGE

struction. Financial Support. Buildings and Other Physical Facilities.
Faculty. Granting of Degrees. Autonomous Status. Student Reform Movement. Student Politics and Violence.

6. THE CHURCH: AN INFLUENCE FOR STANDPATISM OR PROGRESS . . .   146
THE CHURCH IN COLONIAL SOCIETY. THE CHURCH DURING THE WARS OF
INDEPENDENCE. ANTICLERICALISM. REFORM OF THE PRIESTHOOD. EXPROPRIATION
OF THE CHURCH'S GREAT WEALTH. ASSUMPTION BY THE STATE OF THE
CHURCH'S SECULAR ACTIVITIES. SEPARATION OF CHURCH AND STATE. PARTICIPA-
TION BY THE CHURCH IN POLITICS. ROMAN CATHOLICISM'S STRENGTH AND IN-
FLUENCE TODAY. THE CHALLENGE OF PROTESTANTISM. THE CHALLENGE OF
SOCIAL REFORM.

7. THE ARMED FORCES: BIG BROTHER IN ACTION   181
INTERFERENCE IN POLITICS. ALTERNATING TRENDS OF MILITARISM. CAUSES
OF MILITARISM AND MILITARY INTERVENTION IN POLITICS. INFLUENCES TEND-
ING TO LESSEN THE POWER OF THE MILITARY. THE MILITARY AS SOCIAL
REFORMERS. THE MILITARY IN THE SEVERAL NATIONS TODAY. HOW MEXICO
SUCCEEDED IN CURBING MILITARISM.

PART III—PROMOTION OF THE GENERAL WELFARE:
BY EVOLUTION OR REVOLUTION

8. AGRICULTURE AND LAND REFORM: THE CRY FOR LAND AND ITS PORTENT   215
CONCENTRATION OF OWNERSHIP OF LAND. TYPES OF LARGE-SCALE AGRICULTURAL
ENTERPRISES: Corporate Mechanized Farms. Haciendas. PIECEMEAL AT-
TEMPTS AT REFORM. THE CRY FOR LAND: ITS REVOLUTIONARY SIGNIFICANCE.
MEXICO'S REVOLUTIONARY PROGRAM OF LAND REFORM. BOLIVIA'S REVOLU-
TIONARY PROGRAM OF LAND REFORM. CUBA'S REVOLUTIONARY PROGRAM OF
LAND REFORM. THE PROSPECTS FOR LAND REFORM BY PEACEFUL MEANS.

9. INDUSTRY: THE REVOLUTION OF RISING EXPECTATIONS   253
THE DRIVE FOR INDUSTRIAL DEVELOPMENT: BACKGROUND AND MOTIVATIONS.
PROGRESS MADE IN INDUSTRIAL DEVELOPMENT. TRADITIONAL METHODS FOR
PROMOTING INDUSTRY. OBSTACLES TO INDUSTRIAL DEVELOPMENT: Lack of
Capital. Shortage of Engineers and Skilled Labor. High Costs of Produc-
tion and Distribution. Cultural Values and Mores. THE EXPANDED ROLE OF
GOVERNMENT IN ECONOMIC DEVELOPMENT.

10. LABOR: A FAIR SHARE OR ELSE   279
ORIGIN AND DEVELOPMENT OF TRADE UNIONISM. DISTINCTIVE FEATURES OF
THE LABOR FORCE: Underemployment and Unemployment. Employment of
Women. Employment of Minors. GOALS AND GAINS: The Right to Organize
and Strike. Higher Wages. A Shorter Working Day. Better Working
Conditions. Security of Tenure. Other Goals. LABOR-MANAGEMENT RELA-
TIONS AND COLLECTIVE BARGAINING: Labor-Management Relations. Collective
Bargaining. INVOLVEMENT IN POLITICS: Dependence Upon Government.
Supervision by Government. Labor's Weapons.

PART IV—DYNAMICS OF POLITICAL CHANGE

11. CAUDILLOS AND REVOLUTIONS: BULLETS, IF NECESSARY   305
CAUDILLOS: Origin and Duration. Background and Personal Qualifications
for Governing. The *Caudillo's* Rise to Power and Exercise of Governmental
Authority. How the *Caudillo* Maintains His Power Over the Nation. The
Caudillo's Concern for His Safety. Why Dictatorship Has Continued to

CHAPTER   PAGE

Flourish. Effects of Dictatorship. REVOLUTIONS AND VIOLENCE: Types of Revolutions.

12. POLITICAL PARTIES AND ELECTIONS: BALLOTS, PREFERABLY HONEST . . 335
GENERAL ATTRIBUTES OF PARTIES: Personalism. Charismatic Appeal of the Caudillo. Party and Membership Instability. Identification of Government with a Political Party. Intolerance of the Opposition. THE TRADITIONAL PARTIES. THE ONE, TWO, AND MULTIPARTY SYSTEMS: One-Party Systems. Two-Party Systems. The Multiparty System. THE MAJOR PARTIES TODAY: Native Liberal Parties. Christian Democrats. The Communist Party. CAMPAIGNS AND ELECTIONS: Qualifications for Voting. Registration of Voters. The Campaign. The Election.

PART V—STRUCTURE AND OPERATION OF GOVERNMENT

13. CONSTITUTIONS, FEDERALISM, AND PRIVATE RIGHTS: IN THEORY AND IN
PRACTICE 371
CONSTITUTIONS: General Characteristics. Formulation and Adoption. The Many Constitutions Most Nations Have Had. Foreign Influences. Amendment. FEDERALISM: Background. Arguments For and Against. Federalism in Operation. PRIVATE RIGHTS: Respect for Rights Generally. Freedom of Speech and the Press. Freedom of Religion. Physical Liberty. Political Asylum.

14. EXECUTIVES: DEMOCRATIC CAESARS AND DEMOCRATS 393
TYPES OF EXECUTIVES SINCE INDEPENDENCE: Monarch and Emperor. Life President and Life Consul. Parliamentary Government. Committee or Council. THE PRESIDENT TODAY. QUALIFICATIONS FOR THE PRESIDENT. CALIBER OF MEN CHOSEN TO BE PRESIDENT. TERM OF OFFICE. ELIGIBILITY FOR REELECTION. MEANS OF SELECTION. TRANSFER OF THE OFFICE. POWERS OF THE PRESIDENT: Armed Forces. Administration. Appointment and Removal. Legislative. Decree. Finance. Foreign Relations. Judicial. Intervention. State of Siege. THE CABINET. METHODS OF EXERCISING PRESIDENTIAL CONTROL. PRESIDENTIAL RESPONSIBILITY. EXPOSURE TO THE PUBLIC—A RISK OF THE GAME. SUCCESSION TO THE PRESIDENTIAL OFFICE WHEN VACANT. EX-PRESIDENTS.

15. LEGISLATURES: ECHOES AND VOICES 429
LEGISLATIVE-EXECUTIVE RELATIONS. LEGISLATIVE EXPERIMENTATION. SELECTION OF MEMBERS: Qualifications. Apportionment. Method of Election. ORGANIZATION OF THE LEGISLATURE. THE LEGISLATIVE PROCESS. SESSIONS. POWERS AND FUNCTIONS. Legislative. Constitutive. Electoral. Judicial. LEGISLATIVE PRIVILEGES AND IMMUNITIES.

16. COURTS AND LAW: THE LAST WORD, FACT OR FICTION 450
PECULIAR ATTRIBUTES OF LATIN AMERICAN LAW: A Blend of Legal Systems. Extensive Borrowings. Embodiment of the Law in Codes. ORGANIZATION AND OPERATION OF THE COURTS: The Supreme Court. The Lower Courts. Special Courts. INDEPENDENCE OF THE JUDICIARY. CIVIL AND CRIMINAL PROCEDURE. JUDICIAL REVIEW. CRITICISMS OF THE COURTS.

INDEXES

INDEX OF AUTHORS 475
INDEX OF SUBJECTS 479

LIST OF TABLES AND FIGURES

TABLES   **PAGE**

5–1. Absenteeism among Schoolchildren, Ages 7 to 14, in 1950 . . . 112
5–2. Teachers in Certain Countries, 1958 (Trained and Untrained) . 122
8–1. *Minifundios* and *Latifundios* 217
8–2. Land Distribution in Mexico, 1916–1964 234
8–3. Increasing Tempo of Land Reform in Bolivia 241
8–4. Distribution of Land in Venezuela, 1959–1962 248
9–1. Production of Electric Energy 259
9–2. Production of Crude Steel 261
10–1. Distribution of the Labor Force by Major Sectors 282
10–2. Percentages in Three Major Age Groups in Latin America . . 284
12–1. Election Results in Bolivia, 1956–1962 345
12–2. Leading Parties and Their Strength in Recent Elections . . . 346
12–3. Second and Third Parties and Their Strength in Recent Elections 347
13–1. Latin American Constitutions 376
14–1. Executives, February, 1965 397
15–1. Bicameral Legislatures, Senate 436
15–2. Bicameral Legislatures, Chamber of Deputies 438
15–3. Unicameral Legislatures 440

FIGURES   **PAGE**

1–1. Comparative Areas, Latin American Countries and the United
States; Central America and Texas 5
1–2. Relief Map, North and South America 7
1–3. Temperature and Rainfall 13
1–4. Main Airway Systems and Comparative Distances 26
2–1. Density and Spatial Distribution of Population 33
2–2. Ethnic Composition of Each Country 34
2–3. Population Growth Rates in the Americas 46
2–4. Population Growth Rates of Major Regions of the Free World . 46
2–5. Relative Decrease of Indian Population in the Americas . . . 49
3–1. Urban Population, Percentage of Total Population 79
3–2. Urban Population Growing Faster than Total Population . . . 80
3–3. Percentage of Urban Increase Due to Natural Increase and
Migration 81
5–1. Newspaper Circulation in 1960 115

5–2. Distribution of Education Budget for Different Levels 121
5–3. Literacy in Latin America, 1950–1960 131
6–1. Percentage of Population That Is Catholic 170
6–2. Percentage of Population That Is Protestant 173
7–1. National Government Budgets by Category of Expenditure . . 186
8–1. Percentage of Populace Engaged in Agriculture 216
8–2. Size of Labor Force and Worker Productivity 224
9–1. Electric Power Production, 1960 260
9–2. Gross Domestic Product, Percentage by Area of Activity . . . 263
10–1. Percentages in Age Groups in Latin America, United States, and
       Britain 285

CHAPTER 1

THE LAND AND RESOURCES:
Challenges to Ingenuity

IN ADDITION to Canada, our Anglo-Saxon neighbor to the north, the United States has twenty other neighbors which share with it the land and destiny of the western hemisphere. These 20, all lying to the south and southeast of the United States, are Mexico, the six nations of Central America: Guatemala, El Salvador, Honduras, Nicaragua, Costa Rica, and Panama; the three insular Caribbean countries: Cuba, Haiti, and Dominican Republic; and the ten nations of South America: Argentina, Bolivia, Brazil, Chile, Colombia, Ecuador, Paraguay, Peru, Uruguay, and Venezuela.

This vast area, extending from Mexico's northern boundary, the Rio Grande, all the way to Cape Horn on the southern tip of Argentina, has long been called "Latin America." But like many other things about the region, its very name is controversial. The name came into vogue during the nineteenth century, after the young nations had won their independence, and it reflected their admiration for the French (Latin) political idealism and culture—values that still appeal to many intellectuals. To them the name is quite appropriate. As F. García Calderón, one of the region's distinguished writers, expresses it, the Latin Americans ". . . belong to the great Latin family; they are the children of Spain, Portugal, and Italy by blood and by deep-rooted tradition, and by their general ideas, they are the children of France."[1]

However, "Latin America," although generally used, is resented by many who regard it as inaccurate and inappropriate. Among these is Luis Alberto Sánchez, a Peruvian writer. Sánchez, in his book "¿Existe América Latina?" concluded that Latin America in reality does not exist. Its culture, he reasoned, is by no means entirely Latin but is a blend with the Indian.[2]

---

[1] F. García Calderón, *Latin America: Its Rise and Progress,* trans. Bernard Miall (London: T. Fisher Unwin, 1913), p. 288.

[2] *Luis Alberto Sánchez, ¿Existe América Latina?* (Mexico City: Fondo de Cultura Económica, 1945).

Obviously, the name "Latin America" does not adequately designate the region, but neither do the other commonly used synonyms, "Hispanic America" and "Ibero-America," which also fail to recognize the Indian and his contributions to the area's culture. Yet the term "Indo-America," advocated by some, is equally inadequate because it ignores the Spanish and Portuguese altogether. To compound the confusion, all of them are inaccurate because they completely neglect one of the main racial and cultural ingredients—the African.

Yet, just as most Southerners (especially those who have "held onto their Confederate currency") continue to refer to everything north of the Mason and Dixon line as "The North," so do most of us in the United States regard everything south of the border as "Latin America." In the absence of agreement among our neighbors there, that is the name we shall use.

GEOGRAPHICAL ASPECTS

Area

The area of Latin America is approximately 8 million square miles, which amounts to about 10 percent of the world's inhabited continental territory. South America proper is the fourth largest continent—a fairly respectable showing as continents go. The individual countries vary considerably in size. Brazil, with more than 3¼ million square miles, is the giant. Containing almost half the total area of South America, it is larger than the continental United States. At the other extreme is El Salvador, the midget, with only 7,700 square miles, approximately the size of New Jersey. Figure 1–1 which imposes the area of Central America on that of Texas, and that of other nations on the United States, shows the comparative sizes of the countries.

Location

The relative location of Latin America has greatly affected its development and relations with other nations. From the beginning its southerly latitude played a large part in determining that it would be Spanish and Portuguese instead of, perhaps, English. The region is much closer to Spain and Portugal, located in the extreme southwestern part of Europe, than to the British Isles, which are far to the north. Columbus, venturing forth from Spain in his quest to reach the Orient, was somewhat south of his westward course when he landed in the Bahamas, triumphantly planted the Spanish flag, and claimed the territory for Spain, all the while assuming it was India. In somewhat similar fashion, the English explorers sailed westward too, landed in upper North America, and proudly claimed that territory for England.

The location of Latin America was also influential in aiding these colonies to break away from the mother country. Far from the Old

FIGURE 1–1

COMPARATIVE AREAS: LATIN AMERICAN COUNTRIES AND THE
UNITED STATES; CENTRAL AMERICA AND TEXAS

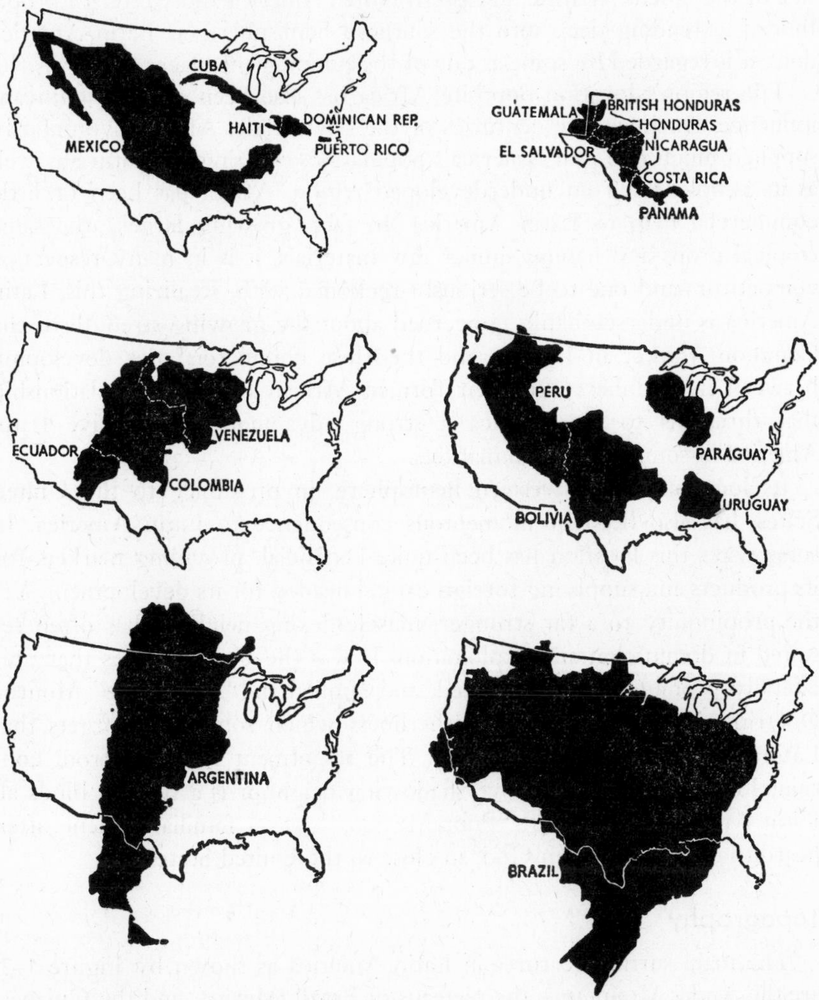

SOURCE: *Center of Intercultural Formation* (CIF), *Study No. 1. Socio-Economic Data—Latin America in Maps, Charts, and Tables* (compiled by Yvan Labelle and Adriana Estrada) (Guernavaca, Mexico, 1963), p. 30. Reproduced by permission.

World, which for decades was convulsed in the Napoleonic struggle, they were able to declare, and successfully assert, their independence. The support of the swashbuckling young United States, embodied in the Monroe Doctrine, was a verbal deterrent against the Old World's henceforth attempting to colonize the New or to extend its political system there. The more tangible support of seasoned British tars and battle-ready British ships was the effective nineteenth century threat of massive retaliation.

From the standpoint of international trade, the location of Latin America is not advantageous. The region is remote from the main centers of commercial activity of the modern world, which are situated on either side of the North Atlantic, in eastern North America and western Europe. Indeed, extending deep into the southern hemisphere, as Latin America does, it is regarded by some as one of the jumping-off places of the world.

The region's location opposite Africa has also been a very significant influence. During three centuries of the slave trade, Africa involuntarily supplied much of Latin America's population, coloring its culture as well as its people. Itself an underdeveloped region, Africa has been of little commercial help to Latin America. In fact, growing largely the same tropical crops and having similar raw materials, it is in many respects a competitor—and one to be seriously reckoned with. Realizing this, Latin America is understandably concerned about the growing strength of the Common Market in Europe and the close commercial ties developing between its members and their former African colonies, a relationship that threatens to give Africa a strong advantage and deprive Latin America of some of its main markets.

Its location in the western hemisphere, in proximity to the United States, has also been of momentous consequence to Latin America. In some ways this location has been quite beneficial, providing markets for its products and supplying foreign capital needed for its development. Yet the propinquity to a far stronger, muscle-flexing neighbor has often resulted in domination and exploitation. It was the United States that unilaterally promulgated, interpreted, and applied the "protective" Monroe Doctrine—in a spirit of big brotherliness which sometimes forgets that Latin America too has grown up. The resentment resulting from continued overexposure to an overshadowing neighbor is a tie that binds all Latin Americans together. "Poor Mexico," goes a familiar lament often heard there, "so far from God, so close to the United States."

Topography

The main surface features in Latin America as shown by Figure 1–2, are the Andes Mountains; the plateaus of Brazil, Mexico, and the Guianas; the tropical jungles or rain forests; and the broad fertile plains or pampas. The Andes and the jungles are as fiercely individualistic and assertive as their Spanish and Portuguese conquerors, and as uncooperative as the Indians. The mountains, with their many defiant peaks, and the jungles, with their overwhelming growth, are antisocial, flaunting their contempt for man. They may appear on the map as belonging to Brazil or Ecuador, but they have never been really conquered. Indeed, a large part of the territory still remains outside the effective control of the states that claim it.

Unlike the mountains and jungle, the pampas and plains are sociable

FIGURE 1–2

RELIEF MAP: NORTH AND SOUTH AMERICA

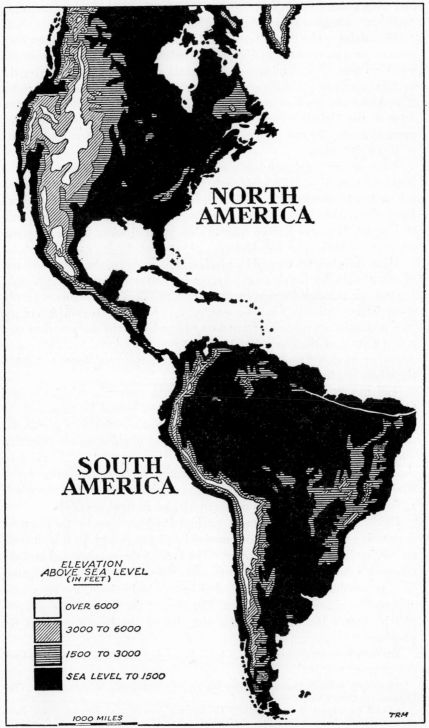

ELEVATION
ABOVE SEA LEVEL
(IN FEET)

OVER 6000

3000 TO 6000

1500 TO 3000

SEA LEVEL TO 1500

1000 MILES

TRM

SOURCE: Hubert Herring, *A History of Latin America from the Beginnings to the Present*, 2d ed. rev. (New York: Alfred A. Knopf, Inc., 1961), p. 9. Reproduced by permission.

and responsive to man's overtures. The fertile, grass-covered expanses meet him with open arms and make him feel welcome.

Mountains. The Andes have the distinction of being the longest continuous mountain chain in the world, extending all the way from the northern part of Colombia and Venezuela to Tierra del Fuego on the extreme southern tip of the continent, a distance of more than 4,000 miles. The Andes are much narrower and much higher than the Rocky Mountains in the United States. Throughout most of their length, they are approximately 200 miles wide, except in Bolivia where they "bulge out" to about 400 miles.

They are among the highest mountains in the world. At least 14 of the peaks are more than 21,000 feet high, and one of them, Mount Aconcagua, which boasts an elevation of 22,835 feet, is the highest in the western hemisphere. Most of the passes across the mountains are above 10,000 feet, making crossings much more difficult than in the Rockies where the passes are only 6,000 to 7,000 feet high.

With their heights capped by glaciers and ice sheets, the Andes in some places are split, by raging river torrents, into several separate ranges, making passage through them even more of a problem. "Colombia is an obstinately perpendicular kind of country," says Kathleen Romoli, describing its topography. "Crossing it from west to east has all the dizzy variety of a roller coaster of the Gods. Sea level to 8,000 feet, down to 3,000, up to 10,000 or so, down to 800, up a mile and three quarters, down to 1,000—the whole in a little over 200 air miles."[3]

Tall and "gangly," the Andes, as well as the mountains of Mexico and Central America, are geologically young, undisciplined by time and the elements. And with all the impetuosity and unpredictability of youth, the obstreperous upstarts occasionally go on a tear, pitching an earthquake, a volcanic eruption, or an avalanche. The narrowness and great height of the young mountains account for potential subterranean stresses and strains that make disasters of nature an ever-present menace in the whole region of the Cordillera from northern Mexico to southern Chile.

Of these cataclysmic scourges, earthquakes have been by far the most devastating in their effects, both material and psychological. It is difficult to imagine how awful they can be. "The face of the country was entirely changed," said W. B. Stevenson, describing a very severe quake, ". . . mountains rose where cultivated valleys had existed, the rivers disappeared or changed their courses. The face of the country was so completely altered that no one knew the site of the largest farm in the province."[4]

Smitten by nature, many cities have been destroyed or virtually wiped

---

[3] Kathleen Romoli, *Colombia: Gateway to South America* (Garden City, N.Y.: Doubleday, Doran Co., 1941), pp. 6–7.

[4] W. B. Stevenson, *A Historical and Descriptive Narrative of Twenty Years' Residence in South America* (London, 1825), Vol. II, p. 267.

out by earthquakes, including Lima, Caracas, Santiago, Arica, Cuzco, Concepción, and Mendoza. Some have been destroyed a number of times: Concepción, in 1570, 1730, 1751, and 1835; and the capital of Guatemala in 1541, 1773, and 1917.

In recent years Chile has suffered two destructive earthquakes that caused great damage and loss of life. In 1939 Chillán was reduced to a pile of rubble and 30,000 of its residents killed. In 1960 the nation was struck by a series of earthquakes, tidal waves, and volcanic eruptions that killed almost 10,000 people.

The 1960 disasters that struck Chile show the full magnitude and extent of seismic destruction. Property losses were fantastic and included damage or destruction of homes and buildings, public utilities, railroad tracks and roadbeds, and highways and roads. Also, large areas of good farmland were sterilized or otherwise damaged, irrigation systems were disrupted, and rivers were even diverted from their courses.

In all, 2 million people, more than a fourth of the population, were left homeless; and half of the nation's farmland was damaged. The total loss was estimated at $500 million, more than the annual national budget.[5] If comparable damage were suffered by the United States, it would be more than $40 billion, the amount of our nondefense expenditures.

The material losses, however large, can be estimated and statistically shown, yet nothing can measure the tragic psychological effects these calamities have on the people. "Mass hysteria and paroxysms of terror," says William Lytle Schurz, "are often followed by a state of fatalism and resignation. The hypertension of panic may result in outbursts of fanatical religious fervor or end in downright madness as the mind breaks from the memory of horrors and the suspense of waiting for the repetition of disaster."[6]

Plateaus. Another important surface feature is the plateau, extensive ones being found in Mexico and Brazil and smaller ones in the southern parts of Venezuela and Argentina.

The Mexican plateau covers most of the country. The northern part, lightly populated and containing much of the nation's mineral resources, is desert and semidesert with a very low or seasonal rainfall. The central part of the plateau is far more important; although containing only about one-seventh of the area of the nation, this includes half of its arable land. And crowded into a series of intermont basins, at elevations of 5,000 to 8,000 feet, are half of the nation's population and most of its industry.

The Brazilian plateau, located in the southeastern part of the country, is one of the major upland masses in the world. Four times the size of Texas, it has an average elevation of 2,500 feet. The highest part, the Great

---

[5] *New York Times*, "Hemisphere Economic Review," January 11, 1961, p. 49, col. 1.

[6] William Lytle Schurz, *This New World: The Civilization of Latin America* (New York: E. P. Dutton & Co., Inc., 1954), p. 30.

Escarpment, extends along the coast for about a thousand miles, rising to a height of 10,000 feet back of Rio de Janeiro. So steep is the escarpment here that a train crossing it can make the ascent only by the aid of cables.

In the highlands, or along the coastal area just over the Great Escarpment, live most of Brazil's population; the region contains, with the exception of Rio de Janeiro on the southeastern coast, and Belem at the mouth of the Amazon, all the large cities. Much of the area is rolling grassland or brushland, except in the southern part where there are large stretches of fine forests.

Jungles or Rain Forests. With three-fourths of its area lying in the equatorial belt, Latin America's many rain forests extend from southern Mexico, through the coastal plains of Central America and the Choco country of Colombia, into the very heart of the continent. By far the largest such forest of all—in fact the largest tropical jungle in the world—is the huge Amazon basin.

All the rain forests follow a similar pattern of tall, thick, tree growth, dense tangled foliage, incessant rain, and debilitating heat. These vast and seemingly endless jungles are like Doctor Jekyll and Mr. Hyde, showing one face to the naturalist but quite a different one to the settler.

To the naturalist they are fascinating and challenging—a tropical paradise. Among the many distinguished naturalists interested in the area was Henry Bates, who spent 11 years there studying and collecting specimens. During this time he collected the enormous total of almost 15,000 species, including 52 mammals, 350 birds, 140 reptiles, 120 fishes, 35 mollusks, and 14,000 insects. Approximately 8,000 of these, according to Bates, were species new to science.[7]

The settler, however, bent on carving out his own small private domain and developing it by courage and *cruzeiros*, has found the jungle to be Mr. Hyde at his worst. Ready and anxious to combat man, his crops, and his domestic animals is a heavy mass of verdure. Stimulated by heat and moisture, the trees and vines rudely trample and elbow one another in a frantic effort to reach the sun, shutting out all sunlight on the vastness below. The settler's hope of substituting crops for creepers and reaping the benefits of a perfervid fertility always seemed a good idea, but the jungle usually won out, closing in again and asserting itself once more.

The profuse vegetation is only one of the many enemies of man in the jungle. There are snakes ready to challenge him on every hand: from the large boa constrictors, reaching 30 feet in length (adversaries to be respected, although they do not usually attack man), to the rattlesnakes, the most poisonous and the boldest of all—who never retreat from humans but daringly crawl toward them and strike with little or no warning.

In the jungle waters, where man bathes (and sometimes has to work), the stinging ray attacks him with its poison and the electric eel with its

[7] Paul Russell Cutright, *The Great Naturalists Explore South America* (New York: The Macmillan Company, 1940), p. 5.

power charge. Also infesting the waters is the piranha, the most ferocious fish in the world, whose sharklike teeth, sharp as a buzz saw, can tear a man to shreds within minutes.

Also ready to pester and torment him are the 14,000 species of insects, including mosquitoes, chigoes, and red ants. Besides causing discomfort, the mosquitoes are carriers of chills and fevers. Although Bates identified many varieties of the insect, according to one traveler in the jungle there are just two kinds: the day shift and the night shift.

About the most dreaded insects of all are the tambochas. When the natives sense their approach they flee in terror and submerge themselves in the nearest stream. Like Sherman's Army on its march to the sea, the tambochas devastate the land, devouring everything in their path, including people, animals, plants, and trees. Before them, even the earth trembles —say some who lived through their awesome destruction.[8]

Pampas. Latin America has an extensive fertile plain, the pampa, that produces most of the grain and cattle raised on the continent. Located in northeastern Argentina, Uruguay, and parts of Paraguay and southern Brazil, it contains about 250,000 square miles. Comprising some of the most fertile land in the world, its soil would do as fertilizer for the poorer land of less favored nations.

Until the middle of the nineteenth century this large plain, lying mostly in Argentina, and sometimes called the Sea of Grass, was inhabited mainly by Indians, outlaws, range cattle, and gauchos. Everything there was wild and tough: the wiry prairie grass, the hardy far-ranging cattle, and the husky lawless gauchos who were so ". . . rowdy that the drinking houses where they caroused had iron grills to protect the bar man from their patrons."[9]

This primitive and undeveloped world of the gaucho was completely transformed by the flood of immigrants who began to pour into the area during the 1870s. They were searching, not for El Dorado, but for good land to farm. For the first time fences were put up, utilizing barbed wire that had been invented only shortly before, and pastures were planted in alfalfa. Purebred English longhorn cattle, with as proud a pedigree as any member of the peerage, were brought over from England; their offspring returned later as choice steaks and roasts on the recently invented refrigerated ships. Supplying English and other European markets, Argentina soon became the world's leading exporter of meat. By 1900, however, wheat and other grains were more important to the nation's economy than meat and other animal products.

Argentina, which in Spanish means "land of silver," was named in the

---

[8] For a graphic account of their onslaught see José Eustacio Rivera, "The Vortex," *The Green Continent: a Comprehensive View of Latin America by Its Leading Writers* (ed., Germán Arciniegas) (New York: Alfred A. Knopf, Inc., 1944), pp. 39–40.

[9] Lewis Hanke, *South America* (Princeton, N.J.: D. Van Nostrand Co., Inc., 1959), p. 64.

expectation that the precious metal would be found there. When none was found, however, Argentina was pitied for its lack of resources and long regarded by its neighbors as a poor relative. But its pampa, although tapped belatedly, has proved to be an asset far more valuable than any mineral resource of the New World.

CLIMATE

One of the many misconceptions we North Americans often have concerns the climate of Latin America. Since most of the region lies within the equatorial zone, we jump to the conclusion that it must be stiflingly hot and humid. This is not the case at all (see Figure 1–3). On the contrary, most of the area has a wide range of climates, especially in the Andes. While there are many local variations there, depending on exposure to sunlight and rain-bearing winds, there are general altitude zones where the temperature decreases as the elevation increases. In fact, in the Andes, climate is primarily a matter of altitude and varies as the elevation increases or decreases.

The differences in climate are so distinct at the different elevations that Latin Americans living in the Andes and toward the equator describe their climate in terms of "vertical zones." The lowest zone, *tierra caliente*, or hot country, extends from sea level to about 3,000 feet. Here the average annual temperature is usually between 75 and 80 degrees, with a difference of only 3 or 4 degrees between the averages of the warmest and coldest months.

Above the hot country, the next zone, *tierra templada*, or temperate country, extends from approximately 3,000 to 6,000 feet. At this elevation the average annual temperature is between 65 and 75 degrees, but the difference between the coldest and warmest months is even less than in *tierra caliente*.

Still higher, a third zone, *tierra fría* or cold country, extends from approximately 6,000 to 10,000 feet. Here the average annual temperature is between 55 and 65 degrees, with practically no difference in temperature from one month to another.[10] Perhaps the extreme of high altitude monotony exists in Quito, located above 9,000 feet. Here the average annual temperature is an invigorating 54.6 degrees, and the average temperatures of the coldest and warmest months vary by only .3 of a degree. Above the cold country, extending from approximately 10,000 feet to the snow line at about 15,000, lies the zone of the Alpine Meadows, or treeless *páramos*.

The vertical zones that exist throughout the long stretch of the Andean chain are especially noticeable in Colombia, located on the equator with mountain peaks reaching up to the snow line. The result? At sea level it is

---

[10] For these zones see Preston E. James, *Latin America* (3rd ed.; New York: The Odyssey Press, Inc., 1959), pp. 79–80.

FIGURE 1-3

Temperature and Rainfall

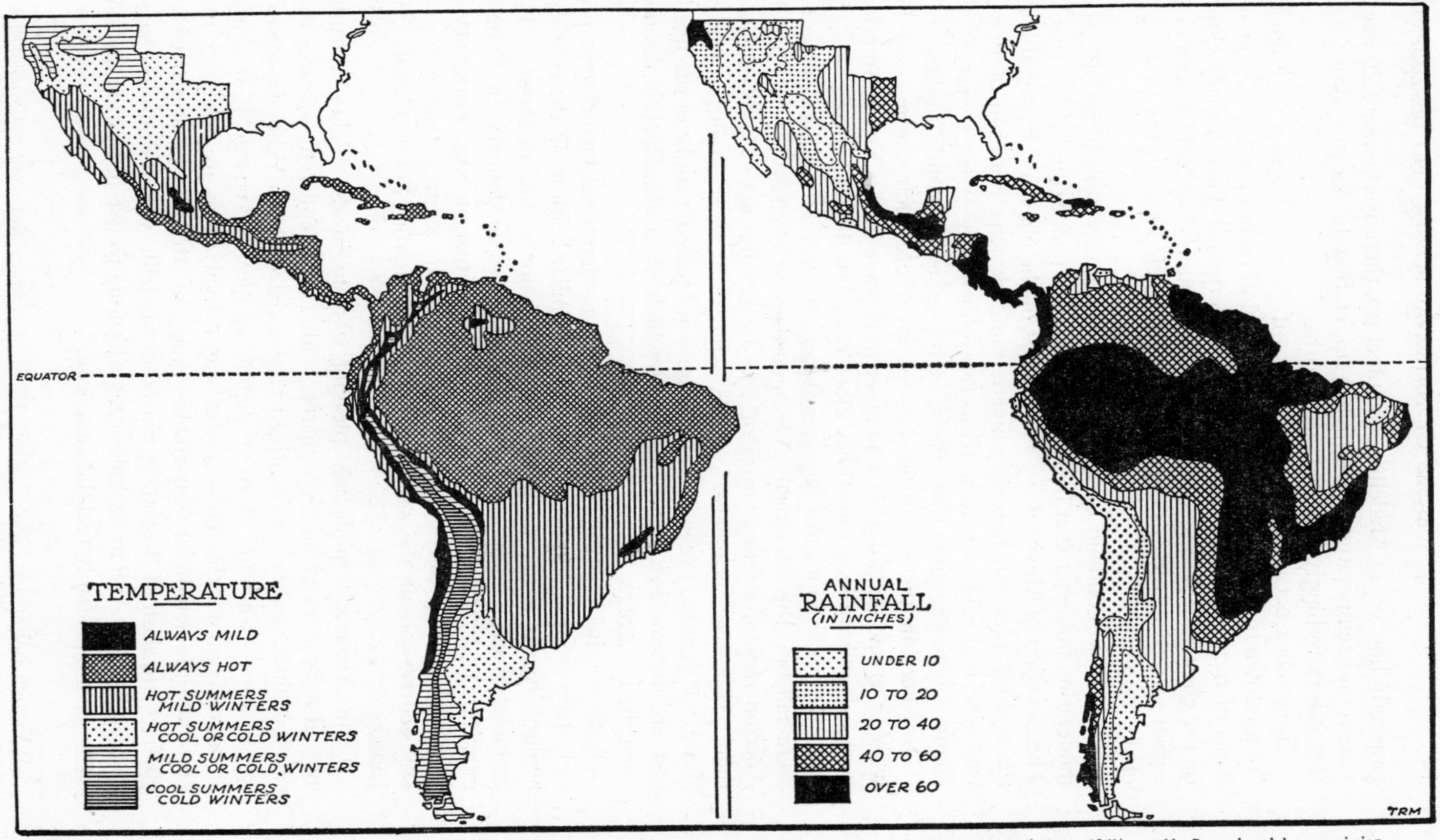

Source: Hubert Herring, A History of Latin America from the Beginnings to the Present, 2d ed. rev. (New York: Alfred A. Knopf, Inc., 1961), p. 11. Reproduced by permission.

gaspingly hot, yet at Medellín, 5,000 feet up, there is a pleasant 70 degree year-round temperature. Still higher up, at Bogotá, located above 9,000 feet, it is refreshingly brisk topcoat weather.

"Bogotanos occasionally take a day off," wrote Vernon L. Fluharty, "to go down to 'hot country' to drive the chill from their bones, and residents of *tierra caliente* who swelter in a perpetual Turkish-bath climate on the coastal littorals, go up to 'temperate country' or 'cold country' for a spell to activate sluggish livers and regain their vigor in the bracing air of the *altiplano*."[11]

The other mountain areas and upland plateaus benefit by the same moderating influence that high elevation has on temperature in the tropics. The elevation of Mexico City and the rest of the plateau is responsible for the region's pleasant, bracing climate. Similarly, the elevation of Brazil's extensive highland assures a temperate climate for a large part of the country, which would otherwise be as tropical as its latitude implies.

Nowhere in the equatorial regions are there such extremes of hot weather as one finds during a summer heat wave in the North American corn belt, where it is sometimes more than 110 degrees. At the equator temperatures rise into the 80s, occasionally the 90s during the day, and at night fall into the 70s or 60s. Yet according to climatic records for the Amazon region, a temperature of 100 degrees has never been recorded there. Moreover, nowhere in Latin America does the temperature go above 110 degrees, except in several areas in Mexico, mainly in the northeast, and in northern Argentina—areas which are a considerable distance from the equator.

In the southern part of South America, a moderate seasonal climate prevails that is roughly comparable to that of similar latitudes in the northern hemisphere yet is neither as cold in winter nor as hot in summer. For example, average temperature of Buenos Aires in January, a summer month there, is 73.6 degrees—about the same as that of New York City in July. But in July, Buenos Aires' cold season, the average temperature is 48.9 degrees—about the same as that of Charleston, South Carolina, in January.

Latin America's moderate, pleasant climate in the higher altitudes located near or even on the equator, with year-round temperatures that vary but little, is very provocative to the social scientist. While he regards temperatures of around 60 to 70 degrees as ideal for energetic, healthful living, he contends that considerable seasonal variations are necessary too. But could the delightful year-round climate of Medellín be improved by the sleet and slush of Boston? A citizen of Medellín would doubtless laugh at the very idea. And most Americans who long to live in Florida or California would probably feel the same way.

11 Vernon L. Fluharty, *Dance of the Millions: Military Rule and the Social Revolution in Colombia, 1930–1956* (Pittsburgh, Pa.: University of Pittsburgh Press, 1957), pp. 11–12.

Despite the moderate climate in large areas, the climate elsewhere has sometimes been a cause of concern. In the opinion of some scholars, the South American continent, by virtue of its size and climate, should be able to support many different species of large animals. Yet instead it has

. . . a prodigality of inferior life, aggressive and useless. . . . Still incipient studies lead to the conclusion that the higher animals degenerate in South American regions, sometimes because of the altitude, as in Bolivia and Peru, sometimes because of the grave disease prevalent in the torrid lowlands of the rest of the country. . . . It has been a struggle for centuries, for the livestock introduced in the Spanish Colonial Period deteriorated in the whole of Colombia, and, a still more disturbing fact, man has slowed up a little, not progressed much in stature nor in ambition to dominate.[12]

Evidence does exist that living in the high Andes was quite difficult for the early conquering whites. Most of them suffered from the bitter cold; some were bothered with acute nervous tensions; and a few were stricken by *soroche* (mountain sickness), becoming so nauseated that they staggered or even threw down their arms.

Another disconcerting problem was male sterility; it was a long time before any Spanish babies were conceived and born in Potosí, high up in the Bolivian Andes.[13] Speaking of Cerro de Pasco, located in the Peruvian Andes at an elevation of almost 15,000 feet, lieutenants Ferndon and Gibbon observed: "The temperature is so rigorous here that the hens do not hatch nor the llamas procreate; and women at the period of their confinement are obliged to seek a more congenial climate or their offspring will not live."[14]

Leaving the subject of temperature, we find that the rainfall of the region varies considerably over its large territory, with its wide range of latitude and elevation. The Atacama Desert on the west coast is one of the driest places on earth. During a 20-year period, Iquique in northern Chile had a total of only 1.1 inches of rain, and in some regions of the Atacama no rainfall has ever been recorded.[15] In these areas, which are very lightly populated, the lack of rain has occasioned but little hardship. But in heavily populated northeastern Brazil, where most of the inhabitants depend on farming for at least a bare sustenance, the long periods of severe drought have caused thousands to perish from sheer starvation and thirst. The result has been mass migration from the region, with its abject poverty and fierce struggle for existence. This part of Brazil is understandably one of the most fertile breeding places for communism in all Latin America.

Some areas, instead of suffering from lack of rain, go to the other extreme. In an average year, the Caribbean side of Nicaragua has a rainfall

---

[12] In Romoli, *op. cit.*, pp. 8–9.
[13] Schurz, *op. cit.*, p. 9.
[14] Quoted, *ibid.*, p. 34.
[15] James, *op. cit.*, p. 256.

of more than 250 inches, or almost 21 feet. But over the main agricultural region, the broad and fertile pampa of South America, fortunately no such extremes exist. There, the rainfall is apt to be 30 to 40 inches a year, enough to insure the region's being one of the great granaries of the world.

NATURAL RESOURCES

Minerals and other natural resources have played an important and often exciting role in Latin America. With their venturesome spirit, the conquerors of the new world were impelled by Gold, God, and Gusto. Gold unquestionably had top billing. The lure of enormous riches, sometimes realized but usually illusory, emboldened men to trudge across blazing deserts, plod through savage jungles, and tackle perilous mountain heights. "Spanish America was born in a gold rush. . . ." says Hubert Herring. "Hunger for precious metal was the propulsive force which cleared the way for the Spanish American empire."[16]

After appropriating, by hook or by crook, the gold treasures of the Indians, the newcomers began an intensive exploitation of the many valuable mineral resources of the region. They discovered, however, that "all that glitters is not gold"; sometimes it is silver. The rich find at Potosí, Bolivia, in 1545 has been called "the most fabulous pile of silver ever uncovered by man. A 2,000 foot hill of silver." The treasure was so vast that the expression, *vale un Potosí* ("worth a Potosí"), came to mean "indescribably wealthy."[17]

More than four centuries later, Latin America is still a colossal storehouse of basic minerals. Chile has the only sizable deposits of natural nitrates known to exist; it is also the world's second largest producer of copper. Mexico is the world's largest producer of silver, and Bolivia's tin deposits are among the largest in the world. Venezuela is now the world's third major producer of petroleum, the new black gold which is found in most of the countries and which provides greater wealth than the early seekers of gold ever dreamed of.

Equally as impressive are the rich deposits of iron ore which are found in many of the countries. Brazil's Itabira deposit is estimated to contain more than a billion tons of ore, and Venezuela has several whole mountains of iron, the largest of which contains an estimated 2 to 2½ billion tons, with an iron content of more than 50 percent. Indeed, it is believed to be the richest iron deposit in the world. These recently discovered ores are now pouring into the United States to make up for the dwindling output of the formerly highly productive Mesabi Range. The production of industrial metals—zinc, mercury, graphite, antimony, arsenic, cadmium,

---

[16] Hubert Herring, *A History of Latin America from the Beginnings to the Present* (2d ed. rev.; New York: Alfred A. Knopf, Inc., 1961), p. 198.
[17] *Ibid.*, p. 109.

cobalt, vanadium, and bismuth, as well as industrial diamonds—is becoming of increasing importance in many of the countries.

These numerous and extensive resources have been of inestimable value in the development of the countries. As exports, they have provided much or most of the foreign exchange needed to pay for imports. Copper represents more than half of Chile's total exports; tin constitutes three-fourths of Bolivia's; and petroleum accounts for 95 percent of Venezuela's.

On the domestic front, the production of minerals stimulates internal development and provides jobs for many people. Moreover, as the mining communities grow into towns and cities, they become important markets for local products. Agriculture benefits as farms and ranches spring up around the mining communities to supply their food. Roads and railroads have to be built to transport the minerals to a port of embarkation, and hauling provides a large part of the freight of the railroads and other carriers.

Moreover, taxes paid on mining enterprises are an important source of government income, sometimes the major source. In Chile, nitrates were a bonanza to the government; during the four decades following the 1880s, they provided most of the national revenue, sometimes as much as 68 percent of the total.

Today, foreigners own the greater part of the mineral resources in Latin America. Much foreign capital has entered the region to speed up and extend exploitation, particularly in the latter half of the nineteenth century. Foreign money was needed because of the relatively little domestic capital accumulated in the countries, and also because of the traditional preference of local investors for putting their money in land and commercial enterprises rather than in mines.

The resulting foreign ownership has caused widespread and bitter resentment that increases as the Latin Americans become more nationalistic. The tirades against foreign "exploiters" are sometimes vehement. You have gotten wealthy . . . built up your own high standard of living at our expense, many Latin Americans charge. You take our invaluable, irreplaceable natural resources . . . pay us little for them—just about whatever you wish . . . and reduce us to economic colonialism. You meddle in our politics too . . . try to tell us what kind of government we should have . . . even the policies we should follow. While these charges are sometimes exaggerated, a student of United States history is apt to conclude that there is considerable justification for the resentment.[18]

Yet, however justified this attitude may be, the intense nationalism that today tends increasingly to shut out foreign investments in Latin American mining has some risky implications. Unable herself to supply the

---

[18] A main area of conflict today is foreign (which means mainly American) exploitation and marketing of petroleum. For the main issues involved and national policies of the several producing states, see Peter R. Odell, "Oil and State in Latin America," *International Affairs*, Vol. 40, No. 4 (October, 1964), pp. 659–73.

capital needed for development, Latin America may tarry too long—miss taking advantage of the brisk world demand for her resources until some new technological advance comes along that makes them obsolete and unneeded.

Chile knows from sad experience the awful impact that a new and radical technological change can have on a national economy. For decades the nation had enjoyed a world monopoly of the production of natural nitrates, an industry which was the backbone of its economy and responsible for its boom-time prosperity. However, the bubble suddenly burst in the 1920s when a process was discovered for making synthetic nitrogen from the air, causing the large demand for natural nitrates—their high price, too—to plummet. New techniques could similarly affect other mineral resources if they are not utilized while the brisk demand for them exists.

In many ways their valuable mineral resources are not fulfilling the expectations of the Latin Americans. Instead of being processed and used by manufacturers at home, their ores are usually shipped to the United States or some other foreign country to be processed and utilized. The prices paid for them, determined in the highly competitive world market, are sometimes disappointingly low and often fluctuate widely—conditions that both hurt and infuriate the Latin Americans. The drop of just one cent per pound in the price of copper on the world market costs Chile a much-needed $6 million a year in its foreign exchange; a drop of a few cents may completely unbalance its national budget and seriously dislocate its economy.

Nevertheless, mineral resources have generally benefited the nations possessing them. In Mexico, says Frank Tannenbaum, ". . . the mines—chiefly silver—paid for most of Mexico's imports for nearly four centuries, made possible the development of Mexico into a modern nation, justified the building of most of the railroads, and gave Mexico its distinctive place in the outside world."[19]

But some nations have not been so fortunate as Mexico—Bolivia, for example. Neither its fabulous deposits of silver at Potosí, exhausted and drained off to Spain before the end of the colonial period, nor its valuable, more recently exploited tin mines have contributed much to the nation's development. In fact, some contend that these misused mineral assets are primarily responsible for its serious economic problems. The legacy of Potosí, they believe, is "responsible for fastening upon Bolivia a pernicious economic-social system which exalted quick profits from the mines and left agriculture so little regarded that its growth was dangerously neglected and a feudal-type society prolonged for centuries."[20]

---

[19] Frank Tannenbaum, *Mexico: The Struggle for Peace and Bread* (New York: Alfred A. Knopf, Inc., 1954), p. 201.
[20] Hanke, *op. cit.*, p. 31.

Bolivia's wealth in tin has served the nation little, if any, better than did its treasure of silver. The tin mines were controlled by Patiño, Hochschild, and Aramayo, a powerful, ruthless alliance popularly known as the *rosco* (a yoke around the neck of oxen). The tycoons dominated the nation's government and economy, dictating to presidents and cabinets alike. Members of the clique and a few others made immense fortunes; Patiño, who owned the biggest share of the tin produced, was reputedly one of the richest men in the world. Yet their sole motive was profit. They paid paltry wages to their underfed, overworked miners, who lived short, wretched lives.

Since Latin America does have many important natural resources, it might understandably be concluded that it will some day be one of the highly industrialized areas of the world, comparable to the eastern United States or to western Europe. Yet much as Latin Americans would welcome this, prospects for its happening are not good at present. Because of the lateness of industrialization or other factors, the nations have been slow in utilizing their deposits of coal and in assessing their reserves. Argentina, which had long been dependent upon Great Britain for coal, was faced with such a serious crisis during World War II, when its fuel supply was cut off, that its railroads were forced to use wood as fuel and sometimes even maize and other grains soaked in linseed oil. The most important deposit of Argentina coal is that of the Rio Turbio, located about 1800 miles from Buenos Aires. The reserve has been estimated at more than 400 million tons, and the exploitation of the deposit is in the hands of the state.[21]

While the total amount of coal available in Latin America cannot be considered small, coal which can be directly converted into coke is scarce. Most of the coal produced is of low quality, having a high ash content and containing sulphur. The iron and steel plants at Volta Redonda in Brazil and Huachipato in Chile manage to operate by mixing, in the ratio of 80 to 20, the low quality coal produced locally with high quality coal imported from the United States. Moreover, to add insult to injury, the coal that exists in the region is usually located far from the iron ore where it is needed.[22]

Due to the lack of coal, water power is regarded by some as the answer to the region's critical need for energy. Thanks to the towering Andes and rushing rivers, the area has a very large power potential, estimated at approximately 120 million kilowatts. But as with coal, there is a catch here too. Most of the sites that are excellent for generating power are located at the narrow parts of the great rivers that flow eastward or south-

---

[21] For Argentina's problem with coal, see Marcelo Isacovich, "*Carbón*," *Argentina Económica y Social* (Buenos Aires: Editorial Quipo, 1961), pp. 103–5.

[22] For the problem of coal in Latin America's industrial development, see Bruno Leuschner, "Technological Research in Latin America," *Economic Bulletin for Latin America*, UNESCO, Vol. 8, No. 1 (March, 1963), pp. 68–69.

ward from the Andes in Venezuela, Colombia, Ecuador, Peru, and Bolivia. Unfortunately, these sites are deep in the remote interior, far from the populated areas and busy industries that need power. Since the cost of transmission and distribution from such distances is virtually prohibitive, only about 7 percent of its potential hydroelectric power has actually been developed to date.

In Brazil, abundant power was obtained by redirecting the Tieté River to flow eastward and plunge 2,000 feet down the Serra do Mar mountain. This engineering feat is one reason why São Paulo has become the industrial center of the nation. Another hydroelectric plant located at the Paulo Alfonso Falls on the São Francisco River, is designed to aid in the economic development of the northeastern section which has suffered so greatly from periodic droughts.

Of all the countries of Latin America, Chile has the best prospects for extensive development of water power. In the central and southern parts of the country, the rapid fall of the rivers from the Andes to the Pacific Ocean provides many possible sites for power-generating installations.[23]

Still another of Latin America's important resources is its farmland. In the absence of extensive land-use studies and soil surveys, it is not definitely known just how much of the land is cultivable. Irrespective of surveys and statistics, the definition of cultivability is itself a pertinent consideration. How do you define "arable land"? Should it include such arid areas as northern Mexico, where the rainfall is too little for crops, yet supports drought-resistant grasses that provide limited grazing for cattle? Should it include large areas that might be cultivated if cleared or irrigated, although at considerable expense?

However arability is defined, it is obvious that large areas in Latin America cannot be so classified. The terrain consists largely of mountains and hills, jungles and deserts, leaving relatively little land with the combination of topography, soil, and climate necessary for agriculture. In fact, this area is estimated to be only 5 percent of the total, or about an acre and a half per person. This figure is small compared with that of western Europe or the United States; it is large, however, compared with that of Asia. There, although 6 percent of the area is estimated as cultivable, this amounts to less than one-half acre per person.[24]

The acre and a half per person for Latin America is of course only a statistical average. Uruguay, blessed with fertile, level land and a favorable climate, can use 86 percent of its land for farming—a whopping 15.1 acres per capita. At the other extreme is Bolivia, saddled with a mountainous terrain and a cold climate; as a result, only .3 percent of its land area is presently used for farming—a mere .2 of an acre per person. Thus Uru-

---

[23] F. Benham and H. A. Holley, *A Short Introduction to the Economy of Latin America* (Royal Institute of International Affairs) (New York: Oxford University Press, 1960), p. 49.

[24] *Ibid.*, p. 20.

guay has about 75 times the amount of arable land per capita as Bolivia, whose situation will improve in time as its fertile Oriente is developed.

South America is sometimes called the Vanishing Continent, and for good reason. Little attention has been given to conservation of the soil since the days of the Incas. As a result of heavy, relentless rains beating down on unterraced cultivated slopes, the topsoil of large areas has been swept down the slopes and into rushing rivers to be deposited far out in the Atlantic—a most difficult region to farm! Completely ruined by erosion or by leaching, as in the Paraná and Amazon River basins, many areas formerly used for agriculture have had to be abandoned entirely.

In striking contrast to such wastage, both Mexico and Paraguay in the last two decades have shown what can be accomplished by good land-use practices. By means of irrigation and better methods of farming, they have expanded their harvested area by almost 50 percent.

The amount of land suitable for agriculture is always important, affecting as it does a region's standard of living and its prospects for economic development generally. Yet of even greater significance at the moment than the amount of arable land in Latin America are such pressing problems as the need for wider distribution of land ownership and the better use of cultivable areas already known to exist. These problems will be dealt with at length in Chapter 8, Agriculture and Land Reform.

TRANSPORTATION AND COMMUNICATION

Railroads

The high mountains, impenetrable jungles, and desert wastes which cover most of the area of Latin America have been great obstacles to transportation, making the building of railroads a very difficult and expensive undertaking. Sometimes the most complicated engineering problems are involved, as in the case of the Peruvian Central Railroad. At a distance of only 106 miles from the sea, its trains laboriously reach an elevation of 15,680 feet, the highest rail line in the world, by the use of 65 tunnels, 67 bridges, and a series of 16 switchbacks over which the trains move alternately forward and backward.

Another engineering marvel—a product of Henry Meiggs, world-renowned builder of railroads—is the rail line to Cerro de Pasco, the famous old silver mine in Peru. Struggling to reach the heights, the little cars cling for dear life to the sides of almost vertical cliffs, teeter around kinky curves, grope their way in dark tunnels through high mountain peaks, gingerly cross bridges above bottomless chasms. In one place they must even spiral upward in a tunnel inside a mountain in order to reach the heights.

Although railroads are the main mode of inland transportation, in many respects they are inadequate for the needs of the region. The mileage is relatively small, comprising only about 80,000 miles of track. This is little more than a third of the mileage in the United States, yet it serves an area more than two and a half times as large. As a result of this small mileage, less than one-fifth of the territory is within 20 miles of a railroad, and many of the older towns that sprang up at road junctions or river crossings are not served by a railroad at all. Moreover, the rail lines which have been constructed tend to be very concentrated within the small populous areas. In Brazil, nine-tenths of the nation's mileage is in a narrow coastal belt 300 miles long, serving the region from Santos and São Paulo to Rio, leaving an area half the size of the United States with only 35 miles of railway.

Another serious shortcoming of the railroads is their haphazard planning and construction. Built decades ago by foreign interests to connect a mine or plantation with a port, they were not designed to develop a region as a whole or to promote intercourse between regions. Consequently, there were few, if any, connections between different railroads. In Argentina, all lines converged on Buenos Aires, often necessitating a long and circuitous journey to cover a short distance as the crow flies. To remedy this, connecting lines have been constructed in recent years between major interior points. In August 1961, Colombia celebrated one of its proudest achievements, the completion of its first through rail line of 418 miles, which connected the seven existing railroads, the major cities, and the Pacific and Caribbean ports.

An even more serious problem is the use of different gauges, necessitating expensive and time-consuming transfers. In many of the countries there are three gauges: the narrow, of one metre; the standard, 4 feet 8½ inches; and the broad, 5 feet 3 inches. Brazil even has five gauges. "Caramba!" you may exclaim. "What a way to run a railroad!" Mexico thought so too, and between 1945 and 1950 she spent a tremendous sum to modernize the railroads and institute a uniform standard gauge.

High freight rates are still another problem of the rail lines. Necessitated by the heavy cost of construction and maintenance and the prevalent pattern of one-way payloads and return deadheading, the rates are so high that some commodities cannot stand the cost. To ship an article from Buenos Aires to Asunción, about 1,000 miles, you pay as much as if you were sending it all the way to Yokohama, halfway around the world.

Besides modernizing and expanding the railroads, the governments have, since World War II, been progressively taking them over from private ownership. The justification? Unprofitable operation by the former owners (with the government often refusing rate increases), needed construction of new lines into undeveloped territory, and promotion of the national interest by an integrated, home-owned system. In Argentina and Uruguay, the railroads have been nationalized; in Brazil, Chile, Mexico, and many other countries, the government lines dominate the railroad systems.

River Steamers

Generally speaking, Latin America is not very well endowed with usable rivers. Those of Mexico, Central America, and the west coast of South America are studded with rapids and falls in their abrupt descent from the mountains. Although possibly useful for irrigation and power, none of them is truly navigable.

The best-known of the rivers, the Amazon, dwarfs all other rivers of the world. Fed by countless thousands of small streams that collect water from snow melting high in the Andes and from the torrential rains constantly drenching the huge basin, it drains an area of more than 2,700,000 square miles—about 40 percent of all Latin America. The volume of muddy water that pours into the Atlantic—five times that of the Mississippi —is so huge that it turns the salt water fresh for 200 miles from shore. When the swollen river goes on a rampage, it sometimes "tears great pieces of the earth loose from their moorings and carries them down stream as floating islands, often complete with trees in whose branches monkeys or birds may sit."[25]

Skirting floating islands is only one of the many challenges to the ingenuity of a river pilot. Unexpected shifts in the channels may land him on a sand bar or trap him in the shallows, or the water level may fall so drastically that a freighter anchored at a dock one evening may find itself high and dry on the bank the next morning. Despite these obstacles, the Amazon is navigable by ocean vessels all the way to Iquitos in eastern Peru, 2,000 miles from its mouth—the longest navigable distance of any river of the world.

Yet for all its mighty volume of water and long navigable distance, the Amazon is of comparatively little value to Brazil or the other countries as a water highway for trade and economic development. For Amazonia is so lightly populated and undeveloped that its output of goods provides only a very small volume of freight to be transported on this remarkable waterway.

Second in size among the river systems of Latin America is the Paraná-Paraguay, which drains an area of about 1,500,000 square miles of northern Argentina, Paraguay, southern Brazil, and Uruguay. Despite many problems of navigation similar to those on the Amazon, oceangoing vessels use the river as far inland as Santa Fe—about 300 miles—and slightly smaller vessels can make it up to Asunción, about 700 miles farther upstream. Although the Paraná-Paraguay is not as large or as long as the Amazon, it is easily the most important river in South America, serving a population of more than 20 million and carrying much of northern Argentina's grain and meat and Paraguay's lumber and *quebracho*.

There are other important rivers, too, including the Magdalena and the Orinoco, but like the Amazon, they are of limited value as highways of

---

[25] Schurz, *op. cit.*, p. 21.

travel and commerce. Often they are in the wrong place or, perhaps, flow in the wrong direction. The São Francisco, for example, rises in southeastern Brazil only a short distance from the coast; yet because of the 10,000 foot escarpment along the coast, it flows northward and away from the populous developed areas of São Paulo and Rio de Janeiro that could well use a navigable river and a supporting inland territory.

For the past two decades, rivers have played a decreasingly important role in transportation, as expanded highway, rail, and airway systems carry much of the traffic formerly handled by ships. Antiquated river vessels which use outmoded towing methods have burdened the shipping lines with high operating costs. To remedy the situation, Argentina and Brazil have given ailing transportation on the Paraná and Amazon a revivifying transfusion by the purchase of modern river barges and efficient "pusher" tugboats.

Ocean Liners

The long coastline of Latin America and the concentration of most of its population near the ocean have made coastwise shipping very important to the region. Much of the trade between the countries is carried by ocean vessels, and some of the nations have sizable merchant marines. Argentina's state-owned fleet, totaling about 1 million tons, visits most of the other Latin American ports, as well as those of many other nations.

As in the case of usable rivers, Latin America has also been noticeably shortchanged in the possession of good natural harbors. At most of the ports on the west coast, ships are forced to anchor in the open ocean a mile or more offshore and load or unload their cargoes by means of lighters—a slow, expensive, and sometimes risky undertaking. In striking contrast is the magnificent harbor of Rio de Janeiro, considered one of the finest in the world. Yet its value as a harbor is greatly diminished by the high mountains which literally rise out of the ocean to hem in the city and make access to the interior both difficult and costly.

Unlike Rio, Buenos Aires does not have a good natural harbor. In order for oceangoing vessels to be able to reach its artificial harbor, dredges must work constantly to maintain a channel across the shallow mudbank of the Plata. Despite this disadvantage, however, Buenos Aires has become the leading port in Latin America. It was established on a strategic site that could benefit from the large inland area served by the Paraná-Paraguay River, which virtually assured its becoming one of the important ports of the world.

Roads

Roads are another main means of transportation. When the early conquerors reached the Andes, they found that the Incas, like the Romans, had magnificent roads to all parts of their far-flung empire. Easy, rapid communication was an important technique of political control; and a swift courier service, maintained by relays of runners, interlaced the country to carry reports and orders. Gaping gorges and raging rapids were easily crossed by bridges built of wood or bamboo suspended from dizzy heights by liana vines. Not appreciating the value of the Inca roads, the conquerors let them deteriorate into complete ruin; travel in the area was not as safe or as fast again until the advent of the airplane.

The construction of highways in modern times has been handicapped by the same geographic obstacles that made the building of railroads so difficult and expensive; consequently, the area is deficient in good roads too. It has only about 20,000 miles of paved road, compared with approximately 300,000 miles in the United States; an additional 150,000 miles are regarded as all-weather roads. Large areas in the region have no roads at all, and in many instances the roads duplicate and compete with existing rail lines instead of taking care of areas not served by trains. Along with its small road mileage, the region has relatively few motor vehicles—only about a million and a half as compared with about 65 million in the United States.

In the past two decades great strides have been made in the building of new roads, which today has a high priority on the region's program of economic development. Indicative of the progress being made is Argentina's ambitious ten-year program, scheduled for completion in 1969, which will give the nation an additional 12,000 miles of new, modern roads.

Since such programs are very expensive, the countries are able to undertake them only with the assistance of large loans obtained from international and foreign agencies. In 1960 and 1961 sizable loans for roads were made by the International Bank for Reconstruction and Development to Chile, Colombia, Panama, Peru, and Venezuela. The Export-Import Bank has also aided in the construction program, and the very first loan of the newly established International Development Association, to Honduras in May 1961, was an interest-free, "soft" loan to extend the nation's roads.

The new roads are proving most beneficial. Those constructed across the Andes into eastern Bolivia, Colombia, and Peru have opened up large virgin tracts whose fertile soil attracts the landless peons spilling over from the high, crowded valleys and whose rich resources greatly increase the national wealth, promising a better life for all. As the roads reach out into new areas, they also stimulate industry by expanding the national market and aid in national unification by facilitating intercourse between formerly isolated regions.

One road of especial interest to us is the Pan-American Highway which extends from Laredo, Texas, in the north to Puerto Montt, Chile, in the south and to Buenos Aires, Montevideo, and Rio de Janeiro in the east, connecting all the capitals of continental Latin America. When completed, this highway is expected to enable tourists to travel freely between the countries, thus providing a powerful stimulus to mutual understanding and hemispheric solidarity.

Airplanes

One of the first successful airlines in the world was established in Colombia in 1920 by an Austro-German group. Since then, airlines, whose main routes and distances are shown in Figure 1-4, have been the fastest-growing form of transportation in Latin America. The region is a natural

FIGURE 1-4

MAIN AIRWAY SYSTEMS AND COMPARATIVE DISTANCES

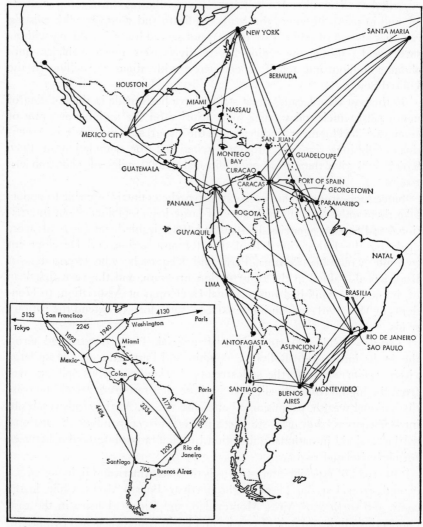

SOURCE: *Center of Intercultural Formation* (CIF) *Study No. 1,* pp. 32, 105. Reproduced by permission.

proving ground for airplanes. "The great distances," said Simon G. Hanson, "meager development of surface transportation, physical barriers to construction of surface facilities, high cost and poor service of existing transportation forms . . . all helped to promote air-mindedness."[26]

The advent of the plane was revolutionary in Latin America, as elsewhere, only more so. A small, level clearing sufficed for takeoffs and landings, without the laborious, backbreaking, or dangerous toil needed to hang a puny railroad line foot by foot onto an Andean precipice—or hewing, clawing, or fighting through a tropical jungle, either. With their three-dimensional simplicity of operation, airplanes take up the challenge of topographical obstacles, shrink distances, and whittle down barriers to man-sized proportions, opening up completely new horizons and bringing all Latin America much closer together. Until the coming of the plane, if you wanted to travel in Peru from Lima to Iquitos, you had to endure a two months' sea voyage around Cape Horn or through the Panama Canal, and then a long river trip of 2,000 miles up the Amazon. Today, you can board a plane in Lima and step off in Iquitos just four hours later.

Although planes carry most of the passenger traffic, their value for carrying freight has been lessened by the high rates they have to charge, rates that make them hardly competitive with other common carriers. According to an analysis made in Central America, the rates charged by such carriers for general commodities per ton-mile has been estimated as follows: $0.845 for interior air transport, $0.65 for inland water, $0.086 for domestic rail traffic, $0.116 for motor transport on the Inter-American Highway, and $0.175 on other roads.[27]

Comparatively a very expensive means of moving freight, air transportation has proved useful mainly for carrying high-value loads that can bear the high charge. Since these constitute such a small volume, freight transported by air is very small in volume compared with that transported by other carriers. In Argentina, while the airways carried only 11,383 tons of cargo in 1958, the railways, in 1959, carried 10,377,000 tons.

Although at a rate disadvantage, planes have proved themselves best as cargo carriers serving areas that are inaccessible by conventional means of transportation. For these areas, airplanes seem the perfect answer. Casting their punctual shadows on jade forests or opal heights that have never known the feet of men, they vie with the condors for use of the rarefied air space, swooping down and landing atop a mountain crag where a village perches with its head in the clouds. There is no road of any kind to the village. The Indian living there would be shocked at the sight of an automobile, for he has never seen one. Yet the sight of a plane is old hat to him. He may hop one every morning to get to his work on a neigh-

---

[26] Simon G. Hanson, *Economic Development in Latin America* (Washington, D.C.: Inter-American Affairs Press, 1951), p. 334.

[27] *Ibid.*, pp. 339–40.

boring height a few minutes away, a trip that by foot or muleback would take days, perhaps weeks.

In these lofty regions of the Andes, many villages and towns have come into existence as a result of the airplane and can endure only with its help. They depend on it for practically everything, even their sustenance. In addition to the passengers, the planes are apt to carry a motley cargo, including ducks and chickens, sheep and goats, llamas and burros.

Years ago pilots in Brazil drew the line at carrying certain things on their planes. Sometimes a native would board a plane, carrying a baby boa constrictor ten feet or so long to sell to a buyer for a zoo. "The pilots got to the point where they flatly refused to carry them unless they were boxed. They didn't like the idea of a boa constrictor chasing around loose in their planes."[28]

EFFECTS OF TOPOGRAPHY

Latin America's mountains may be awe-inspiring to the tourists, its jungles a delight to the naturalists, and its deserts a challenge to the meteorologists, but they have played havoc with the region's political, economic, and social development, which depends so largely upon ease of transportation and communication.

The adverse topography and difficulties of transportation have greatly affected the distribution of the population, causing fragmentation and scattering the numerous fragments, large and small, helter-skelter throughout the country. The main fragments are usually the capital of the nation, the leading seaport, an industrial center or two, and a few, very few, smaller cities and towns. Often the capital overshadows all the other urban areas—sometimes the rest of the country as well.

In most of the nations, a large part of the population is splintered into thousands of tiny villages of only several hundred people. Life there is extremely rudimentary. The little village

has almost nothing that identifies it with the modern world. . . . It has no Spanish, for the people speak *Quechua* [or other Indian dialect]; it has no newspaper for the people are illiterate; it has no books; it may have no school. The people are barefooted or wear homemade sandals; they sleep on the floor; they carry their burdens on their own backs; they have no modern tools; they have few animals. They have retained many of their ancient family customs, such as trial marriage. They may work their land in common if they have any land . . . the individual living in one of these communities belongs to a society and is related through an extended family which will include almost every member of the community.[29]

---

[28] Kathleen McLaughlin, *New Life in Old Lands* (New York: Dodd, Mead & Co., 1954), pp. 132–33.

[29] Frank Tannenbaum, "Toward an Appreciation of Latin America," *The United States and Latin America* (ed. Herbert L. Matthews) (The American Assembly) (2d ed.; New York: Columbia University Press, 1963), pp. 14–15 and 17.

Isolated as the village is, the cleavage between it and the city is almost complete. There is very little rapport between them. City is city and village is village, and it seems that never the twain shall meet.

In fact, the village, a microcosm in itself, has very few contacts with the outside world. Almost completely self-sufficient, it produces practically all the food it eats, the clothing that it wears, and the building materials and furnishings for its homes. It therefore has very little intercourse with the capital of the province or the nation; it knows little about these faraway places, and cares even less.

Isolated from the cities and towns, the many villages stand aloof and detached even from one another. The intervening mountains or jungles are difficult to traverse; much greater barriers, however, are the differences in customs and ideas. In fact, a villager would be most hesitant to forsake the shelter and security of his own group and migrate to another village. For there he would be suspiciously regarded as a stranger; he might not even be allowed to stay.

Topographical obstacles and transportation difficulties, in addition to causing fragmentation of the populace into many small isolated communities, have been primarily responsible for regionalism in Latin America. The provinces or states within a nation are often of less importance than its main regions. These usually have marked differences from one another, and distinctive characteristics which the inhabitants are very proud of. In fact, the inhabitants may feel greater loyalty to the region than they do to the nation. As a result of this loyalty and pride, regions may be very jealous of each other—a jealousy which often leads to keen rivalry, fierce competition, and sometimes outright antagonism.

With these many complications, it is no wonder that topographical obstacles and transportation difficulties have had a great impact on the economic, cultural, and political life of Latin America.

Economically, development has been hindered by the existence of numerous isolated, self-sufficient communities which contain most of the population. These communities have contributed little, if anything, to the national economy or to the advancement of industrialization, which is largely dependent on a wide consumer market.

Culturally too, the effects have been adverse. The isolation of many small communities with a mulish resistance to change of any kind has in the past been a great hindrance to the cultural progress of a nation. Although they account for most of its illiteracy, such communities often opposed the establishment of schools, fearing that education would undermine their local allegiance, traditions, and values.

Politically, loyalty to the region has impeded the development of stable national government, siphoning off loyalty from the nation as a whole. Ruling families or local bosses have been exalted at the expense of strong national leaders and national political parties. And regional antagonisms have sometimes erupted with a fury that convulsed the nation in bloody revolution.

All this is changing, slowly and laboriously. But in view of the many adverse effects of topography on the society, it is easy to see why Latin Americans sometimes say, "We are prisoners of our geography."

SUGGESTED READINGS

ARCINIEGAS, GERMÁN (ed.). *The Green Continent: A Comprehensive View of Latin America by Its Leading Writers.* Trans. HARRIET DE ONÍS and others. Part I. New York: Alfred A. Knopf, Inc., 1944.

BATES, MARSTON. *Where Winter Never Comes: A Study of Man and Nature in the Tropics,* chaps. vi–xiv. New York: Charles Scribner's Sons, 1952.

BENHAM, F., AND HOLLEY, H. A. *A Short Introduction to the Economy of Latin America,* chaps. iv–vi. Royal Institute of International Affairs. New York: Oxford University Press, 1960.

BUTLAND, GILBERT J. *Latin America: A Regional Geography.* New York: John Wiley & Sons, Inc., 1960.

CLINE, HOWARD F. *Mexico: Revolution to Evolution: 1940–1960,* chaps. iv–vi and xxix. Royal Institute of International Affairs. New York: Oxford University Press, 1962.

CUTRIGHT, PAUL RUSSELL. *The Great Naturalists Explore South America.* New York: The Macmillan Company, 1940.

FURTADO, CELSO. *The Economic Growth of Brazil: A Survey from Colonial to Modern Times,* Part III. Trans. RICARDO W. DE AGUIAR AND ERIC CHARLES DRYSDALE. Berkeley: University of California Press, 1963.

HANSON, SIMON G. *Economic Development in Latin America,* chaps. 3 and 11. Washington, D.C.: Inter-American Affairs Press, 1951.

INTERNATIONAL LABOUR OFFICE. *Indigenous Peoples: Living and Working Conditions of Aboriginal Populations in Independent Countries,* chap. vi, "Alcoholism and Cocoaism in South America." Studies and Reports, New Series, No. 35, Geneva, Switzerland, 1953.

INTERNATIONAL BANK FOR RECONSTRUCTION AND DEVELOPMENT. *The Economic Development of Venezuela,* chaps. 1, 8, 11–13. Baltimore: Johns Hopkins Press, 1961.

———. *The Basis of a Development Program for Colombia: Report of a Mission,* chaps. vii, viii, xx, xxi. Washington, D.C., 1950.

JAMES, PRESTON E. *Latin America.* 3rd ed.; New York: The Odyssey Press, Inc., 1959.

KALIJARVI, THORSTEN V. *Central America: Land of Lords and Lizards,* chap. 2. Princeton, N.J.: D. Van Nostrand Co., Inc., 1962.

LEONARD, OLEN E. *Bolivia: Land, People and Institutions,* chap. i. Washington, D.C.: The Scarecrow Press, Inc., 1952.

MAY, STACY (dir.), *et al. Costa Rica: A Study in Economic Development,* chaps. 5 and 7. New York: Twentieth Century Fund, 1952.

MONGE, CARLOS. *Acclimatization in the Andes.* Trans. DONALD F. BROWN. Baltimore: Johns Hopkins Press, 1948.

ODELL, PETER R. "Oil and State in Latin America," *International Affairs,* Vol. 40, No. 4 (October, 1964), pp. 659–73.

OSBORNE, HAROLD. *Bolivia: A Land Divided*, pp. 1–43; 71–82. Royal Institute of International Affairs. New York: Oxford University Press, 1954.

OWENS, R. J. *Peru*, pp. 1–6; 114–32. Royal Institute of International Affairs. New York: Oxford University Press, 1963.

SCHURZ, WILLIAM LYTLE. *Brazil: The Infinite Country*, chaps. 1 and 2. New York: E. P. Dutton & Co., Inc., 1961.

——. *This New World: The Civilization of Latin America*, chap. i. New York: E. P. Dutton & Co., Inc., 1954.

STARK, HARRY. *Social and Economic Frontiers in Latin America*, chaps. 17, 19, and 20. 2d ed. Dubuque, Ia.: W. C. Brown Co., 1963.

TAYLOR, CARL C. *Rural Life in Argentina*, chaps. i and ii. Baton Rouge, La.: Louisiana State University Press, 1948.

WAGLEY, CHARLES. *An Introduction to Brazil*, chaps. 1 and 2. New York: Columbia University Press, 1963.

WHETTEN, NATHAN L. *Guatemala: The Land and the People*, chap. 1. Caribbean Series, 4. New Haven, Conn.: Yale University Press, 1961.

——. *Rural Mexico*, chap. i. Chicago: University of Chicago Press, 1948.

WILGUS, A. CURTIS (ed.). *The Caribbean: Venezuelan Development; A Case History*, Part I. The Caribbean Conference Series, 1, Vol. XIII. Gainesville, Fla.: University of Florida Press, 1963.

——. *The Development of Hispanic America*, chap. i. New York: Farrar & Rinehart, Inc., 1941.

WOLF, ERIC R. *Sons of the Shaking Earth*, chap. i. Chicago: University of Chicago Press, 1959.

WYTHE, GEORGE. *Industry in Latin America*, pp. 29–40. 2d ed. New York: Columbia University Press, 1949.

CHAPTER 2

THE PEOPLE:
Demographic Potpourri of a Society in Ferment

THE REGION'S towering peaks, overwhelming jungles, and spacious plains provide a vivid setting for the drama that is Latin America. Equally interesting and picturesque are the people who live in the 20 republics, numbering about 190 million, or 8 percent of the total population of the world. Brazil has by far the largest number, 70 million; Mexico is next, with 30 million; and Panama is the smallest, with only 1 million.

Considering the large size of the region, its population is relatively small. In fact, it has the lowest density of any major region except Africa and Australia. In 1958 the density was estimated to be 24 persons per square mile, compared with 43 for the world as a whole, 57 for the United States, and 195 for Europe exclusive of Russia. In Latin America the density varies considerably among the 20 nations; Bolivia, with only 8 persons per square mile, has plenty of elbow room, but El Salvador, with 315 persons per square mile, represents one of the most densely populated areas in the world. Figure 2–1 gives the density and spatial distribution of population.

Representing three of the races of mankind—Caucasian, Indian, and Negro—the people of Latin America range in color from alabaster white to bronze red to jet black, with every conceivable variation in between. In some nations the population is decidedly homogeneous: Haiti is approximately 90 percent Negro with most of the rest of the population Negroid; Guatemala is almost 60 percent Indian and 25 percent mestizo; and Argentina is approximately 85 percent white—"the only white country south of Canada," Argentines sometimes like to boast. In striking contrast to these nations is Brazil, whose population is one of the most heterogeneous of all. It is 17 percent Negro, 20 percent mulatto, 8 percent "mixed" (including Indians, Orientals, and many others), and 55 percent

FIGURE 2–1

DENSITY AND SPATIAL DISTRIBUTION OF POPULATION

UNITED STATES 42

Monterrey

Havana

MEXICO 43   CUBA 146   DOMINCAN REPUBLIC 149

HONDURAS 42

GUATEMALA 84   NICARAGUA 24
EL SALVADOR 315

Caracas

COSTA RICA 55   Panama
PANAMA 35   VENEZUELA   GUIANAS
   Bogota   13

COLOMBIA

ECUADOR 9

BRAZIL 19   Recife

Lima   Sao Salvador

PERU 21   BOLIVIA
   8
PARAGUAY 11

CHILE 25   Rio De Janeiro
   Sao Paulo

• 500,000 TO 1 MILLION

Porto Alegre

Santiago

● 1 TO 2 MILLION   URUGUAY 37
   Montevideo
   Buenos Aires

● 2 TO 3 MILLION

● 3 TO 4 MILLION

● 4 TO 5 MILLION

ARGENTINA 19

SOURCE: *Center of Intercultural Formation* (CIF) *Study No. 1,* pp. 57, 59. Reproduced by permission.

white—a veritable demographic potpourri. The ethnic composition of each country is shown in Figure 2–2.

THE WHITES

In general, each of the three racial groups lives in the area most congenial to its physical well-being, culture, and tradition. The whites inhabit Costa Rica and the southern temperate region of South America, consisting

FIGURE 2–2

ETHNIC COMPOSITION OF EACH COUNTRY

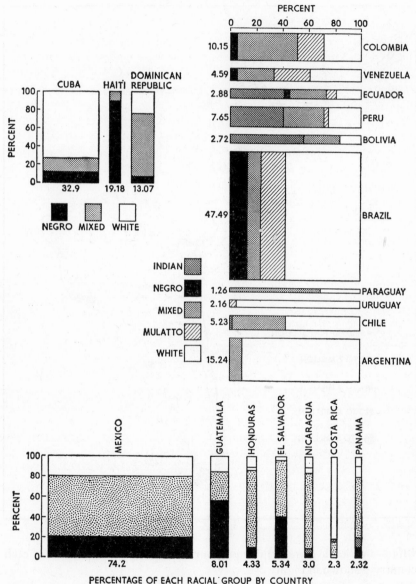

SOURCE: *Center of Intercultural Formation* (CIF) *Study No. 1*, p. 76. Reproduced by permission.

of Argentina, Uruguay, southern Brazil, and Chile. In these areas the climate, crops, and social patterns were not suitable for importing and using large numbers of Negro slaves as in eastern Brazil and the Caribbean nations.

The scattered Indian groups in these countries disappeared long ago. In Uruguay they were assimilated into the predominantly white population. In Costa Rica they succumbed to disease, and the Spanish settlers, instead of importing Negro slaves for the large estates, evolved into a community of mainly small farmers.

In Argentina, after a long series of Indian depredations and killings, the Red Men were exterminated by a military campaign that began in 1879. Its slogan, according to its leader, General Julio A. Roca was, "For the Argentine Republic there is no frontier in the West and the South than the peaks of the Andes and the Ocean." The mere 2,000 Indians that survived the fierce war of extermination were captured, shipped to Buenos Aires, and imprisoned or indentured as domestic servants.

In Chile the whites encountered the roughest going in all Latin America. The Araucanian Indian defiantly risked extermination to avoid the shame and ignominy of being conquered.

His spirit was indomitable. Said an Araucanian prisoner to the Spaniards:

I am your captive, . . . [but] the Araucanian is never subdued. He is born free. You may put chains on his body, but you cannot put chains on his spirit. You may kill our warriors and make our country a desert; but you will marry our women, and your children will have the strong blood of the Araucanian. . . . The Araucanian has always triumphed, and he will still triumph. . . . You may tear us in pieces with your horses; you may burn us with hot irons; you may pull out our tongues by the roots; but the Araucanian will not be conquered.[1]

Fighting with savage ferocity and a contempt for death, the Araucanians made the Spaniards pay dearly for their victories. According to General Indalicio Tellez, the campaign against them cost Spain the lives of more than 42,000 soldiers up until the seventeenth century alone. This was a heavier loss of life than Spain suffered in the discovery and conquest of all the rest of Latin America. The Araucanians continued to inhabit the southern half of the country until 1883, when they were assigned certain lands in perpetuity, similar to the reservations of the United States.

With the Indians largely or completely exterminated and with only a few Negroes imported, the population of these countries is predominantly white because of intensive emigration from Europe. From southern Europe came some 5 million Italians, about 4 million Spaniards, and a little more than 2 million Portuguese. Of the northern European nations, Germany supplied the largest number, which accounts today for the predominantly German populations in southern Brazil and in parts of southern Chile.

These and other groups of hopeful immigrants packed the steerage of passenger boats or worked their way over on freighters to pioneer a new

---

[1] In Bernard Moses, *The Spanish Dependencies in South America* (2 vols.; New York: Harper & Bros., 1914), Vol. I, pp. 358–59.

world frontier—South America. Ships from the west brought Chinese and Japanese to settle in Peru and other nations on the Pacific coast and also in Brazil. Ships from the east brought a large variety of nationals that included the English, Scotch, Irish, Poles, Ukranians, Yugoslavs, French, Swiss, Dutch, Syrians, Lebanese, and others.

There were even a number of disappointed Confederates who went to Brazil, still a slave country, after the South was defeated in the Civil War. There they encountered many perplexing problems, such as the time a large group was expectantly awaiting the arrival of the new United States consul, just appointed by the new Democratic president of the United States, Grover Cleveland. The new consul, they reasoned, must also be a good Democrat, and, of course, white too.

The afternoon he arrived, the entire population of the colony was anxiously waiting at the station platform, with a southern colonel at the head of the deputation. The train rolled up, a first-class compartment door opened, a gentleman stepped out with a suitcase and walked up to the colonel with outstretched hand. It was the consul, but a consul as black as the ace of spades. The colonel rose nobly to the occasion and shook the hand of the consul. He and the other southerners gave the official the time of his life, but when he departed they vowed that never again would they trust a Democratic administration.[2]

The huge swell of immigration, consisting of perplexed Confederates and many others, hardly got started until the middle of the nineteenth century. All during the colonial era, the colonies were practically off limits to Europeans, except those from the Iberian peninsula. And for several decades after independence, the nations were in such political and economic chaos that would-be immigrants were deterred from moving there. But as stability and order were gradually achieved, the immigration to the new world that began as a mere trickle, no bigger than a tiny streamlet that forms the headwaters of the Paraná River, soon picked up volume and shortly became a mighty flood of humanity that poured over the rich farmlands of the pampas. Up to World War II, more than 12 million immigrants entered the area. At least half of them, between 6 and 7 million in all, settled in Argentina, and most of the rest settled in southern Brazil and Uruguay.

Bringing with them their skills, their strong arms, and their eagerness to work, the newcomers contributed much to the prosperity and development of their adopted nations. The Italians for the most part soon became assimilated, transferring their allegiance and loyalty to their new-found home. Most of the other nationalities in time became assimilated too. But there are notable exceptions. The Japanese in Brazil remain separate and organized; and the German colony south of Valdivia, Chile, numbering some 30,000 to 40,000 persons, remains an isolated economic and cultural group, retaining its German language and customs.

---

[2] L. E. Elliott, *Brazil: Today and Tomorrow* (New York, 1917), pp. 65–66.

It is understandable that the newcomers would affiliate with their own national groups and also seek to preserve their traditional customs and values. There is a distinct danger, however, of these groups becoming "cultural cysts." Their failure to melt into the proverbial melting pot and the retaining of their native customs, values, and even political ideologies has strongly influenced the policies of their adopted countries. Some of the emigrants from Italy prior to World War II, as well as many of those from Germany and Japan, were at best only partially assimilated. Susceptible to the totalitarian doctrines of fascism and nazism, they were strongly pro-Axis and vehemently anti-United States. Because of immigrant and other influences, Argentina did not break diplomatic relations with Germany until 1944, but permitted German agents to operate freely in the nation, transmitting vital bits of military intelligence that resulted in the loss of many American ships, and many lives too.

Argentina's domestic policy likewise felt the impact of its many unassimilated immigrants. In the opinion of Ricardo Rojas, an Argentine intellectual, the immigrant hordes were responsible for weakening the very moral fiber of the nation. They came to Argentina solely to make money, and their "get-rich-quick" attitude tainted the national life with their materialistic and unhealthy values. These values, Rojas was convinced, had paved the way for Perón from as far back as the turn of the century.[3]

THE INDIANS

Decidedly in second place now, but earlier the FFV's of Latin America, are the Indians, who are believed to be of Asiatic origin and to have crossed over to Alaska from Siberia many centuries ago when the two continents were connected by a land bridge.

Their number is a matter of conjecture, depending primarily on how you define Indian. If your definition is based on physical characteristics only, as color of the skin, texture of the hair, or shape of the head, you will arrive at a relatively high figure, close to 30 million. If, however, you classify as a mestizo every Indian who has picked up a few words of Spanish, wears sandals, and has adopted some of the customs of the whites you will get a much smaller figure, closer to 14 million.

Two of the recent censuses of Mexico show how widely the figures may vary within a nation, depending on the criteria that are used. In 1921 when "Indian-ness" was based on physical characteristics alone, more than 4 million persons, approximately 24 percent of the population, were classified as Indians. In 1940, however, when Indian-ness was defined in terms of social characteristics, the number dropped drastically to less than a

---

[3] Lewis Hanke, *South America* (Princeton, N.J.: D. Van Nostrand Co., Inc., 1959), p. 66.

million and a half, approximately 7½ percent of the population. In the determination of the number of Indians in the Latin-American nations today, the cultural yardstick is the one that is usually used.

Where do these Indians live? Mostly in Mexico, Guatemala, Honduras and El Salvador, Bolivia, Peru, Ecuador, and Paraguay. Almost no Indians, on the other hand, are found in the insular republics of Cuba, Haiti, and the Dominican Republic or in the predominantly white areas of South America. A few of them are found in the remaining countries.

The reaction of the Indians to the Spaniard's culture and domination is one of the most significant influences in Latin America today. In a few areas they are still wholly beyond the reach of white culture and rule. Such a group is the Camayuras of Brazil, who live near the geographical center of South America in the midst of the dense jungle of the Mato Grosso (thick forest). Most of this country is so wild it is still uncharted and unexplored. Secluded in their isolated refuge, the Camayuras maintain a way of life as primitive as that of the Stone Age. Indeed, neighboring tribes are so hostile to white men that they have been known to shoot arrows at low-flying planes.[4]

Some of the other Indians, as the Otavalos who live on the lower slopes of Mount Imbabura in Ecuador, have gradually adopted many of the ways of the white society but without discarding the values of their ancient culture. The Otavalos fare well from their thriving small farms and a prosperous textile industry carried on in their homes. They are also learning Spanish and seeking an education when schools are available. The achievements of these self-reliant citizens are lyrically described in *The Awakening Valley*, whose authors believe that the success of the Otavalos "could be shared throughout the Andes, for their vitality is born of universal energies."[5]

Most of the Indians, however, react quite differently. Except for those who have moved to urban areas, they shun any association with whites and steadfastly resist their influence.

It is difficult to blame them. Over the centuries of Spanish rule, they have been brutally and heartlessly exploited. Because of this, and because of neglect by the rest of society, the Indian adamantly refuses to be Europeanized. Determined to remain an Indian in his culture and way of life, he clams up in his shell—his native community in the sierra. When necessary to escape the influence of the advancing intruder, he "has climbed to altitudes so high and terrains so barren that white exploiters have found it unprofitable to follow."[6]

Although the high Andes were distasteful to the Spaniards, the Indians have felt as much at home there as Brer Rabbit in the briar patch. Wor-

---

4 "Stone Age Brazilians," *Life*, Vol. 25 (September 20, 1948), pp. 88–91.
5 John Collier, Jr., and Aníbal Buitrón, *The Awakening Valley* (Chicago: University of Chicago Press, 1949), p. 2.
6 W. Stanley Rycroft (ed.), *Indians of the High Andes* (New York: Committee on Cooperation with Latin America, 1946), p. 81.

shipping the Sun God, their ancestors centuries ago ascended the heights to be nearer to him. In the high valleys or on steep mountain slopes, their civilization rose and flourished. With their scientific farming, they could produce enough on one-half acre of land to feed a family. Good conservationists that they were, they built up the soil instead of depleting it.[7] Thus the Indians have become children of the heights, even developing a barrel-like chest with a larger lung capacity to compensate for the lack of oxygen in the rarefied atmosphere.

In the Spaniard's world but not of it, the rural Indian has clung tenaciously and successfully to his ancestral heritage. According to Frank Tannenbaum,

. . . wherever the Indian managed to retain his land and his own community, he remained an Indian, keeping his language, his customs, his family organization, his religious rituals even if he became a Catholic, using the same tools, working the land much the same way as before the conquest, eating the same food, and living in the same kind of house. . . . The result was a nation within a nation, a culture within a culture, two peoples, living in proximity but belonging to two different universes.[8]

As a result of his self-chosen isolation, the Indian in effect is not a citizen or member of the national society. He is not the least interested in politics; in fact, he feels an intense dislike for government. To him, government is simply the tax collector who chisels in on his meager living, or the law who slaps him in the calaboose when he gets too much *chicha* under his belt. But even if the Indians desired to participate in the political life of the nation, they would often be prevented by law from doing so. Thus, they are barred from voting by literacy qualifications in many of the constitutions. Ecuador's Constitution of 1946 contains such a qualification, and since an estimated 95 percent of the nation's Indians are illiterate, they are legally excluded from the suffrage.[9]

In only two countries of Latin America, Mexico and Bolivia, has the Indian really come into his own. Since Mexico's 1917 revolution, he has had a recognized, influential, even honored role in society. He is "a symbol of oppression, and the redemption of the Indian has been a major theme of the Mexican revolution. In sentiment most Mexicans identify their nation with the Indian rather than the Spanish heritage."[10] And since Bolivia's 1952 revolution that completely swept aside the old order, the Indian there too for the first time stands erect and holds up his head in

---

[7] Julian H. Steward and Louis C. Faron, *Native Peoples of South America* (New York: McGraw-Hill Book Co., Inc., 1959), p. 121.

[8] Frank Tannenbaum, "Toward an Appreciation of Latin America," *The United States and Latin America* (ed. Herbert L. Matthews) (American Assembly) (2d ed.; New York: Columbia University Press, 1963), pp. 19–20.

[9] George I. Blanksten, *Ecuador: Constitutions and Caudillos* (Berkeley: University of California Press, 1951), p. 19.

[10] Oscar Lewis, "Mexico Since Cárdenas," *Social Change in Latin America Today* (Council on Foreign Relations) (New York: Harper & Bros., 1960), p. 290.

human dignity, a respected member of society who owns land and participates in the government of his country.

Unlike Bolivia and Mexico, however, most of the other countries with large numbers of Indians continue to ignore or neglect them. However, occasionally the role of the Indian and his value to society are the subjects of bitter debate. Some are convinced that a terrible injustice has been done to him—that if helped and given a chance, he will be a respectable, responsible, and self-reliant member of society. Others, however, even go so far as to hold him responsible for the failure of the nations to achieve their desired progress. "The red man gave up the struggle centuries ago. . . ." said Gabriel René-Moreno. "The Inca Indian is useless. But by some monstrous deformity the Indian is indeed a living force . . . a passive, inert mass, a stone blocking the viscera of the social program."[11]

Whatever has been responsible for their plight, the presence of large Indian populations not assimilated into the Spanish society and culture is one of the greatest problems many of the countries face, a problem that casts a shadow over the societies of Latin America even as some of the awesome mountains cast a shadow over the lands they inhabit.

THE NEGROES

Although the Negroes are the johnnies-come-lately of Latin America, their cultural and biological influence is strongly felt over much of the region.

In colonial days, Negroes in large numbers were found not only in the hot tropical areas but also in many of the other regions. Venezuela with a population of approximately a million is estimated to have had 72,000 Negro slaves and 400,000 mulattoes, who constituted more than 47 percent of the populace. Chile, Ecuador, and Colombia were other areas with large numbers of Africans.[12]

Their number today is variously estimated at between 25 and 30 million, figures that are at best only approximations, for one encounters many difficulties in trying accurately to ascertain the number. Census records are notoriously unreliable, often incomplete or not up to date. Sometimes the census questionnaire is purposely designed to keep from showing the nation's racial composition. Since 1890, the year after the Negro slaves in Brazil were given their freedom, the censuses there have contained no questions whatever relating to racial background. Still another difficulty is the lack of a uniformly accepted definition as to who is a Negro or mulatto; as in the case of the Indian, this depends mainly on the criterion followed, whether physiological or cultural.

Whatever their number, Negroes constitute a large and important part

---

[11] In Lewis Hanke, *op. cit.*, p. 135.
[12] Frank Tannenbaum, *Slave and Citizen: The Negro in the Americas* (New York: Alfred A. Knopf, Inc., 1947), p. 13.

of the population in many of the nations. Brought over from Africa in one of the greatest forced migrations in history, their habitat in the New World is usually the warm tropical areas similar to their native land. Brazil has the largest number, probably 20 million or so, or about a third of the population. Haiti, with a population of more than 3 million, has the largest percentage of Negroes, being almost entirely Negroid. Large numbers are also found in Cuba, the Dominican Republic, Colombia, Venezuela, Mexico, and Panama.

Unlike his colored brother in the United States, the Negro in Latin America has been assimilated to a remarkable degree, especially in Brazil. This has been accomplished peacefully and naturally. No Civil War with its tragic hangover of hate and bitterness . . . no lynchings or segregation . . . no Supreme Court decisions . . . no freedom rides, sit-ins, wade-ins, kneel-ins, or voter registration drives. In Latin America "there was never the question that so agitated people . . . in the United States—the danger of emancipation, the lack of fitness for freedom," says Frank Tannenbaum. "There was never the horrifying spectacle so often evoked in the United States of admitting a morally inferior and therefore by implication a biologically inferior people into the body politic on equal terms."[13]

Among the several factors that have greatly aided assimilation in Brazil are the many opportunities for obtaining freedom; the extensive miscegenation that has taken place; the temperament, physical courage, and ability of the Negroes; and the liberal definition of "white" as applied to race.

Regarding opportunities for freedom, manumission existed from the earliest days, and accounted for the large number of freed men of color. According to some estimates there were actually more Negro freemen than slaves, thanks to the many ways by which freedom could be attained. A slave could buy his liberty by paying the original purchase price. Sometimes liberty was a gift bestowed by the owner either during his lifetime or upon his death. Often the fathers of illegitimate offspring freed their children at the baptismal ceremony, or the owners of female slaves "freed the womb" of servitude, assuring freedom to their offspring.

Manumission was sometimes granted as a reward for faithful service; from 1864 to 1870, many of the male slaves in Brazil were granted their freedom for serving in the prolonged bloody war against Paraguay. But the Negro women had to earn their freedom the hard way. Under the law they were automatically free after rearing ten children;[14] the lucky tenth child was their passport to freedom.

Assimilation by the process of gradualism was furthered primarily by miscegenation, the great social equalizer. The Portuguese pioneer who

---

[13] *Ibid.*, p. 100.

[14] For the many ways by which a slave could obtain his freedom, see Donald Pierson, *Negroes in Brazil: A Study of Race Contact at Bahia* (Chicago: University of Chicago Press, 1942), pp. 51–52.

sought his fortune in the new world usually came without his wife and was apt to pick his Negro slaves, particularly the females, on criteria quite different from those followed by the English colonist in North America. The Englishman, who brought along his wife to be his companion, selected his slaves to work in the field; they had to have plenty of brute strength and stamina—and be cheap.[15]

But the Portuguese colonist had other things in mind. Besides needing all kinds of skilled workers and specialists for his society, including ironworkers, mining technicians, cattle raisers, schoolmasters, and priests, he also needed attractive females—one might end up as the mistress of his house. In his ads for Negroes that he wished to buy, he was unabashedly explicit in his preference for physical attractiveness. He wanted females who were tall, well-built, "comely of face and body," and "with all the teeth in front."[16]

In meeting these exacting requirements, it was no accident that the Portuguese colonists "skimmed off the top-soil of the African people."

Miscegenation in Latin America was basically different from the intermingling that took place in the Old South. There, in spite of stern laws and strong mores against fraternizing, "behind-the-barn" association was widespread. According to some estimates, not more than 10 percent of the Negroes in the United States are racially pure. Reaction to the results of illicit unions was different too. In the South a white father never recognized his illegitimate mulatto offspring but concealed it as a skeleton in the family closet. In Latin America, however, a father is usually proud of his illegitimate offspring, whether blackish, whitish, brownish, or polka dot; it is proof of his virility. Often a strong personal tie develops between the two, a tie that may afford many opportunities to the child and enable him to advance socially.

In brief, "in the United States," according to García Calderón, "union with the aborigines is regarded by the colonists with repugnance; in the south [South America] miscegenation is a great national fact; it is universal."[17]

The temperament and personality of the Negro were also favorable to his assimilation into society. Unlike the Indian, characteristically an introvert with a tendency to withdraw from contact with the European, the Negro was basically an extrovert, sociable, expansive, and easygoing. Also unlike the Indian, he was adaptable, interested in learning the language of his masters, adopting their customs and habits, and in general identifying himself with them.

His physical courage and military prowess won him great respect.

---

[15] Gilberto Freyre, *The Masters and the Slaves: a Study in the Development of Brazilian Civilization*, trans. Samuel Putnam (2d Eng. ed. rev.; New York: Alfred A. Knopf, Inc., 1956), p. 308.

[16] *Ibid.*, pp. 320–21.

[17] F. García Calderón, *Latin America: Its Rise and Progress*, trans. Bernard Miall (London: T. Fisher Unwin, 1913), p. 356.

Henrique Días, one of Brazil's two national heroes, had immortalized himself by the valor he displayed in the early colonial wars against the Dutch. Later, in the wars of independence, other Negroes valiantly aided the cause of freedom by fighting in the ranks of the armies. Still later, in the War of the Triple Alliance, they loyally volunteered in large numbers to aid Brazil in crushing Paraguay.

The Negro has also proved to be an industrious and useful member of society. In Brazil many of them were artisans and skilled workers; some became quite wealthy, owning businesses, mines, or other valuable property. Occasionally they themselves owned slaves and even invested their savings in the slave trade, sending money, tradable goods, and arms to a designated individual in Africa to "get up raids in their old homes or amongst neighboring tribes,"[18] somewhat suggestive of a second year classman at West Point who has somehow survived his freshman year and relishes hazing the plebes.

In the realm of the arts, too, the Negroes and their mulatto offspring often distinguished themselves, contributing many of the leading musicians, artists, and sculptors. The sculpture of Aleijadinho in the churches of Minas Geraes is world renowned for its unique artistry. Aleijadinho, which means "little cripple," was the nickname given Antônio Francisco Lisboa, a poor crippled mulatto. Having no hands, he had to tie the hammer and chisel to his wrists with ribbons to carve painfully and laboriously the stone shapes of angels and saints whose faces bore the mark of his suffering soul. A whole school of art developed around Aleijadinho, a tribute to his rare ability in designing churches and sculpturing.[19]

Contributing much to Brazil's dynamic, mobile society, men of color understandably had access to the culture, political offices, and social life of the country. The royal court established in the colony when Portugal was overrun by Napoleon's armies early set the example for acceptance of the darker Brazilians. Several times the emperor appointed a Negro as president of the cabinet, and at social functions too the royal family made it clear that no color bar existed. On one occasion, when a certain lady declined to dance with André Rebouças at a court ball, Princess Isabel herself danced the next waltz with him "to compensate for the affront to this illustrious man."[20]

The Negro's—especially the mulatto's—rise and acceptance in Brazilian society has also been facilitated by the definition of race. The Brazilian definition of "white" is almost as broad as the definition of "Negro" in the United States, where one drop of Negro blood, if it is known, makes a man a Negro. In Brazil, one may have decidedly Negroid features and still be accepted as white. *"Ele tem dedo na cozinha"* ("He has a finger in the kitchen"), the Brazilians may say facetiously about one suspected of

[18] Pierson, *op. cit.*, p. 68.
[19] Freyre, *op. cit.*, p. 295.
[20] Pierson, *op. cit.*, p. 170.

having Negro blood. But even if it is known that he has a close Negro ancestor, this is not likely to affect his social standing. In his tactful, "So what?" manner, the Brazilian may simply answer, "We never go very far into a person's past . . . that would be impolite."[21]

Although the Negro in Brazil is often handicapped by low income, illiteracy, and a low standard of living, he nevertheless has the opportunity to improve and advance himself—an opportunity that enables him to compete freely in the whole community. In this respect his situation is quite different from that of his racial brother in the United States, who has to be satisfied with competing and rising only within the limits of the Negro world.

Racial prejudice is common in Latin America; it exists to some degree in Brazil too. But the many contributions of the versatile Negro, brought over as a humble slave, are recognized as largely responsible for the progressive new society that Brazilians are so proud of—a society that gratefully recognizes him as "the white man's greatest and most plastic collaborator in the task of agrarian colonization." The whole society, too, feels a close affinity with him. "Every Brazilian, even the light-skinned fair-haired one," says Gilberto Freyre, "carries about with him on his soul, when not on soul and body alike . . . the shadow, or at least the birthmark, of the aborigine or the Negro."[22]

DISTRIBUTION OF POPULATION

In Latin America the population is distributed most unevenly; some areas have far too few people, others have far too many. The huge Amazon basin, almost two-thirds the size of the United States, has a population less than the Dominican Republic—too few people, in fact to develop the area economically. Haiti, on the other hand, has so many people crowded together that they cannot support themselves adequately by the agricultural economy they have to depend on for a livelihood. In the region as a whole, the population tends to be heavily concentrated in certain areas. Most of the people live in communities located near the coast, easily accessible from the sea, or in the highlands that afford a moderate climate.

Although the population of most countries is predominantly rural, the urban population since World War II has increased three times faster than the rural. While all urban areas have grown in size, the larger cities have grown much more rapidly. Today there are at least 71 cities with populations between 100,000 and 1 million—43 in South America, and 38 in Middle America. The number of such cities almost doubled between 1948 and 1958.[23]

---

21 *Ibid.*, pp. 128, 139.

22 Freyre, *op. cit.*, p. 278.

23 Preston James, *Latin America* (3rd ed.; New York: The Odyssey Press, Inc., 1959), p. 9.

In some instances the growth has been spectacular. Mexico City shot up from about 1.4 million inhabitants in 1940 to an estimated 5 million in 1963, and is now vying with Buenos Aires for the distinction of being the largest city in Latin America. There are a number of other large cities: Rio de Janeiro and São Paulo each boast of about 4 million; Santiago and Havana, approximately 2 million; and Bogotá, Caracas, Lima, and Montevideo, over 1 million.

Such statistics, impressive though they are, tell us nothing of the human drama behind them. The phenomenal growth of the cities—some of the most beautiful in the world—is a source of much pride to Latin Americans. But this growth is also the cause of many serious social problems resulting from the vast internal migration to the cities from rural areas that are burdened with poverty, illiteracy, and lack of opportunity.

The trek to the city is often the gamble of a lifetime. "Entire Indian villages," says J. Halcro Ferguson, speaking of Peru, "impelled by the poverty of their highland holdings, pack up and take train or truck, or even walk, to Lima, to them the capital of the world, where they have heard that it is possible to live like human beings. Usually they arrive with little or no money, and knowing nobody except some *compadre* (a word denoting some friendly person from outside) of whose very address they have probably only the haziest notion."[24]

They soon found out, however, that the city is far from the land of their dreams. Everything there is in short supply. There are not enough houses, not enough jobs, not enough schools. There is not enough food, not enough transportation, in fact, not enough of anything! Worst of all, the newcomers feel friendless, lonely, and bewildered in a busy, impersonal society that is too preoccupied with its own interests to know or care about their problems.

"Where do these people go?" asked an editorial in *La Prensa*, one of Lima's daily newspapers. "To fill the crime pages of the daily Press? To . . . live in the primitive and promiscuous condition of animals? . . . To crowd the tubercular wards of the hospitals? To form new gangs of juvenile delinquents? . . . To increase the population of the prisons?"[25]

Flooding the cities and seething with discontent, the newcomers are social dynamite of megaton proportions.

POPULATION TRENDS—GROWTH AND CHANGES IN COMPOSITION

The population explosion, a worldwide demographic phenomenon of our age, has greater significance for Latin America than for any other region. Its population is increasing at the prodigious rate of almost 2.8 per-

---

[24] J. Halcro Ferguson, *Latin America: the Balance of Race Redressed* (Institute of Race Relations) (New York: Oxford University Press, 1961), p. 63.

[25] *Ibid.,* p. 64.

cent a year, the highest in the world. "If our last two censuses are accurate," exclaimed one official in the Dominican Republic, "The period of gestation here is three months!"[26]

In the individual countries, the annual growth rates range from 4 percent in Costa Rica and Venezuela to 1.6 in Uruguay, as Figure 2–3 shows. The rate of increase outside Latin America is smaller, as Figure 2–4 shows.

FIGURE 2-3

POPULATION GROWTH RATES IN THE AMERICAS
(Annual Growth Rates between Last Two Censuses)

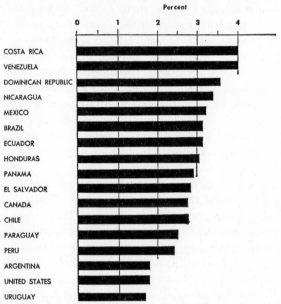

SOURCE: *Américas*, a monthly magazine published by the Pan American Union in English, Spanish, and Portuguese, July, 1964, p. 46. Reproduced by permission.

FIGURE 2-4

POPULATION GROWTH RATES OF MAJOR REGIONS OF THE FREE WORLD

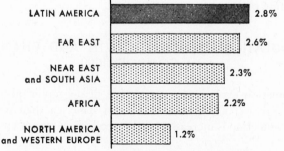

SOURCE: *Américas*, April, 1964, p. 42. Reproduced by permission.

[26] "How Many Babies Is Too Many?" *Newsweek*, July 23, 1962, p. 32.

The significance of Latin America's high rate of increase is seen by comparing its predicted growth with that of the United States. In 1964 Latin America had approximately 200 million people, about equal to the population of the United States and Canada combined. By the year 2000, however, according to a United Nations estimate, it will probably have 600 million, almost double that estimated for the United States and Canada.

This explosive growth in Latin America is primarily the result of a drastic fall in the death rate without a corresponding decline in the high birth rate. For centuries both the birth and the death rates were high. "Women gave birth to children with a frequency close to that possible in the human organism." Indeed, during the last century, the birth rate was probably as high as 40 to 50 per 1,000, and the mortality rate was almost as high; up to half of all the babies died before reaching their first birthday.[27]

The present decline in the death rate is attributable to a large number of modern advances, including better medical facilities and care, public health campaigns stressing the importance of sanitation, more adequate diets, a higher level of living for the masses, and, most important of all, better care and feeding of infants.

In time, increasing urbanization and industrialization will likely lead to lower birth rates—a trend that usually accompanies the change from an agricultural to an industrial economy. For the foreseeable future, however, no reduction is anticipated in the high birth rate or in the high annual population increase. If anything, this increase will probably go even higher as the death rate continues to decline further with improved sanitation, better medicine, and healthier diets.

The vast outpouring of children in a population that is pitifully poor, largely illiterate, and struggling to pull itself up by its bootstraps creates staggering problems. It means more mouths to feed when there is already too little to go around, more schools to build with funds already woefully inadequate.

Viewing the growth rate optimistically, some like to think that the larger population will eventually stimulate economic expansion and more fully utilize the area's potentialities. The results of such growth, however, are almost sure to be uneven. Haiti is already very overcrowded, with little likelihood of providing a desirable standard of living even for its present population, much less for the large probable future increase.

Argentina, on the other hand, would welcome a larger population. It needs millions more people to develop its expansive territory, which is equal in size to all of the United States east of the Mississippi River. When the 1960 census was taken, the population turned out to be only 20 million

---

[27] T. Lynn Smith, "Current Population Trends in Latin America," *American Journal of Sociology*, Vol. LXII (January, 1957), p. 401.

—1 million less than had been confidently expected. The population lag was caused by a sharp decline in immigration due to unsettled political and economic conditions and to a declining birth rate. The lag evoked considerable consternation. Experts doubted that the nation could even effectively carry through its present industrialization and development program without the greater growth of population that was needed.[28]

Unlike Argentina, nations that are overcrowded, poor, and have a high rate of growth will hardly welcome the multitude that is anticipated. And, thinking of Argentina's wealth but slower growth, they probably will agree that "the rich get richer and the poor get children."

The population explosion, whatever its local or general effects and whatever problems it may cause, is like an atomic detonation: once the atom is unleashed, only time can tell the full effects of the fallout.

Besides being much larger, the population of Latin America in the future will probably be quite different racially from what it is today. According to many indications, the proportion of Indians and Negroes is decreasing, while the proportion of whites is increasing. This is attributable to several causes. The upper classes have as large families as the other classes, and, what is particularly significant, with their higher standard of living and better medical care they manage to save a far greater proportion of their children. Also, the mores of Latin America that sanction extramarital relations of the male are responsible for the upper class whites' siring many of the children born to lower class women of color. "The net result of all this is that the population of Latin America is 'bleaching' rapidly. . . ."[29] The Indian population has decreased from 100 percent of the total population to only 4.58 percent, as shown by the table and graphs in Figure 2–5.

Yet in spite of all this "bleaching," the whites may yet fail to assimilate the Indians, who have managed over the centuries to maintain their own race and way of life. Like the captured Araucanian warrior, they may refuse to capitulate.

" . . . the Indian is in all probability increasing more rapidly than the urbanized population . . ." says Frank Tannenbaum. "That the Latin will ultimately absorb the American has been taken for granted from the beginning which is more than four centuries ago. And so it may prove in the end, but the end is a long way off and history has shown itself capable of many an unexpected turn."[30]

Perhaps it is too early to tell yet whether the Indians and Negroes will be bleached or whether the whites will be colored. But from many indications, the race that is emerging in Latin America today will probably be a new breed, different from any of its ancestors. It will likely be part white, part red, and with at least a little "finger in the kitchen."

[28] *New York Times*, September 24, 1961, p. 28, col. 3.
[29] Smith, *op. cit.*, p. 406.
[30] Tannenbaum, "Toward an Appreciation of Latin America," *op. cit.*, pp. 20–21.

FIGURE 2-5

RELATIVE DECREASE OF INDIAN POPULATION IN THE AMERICAS

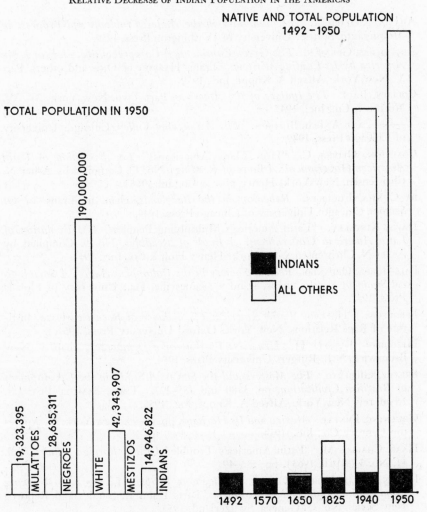

NATIVE AND TOTAL POPULATION
1492–1950

TOTAL POPULATION IN 1950

INDIANS

ALL OTHERS

MULATTOES 19,323,395
NEGROES 28,635,311
WHITE 190,000,000
MESTIZOS 42,343,907
INDIANS 14,946,822

1492 1570 1650 1825 1940 1950

CHANGE IN INDIAN POPULATION

Year	Indian Population	Increase or Decrease	Total Population	Percent Indian
1492	13,385,000		13,385,000	100
1570	10,827,150	−2,557,850	11,229,650	96.41
1650	10,035,000	− 792,150	12,411,000	80.85
1825	8,634,301	−1,400,699	34,531,536	25.10
1940	13,450,387	−4,816,086	273,659,467	4.95
1950	14,946,882	−1,496,435	326,410,029	4.58

SOURCE: Angel Rosenblat, *Poblaciones Indigenas*, p. 22, and *Center of Intercultural Formation* (CIF) *Study No. 1*, p. 73. Reproduced by permission.

SUGGESTED READINGS

ADAMS, RICHARD N. *A Community in the Andes: Problems and Progress in Muquiyauto.* Seattle: University of Washington Press, 1959.

ARCINIEGAS, GERMÁN. *The Green Continent; A Comprehensive View of Latin America by Its Leading Writers.* Trans. HARRIET DE ONÍS and others. Part V. New York: Alfred A. Knopf, Inc., 1959.

COLLIER, JOHN. *The Indians of the Americas,* Part Two. New York: W. W. Norton & Co., Inc., 1947.

———, AND ANÍBAL BUITRÓN. *The Awakening Valley.* Chicago: University of Chicago Press, 1949.

COMPTON, GEORGE C. "How Many Americans?" *The Evolution of Latin American Government: A Book of Readings,* No. 10. Compiled by Asher N. Christensen. New York: Henry Holt & Co., Inc., 1951.

DA CUNHA, EUCLIDES. *Rebellion in the Backlands,* chap. ii. Trans. of *Os Sertões.* Chicago: University of Chicago Press, 1944.

DAVIS, KINGSLEY. "Latin America's Multiplying Peoples," *The Evolution of Latin American Government: A Book of Readings,* No. 9. Compiled by Asher N. Christensen. New York: Henry Holt & Co., Inc., 1951.

FALS-BORDA, ORLANDO. *Peasant Society in the Colombian Andes; A Sociological Study of Saucío,* chaps. 4 and 9. Gainesville, Fla.: University of Florida Press, 1957.

FERGUSON, J. HALCRO. *Latin America: The Balance of Race Redressed.* Institute of Race Relations. New York: Oxford University Press, 1961.

FITZGIBBON, RUSSELL H. *Uruguay: Portrait of a Democracy,* chap. v. New Brunswick, N.J.: Rutgers University Press, 1954.

FREYRE, GILBERTO. *The Masters and the Slaves: A Study in the Development of Brazilian Civilization,* pp. 3–80 and 185–277. Trans. SAMUEL PUTNAM. 2d ed. rev. New York: Alfred A. Knopf, Inc., 1956.

GRUENING, ERNEST. *Mexico and Its Heritage,* pp. 69–90. New York: D. Appleton-Century Co., Inc., 1934.

HAAR, CHARLES M. "Latin America's Troubled Cities," *Foreign Affairs,* Vol. 41, No. 3 (April, 1963), pp. 536–49.

INTERNATIONAL LABOUR OFFICE. *Indigenous Peoples: Living and Working Conditions in Independent Countries,* Parts I and II. Studies and Reports, New Series, No. 35. Geneva, Switzerland, 1953.

KALIJARVI, THORSTEN V. *Central America: Land of Lords and Lizards,* chap. 3. Princeton, N.J.: D. Van Nostrand Co., Inc., 1962.

LEONARD, OLEN E. *Bolivia: Land, People and Institutions,* chaps. ii–iv. Washington, D.C.: The Scarecrow Press, Inc., 1952.

NELSON, LOWRY. *Rural Cuba,* chaps. ii and iv. Minneapolis: University of Minnesota Press, 1950.

OSBORNE, HAROLD. *Indians of the Andes: Aymaras and Quechuas.* Cambridge, Mass.: Harvard University Press, 1952.

OWENS, R. J. *Peru,* pp. 6–23 and 90–100. Royal Institute of International Affairs. New York: Oxford University Press, 1963.

PIERSON, DONALD. *Negroes in Brazil: A Study of Race Contact at Bahia,* chaps. ii–v and ix–xi. Chicago: University of Chicago Press, 1942.

RYCROFT, W. STANLEY (ed.). *Indians of the High Andes.* New York: Committee on Cooperation with Latin America, 1946.

SCHURZ, WILLIAM LYTLE. *Brazil: The Infinite Country,* chaps. 3 and 7. New York: E. P. Dutton & Co., Inc., 1961.

————. *This New World: The Civilization of Latin America,* chaps. ii–vi. New York: E. P. Dutton & Co., Inc., 1954.

SMITH, T. LYNN. *Brazil: People and Institutions,* Part II. Rev. ed. Baton Rouge, La.: Louisiana State University Press, 1963.

STEWARD, JULIAN H., AND FARON, LOUIS C. *Native Peoples of South America.* New York: McGraw-Hill Book Co., Inc., 1959.

TANNENBAUM, FRANK. *Slave and Citizen: The Negro in the Americas.* New York: Alfred A. Knopf, Inc., 1947.

TAYLOR, CARL C. *Rural Life in Argentina,* chaps. iii–vii. Baton Rouge, La.: Louisiana State University Press, 1948.

WAGLEY, CHARLES. *An Introduction to Brazil,* chap. 7. New York: Columbia University Press, 1963.

WHETTEN, NATHAN L. *Guatemala: The Land and the People,* chaps. 2 and 3. Caribbean Series, 4. New Haven, Conn.: Yale University Press, 1961.

————. *Rural Mexico,* chaps. ii and iii. Chicago: University of Chicago Press, 1948.

PART II

SOCIAL FOUNTAINHEADS
OF POLITICAL ACTION

THE CLASS STRUCTURE:
The High Hurdle on the Way Up

CLASSES IN THE COLONIAL ERA

Whites

IN COLONIAL Hispanic America, the society, consisting of various races and nationalities, was highly stratified. In this "Neapolitan social cake," the top layer consisted of the whites, of which one group, the *peninsulares* ("men of the peninsula," or Spaniards born in Spain), was the icing. These men, the bulwark of Spanish rule in the New World, were entrusted by the crown and the papacy with the highest offices in the government, the army, and the Church. Consequently, they became the viceroys, captains-general, governors, indendants, judges, generals, archbishops, and bishops.[1]

The extent to which they monopolized high offices is shown by the record of their appointments during the colonial era. Of the 170 viceroys appointed prior to 1813, only 4 were born in America—all sons of government officials serving in the New World. Of the 602 captains-general and presidents, only 14 were born in the colonies. Of the 706 bishops, only 105 were born in the New World, and most of these served in minor dioceses.[2] The near-monopolization of high offices by the *peninsulares* is even more striking when one recalls how relatively small their number was. In 1800, out of a total of 3 million whites, less than 300,000 were *peninsulares*.

Besides monopolizing the higher offices, they were granted many *fueros* or special privileges, including exemption from taxes, despite their enormous wealth, and immunity from imprisonment for debt, however it had been contracted.

---

[1] J. Fred Rippy, *Historical Evolution of Hispanic America* (3rd ed.; New York: Appleton-Century-Crofts, Inc., 1945), p. 107.
[2] Lucas Alamán, *Disertaciones sobre la história de la república Mexicana desde la epoca de la conquista, México, 1844–49* (3 Vols.), Vol. I, pp. 12–13.

The privileges and preferences bestowed on the *peninsulares* were bitterly resented by the *criollos*, the whites born in the New World who were excluded from most of the responsible and prestigious offices. Although they were children or descendants of Spanish parents, the unfortunate accident of being born on the "wrong side of the tracks," in this case ocean, they felt, unfairly denied them their birthright, no matter how proud their lineage. In Mexico, they derisively referred to *peninsulares* as the *gachupines* (the men with spurs) and in South America as the *chapetones* (the tenderfeet).[3] But this derision was little balm to their pride, often insulted without limit.

"The most miserable European, without education or intellectual cultivation," observed Alexander von Humboldt, "thinks himself superior to all other white men in the new continent." Realizing the resentment of the *criollos*, Don Malchor Macanaz, able minister of the crown, urged a change of policy:

As the natives . . . are equally deserving of filling the principal offices of their own country, it appears reasonable that they should not be divested of all management in their own homes. I am fully persuaded . . . there are many discontented persons, not because they are under the control of Spain, but because they are cast down, and tyrannized by the very persons who are sent over to exercise the duties of the judicature. Let your majesty give these offices to subjects of that country, and by this means disturbances will be avoided.[4]

The crown did not heed this warning, however, and the *criollos*, denied an important role in political administration, became the dominating influence in the *cabildos*, the municipal councils in the colonies. Although these were largely honorific, being sold to the highest bidder, they turned out to be very significant in the wars for independence, since they functioned as legislative bodies in many of the colonies during the protracted struggle. The *criollos*, rebuffed in their frequent demands for self-government, cast in their lot for independence and provided the leadership for achieving it.[5]

Long before the break with Spain, the *criollos*, excluded from most positions of leadership and prestige, entered the professions in increasing numbers, becoming the doctors, lawyers, and traders of colonial society. Many became quite wealthy from their ownership of productive plantations, profitable mines, and lucrative businesses.

Despite the political differences between *criollos* and *peninsulares*, all members of the upper class had one thing in common—their affluence. They very much enjoyed conspicuous consumption, setting the tone for future Latin American society. Indeed, descriptions of their efforts to

---

[3] Hubert Herring, *A History of Latin America from the Beginnings to the Present* (2d ed., rev.; New York: Alfred A. Knopf, Inc., 1961), p. 187.

[4] In Bernard Moses, *South America on the Eve of Emancipation* (New York: Putnam & Sons, 1908), pp. 103–4.

[5] Donald E. Worcester and Wendell G. Schaeffer, *The Growth and Culture of Latin America* (New York: Oxford University Press, 1956), pp. 536–37.

outdo each other in showy displays whet the imagination. Baptism offered just such an occasion. "The traditions relate how it was a customary thing," said Riva Palacio, "for the rich to lay down a path of silver bars from their houses to the nearby parish church or at least from the vestibule to the alcove, for those who carried the capitalist's baby for baptism."[6]

Besides silver sidewalks, silver dishes, and even furniture, there was other impressive evidence that the owners were "as rich as Potosí." With innumerable slaves and servants, is it any wonder that they disdained almost every kind of physical exertion? In Brazil, "some ladies even had themselves borne to church in their hammocks," said Gilberto Freyre, "and would enter, haughty and triumphant, carried by their slaves. This was a true affront to the saints, and it became necessary for the bishops to forbid such a show of indolence."[7]

While the great majority of the upper class were white, some others were accepted into the group. During the colonial period the caciques, Indian chiefs, played an important role by cooperating with the European conquerors in governing the Indian masses. As recognition of their contribution, the Indian aristocracy was accepted as part of the upper class.

Indians

The Indians, the largest group in colonial society, were the strawberry layer of the "social cake." Although free men, at least in theory, they were subjected in reality to a prolonged slavery dating from the first days of the conquest. When the conquistadors landed, triumphantly claiming the territory for Spain, "they fell first on their knees and then on the Indians."

Almost from the very first, the crown was confronted with a puzzling problem. Its empire in the New World depended on the labor of the Indians, yet they would not work unless they were forced to, fleeing to the mountains or forests if necessary to escape their taskmasters. As a result, throughout the colonial period the crown was continually attempting to find a satisfactory policy that would permit the use but not the abuse of the Indians.

In the colonies, several institutional arrangements developed for utilizing this unwilling working force.[8] Under the *repartimiento*, natives could be temporarily allotted to an individual for the purpose of performing some work in the public interest, a purpose interpreted liberally enough to include work on private plantations, mines, or factories. In

---

[6] Vicente Riva Palacio (ed.), *México a través de los siglos* (5 vols.; Barcelona: 1888–89), Vol. II, pp. 724–25, in Bailey W. Diffie, *Latin American Civilization: Colonial Period* (Harrisburg, Pa.: Stackpole Sons, 1947), pp. 482–83.

[7] Gilberto Freyre, *The Masters and the Slaves: A Study in the Development of Brazilian Civilization*, trans. Samuel Putnam (2d Eng. ed. rev.; New York: Alfred A. Knopf, Inc., 1956), p. 361.

[8] For these arrangements see Herring, *op. cit.*, p. 190–92, and William Lytle Schurz, *This New World: The Civilization of Latin America* (New York: E. P. Dutton & Co., Inc., 1954), pp. 58–60.

effect the *repartimiento* was little more than legalized slavery; the authorities would even aid in rounding up the number of Indians needed by the colonists and in compelling them to work.

Another arrangement devised in the colonies was the *encomienda*, a grant of certain land together with the right to work the Indians who lived there. The *encomendero* had extensive legal rights over them, especially when his grant embraced an entire village or district, in effect giving him the great authority of a cacique.

Still another device designed to provide labor for the colonists was the *mita*, a sort of corvée. Under this the Indian communities were required to supply a certain number of workers for a specified task as tilling the fields, digging in the mines, or weaving in the textile plants.

Rapidly reduced to servitude, the Indians were the victims of widespread cruelty and mistreatment. In an effort to protect them, the crown passed many laws and regulations; they were legally regarded as minors, were not subject to military service or the Inquisition, and were exempt from paying taxes except for a small annual personal tax. If they got into trouble, they were entitled to lawyers to defend them free of charge.[9]

Besides being accorded a special status, the Indian was the beneficiary, nominally at least, of many laws specifically relating to his employment, including minimum wages, maximum hours, and provision for adequate food and shelter, as well as an education and religious instruction. Repeatedly declared to be a free man, he was to be given humane treatment and not to be used as a beast of burden without his consent, except possibly in emergencies. Although in some measure effective, the many laws to protect the Indians were essentially just so much verbiage, violated with impunity by greedy, rapacious colonists, overseers, and colonial administrators.

As a result, the enslavement suffered by the Indian was far worse than that of the Negro.[10] Purchased at a high price, the African represented a big investment that a slaveowner or overseer, however cruel, would not willfully destroy. But not so the Indian; he was expendable. When he died in the factory, still holding the weaving in his hands, or collapsed in the mine from overwork or hunger, he was hauled out like cattle and left exposed to the elements.

In the area around the mines in Mexico, the ground was so covered with cadavers and bones that "it was hardly possible to walk except over dead men or bones, and so great were the number of the birds and buzzards that came to eat on the bodies of the dead that they cast a huge shadow over the sun."[11]

---

[9] Alamán, *op. cit.*, pp. 22–25.
[10] For the many brutalities inflicted on the Indian, see Diffie, *op. cit.*, pp. 200–203, 462–64, and 467–69.
[11] In Diffie, *op. cit.*, p. 202.

With the cruel and inhuman treatment often inflicted on them, millions of Indians died from starvation, overwork, and punishment. In fact, the race was exterminated in large areas.

Those fortunate enough to escape such a fate, possibly legal slavery too, usually found themselves entrapped in the most insidious form of servitude of all—debt slavery.[12] It was so easy to become enmeshed in it. The landlord who kept the books knew how to figure—and how to "outfigure" too. He could charge his workers for expenses they did not incur, force them to buy such useless things as silk hose or Parisian hats, maybe advance them money for *chicha* or a *fiesta*.

Easy to get into, debt slavery was most difficult to escape from. For it was in effect a legalized form of servitude. The law upheld the right of creditors to obtain payment for such debts, which usually lasted for the full lifetime of the worker and could even be passed on to his children, putting them too into legal servitude.

The mistreatment of the Indian is the most unsavory chapter of the colonial era, and its aftermath persists even today in the "Indian Problem" that is such a burden to much of Latin America.

Negroes

Furnishing the chocolate, the bottom layer of the "Neapolitan social cake," were the Negroes, most of whom were slaves during the colonial era. Negro slavery in the New World followed close on the heels of the conquistadors. In 1502, Nicolás de Ovando, commissioned governor of Hispaniola, was authorized by the Spanish crown to take to the New World a few Christian Negroes born in the Iberian peninsula. The number of blacks was destined to increase greatly as the slave trade expanded.

The Indians on whom the colonists depended for labor on plantations proved unable to stand the hot sun; as a result, many died from heatstroke and exhaustion. The Negroes, on the other hand, were inured in their native Africa to working long hours under the tropical sun, growing crops in an agrarian society. In the New World large numbers were needed on plantations for growing sugarcane and for operating the many sugar mills, each of which required from 50 to 100 hands.

With so much labor needed, the slave trade increased in volume like the fierce tropical hurricanes that spawn in the Caribbean. For the next three centuries the tropical winds when calm were to slowly waft many slavers' ships, burdened with their suffering human cargo, to their destination in the New World. Not only were large fortunes to be made in sugar but also in the slave trade itself. Hardy adventurers, risk capital too,

---

12 See Diffie, *op. cit.*, pp. 471–72, and Frank Tannenbaum, "Toward an Appreciation of Latin America," *The United States and Latin America* (ed. Herbert L. Matthews) (American Assembly) (2d ed.; New York: Columbia University, 1963), pp. 34–35.

enthusiastically engaged in it; slaves were sold in the New World for as much as 30 times what they cost in Africa![13]

Originating in economic necessity, the slave trade in its early years was sanctioned by the Church. The importation and use of Negro slaves were designed to protect the Indians, a purpose regarded as wholly compatible with Christian ethics.[14] In later years, however, the Church condemned the slave trade and prohibited Catholics from engaging in it, but did not interfere with slavery itself where domestic law permitted it. In fact, the Jesuits themselves owned a considerable number of slaves; these comprised much of their property when they were expelled from America in 1767.

While there were undoubtedly many instances of cruelty and brutality to slaves in Latin America, laws did exist to protect them and give them certain rights. For slavery had been recognized for centuries by both Spain and Portugal, and such codes as *Las Siete Partidas*, adopted about 1265, recognized the slave as a human being whose moral status was equal to that of his master; his spirituality might be even greater. When the Negro was transplanted to the New World, he automatically became the beneficiary of this ancient legal heritage.[15]

This heritage and its protection were invaluable to the slave, as Frank Tannenbaum concludes.

He was no stranger to the law. His obligation and freedom within the code were both known. In fact, the element of human personality was not lost in the transition to slavery from Africa to the Spanish or Portuguese dominions. He remained a person even while he was a slave. He lost his freedom, but he retained his right to become free again, and, with that privilege, the essential elements in moral worth that make freedom a possibility. He was never considered a mere chattel, never defined as unanimated property, and never under the law treated as such. His master never enjoyed the powers of life and death over his body, even though abuses existed and cruelties were performed. Even justice proved to be blind, and blindness was not incurable. The Negro slave under this system had both a juridical and moral personality, even while he was in bondage.[16]

Aided by law and custom, the slave in time came to enjoy many of the rights of a free man. He had two days a week to work for himself, could accumulate property which might be inherited by his children, and could defend the chastity of his wife even against his owner.

The possibilities of obtaining freedom were many. In Brazil he could compel his master to free him by reimbursing the original purchase price. In Cuba and other areas, he might purchase his freedom by installments. Sometimes a slave would purposefully pay all but the last installment or

---

[13] For a vivid account of the slave trade with its incredible profits and horrible brutalities, see Herring, *op. cit.*, pp. 100–109, and Frank Tannenbaum, *Slave and Citizen: The Negro in the Americas* (New York: Alfred A. Knopf, Inc., 1947), p. 33.

[14] Diffie, *op. cit.*, pp. 192–93 and 473.

[15] Tannenbaum, *Slave and Citizen: The Negro in the Americas, op. cit.*, pp. 48–52.

[16] *Ibid.*, pp. 97–98.

two, thereby obtaining most of his freedom, but by remaining partially a slave, escaping the payment of taxes on his property and the obligation of military service.[17]

Thus Negroes became free men, but their color, like a haunting refrain, continues to be associated with the taint of slavery.

Mestizos, Mulattos, and Zambos

Following the arrival of the conquistadors and colonists in Latin America and the introduction of Negro slaves, miscegenation became so common and widespread as to change radically the character of the component groups. The indiscriminate sexual activity of Spaniards and Portuguese with Indians and Negroes produced so many varieties of racial mixtures as to defy complete classification. The offspring of the unions were of three general castes: the mestizo, a cross between a white and an Indian; the mulatto, between a white and a Negro; and the zambo, between an Indian and a Negro.

What were the reasons for this widespread miscegenation?

For one thing, white women were very scarce. Since the conquistadors were engaged in a military mission of exploring and conquering a vast, hitherto unknown region, they did not take their wives and families with them in the first stages of the conquest. To alleviate the shortage of women, the government sent some from the mother country, mainly prostitutes and girls from orphanages.

Miscegenation was also facilitated by the fact that Moors had ruled the Iberian peninsula for centuries, tending to remove any racial prejudice on the part of both the Spanish and Portuguese. Indeed, even members of the royal family regarded it as an honor to mate with the dark-skinned Moors who not only exercised political control but also possessed a superior culture.

Also contributing to miscegenation were the easy standards of sexual relations characteristic of many of the Indian tribes. The principal Indians have more than one wife, wrote Gabriel Soares of the Tupinambás around Bahia, and the one who had the most wives was the most honored and esteemed of the tribe. The men were so lustful that they seldom respected sisters and aunts or even their own daughters, and they were not content with one woman but had many. "The men," according to Soares, "are not jealous and even when they find another with their wives, they kill no one . . . the most they do is spank the woman. . . . Women who love their husbands well, in order to please them, look for young girls with whom the husbands may divert themselves. . . ."[18]

Indian standards and mores had quite an impact on the early Portuguese

---

[17] For the Negro's rights and status see *ibid.*, pp. 53–54, and Donald Pierson, *Negroes in Brazil: A Study of Race Contact at Bahia* (Chicago: University of Chicago Press, 1942), pp. 83–88.

[18] In Diffie, *op. cit.*, p. 695.

soldiers and colonists. "The milieu in which Brazilian life began," wrote Gilberto Freyre, "was one of sexual intoxication." Continuing, he quotes Father Anchieta: "The women go naked and are unable to say no to anyone but they themselves provoke and importune the men . . . for they hold it to be an honor to sleep with the Christians."[19]

Fraternization between the races was so unrestrained that the mestizos increased much more rapidly proportionately than either the whites or the Indians. These *naturales*, or bastards, did not have the status of either the Spaniards or natives. And when unacknowledged by their fathers—often unknown in the many "casual unions"—or ignored by their mothers, they were so many pack rats having to fend for themselves at the expense of society.

The importation of Negro slaves inevitably resulted in sexual depravity, a concomitant of slavery wherever it exists. The woman slave, subject to the commands or desires of young sons of the family, usually initiated them precociously into physical love. The owner too used them to satisfy his sexual desires, and encouraged dissoluteness in order to increase the number of his *crias* (young slaves). "The most productive feature of slave property," said Joaquim Nabuco, "is the generative belly."[20]

With the onsurge of miscegenation, the determination of whiteness was largely a legal fiction that blurred or eliminated the distinction between whites, Negroes, and Indians. In both Paraguay and Chile all mestizos were recognized by law as being white and entirely of European origin. Where law did not whiten, money often did. A swarthy mulatto who had struck it rich was able to buy a certificate of purity of blood which attested that he was entirely of European origin. If the petitioner was so black that such a statement was obviously incredible, he could still receive the more equivocal verdict, "that such individuals may consider themselves as whites."[21]

SOCIAL CLASSES TODAY

In most of the Latin American nations the class structure has changed little since the days of the colonial era. The boldly proclaimed declarations of independence and idealistically inspired professions of equality and rights scarcely made a dent in the hard-shell social structure. As a result, the classes today have many characteristics that one would hardly expect to find in democratic nations, especially after almost a century and a half of democratic ideology.

Except in a few countries, the classes are sharply stratified, and their standards of living, values, and aspirations reflect almost unbelievable extremes. There is little vertical mobility. Indeed, the social barriers between the upper and lower classes are as formidable as the physical ones formed

---

[19] Freyre, *op. cit.*, pp. 85–86.
[20] *Ibid.*, p. 324.
[21] Diffie, *op. cit.*, p. 481.

by the high wall topped by barbed wire or jagged pieces of broken glass that often safeguards the older luxurious homes of the wealthy.

Determinants of Social Status

Education and Culture. Among the several determinants of one's social status in Latin America today, education and culture are easily the most important. In fact they are the "open sesame" to achievement and prestige. Illiteracy and little or no schooling, on the other hand, are characteristic of the large lower class and virtually destine its members to poverty, meniality, and servility.

Language is one of the most important cultural criteria of status. Throughout Hispanic America, Spanish is the accepted language of polite society; in Brazil, it is Portuguese; in Haiti, it is French. The millions of Indians who speak nothing but one of the hundreds of Indian languages or dialects are in effect social outcasts beyond the pale of polite society.

Of all these Indian languages, only Guaraní spoken in Paraguay is sanctioned by polite usage. It is one of the principal Indian contributions to Paraguayan culture, and gives the nation the distinction of being the only truly bilingual country in Latin America. While Spanish is the official language of the country and is used on more formal occasions, even the best families speak Guaraní at home. "The Paraguayans love, hate, and fight in Guaraní. In this tongue they shout on the football field and whisper their declarations of love in the dark corners of the patios of their old colonial houses."[22] When debate becomes heated in Parliament, the members may suddenly lapse into their ancestral tongue.

Religion. Another cultural requirement for social status is that one belong to the Roman Catholic Church. Although it has lost much of its earlier influence and has been the target of widespread anticlericalism, Catholicism is nevertheless regarded as the religion of higher status.

Dress, Home, and Manners. As in other societies, the Latin American's dress, home, and manners are also important in determining the class he belongs to. To achieve a higher status he must wear the conventional attire of the West, live in one of the better neighborhoods in a substantial home or at least a dwelling of permanent construction with its floors made of something better than packed earth. He must also use polite language, as well as have good manners and social *savoir-faire*. If he is not sure of himself, the aspirant for higher social status would do well to bone up on his Hispanic "Amy Vanderbilt."

Occupation. As in other socially conscious societies, occupation is another important determinant of social status. The ideal is not to have any occupation at all. For work is regarded as simply a means to an end—a sort of necessary evil to obtain a livelihood. There is nothing noble or dignifying about it.

---

[22] George Pendle, *Paraguay: A Riverside Nation* (The Royal Institute of International Affairs) (London: Oxford University Press, 1954), p. 93.

But if one has to work for a living, he should select something dignified, possibly enter one of the professions as law, medicine, teaching, writing, artistic achievement, military service, or the priesthood. Only as a last resort would he choose manual labor; it would immediately stamp him as belonging to the lower class. As an aphorism in Brazil tersely expresses it, *"Trabalho é para cachorro e negro"* ("Work [manual labor] is for Negroes and dogs").

Wealth. "Money talks" is a saying that we often hear in the United States. In Latin America it shouts in a stentorian voice. Money alone does not assure a high social status, but if one has even a modicum of culture and social graces, he will find that having plenty of money will get him nowhere socially but to the top.

Money can even change one's color, too. In Brazil with its large Negro and Negroid population, it changes black to white and white to black. *"Negro rico é branco, e branco pobre é negro"* ("A rich Negro is a white man, and a poor white man is a Negro").[23]

In Colombia, the lack of money can change white to red. "The term 'Indian' designates a social status, and not an ethnically identifiable biology," asserts Gerardo Reichel. "An individual with predominantly Caucasian physical characteristics [still] is designated as an 'Indian' if he lives on an aboriginal cultural level, or if he *occupies a low rung on the social scale.*"[24]

Race. Race also has an important bearing on a person's social position. While there is no "race problem" in the same sense that it exists in the United States and many other nations, in every country of Latin America the ruling classes are whiter than the lower classes; and usually the whiter the individual is, the higher his status is in the social hierarchy.

White blood is highly prized by the ruling classes who sometimes boast of *pureza de sangre* (purity of blood). "The concupiscent conquistadors and their descendants," wrote Vernon Fluharty, "took the native and slave women to their beds, but scarcely ever to their bosoms; they used them, but did not marry them. Rather, they made of 'whiteness' a yardstick by which all social, economic, and political preference was measured. Children of cross-matings had better social chances than did the aborigine; and further 'whitening' might bring them even closer to the select circle. Still, from the beginning down to the present in Colombia, the circle has been select."[25]

White blood is prized too by the dark-skinned persons in the lower classes. In Brazil, for example, a Negroid woman who bears a whiter child considers herself fortunate; her status and her child's are improved. "I

---

[23] Pierson, *op. cit.*, p. 152.
[24] In Vernon L. Fluharty, *Dance of the Millions: Military Rule and the Social Revolution in Colombia, 1930–1956* (Pittsburgh, Pa.: University of Pittsburgh Press, 1957), p. 179.
[25] *Ibid.*, p. 175.

don't want to go back to Africa," she may say to express her preference for lighter offspring. And as a sort of justification for her action, if any were needed, she is apt to add, *"Estou limpando a minha raça"* ("I am cleansing [i.e., 'whitening'] my race"), or *"Melhorando a raça"* ("improving the breed").[26]

In most of the Latin American countries, being either Indian or Negro is a distinct handicap because these racial groups have been relegated to the lower classes through the denial of social and economic opportunity. As a result, their very physical characteristics continue to be symbols of low social rank, of descent from slaves or peons.

Yet in the rigidly stratified society, class lines are actually greater barriers than racial differences. Since Latin America defines "race" in terms of cultural traits rather than physical differences, and since culture is such an influential factor in determining social status, neither Negro nor Indian blood has been an insuperable bar to acceptance in high social circles. Individual competence is more important than social background in the determination of one's status, according to Donald Pierson. "Color is undoubtedly a handicap. But it always tends to be discounted if the individual in question possesses other characteristics of upper-class identity, such as professional competence, intellectual ability, educational achievement, wealth, an 'engaging' manner, personal 'charm,' poise, 'breeding,' and, especially with the females, beauty."[27]

Even in the sensitive area of marriage, class is a more important consideration than race. Where there is opposition to marrying a black, it is based on class rather than on racial grounds concludes Donald Pierson speaking of the Negroes in Brazil. Indeed, when the color black does not ". . . identify an individual as a member of the lower class, opposition to him tends to disappear. Virtually no opposition attaches to the marriage of light mixed-bloods into even the upper class, especially if they do not show in their features or color too obvious evidence of Negro origin."[28]

Indeed, the Moreno is regarded in Bahía as the ideal type of feminine beauty. With her dark-brown eyes, dark wavy hair, and *café com leite* (coffee with milk) complexion, she is the toast of poets and songwriters and the overwhelming preference in marriage over mulatto or even white girls.

The Several Social Classes

The Upper Class. The Old Landed Aristocracy. This upper class consists of two groups—the old landed aristocracy and the new moneyed elite. Most members of the former, who own the *haciendas* and plantations, enjoy their status by virtue of birth, *el privilegio de la cuna* (the

---

26 Pierson, *op. cit.*, pp. 120–22.
27 *Ibid.*, pp. 204–5.
28 *Ibid.*, p. 151.

privilege of the cradle).[29] Some, however, have entered the group by virtue of a fortunate marriage. But since its members have strongly tended to intermarry, it has been virtually a closed circle, almost as select as that of the earlier Inca whose status was so exalted that only his full sister was qualified to be his wife.

Belonging to this closed circle, however achieved, was all-important. Its members had a monopoly of the political power, wealth, education and culture, prestige and influence in the countries. Belonging to it meant the difference between being master or servant, living in the "big house" or in a hut, giving orders or taking them.

The baby of the aristocrat is born with something better than a silver spoon in his mouth—he holds a scepter in his tiny hand.[30] Even as a child he rules his little world, gives orders to servants who carry them out with a respectful "sí, sí." He has no responsibilities, performs no chores; he has a servant who accompanies him to school in the morning and back home in the afternoon just to relieve him of the schoolboyish task of carrying his books.

As a student he is well educated, probably studying the humanities and the arts at one of the European universities and traveling extensively in Europe. During vacations, he learns from his father how to manage the ancestral estate. Never a dirt farmer, he does not know how to plow a straight furrow or even how to saddle his own horse. But he learns quite thoroughly how to plan, give orders, and assume his responsibilities as a *hacendado*.

In later life, he and his family spend much of the year at their home in the city where there are many social and cultural activities, occasionally interrupted by a visit to the hacienda, or by a trip to Paris or Rome to whet their appetites for continental culture and living.

Capable, cultured, and cosmopolitan, the landed aristocrats are versatile individuals.[31] Besides managing their haciendas, supervised in their absence by overseers, they sometimes become interested in urban economic opportunities—no ordinary jobs, of course, but something befitting their status, such as president of a bank or director of a railroad. Sometimes they enter politics, playing a prominent role in the national congress or perhaps in the president's cabinet. Sometimes they prefer to dabble in a profession, delving deeper into law, philosophy, or some other love of their student days. But whatever they do, it is with the love of a dilettante who does not have to depend on it for a living.

Born as they were to rule, with a hereditary scepter in their hands, the

---

[29] Ironically, among the poorer classes where infant mortality is very high, *cuna*, cradle, means "coffin."

[30] For a vivid portrayal of the young aristocrat, see George McCutchen McBride, *Chile: Land and Society* (American Geographical Society Research Series, No. 19) (New York, 1936), pp. 10–11.

[31] For a sympathetic, yet penetrating, critical evaluation of the privileged upper class, see Fluharty, *op. cit.*, pp. 183–87.

landed aristocrats were not dependent on anything except their vast landed estates. Some of their haciendas were larger than many American states, had a larger population of peons than some American cities, were governed by a power as absolute as that of any medieval feudal lord.

In Brazil, the landed aristocrat's gigantic plantation with its large retinue of Negro slaves was an independent, self-sufficient world of its own. The Big House, his palatial residence with its thick walls, deep foundations, and massive proportions, embodied the pomp and power of the Middle Ages. As the command post and nerve center of the principality, "the Big House was . . . at one and the same time a fortress, a bank, a cemetery, a hospital, a school and a house of charity, giving shelter to the aged, the widow, and the orphan."[32]

The lords and masters of all they surveyed (most of the farm land in Latin America and practically all of the good land), the *hacendados* have been a powerful force in the painful evolution of Latin America.

A few of them, able to see beyond their own immediate interests, have been idealistic champions of reform. Galo Plaza, a wealthy liberal land-owner and president of Ecuador from 1948 to 1952, was a model president, promoting democracy, prosperity, and progress. And Pedro Aguirre Cerda, a wealthy intellectual radical and president of Chile from 1938 to 1941, promoted an extensive program of social legislation that made his nation one of the model welfare states of the world.

Yet even several swallows do not make a spring, nor do several liberal aristocrats make a democratic party. The *hacendados*, ensconced in their feudal domains, have strenuously and successfully opposed any changes that would diminish their status. Their philosophy concerning social problems was well stated by the president of the Chilean Conservative Party at its 1933 convention: He could understand, he said, why the terrible gulf between the rich and the poor would be the despair of the socialists and why it should drive them mad. From their materialistic point of view, which envisaged that man should live as comfortably in this world as is humanly possible, poverty did not make sense and was the worst scourge of humanity. "But," he insisted, "that there are few rich and many poor is an inevitable natural fact . . . all our efforts to change it will turn out to be fruitless. And if our efforts should bear fruit, we would so alter the natural order of things that humanity would be condemned to disappear. . . ."[33]

To the aristocrats, the disappearance of humanity meant the loss of their traditional power and entrenched position. It also meant upsetting the time-hallowed scheme of things; centuries of rule had established that the aristocrats were a superior class to the manner born, educated and trained to manage not only their own destiny but also that of the large

---

[32] Freyre, *op. cit.*, p. xxxiii.
[33] In Lewis Hanke, *South America* (Princeton, N.J.: D. Van Nostrand Co., Inc., 1959), pp. 147–48.

inferior masses who were destined to cook and clean, serve and sew, bow and scrape. It further meant upsetting their political control, too. Their peons, no longer bound to the soil, would become citizens, free men of the nation who could say "no, no" to them instead of the invariable and servile "sí, sí."

Worse still, social reforms would cost a lot of money: money for schools, hospitals, medical clinics, housing, and social security—and also for higher wages that would enable the peons to live like human beings. The cost would inevitably have to be borne mainly by the aristocrats, since they possessed most of the wealth.

No wonder the aristocrats have regarded social reform as disastrous. Proposals for reform inevitably touched the "pocketbook nerve," unusually raw and sensitive with the gentry, since they paid very little taxes. Juan Luis Sanfuentes, elected president of Chile in 1915, well expressed the outrage of the big landowners at the very idea of change. According to him, ". . . social change was not only bad for business but an insult to Almighty God."[34]

Determined to safeguard their privileges, they have used every weapon in their aristocratic arsenal. They have organized powerful pressure groups, such as the Sociedad Nacional de Agricultura, to elect members to the national congress and to fight any proposed legislation considered inimical to their interests. They have also cultivated the armed forces, winning their support by granting them privileges and large budgets. And whenever it served their interests, which was often, they have openly or tacitly supported dictators who could be counted on to preserve the status quo and, although repressive in their rule, to stave off the hideous specter of change.

In some countries the aristocracy has had notable reverses; in Paraguay it never recovered from the body blows inflicted by Francia, in Venezuela it was reduced to virtual impotence by the long ruthless dictatorship of Gómez, and in Brazil its economic base was obliterated by the abolition of slavery. There, the Big House, for all its pomp and planning for posterity, is an empty, decaying reminder of a slave society that, like our own, has "gone with the wind."

The whirlwinds of social change have had their effects, too. The social revolutions in Mexico, Bolivia, and, most recently, Cuba, have apparently jolted the complacency of the oligarchs, creating some misgivings about their traditional opposition to social reform. In Peru the oligarchy played an important role in ending the military dictatorship of General Manuel Odría in 1956, possibly fearing that change is inevitable and that it had better come gradually through the democratic process rather than by violent revolution as in neighboring Bolivia.

In most of the countries, however, the oligarchy remains an adamant, usually decisive force in determining national policies and objectives. Even

---

[34] Herring, *op. cit.*, pp. 590–91.

when it has been unable to muster large blocks of votes and has lost direct control of government, it usually manages, with its great economic power, influence, and prestige to exercise an effective veto over any measures it opposes. Its intransigent attitude toward social reform, especially land and tax reform, threatens to defeat the ambitious objectives of the Alliance for Progress, the projected ten-year partnership between the United States and Latin America for achieving social development.

The Indian, as you recall, has been belittlingly described as ". . . a stone blocking the viscera of the social program." The entrenched oligarchs are not stones—they are veritable roadblocks to progress. In fact a seasoned United States diplomat has concluded, after long service in the region, "They are willing to tie down the safety valve and to wait for the boiler to burst."[35]

The New Moneyed Elite. In addition to the aristocratic landed elite, many of the countries have a new upper class that consists of industrialists, entrepreneurs, businessmen, and bankers who have risen to prominence in the more industrially developed nations. Often from humble backgrounds, they are self-made men who had no family name or prestige to rely on, only their ability, vision, and driving ambition for success and recognition. Many of them are *arrivistas*, or recent arrivals—European immigrants who despaired of their opportunities in the old world and were attracted to Latin America by the chance to begin a new life, setting up their own small businesses, becoming financially independent, possibly even amassing a fortune.

With seemingly unlimited resources ready to be exploited and with insatiable wants for new products and services, Latin America offered boundless opportunity—the proverbial "tide in the affairs of men"—for those astute and daring enough to grasp it. Staking their all on hard work, ingenuity, and unscrupulous methods if necessary, they sometimes succeeded beyond a young hopeful's wildest dreams. The sagas of their rise from rags to riches are Horatio Alger exploits in a Latin American setting.

Among those particularly favored by fortune's wide smile was Francisco Matarazzo, an energetic, imaginative emigrant from Italy. On his trip over in 1881, he lost his initial capital, the merchandise he was bringing with him. Undaunted by this setback, after settling down in Sorocaba, Brazil, he began to experiment with new methods for processing and putting up foods. As each new venture succeeded, he branched out into others. During World War I, already one of the nation's leading industrialists, he plunged headlong into many new enterprises, reaping such great profits that he was accused by his countrymen of desiring to aid both sides so as to prolong the conflict and pyramid his profits.[36]

---

[35] John M. Cabot, "Social Evolution in Latin America—the Necessity for Mutual Understanding," *Toward Our Common American Destiny* (Fletcher School of Law and Diplomacy, 1954), p. 21.

[36] Richard M. Morse, *From Community to Metropolis: A Biography of São Paulo, Brazil* (Gainesville, Fla.: University of Florida Press, 1958), pp. 176 and 228-29.

His sprawling industrial empire, United Industries, included chemicals, distilling, artificial silk, meat packing, metallurgy, salt and sugar refining, as well as many others. In addition, it controlled railroads and ship lines, banks and insurance companies. Before his death in 1937, Matarazzo was reputedly the wealthiest man in Latin America, heading the world's largest personally managed industrial empire.[37]

Other enterprising individuals were eminently successful too, and soon came to constitute a new upper class, a respected and envied plutocracy. With the prestige of their wealth and influence, they sometimes marry members of the landed aristocracy. Like other established Latin Americans, the *nouveaux riches* enjoy ostentation, and sometimes flaunt their lavish means in flamboyant displays of elegance and extravagance. The home reportedly being built for his fiancée by a wealthy young industrialist was described as a "million-dollar house . . . with two Turkish baths, a shooting gallery, a bowling alley and an outdoor swimming pool. It will also have a 130-foot indoor swimming pool with a cascade of water 30 feet wide and 21 feet high at one end. By swimming through his waterfall [the owner] will find himself in a grotto equipped with bar, bath, and bed."[38]

With his grandiose personal and business plans, the aggressive industrialist is giving a momentum to economic development that augurs well for the future of the countries. All segments benefit from his goals. In order to develop a larger internal consumer market that will buy his products and augment the profits of his enterprise, he is interested in increasing the purchasing power of the mass, developing new wants of many kinds, and promoting a higher standard of living for all.

And just as he has taken over some of the prestige formerly monopolized by the old landed elite, he has also made inroads on its political power and influence. To further his objectives, he usually allies himself with the liberal parties that champion social reform. In Brazil he has often supported the Partido Social Progressista led by Adhemar de Barros, and the Partido Trabalhista Brasileiro founded by Getulio Vargas, both of which are strongly supported by the urban lower class. It is "an unusual political alliance," observes Charles Wagley, "an alliance . . . between the wealthiest segment of the population, the new business and industrial groups, and the urban lower class who often live in outright misery. For different reasons, both seem to be united against what they consider the special privileges of the old oligarchy."[39]

The Middle Class. Its Size, Composition, and Characteristics. The rise and growth of the middle class in Latin America have been very uneven

---

[37] *Ibid.*, p. 229.

[38] In *ibid.*, p. 218.

[39] Charles Wagley, "The Brazilian Revolution: Social Changes Since 1930," *Social Change in Latin America Today* (Council on Foreign Relations) (New York: Harper & Bros., 1960), pp. 226–27.

among the twenty countries. In five of them—Argentina, Brazil, Chile, Uruguay, and Mexico—the class is growing rapidly, as shown by the great increase in the demand for consumer goods and services, and is playing an important role in the progress of these nations. In Argentina, Chile, and Uruguay, the class is estimated to be 50 percent or more of the population; in Mexico and Brazil, about 30 percent.[40] These countries are the most progressive in the region, and also the most important in terms of population, area, wealth, and international prestige.

Studying the middle class in other countries, one is tempted to ask: "*¿Existe la clase de media?*" One scholar after spending a year observing and investigating in Cuba was not sure that it did. "One has the general feeling," said Lowry Nelson, "that Cuban society has not 'set' or 'jelled.' "[41] Another scholar was apparently even more frustrated. "The most difficult task in studying the Colombian middle class," wrote Vernon Fluharty, "is to find it."[42]

In those countries, the less advanced ones burdened by illiteracy, poverty, and dictatorship, as well as the more progressive ones having large Indian populations, the embryonic middle class has had difficulty pecking its way through the hard shell of social stratification. Between the extremes of wealth and culture, there is no sizable middle group that even resembles a class.

Even in the five countries where the middle class constitutes a sizable part of the population, it is not a middle class in the sense that we think of ours—a group politically dominant, economically powerful, numerically large, and typical of our values, the group to which most members of society belong emotionally as well as economically. Since the middle group in Latin America differs so markedly from our own, even in those countries where it is most powerful, some writers prefer to use other terms to describe it, such as "middle sectors," "middle groups," "middle segments," "middle components," "middle elements," and the like. Yet since we are accustomed to thinking of a middle group as a class, however much it differs from our own, we will use the accepted term "middle class."

In several respects the middle class does not have the usual characteristics of a social class. For one thing, it lacks a class consciousness that results from a common background and similar interests. This is partly the result of the great difference in the income and standard of living among members of the class. In Mexico some earn 50,000 pesos a year or more, enabling them to live opulently in the finest mansions in the city; most of

---

[40] The Brazilian social pyramid, according to L. C. Bresser Pereira, is as follows: upper class, 1 percent; upper-middle, 2 percent; middle, 6; lower-middle, 18; and lower, 70 (leaving 3 percent undistributed). See L. C. Bresser Pereira, "The Rise of Middle Class and Middle Management in Brazil," *Journal of Inter-American Studies,* Vol. IV, No. 3 (July, 1962), p. 320.

[41] Lowry Nelson, *Rural Cuba* (Minneapolis: University of Minnesota Press, 1950), p. 139.

[42] Fluharty, *op. cit.,* p. 187.

them, however, have very modest incomes, as little as 5,000 pesos or less, forcing them to live in undesirable sections.[43]

The family backgrounds of members differ even more than their economic circumstances. In fact it is a very heterogeneous group consisting of mestizos, mulattos, and Negroes; white emigrants from Europe; members of the old aristocracy whose families have lost their landed fortunes; and the spillover from the aristocracy whose wealth, however great, was limited as to the number it could support in elite fashion.

Besides lacking a class consciousness, the middle class is far from united on common purposes and ideals. While many would like to identify themselves with the upper class, the "bootstrappers," members of the first two groups, strongly sympathize with the underdog and actively support social reform. A mulatto in Brazil remembers how his Negro mother had to scavenge through the garbage heap in São Paulo to find scraps of bread to feed her children, or scraps of paper to sell for a few *cruceiros*. A mestizo in Peru remembers how his father, a peon on a hacienda, was paid his meager wages in wooden tokens, worthless except at the hacienda store that charged exorbitant prices for its black beans and heady *chicha*. Having no real money to spend, he could not look for work elsewhere. "He who doesn't go anywhere doesn't stumble," was an adage the *hacendado* enjoyed repeating. The mestizo's father, however, had never been able to see anything to appreciate in these sentiments.

The more privileged members of the middle class, despite their limited means, still continue to identify themselves with the upper class and to oppose social change. The loser-out from the upper class takes pride in stories of the old days when the family Big House was the envy of the country, when a retinue of servants jumped at the master's beck and call, and when a member of the family could pursue his dilettante interests to his heart's desire. The loser-out is apt to cherish forever the memories of Paradise Lost, no matter how slim his chances are of realizing Paradise Regained.

The overflow or spillover, the offspring of large aristocratic families, have been crowded out from the top and "pushed down the economic ladder by the inexorable pressure of mathematics"—the limit to which family wealth in land and cattle, apartments, stocks, and other properties could be divided and subdivided. They lament their misfortune in being deprived of el *privilegio de cuna*, and continue to retain the values, beliefs, and prejudices of the class from which they descended. Convinced they were meant for better things, they feel they have little in common with other members of the middle class. They are strongly opposed to any egalitarian philosophy, for this would lessen their chances of regaining their birthright. In brief, they are conservatives—albeit poor ones—and as Vernon Fluharty philosophized, "There is nothing more conservative than

---

[43] Oscar Lewis, "Mexico since Cárdenas," *Social Change in Latin America Today*, *op. cit.*, p. 336.

a poor conservative with hopes of becoming a rich one."[44] Bootstrappers . . . losers-out . . . spillovers—is it any wonder that such odd bedfellows would lack a class consciousness, not be united on common purposes and ideals?

Several factors are responsible for the rise of the middle class, probably the most important being industrialization. The industrial revolution was slow to get to Latin America, but when it did, technology and machines went far toward recreating society and its values. In the new industries that were established, a wide range of new positions was provided—clerical, supervisory, statistical, analytical, research, and many others. The white collar, the trademark of the middle class, was as symbolic of the new order as was the machine.

The great expansion of government resulting from its assumption of many new activities was also a powerful stimulus to the rise of the new class; as in the case of industry, it created many new white-collar positions. The spread of public education also served to promote the new class. By obtaining a high school, technical school, or perhaps university education, large numbers could prepare for the professions or the many desirable new jobs in industry and government.[45]

There are many occupational opportunities that are open to members of the class. Professional men and intellectuals play a prominent role as doctors, lawyers, professors and school teachers, writers and journalists, painters, scientists, actors, and radio and television performers. Others in the class are associated with industry and trade, including small industrialists, businessmen, salesmen, engineers, technicians, and mechanics. The more influential labor leaders, although beginning as proletarians, move up into the class by acquiring skills and symbols that are mandatory for the national influence they need.

Still other members are engaged in politics or are employed by the large governmental bureaucracy as administrators, supervisors, clerks, and a wide range of specialists, including farm extension workers, labor advisors, nurses, and hygienists and social workers. Many other occupational groups, such as army officers and clergymen, belong to the class.

There are no set criteria to determine precisely who will be in the middle class. In most countries, however, it does not include persons engaged in any kind of manual labor. But this is not true in Mexico. Due to the country's industrial expansion and constant upgrading of labor, the Mexican blue-collar worker performing skilled labor is considered middle

---

[44] Fluharty, *op. cit.*, p. 191.

[45] The spread of public education has also benefited the middle class by providing many new jobs for its members, who fill a large majority of the teaching positions in both primary and secondary schools. According to a study made in the state of Rio de Janeiro, Brazil, the upper and upper middle class contributed 26 percent of the primary teachers and 40 percent of the secondary; the lower middle, 53 percent of the primary and 56 percent of the secondary; and the lower class, 20 percent of the primary and 3 percent of the secondary. (Robert J. Havighurst y colaboradores, *La sociedad y la educación en América latina* [Buenos Aires, 1962], p. 328.)

class. Similarly, although in most countries the farmer of a few acres is relegated to the rural lower class, in Mexico the small landowners and *ejidatarios* are regarded by some as belonging to the middle class. The radical agrarian programs instituted since the 1910 revolution have aimed at creating many small independent land owners. Indeed, ownership of even a few acres has been one of the main routes by which members of the lower class could move up the social scale.

Frustrations and Ambitions of the Middle Class. Most members of the middle class, regardless of their backgrounds, aspire to the old aristocratic values of the landed gentry. For the great majority, this "beer income but champagne appetite" is the cause of much frustration. They regard telephones, electric stoves, refrigerators, and washing machines as not merely conveniences but necessities, yet the cost of these products is extremely high when compared with their income. A small electric refrigerator, for example, may cost the equivalent of five or six months' salary; the prices of other conveniences are likewise very high.[46]

As in the United States, better housing is an important status symbol, but it is often impossible for a family to obtain a home befitting its status. Building or buying one is very difficult. A prospective builder or buyer can get a loan for only 40 to 60 percent of the value, must pay 20 percent interest a year, and must repay the entire mortgage within five or six years. As a result of inadequate long-term financing, most of the urban property in many cities is rental, and many middle class families have to live cramped in one or two-room apartments. In the fast-growing cities, building has not been able to keep up with population growth and millions of new dwellings are urgently needed. Families that could afford better places are often forced to live in undesirable quarters because nothing else is available.[47]

The disdain of Latin Americans for manual labor makes it even more difficult for them to live within their income. Regardless of the tight squeeze on its budget, the family must have at least one domestic servant, preferably several, since they are visible proof to the world that it has arrived. To be able to afford them and keep up appearances, the husband may have to work long hours, possibly moonlight too, with at least one other job in addition to his regular one.

His ancestors, the "radish-eaters" of the Iberian peninsula, would understand completely. In order to afford servants, they had to cut down on the grocery bill and were reduced to eating radishes. But they had plenty

---

[46] Wagley, *op. cit.*, p. 219.

Moreover, to aggrevate the financial difficulties of the middle class, its savings, if any have possibly been accumulated, are often wiped out by inflation. Sometimes too, its jobs, which are the basis of any real security, are jeopardized by political instability. (Charles Wagley, "The Dilemma of the Latin American Middle Classes," *Proceedings of the Academy of Political Science* (Economic and Political Trends in Latin America), Vol. XXVII, No. 4 (May, 1964), pp. 2–10.

[47] "Needed: Millions of Houses," *Américas,* Vol. 13, No. 7 (July, 1961), pp. 19–23.

of servants. When they pompously ventured outside, they "were accompanied by one to remove their hats, another to take their capes, a third with a brush to dust their clothing, and a fourth with a comb for their hair."[48]

Caught between the squeeze of extravagant wants and limited financial means, the middle class is being forced to modify some of its traditional values and to discard some of its long-standing prejudices. The woman's place is in the home, they have long believed, yet in order to afford a higher standard of living, wives and daughters in increasing numbers have had to go to work to supplement the family income.

Despite his frustrations, the member of the middle class is undaunted. Statistics may accurately reflect his income, level of education, or number of rooms in his home, including of course "inside plumbing," our criterion for evaluating any society. But there is one thing that cold impersonal figures can never measure—the most distinguishing characteristic of his class—his burning ambition to get ahead, to be a Somebody instead of a Nobody.

Often he has as much difficulty in rising from his humble, maybe lowly, background as does the Peruvian train that laboriously struggles up the Andean heights. And like the determined train, he triumphs over every obstacle. For besides having determination, perseverance, and dedication, he is willing to work hard, overcome any handicap, make any sacrifice, especially in order to obtain an education.

Sometimes he will settle for nothing short of the very top. A true social climber, he may regard the middle class as not an acceptable end in itself but merely as a steppingstone on his way to the upper class, to which he dreams of belonging at the earliest opportunity and at whatever cost is required.

The Program of the Middle Class. Owing its very existence to change and progress, the middle class supports a broad program of social change:[49]

1. It strongly supports public education, which is probably the most revolutionary single force operating to remake the society. For public education affords an opportunity to underprivileged citizens to improve their status—in time will even refashion the centuries-old social structure.

2. It accepts the need for industrialization as a self-evident truth, the one accomplishment most likely to solve all national problems and insure economic progress. This will also give the class a deciding voice in national affairs.

3. Intensely patriotic, it stresses national goals and interests, and embraces nationalism as a major ideology in its efforts to assert national

---

[48] Freyre, *op. cit.*, p. 245.

[49] See especially John J. Johnson, *Political Change in Latin America: The Emergence of the Middle Sectors* (Stanford, Calif.: Stanford University Press, 1958), pp. 5–11; and Victor Alba, "The Latin American Style and the New Social Forces," *Latin American Issues: Essays and Comments* (ed. Albert G. Hirschman) (New York: Twentieth Century Fund, 1961), pp. 50–51.

sovereignty and dignity. Pursuing these ends, it is often anti-foreign and particularly anti-American.

4. Rejecting the laissez-faire philosophy, it accepts the concept of the welfare state and advocates a strong, active role for government in the attainment of social goals. Government should plan for the public welfare, and where necessary, should provide the machinery and investment for establishing any enterprise needed by the nation. Also, where necessary for the public interest, government should nationalize basic industry, mining, or public services.

5. Aiming to help all the broad segments of society, it supports agrarian reform and improvement of the lot of the rural masses, collective bargaining and other rights for labor, and a comprehensive program of social security to aid the aged, unemployed, sick, and disabled.

Power and Influence of the Middle Class. Prior to the twentieth century, the elite generally made the decisions and the middle class carried them out. Its role in the formation of policy is thus rather recent. Increasing in numbers as urbanization and industrialization spread, members of the class are vitally interested in the problems inherent in the transition from feudal agriculture to semi-industrial capitalism, and are assuming leadership of the new political amalgams advocating change. Since 1920 every president of Mexico has come from this class.

Its members, the intellectuals and professionals, are the articulate people, says John P. Gillin, who "speak to the outside world for Latin America, and the outside world must speak to Latin America through them." And, despite their heterogeneity and other problems, "the middle groups constitute beyond doubt the segment of society most in touch with the modern world, most susceptible to influences for change, and most potent in the internal and international affairs of their own nation."[50] The middle class, committed to economic progress and to social and political democracy,[51] is Latin America's hope for the future.

The Lower Class. The lower class, popularly referred to as the masses, has been intensively studied by reformers and graphically portrayed by writers. It is definitely the class to be from, not in. Usually illiterate, its members are ordinarily unskilled and can perform only some sort of manual labor which automatically consigns them to the class. They are the most poorly paid in society, earning so little that they are not an effective part of the consumer economy. Unlike members of the middle class who

---

[50] John P. Gillin, "Some Guideposts for Policy," *Social Change in Latin America Today, op. cit.,* p. 26.

[51] The middle class strongly supports representative and party government. Speaking of Central America, Charles W. Anderson says, "the political party is the instrument through which the middle sectors strive to attain a power capability which will be recognized by other contenders in the political process, thereby winning for them admission to the arena in which the power structure is determined by manipulation among those possessing important power capabilities." (Charles W. Anderson, "Central American Political Parties: A Functional Approach," *Western Political Quarterly,* Vol. 15, No. 1 (March, 1962), pp. 133 and 135.)

ambitiously strive to get an education and maintain a minimum standard of decency, they are too busy scratching for a living to have time or thought for the niceties and amenities of life.

Sociologists and others sometimes divide the upper class into the upper upper and lower upper; similarly the middle class into the upper middle, middle middle, and lower middle. While there is much variation in the lower class also, its status is so low and so little is known about it that nobody has bothered to divide it into the upper lower, middle lower, and lower lower. However, it is by far the largest class in most countries, and it has two clearly ascertainable groups, the rural and the urban.

The Rural Lower Class. Since most of the countries of Latin America are predominantly rural, and since a few wealthy persons own most of the land, the largest group in the whole population is the landless peons and others working on the haciendas and plantations. The peon is a stable, permanent worker. Usually in debt to the *hacendado* who keeps the books, he stays put like his forefathers, who have lived on the same hacienda for generations. Obedient and uncomplaining, he is the work horse of the hacienda, laboring from "can till can't." He patiently performs all his tasks by hand just as his ancestors have done for centuries before him, eking out a meager existence for himself and his family.

He nevertheless enjoys a warm personal relationship with the *hacendado* who is his *patrón* (*patrão* in Brazil) and who shows a paternalistic regard for his problems and welfare. This relationship affords a sense of security to him; he knows that in time of extreme need or trouble, he and members of his family will receive the help they ask for.

Another segment of the rural class consists of laborers who are employed on the large, corporate, highly mechanized farms, sometimes called "factories in the field." There the worker, enjoying stable employment, punches a time clock, works regular hours, and is paid fairly and honestly in coin of the realm that is good anywhere he may choose to spend it.[52]

Often he is there only for a harvest season or so and then moves on, usually in the hope of somehow bettering himself. During his stay, his relations with management are businesslike and impersonal, with no tinge whatever of paternalism. Lacking an understanding *patrón* to turn to in time of trouble, he feels unsure and insecure, rootless and alone. As a result he is apt to respond readily to the labor leader or political radical who promises to befriend him. He also tends to look increasingly to government as a new *patrón* who will take care of his problems.

Another group of rural workers only spasmodically employed would doubtlessly be in the lower lower class. The *macaqueiros* of Brazil, for example, toil as water carriers, road workers, field hands, or washerwomen; others are prostitutes or beggars. As their jobs are menial,

---

[52] The new pattern of work on a large corporate farm is described by Harry W. Hutchinson in *Village and Plantation Life in Northeastern Brazil* (Seattle: University of Washington Press, 1957), p. 107.

seasonal, intermittent, and unpredictable, they jump from one job to another—hence the term *macaqueiro* which means, "like a monkey."[53]

Submerged in poverty and squalor, they are complete social outcasts. "Their clothes are so torn and few in number," says Marvin Harris, "that they are even ashamed to go to church. Partly for the same reason their children do not attend school. At the religious and secular *fiestas* the *macaqueiros* appear on the fringes, unable to bid at the auctions, dance at the dances, or walk in the processions." This outcast group, he continues, "manages barely to meet the basic requirements of metabolism by abstaining from a series of social requirements deemed by the rest of the society to be as necessary as food itself."[54]

The Urban Lower Class. Since early colonial days there has also been an urban lower class; a mudsill society always needs plenty of hewers of wood and drawers of water. The urban group, although not presently as large as the rural in most of the nations, is increasing much faster than the total population, as Figures 3–1 and 3–2 show, whether from natural increase or from migration, as reflected in Figure 3–3.

The cities are growing at a fantastic rate. From one end of Latin America to the other, peons and other farm workers have been leaving the farms by the millions and pouring into the cities, drawn to them as irresistibly as Mohammedans to Mecca. They come in droves, on foot, by cart, bus, train, and river boat, bringing their belongings, usually only what they wear on their backs and a few pesos they have managed to save, but bringing mainly a "pocketful of dreams."

Although never seeming to have enough jobs, the city does offer a wide variety of work for persons in the lower class. The construction going on everywhere on public buildings, factories, and homes provides many jobs for skilled and unskilled laborers. The increasing number of factories too provide many such jobs. And there are various other employment opportunities for manual laborers, as stevedores and truck drivers, domestics and laundresses, candy peddlers, newsboys, and shoe shiners.

While their jobs pay three or four times as much as those in the rural areas, the cost of living is much higher and housing is a critical problem, especially for the new arrivals. As a result they usually end up as squatters in one of the many *favelas* mushrooming like cancerous growths on the periphery of the cities. These slums cling to the hillsides in Caracas, Rio de Janeiro, and São Paulo, rest on the mud flats in Recife. As rude shelter for protection against the elements and for providing a semblance of family living, *favelados* throw up a one-room shack of whatever material is available: scraps of lumber, found or stolen; flattened gasoline cans; poles,

---

[53] Marvin Harris, *Town and Country in Brazil* (New York: Columbia University Press, 1956), pp. 104–5.
[54] *Ibid.*

FIGURE 3-1

PERCENTAGES OF URBAN POPULATION

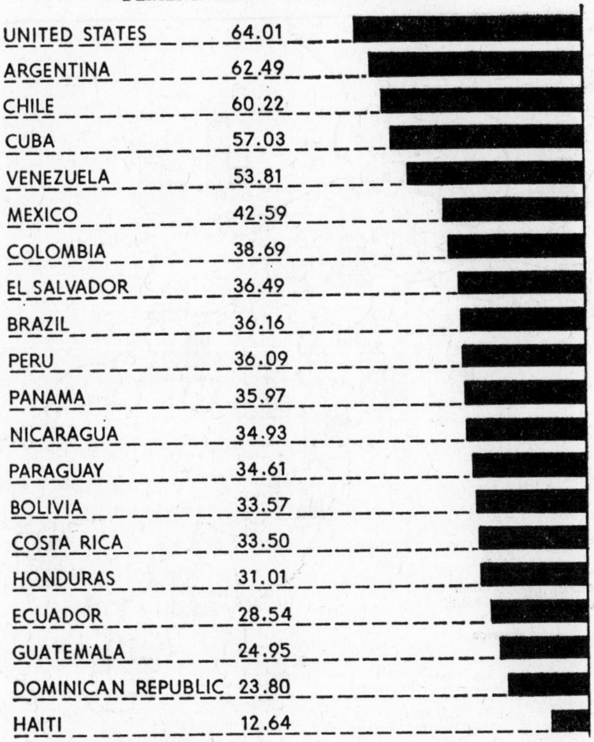

70%

UNITED STATES	64.01
ARGENTINA	62.49
CHILE	60.22
CUBA	57.03
VENEZUELA	53.81
MEXICO	42.59
COLOMBIA	38.69
EL SALVADOR	36.49
BRAZIL	36.16
PERU	36.09
PANAMA	35.97
NICARAGUA	34.93
PARAGUAY	34.61
BOLIVIA	33.57
COSTA RICA	33.50
HONDURAS	31.01
ECUADOR	28.54
GUATEMALA	24.95
DOMINICAN REPUBLIC	23.80
HAITI	12.64

SOURCE: *Center of Intercultural Formation* (CIF) *Study No. 1*, p. 63.
Reproduced by permission.

thatch, and mud. Crates, drums, and boxes usually serve as furniture.
Maybe there is one old iron bed on which six sleep, three at the head and
three at the foot. Others sleep in hammocks hung over the bed or on mats
strewn about the earthen floor. "There they endure their afflictions, pains,
and personal dramas in silence . . . the sadness etched on every face."[55]

Yet whatever the privation and discomfort, migrants from the country,
having once tasted city life, seldom go back to the farm.

Power and Influence of the Lower Class. In most of the countries the
large lower class has very little political power or influence. Most of the
members are illiterate, a handicap which precludes an effective awareness
of the ramifications of economic and political problems. And since in
many countries literacy is a requisite for voting, they are prevented from
participating in politics. But even when given the suffrage and possibly
encouraged to exercise it, they often show very little interest. Their

---

[55] Walmyr Maranhão, "Recife Carnival," *Américas*, Vol. 12, No. 3 (March, 1960),
p. 17.

FIGURE 3–2

URBAN POPULATION GROWING FASTER THAN TOTAL POPULATION

SOURCE: *UN Statistical Yearbook; Economic Commission for Latin America,* as given in Chase National Bank, *Latin American Business Highlights,* 3rd Quarter, 1964, p. 5. Reproduced by permission.

struggle for sheer existence leaves little time or concern for the privileges and duties of an articulate, politically conscious citizen.

The peons on the haciendas and plantations are the ones who have the least political power and influence. In most countries where the big land-owners still determine public policy or at least effectively veto reforms,

FIGURE 3-3

PERCENTAGE OF URBAN INCREASE DUE TO NATURAL INCREASE AND MIGRATION

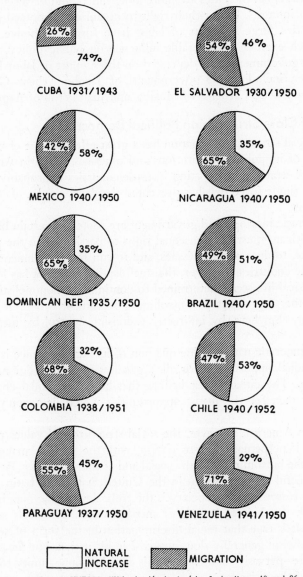

CUBA 1931/1943 — 26%, 74%

EL SALVADOR 1930/1950 — 54%, 46%

MEXICO 1940/1950 — 42%, 58%

NICARAGUA 1940/1950 — 35%, 65%

DOMINICAN REP. 1935/1950 — 35%, 65%

BRAZIL 1940/1950 — 49%, 51%

COLOMBIA 1938/1951 — 32%, 68%

CHILE 1940/1952 — 47%, 53%

PARAGUAY 1937/1950 — 55%, 45%

VENEZUELA 1941/1950 — 29%, 71%

☐ NATURAL INCREASE   ▨ MIGRATION

SOURCE: UNESCO, "Urbanización in América Latina," pp. 18 and 96, as given in (CIF) *Study No. 1*, p. 62. Reproduced by permission.

the rural workers have been prevented by law from organizing and presenting a united front. Thus disorganized and weak, they are easily controlled, even used to promote the interests of the *hacendados*. In fact, the strong conservative parties in Brazil, Chile, Colombia, Ecuador, Nicaragua, and Uruguay, representing the interests of the big landowners, ". . . get their electoral strength mainly from the ability of landowners to march their peons to the polls to vote as their masters instruct them."[56]

The workers in the cities are more independent and better able to promote their interests. Under their right to organize, guaranteed in most of the countries, large segments of labor have formed cohesive, powerful units which exercise considerable influence on public policy. In several countries, governments that depended on the support of labor have come into power, including the governments of Jacobo Arbenz Guzmán of Guatemala, Lázaro Cárdenas of Mexico, and Juan Perón of Argentina.

Effects of Class Structure on Political Democracy

The social structure of a nation has a great effect on the character and evolution of its political institutions and practices. In Latin America the rigid social stratification existing in most countries is probably the most important single force that has prevented the development of democratic government.

Democratic ideology and government are rooted in certain basic premises. All citizens must have an equal right to participate in the public life of the state, to decide public issues, and to run for government office. In most of the countries, however, the small landed elite that has long dominated political life seems determined to continue its monopolistic hold on power, either by directly controlling government where it is strong enough, or, elsewhere, by indirectly exercising control by means of the veto.

In a democratic nation a sine qua non of its very existence is the guarantee of equal opportunity for all, regardless of race, religion, or other differences. The citizen must believe that he has an equal chance with his fellow men for the many opportunities which democracy seeks to provide.

In Latin America, however, the social structure and values practically assure a self-perpetuating caste system, with the mass permanently consigned to the bottom rung of the social and economic ladder. Referring to the disgraceful racial problem in the United States, the Latin American sometimes reasons that his society is the truly democratic one; because he sleeps with the Negro, Indian, or mestizo woman, he feels an aura of tolerance. It is true that racial discrimination in the form of segregation or Jim Crowism generally does not exist in his nation, but the real segregation there—pervasive and effective—is denial of opportunity to the great majority of the citizens.

In a democratic state, too, men must be able to move easily from one social class to another on the basis of individual merit and ability. Democracy does not and cannot prevent the existence of classes; because of differences in environment and other influences, social classes are inevita-

---

[56] Charles O. Porter and Robert J. Alexander, *The Struggle for Democracy in Latin America* (New York: The Macmillan Company, 1961), p. 27.

ble. Yet the class lines should not be rigid and inflexible. If they tend to be, as is the case in Latin America, they are the very antithesis of a democratic society. ⟩

Only time itself can tell which class will ultimately control the destiny of Latin America. If the middle class is too slow in emerging and asserting itself, and if the powerful oligarchy continues to thwart social reform, control may pass by default to the lower class.

Anticipating this possibility, Francisco Julião, the rabidly communist leader in northeast Brazil, succinctly proclaims, "I've got a General on my side—Hunger!"

Perhaps this is an exaggerated boast. But, paradoxically, this hunger is food for thought.

SUGGESTED READINGS

ADAMS, RICHARD N., *et al.* *Social Change in Latin America Today*. Council on Foreign Relations. New York: Harper & Bros., 1960.

ALBA, VICTOR. "The Latin American Style and the New Social Forces," *Latin American Issues: Essays and Comments* (ed. ALBERT O. HIRSCHMAN), pp. 43–53. New York: Twentieth Century Fund, 1961.

AZEVEDO, THALES DE. *Social Change in Brazil*, chap. ii. Latin American Monograph Series, No. 22. Gainesville, Fla.: University of Florida Press, 1963.

BIESANZ, JOHN, AND BIESANZ, MAVIS. *The People of Panama*, pp. 202–70. New York: Columbia University Press, 1955.

BRESSER, L. C. Pereira. "The Rise of Middle Class and Middle Management in Brazil," *Journal of Inter-American Studies*, Vol. IV, No. 3 (July, 1962), pp. 313–26.

CLINE, HOWARD F. *Mexico: Revolution to Evolution: 1940–1960*, chap. xi. Royal Institute of International Affairs. New York: Oxford University Press, 1962.

FLUHARTY, VERNON L. *Dance of the Millions; Military Rule and Social Revolution in Colombia: 1930–1956*, pp. 174–201. Pittsburgh: University of Pittsburgh Press, 1957.

FREYRE, GILBERTO. *New World in the Tropics; The Culture of Modern Brazil*, chap. iv. New York: Alfred A. Knopf, Inc., 1959.

HARRIS, MARVIN. *Town and Country in Brazil*, pp. 96–146. New York: Columbia University Press, 1956.

HUTCHINSON, HARRY W. *Village and Plantation Life in Northeastern Brazil*. Seattle: University of Washington Press, 1957.

LEWIS, OSCAR. *Five Families; Mexican Case Studies in the Culture of Poverty*. New York: Basic Books, Inc., 1959.

MCBRIDE, GEORGE MCCUTCHEN. *Chile: Land and Society*, chap. i. American Geographical Society Research Series, No. 19. New York, 1936.

NELSON, LOWRY. *Rural Cuba*, chaps. vii and ix. Minneapolis: University of Minnesota Press, 1950.

PIERSON, DONALD. *Negroes in Brazil: A Study of Race Contact at Bahia*, chaps. vi–viii. Chicago: University of Chicago Press, 1942.

PORTER, CHARLES O., AND ALEXANDER, ROBERT J. *The Struggle for Democracy in Latin America*, pp. 44–60. New York: The Macmillan Company, 1961.

TUMIN, MELVIN M. *Social Class and Social Change in Puerto Rico.* Princeton University Press, 1961.

WAGLEY, CHARLES. *Amazon Town: A Study of Man in the Tropics*, chap. iv. New York: The Macmillan Company, 1953.

——. "The Dilemma of the Latin American Middle Classes," *Proceedings of the Academy of Political Science, Economic and Political Trends in Latin America*, Vol. XXVII, No. 4 (May, 1964), pp. 2–10.

——. *An Introduction to Brazil*, chap. 3. New York: Columbia University Press, 1963.

WHETTEN, NATHAN L. *Guatemala: The Land and the People*, chap. 4. Caribbean Series, 4. New Haven, Conn.: Yale University Press, 1961.

——. *Rural Mexico*, chap. 4. Chicago: University of Chicago Press, 1948.

CHAPTER 4

THE FAMILY:
A Loyalty Still Strong but Waning

THE FAMILY is easily one of the most important institutions in Latin America. As the primary group in society it exerts a greater influence on the individual than does any other group. It determines what class he will belong to, what rank he will have within his class, and what cultural background he will be exposed to during the most formative years of his life.

The family is of interest to us not only as a key social unit but also as one of the major influences shaping the nations' political and economic development.

THE TYPES OF MARITAL UNIONS

In Latin America there are three usual types of marital unions: civil marriages, church marriages, and consensual or free unions. The three, very different in their contraction and sanction, reflect in many ways the social and economic chasm between the haves and the have-nots, the some-bodies and the nobodies. They reflect too the long struggle of the state to circumscribe the powers of the church and to put the family under its control and protection.

The civil marriage is performed in accordance with the laws of the state and by a government official, usually a justice of the peace, in a ceremony that is simple, brief, and inexpensive. If he and his clerk, how-ever, have to go out to a village to perform the ceremony, their traveling expenses together with the fee, cost of papers, and stamps may amount to more than a small farmer or sharecropper earns in a month.[1]

The civil marriage is popular with many in the rising middle class and

---

[1] Marvin Harris, *Town and Country in Brazil* (New York: Columbia University Press, 1956), p. 161.

is almost invariably the one that members of the lower class have, if they have any formal ceremony at all. With its modest, unpretentious, egalitarian background, however, it does not ordinarily enhance one's social status; no ambitious social climber would think of going to a justice of the peace to be united if he could possibly do better.

Since their attainment of independence, the republics have strongly promoted civil marriage. In Mexico it is the only form recognized by the state since the 1910 revolution, which drastically limited the influence and activities of the Roman Catholic Church. According to the constitution of 1917, "Marriage is a civil contract. This and other acts of a civil nature concerning persons are within the exclusive competence of the civil officials and authorities."[2] In other Latin-American nations the church ceremony must be supplemented by a civil ceremony, which usually must be held first; and in still others, the religious service alone is sufficient when it is properly registered with the authorities. In Guatemala, under a law of June 2, 1959, priests and ministers may obtain authorization to perform marriages that are legally recognized by the government.[3]

If most Latin Americans about to be married "had their druthers," doubtlessly they would choose a church wedding, with all its solemnity, pomp, and prestige. This is the only marriage that has the blessing and sanction of the Catholic Church. According to Catholic doctrine, the family has a divine and natural origin, which gives the Church alone the authority to perform marriages. The state, it contends, has no right to require only a civil ceremony.[4]

Yet despite the Church's emphasis on religious marriage, the number of persons united in wedlock by the priest is but a very small minority of the total population. Since a church wedding is the marriage of status, why do not more Latin-American couples marry in the church, especially since it is the only ceremony sanctioned by the Church and Latin America is predominantly Catholic?

Some persons just do not care for a "big wedding," which a religious ceremony usually entails, but instead prefer the simplicity of a civil ceremony. Others with an anticlerical bent are content to have their marital bond tied and recorded with the seal of approval of the state. But apparently most of those who might be expected because of their social and religious background to prefer a religious ceremony are deterred from it by one thing only—the cost.

To the wealthy, the expense of a church wedding, with its concomitant glamour and ostentation, presents no problems at all—rather it is welcomed as another opportunity to impress society with their affluence. In this

---

2 Mexican Constitution of 1917, Article 130.

3 Nathan L. Whetten, *Guatemala: The Land and the People* (New Haven, Conn.: Yale University Press, 1961), p. 244.

4 John J. Kennedy, *Catholicism, Nationalism, and Democracy in Argentina* (Notre Dame, Ind.: University of Notre Dame Press, 1958), p. 202.

respect Brazil's *nouveaux riches* set a fast pace for any society. When Francisco Matarazzo's granddaughter married in 1945, the wedding was preceded by 8 receptions, 26 dinners, and 23 suppers; the ceremonies proper lasted three days and cost $300,000.[5]

The rural families, mere bush leaguers by comparison, cannot afford to pitch such a lavish show, but they do the best they can. "The *campesinos* who marry celebrate the occasion in high style . . . The bride's father rides through the streets inviting friends to the feast and loudly announcing the menu: rice with chitterlings, chicken, pork, *sancocho,* six roast suckling pigs, liquid refreshments, meringues, *chicas,* white rolls, and painted tortillas."[6]

The menu is enough to make anyone's mouth water, especially a country bumpkin who is apt to favor his stomach. It is also expensive enough sometimes to keep the bride's father in hock for years.

Much as the state stresses civil marriage and much as the church stresses religious marriage, both types are limited mainly to the upper and middle classes of society. In the lower class, which is by far the largest in most countries, the great majority of persons live in what is known as the consensual or free union. In effect it is a common-law marriage where the man and woman live together as husband and wife, exhibiting toward each other and also toward the community the responsibility that a legal marital relationship imposes. Neither sanctioned by the state nor blessed by the church, this do-it-yourself union is sometimes known as "living in friendship."

Sometimes the friendship is quite stable, and the couple live together as blissfully and loyally as though they had been married by the justice of the peace, the priest, or perhaps both. Sometimes in fact, after having lived together many years, they finally get married. This may be the consequence of some good fortune, as getting a better paying job; persuasion on the part of their grown children, who regard marriage as important; or possibly the refusal of the priest to give extreme unction unless they are married. Other free unions may last for years and then for some reason or another break up. Still others are so short term as to be mere passing fancies and, whether by design or by accident, are little more than shacking up.[7]

This living in sin, as the more strait-laced brand it, or in friendship, as the sympathetically inclined term it, is an embarrassing and frustrating social problem for Latin America. A high degree of illegitimacy is hardly a credit to any society, especially an overwhelmingly Catholic community

----

[5] Richard M. Morse, *From Community to Metropolis: A Biography of São Paulo, Brazil* (Gainesville, Fla.: University of Florida Press, 1958), p. 218.

[6] John and Mavis Biesanz, *The People of Panama* (New York: Columbia University Press, 1955), p. 282.

[7] For a good account of the several types of marital unions, see Elman R. and Helen S. Service, *Tobatí: Paraguayan Town* (Chicago: University of Chicago Press, 1954), pp. 142–44 and 158–61.

that puts great stress on the sanctity of the family. But since such a large part of the populace lives in free union and has never been married by either a civil or religious ceremony, up to seventy percent of the children in some countries are *naturales,* a euphonious word meaning bastards.[8]

Why do so many couples in the lower class live together in consensual union instead of being married by the priest or justice of the peace? For one thing, the cost of either kind of ceremony is often a big deterrent to getting married. Besides the fee for the justice of the peace or offering for the priest, there is the far larger expense of the wedding party, a lavish feast that is regarded by most persons as a "must" for any wedding. But a more important consideration than cost is the sanction that is given the free union by public opinion. Within the community, whether rural or urban, the relationship is accepted with little or no disapproval by the rest of society. No social stigma results from living *amancebados* (in concubinage) or *apalabrados* (promised). In fact, in many areas either relationship is considered to be almost as respectable as a legal union itself.

Apparently more important, however, than either the high cost of marriage or the social acceptance of free union is the nature of the marital bond and the attitude of most lower-class persons toward it. Since divorce is forbidden in most countries except on very narrow grounds, marriage is generally regarded as indissoluble. But while "till death do us part" may express the idealistic concept of marriage, it is not accepted as a realistic solution to the problem of marital incompatibility. As a result, the man and the woman both shy away from a relationship that neither one of them can leave if it turns out badly. Buying a lottery ticket with a 1 in 10,000 chance of winning is not regarded as a bad risk, but a 1 in 2 chance of winning on "for better or for worse" is a gamble that frightens many away from formal marriage.

---

[8] In Cali, Colombia, an analysis of 168 families according to married status revealed the following percentages in each group with from 1 to 11 children:

Number of Children	Married Percent	Widowed, Separated, Abandoned with Children—Percent	Free Union Percent
1	6.7	35.8	17.1
2	25.8	15.4	19.5
3	22.0	20.5	26.8
4	18.0	10.2	19.5
5	11.3	7.7	2.4
6	4.5	2.6	4.9
7	3.4	2.6	...
8	2.2	...	4.9
9	2.2	2.6	4.9
10	...	...	...
11	1.2	...	...

SOURCE: Juan Luis de Lannoy and Gustavo Pérez, *Estructuras Demográphicas y Sociales de Colombia* (Serie Socio-económica); (Bogotá, Colombia: Centro de Investigaciones Sociales, 1961), p. 172.

Although consensual unions are formed outside the purview of the law, it is forced to take cognizance of the common-law relationship that has been freely assumed by such a large part of the populace in every country. Once the relationship is legally recognized, its status under law is definite and enjoys most of the advantages of a legal marriage. The difficulty, however, has been to decide when and under what conditions such a union becomes a legally recognized relationship.[9]

The constitutions and laws of the different nations have established various criteria for determining this. A provision in the Panamanian constitution of 1946 specifies: "A union in fact between persons legally capacitated to contract matrimony, maintained during ten consecutive years in conditions of singularity and stability, will have all the effects of civil matrimony."[10] Other countries have similar laws that differ mainly in the duration required of the union. Guatemala, for example, specifies three years[11] and Bolivia, only two.[12]

THE PATRIARCHAL UPPER AND MIDDLE CLASS FAMILY

Role of the Husband

In the upper and middle classes, the family is strongly authoritarian and patriarchal. The father is the unquestioned head of his brood; his word is law with his wife, his children, his relatives that live with them and, of course, with his servants. Virtually on his own he makes the important decisions for the group or any one of its members, ruling with an iron hand if necessary.

The highly authoritarian control he exercises is the result of several historic influences. On the Iberian peninsula the father was a little dictator within the family circle, a tradition that was brought over by the colonists to the New World. Here, the father on occasion even exercised the momentous power of life and death, and there are cases where he actually had his own son put to death. "It was that God's will might be done that I had my son killed," wrote patriarch Pedro Vieira, who ordered an older son to slay his younger brother. "God's will" with Vieira was his jealous discovery that one of his sons was having relations with his favorite slave girl.[13]

Catholicism has also contributed to the strong role of the father, stressing as it does the necessity of obedience and submission on the part of other members of the family.

[9] Melvin M. Tumin, *Social Class and Social Change in Puerto Rico* (Princeton, N.J.: Princeton University Press, 1961), p. 249.

[10] Constitution of 1946, Article 56.

[11] Whetten, *op. cit.*, p. 240.

[12] Constitution of 1961, Article 131.

[13] Gilberto Freyre, *The Masters and the Slaves* (2d Eng. ed. rev.; New York: Alfred A. Knopf, Inc., 1956), p. xxxix.

There are a number of ways by which the father maintains his position and asserts his authority within the family. For one thing, he would not deign to perform any of the household chores that American husbands commonly do. He would not think, for example, of lowering his dignity by mowing the grass, putting up storm windows, or washing the automobile; these are menial tasks to be performed by a servant. Even more abhorrent to him would be the very idea of changing a diaper or pushing a stroller along the sidewalk, tasks too utterly sissified for the he-man that he is.

A quip that "the honeymoon is over when he stops helping her with the dishes—and begins doing them himself" is usually good for a laugh in the United States. The Latin American male, however, would think it quite nonsensical. And as the undisputed master of his household, he vaunts his authority and independence in yet another way—the many extramarital affairs he engages in. Convinced that he is more virile than men of other races, he worships at the shrine of *machismo* (masculinity) and takes great pride in his feminine conquests. Whether he is the driver of a bus or president of a bank, he is apt to show his sexual prowess not only by occasional forays of seduction but also by supporting a *querida* (mistress) or a *casa chica* (little house).

He has ample time to maintain one, maybe several, of these extramarital relationships outside the home. Sharing few diversions with his wife, he seldom takes her anywhere except possibly to family parties, to weddings, or to formal receptions. Most evenings she baby-sits at home, uncomplainingly and unquestioningly, while he steps out with his girl friend to the races, cabarets, and night clubs.

With the modest income that most husbands have, supporting an additional household or two is often a heavy financial burden. This is another frustration of the middle class, just like the cost of servants, refrigerators, washing machines, homes, and automobiles—all things that members of the class desire but find very difficult to afford. But the *querida* and *casa chica*, like the servant, are such symbols of status and personal pride that the male somehow manages to include them in his budget, possibly by holding down an extra job, by working longer hours, and more especially by cutting down on what he allows his wife for running the home.

Neither limited income nor personal prominence is a serious deterrent to extramarital ventures. Indeed, even statesmen and high governmental officials indulge in them without any apparent loss in public esteem. Quite to the contrary, as one observer facetiously notes: "So generally accepted among Latin Americans is the extra-marital lark that it is dirty politics to hint that a *político* is faithful to his wife."[14]

In Guatemala President Miguel Ydígoras Fuentes took the unprecedented step of trying to curb the extramarital interests of governmental personnel. In a memorandum quietly circulated to all government min-

---

[14] *Newsweek*, August 28, 1961, p. 40.

isteries and departments, he cautioned: "There have been public whispers, and with reason, some government officials not only maintain mistresses but are seen in public with them. Since on a public employee's salary it is impossible to support two homes, will you please warn your personnel that he on whom this is proved, will be removed in the interest of the state." Department heads read the circular and signed it as instructed, but they did not take it seriously. "If Ydígoras really meant business," one observer exclaimed, "you would see whole government agencies deserted for lack of personnel to man them!"[15]

From many indications, *machismo* is more prevalent in the cities than in the rural areas and in the middle and upper classes than in the lower. Sometimes it expresses itself in husbands' continuing after marriage to visit prostitutes, though "with lessened frequency and increasing circumspection." Apparently most wives expect and even tolerate such behavior so long as their husbands make a reasonable effort to keep it secret from them and the rest of the community.[16] More often, however, *machismo* expresses itself in the *querida*, who bestows her favors on a low income paramour in return for help with the rent and grocery bill, or on a wealthy lover in return for a lavish apartment, flashy automobile, and charge accounts at all the best stores.

Often the most conspicuous feature in a society that enjoys conspicuous consumption, "the *querida* is a prestige item, like a Cadillac. Men flaunt their mistresses, take other men to call on them, provide them with luxuries usually far more expensive than those they give their wives. Panamanians boast, 'We do not hide our mistresses like the Costa Ricans.' *Queridas* are the subject of gossip at the market and in the park; everyone seems to know all about such relationships and to tolerate them. It is generally agreed that a man has a right to as many mistresses as he can afford."[17]

Attributing his successes to his virility and irresistible charm—to his being a Rudolph Valentino, Clark Gable, and Rock Hudson all rolled into one—the *macho* (he-man) would be the last to admit the real explanation for his easy conquests—the existence of a large number of underprivileged women who can be exploited for pesos or *cruzeiros*, especially enough of them.

As the position of women continues to improve in Latin America, however, *machismo*, *queridas*, and *casas chicas* are expected to be less and less prevalent until they cease to be institutions that are characteristic of the society. In fact, changes are already in evidence, as in Panama, where women enjoy a relatively independent role, thanks largely to the foreign influences to which the society has been exposed. From the observation of John and Mavis Biesanz,

---

[15] *Ibid.*, pp. 40, 44.
[16] Harris, *op. cit.*, pp. 166–67.
[17] Biesanz, *op. cit.*, p. 300.

More and more in Panama . . . young men are coming to believe that wife and sweetheart can be one and the same, for they have increasing freedom of choice in marriage and less likelihood of social ostracism and disinheritance if they marry a pretty lower-class sweetheart. Also, with increasing education and freedom of action, women are better companions to their husbands; since they practice birth control they are less tied down. They are also less resigned to male infidelity.[18]

Status and Role of the Wife

In decided contrast to the husband, the typical upper or middle class wife in Latin America leads a very circumscribed life. Her place is in the home and she seldom goes outside except to do the shopping, visit relatives, or go to Mass. Her principal duties are to adore and obey her husband, to bear and raise his children, and to supervise the domestic operation of the household. In fact, most of her time is spent in running the home. The cooking, cleaning, laundering, and other domestic tasks are all done by a servant or servants. She would not think of doing these, for it would lower her to the status of a servant. Moreover, she knows that her husband expects her to be radiant and lovely, with no semblance of dishpan hands or housemaid's knee.

Confined to her home, she does not share in the freedom of Hispanic-American individualism so enjoyed by her roving-eyed, footloose husband. Put on a pedestal by him, she is always expected to be a model of virtue and feminine behavior. In this exalted status, she is under constant social pressure to avoid doing anything, however slight, that might make her honor subject to the least suspicion.

For all practical purposes the wife is kept in a chastity belt.

Her husband may be carrying on an affair that is the gossip of the town, but her conduct at all times must adhere to the strictest moral standards and be beyond reproach, even by the exacting demands of the understandably suspicious Latin-American males. When she goes to market, accompanied by a servant, she would not dare to stop and chat briefly with a man on the street, even though he is a good friend of the family; anyone else seeing the friend talking to her would immediately assume that he was attempting to proposition her. He probably would be, too!

Although they lead very circumscribed lives, wives have appeared to be contented with their lot and to accept gracefully their confining, double-standard existence. They value the love and devotion of their children—the passionate affection of their philandering husbands too, even though this affection, according to Charles Edward Chapman, ". . . is a love, not so much for an equal partner, as for a possession, though prized far more highly than one's favorite dog or horse, for example." Yet

---

[18] *Ibid.*, p. 299.

despite wives' chattel-like existence, Chapman concludes that ". . . they seem to be happy, and to have the kind of life they want."[19]

What may perhaps seem most surprising, Latin-American women do not appear to attach great importance to fidelity on the part of the husband. Indeed, according to some opinions, "Women expect their husbands to have *queridas* just as they expect their children to have measles."[20] According to a poll conducted in Costa Rica to ascertain feminine attitudes on the subject of traits desired in a husband, the married women rated fidelity fourteenth! In their scale of feminine values the most important quality was believed to be culture, defined as "manners, courtesy, some degree of formal education."[21]

What could account for such values, so difficult for us to understand? They result from centuries of conditioning by the home, the church, and society generally. From early girlhood, females are imbued with the conception of a double standard of marital fidelity and with the expectation of philandering by the mate. The Catholic Church, too, is partly responsible for the situation; although in theory it condemns infidelity, in practice it has done little to enforce this condemnation. As a matter of fact, by counseling patience, submission, and resignation on the part of the wife, and by denying her right to a divorce, the Church in effect buttresses the husband's libertinism.

Despite the strong social and religious sanctions, however, all wives are apparently not so submissive. Some retaliate against their unfaithful husbands with extramarital ventures of their own. What is sauce for the goose is sauce for the gander, they reason.

Yet while society is quite willing to overlook male infidelity, dismissing it with the attitude that boys will be boys, unfaithfulness on the part of the wife is abhorred as a cardinal sin. In fact, the husband considers it such an unforgivable insult to his masculine dignity that he feels compelled to divorce an unfaithful wife to preserve his "good name" before society.[22]

Whether unfaithful or faithful—and the great majority of middle and upper class wives are no doubt the latter—wives in these groups paradoxically "live with much more marital distress" than do wives in the lower class. The latter are accustomed to working for a living and know they can support themselves. Being financially independent and bound only by ties of "friendship," not law, they are the equals and partners of their husbands; if the friendship terminates, the wife is as free as the husband in deciding to separate.

In striking contrast, however, are most middle and upper class wives,

[19] Charles Edward Chapman, *Republican Hispanic America: A History* (New York: The Macmillan Company, 1937), p. 15.

[20] Biesanz, *op. cit.*, p. 300.

[21] John and Mavis Biesanz, *Costa Rican Life* (New York: Columbia University Press, 1944), p. 62.

[22] Biesanz, *The People of Panama, op. cit.*, p. 301.

who are unable to earn their own way and would not be interested in doing so if they could. Accepting their chains, even coming to love them according to some, they are willing to swallow their pride and continue on their lofty, lonely pedestal; a breakup of the home must be avoided at all costs.[23]

This attitude is doubtlessly held by most upper and middle class wives. But one country in particular does not conform to the prevailing pattern in Latin America. In Uruguay "its women, especially those of Montevideo, have a much better psychological, economic, and legal status than is true of those in almost any other country in Latin America . . ." says Russell Fitzgibbon. "The roving and appraising masculine eye is not nonexistent in Uruguay, but it is much less in evidence than elsewhere in Latin America. Women have achieved a highly commendable degree of social emancipation." They have played quite an active role in politics as well as in business and professional life. Too, they have won the right to own property, seek a divorce, and in general to be recognized as "equals capable of taking an intelligent part in a conversation, a business deal, a governmental enterprise, or a cultural activity."[24]

Some other countries have attempted to provide legal equality of the sexes. In Cuba, according to the 1940 constitution, there is an "absolute equality of rights of both husband and wife . . . The married woman enjoys the full advantages of equal civil capacity, with no necessity for marital permission or authorization in order to manage property, freely to engage in trade, to enter industry or a profession, to practice an art, to hold office, and to dispose of the product of her work."[25]

Other countries too have given attention to the legal equality of the sexes. In Paraguay the constitution provides: "The civil rights of women shall be regulated by law, taking heed of the unity of the family, the equality of woman and man, and the diversity of their respective functions in society."[26]

In addition to these broader provisions designed to give greater rights to women, the countries usually attempt to protect working women during the early period of maternity. In Guatemala, for example, working mothers are guaranteed by the constitution a paid rest for 1 month before childbirth and 45 days afterward. During the period of breast feeding, moreover, they are entitled to two half-hour daily periods of special rest for feeding the child.[27]

With the many social changes that are sweeping over Latin America today, the status and role of women are inevitably changing too. In decided contrast to earlier times, many women have shaken off the confines

---

[23] Tumin, *op. cit.*, p. 256.
[24] Russell Fitzgibbon, *Uruguay: Portrait of a Democracy* (New Brunswick, N.J.: Rutgers University Press, 1954), p. 267.
[25] Constitution of 1940, Article 43.
[26] Constitution of 1940, Article 23.
[27] Constitution of 1956, Article 116.

of the home and have taken jobs of one sort or another. In Panama approximately a third of them work—about the same percentage as in the United States. Women seek employment for several reasons: sometimes they are forced to provide the entire livelihood for the family; sometimes they supplement the family income so they can have things they could not otherwise afford; often they go to work simply because they are bored and desire challenging interests to be found outside the home.

In their newly found freedom they are following a wide variety of occupations. Many are white-collar workers who are employed as secretaries or clerks in government offices, businesses, or industries. Others have invaded the professions and are making contributions to their society as teachers and journalists, doctors and lawyers.

In the realm of politics, too, they are becoming increasingly active. Some have been elected mayors, as in San Juan, Puerto Rico, and Santiago, Chile, or elected members of the national congress. Others have held some of the highest appointive positions in their countries, including membership in the cabinet, judgeships, or diplomatic assignments.

In at least one country, the new role and influence of women in politics has been the cause of publicly expressed concern. In an attempt to stem the obvious tide of feminine influence, the Panamanian constitution of 1946 expressly forbids the formation of any political party established solely on the basis of sex, race, or religion.[28] This constitutional restriction was regarded by some feminist leaders as a masculine trick to prevent them from forming a militant reform party that might put an end to governmental corruption and inefficiency.[29]

Care and Training of Children

The training of girls and boys is changing with the greater freedom enjoyed by women, but still tends to conform to the traditional pattern for middle and upper class families. Since the sexes are believed to be basically different psychologically as well as physiologically, great emphasis is put on each sex developing its proper attitudes and values. To this end, at an early age boys and girls are separated in their educational and social activities, and each group is given training that is appropriate for the role it is expected to play in later life.

The father assumes most of the responsibility for the training of the son, who while still very young has instilled in him the masculine traits of self-reliance, aggressiveness, and self-expression. The male, he learns early, is the dominant sex. It is all right for him to strike his older sister who cowers before him and tries to protect herself from his blows. She dare not strike back, as she has learned from long conditioning. By the time the boy is a teen-ager, he accompanies his father to important conferences to acquire confidence and poise. And if he has not already shown an interest

---

[28] Constitution of 1946, Article 103.
[29] Biesanz, *The People of Panama, op. cit.,* p. 164.

in sex, he may be encouraged by his father to take advantage of the nurse or the maid. For the father knows that the *virgo* (the male virgin or even one who is suspected of being virgin) is apt to be the object of derision by his fellows.

The daughter, too, has her own distinctive training. She is taught how to manage the household and see that the servants perform their tasks properly. More importantly, she is taught how to act and think as a lady so that she may be pleasing to men and attractive to her future husband. For the son, premarital sex experience may be condoned or even encouraged, but it is strictly forbidden for the daughter. Any such activity on her part, particularly if she is caught through pregnancy, brings disgrace upon the family.

Consequently, she is always kept under the closest surveillance to protect her virtue and reputation. In the Big House in Brazil, during the day she was under the watchful eye of her mother or a trusted servant, and during the night the vigilance to safeguard her was redoubled. Her small bedroom, located in the center of the house, was surrounded on all four sides by those of her elders. It was "more of a prison than the apartment of a free being."[30] Today as formerly, the daughter is safeguarded as carefully as though the whole family honor depended on her. Among many other restrictions imposed on her, she is never permitted in the company of a young man without the presence of a chaperone.

The romanticist is convinced that marriages are made in heaven. But the Latin American knows otherwise—at least for his part of the globe. There, most of the marriages are arranged by fond parents who pair off their sons and daughters according to their parental conception of status, family congeniality, and, especially, family interests to be served. This selection of mates by parents has hardly been conducive to romance and largely accounts for the lack of basic congeniality between married couples and the philandering role that the husband assumes early in their married life.

The age at which couples marry has changed considerably. In former times it was quite early; in Brazil girls usually married at the age of 14, 13, or even 12. "With an unmarried fifteen year old daughter in the house, the parents already began to be worried and to make promises to Saint Anthony and Saint John. Before she had reached the age of twenty, the girl without a husband was a spinster. Today she would be green fruit, but in those days it was feared that the fruit would spoil from overripeness if no one plucked it in time."[31]

Today the fruit apparently ripens more slowly, and is allowed to hang on the vine much longer. The legal age for marriage is still sometimes quite low; in Cuba it is 14 for boys and only 12 for girls. However, parents must give their consent for marriages between those ages and age 21; and

---

[30] Freyre, *op. cit.*, p. 353.
[31] *Ibid.*, p. 361.

marriages at such early ages are not very common, especially among the males.[32] In fact, the large majority of girls in Latin America are not married until after the age of 20. The boys have a tendency to marry even later.[33]

THE CONVENTIONAL FAMILY IN THE LOWER CLASS

In the lower class conventional family, as in the middle and upper class family, the husband is the undisputed head. He makes all the important decisions for the group, and enforces obedience on the part of his wife and children. Occasionally he even exercises his masculine prerogative of giving the wife a beating, especially if he suspects that she may have been flirting, or worse still, possibly seeing another man.

In running the household the wife does the cooking, the washing, the cleaning, as well as helping with the garden. In some rural areas she is not expected to work in the field, but in others she helps her husband with the planting and harvesting.

The raising of children, too, is quite different in this class. As might well be imagined, they are not pampered in any way. Often they are served last at mealtime and they seldom get a second helping. As an important part of their training, they are taught to obey, respect, and fear their father—an attitude that remains even in adulthood.

At an early age the boy is trained to be industrious and helpful to the family in many ways. He performs certain chores about the house or farm, as running errands to the *tienda* (store) or fetching water from the spring. In fact, according to an old saying, "the last slave in Brazil is a little boy." When he reaches the age of ten or eleven, he is required to work in the garden; and several years later he begins to help in the field with the planting, cultivating, and harvesting of the crops.

Meanwhile, the girl is kept busy in the house helping her mother in a variety of ways; she learns to cook, sew, and do many other feminine tasks for the family. When she reaches her teens, she is watched with particular vigilance by her parents, who eye very suspiciously a boy who pays her any attention. No doubt the father, remembering his own youthful experience, has a point in suspecting the intentions of a boy toward his daughter. They are not likely to be honorable, certainly not if he has the choice.

Any courting during these early years has to be done secretly to avoid

---

[32] Lowry Nelson, *Rural Cuba* (Minneapolis: University of Minnesota Press, 1950), pp. 187–88.

[33] Richard N. Adams, *A Community in the Andes* (American Ethnological Society) (Seattle: University of Washington Press, 1959), p. 158; T. Lynn Smith, *Brazil: People and Institutions* (rev. ed.; Baton Rouge, La.: Louisiana State University Press, 1963), p. 468; and Orlando Fals-Borda, *Peasant Society in the Colombian Andes* (Gainesville, Fla.: University of Florida Press, 1957), pp. 49–50.

the watchful eyes of parents. But as the daughter enters her twenties, they are apt to be less vigilant. It is time for her to get married and the bars are lowered a bit. In the ideal situation a boy interested in her would come to the family and ask permission to visit her. If this was granted, the courtship would in time probably lead to an engagement and marriage.

While the girl is expected to be a virgin when she marries, this is often not the case. Sometimes she sacrificially gives herself before the altar of love. In Panama, "the boy may promise marriage, but usually she is satisfied if he professes love. The Panamanians have a saying, 'The best marriage is love.' "[34] Sometimes the girl cheerfully "proves herself" by producing a child before she expects her suitor to consider her seriously for a wife. Yet often in such cases, the boy tends to vanish magically when the subject of marriage is brought up.

When a couple do not intend to marry legally, they may simply elope. In Paraguay the elopement is popularly known as "marriage by capture." Although the girl has encouraged and even helped to plan the venture, which makes her an accessory before as well as after the fact, it is nevertheless called a "capture" and she is regarded as an unwilling, helpless victim.[35] In some areas there is a premarital period of sexual adjustment called *amancebamiento* when a couple may live together on a sort of trial basis, as in a common-law union.[36] If it lasts longer than several months, however, it is frowned upon as cheating on the honor system.

When a boy has deflowered a girl but shows symptoms of being allergic to getting married, he is oftentimes persuaded with the assistance of the local police. In some areas this occurs so frequently that it is the normal way of getting married. The procedure is quite simple; when the father finds that his daughter has been deflowered, he makes a complaint to the police who forthwith proceed to round up the miscreant. Usually the very threat of jail is enough to cure his allergy in a hurry. But despite its coercive aspect, marriage "by the police" actually has one big advantage. All the fees charged by the justice of the peace and the civil registrar are waived. The marriage is strictly "on the house," more specifically on the government, giving the groom quite a financial break.[37]

With the boys, it is always open season for seduction. With the girls, the time when they are most apt to run into trouble is at the fiestas. Parents are too busy whooping it up then to watch over them very closely. The emotions of daughters—of everybody else, too—are apt to run wild, with no thought whatever of *mañana*.

If the girl loses her virginity, the boy sometimes has the choice of either

---

[34] Biesanz, *The People of Panama, op. cit.*, p. 293.
[35] Service, *op. cit.*, p. 272.
[36] Fals-Borda, *op. cit.*, p. 205.
[37] Charles Wagley, *Amazon Town: A Study of Man in the Tropics* (New York: The Macmillan Company, 1953), pp. 171–74.

marrying her or paying her an indemnity. He usually chooses to do the latter, but often gets out of paying by hurriedly ducking out of town. If the girl becomes pregnant, however, he has no choice but to marry her if she wishes it. Should he raise any objections or shirk doing his manly duty, her father and brothers usually seek him out and use whatever force is necessary to persuade him to change his mind.[38] In the United States, this is popularly known as Ye Olde Shotgun Wedding.

THE MATRIFOCAL OR MATRILINEAL FAMILY IN THE LOWER CLASS

A large percentage of the households, mostly in the lower class, are matrifocal or matrilineal families headed by women. In some communities women head almost half the total number of households.[39] In such cases the mother earns the living, usually working in some menial capacity as a cook, maid, washerwoman, or the like. And on her meager income she has to support her children, sometimes a houseful of them, possibly one or both of her parents, and maybe even some of her other relatives. A big order, by any stretch of the imagination.

There are several causes for the widespread existence of the matrifocal family. Foremost among these is the popularity of the "free union," a large majority of which are quite unstable. The "husband" lives with the "wife" only long enough to have a child or two, often as a freeloader, then heads for some greener pasture, leaving her with the offspring. Sometimes, while living with his common-law wife, known as a *conviviente*, he may even have another woman or two with whom he maintains a similar relationship and who also bears him children.[40]

Another cause of the matrifocal family is the decided imbalance between the number of men and women in some areas. Paraguay has long been regarded as a "land of women" because of a very real shortage of men at different times. In early days there were so many more women than men—about ten to one in Asunción, the capital—that the Spaniards acquired "harems" of Guaraní women. Some of these harems contained as many as 40 to 50 females.[41]

In more recent years the tragic War of the Triple Alliance, 1865–70, consumed most of the manpower of Paraguay, leaving many women but few males except very young boys and doddering old men. The more recent bloody war over the Chaco, 1928–35, again cost Paraguay many thousands of casualties. And still more recently, the cruel tenacious dic-

---

[38] Fals-Borda, *op. cit.*, p. 205.

[39] Service, *op. cit.*, p. 45.

[40] Richard W. Patch, "The Role of a Coastal Hacienda in the Hispanization of Andean Indians," *American Universities Field Staff*, March 15, 1959, pp. 8–9.

[41] Service, *op. cit.*, p. 44.

tatorships and economic stagnation have driven many thousands of young
men to Argentina, Uruguay, or Brazil in search of political exile or economic opportunity, again resulting in a noticeable imbalance of the sexes
and a predominance of women in Paraguayan town life.[42]

Another cause of the matrifocal family generally is the fact that the
women tend to live longer than the men, especially among the lower
classes. There the males often burn themselves out in early middle age by
grueling manual labor. As a result there are a large number of widows
who automatically become the heads of their households.[43]

THE EXTENDED FAMILY AND THE
COMPADRE RELATIONSHIP

When you speak of your family, you are probably referring to the
small group at home consisting of your parents and one or several brothers
and sisters. You may also have in mind the close relatives that you ordinarily keep up with. But when the Latin American speaks of his family, he is
referring to a large group, a sort of a clan, that is termed by United States
scholars the "extended family." This consists not only of the immediate
family—the parents, the children, and possibly one or several grandparents
living with them—but also of a host of other relatives, including possibly
great-grandparents, uncles and aunts, nieces and nephews, as well as numerous cousins, from the first cousin close by on the family tree to distant
twigs that the family genealogist might refer to as sixth cousins, or is it
fifth cousins once removed?

So great is the Latin American's interest in his family that it is not unusual for him to keep up closely with 100 or more relatives. According to
a survey made in São Paulo, he might even be able to identify as many as
500![44] Both in the city and in the country, the large extended family is the
rule. Indeed, the small immediate family consisting of the husband, wife,
and children who live isolated from their relatives is quite the exception
throughout Latin America. And anyone who has no kin, such as in the
case of an abandoned orphan, is regarded as one of the most pitied members of society.

In addition to its large size, the traditional family in Latin America is
also notable for its cohesiveness and closeness. It is by far the most tightly
knit unit in society, without even the semblance of a rival. Indeed, its
strength and cohesiveness are among the most cherished traditions of the
region. In the aristocratic, patriarchal society of Brazil, the wishes and
interests of the family predominated over individual desires when in-

---

[42] *Ibid.*, pp. 44–45.
[43] Raymond T. Smith, "The Family in the Caribbean," *Caribbean Studies: A
Symposium* (ed. Vera Rubin) (Seattle: University of Washington Press, 1960), p. 70.
[44] Morse, *op. cit.*, p. 216.

heritance or property was involved; and the collective interests of all were safeguarded by the family council, an institution that is still powerful in the nation.[45]

The closeness of the family is also shown by the frequent marriages that take place between members of the group. In Brazil consanguineous marriages have been common since the first century of colonization. Often a man married a niece or a cousin, usually for the purpose of preventing the dispersal of the family property or to preserve the purity of the family bloodstream of noble or illustrious origin.[46] Marriage between first cousins still occurs occasionally, more frequently in the upper class than in the lower, sometimes to keep estates from being dispersed and sometimes because mates of equal social position are just not available.[47]

Besides marrying close relatives, members of the family often show their cohesiveness by living closely together. In the rural areas on the big plantations or ranches, whenever a son married it was a simple matter to provide for family proliferation. Another wing would be built onto the main house for the new family that still drew its succor from the main taproot, or a separate home would be built nearby. But all members of the family would usually eat together and spend most of their time together.

In the country the large landowner also takes cognizance of the family relationships among his workers. They too are apt to have families of the extended type, with grandparents, uncles, aunts, nephews, nieces, cousins, or godchildren living with the husband, wife, and children. Often several families will be related, and the hacienda will accordingly arrange for them to live in adjacent quarters in the housing that it provides for its help.[48]

The closeness and devotion treasured by members of the family are poignantly shown by some of their customs. In Brazil the patriarchal family that lived in the Big House customarily buried its kin underneath the sheltering expanse of the home—more specifically, beneath the chapel which was an annex to it.[49] In this way those who had passed on continued to remain under the same roof with the living. Not even death could separate the members of the family from one another.

Another traditional family custom in some areas is intended to bind the child as closely to his family as though tied to his mother's apron strings. When a baby is born, its umbilical cord is carefully saved and preserved, because if it is lost it is feared that the child will be stubborn or forgetful. And when the child reaches the age of 14 or so, the cord is lovingly removed from its safe depository and buried in a corner of the

---

[45] Lewis Hanke, *South America* (Princeton, N.J.: D. Van Nostrand & Co., Inc., 1959), p. 81.

[46] Freyre, *op. cit.*, p. 356.

[47] Harris, *op. cit.*, p. 103, and Service, *op. cit.*, p. 165.

[48] Patch, *op. cit.*, p. 8.

[49] Freyre, *op. cit.*, p. xxxvi.

house. With it there, it is believed that the child will always be very close to the family circle.[50]

As large and closely knit as it is, the extended family is socially self-sufficient and does not have to look outside for its social interests or gratifications. In fact most of the social activities of its members are carried on strictly within the family circle and between its many members. Whenever there is an anniversary or birthday to be celebrated, or perhaps a graduation to be honored, the members of the group gather together to celebrate the occasion, renew family ties, and enjoy themselves. In between times, too, they maintain close relationships, visiting each other regularly and spending so much time together that they do not feel the need for friends.

With their many close ties and deeply rooted loyalties, the members of a family have a strong sense of responsibility for one another. Standing together one for all and all for one, they help to bear each other's burdens and also to share in each other's successes. If a member of the family is stricken with a serious illness or loses his job, the other members will all pitch in and render aid in every possible way. The whole family would lose caste, as well as its own self-respect, if any one of its members in dire need were compelled to ask for public charity.

In similar fashion, if a member of the family is fortunate enough to acquire wealth or high position, he is expected to spread the benefits of his good fortune among all his relatives. If he becomes a government official, for example, he is expected to use his influence and whatever authority he may have to get them appointed to good positions in the government service.[51]

With its cohesiveness, close ties, and deeply rooted loyalties, the family in Latin America is frankly an enigma to most of us in the United States. Its self-sufficiency and lack of need of outsiders seem to present a cold shoulder to the rest of the world. Architecturally the home is an enclave, virtually shut off from the rest of society. A high wall completely surrounds it, preventing the passerby from seeing the lovely patio and exquisite garden, or even in fact from knowing that a home actually exists there. The latchstring is never out, and very few outsiders, whether foreigners or even intimate business associates, are ever invited into the sanctum sanctorum.

Judged by our neighborly standards, the home never lets down its hair in good fellowship, or joins hands with what might be a neighborhood. No neighbor, even one right next door, may go in and ask such a small favor as borrowing a cup of sugar . . . friends never casually drop by for a coke, coffee, or a highball . . . there is never open house to which a wide circle of friends and acquaintances are invited.

---

[50] Service, *op. cit.*, p. 270.
[51] Nelson, *op. cit.*, p. 184.

Another distinctive characteristic of the family in Latin America is *compadrazgo*, the relationship of coparenthood, and *padrinazgo* or godparenthood. Godparents are known as *padrinos* (masculine) and *madrinas* (feminine) by their godchildren, and as *compadres* (masculine) and *comadres* (feminine) by the parents.

These coparents, honored by being invited into the close family circle, are carefully selected by the parents for certain important ceremonial occasions within the family. There are a number of these—as many as 14 in some communities. Some are ceremonies that were instituted by the Christian missionaries, the main ones being the sacraments of baptism, confirmation, and marriage. Others are special occasions long revered and scrupulously observed by the indigenous population, occasions such as the first cutting of hair, the opening of ear lobes, and the first cutting of fingernails.[52] These ceremonies have long been of great significance to primitive and superstitious peoples of the world;[53] how to dispose of the shorn hair or cut nails was as critical a problem to them as how to dispose of the dangerous waste resulting from the production of fissionable materials is for us today.

Selected for these special occasions, the godparents assume a weighty responsibility for the concern and welfare of their godchild. If death or other serious misfortune to the parents should leave the child sorely in need of help, the godparents would step in as auxiliary or substitute parents willing, ready, and able to assume the responsibility of parenthood. In appreciation of this broad commitment on his behalf, the godchild is expected to show respect, affection, and devotion toward his *padrino* and *madrina*. The godfather, or *compadre* and the godmother, or *comadre*, as coparents assume responsibilities toward the parents as well as the child, providing advice, or even material assistance if perhaps they fall on hard times and badly need it.

In reality, the significance of the godparenthood relationship depends largely on the relative social status of the *compadres*, and whether they live in the country or in the city. In the lower class the parents usually select as godparents some wealthy or influential persons who are in a position to help their children, and themselves, too, if help is needed. In rural areas the owner of the hacienda or the *tienda* or the cacique (local political boss) is very often invited to assume this responsibility.

Where the *compadre* and his godchild are separated by class barriers, the coparents do not refer to each other as such because this would imply an inadmissible equality. Yet if the parents die, the godparents would nevertheless rear the orphaned child as an *hijo de casa* (child of the

---

52 Fals-Borda, *op. cit.*, p. 197. For a vivid description of the *quitanaqui*, celebrated at the first haircutting of a child, see Patch, *op. cit.*, p. 6.

53 For the great significance of these ceremonies, see Sir James George Frazer, *The Golden Bough: A Study in Magic and Religion* (1 vol. abridged ed.) (New York: The Macmillan Company, 1951), pp. 272–76.

house), being rewarded for this charitable act by services that he would render about the house until adulthood.[54]

Sometimes a prominent person in the community, such as a doctor or a politician, may have dozens or even a hundred or more godchildren. When this is the case, the bond is understandably rather flimsy and superficial. Not even the most sincere godfather could be expected to raise a hundred or so godchildren. Yet being invited to be a godparent is an honor that one cannot gracefully and in good conscience decline. Sometimes only a small gift of baby clothes or perhaps a toy on birthdays or at Christmas has to suffice as at least a token of a godparent's interest and concern for his godchild.[55]

Among persons of the middle and upper classes, the parents usually select another member of the family or possibly a close friend to act as the godparent of their child. The only considerations in the selection are affection, congeniality, and trust; and ordinarily the responsibility that the godparent assumes is fairly light and nominal. He pays for the cost of the baptism or other ceremony which he is godparent for, and sends gifts to his godchild on birthdays, graduations, and other special occasions. While he assumes the nominal obligations to care for the child if the parents should die, the financial means necessary for the support of the child would be provided by the child's inheritance.

In short, the godparenthood relationship as it exists in the middle and upper classes is primarily one of affection and friendship between equals, and the ties created by the relationship are strong, intimate, and inviolate. The couples visit each other freely without fear of jealousy or design within the family circle. In fact, the relationship is so close and intimate that a godchild cannot marry a child of his *padrinos*,[56] and any sexual relations between the godchild and the godparent or between the parent and the coparent would be considered incestuous.

THE DECLINING INFLUENCE OF THE FAMILY

Although its influence has been great in Latin American society since the early days of colonization, the family is obviously declining in importance. Urbanization, industrialization, the expansion of government, the rise of political parties, and the increasing emancipation of women are all contributing to this decline.[57]

---

[54] Whetten, *op. cit.*, p. 252.

[55] Harris, *op. cit.*, p. 154.

[56] Whetten, *op. cit.*, p. 254.

[57] See John J. Johnson, *Political Change in Latin America: The Emergence of the Middle Sectors* (Stanford, Calif.: Stanford University Press, 1958), pp. 10–11; William Lytle Schurz, *This New World: The Civilization of Latin America* (New York: E. P. Dutton & Co., Inc., 1954), p. 325; and Biesanz, *The People of Panama, op. cit.*, p. 273.

Social forces since 1850, and especially since 1900, have stripped the family of a large part of its earlier functions, and transformed it mainly into an institution limited

The growth of cities has proved to be the "natural enemy" of the Latin American family. Concludes John J. Johnson:

. . . the family as a political entity probably never operated as effectively in the cities as it did in the country. In this century it has been progressively less successful as new social and economic forces have undermined the interdependence of the member. The mobility offered by modern means of transportation has encouraged the younger generation to make associations outside the family. Cinemas, clubs, public parks and beaches, and social activities sponsored by the schools increasingly compete with the family for the leisure time of its members.[58]

Even the umbilical cord so carefully and lovingly buried in a corner of the homeplace is not a strong enough tie for children who move hundreds, perhaps thousands, of miles away from home and become immersed in the manifold activities of the city.

Industrialization and the growth of large impersonal businesses likewise tend to lessen the influence of the family. No longer can its patriarchal head be sure of putting his relatives in desirable positions in business solely on the basis of a family relationship. With the increasing emphasis on profits and performance by business, family name and background are inevitably of less importance to personnel managers than are personal qualifications, whether administrative, fiscal, legal, technical, or scientific. Individual qualifications are what count most today, not just family credentials.

The great expansion of government necessitated by the many new responsibilities undertaken has also dealt a strong blow to family ties. As governmental functions increase and expand, more reliance is placed on a civil service that is both professional and impersonal. The trend is to select government employees on the basis of merit and ability to discharge responsibilities rather than on family name or influence. Even with changes of administration, nepotism and the awarding of positions solely on the basis of family or friendship are becoming less and less prevalent.

The rise of political parties is also responsible for loosening family ties by undermining the hitherto strong and united political allegiances inculcated in all members of the family. More and more on their own in making their way in business or government, members of the family tend to think and vote as they please, and to transfer their allegiance to political parties that "provide a common background for those who have similar objectives based on educational and occupational interests and on social relationships outside the home."[59]

Last but by no means least, the increasing emancipation of women is

---

to raising children and regulating relations between the sexes. (Robert J. Havighurst y colaboradores, *La sociedad y la educación en América latina* [Buenos Aires, Argentina: Editorial Universitaria de Buenos Aires, 1962], p. 151. Chapter 9, "La familia y la mujer en América latina," treats the evolution of the family and its status today.)

[58] Johnson, *op. cit.*, p. 10.

[59] *Ibid.*, p. 11.

lessening the stability of the supposedly sacrosanct male-dominated family. As wives and daughters in larger numbers venture out into the world with occupations and careers that assure them financial independence, they demand a greater voice in family decisions and challenge the assumed prerogative of husbands to do as they please, especially in extramarital relationships. Indeed, when wives are convinced that the marital bond is too onerous or one-sided, they often free themselves from it.

The divorce laws of some countries well reflect the increasing emancipation of women. In Cuba, for example, under the Spanish civil code which prevailed until 1918, divorce was very difficult to obtain, especially by a wife. Adultery was the main grounds for a divorce, but particularly adultery on the part of the wife; as Article 105 of the code succinctly put it, "The adultery of the wife in any case, and of the husband when it results in a public scandal, or the neglect of the wife."[60] In 1918 Cuba passed its first law which authorized divorce, and its constitution of 1940 put husbands and wives in a position of legal equality regarding dissolution of the marital bonds. "Marriage may be dissolved," reads the constitution, "by agreement of the husband and wife, or in the petition of either of the two, for the reasons and in the form established in the law."[61]

Besides giving women an equal right to obtain a divorce, the Cuban constitution went even further in establishing their rights. In the event of a divorce, where the wife was not at fault and had no adequate means of support, she and the children were entitled to allowances for their maintenance that would have precedence over all the husband's other obligations.[62]

The equal right of the wife to obtain a divorce is like the tenth child borne and raised by the Negro slave mother in Brazil. It is her passport to freedom.

ECONOMIC, POLITICAL, AND SOCIAL IMPLICATIONS

The strong influence of the family has greatly affected economic development in Latin America. Since early colonial days, the family has been largely responsible for the intense concentration of land in a very small part of the population. Furthermore, family cohesiveness and exclusiveness have actually tended to hinder the formation of adequate capital that is so necessary for an industrialized society. "Partly because of the continuing vitality of the extended family," says Richard M. Morse, "so typically modern an institution as the stock market has failed to develop in urban Brazil; 'the most important joint stock companies are owned by kin groups which handle transfer of stocks as a purely domestic matter.

---

[60] Angel C. Betancourt, *Codigo Civil* (3rd ed.; Havana: Imprenta y Papeleria de Rambla, Bouza y Cia, 1934), p. 93.
[61] Constitution of 1940, Article 43.
[62] *Ibid.*

In fact, despite heavy industrialization, a stock market comparable to that of other industrialized countries does not exist at all.' "[63]

From the standpoint of government and politics, the structure and values of the family have not been conducive to the development of democratic institutions. For the domination of the family by the father tends to condition all its members to submissiveness and the unquestioning acceptance of authority. Moreover, the preference for governmental positions given when possible by members of the family to each other and to close friends is undisguised nepotism, favoritism, and paternalism, all of which thwart the development of an effective civil service and an efficient public administration.

Sometimes one or several families manages to get control of a branch of the armed services, thereby enjoying an influential, possibly decisive, role in the exercise of the nation's armed might. In Cuba control of the military in support of dictator Batista was practically a family affair. General In Chief Francisco J. Tabernilla had three sons, Francisco, Carlos, and Marcelo, all of whom were commanding officers of critical components of Cuba's military forces. Brigadier General Francisco H. Tabernilla was commanding officer of the Mixed Tank Regiment, which included all the tanks in the nation's armed forces; Brigadier General Carlos M. Tabernilla was commanding officer of the Cuban Army Air Force, which contained almost all of the military aircraft; and Lieutenant Colonel Marcelo Tabernilla, "the baby of the family," was commanding officer of the Army Air Force Bomber Squadron. In addition, the General In Chief's sister was married to Brigadier General Alberto Del Rio Chaviano, commanding officer of the southern military zone of Oriente Province, which included the city of Santiago (Cuba's second largest) and the Sierra Maestra Mountains, the center and heartland of Fidel Castro's operations.[64]

In Venezuela, too, one of the branches of the armed forces was virtually controlled by a single family. In 1962 the Venezuelan Navy had six admirals: two of them were the Larrazábal brothers, Carlos and Wolfgang; a third, Sosa Ríos, was married to a sister of the Larrazábal brothers.[65]

As a social pillar of democracy in Latin America, the family is a sagging support that rests uneasily on the quicksands of *queridas, casas chicas,* and *naturales.* These are hardly compatible with the love, loyalty, and devotion that closely bind members of the family together. The prohibition of

---

[63] Morse, *op. cit.,* pp. 216–17.

But the Asimow Plan (named after Morris Asimow, a professor of industrial engineering at UCLA who supervised the project), designed to establish many small industries which could benefit by the giant hydroelectric plant on the Rio São Francisco in Brazil, revealed that professional groups, merchants, and farmers would be willing to invest their savings in corporative enterprises if they were convinced of the viability of the new ventures. (Hilgard O'Reilly Sternberg, "Brazil: Complex Giant," *Foreign Affairs,* Vol. 43, No. 2 [January, 1965], pp. 306–7.)

[64] John J. Johnson, *The Military and Society in Latin America* (Stanford, Calif.: Stanford University Press, 1964), pp. 111–12.

[65] *Ibid.,* p. 111.

divorce decreed by the Roman Catholic Church has in some respects actually aggravated the situation.

Moreover, the duplicity surrounding the supposedly monogamous, indissoluble, and divinely ordained family affects other aspects of life in the society. "Perhaps the double standard of sexual morality," says William S. Stokes, speaking of upper and middle class families, "has contributed to the development of hypocrisy in Latin American politics. It is assuredly anomalous to witness the head of a Latin American family expressing almost pathological concern over the protection of the honor of his family at the same time that he is supporting a mistress and has campaigns under way to seduce females of friends and associates."[66]

The condition of the family in the lower class is a cause of especial concern. "The virtual breakdown of the traditional family [in this group] . . ." observes Richard Patch, "is a phenomenon richly deserving further study."[67]

Can the family in Latin America be rehabilitated to comport with its professed ideals? Or will it continue to be an erosive force that weakens a would-be democratic society?

SUGGESTED READINGS

AZEVEDO, THALES DE. *Social Change in Brazil*, chap. i. Latin American Monograph Series, No. 22. Gainesville, Fla.: University of Florida Press, 1963.

BIESANZ, JOHN, AND BIESANZ, MAVIS. *The People of Panama*, pp. 271–323. New York: Columbia University Press, 1955.

FALS-BORDA, ORLANDO. *Peasant Society in the Colombian Andes: A Sociological Study of Saucío*, chap. 13. Gainesville, Fla.: University of Florida Press, 1957.

FREYRE, GILBERTO. *The Masters and the Slaves: A Study in the Development of Brazilian Civilization*, pp. 81–184 and 278–467. Trans. SAMUEL PUTNAM. 2d Eng. ed. rev.; New York: Alfred A. Knopf, Inc., 1956.

HARRIS, MARVIN. *Town and Country in Brazil*, pp. 147–78. New York: Columbia University Press, 1956.

LEONARD, OLEN E. *Bolivia: Land, People and Institutions*, chap. ix. Washington, D.C.: The Scarecrow Press, Inc., 1952.

LEWIS, OSCAR. *The Children of Sánchez: Autobiography of a Mexican Family*. New York: Random House, Inc., 1963.

———. *Five Families: Mexican Case Studies in the Culture of Poverty*. New York: Basic Books, Inc., 1959.

NELSON, LOWRY. *Rural Cuba*, chap. x. Minneapolis: University of Minnesota Press, 1950.

SCHURZ, WILLIAM LYTLE. *This New World: The Civilization of Latin America*, chap. viii. New York: E. P. Dutton & Co., Inc., 1954.

---

[66] William S. Stokes, *Latin American Politics* (New York: Thomas Y. Crowell Co., 1959), p. 39.

[67] Patch, *op. cit.*, p. 9.

SERVICE, ELMAN R., AND SERVICE, HELEN S. *Tobatí: Paraguayan Town*, chaps. ix–xii. Chicago: University of Chicago Press, 1954.

SMITH, RAYMOND T. "The Family in the Caribbean," *Caribbean Studies: A Symposium* (ed. VERA RUBIN). Seattle: University of Washington Press, 1960.

SMITH, T. LYNN. *Brazil: People and Institutions*, chap. xviii. Rev. ed.: Baton Rouge, La.: Louisiana State University Press, 1963.

STOKES, WILLIAM S. *Latin American Politics*, chap. 3. New York: Thomas Y. Crowell Co., 1959.

TAYLOR, CARL C. *Rural Life in Argentina*, chap. xiii. Baton Rouge, La.: Louisiana State University Press, 1948.

TUMIN, MELVIN M. *Social Class and Social Change in Puerto Rico*, chaps. 15 and 16. Princeton, N.J.: Princeton University Press, 1961.

WAGLEY, CHARLES. *Amazon Town: A Study of Man in the Tropics*, chap. v. New York: The Macmillan Company, 1953.

———. *An Introduction to Brazil*, pp. 184–203. New York: Columbia University Press, 1963.

WHETTEN, NATHAN L. *Guatemala: The Land and the People*, chap. 12. Caribbean Series, 4. New Haven, Conn.: Yale University Press, 1961.

———. *Rural Mexico*, chap. xvi. Chicago: University of Chicago Press, 1948.

CHAPTER 5

EDUCATION:
The Open Sesame
to Individual Advancement

ELEMENTARY AND SECONDARY EDUCATION

A GOOD EDUCATION and cultural background have long been valued in Latin America. Since the time of the conquest, they have been the main distinctions between the upper class and the lower. Besides having a definite snob value, an education was an important asset for succeeding in the rough and tumble of colonial society. In colonial Brazil, so many of the white colonists were illiterate or semiliterate that "not rarely, rich *fazendeiros* in the interior requested their friends on the coast to arrange a son-in-law who, although he had no other possession, did know how to read and write."[1] As a result of the premium on learning, some of the sons-in-law who were cheerfully welcomed into the families of the wealthy white landowners were light mulattoes.

The achievement of political independence by Latin America was regarded at the time as the dawn of a new democratic society in which education would have a most important role. "Public instruction is the primary need of all pupils," declared San Martín in a decree of February 23, 1822. "Any government that does not promote it is guilty of a crime which later generations, however long after, have the right to avenge while cursing its memory."

Constitutional and Legal Provisions

In keeping with San Martín's ideal, the many constitutions of Latin America formulated since independence have boldly and unequivocally

---

[1] Henry Koster, *Travels in Brazil, 1809 to 1815*, in Donald Pierson, *Negroes in Brazil: A Study of Race Contact at Bahia* (University of Chicago Sociological Series) (Chicago: University of Chicago Press, 1942), pp. 144-45.

proclaimed that the state has a vital interest in popular education. Asserts Bolivia's 1961 constitution, "Education is the highest function of the State." Panama's constitution of 1946 recognizes that providing an education is one of the main responsibilities of government. "It is a fundamental duty of the state," it says, "to subserve national education in all its aspects —intellectual, moral, civic, and physical." El Salvador's constitution of 1950 goes a step further: while providing a popular education is the duty of the state, receiving it is both a right as well as duty of the citizen. "All inhabitants of the Republic," it says, "have the right and duty of receiving such basic training as shall fit them to play their part conscientiously and effectively as workers, parents, and citizens. . . ."

Besides containing these strong statements of principle, most constitutions have provisions that pertain to a wide range of educational matters, such as organization of the system; central control; financial support; religious instruction; the training, salaries, and tenure of teachers; and aid to needy students.

The many constitutional provisions have been the bases of innumerable national laws purportedly enacted to carry out the constitutions' expressed intentions of providing an education for all citizens. Among the most important of these were the many laws which stated that education would be compulsory. According to their terms, attendance was required of all children between certain ages, usually 7 and 14, with such variations as 7 to 12 in Colombia and 6 to 14 in Ecuador. In Peru, compulsory attendance extended even to adults between the ages of 16 and 40 who were illiterate.[2]

In addition to detailing the ages of those affected, the compulsory attendance laws have usually specified that pupils must complete the six-year course that comprises primary schooling in urban areas, or the four-year course in rural communities. These laws also brandish various penalties, which include fines on an ascending scale imposed on parents or guardians of children who fail to comply with requirements of the law and on the heads of commercial, industrial, and farming enterprises which employ children during school hours for purposes not connected with education. Under these laws, violators can even be imprisoned in extreme cases.

Among the nations that have often expressed solicitude in their constitutions and laws for the educational welfare of their whole populations is Ecuador. Its first decree making primary education compulsory was issued on August 2, 1821, and later laws or decrees intended to accomplish the same purpose were promulgated in 1833, 1871, 1906, and 1938. In addition

---

[2] UNESCO, *Basic Facts and Figures; 1960* (International statistics relating to education, culture and mass communication) (Paris, 1961), pp. 168–69. For a compilation of the laws of the several countries pertaining to compulsory education, see UNESCO, *World Survey of Education, II: Primary Education* (Paris, 1958).

to these, there were many administrative rulings supposedly intended to further popular education.[3]

Lack of Progress and Reasons for This

In most of the countries, despite the many laws regarding compulsory education, only a relatively small percentage of school-age children are actually attending school. In Haiti, a poor, retarded nation, only 23 percent of the children from ages 5 to 14 are enrolled in school, the lowest percentage in all Latin America. But in Brazil, one of the most dynamic and progressive nations of the region, the record is not much better: there, only 33 percent of children of primary school age are enrolled in school.[4] Even with the low enrollments, the rate of absenteeism is high, as Table 5-1 shows.

TABLE 5-1

ABSENTEEISM AMONG SCHOOLCHILDREN, AGES 7 TO 14, IN 1950

Country	7	8	9	10	11	12	13	14
BOYS								
Costa Rica	43.9%	29.7%	24.2%	24.5%	27.1%	37.1%	50.9%	70.3%
Cuba (1953)	52.0	43.7	37.6	36.2	33.5	36.6	40.5	48.7
El Salvador	64.3	57.4	50.7	51.2	48.5	55.9	59.3	67.6
Guatemala	77.9	73.0	62.9	76.5	66.3	74.0	73.1	82.3
Nicaragua	79.4	76.3	71.1	71.8	66.8	72.0	72.5	77.8
Panama	49.5	30.8	23.4	23.0	20.5	28.6	36.3	53.5
Paraguay	66.9	48.3	35.8	31.8	27.1	28.6	28.4	37.9
Venezuela	57.3	50.1	44.2	44.6	41.4	47.6	47.7	56.6
GIRLS								
Costa Rica	43.3	29.4	23.6	24.6	27.5	38.1	54.2	73.1
Cuba (1953)	49.3	42.0	35.6	33.0	33.0	36.2	44.6	57.6
El Salvador	64.6	57.7	51.6	50.6	47.7	53.9	56.7	61.9
Guatemala	80.3	76.7	67.9	79.1	70.7	78.6	78.9	86.6
Nicaragua	79.0	74.4	69.5	69.5	62.0	67.5	66.6	77.6
Panama	46.8	29.8	21.7	21.0	19.0	27.0	39.4	60.0
Paraguay	65.6	48.9	37.0	32.4	28.2	30.9	32.7	42.7
Venezuela	57.7	50.2	44.5	43.6	40.6	45.6	46.7	56.2

SOURCE: UNESCO, *La Situación Educativa en América Latina*, pp. 211, 225, as given in CIF *Study No. 1*, p. 217. Reproduced by permission.

Additional evidence on the question of the effectiveness of compulsory education is the high rate of dropout in most of the countries. In Colombia, where an analysis was made in 1950 of the cohort of all children enrolled in the first grade, it was found that for every 100 children who started in the first grade, only 59 entered the second grade the next year. The percentage that continued in school declined in each succeeding year, to 25 in the third grade, 18 in the fourth, and 11 in the fifth. These figures, incidentally, included pupils in both urban and rural areas. In rural areas,

---

[3] Emilio Uzcátegui, *Compulsory Education in Ecuador* (UNESCO: Studies on Compulsory Education Series—VII) (Paris, 1951), pp. 13–16 and 23–26.
[4] UNESCO, *Basic Facts and Figures; 1960, op. cit.*, p. 27.

the dropout rate was especially high; there, the percentages left in successive grades after the first were: 50 in the second, 6 in the third, 1.2 in the fourth, and 0.2 in the fifth.[5]

As a result of the low percentage of school-age children enrolled in school and the high rate of dropout, illiteracy is high in most of the nations. Haiti has the unenviable record of heading the list, with 89 percent of its populace illiterate. At least eight of the nations have a rate of more than 50 percent, and only five of them are under 25 percent. In general, the rate is higher in the less influential countries, such as Guatemala with 71 percent and Honduras with 65 percent. But the rate is also high in some of the most important states, such as Brazil with 51 percent, Venezuela with 47 percent, and Mexico with 43 percent. Argentina has the best record of all, with only 13 percent of its populace illiterate.[6]

From all reliable indices, Latin America's progress in education has been ✓ disappointingly slow. You are probably wondering just why this is so.

It is certainly not because of the lack of solicitude of constitution makers or lawmakers. Indeed, if constitutional provisions or laws could by themselves educate persons, Latin Americans would be the best educated peoples in the world today. In fact, not a single additional law would be needed to accomplish this result; all that is necessary is for the laws already on the statute books to be enforced.

Many motives have been behind these many "laws" relating to education for the whole populace, motives ranging from the idealism of visionaries to the selfishness of vested interests. But whatever the motive, enforcement of the law has encountered tremendous obstacles for which almost every segment of society is partly to blame.

The large landowners, the most politically powerful group in most of the countries, have been unalterably opposed to educating the large mass of peons, since this would only make them dissatisfied with their lowly status, demand higher wages for their work, and very likely leave the plantation to go to the city where they would have an opportunity of bettering themselves. "We need peons, not *alumnos* or *estudiantes*," reasoned the big landowners. Many of them were so opposed to any program aiming to educate rural children that they offered to pay in taxes double what the maintenance of the school would cost them in return for being exempt from the provisions of the law.[7]

The sheer poverty of peon families has made an education a luxury which they simply cannot afford. Each member of the family is expected

[5] UNESCO, *World Survey of Education*, 1958, *op. cit.*, p. 265.

In Ecuador an analysis of the cohort beginning school in 1947 showed almost as high attrition, with a successive decline each year from the first grade to the fifth as follows: 100, 54, 43, 28, and 18. (*Informe a la nación, 1962* [Republica del Ecuador; Ministro de Educación Publica] [Quito, Ecuador: Editorial del Ministerio de Educación Publica, 1962], p. 55.)

[6] UNESCO, *Basic Facts and Figures; 1958* (Paris, 1959), pp. 27–28.

[7] Uzcátegui, *op. cit.*, p. 24.

to contribute his share, however small, to its support. The children can help by minding the sheep or cows or llamas; if not baby-sitting with animals, they can do light chores in the fields or at home. In the urban areas, they can help by selling fruit, magazines, or candy bars, or by shining shoes, which they do with much gusto and pride, determined to make a visitor's shoes sparkle as they never did after a shine in New York, Kalamazoo, or even in Johnson City, Texas.

Another discouragement to public education—a considerable one—is the lack of incentive on the part of the child to acquire an education. Regardless of how well he does at school, he has no opportunity at home to display proudly his hard-acquired knowledge to his illiterate parents. Moreover, why should he make the effort to learn to read if there isn't anything to read? He has never owned a single book in his life, a text or otherwise, and there is no local library where he can borrow books to exercise his reading skill, quench his thirst for knowledge, and keep alive his eagerness for learning. Nor does he have access to a single newspaper or magazine, exciting means of finding out what is going on in the world. In seven of the nations, there are only 35 or less copies of newspapers circulated per 1,000 inhabitants, as Figure 5-1 shows.

Another big deterrent to the realization of popular education is the woefully inadequate number of schools in most of the countries. This is especially true of the rural areas, where a child may have to go four, five, or six miles or more in order to attend school, with no roads or school buses or other means of public transportation as we have in the United States. In these areas, a child is fortunate if he has a burro to ride; more than likely he gets to school by walking. In an effort to reach the more inaccessible areas, several of the nations have established mobile schools which attempt to provide the rudiments of an education.

The language barrier is another formidable obstacle to education in much of Latin America. In Mexico, Central America, and the Andean region, a large part of the populace consists of Indians who speak and understand only their own native dialect. In fact, in all Latin America there are several thousand of these dialects.[8] Consequently, a student teacher in Peru who plans to teach in the upland area or in the tropical forest region should acquire at least a speaking knowledge of Quechua, Aymara, Huancha, or other dialect that is spoken in the region.

Recognizing that instruction should be given in the local dialect, Ecuador has specified by law that "in schools established in predominantly Indian zones, Quechua or the native tongue shall be used in addition to Spanish." Accordingly, Quechua was made a required subject in the rural teachers training colleges in the sierra, catering mainly to trainees from the city.[9] However, the legal requirement never became really effective,

---

[8] For an interesting account of the many languages, see Clarence W. Hall, "Two Thousand Tongues to Go," *Reader's Digest*, August, 1958, pp. 195–215.

[9] Uzcátegui, *op. cit.*, p. 55.

FIGURE 5-1

NEWSPAPER CIRCULATION IN 1960

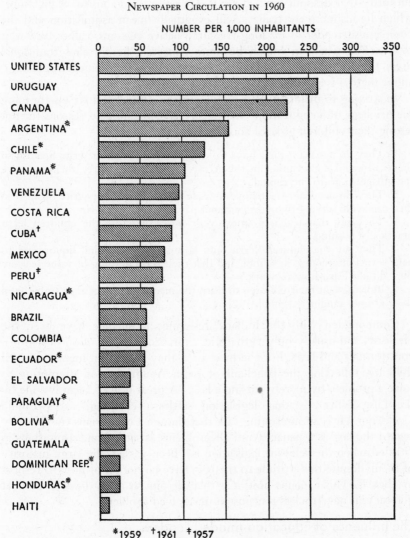

NUMBER PER 1,000 INHABITANTS

*1959 †1961 ‡1957

SOURCE: *Américas*, November, 1963, p. 43. Reproduced by permission.

since almost none of the student-teachers had any knowledge of Quechua or other native tongues, and they were not the least interested in learning them.

Another obstacle to popular education, in addition to the language barrier, is the Indian's attitude of passive, and sometimes active, resistance to getting an education. Deeply resentful of centuries of despoliation at the hands of his white conquerors, the Indian is usually suspicious of any overtures made to him. "He hates all that might destroy his age-long traditions," observed García Calderón, "schools, military training, and the authority that despoils him."[10] He is especially suspicious of "education," which he instinctively realizes will eventually mean assimilation and the complete surrender of his long-treasured native customs, values, and way of life. For when an Indian becomes educated, he forsakes traditional dress, fails to listen to Indian voices and customs, and often even refuses to admit that he is an Indian.

In striving to maintain their native culture, although it means forgoing the privilege of an education, the Indians have given many reasons for not letting their children go to school:

1. They do not want their boys to learn to speak, read, or write Spanish so they can avoid conscription in the Army, which would force them to leave the village to go to the capital.
2. They do not want their boys to learn to speak, read, or write Spanish so they can avoid serving two years without pay as village officials.
3. They say that teachers 'know very little, therefore the children learn practically nothing.'
4. They say the children 'learn only how to play, to drink liquor, and to have sexual intercourse in school, and that they learn nothing of value because they do not learn how to work.'
5. Indians want their children to learn the manual arts necessary to life, and these are not taught at school.[11]

Compounded with the Indians' resistance to change have been the idealistic, and usually only verbalistic, expressions of intention in national constitutions and laws. For the most part, they have been merely wishful thinking, reflecting the penchant of Latin Americans for attempting to solve a problem by merely passing a law. "A great deal of harm is done by the false belief . . . that legislation settles everything," says Emilio Uzcátequi. "It is an interesting fact that though Ecuadorians traditionally regard the law as a panacea and all problems as settled and aspirations as satisfied when the relevant legislation has been passed, the large majority of them, despite this attitude to the law, have no notion of how to respect or obey it. This explains how it is that, despite so many laws to combat illiteracy, it nevertheless remains an unresolved problem. . . ."[12]

The Influence of Education-minded Leaders

On rare occasions, however, some idealist who sincerely believed in the objectives of the laws and was determined to enforce them managed to slip into power. Just such an individual was García Moreno, who dominated Ecuador's politics as president or power behind the scenes from 1860 until his assassination in 1875.

---

[10] F. García Calderón, *Latin America: Its Rise and Progress*, trans. Bernard Miall (London: T. Fisher Unwin, 1913), p. 354.
[11] Morris Siegel, "Problems of Education in Indian Guatemala," *Journal of Experimental Education*, Vol. IX, No. 4 (June, 1941), p. 293.
[12] Uzcátegui, *op. cit.*, p. 26.

At the urging of President García Moreno, another comprehensive law was passed to establish a program of compulsory education for the nation. So many such laws had been enacted in the past that the new one was not taken seriously until the ruling class suddenly realized that this time the president was really going to enforce it. The results of enforcement were phenomenal. School attendance jumped from 14,731 in 1871 to 22,458 in 1873 and to 32,000 in 1875. The number of schools greatly increased too, from about 200 in 1869 to 531 in 1875.[13]

According to Hubert Herring, García Moreno contributed more to the economic and cultural well-being of his nation than any other president of the nineteenth century.[14] Such astonishing progress made in such a short time in Ecuador shows the progress that might well have been made generally in popular education if the many constitutional provisions and laws on the subject had actually been enforced.

The several nations in Latin America which have made the greatest progress in education owe their achievement largely to the idealism and inspiration of a few native sons who were as much concerned with the practice of democracy as with its profession. Argentina's admirable progress is largely attributable to the guiding genius of Domingo F. Sarmiento, who served as president from 1868 to 1874 and is revered as the schoolmaster of his country. Believing ardently in the value of an education, he set as his standard, *"educar al soberano"* (to educate the sovereign people). To Sarmiento, the education of the mass in his beloved Argentina was the very meaning of his life. "A million owe it to me, in part, that their children have been saved from the most grievous afflictions of life, destitution, and hunger," he wrote to a friend several months before his death on September 11, 1888. "There were thick bandages of ignorance and barbarity on the people and I tried to pull them off; I heard noise around me, the noise of still-unbroken chains, and I joined with those who were striving to shatter them."[15]

While most of the nations of Latin America, as elsewhere, revere generals who won wars at the expense of human life and suffering, Argentina reveres Sarmiento as " 'a soldier in the never-ceasing war for the liberty of men's minds,' who considered the schoolroom the most important battlefield in America."[16]

In Uruguay, another inspired leader was mainly responsible for laying the foundation for the nation's great progress in education. José Varella,

---

[13] *Ibid.*, p. 15.

[14] Hubert Herring, *A History of Latin America from the Beginnings to the Present* (2d ed. rev.; New York: Alfred A. Knopf, Inc., 1961), p. 531.

[15] Rodolfo Vinacua, "Sarmiento, Man of Action," *Américas*, Vol. 13, No. 8 (August, 1961), p. 15.

[16] Lewis Hanke, *South America* (Princeton, N.J.: D. Van Nostrand Co., Inc., 1959), p. 63. For the program of education that Sarmiento initiated in Argentina, see Allison Williams Bunkley, *The Life of Sarmiento* (Princeton, N.J.: Princeton University Press, 1952), pp. 372–79.

whose life span was short, from 1845 to 1879, was an ardent scholar, very much impressed by the progress in education made by the United States. Aspiring to give all his fellow countrymen the benefit of a popular education, he wrote two books on the subject, the first treating only theory, but the second proposing a practical, comprehensive new school law for the nation. When Latorre became dictator in 1877, he put into effect by executive decree the Law of Common Education which was based almost verbatim on Varella's recommendations.

In recognition of his service to the nation, Varella was made national inspector of primary instruction, and undertook the difficult job of overhauling Uruguay's whole school system, which was pathetically inadequate. The three principles which he followed in reshaping the nation's educational system were: (1) free schooling from the bottom to the top, (2) secular control of education, with no teaching of religion in the public schools, and (3) more modern educational methods. Thanks to José Varella's idealism, dedication, and foresight, Uruguay today enjoys one of the most democratic and progressive school systems in Latin America.[17]

The Desire of Most Citizens for an Education

Most of the countries of Latin America, however, have not been so fortunate as to have a Sarmiento or Varella to guide their educational destinies. In fact, even today there are skeptics who seriously question the wisdom of educating the mass. It is revolutionary, they argue; it will inevitably mean the end of the established order, with its long heritage of graceful living and privilege. What is more, they contend, the mass of citizens would not appreciate the value of an education, even if they had the opportunity to obtain it.

Old prejudices die hard, whether held by big landowners, suspicious Indians, or any other segment of the society. But wherever you travel in Latin America today, one of your most vivid impressions is the yearning for learning. If you visit a library open to the public on a weekend or even a holiday, you will probably find that every chair is occupied, with an air of quiet earnestness pervading the large reading room. Or, visiting the *altiplano*, you may run up on an Indian community, not a single one of whose members can read or write, but which is so eager to provide an education for its children that all are eagerly pitching in to build a simple adobe schoolhouse, maybe even furnish a teacher too, for the national government to take over as a going concern.

A vivid example of how underprivileged citizens will respond to the opportunity of obtaining an education is the experience of Vicos, one of the more isolated communities in Peru. There, Cornell University with the cooperation of the Peruvian government has for more than a decade been

---

17 Russell H. Fitzgibbon, *Uruguay: Portrait of a Democracy* (New Brunswick, N.J.: Rutgers University Press, 1954), pp. 198–204.

engaged in one of the boldest experiments in all Latin America.[18] Realizing that land reform is bound to come, even if by violence and revolution, the experiment was launched to see if the needed agrarian reform might be accomplished peaceably and democratically. For this purpose, a large run-down hacienda was obtained at Vicos, and a supervised cooperative farming program was instituted in which the peons, benefiting by the fruits of their own labors, would in time become the proud owners of their own small farms.

But for such an audacious project to succeed—a project so significant that it might lead the way to agrarian reform by evolution instead of revolution—it was necessary to enable the former peons and their children to obtain an education. In 1951, a year before the project was launched, only 18 pupils attended the rudimentary elementary rural school on the hacienda, staffed by just one teacher. But after taking over managerial control of the rundown hacienda, the new administration as one of its top priority projects mobilized the resident Indian labor force to build a new school large enough to accommodate the whole school-age population. As the Indians prospered and their horizons broadened, pupil enrollment shot up. In the first six years alone, it jumped from 18 pupils to more than 250 and is still rising sharply. This necessitated the construction of a second wing, consisting of auditorium, dining room, kitchen, three more class-rooms, and a shop, to the building.[19]

The statistics from Vicos are impressive, but they tell only a part of the story. Of even greater significance is what the pupils' education really means to them.

In many instances the acquiring of skills has enabled them to enjoy new prestige at home and to compete successfully in the outside world. This in turn has led to an increasingly optimistic outlook on life and on their prospects for the future. Perhaps more than any other aspect of the Vicos program, the school has become a symbol of progress and of hope for the future.[20]

---

[18] For a concise explanation of the background, objectives, contractual arrangement, problems, and achievements of this challenging project, see Richard N. Adams and Charles C. Cumberland, *United States University Cooperation in Latin America* (A study based on selected programs in Bolivia, Chile, Peru, and Mexico, Institute of Research on Overseas Programs) (East Lansing, Mich.: Michigan State University, 1960), pp. 187–96.

[19] Allan R. Holmberg, "Changing Community Attitudes and Values in Peru: A Case Study in Guided Change," *Social Change in Latin America Today* (Council on Foreign Relations) (New York: Harper & Bros., 1960), pp. 80–84. See also Allan R. Holmberg and Henry F. Dobyns, "The Process of Accelerating Community Change," *Human Organization*, Vol. 21, No. 2 (Summer, 1962), pp. 107–9.

[20] Holmberg, *Social Change in Latin America Today, op. cit.,* pp. 93–94. Mexico's rural education program of sending "missionaries" on horseback to preach the gospel of learning to the remote rural communities also brought very gratifying results. In a short time, more than 6,000 rural schools were built by the communities, without any cost to the central government but with a tremendous boost to local pride and initiative. See Frank Tannenbaum, "The Mexican Experience," *Ten Keys to Latin America* (New York: Alfred A. Knopf, Inc., 1962), pp. 103-9.

Financial Support of Public Education

However ardently the liberals espouse the cause of education for all, and however eager the many underprivileged are to learn, the goal of giving all citizens the opportunity to obtain an education poses tremendous problems, as any government in power soon realizes. An adequate educational system costs money, a great deal of it, and if Latin America is to attain its goal of providing an education for all, it must allocate a much larger proportion of its resources to education. Specifically, by 1965 it should be allocating not less than 4 percent of its gross national product to education. This is a tremendous order for the region. In 1960 only one country allotted more than 4 percent; three countries allotted between 3 and 4 percent; seven, between 2 and 3 percent; and eight, less than 2 percent.[21] Even with limited budgets, the proportion spent for administration is sometimes quite high—about 33 percent in the Dominican Republic, as Figure 5-2 portrays.

Although the nations are increasing their budgets for education, they are spending much less for it than is critically needed. In fact, they usually spend less for education than for defense,[22] despite the fact that they have seldom had to resort to war to settle an issue with one another, and despite the fact that communism, a great threat to their existence, is more likely to well up from within as a result of the ignorance, poverty, and frustration of the large mass of citizens rather than from a frontal attack from outside the hemisphere. Although the large landowners and other vested interests have the most to lose if either communism or national social revolution takes over in their country, they are willing to risk everything on a bold gamble that such drastic change will not occur, and they refuse to make any real sacrifice to educate their less privileged fellow countrymen.

Construction of Schools

Another big problem which school administrators and planners face in Latin America is the pressing necessity to construct a tremendous number of new schools which are needed to take care of all pupils adequately. Until relatively recently, public education was not taken seriously enough to justify the building of schools as such, and most classes were held in old private homes, in buildings constructed for offices, or in any other space that the government might acquire by leasing or renting. With such makeshift arrangements, the accommodations provided for the schools were often run-down and ill-kept, since neither the state nor the private owner felt responsible for making repairs. Even Chile, one of the most progressive

---

[21] Gabriel Betancur-Mejía, "Education: Backbone of the Alliance for Progress," *Américas*, Vol. 15, No. 9 (September, 1963), p. 6.

[22] Brazil, for example, considerably shortchanges education, allocating far less than the 10 percent of the budget specified by the constitution, while at the same time spending four or five times as much for the armed forces. See William Lytle Schurz, *Brazil: The Infinite Country* (New York: E. P. Dutton & Co., Inc., 1961), p. 210.

FIGURE 5–2

Distribution of Education Budget for Different Levels

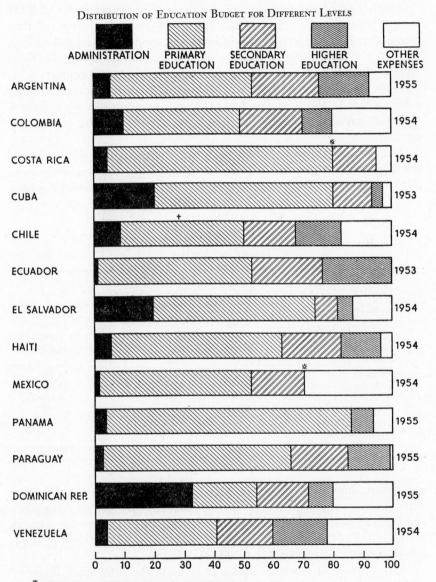

* DOES NOT INCLUDE HIGHER EDUCATION
† INCLUDES FORMATION

Source: *Center of Intercultural Formation* (CIF) *Study No. 1*, p. 216. Reproduced by permission.

nations of Latin America, did not awaken until 1937 to the need of modern, utilitarian buildings, designed for the particular needs of students, with sufficient light and ventilation, adequate space for teaching and recreation activities, and easy egress in case of fire, earthquake, or other emergency.

Training of Teachers

Another problem which is stymieing the goal of education for all is the critical shortage of teachers. Colombia, for example, is better off than many other Latin-American nations in its educational facilities and staffing, with 40,175 teachers in its primary grades. But the nation needs 25,000 additional primary teachers now; and while the number of teachers is increasing, the increase is barely able to keep up with the increase in pupil enrollment.[23] In the whole of Latin America, at least 400,000 additional qualified teachers are critically needed to educate the region's young citizens.

As a result of this severe shortage, a large percentage of those who are teaching are not prepared for their responsibility. Approximately one-third of them, as Table 5-2 reveals, do not have professional teaching

TABLE 5-2

TEACHERS IN CERTAIN COUNTRIES: 1958
(Trained and Untrained)

Country	With a Degree	Without a Degree		Total
		Number	% of Total	
Argentina	105,333	17	0.016	105,350
Bolivia	4,019	18,617	82	22,636
Brazil	94,560	77,262	44	171,822
Colombia	8,396	25,478	75	33,874
Chile	19,132	147	0.76	19,279
Mexico	49,889	8,912	15	58,801
Peru	16,348	15,769	49	32,117
Uruguay	7,880	738	9	8,618
Venezuela	8,604	11,617	57	20,221
Totals (including 9 smaller nations and Puerto Rico)	369,232	187,157		556,480

SOURCE: UNESCO, La Situación Educativa en América Latina, pp. 240 and 246.

certificates. Indeed, "lay" or "provisional" teachers are so common that often there is not a single teacher in a school really qualified by recognized standards to hold a teaching position. In Bolivia, 82 percent of the teachers are classified as "provisional." Many of these have only finished primary school, a pretty meager background for teaching.

This shortage of teachers, especially acute in the rural areas, is attributable to a number of causes. The salary is usually miserably low; in four countries it averages only $60 a month, and it is as low as $18 a month in Haiti. In fact, teaching in much of the region pays so poorly—hardly enough to live on—that people sometimes say when they are very hungry, "I am as hungry as a school teacher."

---

[23] International Yearbook of Education, 1961, Vol. 23 (Geneva: International Bureau of Education, Publication No. 236) (Paris: UNESCO, 1962), pp. 94–95.

But the small financial remuneration of the rural teacher is in almost inverse ratio to the many hardships she is expected to endure. In most of the rural areas, she lives a dull, drab, isolated existence, with no inside plumbing, no outside interests. She has to endure the discomfort of poor and unhealthy housing, also the lack of a regular supply of such expected things as meat and vegetables, as well as books, magazines, newspapers, and broadening contacts with the outside world. Medical care and medicine are almost wholly lacking, a lack which may endanger her very life.[24]

Confronted with these privations and hazards, it is no wonder that ". . . teachers raised in an urban environment, unless moved by missionary zeal, find the rural community, where no Spanish is spoken, where there are no electric lights, no moving picture houses, and no newspapers, a place of exile. To be a rural school teacher . . . calls for a high degree of self-sacrifice and devotion to an ideal."[25]

Even Vicos, one of the most practical as well as idealistic experiments in all Latin America, has difficulty in obtaining the teachers it needs to further its ambitious program. In fact, Vicos is not regarded as a preferred assignment for the typical Peruvian teacher, who aspires to teach in Lima, the national capital and metropolis, with its bright lights, comfortable living, and many cultural and recreational attractions. In fact, a teaching stint in Vicos is regarded as the necessary and temporary step toward a more desirable teaching position in the city.

As a result, most of the teachers at Vicos are perforce natives of the region and not very reliable. They are frequently absent from class, taking long weekends to go home, or getting leave to go to the provincial capital or to visit a "deathly ill relative." They often go on binges at the numerous fiestas, or simply when two of them get together, often needing the next day to sober up.[26]

Even the most dedicated teacher venturing out into the hinterland is apt to be overwhelmed by the responsibilities she is charged with. In Brazil, for example, the teacher in the rural school has had to comply with at least 29 positive requirements. These include: zealously cleaning and caring for the classroom and its equipment; covering every day's assignment exactly as the guidebook specifies; correcting all papers every day and filing them away to be returned to the pupils at the end of the year; keeping a daily record of school work "without erasures, deletions, or additions"; treating her pupils with tenderness, care, and politeness; maintaining discipline, though forbidden to administer physical punishment of

24 M. B. Lourenço Filho, *et al., The Training of Rural School Teachers* (UNESCO: Problems in Education Series—VII) (Paris, 1953), p. 12.
25 Frank Tannenbaum, "Democracy and Rural Education in Latin America," *Responsible Freedom in the Americas* (ed. Angel del Río) (Columbia University Bicentennial Conference Series) (Garden City, N.Y.: Doubleday & Co., Inc., 1955), p. 13.
26 Holmberg and Dobyns, *op. cit.,* p. 108.

any kind, however much it might be deserved; and setting an example in the community for morality, politeness, punctuality, assiduity, and love of work.[27]

Isolated in the rural community, the teacher cannot even take refuge in "Thank God for Friday!"—a sustenance that enables many an American teacher to keep going. Denied even this respite, the rural teacher in Latin America is expected to appear, if invited, at all school celebrations and civic educational gatherings, even when they occur on weekends or holidays.[28]

Yes, the rural school teacher in the drab, uninspiring backwoods community has plenty of responsibilities—plenty of pupils too. The ideal is 30 or so pupils per class. But sometimes, as in Haiti, a teacher may find to her dismay that she has more than 200 in her classroom. "It is understandable," explain Haitian authorities, "that in such conditions the task of the teacher becomes extremely difficult."[29]

The reluctance of city-born and educated young people to go to the sticks to teach is only one aspect of the problem of getting teachers for rural areas. Another aspect is the unwillingness of most rural boys and girls, educated at rural teacher-training colleges, to remain in the country to teach. After graduation, they head out for the city to enjoy its bright lights and many attractions.

Many of those who matriculate at the rural training colleges do so only to enjoy its residential facilities while completing their secondary education. They have no intention of getting a college degree and actually teaching. Thus in Mexico in 1951, the 21 rural teacher-training colleges of the nation had a total enrollment of 4,872 students, but only 228 graduated that year, presumably to become teachers in rural schools.[30]

In striking contrast to other nations that are handicapped by the serious shortage of teachers is Argentina, which has more teachers than it needs. Seeking to alleviate the shortage elsewhere in Latin America, the Argentine government has offered to send some of its teachers to other countries and to train their student-teachers in its normal schools. The government's "Teachers for the Americas" plan was enthusiastically received by the people; more than 7,500 Argentine teachers volunteered their services. Under the first phase of the program, 50 of them will serve for one year in other Latin-American countries, with all expenses borne by the Argentine government.[31]

---

[27] T. Lynn Smith, *Brazil: People and Institutions* (rev. ed.; Baton Rouge, La.: Louisiana State University Press, 1963), pp. 497–99.

[28] *Ibid.*

[29] UNESCO, *World Survey of Education, 1958, op. cit.,* pp. 504–5.

[30] Isidro Castillo, "Rural Teacher Training in Mexico," *The Training of Rural School Teachers, op. cit.,* p. 162.

[31] "The OAS in Action: Socio-Economic Affairs," *Américas,* Vol. 15, No. 10 (October, 1963), p. 45.

The Curriculum Taught

Another problem which educators in Latin America have had to cope with is the kind of curriculum to be taught in the schools. Traditionally, the schools were designed to serve only the privileged elite, to give them a cultural background befitting their status. Consequently, under the modern democratic, egalitarian philosophy of education for all, the curriculum from the bottom to the top has undergone extensive revision.

In the elementary school, which provides the only educational opportunity that the vast majority of citizens enjoy, the emphasis is strongly and unabashedly on practicality. "If the Indian is to become a free human being, a full citizen of his country," said Galo Plaza, commenting on Ecuador's problem, "and if his country is to become a true democracy by incorporating into political and civic activities a large sector of its population, the only effective course of action is to give the Indian an education along practical and sensible lines."[32]

Accordingly, in Ecuador—and in the rest of Latin America too—the trend in elementary education has been to emphasize practical instruction, especially in rural areas. In Bolivia with its revolutionary program of education designed to benefit the rural mass, the guidebook for rural teachers contains the following subjects calculated to be very helpful and appealing to the rural people: Our Cleanliness; How We Protect Ourselves from Disease; Cultivation of the Potato, Maize, Rice, the Banana, and Sugar Cane; Manures and Fertilizers; The Care of the Rabbit, the Ewe, the Cow, and the Bee; also, How We Improve Our Home.[33]

Thus, in response to the needs of farm youths, as well as to those of many in the city, the curriculum of the primary school has been tailored primarily to practical needs. But in the secondary schools, which serve mainly to prepare students for the professions, changing the traditional classical curriculum has been a more difficult but necessary task. Earlier, the primary aim of the schools was to weed out students by one means or another so that the number of graduates would be no more than government, business, and the professions could absorb. But today, the democratic philosophy of public education aims to give all students the opportunity for an education from the elementary grades all the way through the university.

Under this program, the secondary schools have many pressing problems, including the problem of a tremendous influx of students. During the period 1955–60, the number of students in secondary schools grew from 2,194,000 to 3,837,000, an increase of about 15 percent each year. The increase is impressive, but 78 percent of the students enrolled do not

---

[32] Galo Plaza, "Two Experiments in Education for Democracy," *Responsible Freedom in the Americas, op. cit.,* p. 69.

[33] *Guia Didactica de Educación Rural No. 2* (Preparada por la Dirección General de Educación Rural en Cooperación con el SCIDE, Ministerio de Asuntos Campesinos) (La Paz, Bolivia: Alianza Para El Progreso, 1963), p. 233.

finish the whole program of six years that most countries offer; for financial or other reasons, they drop out to get jobs, usually ones requiring technical competence or know-how that can utilize their level of educational progress.

The drop-outs and the pressing needs of the society pose thorny problems for the secondary schools. What should their curriculum be? Moreover, how can students be steered to major in fields of learning and training which the nations really need? In spite of the fact that Latin America needs a huge number of trained technicians to aid agricultural and industrial development, and in spite of the fact that four out of five students drop out during secondary school, the enrollment pattern there, as shown in 1960, was not geared to this reality. Of the total number of students, 15 percent were taking a commercial course; 10 percent, teacher training; 9 percent, industrial studies; 2 percent, home economics; and only 1 percent, agriculture and animal husbandry. But 63 percent, almost two-thirds of the total number, were taking the general secondary education courses[34] in the expectation of becoming white-collar workers, with which Latin America is already surfeited.

Increase in Enrollment and Segregation of Sexes

By all odds one of the biggest headaches confronting the educational system is the tremendous increase in the number of children to be educated. The average annual increase in population is 2.7 percent, the highest of any major region in the world. The population explosion, added to the region's many other problems, makes it daily more difficult to educate the burgeoning young population. From 1950 to 1960, the primary school enrollment in the 19 Latin-American countries, exclusive of Cuba, increased from 14,312,305 pupils to 24,794,000, an increase of more than 73 percent. Demographers estimate that by 1970 Latin America will have a population of approximately 270,000,000; according to this projection, the schools must be prepared to receive an additional 5 million children each year.[35]

The heavy pupil fall-out from the region's population explosion is already resulting in a critical shortage of funds, schools, and qualified teachers. As a result, many of the educational systems are having to hold double sessions of school. Sometimes one group of students comes in the morning, and another in the afternoon; sometimes one group attends school on Monday, Wednesday, and Friday, while another group attends on Tuesday, Thursday, and Saturday. The situation is so critical in Brazil, due mainly to the fact that very few schools were built during the period 1935–50, that some schools have three sessions a day.

The shortage of facilities and teaching staff is complicated by the prevailing mores requiring that boys and girls be separated in their instruc-

---

[34] Betancur-Mejía, op. cit., p. 3.
[35] Ibid.

tion, a practice that is rigidly followed in private schools and in most public schools as well. Separation of the sexes is deeply ingrained in the educational tradition of Latin America. "The ideal of education," said a member of the Secretariat of Public Education in Mexico, "is to make woman more feminine and man more masculine; in other words: education should enable the boy and the girl to emphasize the characteristics proper to their sex instead of blunting, nullifying, or substituting them."[36]

Separation of the sexes is not much of a problem in the cities, whose large enrollments and many schools can fairly easily be divided between members of both sexes. But in rural areas, fortunate to have even one school, separation of the sexes often works a real hardship; as a result, many of these schools teach boys and girls together.

For one reason or another, coeducation has gotten a firm toehold, and threatens to make further inroads on the traditional pattern of separation of the sexes. Some Latin Americans have even given coeducation enthusiastic approval. "The boys and girls of our school go to class, study and play together, as well as participate in an active social program," said Galo Plaza, referring to the American School in Quito, an Ecuadorian institution, 80 percent of whose student body is Ecuadorian. "Coeducation has made possible a wholesome, normal, and happy relationship between girls and boys that was not thought possible before."[37]

The Roman Catholic Church, however, is strongly opposed to coeducational schools. A decree issued by the Sacred Congregation of the Religious in 1958 forbids "any member of a religious order from becoming head of an elementary or secondary coeducational school except in case of dire necessity." And where coeducation is unavoidable, "there should be scrupulous separation of the sexes for lessons on the Sixth Commandment which forbids sins of the flesh and on biological and psychological subjects." Boys and girls should never participate together in gymnastics, sports, or games; moreover, they should be seated separately in class and have separate doors and gateways for entering and leaving school.[38]

Methods of Instruction

One of the most distinctive features of Latin American education is the method of instruction. Some of the countries, the more progressive ones, are stressing methods that are followed today by nations with advanced educational systems. In Costa Rica, for example, work in class is supposed to take the most active form possible, with full use being made of observation and expression. In Uruguay, it is recognized that teachers should give their pupils individual attention and allow the most able to progress as rapidly as their abilities permit.[39]

---

[36] In William S. Stokes, *Latin American Politics* (New York: Thomas Y. Crowell Co., 1959), p. 54.
[37] Galo Plaza, *op. cit.,* p. 76.
[38] *New York Times,* March 11, 1958, p. 7, col. 6.
[39] UNESCO, *World Survey of Education, 1958, op. cit.,* pp. 271 and 1319.

However, most of the countries, probably many of the schools in Costa Rica and Uruguay too, continue to follow the traditional methods of instruction. The teacher dominates the classroom, dictating materials that the pupils painstakingly write down in their notebooks or on slates. There is no opportunity for the pupils to ask questions, tell about their "experiences," or report on the results of their observations. They are not encouraged to think for themselves, but rather to memorize the information imparted by the teacher. When she asks questions, she expects to receive verbatim answers from the information she has dished out. Moreover, she pays little attention to the individual aptitudes or differences of her pupils or to their widely varying proficiency in reading.

Ability to cram (without necessarily understanding the content) has long been the accepted criterion of scholastic achievement. "It was considered an evidence of high academic standards," wrote William Griffith, describing Guatemala's educational system, "to force difficult subject matter farther and farther down in the curriculum without regard for the ability of the child to grasp the principles which the instruction involved. The proposed reform of the elementary school curriculum after the revolution, for example, included geometry for the first grade."[40]

Centralized Control

Another distinctive feature of education in Latin America is its highly centralized control. The national government dominates all phases of education at all levels. Ordinarily it makes all decisions of any importance: the school buildings to be constructed, the curriculum to be taught, the textbooks to be used, the teachers to be employed, the teaching guides to be used, the timetable of instruction to be followed, and even the tests or examinations to be given. So extensive is the national control exercised from the top that teachers are usually expressly forbidden to omit any part of the instructional program, alter the order of recitations, or even change the distribution of time among the various subjects.[41]

The tight control from the top precludes the development of much local concern with the activity and welfare of the local school. There is no locally elected school board whose public discusssions and decisions tend to whip up interest on the part of the community. There is seldom a parent-teacher association to give the school strong grass-roots support.

Moreover, centralized control has many directly harmful effects on the educational system. The minister of education is usually a political appointee with no training or experience in education. When this is the case,

[40] William Griffith, "A Recent Attempt at Educational Cooperation Between the United States and Guatemala," *Middle American Research Records*, Vol. 1 (1949), p. 175.

[41] For a chart showing Chile's highly centralized organization of education, which other national systems resemble, see UNESCO, *World Survey of Education, 1958, op. cit.*, p. 233.

as in Panama for example, the entire system is vulnerable to political influence, as is shown by the disproportionate amount of funds allocated to administration as compared with teaching. Political considerations are also evident in the rental of buildings and in the arranging of contracts for equipment and supplies. The minister and his staff change with each new administration, which, because of the region's political instability, means frequently. Consequently, the planning and execution of a program hardly get under way before a new minister takes office, scraps the old plan, and institutes one of his own, which is also likely to be short-lived. Thus, there is little continuity in organization and planning, as a result of which much of the money and effort expended on education are wasted.[42]

A significant development today is the emphasis that public education is receiving. During the colonial period, the Catholic Church enjoyed an almost complete monopoly on education and for many years after independence dominated the educational programs of the countries. Consequently, the concept of free public education available to all children was slow in taking hold. In recent decades, however, the number of public primary schools and pupils far exceeds the number of private primary schools and pupils. In secondary education, however, the picture is different; here, there is a much larger proportion of both private schools and enrollments. In fact, in several of the countries, private secondary schools play the major role in the educational system. In Brazil, for example, there are 1,843 private secondary schools with 369,881 students, as compared with only 669 public schools with 261,121 students.

Adult Education and Literacy Campaigns

The high rate of illiteracy that prevails over most of Latin America has been the cause of much concern, as evidenced by the many national campaigns which have been launched to teach adults to read and write.

In 1944, Mexico began a dramatic, nationwide campaign to reduce illiteracy. According to the program, every literate person between the ages of 18 and 60 was to teach one illiterate how to read and write during the period of one year. If the program had worked out as planned, it would have eliminated illiteracy within a short time. But this high goal was not achieved, and the nation periodically undertakes another nationwide literacy drive.[43]

Another nation which has attempted to reduce illiteracy by nationwide campaigns is Ecuador. In 1945, a sweeping literacy law was enacted, under which all illiterate Ecuadorians between the ages of 16 and 50 were required to learn to read and write and to understand the elements of

---

[42] John and Mavis Biesanz, *The People of Panama* (New York: Columbia University Press, 1955), p. 326.

[43] For the one planned in 1959, see *New York Times*, December 27, 1959, p. 22, col. 1.

arithmetic within five years. All persons having illiterates in their employ were to send their names to the appropriate authorities and to assist in their attending classes. But the great mass of illiterates were not noticeably affected by the law. Unable to read even the simplest government posters or pronouncements, they never knew anything about it! And many of those who could read did not bother to tell them about it![44]

In 1950, Ecuador launched another extensive campaign to teach illiterates to read and write. This time, a mobile rural cultural division was established, consisting of ten motor vans and two launches elaborately equipped with loudspeakers, recorded music, movie projectors, and library material. The crew of each van and launch included at least one or more doctors, nurses, and engineers, also census takers and schoolgirls. The mornings were devoted to such practical activities as giving vaccinations or building latrines; the afternoons, to discussions regarding the problems and needs of the community; and the evenings, to entertainment provided by music and movies.[45] But despite these imaginative efforts, illiteracy continues to be high in the nation.

An especially bold attack on illiteracy is Acción Cultural Popular (Popular Cultural Movement), undertaken from Sutatenza, Colombia, by Father José Joaquin Salcedo. A radio enthusiast and ham operator, Father Salcedo conceived the idea of teaching the peasants to read and write by means of lessons given over radio. After much experimentation, and with UNESCO assistance, Radio Sutatenza has become a most effective and world-renowned medium for educating people in the remote backwoods, also giving them religious instruction and entertainment to boot. The more than 42,000 receivers of Acción Cultural Popular distributed throughout the rural areas of the nation are all one-station receivers and can get only broadcasts from Radio Sutatenza. But its programs are a potent cultural and religious influence in the life of rural Colombia.[46]

Many other imaginative steps have been taken to reduce illiteracy. In Bolivia, the compulsory military service required of all male citizens at age 19 has been utilized for this purpose, the captive audience being given educational instruction which has taught many an Indian youth how to read and write.[47] Thanks to such imaginative and constructive measures, some of the nations are making impressive gains in reducing illiteracy, as Figure 5–3 indicates.

---

[44] Uzcátequi, op. cit., pp. 34–35.

[45] Ibid., pp. 27–29.

[46] Pablo M. Ozaeta, "The Radiophonic Schools of Sutatenza, Colombia," Communication Media and the School: The Yearbook of Education: 1960 (eds. George Z. F. Bereday and Joseph A. Lauwerys) (University of London Institute of Education, 1960), chap. 13, pp. 557–64. See also John J. Considine, New Horizons in Latin America (New York: Dodd, Mead & Co., 1958), pp. 219–27.

[47] Olen E. Leonard, Bolivia: Land, People and Institutions (Washington, D.C.: The Scarecrow Press, Inc., 1952), p. 167.

FIGURE 5-3

LITERACY IN LATIN AMERICA: 1950–60

PERCENTAGE OF LITERATES AMONG POPULATION AGE 15 OR OVER
(TEN YEAR COMPARISON IN CASES WHERE DATA WERE AVAILABLE)

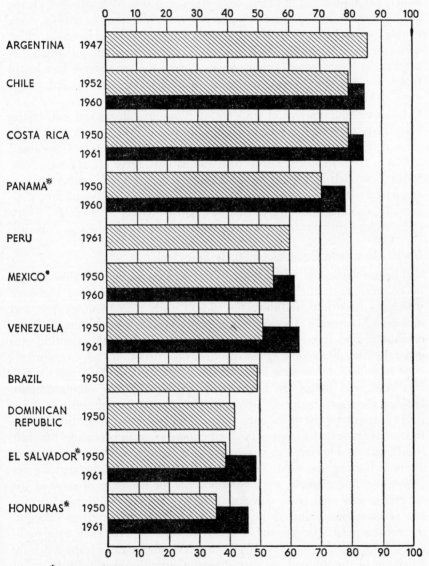

* POPULATION AGE 10 OR OVER
• POPULATION AGE 6 OR OVER

SOURCE: *Américas*, May, 1964, pp. 46–47. Reproduced by permission.

HIGHER EDUCATION

Number of Institutions and Students

There are 527 institutions of higher education in Latin America, of which 243 are located in Brazil, 68 in Argentina, and 61 in Mexico. Of the 527 institutions, about 90 are of university rank. In ten of the nations, there is only one university; in Brazil, Colombia, and Mexico, however, there are 12 or more in each of the countries. The total number of colleges and universities has increased tremendously during the last several decades. In Brazil, for example, it was not until 1920 that the first university was created; but by 1959 there were 19 in the nation.

Likewise, the number of students studying at colleges and universities has greatly increased in recent decades. In Brazil, which well reflects the general trend, the number increased from about 26,000 in 1935 to about 75,000 in 1955. In all the Latin American nations, there are approximately 500,000 enrolled in institutions of higher learning. This number is small compared with the 4 million in the United States, whose population, incidentally, is about the same as that of Latin America. In short, for every eight college students in the United States, there is one in Latin America.

Curriculum and Courses of Study Selected

The curriculum in Latin America has undergone considerable change. In colonial days, the universities were primarily schools of theology which trained priests, and the main fields of study were theology, law, and medicine. Sometimes other courses were given, such as astronomy, botany, chemistry, and mineralogy. In recent decades, as man's scientific and general cultural horizons have expanded, the curriculum has been broadened to include many new fields of study, such as electrical, mechanical, aviational, and petroleum engineering, geology, public administration, business administration, even oceanography and nuclear physics.

As a result of the broadened curriculum, students in Latin America today have many challenging fields to choose from in preparing for their future careers. However, as in the case of secondary school students, they are not choosing the fields that will contribute most to the region's development. For example, since agriculture is the mainstay of most of the countries, and since poor farming practices are largely responsible for low productivity, abuse of the soil, and calamitous effects from drought, the nations need a large number of agricultural experts, such as agronomists, soil specialists, and conservationists. Yet despite this great need, only 2 percent of the students are specializing in agriculture; it is not regarded as having high status, being too closely associated with manual labor and dirty hands.

Not even all this 2 percent would be studying agriculture were it not for the more dignified title of "agricultural engineer" which graduates of colleges of agriculture now receive. "What's in a name?" Maybe not much to a rose, which by any other name would smell as sweet. But it means a great deal to an "agricultural engineer" south of the border.

The plight of the field of education is similar to that of agriculture. Despite the bumper crop of babies every year from the population explosion and the critical shortage in most countries of qualified teachers, only 4 percent of the students in higher education are studying to be teachers. As a result, instead of making headway in alleviating the shortage of teachers, some of the nations are actually falling still further behind.

But while agriculture and education are suffering from the lack of interest of students, certain other fields are booming. Eleven percent of the students are specializing in the humanities; 17 percent, in the social sciences; and 20 percent, in law.[48] Thus regardless of the region's primary needs, more than three times as many students are studying law as agriculture and teacher education combined. Ironically, the society is glutted with lawyers; they are a dime a dozen, and their economic straits are relieved only by their pride of being recognized as Doctor—a title which is proudly displayed to the world on calling cards, name plates at residences, telephone directories, or anywhere else it may be advertised.

The unwillingness of students to enter fields in which they are critically needed is the cause of much concern. "Latin America has a fertile University tradition," concluded the Task Force Report of the OAS Special Commission for the Programming and Development of Education, Science, and Culture in Latin America. "Since colonial days, the universities have molded the leading social sectors and have played an important part in political life. At present, however, it may be said that the university has failed to keep pace with the social and economic evolution of the Latin American countries, and has made little effort to promote the 'new' professions needed for accelerating development. Although there is a critical shortage of trained, high-level manpower, Latin American universities continue to emphasize the traditional professions, many of which are neutral towards development and have failed to train enough persons capable of leadership or to contribute to the mobility of societies. . . ."[49]

---

[48] Betancur-Mejía, *op. cit.*, p. 4. The other fields of student specialization are as follows: fine arts, 3 percent; exact and natural sciences, 4 percent; engineering, 18 percent; and medical sciences, 21 percent.

Specialization in the "status fields" is also shown by a breakdown of the 1959 enrollment at 62 Latin-American universities. The field of specialization and number of students in each is as follows: law and political and social science, 69,584; medicine, 64,102; engineering, architecture, and urban planning, 51,909; economics, 45,254; the humanities, liberal arts, and education, 40,837; exact and natural sciences, 29,013; dentistry, 12,388; pharmacy and biochemistry, 10,722; and agronomy and veterinary medicine, 9,917. (Luis Reissig, *Educación y Desarrollo Económico* [Buenos Aires: Editorial Losada, S.A., 1961], p. 73.)

[49] Betancur-Mejía, *op. cit.*, p. 4.) The report and recommendations of the OAS Special Committee are embodied in *Latin American Higher Education and Inter-American Cooperation* (Washington, D.C.: Pan American Union, June, 1961).

Methods of Instruction

The methods of instruction at the colleges and universities are usually quite outdated. Just as in the primary and secondary schools, most instruction is given by lectures only, with the students assiduously taking notes and memorizing them. This procedure is followed even in such courses as engineering and medicine, which are taught primarily from a theoretical point of view, with little or no opportunity of practical application. As a result, most medical doctors get their degrees without ever having actually performed, assisted in, or even seen an operation. The theoretical tenor of instruction is adequate for the purposes of most "med students," who obtain an M.D. degree only because of the prestige that it confers without any intention of ever practicing medicine. If they should later change their minds, there are plenty of peons to practice on, without any bother of postmortems or vital statistics to show whether their guesses were right or wrong.

Financial Support

One of the big problems of higher learning in Latin America is lack of adequate financial support. Most of the institutions, publicly supported, are resigned to an economically precarious existence, since the government is apt to be very closefisted with its appropriations. While some nations are more generous than others, the total expenditure of the whole region is piddling. All the countries of Latin America combined spend only about $70 million a year on higher education, which is only about 2 percent of the $3.5 billion dollars which the United States spends annually on its students.

Sometimes a university in Latin America lives a hand-to-mouth existence, facing the prospect of having to dismiss classes and close its doors any day because the governmental appropriation which it depends on has not been received. The University of San Carlos, Guatemala's only institution of higher learning, was confronted with just such a prospect in 1960, when government payments for its support were three months overdue.[50]

Buildings and Other Physical Facilities

The buildings and physical plant of the typical Latin American institution generally are quite different from what one visualizes as those of a college or university. In Latin America, only a few of the schools have campuses where students can go out to enjoy a breath of fresh air, and possibly to do a bit of courting, between classes. Among these are the National University of Mexico, with its many magnificent buildings, and the Universities of Panama and Colombia.

Most of the institutions, however, are located in business districts, noisy and crowded parts of the cities. Indeed, the typical college or university, with its classrooms, administrative offices, and few cubbyholes for pro-

---

[50] *New York Times,* January 18, 1960, p. 12, col. 8.

fessors, is housed in a single building in the downtown area—just another building, one would conclude, seeing it from the outside. The University of San Marcos in Lima is so housed, and it faces a public plaza where there is always much activity. The lack of student unions with their various facilities, of stadia for intercollegiate athletic events, as well as of dormitories and organized houses where students eat, sleep, and learn to live together, has made higher education in Latin America profoundly different from that in the United States.

Student life in the National University and in other Mexican schools of higher education is characterized by a lack of sociability and conviviality which permeate college life in the United States. Social gatherings, dances, and entertainment are infrequent. . . . The relationship of faculty members to students is therefore inclined to be of a business and scholarly nature rather than of personal interest and friendship. Indeed, student association with faculty members is rare.[51]

Carefully weighing the effects of the lack of physical facilities in Latin American universities, the OAS commission studying the educational needs of Latin America included among its recommendations: "Provision of adequate means to students to integrate them into university life . . . thus improving their social and educational status. . . . Preference would be given to the establishment of cafeterias, dormitories, gymnasiums, and centers of artistic recreation, and other common services. . . ."[52]

Faculty

In most of the Latin American colleges and universities, only a small part of the teaching staff are full-time professors who have no other outside jobs and devote to the institutions their full time and energy. At the Greater University of San Simón, in Cochabamba, Bolivia, for example, there are only four full-time professors, and 164 who teach part time. The part-time staff members are often called "taxi" professors because they rush to the classroom for an hour or so, read a prepared lecture that has not been brought up to date for years, then rush away to another job they depend on for a livelihood to make up for the meager salary they are paid for teaching.

The full-time professors, rare in most Latin American nations but the usual practice in the United States, have often brought disrepute on the profession. "Proprietors of a chair," as they are commonly dubbed, they seldom take the trouble to go to class; instead, they simply send their students mimeographed lectures that were prepared many years ago. And they probably get back answers of many years ago that some enterprising student mimeographed and sold for a few pesos to pay his way through college.

---

[51] George F. Kneller, *The Education of the Mexican Nation* (New York: Columbia University Press, 1951), p. 177.
[52] *Latin American Higher Education and Inter-American Cooperation, op. cit.,* pp. 15–16.

Several nations are trying hard to make teaching a full-time profession. Venezuela is outstanding in this respect, having one of the highest percentages of full-time faculty members. But even there, absenteeism of professors has become such a problem that regulations put into effect specify that any professor who is absent for more than 25 percent of the time is subject to dismissal.[53]

Granting of Degrees

Most universities in Latin America are public institutions, supported by public funds. And in most of the countries, these are the only bodies authorized by law to grant degrees. In Argentina, the monopoly of the public universities was ended in August 1959, after a hectic battle in the national congress. The Catholic colleges which would benefit were jubilant. Almost a year later, the government authorized the opening of the Catholic University of Córdoba, the first private university in the nation, with colleges of law, medicine, and engineering.[54]

Autonomous Status

In Latin America the university prides itself on having a unique status popularly known as "autonomy." Under this status, the universities, although supported by public funds, traditionally claim the right to be completely independent in their operation and control, immune from any interference by the government, even by law enforcement authorities. In deference to this tradition, the government does accord unusual respect to the university and its students. In Cuba, for example, although strongman Fulgencio Batista who dominated the island's politics from 1934 to 1959 did not hesitate to crack down on the rest of the nation, he nevertheless respected the autonomy of Havana University, the center of learning in the nation. In effect, it was "off limits" even for his dictatorial regime. In El Salvador, where the National Autonomous University had been closed after violent demonstration against the government, it refused to reopen until President Lemus agreed to apologize for the government's attacks and to pay for all damages that had been inflicted.[55]

The much-vaunted autonomy, however, is often more theoretical than real. When the chips are down and a government's very survival is at stake, it has little compunction about taking over the "autonomous" university, which in all probability instigated the crisis or at least is aiding and abetting it. Juan Perón was one of the strong-men in Latin America who moved boldly to destroy the autonomy of the universities and the academic freedom of professors. After some professors in Argentina were

---

[53] George I. Sánchez, *The Development of Education in Venezuela* (U.S. Department of Health, Education, and Welfare) (Washington, D.C.: U.S. Government Printing Office, 1963), pp. 107–8.

[54] *New York Times,* September 21, 1958, p. 33, col. 4, and August 22, 1959, p. 4, col. 6.

[55] *Ibid.,* October 2, 1960, p. 28, col. 7.

removed for political reasons, a total of 1,250 withdrew or resigned their posts. Shortly afterward, the universities came under the complete control and direction of Perón.

The university became a vehicle of propaganda, observed Juan Mantovani; "it became partisan, dogmatic, accepted impositions as a method of teaching, lost the objective meaning of truth, and many times in lectures the 'official truth' was uttered—the truth convenient to the regime. . . . In nearly all subjects, even in those very far removed from it, the party view was expressed. . . ."[56]

Student Reform Movement

Origin and Objectives. One of the most significant developments in the history of Latin American education is the University Reform Movement, born at the university at Córdoba, Argentina in June 1918. Picking up momentum as its objectives were publicized, it spread in time to Lima, to Santiago, and eventually to all the institutions of higher learning in Latin America. In essence, the movement was the outgrowth of the region's antiquated system of higher education and the determination of students to force basic, much-needed measures of reform.

The University Reform Movement as espoused by the students was a very ambitious program. Its main objectives were: (1) to make the university democratic and open to all students, regardless of class, race, or family; (2) to enable the students to participate in the government of the university in order to end the monopoly over professorships which the upper class had long enjoyed; (3) to limit a professor's term of appointment to from five to ten years in order to afford a periodic review of his competence, and to "break down the impermeability of a dogmatic faculty that failed to reflect changes in its respective disciplines"; (4) to encourage seminars, round tables, and group discussions to stimulate thought among students and professors alike; and (5) to involve the university more closely with the actual problems in each country and locality.[57]

Accomplishments. Thanks to the Reform Movement, many much-needed changes have been made in the universities of Latin America. No longer the private preserve of the elite, their doors are now open to all students, usually at modest or practically no costs; as a result, the university today, with its many students from the lower and middle classes, is one of the most democratizing influences in society. Moreover, students are represented on the ruling council of the university, along with the rector, deans, and representatives of the faculty and alumni, thus having

---

[56] Juan Mantovani, "Freedom of Argentine Universities Before and After the Perón Regime," *Higher Education: The Yearbook of Education* (eds. George Z. F. Bereday and Joseph A. Lauverys) (University of London Institute of Education, 1959), p. 410.

[57] Luis Alberto Sánchez, "The University in Latin America: Part III: The University Reform Movement," *Américas,* Vol. 14, No. 1 (January, 1962), pp. 13–14.

a voice in all decisions made on university policy and operations. Also, professors are now often selected and promoted on the basis of competitive examination, administered by a tribunal on which students are represented. This method of selection and promotion, and the limitation of tenure, would hardly be palatable to the academic profession in the United States. In Latin America, however, these measures have served to renovate the faculties and get rid of much deadwood, as well as to terminate the centuries-old monopoly of families and classes on university professorships. Furthermore, instruction has been vitalized and enlivened by seminars and group discussions, and the curriculum has been vastly augmented and broadened to reflect an awareness of social problems and a social emphasis which it never had before.

Shortcomings and Abuses. The Reform Movement must thus be given credit for many of the needed changes made in Latin American universities during the past four decades. But it can also be held responsible for many questionable practices, even grave abuses. Largely because of student pressure, standards of admission have been lowered, with no attempt to weed out students who are not of university caliber. Also, examinations have either been abolished or so watered down as to be of little value in measuring accomplishment. Indeed, if a student fails to pass an examination, he is authorized to take it again in a few months; and if he fails then, he can keep on taking it until he finally passes it or loses interest and leaves the university. Some students doggedly persist in taking the examination for a course a dozen times or more. Largely because of the retake privilege, a majority of the students spend six years or longer at the university; occasionally a student hangs on for so long that he is almost ready for social security by the time he receives his degree.

Another unfortunate consequence of the university reforms, the representation on university governing bodies often involves consideration of academic problems which students are not familiar with and are not qualified to handle. Thus, they exercise a strong voice in setting up new courses of study or throwing out others as "useless"—in Latin American lingo, courses which made them study and dig for themselves, or possibly courses on which they received low grades, maybe flunked.

To force acceptance of their point of view, students often resort to very crude, rough tactics. If a professor or administrator rubs them the wrong way, he is likely to incur their full wrath, vented by tactics ranging from badgering and hectoring to demonstrating, striking, and burning in effigy.[58]

Student obstreperousness expressed in such irresponsible fashion often has quite unfortunate consequences. In October, 1959, for example, the

---

[58] According to Focion Febres Cordero, the enemies of the reform which have largely thwarted its fulfillment are: university factions; timid, unsuitable professors interested only in the prestige of their position; "academic feudalism"; and abuses on the part of the students. (Focion Febres Cordero, *Reforma Universitaria* [Caracas: Universidad Central de Venezuela, 1959], pp. 73–79.)

strong resentment of the left-wing University Student Federation at the University of Buenos Aires, terming the United States-financed technical assistance program to the universities "cultural imperialism," put on so much pressure that the carefully planned and much needed program had to be abandoned.[59]

In Brazil, a visiting American professor of geology at the University of Recife incurred the wrath of students in his class in economic geology when he gave some of them low grades. The students retaliated by striking, hoisting banners reading "Down with the Dishonest Professor," refusing to go on a field trip, and, finally, issuing an ultimatum to the university rector demanding that the grades be raised. Student pressure became so great that the United States, in February 1960, finally had to withdraw all three American professors engaged in a technical assistance program of the greatest importance to Brazil. Striving to develop her subsoil resources, the nation critically needs trained geologists, of which there are only about 100 in the country. Yet this important program, too, as in the case of the one in Argentina, had to be abandoned because of student opposition.[60]

Such irresponsible actions by students of Latin America have often been deplored in both Latin America and the United States.

". . . one of the greatest needs of Latin America is the establishment—and strengthening—of private universities which can set standards," concludes William Benton. "Most Latin American universities are national universities, financed by their governments. The problems of improving their standards are often exacerbated by the powerful role of the students in their management. Characteristically, student representatives sit on their ruling councils, often in such numbers as to make effective faculty control of curricula and discipline exceedingly difficult if not impossible. A proposal that I believe has great merit calls for an attempt to help a single privately run Latin American university, free of political or student control, reach such a peak of distinction that it will serve as an example for others. This was the theory on which Johns Hopkins was founded and on which John D. Rockefeller later founded the University of Chicago. Such a private university in Latin America could quickly exercise a powerful influence over the course of higher education."[61]

Student Politics and Violence

In Latin America, university students are one of the most politically conscious and politically active groups in society. This had been the case ever since the wars for independence, which began in the early part of the nineteenth century. In the struggles to throw off the yoke of Spanish rule,

[59] *New York Times,* October 26, 1959, p. 1, col. 6.
[60] *Ibid.,* February 15, 1960, p. 6, col. 3.
[61] Committee for Economic Development, *Cooperation for Progress in Latin America* (New York: April, 1961), p. 24.

the university was the "cradle of republican thought." In fact, students and professors alike were among the principal promoters of independence for Latin America.[62]

Since independence, the university has continued to live up to its tradition of liberal, freewheeling thought and action. It is the spawning place of political philosophies. Thus, it was at the venerable University of San Marcos in Lima that Aprismo was conceived—a liberal political philosophy and program of action that has influenced the development of much of Latin America.

But students and professors do more than philosophize; they often aid or maybe foment revolutions. Sometimes in fact they are the sole intransigent force in the nation that dares to oppose a dictator—an opposition that is apt to mean imprisonment, torture, or liquidation. Even when such sacrifices are not immediately successful, they leave their mark. For even the worst dictators have learned to respect and fear students, and because of their efforts, a later revolution often succeeds. Perón in Argentina and Jiménez in Venezuela were both overthrown largely as a result of the determined opposition of the students. And many another dictator has been discredited and finally dislodged by their persistent, uncompromising tactics.

Just as the university is the cradle of political philosophies, so is campus politics the cradle of national politics. And whether a student majors in political science, veterinary medicine, or architecture, he participates in campus politics as a matter of absorbing interest. "Politics is not a game in the university," concludes Richard Patch, "it is a completely serious business for students and professors alike. Student politicians are playing for larger stakes than campus offices. They are beginning careers which may take them to power or exile within a few years. Most student politics is directed to national goals and the students expect to become national figures."[63]

A student election is therefore regarded as a serious test of strength between rival political parties and candidates. And in the absence of local elections that would reflect grass-roots sentiments, an election at the university is regarded as a political weather vane, a sort of Latin American New Hampshire primary. Interest is heightened by the realization that student parties in effect are national parties; they are generously aided financially by the national party organizations, which may even specify the strategy and tactics to be followed. The student election thus becomes a matter of national interest and is followed closely by the public via all

62 Luis Alberto Sánchez, "The University in Latin America: Part II: Cradle of Republican Thought," *Américas*, Vol. 13, No. 12 (December, 1961), pp. 20–23.
63 Richard W. Patch, "Fidelismo in Peruvian Universities: Part I: A New Platform for Old Causes," *American Universities Field Staff Reports Service* (West Coast South American Series, Vol. VIII, No. 2—Peru), (New York: AUFS, Inc., January, 1961), pp. 2–3.

the nation's media of mass communication, including radio and television stations, newspapers, and magazines.[64]

Taking his politics as seriously as he does, the student in Latin America would guffaw at the very idea of "mock elections," which are often held perfunctorily on our campuses to ascertain student attitudes toward national issues or candidates. Indeed, the serious interest of the Latin American student in politics is quite different from the noticeably indifferent attitude of the student in the United States. What accounts for the difference? According to some, the Latin American does not have any "normal" means of letting off steam, such as intercollegiate football games, intramural athletics, or panty raids.

But his absorbing interest in politics and his pronounced revolutionary spirit cannot be accounted for by such superficial explanations. Sagely observes Luis Alberto Sánchez, Rector of the venerable San Marcos University in Lima:

. . . a Latin American student . . . is, above and beyond everything, a young person who is dissatisfied with the society in which he lives, with the way he is developing as an individual, with the means available to him for achieving his objectives. A student like this may try to learn by himself and to find the truth by his own methods, but he will be dominated by the feeling of protest against the injustice that he feels binds him, and he will be carried away by the impulse to rebel against the powers that block the way to what he thinks are his ultimate goals. If one does not understand this, one can not understand anything about today's Latin American universities. . . .[65]

With his built-in impulse to rebel, the student has usually been the underdog, particularly when an oppressive dictatorship gripped his nation. For then he bore the full brunt of its determination to stamp out intellectuality, its most dangerous enemy. "Kill a student for the good of the country!" a regime such as Juan Perón's might openly advocate. "Close the university! This will contribute to the nation's progress!," another regime might have for its watchword.

Whatever the reason for the student's antagonistic attitude, "student violence in politics has a romantic appeal in Latin America," says William S. Stokes. "In practice, the idea of direct action means the use of pistols, rifles, bombs, machine guns, even light artillery. It means that students

---

[64] For an interpretative account, see *ibid.*, and Richard W. Patch, "Fidelismo in Peruvian Universities: Part II: "The Fidelistas Take Power," *op. cit.*, No. 3, February, 1961.

[65] Luis Alberto Sánchez, "The University in Latin America: Part IV: As It Looks Today," *Américas*, Vol. 14, No. 2 (February, 1962), p. 16.

Three conditions incline Latin-American students to political activity, according to S. Walter Washington: Latin Americans have respect for the educated; many students, coming from the poorer classes, are impatient for social reform; the population is young—more than 70 percent of the Venezuelans, for example, are under 30 years of age. (S. Walter Washington, "Student Politics in Latin America: The Venezuelan Example," *Foreign Affairs*, Vol. VII, No. 3 [April, 1959], p. 463.)

have to become arsonists, murderers, and assassins in order to achieve their political ideals."[66]

The willingness of students to resort to violence on the least provocation has made them very vulnerable to criticism, even by those who agree with their objectives. As another scholar, George I. Sánchez, concludes:

Factional politics, often without convincing rhyme or reason, run rampant on university campuses and in the *liceos*. The political parties, the most active of which have been communists or pro-communists on the campuses, vie for dominance in university elections, and the demonstrations of students. *Liceo* students are led into riots hither and yon; some are employed to manufacture Molotov cocktails and to engage in terrorism and guerrilla activities. Strikes are called; marches are organized—these often being expressions of sympathy for the little understood issues being argued. Irresponsible and unbridled, the political action of some groups of students in Venezuela are making a mockery of university autonomy and educational discipline, at both the university and secondary levels. The power of the students has been allowed to get out of hand, the place of political democracy in educational institutions has been vitiated by political irresponsibility.[67]

Unfortunately, student violence and destructiveness have almost become trademarks of student activity. And sometimes their violence and destructiveness are so flagrant as to be most offensive and harmful to the rest of society. The crippling of Mexico City's bus system in September, 1958, shows how absurdly far supposedly mature students will go in giving vent to their wanton urge to create sheer havoc.

The trouble began when the city government announced a one-cent increase in bus fare to help pay for increases in drivers' wages and for 1,400 new buses that were needed. University students were specifically exempted from the higher fare. However, proclaiming themselves to be "defenders of the working class," they seized a number of buses, playing "dodge-'em, bump-'em, hot-rodding the buses back and forth. . . ." They then looted and burned a bus terminal, beating up drivers and seizing many more buses, which they drove onto the university campus for the purpose of methodically wrecking them. As student rioting spread throughout the city, the campus took full advantage of its inviolability. While troops ringed its borders, not daring to set foot on its soil, "students danced around blazing buses as white-clad medical students set up first-aid sta-

---

[66] Stokes, *op. cit.*, p. 82.

For many acts of violence by and against university students in Cuba, see William S. Stokes, "National and Local Violence in Cuban Politics," *Southwestern Social Science Quarterly*, Vol. 34, No. 2 (September, 1953), pp. 59–60.

[67] George I. Sánchez, *op. cit.*, pp. 108–9.

Chilean students, on the other hand, have been a beneficial influence. "Students have been a force for progress within the university," concludes Frank Bonilla; "their dedication to democratic ideals, their readiness to protest injustice, and their resistance to political repression have helped keep Chile politically moderate." (Frank Bonilla, "The Student Federation of Chile: 50 years of Political Action," *Journal of Inter-American Studies*, Vol. 11, No. 3 [July, 1960], p. 315.)

tions, home economics coeds perspired prettily over soup kettles, and chemistry aspirants continued to make Molotov cocktails."[68]

The damage from the senseless rioting and wholesale vandalism was estimated at $160,000. The students had stolen some 340 buses, leaving more than 200 of them in need of major repairs. The bus drivers who were supposed to benefit by the higher fare got no increase in salary at all; rather, because of the loss of their buses, many of them were reduced to part-time work or laid off entirely. And the city bus industry was bankrupt.[69]

Higher education ordinarily implies greater maturity and a more developed sense of responsibility. Unfortunately, as the Mexican bus strike of 1958 clearly shows, this is not always the case. Yet paradoxically, many an obstreperous, destructive student of yesterday has turned out to be the dynamic constructive leader of tomorrow.

SUGGESTED READINGS

ADAMS, RICHARD N., AND CUMBERLAND, CHARLES C. *United States University Cooperation in Latin America.* Institute of Research on Overseas Programs. East Lansing, Mich.: Michigan State University, 1960.

ARCINIEGAS, GERMÁN (ed.). *The Green Continent; A Comprehensive View of Latin America by Its Leading Writers,* pp. 337–53. Trans. HARRIET DE ONÍS and others. New York: Alfred A. Knopf, Inc., 1959.

BETANCUR-MEJÍA, GABRIEL. "Education: Backbone of the Alliance for Progress," *Américas,* Vol. XXV, No. 9 (September, 1963).

BIESANZ, JOHN, AND BIESANZ, MAVIS. *The People of Panama,* pp. 157–61, 324–51. New York: Columbia University Press, 1955.

BONILLA, FRANK. "The Student Federation of Chile: 50 Years of Political Action," *Journal of Inter-American Studies,* Vol. 11, No. 3 (July, 1960), pp. 311–34.

BUNKLEY, ALLISON WILLIAMS. *The Life of Sarmiento.* Princeton, N.J.: Princeton University Press, 1952.

CLINE, HOWARD F. *Mexico: Revolution to Evolution: 1940–1960,* chaps. xx and xxi. Royal Institute of International Affairs. New York: Oxford University Press, 1962.

FILHO, M. B. LOURENÇO, *et al. The Training of Rural School Teachers;* "Part I, Rural Teacher Training in Brazil," pp. 15–54; "Part IV, Rural Teacher Training in Mexico," pp. 131–64: UNESCO: Problems in Education Series—VII. Paris, 1953.

FITZGIBBON, RUSSELL H. *Uruguay: Portrait of a Democracy,* chap. xiv. New Brunswick, N.J.: Rutgers University Press, 1954.

GRUENING, ERNEST. *Mexico and Its Heritage,* pp. 515–32. New York: D. Appleton-Century Co., Inc., 1934.

HOLMBERG, ALLAN R. "Changing Attitudes and Values in Peru: A Case Study in Guided Change," *Social Change in Latin America Today,* chap. 2. Council on Foreign Relations. New York: Harper & Bros., 1960.

---

[68] *Time,* September 8, 1958, pp. 30–31.
[69] *Ibid.,* September 29, 1958, p. 33.

INTERNATIONAL BANK FOR RECONSTRUCTION AND DEVELOPMENT. *The Basis of a Development Program for Colombia: Report of a Mission*, chaps. xii and xxv. Washington, D.C., 1950.

————. *Economic Development of Venezuela*, chap 14. Baltimore: Johns Hopkins Press, 1963.

KNELLER, GEORGE F. *The Education of the Mexican Nation*. New York: Columbia University Press, 1951.

LABARCA, AMANDA H. "Women and Education in Chile," *Women and Education*, Part I. UNESCO: Problems in Education Series—V. Paris, 1953.

LEONARD, OLEN E. *Bolivia: Land, People and Institutions*, chap. x. Washington, D.C.: The Scarecrow Press, Inc., 1952.

MACGAFFEY, WYATT, AND BARNETT, CLIFFORD R. *Cuba: Survey of World Cultures*, chap. 8. New Haven, Conn.: American University: HRAF Press, 1962.

NELSON, LOWRY. *Rural Cuba*, chap. xii. Minneapolis: University of Minnesota Press, 1950.

ORGANIZATION OF AMERICAN STATES. *Latin American Higher Education and Inter-American Cooperation*. Washington, D.C.: Pan American Union, June, 1961.

OZAETA, PABLO M. "The Radiophonic Schools of Sutatenza, Colombia, *Communication Media and the School: The Yearbook of Education: 1960* (ed. GEORGE Z. F. BEREDAY AND JOSEPH A. LAUWERYS), chap. 13. University of London Institute of Education, 1960.

PATCH, RICHARD W. "Fidelismo in Peruvian Universities," *American Universities Field Staff Reports Service*. West Coast South American Series, Part I: "A New Platform for Old Causes," Vol. VIII, No. 2 (Peru); January, 1961. Part II: "The Fidelistas Take Power," Vol. VIII, No. 3 (Peru), February, 1961.

PIERSON, WILLIAM W., AND GIL, FEDERICO G. "Education," *Governments of Latin America*, chap. 16. New York: McGraw-Hill Book Co., Inc., 1957.

RIO, ANGEL DEL (ed.). *Responsible Freedom in the Americas*, "Part One: Elementary, Primary, and Secondary Education"; "Part Two: University Education"; "Part Five: The Government in Education." Garden City, N.Y.: Doubleday & Co., Inc., 1955.

SÁNCHEZ, GEORGE I. *The Development of Education in Venezuela*. United States Department of Health, Education, and Welfare. Washington, D.C.: U.S. Government Printing Office, 1963.

SÁNCHEZ, LUIS ALBERTO. "The University in Latin America," *Américas:* "Part I: The Colonial Period," November, 1961; "Part II: Cradle of Republican Thought," December, 1961; "Part III: The University Reform Movement," January, 1962; "Part IV: The University As It Looks Today," February, 1962.

SCHURZ, WILLIAM LYTLE. *Brazil: The Infinite Country*, chap. 10. New York: E. P. Dutton & Co., Inc., 1961.

SMITH, T. LYNN. *Brazil: People and Institutions*, Part 5, chap. xix. Rev. ed. Baton Rouge, La.: Louisiana State University Press, 1963.

STOKES, WILLIAM S. *Latin American Politics*, chaps. 5 and 6. New York: Thomas Y. Crowell Co., 1959.

TANNENBAUM, FRANK. *Mexico: The Struggle for Peace and Bread*, chap. 10. New York: Alfred A. Knopf, Inc., 1954.

———. *Peace by Revolution: An Interpretation of Mexico*, chaps. 24–26. New York: Columbia University Press, 1933.

———. *Ten Keys to Latin America*, chap. 6. New York: Alfred A. Knopf, Inc., 1962.

TUCKER, WILLIAM P. *The Mexican Government Today*, chap. 24. Minneapolis: University of Minnesota Press, 1957.

UNESCO. *World Survey of Education, II: Primary Education*. Paris, 1958.

———. *World Survey of Education, III: Secondary Education*. New York: Columbia University Press, 1961.

UZCÁTEGUI, EMILIO. *Compulsory Education in Ecuador*. UNESCO: Studies on Compulsory Education Series—VII. Paris, 1951.

WAGLEY, CHARLES. *An Introduction to Brazil*, pp. 204–31. New York: Columbia University Press, 1963.

WASHINGTON, S. WALTER. "Student Politics in Latin America: The Venezuelan Example," *Foreign Affairs*, Vol. VII, No. 3 (April, 1959), pp. 463–73.

WHETTEN, NATHAN L. *Guatemala: The Land and the People*, chap. 13. Caribbean Series, 4. New Haven, Conn.: Yale University Press, 1961.

———. *Rural Mexico*, chap. xvii. Chicago: University of Chicago Press, 1948.

WILGUS, A. CURTIS (ed.). *The Caribbean: Venezuelan Development, A Case History*, Part II. Gainesville, Fla.: University of Florida Press, 1963.

CHAPTER 6

THE CHURCH:
An Influence for Standpatism
or Progress

THE CHURCH in Latin America, meaning until recent decades the Roman Catholic Church, has been one of the strongest influences on the development of each nation and the lives of its citizens. This influence began in the very first days of conquest and colonization and has continued until today. In fact, the questions of just what authority the Church should enjoy in the society and what functions it should exercise have been very controversial issues ever since independence, and have not been completely settled to date.

THE CHURCH IN COLONIAL SOCIETY

At the time that America was discovered, the Roman Catholic Church enjoyed a position of great power and prestige in both Spain and Portugal. The successful campaigns which had been waged to oust the Moors and crush Mohammedanism had long been a holy crusade, greatly aided by members of the clergy. Exhorting their parishioners to fight as a Christian duty and threatening punishment to those who shirked, members of the clergy could justifiably claim much of the credit for victory. As a reward for their invaluable assistance, they were given a large part of the land that was reconquered. Consequently, the Church became exceedingly wealthy, with a prestige and influence commensurate with its great wealth.

After Columbus accidentally bumped into America in his quest for the East Indies, the Spanish and Portuguese crowns lost no time laying claim to this new, large, hitherto undiscovered part of the world. In conquering its vast domain and exploiting its rich resources, even more valuable than those of the East Indies, the monarchy and the papacy worked hand in hand as a close partnership, the crown furnishing the manpower and material necessary for conquering the region, while the Church assumed the responsibility of Christianizing and educating the heathen natives.

While the partnership between the monarchy and the Church was very close, the monarchy was unquestionably the senior partner, determined to enjoy the temporal power which Spain as a new nation-state could exercise independently of the papacy. In effect, the king was the secular head of the Church, with control over most of its activities in the new world. This control was recognized in three papal documents issued soon after the discovery of America. A bull of Alexander VI issued in 1493 divided the New World between Spain and Portugal, granting to them the exclusive privilege of Christianizing and civilizing the natives. Another bull of Alexander VI in 1501 granted to the Spanish monarch the right to ecclesiastical tithes in all his New World dominions on condition that he be responsible for establishing and maintaining the Church. Still another bull, issued by Julius II in 1508, conferred upon the king the right of universal patronage over the Church in the New World.

These three papal documents constituted a firm basis upon which the Spanish crown was able to maintain its control over the Church. The first bull gave papal confirmation of the crown's territorial claims, making a contest with Portugal less likely; the second vested in the crown the all-important power of the purse; and the third, probably the most significant of all, in effect gave the crown the power to select all the clergy in America—the archbishops, bishops, and abbots, as well as lower members of the clergy.

Known as the *Patronato Real*, or royal patronage of the Church, the king had the authority to nominate a cleric for any benefice that was vacant. If an archbishop, bishop, canon, or other high officer was to be selected, the king's nomination was made to the pope. However, if an individual was to be selected for one of the lower benefices, the royal nomination was made to the archbishop or bishop of the diocese containing the vacancy. Until 1574 the king himself made all nominations for vacant clerical offices. But as the administration of the colonies became more complex, the crown delegated to the viceroys, presidents, governors, and captains-general the authority to make nominations for the lesser benefices.

The crown's control over the patronage was one of its most highly prized powers. As "the richest stone, the most precious pearl in the royal diadem," it was a prerogative that was zealously guarded, and any threatened infringement was sure to evoke vigorous royal action.[1]

In the joint exploitation of Latin America, the king was determined to sit in the driver's seat, holding the reins tightly to control the temporal

---

[1] For the significance and exercise of the patronage, see J. Lloyd Mecham, *Church and State in Latin America* (Chapel Hill, N.C.: University of North Carolina Press, 1934), pp. 16–27; also Carlos E. Castaneda, *Church and Society: Catholic Social and Political Thought and Movements* (ed. Joseph N. Moody) (New York: Arts, Inc., 1953), pp. 735–52.

and ecclesiastical team in the new domain. Referring to the crown's control over the Church, J. Lloyd Mecham concludes, ". . . it is difficult to conceive of a more absolute jurisdiction than that which the kings of Spain exercised over the ecclesiastical affairs of the Indies. . . . Never before or since did a sovereign with the consent of a pope so completely control the Catholic Church within his dominions."[2]

During the colonial period, the crown had the deciding voice in practically all of the Church's many activities. Not a single church or monastery or hospital could be built by the Church unless the crown approved it; no priest could come to the New World unless licensed by the government and directed where to serve; no church councils could be held or papal bulls issued applying to the new world unless the monarch first gave his stamp of approval.

But while the state in its impersonal way governed the people, the Church by its close personal touch with them actually ruled them, catering to their everyday needs from the cradle to the grave. "The Church was everywhere and with every individual all his life," says Frank Tannenbaum. "The day began with early morning mass and ended with Ave Maria. . . . The Church was . . . the school, the university, the hospital, the home for the aged, the sick, and the abandoned. It served the individual and the community in many ways. In the absence of newspapers, libraries, museums, and theaters, the religious ritual of the churches . . . gave the individual a place in an enchanted and meaningful world."[3]

In addition, the Church was a strong influence in trying to protect the helpless Indian against the predatory conquistador. Las Casas, the bishop of Guatemala, made more than a dozen trips across the Atlantic to plead with the king for justice to the Indians, asserting that the conquistador was not different or better by nature than the Indian, and that "all men are men and nothing more."

The Indian, thanks to the Church's interest in Christianizing him and interceding for him against the conquistador, certainly enjoyed a much more humane treatment than he would have otherwise received. Consequently, many Indians flocked to the priests, quite willing to be converted in return for protection which they sorely needed. When the spirit was willing, conversion was a relatively easy process, often accomplished en masse.

But when the spirit was not receptive, conversion was often an ordeal for both the priests and members of their refractory flock. Sometimes the Indians had to spend five to seven years in a mission before they were ready for baptism. It was difficult for the priests to hold them that long, as they were not accustomed to such a sedentary life. As a result, they often tried to escape. Occasionally, the entire mission population of Indians

---

[2] Mecham, *op. cit.*, pp. 12 and 43.
[3] Frank Tannenbaum, *Ten Keys to Latin America* (New York: Alfred A. Knopf, Inc., 1962), p. 57.

quietly decamped, heading back for the forests and hills. The missionaries would go after them in hot pursuit with one or two soldiers and perhaps a few "trusties." Sometimes it was a long chase before the fugitives were caught and persuaded or forced to return.[4]

In addition to aiding the Indians (sometimes rather against their will), the Church did much to ease the lot of the Negro slaves. In the early days of the conquest, the Church advocated the importation of slaves from Africa, intending thereby to protect the Indians from exploitation at the hands of colonists. But as the slave trade became more inhumane and barbaric, the Church forbade any of the faithful to engage in it. Regarding slavery itself, opinion within the Church was sharply divided as to whether it was justifiable or should be abolished.[5] Some of the religious orders themselves owned slaves, who were invariably treated most kindly.

In its overall policy regarding slavery, the Church was one of the most influential forces in ameliorating its effects and standing up for the human dignity and rights of the slave. It emphasized the moral equality of all persons, including the slave, and stressed the obligation of protecting his rights, even that of manumission itself.[6]

Thus, the Church played a leading role during the long colonial period, performing many functions which the society very much needed, and enjoying great influence and prestige. Its influential, privileged position was to bring it into bitter conflict with the new states after they had won independence from Spain.

THE CHURCH DURING THE WARS OF INDEPENDENCE

The outbreak of the revolutions against Spain found the clergy bitterly divided in their sympathies and support. Most of the hierarchy were unswerving in their loyalty to the crown, loyalty that is quite understandable. For although exercising a strong degree of control, the king had nevertheless been a faithful friend and ally, furnishing protection to the Church and granting it many valuable privileges for which it was very grateful. Moreover, its prestige and privileged position were assured under the dominion of the crown. But how well would they fare under a new revolutionary regime bent on change?

As a longtime copartner in the whole colonial undertaking, the hierarchy threw its great influence and power solidly behind the royal cause, determined to make it a battle to the death, if necessary, to win. By impassioned exhortations or fearful threats, the members of the higher

---

[4] Clarence H. Haring, *The Spanish Empire in America* (New York: Oxford University Press, 1947), p. 197.

[5] For the difference of opinion in Brazil, see Donald Pierson, *Negroes in Brazil: A Study of Race Contact at Bahia* (Chicago: University of Chicago Press, 1942), pp. 54–57.

[6] Frank Tannenbaum, *Slave and Citizen: The Negro in the Americas* (New York: Alfred A. Knopf, Inc., 1947), pp. 62–64, 92, and 98–99.

clergy strove to prevent defections from allegiance to the crown. Their financial contribution to the cause was considerable too.

A very large part of the lower clergy, however, ardently espoused the aspirations of the revolutionists, giving them invaluable encouragement and assistance, and often capable leadership. Most of the members of the lower clergy were Creoles who greatly resented the favoritism shown by the crown to the *gachupines*, or clergy born in Spain and sent over to monopolize the higher church offices. Also, the great majority of the Creole clergy were very poor, with incomes of only a hundred or so pesos a year—pathetic when compared with the very large incomes—often in the hundreds of thousands of pesos—of the higher clergy, whose affluence enabled them to live like princes. Another tie that bound many of the Creole clergy to the revolutionaries was that they had risen from the humblest ranks of society and were bitter about the many discriminations and exploitations inherent in the colonial system.

Dedicated to the ideals of the revolution, many of the lower clergy aided it in various ways. After celebrating Mass, they explained the principles and ideals of the struggle and exhorted the faithful to give it their full support. Besides supporting the fight verbally, they greatly aided it materially, donating personally a large part of the funds needed to sustain the armies in the field. Some of the priests went even further. Forsaking their parishes and congregations, they took up arms to join the armies on the firing line or possibly to lead them.

In Mexico alone, besides the revered national heroes, Father Hidalgo and Father Morelos, more than 100 parish priests and some 50 members of the religious brotherhoods left the pulpit or cloister and took to the field. Many of these, including Hidalgo and Morelos, were to lose their lives in battle or before a firing squad. Indeed, so active were the clergy of Mexico in fighting for independence that Lucas Alamán, the distinguished Mexican scholar, credits them with sustaining the revolution almost alone.[7]

ANTICLERICALISM

When independence was finally won after years of bitter, bloody fighting, it was almost inevitable that the newly independent states and the Church would clash headlong on many crucial issues. For one thing, the Church as an institution was on the losing side, which hardly helped its position in the new states. More importantly, its privileged position, affluence, and influence were matters of serious concern to many leaders of the new states. Anticlericals, as they are commonly referred to, were opposed to the influence of the Church in political and social affairs, and

---

[7] For the role of the clergy as portrayed here, see Mecham, *op. cit.*, pp. 59–73; and Ernest Gruening, *Mexico and Its Heritage* (New York: D. Appleton-Century Co., Inc., 1934), pp. 184–89.

advocated separating religious authority completely from civil government, with the ultimate goal of subordinating the Church to the control of the state.

The anticlerical liberals were by no means anti-Catholic or antireligious. In fact, they usually regarded themselves as devout members of the faith, with a mission of reforming the Church and adapting it to contemporary society. Bernardo O'Higgins, Chile's national hero, was just such a Catholic from his point of view. Many other national leaders, such as Benito Juárez of Mexico and José Batlle y Ordóñez of Uruguay, were too.

While some of the anticlericals were undoubtedly mere opportunists, seeking to benefit themselves at the expense of the Church, others were very sincerely concerned about the status and role of the Church, as well as its many activities. They deplored the Church's extensive ownership of land that could never be privately owned or developed, as well as its operation of many commercial enterprises. This control of so much of the national wealth, all exempt from taxation, would in the opinion of the anticlericals make it difficult, if not impossible, for the state to have a sufficiently large economic base to maintain its very existence.

Also, the anticlericals were convinced that the Church should devote itself solely to spiritual matters, and that many of its activities, especially those of education, welfare, and control over the family, should be taken over by the state. Furthermore, they were determined that religious authority should be separated completely from that of the civil government, that the Church should be subordinated to state control, and that the Church as an organization should stop interfering in politics. J. Fred Rippy succinctly summarizes the issues:

> The conflict involved both ideals and interest. In part it was a struggle for revenues, power, property, and prestige and for the creation of conditions that would attract immigrants accustomed to religious toleration; in part it was a struggle for greater intellectual freedom, the curtailment of special privileges, and the creation of wider opportunities for at least some of the people. In the end, the functions, privileges, and wealth of the Church were reduced in the interest of the State, and in the interest of those it governed. . . .[8]

Since independence, the concern and activities of the anticlericals have been directed mainly toward the following: reform of the priesthood, expropriation of the Church's great wealth, assumption by the state of the Church's many secular activities, separation of church and state, and preclusion of the Church from participating in politics.

REFORM OF THE PRIESTHOOD

One of the oft-stated objectives of the anticlericals was to reform the priesthood. Many of the clergy and members of the religious orders—

---

[8] J. Fred Rippy, *Latin America: A Modern History* (Ann Arbor: University of Michigan Press, 1958), p. 185.

probably a very large majority of them—were persons of excellent character, wedded to the Church and consecrated to a life of celibacy. But many of the priests and members of the religious orders were opportunists of low morals who regarded their vow of chastity very lightly. The resulting licentiousness among the clergy may have been aggravated by the primitive conditions of the frontier and the many native women of a submissive people who could easily "be had."

However, the moral laxity of many of the clergy did not originate in the New World. In Spain, Queen Isabella herself attempted to cleanse the monasteries, convents, and secular clergy of violations of the rule of celibacy, which were common. For there had grown up in Spain, in spite of all the laws against it, a system of clerical "marriage," simply concubinage, known as "*barragania.*" The practice was so strongly embedded, however, that it was impossible to eradicate.[9]

In Argentina, soon after independence, Bernardino Rivadavia instituted a "Civil Constitution of the Clergy" patterned after the French prototype and intended to remedy the degraded condition of the clergy. When Rosas became dictatorial head of the nation in 1829, he acted summarily to end licentiousness in the lower clergy. Instituting a thorough housecleaning, he issued numerous decrees which suspended, removed, and even jailed priests for immoral conduct.[10]

In Brazil, the ancient question of sacerdotal celibacy was widely debated during the time of the Empire. A large part of the Brazilian clergy had never made the least pretense of observing the rule of clerical chastity; in fact, they had lived quite openly with their wives or concubines. Accustomed to such clerical hypocrisy, the general public was prone to accept such arrangements as being in accord with human nature, the climate, and long-established custom. Indeed, many persons, both lay and clerical, openly declared themselves in favor of legitimizing the practice, even if it meant setting up a separate Brazilian church divorced from the authority of the Vatican.[11]

Another condition among the clergy which the anticlericals aimed to correct was their widely known venality. Many of the clergy had apparently entered the priesthood in the New World solely because of the opportunity it offered for making an easy living. Indeed, if a priest could wangle a concession from the crown to build a church or monastery,

---

[9] Bailey W. Diffie, *Latin American Civilization* (Harrisburg, Pa.: Stackpole Sons, 1945), p. 266.

[10] Mecham, *op. cit.,* pp. 284–85. Though posing as a champion of the Catholic faith, Rosas ruled the Church with an iron hand, appointing all the members of the Argentine Church from the highest to the lowest, and forcing them to serve his regime of absolutism. For a detailed account of his relations with the Church, see A. Curtis Wilgus (ed.), *South American Dictators During the First Century of Independence* (Washington, D.C.: George Washington University Press, 1937), pp. 473–88.

[11] William Lytle Schurz, *Brazil: The Infinite Country* (New York: E. P. Dutton & Co., Inc., 1961), p. 192.

obtain a grant of land to go with it, and then gather a group of Indians whose labor he could exploit without charge, his comfort was assured.

Posing as the protector of the Indians, he was often in reality a burdensome oppressor, collecting stiff fees from them for each and every clerical service which he performed, especially the high fee for High Mass on the saints' days, with an equal amount collected for the sermon.

To this is to be added the customary offering which the overseers are compelled to make to the curate on every saint's festival, which consists of two or three dozen hens, as many chickens, guinea-pigs, eggs, sheep, and a hog if they happen to have any; so that when the saint's day arrives, the curate sweeps off all that the Indian has been able to collect in money during the whole year, and also all the fowls and animals which his wife and children have reared in their huts, so that his family are left almost destitute of food, and are reduced to wild herbs and to the grains which they cultivate in their small gardens.[12]

The venality of many of the priests was recognized by the more conscientious ones as imposing an extreme hardship upon the natives. The Augustinian friar, Júarez de Escobar, advised Philip II that the clergy should not charge for the sacraments because, "besides smacking of simony, it works great injury to the Indians, since, if two *reales* is charged and the native has not that to give, he must remain without the sacrament; or requiring a *tostón* for marrying, the natives remain unmarried for lack of money; and the children die without baptism simply because the parents have not the four or five *tomines* which is charged for the rite."[13]

The lack of genuine spirituality among many members of the clergy at an earlier time was another matter of concern to the anticlericals. In Mexico, the clergy sometimes took advantage of the credulity and ignorance of the faithful to interpret wholly natural phenomena to their own selfish ends, even using trickery and deception on occasion. In May 1912, the "miracle" of the swaying Virgin in the heart of Mexico City aroused the faithful to a delirium of excitement until a carefully laid plant of wires under the church floor connected with the machinery of a neighboring mill was uncovered.[14]

"The fact is," says Ernest Gruening, "that the Mexican clergy has rarely taught anything but the externals of the cult. The ethics, the essence, and spirit of the religion of Jesus have been lost in the process. The responsibility to family and neighbor, the duties of citizenship, as they are inculcated by the Catholic clergy in the United States, have never reached the Mexican people."[15]

---

[12] In Bernard Moses, *South America on the Eve of Emancipation* (New York: G. P. Putnam's Sons, 1908), 186–87.

[13] "Colección de Documentos Inéditos Relativos al Decubrimiento Conquista y Colonización de las Posesiones Españoles . . . ," Sacadas en su Mayor Parte del Real Archivo de Indias. 1 Series, 42 vols., Madrid, 1864–84, in Charles S. Braden, *Religious Aspects of the Conquest of Mexico* (Durham, N.C.: Duke University Press, 1930), p. 218.

[14] Gruening, *op. cit.*, p. 254.

[15] *Ibid.*, p. 253.

Still another condition which has sometimes aroused resentment against the Catholic Church is the foreign character of the priesthood. During colonial days most members of the clergy were foreigners; the king preferred to nominate persons from Spain whose loyalty and dependability could be counted on for carrying out the crown's policies. However, the appointment of Spaniards for the more responsible positions meant that the Creoles were eligible only for the lower church offices, while the mestizos and Indians were excluded altogether.

Since independence, the Church has continued the practice of appointing foreigners as members of the hierarchy, as well as of the lower clergy. Such appointments have been necessary, the Church has explained, because of the high level of illiteracy in most of the Latin American nations, which has seriously hampered efforts to establish seminaries in the region for the training of native-born priests.

However much justified, the foreign character of many of the clergy has greatly impaired their effectiveness, since Latin Americans tend to regard their presence as a hangover of colonial days and a reminder of colonialism which they would like to forget. Indeed the appointment of foreigners has sometimes been met with deep and outwardly expressed resentment, as in 1954 when the Vatican announced the appointment of three bishops to Guatemala, two of whom were foreigners. The clergy of the nation openly expressed their disappointment and resentment, pointing out that there were Guatemalans who were qualified and who deserved the appointments.[16]

In recent years the papacy has frankly recognized that the sending of priests from Spain, Italy, the United States, or elsewhere to the Latin American nations, very nationalistic and sensitive about their sovereignty, is a practice to be discontinued at the earliest possible moment. In his fourth encyclical letter, Pope John XXIII expressed confidence in the native clergy at a time when "the aspirations of the peoples to self-rule and independence is becoming general." The missionary bishops and priests sent to the underdeveloped areas, asserted His Holiness, must educate the native clergies so that they can "take the government of the new churches in their own hands as soon as possible."[17]

The earlier shortcomings of the priesthood have been fully recognized and corrected by the papacy. But their existence at an earlier date is a fact of life which the Catholic Church must reckon with in its relations with the region's 200 million inhabitants, most of whom are at least nominal Catholics. Expecting them to overlook earlier shortcomings is about like asking Southerners to forget the Civil War. But under more benign influences, Latin Americans, like even the most intransigent Southerners, will in time forget.

---

[16] *New York Times,* February 4, 1956, p. 5, col. 6.
[17] *Ibid.,* November 29, 1959, p. 1, col. 5.

EXPROPRIATION OF THE CHURCH'S GREAT WEALTH

The tremendous wealth of the Church was another problem which worried many of the new leaders. When the colonial period ended and the young nations achieved independence, the Church was a fabulously wealthy institution. In Mexico, it owned at least half of the total real estate of the entire nation, and held mortgages on much of the remaining property. Its financial interests were quite varied, and consisted of all kinds of commercial enterprises, including cattle ranches, corn and wheat farms, sugar and flour mills, and even factories and silver mines.

This great wealth came from a number of sources. In addition to large gifts of land or money made by the crown or affluent philanthropists, the Church benefited greatly by bequests. In fact, most of the extensive domain possessed by the monasteries had been willed to them, for as the Chilean, Barros Arana, remarked, "a will which did not include some legacy in favor of the monastery passed for an act against religion."

In an effort to prevent members of the religious orders from unduly influencing their parishioners or charges, the crown in 1774 expressly forbade ecclesiastics from interfering in the drawing up of wills, and in 1775 forbade confessors or their converts to be heirs or legatees. The decrees were not enforced, however, and the Church continued to amass a fortune in real estate and other valuables.

This great wealth of the Church posed serious problems for the development of the new nations. Ownership of such a large part of the land aggravated the effects of the economically unsound *latifundios* or large estates by further reducing the amount of land available for small independent farmers. This discouraged the best use of the land and also the immigration which the region greatly needed. The legal principle of mortmain further aggravated the scarcity of land available for small owners. Under the principle of mortmain ("dead hand" in French), once property was acquired by the Church, it could never be alienated or distributed to other owners. Moreover, since all the Church's properties, including its commercial enterprises, were exempt from taxation, the government did not have a sufficiently large economic base from which to obtain the taxes it needed.

As a result of these problems, in nation after nation the extensive properties of the Church were in time expropriated by the government, which sometimes took over even the churches and other buildings used solely for religious purposes. These buildings were used for a variety of purposes. In Guatemala many of them became public schools or military academies. Others became mental asylums, reformatories, or prisons. Still others were used for government offices or barracks for the army.[18]

---

[18] Mary P. Holleran, *Church and State in Guatemala* (New York: Columbia University Press, 1949), pp. 59–60.

While the society as a whole derived some benefit from the properties taken over, this benefit was apparently small compared with the heavy loss which the Church suffered. In Guatemala the Church was so financially despoiled that it has not even been able to keep its buildings in good repair or to restore them completely after severe earthquake damage. The gain which accrued to society as a whole was far from proportionate to the Church's loss. If the properties expropriated had been administered in such a way as to avoid the temptations of public and political greed, concluded Manuel Montufar y Coronado, they would have served to "repair the losses of the state, substituting in place of the convents . . . loans for the development of agriculture, commerce and highways; but the disorders of the first days and the confusion of the first measures taken impaired everything, and finally only a small number of individuals profited by it."[19]

In brief, it was much easier for the anticlericals to tear down the Church's financial empire than to conserve its valuable assets for the benefit of the nation. For as might have been suspected, some of the anticlericals were merely selfish opportunists, interested only in feathering their own nests.

ASSUMPTION BY THE STATE OF THE CHURCH'S SECULAR ACTIVITIES

Another goal of the anticlericals was to divest the Church of what are commonly regarded in democratic countries today as secular functions and activities, transferring them to the jurisdiction of the state. The main ones which they strove to have secularized were the following: the family, particularly its establishment by marriage and its dissolution by divorce; education at all levels; welfare programs for the less fortunate; cemeteries available to all; banking and credit; and civil registry of wills, deeds, and contracts.

In most of the nations today, a couple that marries must have a civil ceremony, performed by a justice of the peace or some other official of the government in a simple, inexpensive ceremony. This civil ceremony, performed under the auspices of the government, constitutes a legal marriage entitled to the full protection and support of law. The couple may desire to have a religious wedding performed by a priest in the Church, but this can take place only after the civil ceremony and is in no wise a substitute for it. Indeed, a priest joining a couple in wedlock before they have already been married in a civil ceremony is in most countries subject to fine or other punishment by the state.

An exception to the requirement of a civil ceremony is sometimes made for Indians. In Bolivia, a law passed in 1920 allows them to be married by

---

[19] In *Ibid.*, p. 58.

a religious ceremony alone, without the necessity of a civil marriage. This exception was made because of "the fanatical attachment of the ignorant Indians to the priests, and their inability to regard anything other than the religious ceremony as being binding."[20]

In Guatemala, the Indians are so suspicious of government officials that they avoid having any dealings with them whenever possible, even for a civil wedding to legitimize their union in the eyes of the law. But because of the relatively heavy expenses of the religious ceremony, they are unable to afford being married by the Church. As a result, very few of them are married in the eyes of the state or the Church.[21]

Another form of union which most states recognize as legal marriage under certain conditions is the consensual or common-law marriage discussed in Chapter 4. This recognition was dictated by the very large percentage of couples in most of the countries who live together without the blessing of either a civil or a religious ceremony. In order for these common-law unions to be regarded as legal, the couple must have lived together as man and wife for a specified minimum number of years.

The state has further exercised its control over the family by providing for its dissolution under certain conditions. Divorce is now permitted in many of the nations; sometimes, as under the Cuban constitution of 1940, the wife has about the same grounds for divorce as does the husband.[22]

Another function of the Church which the state usually decided to take over is that of providing an education for students at all levels, with religious instruction being forbidden in the public schools. This policy has invariably provoked bitter controversy, for the Church and its partisans were loath to surrender this important function. In states where the Church enjoyed a privileged status, it was sometimes given control of the educational system. In Colombia, the constitution of 1886 empowered the Church to exercise such control, which it did until 1936 when the Liberals succeeded in revising the constitution.

Argentina has traditionally followed quite a different course from Colombia. After a prolonged and bitter church-state controversy, it was finally settled in 1884, or so the nation thought, that the public schools were to be completely secular, with the Church exercising no control over them. No religious instruction could be given in public schools during the regular school day but could be given at the end of the day to children who voluntarily chose to remain at school to receive it. The sensitive issue of compulsory religious instruction in the public schools was revived in 1943

---

[20] Mecham, *op. cit.,* p. 229.

[21] In some parts of Guatemala, only an estimated 2 percent of the Indians are formally married, according to Mary P. Holleran. The complication of having to use *ladino* agents for making all arrangements, also being very discourteously treated by them, discourages Indians from desiring to have a formal marriage, civil or religious. (Holleran, *op. cit.,* p. 245.)

[22] For a survey of divorce in the several republics, see Gordon Ireland and Jesús Galíndez Suárez, *Divorce in the Americas* (Buffalo, N.Y.: Dennis and Co., Inc., 1947).

when the military junta, after taking over the government, reversed the act of congress of 1884 providing for "religious neutrality" in the public schools and instituted compulsory instruction in the Catholic religion for all primary and secondary schools. Only those pupils would be exempted whose parents professed other religions and asked that their children be excused. Those exempted would receive "moral instruction."[23]

In addition to the family and the school, another area to which the government often extended its authority was the welfare program for helping the less fortunate members of society—the orphanages, hospitals, and other agencies of mercy. Argentina was one of the first nations to take over these eleemosynary institutions from the Church. Bernardino Rivadavia, one of the ablest leaders in the early days of the republic and president from 1826–27, confiscated the properties of several religious orders engaged in welfare activities of one sort or another; in his opinion their zeal for discharging these functions was flagging. Rivadavia, a humanitarian, established *La Sociedad de Beneficencia* (Society of Charity) to have jurisdiction over orphanages, hospitals, and other welfare agencies, entrusting its direction to prosperous, socially conscious matrons of Buenos Aires society, who did an excellent job in discharging their responsibility.[24]

Flexing the muscles of their sovereignty, the states also took over other important functions which had previously been performed by the Church. Banking was one of these. Recognizing that credit was the economic lifeblood of society, governments established public banks which would operate directly under their control or authorized private ones which would function under their close supervision. No longer were loans to be a monopoly of the Church, granted under its own terms and conditions— lenient and considerate, it should be noted—but would be provided by agencies which the state either controlled or regulated.

Another church activity which the state decided to take over was control of the cemeteries. At first glance, the government's action may appear to be picayune and its interest in cemeteries provocative and contentious. Far from it; the Church's ownership and operation of cemeteries had long been one of its most effective controls over society. Burial of a loved one in consecrated ground is essential to a family's peace of mind; according to popular belief in Latin America, unless the dead are buried in such ground, they cannot go to heaven. Thus, denying the deceased the privilege of being buried there was tantamount to consigning his soul to hell. But interring him in the cemetery involved a continuing expense that bore heavily on the poor.

To eliminate possible abuses, the governments have provided for the

---

[23] For a discussion of the justification and impact of this law, see George I. Blanksten, *Perón's Argentina* (Chicago: University of Chicago Press, 1953), pp. 188–90.

[24] Hubert Herring, *A History of Latin America from the Beginnings to the Present* (2d ed. rev.; New York: Alfred A. Knopf, Inc., 1961), p. 623.

establishment under municipal supervision of public cemeteries open to all without restrictions, and providing a respectable resting place at very modest cost.

Whatever the activity which the government sought to take over, whether control of education or of cemeteries, it was sure to provoke a vehement, no-holds-barred struggle. The Church, regarding each new design of the government as a further encroachment on its hallowed prerogatives, fought back with every weapon at its disposal. Thus, when the Congress of Chile in 1875 abolished the Church courts and gave the civil courts jurisdiction over priests, the Church excommunicated every congressman who voted for the measure; and when civil marriage was legalized in 1883, the Church excommunicated the president, members of his cabinet, and all congressmen who supported it.[25]

In earlier times excommunication or even the threat of it was such a potent weapon as to make a powerful monarch crawl on his knees to the papacy seeking pardon. But the formerly potent weapon apparently has had little effect on the undisciplined, ultra-individualistic society of Latin America. Moreover, in the strong secular social current, time and tide were on the side of the state.

SEPARATION OF CHURCH AND STATE

Another measure ardently advocated by anticlericals was separation of church and state, which has been accomplished in a number of the countries. Colombia in 1853 was the first to proclaim separation, a radical step proposed by President José Hilario López and approved by his liberal adherents in the Congress; but this action was reversed in 1887 when the Conservatives managed to regain control of the government. Mexico was the first nation to disestablish the Church permanently, and its lead was followed by several of the Central American republics. In reality, however, the Church was usually not actually separated from the state and allowed to operate independently; rather, it was kept under the thumb of the state and often subjected to very oppressive controls.

Brazil, however, in its Federal Republican Constitution promulgated in February, 1891, proved that disestablishment could be accomplished peaceably and amicably. In accordance with the constitution, church and state are completely separated. The government relinquished its control over the national patronage and has no voice whatever in the selection of the Church's personnel. The Church has title to its properties, and all buildings used exclusively for religious purposes are exempt from taxation, although other realty owned by the Church is not. Religious instruction may be given in the public schools after school hours to any children who

---

[25] *Ibid.*, p. 583.

desire it, but the government does not pay the teachers for this service.[26]

The solution of the knotty, complex problem of the relationship between church and state by amicable separation of the two was typically Brazilian. "As one student of colonial art remarked: 'In Brazil, even Christ hangs comfortably on the cross.' In keeping with the general absence of violence and extremes of passion in Brazilian history and with the generally mild and non-political role the Church has played in society, the pattern of violent clericalism and anti-clericalism found elsewhere in Latin America simply does not exist in Brazil."[27]

Friendly separation of church and state has taken place in other nations too: in Cuba in 1902; Panama in 1904; Uruguay, 1919; and Chile, 1925.

Contrasting with the peaceable disestablishment of the Church in the above states is the long-drawn-out, bitterly fought battle over separation in Mexico, which began in 1855 and still has not been settled. The Reform Movement led by Benito Juárez, a full-blooded Zapotec Indian and the nation's venerated national hero, aimed to establish a secular state with democratic, constitutional government. A number of far-reaching reforms were adopted, including: expropriation of the Church's immense holdings, dissolution of the religious communities, public control of education and cemeteries, civil marriage, civil registry of births and deaths, and restrictions on political activities of the clergy.

These reforms were adopted over the most vehement ecclesiastical opposition, which culminated in open revolt against the government. "The War of the Reform was essentially a religious conflict," according to J. Lloyd Mecham, "and for that reason, perhaps, it was characterized by excessive plunder, rapine, brutal reprisals, and a general spirit of extermination. Prisoners were slaughtered in cold blood, doctors and nurses were killed, and churches were sacked. The clergy made it a holy war."[28]

During the long dictatorship of Porfirio Díaz which lasted from 1876 to 1910, the transference of many of the Church's functions to the government and the imposition of various restrictions on the Church were not enforced, as a result of which the Church regained most of its former power and influence. It owned property; operated schools, convents, and monasteries; and in general ignored the laws of the Reform with the tacit acquiescence of Díaz.

But the revolution of 1910, the first social revolution to occur in Latin America, once again put relations between church and state to the acid test. The constitution of 1917, like its predecessor of 1873, contained many provisions designed to increase the power of the state at the expense of the Church; but until 1926 these provisions were practically ignored. Once more, the state's bark seemed to be fiercer than its bite.

---

[26] Mecham, *op. cit.*, pp. 326–27.
[27] In Lewis Hanke, *South America* (Princeton, N.J.: D. Van Nostrand Co., Inc., 1959), p. 89.
[28] Mecham, *op. cit.*, p. 441.

Yet when the archbishops and bishops of Mexico in a joint statement issued in January, 1926, criticized the articles in the constitution relating to religion, President Calles acted swiftly and decisively, throwing the book at the Church. The government promptly nationalized all property that the Church held, closed all church schools, required all private schools to register with a stern prohibition against religious instruction, and deported the foreign-born clergy.

Many of the laws passed by the state governments were minutely restrictive, as those which set such low limits on the number of priests to be allowed as to make impossible the performance of their clerical duties. The state of Tabasco even went so far as to require that all priests must marry. "It was merely an effort to legitimize the existing children," Governor Tomás Garrido alleged.

Once again Mexico became an open battlefield between the intransigent forces of those who championed the cause of the state or of the Church. A nationwide economic boycott instituted by the Catholic League for the Protection of Religious Liberty was a peaceful movement that petered out. But the *cristero* revolt that broke out cost many lives and required more than a year to subdue.

After 1930, relations between the Church and the state began to improve under an unwritten "gentlemen's agreement" whereby it was understood that each would try to avoid as far as possible provoking any open conflict with the other. This arrangement has apparently proved satisfactory to most Mexicans. While the constitution contains many restrictive provisions against Catholicism or any other religion, its provisions are not rigidly enforced. Consequently church schools and seminaries have quietly been allowed to reopen throughout the country,[29] and church buildings and other properties have been quietly returned. In fact, there has been such an increased attendance at Mass as to burden the priests limited in number by law.

From surface indications, relations between the Church and the Mexican state have improved; but it is an uneasy truce at best which can be upset by any one of many highly inflammatory issues. Just such an issue was the government's establishment in 1959 of a free textbook commission, designed to improve instruction in the schools by providing textbooks at government expense, since three-fourths of the pupils cannot afford to buy them. However, the program of providing uniform free textbooks aroused vehement opposition on the part of the Church and many Catholic organizations, which claimed that the program of "one text" is totalitarian and dangerous, is Marxist-oriented, attempts to separate the child from the family, and indoctrinates the students with the supremacy of the state.

The Church expressed its opposition in mass demonstrations; 150,000

---

[29] In 1962, some 30,000 church schools flourished as private institutions, according to the Copley News Service. (*Hispanic American Reports,* Vol. XVI, No. 4 [July, 1963], p. 431.)

participated in the one at Monterrey in February, 1962. The government met this opposition head-on by organizing counterdemonstrations in support of its program. President Mateos himself departed from his usually mild, conciliatory attitude toward the Church by castigating its efforts to thwart his program, terming the Church and its related Catholic organizations "the forces of darkness."[30]

Although the 20 Latin American republics are all predominantly Catholic, there are great differences in their relationships with the Church. On the basis of these relationships, the states may be classified into three general groups.

1. States which have expressly or implicitly retained Catholicism as the established privileged religion in the society. There are seven states in this group: Argentina, Colombia, Costa Rica, Ecuador, Paraguay, Peru, and Venezuela. In these states, the constitutions may require that the president and other officials be Roman Catholics, a requirement that is broadly interpreted and is apparently satisfied by their having been baptized in the Church. Moreover, the Church is the recognized protector of the family; consequently, in accordance with Catholic doctrine, divorce is either difficult or impossible to obtain. The Church may also administer the national program of education or give religious instruction in Catholicism that is compulsory for all students, sometimes with specified exceptions. The government usually has certain peculiar functions, such as nominating members of the clergy, levying and collecting tithes, and using tax money for the support of the Church.

2. States that have dissolved their former union or close association with the Church, which is recognized as nominally independent, or actually so—"a free church in a free state," as we have in the United States. Comprising this group are the following 12 nations: Bolivia, Brazil, Chile, Cuba, the Dominican Republic, El Salvador, Guatemala, Haiti, Honduras, Nicaragua, Panama, and Uruguay.

3. One state, Mexico, where the Church has been separated from the state but kept under its close control. In addition to the restrictions already mentioned, members of the clergy in Mexico may not wear clerical garb in public, engage in politics, hold office, or even vote.

PARTICIPATION BY THE CHURCH IN POLITICS

The Catholic Church in Latin America has since early colonial days been accustomed to taking an active role in the government and politics of the region. Often the archbishops and bishops were assigned governmental responsibilities by the crown, and their discharge of these duties greatly contributed to the effective administration of the colonies. After independence, members of the clergy continued to play a prominent role in government. Among the best-educated and most qualified members of society, they participated in the constituent assemblies which formulated the constitutions of the new nations. Besides playing this important role,

---

[30] For these details regarding the uniform free textbook controversy, see *ibid.*, April, 1962, p. 112; October, 1962, p. 962; March, 1963, p. 19; and July, 1963, p. 431.

they took an active part in both local and national government. Sometimes in the selection of members of congress, it was simply a question of whether to send educated members of the clergy or settle on rural "clod-hoppers."

In Oaxaca, Mexico, a citizen contemplating the election for members of Congress moaned:

In my Department you have . . . three kinds of men: first, the rich, usually ignorant . . . and egotistical; second, persons more or less well-known, who are the only ones suitable to discharge public duties, and who for this reason are almost all employed in public office; and third, those absolutely without property, who, destitute of all knowledge, are useless for public affairs. Except, then, the second class and Oaxaca will have to send to the general Congress a representation of asses, or else ten good clergymen to make up a delegation.[31]

As the Church's temporal activities have been increasingly circumscribed by the state, ministering to the spiritual needs of the faithful has taken up a larger share of the clergy's time, and there is less opportunity for them to be personally involved in dispensing personal ideas and expressing personal convictions on nonspiritual issues. Consequently, clergymen are usually not as politically influential in most of the nations today as earlier, except insofar as they reflect the policies of the hierarchy, which may or may not conform to the thinking of the politically dominant segments of the society.[32]

But although the Church's spiritual role is unquestionably its main concern today, the Church sometimes still finds it as difficult to give up its earlier political role as does a tot to discard his frayed baby blanket. The unfortunate interference of the Church in the Puerto Rican election of 1960 shocked most Americans, and set the Church back on its heels.

It had been known for some time that the Catholic Church was far from happy with the situation in the island commonwealth. Only an estimated one-fourth of the 2 million Catholics practiced their religion, and less than 10 percent of the children attended parochial schools. Over the years, differences on issues which had arisen between the Church and the government had ranged from contraception to sterilization, from bingo in the churches to taxes on charities, from tolerance of divorce to time off from school for religious training. Because of his having sponsored or opposed these measures—also because of having been divorced—Governor Muñoz Marín was a thorn that had long irritated the Church.

The Church's involvement in the 1960 election was triggered by the defeat in the legislature of a bill that would have enabled schoolchildren

---

31 Fran co Bas [?] met to Valentín Gómez Farías, August 16, 1846, Farías Papers. In Wilfrid Hardy Callcott, *Church and State in Mexico: 1822-1857* (Durham, N.C.: Duke University Press, 1926), p. 180.

32 John J. Johnson, *Political Change in Latin America: The Emergence of the Middle Sectors* (Stanford, Calif.: Stanford University Press, 1958), pp. 12–13. His observations regarding Argentina, Brazil, Chile, Uruguay, and Mexico are applicable to the other nations of Latin America.

to receive one hour of religious instruction daily. While this bill actually died in committee, Governor Muñoz had opposed it, contending that the time for such instruction could not be spared, since most children received only three hours of schooling a day.[33]

The reaction of the Catholic hierarchy was immediate and vigorous. The bishop of San Juan (soon to be made archbishop) told a meeting of nearly 100,000 Catholics that they were free to form their own political party. Accordingly, the Christian Action Party was forthwith organized, and a drive undertaken to obtain 70,000 signatures necessary to enable it to participate in the November election on an island-wide basis. The Church was so closely associated with the party that parish churches were used to promote the drive for obtaining the required number of signatures.

The very formation of a Roman Catholic political party within the jurisdiction of United States territory was unprecedented. But the hierarchy in the zeal of its all-out effort took a further step which antagonized not only most Puerto Ricans but many of their own Christian Action Party. In a pastoral letter read in all Catholic churches on the island, the three highest prelates of the commonwealth forbade clergy and members of the faithful alike to vote for the Popular Democratic Party headed by Governor Muñoz.

Denouncing this party as unchristian and undemocratic, the letter said: "It is not our intention to impose Catholic morality on the Government or on the citizens, but it is our duty to prohibit Catholics to vote in favor of a party that accepts as its own the morality of 'the rule of freedom,' thus denying Christian morality."[34]

Reaction to the Church's interference in the electoral campaign was immediate and vehement. Governor Muñoz termed the letter an "incredible, medieval interference in a political campaign" that might lead to violence and bloodshed on election day and afterward. The Church's intervention, he declared, was "the gravest problem that had arisen in the island's four-hundred-year history."[35]

Criticism of the hierarchy's action was widespread. Hundreds of protesting telegrams were sent to newspapers; Catholic churches were picketed; Archbishop Davis was booed; and many, including Governor Muñoz' wife, walked out of church when the offending pastoral letter was read.

Perhaps even more confusing than the action of the Puerto Rican hierarchy was the final pronouncement rendered by the Vatican. Bishops in all countries, said the Vatican, not only have the right but also the duty to advise voters at election time, because voters elect legislators who adopt laws that may be either "good or bad" from a Catholic point of view. But

---

[33] *New York Times*, June 11, 1960, p. 11, col. 4.
[34] *Ibid.*, October 22, 1960, p. 1, col. 8.
[35] *Ibid.*, October 26, 1960, p. 26, col. 3.

bishops might refrain from exercising this duty if they wished. Expediency would determine their decision.[36]

But as the Church found out, expediency hardly paid off in the election. For when the ballots were tabulated, the Popular Democratic Party won handily, receiving more than 58 percent of the total vote. The Christian Action Party, sponsored by the Church, was "clobbered," receiving only 51,072 votes, far less than the 82,027 persons who had earlier signed petitions in the churches for it to be certified as a political party.

When the Church-sponsored party received a vote equal to only two-thirds of the number of signatures on the registration petitions, an investigation was undertaken by the Legislature which uncovered forgery of signatures and various other irregularities. On the basis of its investigation, the Legislature in May, 1961, took unprecedented action. The House by a vote of 49–0 unseated Representative José Felice Pesquera of the Christian Action Party, who incidentally had sponsored the religious instruction bill defeated the year before. The next day by a vote of 25–2, the Senate ousted Senator Mario Davila, chairman of the Christian Action Party. Both actions were taken on the basis of the registration frauds perpetrated and the unconstitutional coercion of the voters by the Roman Catholic bishops of Puerto Rico.

The hierarchy's intervention in Puerto Rican politics, so distasteful to Puerto Ricans and other Americans alike, could hardly have occurred at a more inopportune time. Ironically, it occurred at the crucial moment when a courageous Roman Catholic in the United States was making an uphill yet successful bid for the presidency, a success based largely on managing to allay the fears of Protestants that the Roman Catholic Church presumes to dictate in politics.

In the United States, the blatant interference by the Catholic Church in the Puerto Rican election bewildered Catholics as well as Protestants. Editorialized *America*, the Jesuit weekly magazine:

. . . whatever the record may show elsewhere, such a prohibition is unprecedented in American Catholic history. It has always seemed unnecessary, improper, even something of a profanation, for the authority of the Church to be extended, through the pulpit, to the point of a formal prohibition against voting for one particular party, or for an individual candidate. The record of the Catholic Church and of her priests has been without blemish in this respect.[37]

Regarding its policy of interfering in politics in Latin America, the Catholic Church might do well to ponder the conclusion of a prominent scholar. "Perhaps it is too much to expect," concludes Mary P. Holleran, "but it would seem that after all that time, cognizance would be taken of the lessons that history teaches. One of the greatest of these lessons is that when the Church acts like a political party, it will be treated like one.

---

[36] *Ibid.*, October 28, 1960, p. 19, col. 3.
[37] *America*, Vol. 104 (November 5, 1960), pp. 163–65.

When churchmen become politicians, they will be regarded as politicians."[38]

The Catholic Church, besides participating in politics generally, and sometimes, as in the Puerto Rican election of 1960, getting its fingers burned, has also on occasion supported dictators. This support in no sense represented a preference for dictators as such. Rather, the interests of the Church were often best served by a strong ruler who maintained the status quo and respected vested interests or who gave the Church favored treatment.

A classic example of such support was the Church's policy toward the regime of Juan Perón. There is no valid evidence to show that the Church did anything to help establish the dictatorial regime which governed Argentina's destiny from 1943 to 1955. But the decision of the military junta in late 1943 to make the teaching of Catholicism compulsory in all public schools was enough to win the sympathy and support of the Catholic Church. To show its appreciation, it gratefully thanked the government for the largess it had received. However, the government, which soon meant Colonel Juan Perón, needed more than thanks—it critically needed help in the presidential election scheduled for February 7, 1946.

Whether or not the Church intended to do so, it virtually decided the outcome of the election. Throwing its influential weight solidly behind Perón, the Argentine Espiscopate addressed a pastoral letter to all the clergy and faithful, forbidding them to vote for any parties or candidates that advocated measures contrary to the interests of the Church. This letter was the kiss of death to the moderate, anti-Perón, Democratic Union, generally conceded to be the only party that had a chance of defeating Perón. In appreciation for this support, Perón's government later gave the Church many unusual privileges, such as that of staging religious parades in Buenos Aires during religious week and of unrestrictedly using loudspeakers to cover neighborhoods with hymns, slogans, and sermons—activities which until then had been strictly forbidden.

Whatever the *quid pro quo*, if any, the Church displayed an obvious bias thereafter in its attitude toward Argentine politics. It saw nothing wrong with permitting Father Virgilio Filippo to campaign actively for Perón in 1946 as an ecclesiastical firebrand whose fervent and fanantical support was recognized in 1948 when he was elected a Peronista member of the Chamber of Deputies from Buenos Aires. But while condoning, if not sanctioning or even promoting, this sort of pro-Perón activity, it was at the same time throttling any ecclesiastically expressed opposition to the regime.

When Perón in September, 1948, threatened to hang the enemies who opposed his proposals for constitutional reform, Father José María Dunphy had the courage to chide the dictator-president from his pulpit and in his letters to the Catholic newspaper *El Pueblo.* "It is not Christian for

---

[38] Holleran, *op. cit.,* p. 243.

those in high places to foment or incite to civil war," he said. "Nor is it Christian to elevate hatred to the extreme of wanting to annihilate those who hold differing opinions."

For his bold stand which ran counter to Church policy, Father Dunphy was summarily removed from his parish; Cardinal Copello even refused to put in writing the reasons for his dismissal. An appeal for an ecclesiastical trial in accordance with canon law was not answered, nor was an appeal made directly to the Vatican.[39]

But when Perón toward the end of his administration committed such blasphemies as legalizing divorce and even prostitution, the Church reappraised its position. It excommunicated Perón, adding its weight to help topple a regime that was already beginning to fall.[40]

If the policy of supporting Perón and other dictators was a shortsighted one, we must remember that the Catholic Church was not alone in pursuing this policy. Until 1961, the government of the United States often followed the same course. President Franklin Roosevelt, apologetic for his support of Trujillo, the long-time dictatorial boss of the Dominican Republic, is said to have remarked: "I know he is an S.O.B., but at least he is OUR S.O.B."

Since 1955, the Catholic Church in Latin America, reversing its course, has opposed dictators and time after time has helped to overthrow them. In Colombia, in 1957, it was in the forefront of the fight against Rojas Pinilla. During High Mass on a fateful Sunday morning, Father Severo Velásquez delivered a fiery denunciation of the repressive regime. Before a packed congregation, with many standing in the doorways, he proclaimed: "It is the duty of all Catholics, with the pastors at their heads, to fight against criminals, and not only those from below, but also, and principally, those from above." After the service, with Father Velásquez leading them, the congregation poured out of the edifice chanting "Cristo, si! Rojas, no!" to face a barrage of tear gas from the police and sprays of red dye from tank trucks standing nearby.[41]

In others nations, too, the Catholic Church has had a principal role in helping to topple dictators such as Pérez Jiménez of Venezuela in early 1958, and Fulgencio Batista of Cuba not long afterward. Moreover, it has not hesitated to express its strong disapproval of other dictatorial regimes, such as those of Fidel Castro in Cuba and François Duvalier of Haiti, where members of the clergy, boldly speaking out against the government at great personal risk to themselves, were expelled from the country.

The Catholic Church's new look at dictators extended even to Paraguay, whose government for many years has been so dictatorial that an

---

[39] *New York Times*, September 27, 1948, p. 13, col. 4; and *Time*, January 17, 1949, p. 28.

[40] For a detailed account of the relationship between the Church and the Perón government, see Blanksten, *op. cit.*, pp. 229–37.

[41] John D. Martz, *Colombia: A Contemporary Political Survey* (Chapel Hill, N.C.: University of North Carolina Press, 1962), pp. 238–39.

estimated one-third of the total national population lives abroad as exiles in a "continual state of tourism." In Asunción, a young priest, Father Ramón Talavera, at great danger to himself defied the government by making a public appeal from a loudspeaker-equipped truck before a large crowd in front of the National Pantheon of Heroes, pleading for the restoration of freedom. Citing the many evils in the country that needed to be corrected, the priest urged "active resistance against acts of tyranny."[42]

The Catholic Church has often been criticized for its earlier support of dictators. But after its change of policy in the mid-1950s, while the government of the United States continued for several years longer to support dictators, the question was sometimes facetiously asked with as much truth as humor, "Why can't the State Department be as democratic as the Vatican?"

ROMAN CATHOLICISM'S STRENGTH AND INFLUENCE TODAY

Any attempt to evaluate accurately the strength of the Roman Catholic Church in Latin America as a whole or in any specific nation is at best an estimate. One fact is obvious—its strength varies considerably among the 20 republics, being notably strong in some and weak in others. Colombia has staunchly remained one of the strongest bastions of the Church. Its loyalty might be deflected during liberal regimes, but over most of its national history the nation has been a dedicated supporter of Catholicism. Many of the other nations too, especially Peru and Paraguay, have given the Church strong support.

But in some of the other nations, the Catholic Church is undeniably quite weak. In Bolivia, it has had such slight prestige that it has never been persecuted. In Brazil, it was completely overshadowed by the Big House, an expression of enormous feudal might with an "arrogant solidity of form and material." Yet it must be noted that the pomp of the Big House has turned to dust, gone with the wind, while the Church has survived and is continuing with its work.[43]

In Cuba, although approximately 85 percent of the people are nominally Catholic, only about 10 percent of them are active, informed members, and at least 25 percent are agnostics. In fact, in order to bolster the position of the state, the rationalist opponents of Catholicism deliberately created their own heroes to challenge those which the Church venerated.

[42] New York Times, March 3, 1958, p. 10, col. 3.

[43] Gilberto Freyre, The Masters and the Slaves: A Study in the Development of Brazilian Civilization, trans. Samuel Putnam (2d Eng. ed. rev.; New York: Alfred A. Knopf, Inc., 1956), xxxv, and p. 192.

Thus settlements were named after José Marti and Máximo Gómez and other heroes of the struggle for independence.[44]

In Panama too, religion has not been a very influential factor in national life. The clergy does not play an important role, nor do religious issues often disturb the populace. Most Panamanians tend to keep church and state strictly separated in their thinking.[45]

Uruguay is another nation where Catholicism is weak. In large measure this situation reflects "the lengthened shadow of a man," writes Russell Fitzgibbon, "that of José Batlle y Ordóñez—which helps account for how Uruguay worships, or fails to worship, today. Batlle early developed a skeptical and questioning attitude toward the Catholic Church."[46] Through the medium of his newspaper, *El Dia*, Batlle took advantage of his opportunity to minimize the influence of the Church. As a result of his persuasiveness, a divorce law was passed in 1907, the teaching of religion in public schools was prohibited in 1909, and finally, in 1917, church and state were completely separated. "His measures against it [the Church] set a pattern of anticlericalism that has persisted to the present day and has left the Catholic establishment in Uruguay in as debilitated a position as it is anywhere in Latin America."[47]

In Latin America as a whole, the population is sometimes referred to as being 90 percent or so Catholic—a Catholic stronghold, in fact, where approximately one-third of the total Catholic population of the world resides. Figure 6-1 gives an estimate of the percentage of Catholic population in each country. But according to other estimates, probably no more than 10 to 20 percent of the population are actually "practicing" Catholics who understand the teachings of the Church and apply them in their daily lives. Divorce, for example, is strictly forbidden by the Church, yet many of the nations sanction it. The family is a sacred institution according to the teachings of the Church; yet most of the nations have a disgracefully high rate of illegitimacy, which includes as much as 70 percent or more of the population in some of them. Moreover, *machismo*, a publicly accepted sanction of the husband's right to philander, hardly comports with the Church's teachings regarding the sanctity of the family.

Several factors account for the fact that the great mass of the population ✓ is only nominally Catholic. The region has long suffered from a severe shortage of priests; it has only about 35,000 of them, and according to officials of the Church, from four to five times that many are urgently

[44] Wyatt MacGaffey and Clifford R. Barnett, *Cuba* (Survey of World Cultures; New Haven, Conn.: HRAF Press, 1962), pp. 197 and 203-4.

[45] John and Mavis Biesanz, *The People of Panama* (New York: Columbia University Press, 1955), pp. 161-62.

[46] Russell H. Fitzgibbon, *Uruguay: Portrait of a Democracy* (New Brunswick, N.J.: Rutgers University Press, 1954), p. 231.

[47] Johnson, *op. cit.*, p. 51.

FIGURE 6-1

PERCENTAGE OF POPULATION THAT IS CATHOLIC

SOURCE: *Decision*, October, 1963, p. iv/8 as given in CIF *Study No. 1*, p. 255. Reproduced by permission.

needed. In North America there is one priest for approximately 700 Catholics, but in Latin America there is only one priest for 5,000 of the faithful. In some areas there, a priest may have as many as 30,000 or more people in his nominal flock, and there are thousands of villages and towns that have no church or resident priest. In many of the more remote communities, the priest does well to get around at least once a year. As a result, a formal burial service may have to be postponed for months until the priest can officiate at the ceremony; the first baby may have come and the second be well on its way before the marriage rites can be performed.

Besides suffering from a shortage of priests, the Catholic Church has also been greatly hampered by the lack of funds needed to carry on its work, a condition resulting mainly from the expropriation of its properties and the prevailing poverty of many areas. In Venezuela, the plight of the Church was so serious that President Gómez restored some of its former properties to improve its financial condition. In Guatemala, to help relieve its financial distress, President Ydígoras in July, 1959, decreed that the Church could own property designed exclusively for religious, social welfare, or educational purposes—the first time since 1879 that the Church has been allowed to own property.

The needs of the Church in Latin America have worried not only the Vatican, but also the faithful in many countries. The situation has been soberly surveyed by a number of conferences held in Rome, the United States, Latin America, and elsewhere to consider measures urgently needed for strengthening the Catholic Church in Latin America. The call to action was sounded by Pope John XXIII in his fourth encyclical letter, when he urged all Catholic missions throughout the world to increase their missionary efforts. In response, the Church has planned and is executing a worldwide program calculated to give the spiritual, educational, and material assistance which are so greatly needed in Latin America. Under the program of Papal Volunteers for Latin America, many members of the faithful have been encouraged to go to the region to aid the lay organizations there. Moreover, the Grail, an international group of lay-women, has been training young women for the lay apostolic in the region.

THE CHALLENGE OF PROTESTANTISM

For centuries Catholicism was the only faith recognized in Latin America. Even when freedom of conscience was recognized, as in Argentina's first constitution, in effect it meant freedom only from a Catholic conscience and point of view. One of Perón's greatest insults to the Church, ranking with legalized divorce and prostitution, was authorizing the Seventh-Day Adventists to come in and compete with the Catholic Church.

Protestantism was relatively late in entering Latin America. In fact, during the first three centuries of the colonial era there were no Protestants to speak of in the region. "In those brave days, to get aboard a ship for America a man had to prove that no member of his family had been condemned by the Inquisition for two generations." But conditions changed after independence. Some of the new national leaders, such as O'Higgins of Chile, Rivadavia and Sarmiento of Argentina, and others welcomed Protestant missionaries, sometimes relying on them to reform the nation's educational system. In whatever capacity they entered, however, whether as missionaries or educational advisers, their reception was in effect a rebellion against the established Church and its practices.[48]

The Protestant churches founded in most nations have flourished. In Mexico, they generally endorsed the principles of the social revolution which the nation was aspiring to achieve. As a result of their sympathy, their properties were usually respected, and many of the Protestants became educational leaders or held positions of prominence.[49]

Of all the 20 nations, Brazil has been one of the most receptive to Protestantism. According to reliable reports, Protestantism is growing faster there than in any other country in the world. Figure 6–2 gives its strength there and in the other nations. In spreading the gospel, Protestant groups are carrying it to the neglected lower classes and to the rural areas which priests with their large parishes have found it difficult to take care of. From its humble beginnings in the lower classes and in the rural areas, Protestantism has become respectable among the upper class as rural Protestants migrated to the cities. Many of them have entered the professions or risen to positions of responsibility in government and politics. Although they constitute only about 4 percent of the total population of Brazil, they increased approximately 600 percent between 1940 and 1950.[50]

Protestant missions and missionaries are making many contributions in Brazil and elsewhere to social welfare and educational progress.[51] In proselytizing, they have emphasized the physical and intellectual needs of the people. To this end, they have built many hospitals, as in Quito, that are among the most modern in Latin America and whose facilities are available to even the humblest peon who does not have a peso in his pocket but who needs treatment. In the vast Amazon region, it is often most difficult for patients to reach a doctor or a hospital. To help them, some of the churches have set up medical facilities in the most remote parts of the back country. The Seventh-day Adventists maintain a mobile medical service on the rivers by means of a fleet of nine well-equipped launches, treating from 25,000 to 50,000 patients a year. Their itinerant doctor-dentists in 1958 extracted a total of 13,663 teeth.[52]

The Protestant denominations have also established a large number of schools, sometimes in the cities but often in the remote hinterlands where

---

[48] John J. Considine, *New Horizons in Latin America* (New York: Dodd, Mead & Co., 1958), p. 235.

[49] Wilfrid Hardy Callcott, *Liberalism in Mexico: 1857–1929* (Stanford, Calif.: Stanford University Press, 1931), pp. 251–52.

[50] Thales de Azevedo, *Social Change in Brazil* (Inter-American Studies Monograph Series No. 22) (Gainesville, Fla.: University of Florida Press, 1963), p. 78. For the reasons for the Protestant gains, see pp. 78–80.

[51] For an interesting and detailed discussion of the history of Protestantism in Latin America and the activities engaged in, see Considine, *op. cit.*, pp. 234–75.

[52] Schurz, *op. cit.*, p. 197.

FIGURE 6–2

PERCENTAGE OF POPULATION THAT IS PROTESTANT

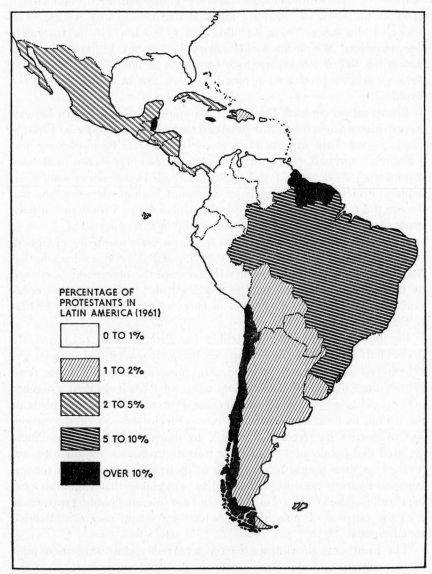

PERCENTAGE OF
PROTESTANTS IN
LATIN AMERICA (1961)

0 TO 1%

1 TO 2%

2 TO 5%

5 TO 10%

OVER 10%

SOURCE: *Center of Intercultural Formation* (CIF) *Study No. 1*, p. 261. Reproduced by permission.

illiteracy is high and schools are a rarity. They have established many
colleges, too, some for providing a general cultural education but others
for affording training in specialized fields. The Presbyterian Mackenzie
College in São Paulo is a leading institution providing technical instruction, and the Presbyterian Experiment Station and Agricultural Training

School at Lavras, Minas Gerais, give scientific training to many a future farmer.

Most of the Protestant activities are conducted as denominational projects, but some of them are interdenominational. Voz Andes, "The Voice of the Andes," was established in Quito in 1931 by the interdenominational World Radio Missionary Fellowship. Its powerful radio station has five transmitters which broadcast 24 hours a day and seven days a week; its programs, in nine languages, can be heard all over the world.

Protestantism entering Latin America could hardly expect to be welcomed with open arms by the long-entrenched Roman Catholic Church, which regarded the area as its own special preserve. Its displeasure was sometimes expressed quite gently, as when Archbishop Pierini of Bolivia, commenting on the very few Protestant schools in the nation, said, ". . . happily, Protestantism among us, as a religion, is an exotic plant, and this despite the fact that for some years the emissaries of Protestantism have made supreme efforts to establish a foothold in this country."[53]

Sometimes, however, antagonism has been very pointedly expressed, as when Cardinal Garibi Rivera of Mexico asserted, on one occasion, that the two greatest problems facing Mexico were the obscurantism created by illiteracy and the expansion of Protestantism[54] and, on another occasion, that Mexico faces the "twin menaces of Communism and Protestantism."[55]

But in only one nation—Colombia—has Protestantism been severely persecuted, with many of its churches being destroyed and its ministers or converts being beaten or killed. The persecution began in the early days of the Rojas Pinilla dictatorship when, in 1953, it decreed a number of legal disabilities designed to eliminate Protestantism in two-thirds of the nation, to limit its freedom to evangelize in the rest of the nation, and to restrict its freedom to teach. In short, President Rojas Pinilla declared that his country would not tolerate Protestant missionaries, implying that they should be sent only to barbarous regions. The foreign minister, Evaristo Sourdis, elaborated by explaining that Colombia permits "full freedom of worship" but would not tolerate "public propaganda with the purpose of proselytizing, which we would consider offensive to our dignity."[56]

The many acts of violence which occurred against Protestant ministers, converts, and churches, usually in the rural areas, were often the result of the bitter civil war which wracked the nation for many years after 1948. While the Catholic hierarchy never condoned acts of violence against Protestants, it sometimes charged that "more often than not, they

[53] Mecham, *op. cit.*, p. 229.
[54] *New York Times*, August 9, 1959, p. 34, col. 1.
[55] *Hispanic American Report*, Vol. XV, No. 7 (September, 1962), p. 590.
[56] *New York Times*, April 12, 1954, p. 23, col. 7; and April 6, 1958, p. 7, col. 1.

are caused by the provocative words and actions and by the illegal propaganda of the proselytizing of the Protestants."[57]

But after the overthrow of Rojas Pinilla, a zealous friend of the Catholic Church during his early years in office but later an oppressor, the persecution of Protestants practically ceased. The call of Pope John XXIII for an ecumenical approach to all Christians for settling their differences in brotherly fashion, without resorting to "the stick and the stone," was mainly responsible for ending the persecution of Protestants in the nation. Another favorable circumstance was the elevation, in December, 1960, of Luis Córdoba Concha, archbishop of Bogotá, to the Sacred College of Cardinals. A scholar, humanist, and liberal who had long worked for peaceful spiritual-secular relations, he inaugurated a policy of promoting religious unity within the nation and undertaking a cooperative defense against the common enemy, communism.[58]

From the viewpoint of the Protestant churches, Latin America, although traditionally and nominally Catholic, is nevertheless a great religious vacuum where ministers and missionaries as well as priests will have all they can take care of without treading on each other's toes. Protestantism's concentration on Latin America since 1938 was apparently largely determined by the difficulties of mission work on the world's largest continent, Asia—difficulties which arose from the presence of exacerbated nationalism and communism.[59] The course of world events has doubtlessly done much to determine the Protestant churches' interest in Latin America, but, from their survey of the region, it is a wide-open field for evangelism and proselytism.

From many indications, the large mass of Indians and other rural citizens are worshiping pretty much as they did five centuries ago, before the advent of conquistador and priest. Conversion to Catholicism has often been more of a formality than a living reality. "The Indians, as a rule," says J. Halcro Ferguson, "either added the Christian God to their own pantheon, as being a more powerful divinity (for the time being, at any rate), or rejected the new religion altogether, though sometimes pretending to accept it to avoid being bothered any more."[60]

From other indications, too, a large part of Latin America's population has at most merely a thin veneer of Catholicism, often so thin in fact that scholars cannot be sure whether their religious practices are really Catholic

---

[57] *Ibid.*, October 18, 1959, p. 71, col. 3.

[58] Martz, *op. cit.*, p. 318.

[59] Considine, *op. cit.*, p. 239.

[60] Halcro J. Ferguson, *Latin America: The Balance of Race Redressed* (Institute of Race Relations) (New York: Oxford University Press, 1961), p. 21.

The Indian understands very little of Roman Catholicism; he listens to Mass, yet does not comprehend it. But Catholicism with its pageantry, ceremonies, and *fiestas*, especially the latter where he gets tight, does provide him with a needed emotional release. (W. Stanley Rycroft, *Religion and Faith in Latin America* [Philadelphia: Westminster Press, 1958], pp. 122–23.)

or simply pagan. In the opinion of some thoughtful observers, the influence of the Catholic Church among the Indians is even less now than it was formerly.[61]

Another indication of the wide-openness of Latin America as a fertile field for proselytizing is the baffling resurgence in some of the nations of the African pagan fetishistic cults. These pagan cults and rites which are hundreds, perhaps even thousands of years old, have long been practiced by many members of the poor, illiterate lower class. But in recent years spiritism and cultism have spread to embrace many in the middle class and even the very top of society. President François Duvalier of Haiti, even after expelling the Catholic clergy and being excommunicated by the Church, still regards himself as a faithful Catholic. But he makes no bones about also practicing voodoo.[62]

Saving souls is the primary goal, as all the churches agree, but just how they should be saved is a doctrinal matter of great importance. The Roman Catholic Church, convinced that it has the answer, is understandably reluctant to share its traditional preserve with Protestant faiths which are equally convinced that they too have the answer. As a stronghold of Catholicism for almost five centuries, Latin America is of monumental significance to the Catholic Church, which has a great deal at stake there, as it frankly recognizes. Within forty years, ". . . if the Church loses Latin America, she loses one-half of her world-wide population," says Roger E. Vekemans, Director of the School of Sociology of Chile's Catholic Pontifical University. "And that could be a crisis within the Church even more serious than the Oriental Schism or the Protestant Reformation."[63]

THE CHALLENGE OF SOCIAL REFORM

Another great challenge which the Roman Catholic Church faces in Latin America is the critical need for social reform, which is largely responsible for the widespread unrest and instability throughout the region. In the past, the Church has been a staunch supporter of the status quo, frequently aligning its great power and prestige with the economic strength of the *hacendados* and the weapons of the military to prevent any "radical" change in the existing order. In its role as spiritual mother to the large underprivileged mass, it was the most influential of the three. By stressing the rewards to be obtained in the hereafter rather than in the

---

[61] José R. Sabogal Wiesse, "The Saints and the Good Earth," *Américas*, Vol. 14, No. 4 (April, 1962), p. 24.

[62] For an extensive account of the nature and impact of such pagan cults in Brazil, see T. Lynn Smith, *Brazil: People and Institutions* (rev. ed.: Baton Rouge, La.: Louisiana State University Press, 1963), pp. 531–49. For their practice in Cuba, see MacGaffey and Barnett, *op. cit.*, pp. 205–10.

[63] *Ave Maria*, in *Time*, January 18, 1960, p. 58.

present life, it used its great spiritual influence to get the mass to accept its lot in society as its Christian duty.

If the Church's interests were threatened, priests or members of the hierarchy might resort to drastic measures. When Mexico was struggling to introduce land reform in the La Laguna region, priests in the area carried on an intensive campaign of propaganda against it. A peasant union (*Sindicato de Campesinos de Durango*) complained in 1922 to the archbishop of the state because of the biased political activities of the priests. "Fr. Reyes of Gómez Palcio is so violently anti-agrarian that he refused to administer the last rites to Eulalio Martínez merely because in life he had been an agrarian," charged one complaint. "Fr. Santiago Zamora of Mapimí sustains on every occasion that taking possession of idle land is theft, and that the government which authorizes it as well as the *campesinos* and their families who benefit by it, are bandits," alleged another complaint.[64]

The seemingly inflexible attitude of the Church toward social change was, in the opinion of many, a serious portent for the future of democracy and of the Church as well. "Since Hispanic Catholicism doesn't seem to be able to make the continent suitable for normal human life," concluded Roger E. Vekemans, "and since, despite the papal encyclicals, the social situation in Latin America is one of the worst in the world, it is obvious that the people of Latin America look for other solutions."[65]

But whatever policy the Church has followed in the past, others are convinced that Catholicism will successfully meet the challenge of the pressing need for reform in Latin America. "Even though the Church stresses the eternal and the intemporal," said Jorge Mañach, professor of philosophy at the University of Havana, "and keeps its doctrine aloof from historic relativity, in practice it has always shown itself much more flexible than its own theories imply. Just because it feels that its vocation is that of eternity, it will take care to adjust itself to the will of the world, to the inescapable design of history."[66]

During the past decade, Roman Catholicism in Latin America has been busy "adjusting itself to the will of the world." By precept and by practice, it is using its great influence in the region to promote social reform. In the several Rural Life Conferences held in Latin America, the Church, with the aid of Protestant and Catholic experts, has studied the problems of the area at the grass roots to attempt to build a solid basis for future policy and activities.

Mobilizing its resources throughout the region, the Catholic Church is giving its strong support to a wide range of social reforms. In Ecuador,

[64] Clarence Senior, *Land Reform and Democracy* (Gainesville, Fla.: University of Florida Press, 1958), p. 60.

[65] *Ave Maria*, in *Time, op. cit.*, p. 58.

[66] Jorge Mañach, "Religion and Freedom in Latin America," *Responsible Freedom in the Americas* (ed. Angel del Rio) (Columbia University Bicentennial Conference Series) (Garden City, N.Y.: Doubleday & Co., Inc., 1955), pp. 359–60.

the clergy in a pastoral letter dealing with agrarian reform advocated the immediate elimination of both *latifundios* and *minifundios*. Emboldened by Pope John XXIII's papal encyclicals, "Mater et Magistra" and "Pacem in Terris," they reaffirmed man's rights to private property, but firmly asserted that the state could rightfully expropriate any land if the action was necessary for the common good, since human dignity had precedence over the right of private property. Going even further, they advocated a progressive income tax and stressed the social obligations of businessmen and property owners toward labor.[67]

In addition to exerting their influence collectively, priests as individuals have often initiated their own personal crusades to accomplish social reforms and improve the condition of the masses. In Brazil, Father Antonio Melo, plugging for a program of farm cooperatives in which the peasant could own and cultivate expropriated land, also receiving training and machinery from the government, has personally organized Catholic peasant leagues with a membership estimated at more than 60,000 landless peasants.[68]

The visitor to Latin America will have certain pictures indelibly etched on his memory: the Maryknoll padre in Cochabamba, Bolivia, who taught his humble flock how to raise a better breed of chickens and how to market their native products quite profitably through their cooperative named Fotrama; or the Seventh-day Adventist medical missionary in Belem, Brazil, who proudly shows visitors through the motor launch, a veritable floating clinic, which he uses to treat patients along the far-flung solitary expanse of the Amazon and its tributaries.

Here at the grass roots, priests and ministers are devoting their lives to helping the many underprivileged in society. It is obvious that here there are no Ugly Americans. There are no ugly Catholics or Protestants either—only servants of the Universal Church, working toward a common goal, to save the Man as well as his Soul, and make Christianity a living reality for all Latin Americans.

SUGGESTED READINGS

AZEVEDO, THALES DE. *Social Change in Brazil*, chap. iii. Inter-American Studies, Monograph Series No. 22. Gainesville, Fla.: University of Florida Press, 1963.

BLANKSTEN, GEORGE I. *Perón's Argentina*, pp. 65–66; 188–90; 229–37. Chicago: University of Chicago Press, 1953.

CALLCOTT, WILFRID HARDY. *Church and State in Mexico: 1822–1857*. Durham, N.C.: Duke University Press, 1926.

---

[67] *Hispanic American Report*, Vol. XVI, No. 4 (July, 1963), p. 482.

[68] *Ibid.*, Vol. XIV, No. 7 (September, 1961), p. 632; and Vol. XV, No. 8 (October, 1962), pp. 758–59.

————. *Liberalism in Mexico: 1857–1929.* Stanford, Calif.: Stanford University Press, 1931.

CASTANEDA, CARLOS E. "Social Developments and Movements in Latin America," *Church and Society: Catholic Social and Political Thought and Movements* (ed. JOSEPH N. MOODY). New York: Arts, Inc., 1953.

CONSIDINE, JOHN. J. *New Horizons in Latin America.* New York: Dodd, Mead & Co., 1958.

DEWART, LESLIE. *Christianity and Revolution: The Lesson of Cuba.* New York: Herder and Herder, 1962.

FITZGIBBON, RUSSELL H. *Uruguay: Portrait of a Democracy,* chap. xvi. New Brunswick, N.J.: Rutgers University Press, 1954.

GRUENING, ERNEST. *Mexico and Its Heritage,* pp. 171–286. New York: D. Appleton-Century Co., Inc., 1934.

HOLLERAN, MARY P. *Church and State in Guatemala.* New York: Columbia University Press, 1949.

JORRÍN, MIGUEL. *Governments of Latin America,* pp. 23–27; 206–15. New York: D. Van Nostrand Co., Inc., 1953.

KENNEDY, JOHN J. *Catholicism, Nationalism, and Democracy in Argentina.* Notre Dame, Ind.: University of Notre Dame Press, 1958.

LEONARD, OLEN E. *Bolivia: Land, People and Institutions,* chap. xi. Washington, D.C.: The Scarecrow Press, Inc., 1952.

MACGAFFEY, WYATT, AND BARNETT, CLIFFORD R. *Cuba,* chap. 11. Survey of World Cultures. New Haven, Conn.: HRAF Press, 1962.

MAÑACH, JORGE. "Religion and Freedom in Latin America," *Responsible Freedom in the Americas* (ed. ANGEL DEL RIO), pp. 349–60. Garden City, N.Y.: Doubleday & Co., Inc., 1955.

MARTZ, JOHN D. *Colombia: a Contemporary Political Survey,* pp. 24–27; 214–17; 219–21; 238–40; 317–19. Chapel Hill, N.C.: University of North Carolina Press, 1962.

MECHAM, J. LLOYD. *Church and State in Latin America.* Chapel Hill, N.C.: University of North Carolina Press, 1934.

PATTEE, RICHARD. *Catholicism in Latin America.* National Catholic Welfare Conference, Washington, D.C., 1945.

PIERSON, WILLIAM W., AND GIL, FEDERICO G. *Governments of Latin America,* chap. 17. New York: McGraw-Hill Book Co., Inc., 1957.

PIKE, FREDRICK B. (ed.). *The Conflict Between Church and State in Latin America.* New York: Alfred A. Knopf, Inc., 1964.

RICE, SISTER M. ELIZABETH. *The Diplomatic Relations Between the United States and Mexico, as Affected by the Struggle for Religious Liberty in Mexico, 1925–1929.* Washington, D.C.: Catholic University of America Press, 1959.

SCHURZ, WILLIAM LYTLE. *Brazil: The Infinite Country,* chap. 9. New York: E. P. Dutton & Co., Inc., 1961.

SEJOURNE, LAURETTE. *Burning Water: Thought and Religion in Ancient Mexico.* Trans. IRENE NICHOLSON. New York: Vanguard Press, 1956.

SMITH, T. LYNN. *Brazil: People and Institutions,* chap. xx. Rev. ed. Baton Rouge, La.: Louisiana State University Press, 1963.

STOKES, WILLIAM S. "Catholicism and Democracy in Latin America," *Responsible Freedom in the Americas* (ed. ANGEL DEL RIO), pp. 361–80. Garden City, N.Y.: Doubleday & Co., Inc., 1955.

TANNENBAUM, FRANK. *Mexico: The Struggle for Peace and Bread*, chap. 8. New York: Alfred A. Knopf, Inc., 1954.

————. *Peace by Revolution: An Interpretation of Mexico*, pp. 34–67. New York: Columbia University Press, 1933.

————. *Ten Keys to Latin America*, chap. 3 and pp. 53–65. New York: Alfred A. Knopf, Inc., 1962.

TUCKER, WILLIAM P. *The Mexican Government Today*, chap. 3. Minneapolis: University of Minnesota Press, 1957.

WAGLEY, CHARLES. *An Introduction to Brazil*, chap. 6. New York: Columbia University Press, 1963.

WHETTEN, NATHAN L. *Guatemala: The Land and the People*, chap. 14. Caribbean Series, 4. New Haven, Conn.: Yale University Press, 1961.

————. *Rural Mexico*, chap. xix. Chicago: University of Chicago Press, 1948.

CHAPTER 7

THE ARMED FORCES:
Big Brother in Action

IN AN INTERNATIONAL order where each nation may have to rely ultimately upon its own resources for survival, the armed forces perform very useful functions. They serve as a bulwark against aggression by other nations and also as a backstop for the police in maintaining internal order. In Latin America they also discharge other responsibilities, such as assisting with the periodic censuses, presiding over elections, and engaging in a wide variety of public works.

INTERFERENCE IN POLITICS

Despite the many useful services they perform, the armed forces, traditionally the army, have been one of the greatest impediments in the laborious, century-and-a-half struggle of the region to attain democracy. Unlike the armies of other democratic nations, the military establishments in most of Latin America have a record of frequent interference in politics.

This interference is evidenced in a number of ways: the military's active, often decisive, role in the selection of the president; its strong voice in the determination of national policy; its recognized right to decide virtually all matters that pertain to itself, a right that in effect amounts to self-regulation; and its large proportion of the national budget.

Accustomed as a rule to throwing its weight around, the military nowhere enjoys this more than in the selection of the nation's executive. It has a more enviable record of president-making than does Tammany Hall or any other political machine in the United States. In fact, if Mr. Gallup were making a public opinion survey in Latin America to determine popular attitudes toward presidential candidates, he would be as far off as the pollsters were in 1948 if he neglected to consider the one opinion that counts most in many of the countries—that of the entrenched military leader or dominant clique in the nation.

Does the military boss desire the presidency for himself? If so, he not only has the inside track but also the only sure one to the presidential palace. Old soldiers never die or fade away either. In Latin America, they become presidents.

The recent history of several of the republics shows this quite well.

Venezuela has a most unenviable record of being governed by ambitious generals who aspired to crown their military careers by occupying the presidential office. When the civilian statesman Rómulo Betancourt was elected president in 1958, it was a welcome phenomenon; in the preceding 50 years the nation had been governed by military men for all but 3 years, the short period 1945–48. The long drought for civilian government was finally broken by the revolution of 1945, led by a coalition of young army officers and the nation's leading political party, Democratic Action, headed by Betancourt. But the government of this civilian regime was abruptly cut short in November, 1948, when the army revolted and ousted President Gallegos, installing a military junta at the nation's helm.

Paraguay, Nicaragua, and the Dominican Republic are other nations in which the military have been able virtually to corner the presidential office. In Paraguay military dictators have been presidents or have controlled civilians who were presidents since the end of the Chaco War with Bolivia in 1936.

In Nicaragua the military has exercised unquestioned control ever since the withdrawal of the United States Marines in the early 1930s. General Anastasia Somoza, head of the armed forces, either governed as president or exercised a controlling voice until his assassination in 1956. Since his death the Somoza family continues to maintain its tight grip on the country, with Luis, a civilian, filling the office of president for the six-year term May 1957–May 1963, succeeded then by René Schick Gutiérrez, who has been careful to respect the interests of the Somoza family. The real power, however, rests with Luis' brother, Colonel Anastasia Somoza, Jr., who is commander in chief of the National Guard.

Instead of assuming the presidency himself, the military leader who has the office within his grasp may prefer to call the tune from behind the scenes and exercise control through a civilian who is president in name only, a mere puppet who moves precisely as the military puppeteer manipulates the strings. In 1947, when General Somoza assumed command of the National Guard in Nicaragua after stepping down from the Presidency, he in effect allowed a civilian, Leonardo Arguello, to be elected president of the nation. But when Arguello attempted to undermine the position of Somoza, the general did not hesitate to pitch him out after only 27 days in office and install another civilian in his place.

Sometimes the military leader who remains in the background may exercise control over the government through the office of the secretary of war. This is a very powerful post which is usually filled by a general who can speak authoritatively for the military. Ensconced in his cabinet office, strategic vantage ground, he is a sort of fifth column within the civilian stronghold, in a position to keep the closest tab on the president.

Sometimes the control exercised by the military takes the form of a veto to prevent someone distasteful to them from attaining the presidential office, even though he has been elected to it or is constitutionally entitled to it by virtue of being the nation's vice-president. When Jânio Quadros unexpectedly resigned as president of Brazil in May, 1961, military leaders took steps to prevent João Goulart, the vice-president, from assuming the presidential responsibilities because of his alleged leftist tendencies. They finally allowed him to take office only to avert the serious threat of imminent civil war, after requiring the establishment of a parliamentary government where most of the executive power was exercised by a prime minister responsible to congress instead of by the president.

While control of the presidency is undoubtedly the *pièce de résistance* in Latin America, the military bosses are sometimes content to dine on lesser fare—the less spectacular but equally meaty formulation of national policy. In democratic nations this is a responsibility of the legislative branch of the government, which has been popularly elected and represents the opinions and desires of the majority of the citizens.

In most of the Latin American nations, however, public policy is formulated quite differently. While there are other politically strong pressure groups, such as political parties and organized labor, ordinarily the decisive voice is that of the armed forces.

The issues that confront the country may be of the greatest importance. Should foreign companies be allowed to develop the nation's petroleum resources, so critically needed, or should development be postponed until and if domestic capital is able to do it? Should the nation maintain economic and diplomatic ties with the United States and other Western countries only, or should it have relations with the Communist nations as well, deriving the benefits that might come from dealing with both groups? Although these are critical questions that tax the wisdom of the most dedicated Latin American statesmen, for them to make a decision without first consulting the military is like playing Russian roulette with their careers at stake—possibly their lives, too.

Perhaps no Latin American statesman in recent times has so stood up to the fierce pressures of the military as did Arturo Frondizi, president of Argentina from 1958 until his overthrow by the military in March, 1962. After withstanding onslaught after onslaught on his presidential prerogatives, and after making one concession after another, he finally took his stand, a brave and bold one: while he welcomed the military's suggestions regarding national problems as a contribution to the government's policies and course of action, he did not intend to give up his prerogative of "directing policies in the economic and social area, in the national affairs, and in those matters that are properly in the President's domain."[1]

---

[1] *New York Times,* October 16, 1960, p. 36, col. 1.

Frondizi's bold stand against the military, even though he was eventually forced out, is in striking contrast to the subservient attitude of presidents in some of the countries, who dare not make any decision of importance without first consulting the military powers that be.

In one area of public policy in particular, the military exercise virtually complete and unchallenged control. This is the important area of matters that relate solely or primarily to the armed forces themselves. In such questions as rank, salary, promotion, and retirement benefits, the desires of the military leaders are determining and final.

Whatever the armed forces may be lacking, it certainly is not in high rank. Military back scratching assures that there will be suitable top brass positions for all the deserving. In this respect Paraguay easily takes the lead. Although its navy consists of only three small river gunboats, there are seven admirals to assume responsibility for them. Like the lord of the admiralty in *H.M.S. Pinafore*, apparently four of the admirals stick close to their desks and never go to sea.

The armed forces, besides deciding matters that relate only to their internal organization and functioning, also preempt for themselves such critical decisions as how large the several branches should be and what weapons and equipment they should have—basic questions of defense policy that are decided by civilian authorities in democratic nations.

In Latin America, however, any interference by civilian officials in the broad area of military interests is regarded as a presumptuous invasion of the military's prerogatives. Several presidents, including Bustamente of Peru and Gallegos of Venezuela, have burned their fingers and been summarily thrown out of office for presuming to make decisions relating to the military establishment. As a consequence, however strongly reform regimes may feel about the need for change in this area, they are obliged to confine their reform activities to nonmilitary matters.

In still another way do the military show their interference in politics— by the large amount of their annual appropriations, a disproportionately large share of the national revenue. Operating on the premise that to the victor belongs the spoils, they in effect cut the budget pie, or at least one large slice for themselves.

As a result, the armed forces in most of the nations receive by far the largest share of the budgetary "take," a share that averages as much as 20–25 percent annually. Sometimes it is considerably larger. As poor as Paraguay is, virtually bankrupt and dependent on the largesse of international financial institutions to keep her afloat, the nation under its military dictatorship has spent more than half its total revenue on the armed forces. Even these reported expenditures in Paraguay and elsewhere, large as they are, do not reveal the full picture. For much of the appropriations designated for public works, interior, and communications actually goes to support the military establishment and its activities.

The extravagant financial demands of the military, a sort of fiscal hijacking, have had a very harmful effect on the social and economic progress of the nations. Although most of the nations have a high rate of illiteracy, they spend more for the armed forces than for public education, as Figure 7–1 shows.

Forced to divert much of their limited resources to appease the military, they do not have the money needed to build more schools, provide additional teachers, or build roads that are necessary for pupils to get to school. As a result, millions of children throughout Latin America are denied the benefit of an education because the demands of the military have to be met, regardless of other pressing needs of society.

Thus, as the record shows, the military in Latin America frequently interfere in politics by the positive means of controlling the presidency, determining national policy, especially as regards the military establishment, and demanding and receiving huge annual appropriations.

Paradoxically, the military's interference in politics may take the form of no action whatever—a sort of sit-down strike. Just such a situation in the Dominican Republic in 1930 was responsible for initially putting Raphael Leonidas Trujillo in the presidency—the first act in the nation's drama of prolonged dictatorship. Thanks to his military ingenuity and driving ambition, Trujillo had been able to rise through the ranks until he became commander in chief of the armed forces, transformed by United States Marine training into a well-equipped, highly disciplined army. When a revolutionary horde moved against President Horacio Vásquez in 1930, the army under the leadership of Trujillo stayed in its barracks, refusing to give help to the beleaguered president, who was consequently overthrown. Soon afterward, Trujillo became president in a thoroughly rigged, "democratic" election.

ALTERNATING TRENDS OF MILITARISM

The intense militarism so characteristic of Latin America has by no means followed an even course; on the contrary, it has ebbed and flowed like the tides that rise and fall upon the seashore.

During the first half-century of independence, characterized by disorder sometimes bordering on chaos, militarism was at flood tide throughout most of Latin America. Then, as the prevalent political instability and turmoil slowly subsided, an ebb tide set in and militarism began to decline. A substantial evidence of this was the long period of international peace which began during the second half-century after independence. Although five major wars were fought in South America during the tumultuous period from 1825 to 1883, none occurred after the latter date until the Chaco War began in 1932.

FIGURE 7-1

NATIONAL GOVERNMENT BUDGETS BY CATEGORY OF EXPENDITURE*
Percentage Expended in Year Shown

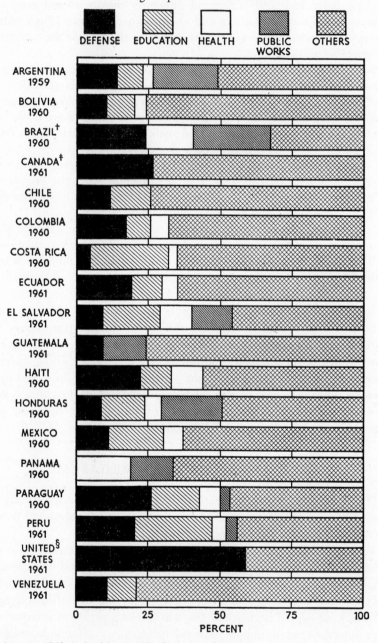

* Data not available for Dominican Republic, Nicaragua, and Uruguay.

† Education and health included in one category.

‡ Percentages for specified categories, in addition to defense, are: debt interest, 13.0; subsidies, 2.1; social security, 11.4; veterans' benefits, 5.1; and transfers to provincial governments, 9.4.

§ Percentages for specified categories, in addition to defense, are: debt interest, 11.2; agricultural subsidies, 4.6; veterans' benefits, 6.6; health, education, welfare, social security, labor, 5.6; foreign aid, 2.2.

SOURCE: *Américas,* July, 1963, pp. 42, 43. Reproduced by permission.

The decline of militarism, so welcome to the region and lasting until the beginning of the Great Depression, is attributable to many causes.

Perhaps as Herbert Spencer and some others believed, the transition from a military to an industrial period was natural and inevitable. In Latin America, wrote F. García Calderón, "invariably we find the sequence of the two periods, one military and one industrial or civil. The independence realized, the rule of militarism sets in throughout the republics. After a period of uncertain duration the military caste is hurled from power, or abdicates without violence, and economic interests become supreme. Politics are then ruled by 'civilism.' "[2]

While evolution was doubtlessly a factor in the decline of militarism, other causes were at work too.

Militarism partly consumed itself through its own outrageous excesses, partly it was mitigated by rising new civilian forces. Much of Latin America began to enter a new epoch. The chaotic aftereffects of the long wars for independence began to subside. Political experience was accumulated, culture diffused, illiteracy reduced. Immigrants began to come in. A heavy influx of foreign capital financed construction of telegraph lines and railroads. And along with people, capital, and technology came modern European ideas.[3]

Still other causes contributed to the decline. The unification of the armed forces into truly national bodies tended to lessen the strength of regional military factions. Also, the acquisition by the armed forces of new weapons, including artillery and planes, tended to give them a preponderance of strength over most would-be insurrectionary groups. The beginning of professionalism in the armed forces was an important influence too: members of the officer corps now began to concentrate on their military functions rather than on political interests, and to regard themselves and their troops as the servants rather than the masters of the state.[4]

Militarism continued to decline until the end of the 1920s when it reached neap tide. At that time military regimes exercised control in only six of the countries, and these represented only about 15 percent of the total population.

Then, following the onset of the depression of 1929, there abruptly began a striking relapse into militarism. This relapse, which saw new military regimes instituted in many formerly democratic countries, was due to several conditions. The devastating effects of the depression, acutely felt in the form of economic stagnation, unemployment, and even hunger, resulted in widespread demands for social reform. While some army officers, particularly the junior ones, sided with the advocates

---

[2] F. García Calderón, *Latin America: Its Rise and Progress*, trans. Bernard Miall (London: T. Fisher Unwin, 1913), pp. 86–87.

[3] Edwin Lieuwen, *Arms and Politics in Latin America* (Council on Foreign Relations) (rev. ed.; New York: Frederick A. Praeger, Inc., 1961), pp. 28–29.

[4] *Ibid.*, pp. 30–31.

of reform, the conservative ranking officers not only backed the oligarchs and other entrenched interests but sometimes even moved into the presidency to assure continuance of the status quo.[5]

As a result of the bitter schism within the society, militarism was once again in the saddle.

The advent of World War II served to further aggravate the region's unfortunate relapse into militarism.

The net effect of the War upon Latin American politics was to freeze traditionalist regimes in power as long as the security of the hemisphere was threatened. The wartime emergency provided dictatorial regimes with justification for outlawing social experimentation and major social or economic reform for the duration. Also, the United States, whose overriding consideration was strategic, did its best to maintain stability in Latin America, sought the cooperation of incumbent regimes which were willing to help the war effort, and provided them with military and economic aid.[6]

Although World War II served to strengthen the control of the military, it paradoxically resulted in a new cycle of revolt against the old vested interests. In some cases the revolt was led by a civilian leader, such as Rómulo Betancourt of Venezuela; in other cases it was led by a reformist military officer, such as Juan Perón in Argentina. Then, as the strokes of the pendulum became shorter, the few years of revolt and reform were hurriedly followed by a period of counterrevolution and opposition to social change. This counterrevolution, lasting from approximately 1947 to 1957, reached a crest in 1954 when 13 of the 20 republics were ruled by military presidents.[7]

One of the most dramatic developments in the recent history of Latin America has been the liquidation of many of the military regimes since 1954.

Three of the military presidents, in Panama, Nicaragua, and Guatemala, were removed by assassination; six others, in Argentina, Haiti, Colombia, Venezuela, Cuba, and El Salvador, were overthrown by revolutions; another, in Chile, was ousted by constitutional means; and still another, in Peru, whose candidate was defeated at the polls, withdrew from politics. In January, 1965, seven of the nations—Bolivia, Brazil, Ecuador, El Salvador, Guatemala, Honduras, and Paraguay—were ruled by a military officer or a military junta.[8] In several other nations, especially Argentina

---

[5] *Ibid.*, p. 59.

[6] *Ibid.*, pp. 62–63.

[7] *Ibid.*, pp. 59–60 and 122.

[8] There were four takeovers of government by the military in 1963, and two in 1964, all disappointing setbacks for democratic government. However, President Humberto Castelo Branco of Brazil, former army chief of staff before the military-civilian uprising of April 1 and his election to the presidency by the Congress, is making heartening progress toward eliminating corruption in government and stemming inflation. (Juan de Onís, *New York Times*, December 26, 1964, p. 1, col. 3.)

But many grave problems lie ahead, including unemployment, slowdown in economic growth, and land reform. (John J. Johnson, "Brazil in Quandary," *Current History*, Vol. 48, No. 281. [January, 1965], pp. 9–15 and 51.)

and Peru, a civilian occupied the presidential office on the suffrance of the military and with their hot breath almost constantly on his neck.

Does this great reduction in the number of military regimes mean that Latin America is about to forsake militarism? Not by a long shot. While it is true that generals occupy only six of the presidential offices, the military still play a strong and aggressive role in most of the nations. And volatile as the Latin American scene is, a swing toward militarism could easily set in again, just as abruptly and extensively as the recent swing away from it.

CAUSES OF MILITARISM AND MILITARY INTERVENTION IN POLITICS

Militarism and the interference of the military in politics have been persistent and tenacious characteristics of the Latin American society. In only a small minority of the nations is democratic government so firmly established that the civilian authorities can govern with assurance that the military are their loyal, obedient servants. Since Latin America was one of the first large areas in the world to embrace democratic government, how can we account for this continued prevalence of militarism, which is the very antithesis of true democracy?

Among the many causes of militarism and the active role of the military in politics, the most important are: (1) the effects of the wars of independence; (2) the lack of a tradition of separation of civil and military power; (3) the social environment, including especially poverty, illiteracy, and localism; (4) the better social status which could be gained by military service; (5) the economic perquisites available to the military; (6) the influence of German, Italian, and certain other military missions; (7) the few wars in Latin America, with politics as a needed outlet for activity; (8) the tradition of the military's serving as guardians of the nation's honor; (9) the social and economic crises that invite military intervention; and (10) the established role of the military as arbiters in national life.

1. In the long struggle for independence, dynamic military leaders of the revolutionary armies rose to the forefront in the rough and tumble of combat. Renowned in their regions, or perhaps in the entire nation, for their prowess and heroic exploits, they were the recognized leaders in the young republics. For the *peninsulares*, who represented Spanish authority, had already fled or been liquidated, leaving a power vacuum which the victorious leaders of the revolution would naturally be the ones to fill. The draughts of victory and power were heady wine for leaders and soldiers alike. "The Generals could not be reconciled to the obscurity of private life under civilian rule," says J. Fred Rippy, "and the common soldiers, accustomed to the adventure, the plunder, and the

excitement of military combat, were loath to exchange the camp for the field and the shop."⁹

2. Unfortunately for the newly established republics, there was no deeply rooted tradition that the civil and military power should be separate and distinct entities, with the military being subordinate to the civil. Bifurcation of the two authorities and the assured supremacy of civil power were part of the American colonies' treasured political heritage from England. Lacking such a tradition, however, the liberators of Latin America were seldom willing to follow the example of George Washington in the United States, and they did not hesitate to seize control of the nation when they had the military force to do so.

3. The social environment, especially poverty, illiteracy, and localism have also taken their toll. In their battle with poverty, the masses were forced to spend most of their time grubbing for the bare essentials of existence. Unable to read, they knew little if anything about the civil rights established in the new constitutions and had not the least conception of civic responsibilities, so essential if democratic government is to be effectual.

4. One's social status could be immeasurably improved by service in the army. Authoritarian and hierarchical though it was, the army was paradoxically one of the region's most democratizing influences. In all the countries, military service was one of the main avenues to a higher social position in the society. Civilians were taught to look up to members of the military, who were among the respected Somebodies in society. "In Francia's time," says C. D. Mansfield, "everybody was forced to take off their hats to every soldier, and the country boys, who wear no clothes at all, were obliged to wear hats for the purpose of saluting them."¹⁰

Even the most ignorant recruit whose Indian race and culture had always been a millstone around his neck would emerge from his military service magically transformed into a cultural mestizo. Indeed, the army was the one means of social mobility in the highly stratified, class-conscious society. And however humble one's background might be, it offered unlimited possibilities for advancement and improvement of his status. The ambitious, intelligent son of even a peasant or ranch hand had one sure opportunity for displaying his ability and talent—his service in the army. Either by distinguishing himself in combat or by obtaining an appointment to the nation's military academy, he could become an officer, possibly rise to a high rank. In fact, he might conceivably achieve the very last step in an eminently successful military career—the presidency of the republic.

An especially prized privilege of the military is the *fuero militar*, which

---

⁹ J. Fred Rippy, "Dictatorships in Spanish America," *Dictatorship in the Modern World* (ed. Guy Stanton Ford) (Minneapolis: University of Minnesota Press, 1935), pp. 54–55.

¹⁰ In George Pendle, *Paraguay: A Riverside Nation* (Royal Institute of International Affairs) (London: Oxford University Press, 1954), p. 20.

in effect gives them a status above the law. The *fuero*, which exempts them from the jurisdiction of the civil courts, tends to create a privileged caste that is exempt from public liability and from civil responsibility. In Mexico, says Henry Bamford Parkes, the officers "resplendent in blue and white uniforms, enjoying, like the clergy, the *fuero* of being tried only in their own military courts . . . soon began to think of themselves as an independent and privileged caste."[11]

5. Important as were the social opportunities open to members of the military, the economic perquisites weighed more heavily. Oftentimes a peon got his first decent suit of clothing, his first pair of shoes, when he joined the army. For the poor and humble, the army was by far the safest and most lucrative career. And, what made it particularly appealing, no special training was needed to enter it.

While the enlisted man had "never had it so good," the officers were naturally the ones favored with the "gravy." Besides receiving high salaries, they were given such valuable additional benefits as housing, medical care, recreational facilities, and commissary privileges which enabled them to buy many items not generally on the market at a relatively low cost. They also enjoyed membership in a luxurious officers' club, and had many opportunities for travel to the United States, Europe, or elsewhere. Early retirement was encouraged to provide opportunities for younger officers, and sometimes the retirement pay was actually larger than the regular salary.

6. The German, Italian, and certain other military missions have also had considerable influence on the development of militarism in Latin America. Not only did they increase the efficiency and fighting ability of the Latin American armies, but they also noticeably affected the thinking of the officer corps. Thanks to their influence, officers often felt even greater contempt for democratic government than before and were convinced that they had an extramilitary responsibility and destiny to fulfil.

7. The Russian grand duke who said that he hated war "because it spoils armies,"[12] hardly expresses the sentiments of the Latin American military. They fairly spoil for a fight. Wars have occurred so rarely in Latin America that the life of the officer has tended to become, oh, so humdrum! Peaceful settlement of boundary disputes may be good for the statesmen and the nation as a whole, but they tend to put the armed forces out of business. Barrack fatigue, the officers find, is more damaging to morale than battle fatigue. As a result, a little war now and then is relished by the military men. It gives them an opportunity to show their daring, their skill with strategy, their mastery of military tactics.

Consigned to barracks boredom, the officers crave a means of self-

---

[11] Henry Bamford Parkes, *A History of Mexico* (3rd ed.; Boston: Houghton Mifflin Co., 1960), p. 117.

[12] Alfred Vagts, *A History of Militarism* (New York: W. W. Norton & Co., Inc., 1937), p. 13.

expression, a feeling quite akin to the creative urge of the artist. The outlet that most of them seize upon is plotting a little revolution or drawing up demands to be made on the president.

8. The military also take pride in their tradition of being guardians of the nation's honor. Feeling their deep responsibility for defending its territorial integrity and sovereignty, they are particularly conscious of the nation as an ideal and as a concept of value. Consequently, they feel very strongly about its sacred honor, and are convinced that they are responsible for preserving it. If the politicians use power in any way that detracts from the dignity of the nation, the military feel they must intervene and set things right. Such intervention is as natural for them as writing a strong letter to his congressman is for a U.S. citizen.

9. The fundamental social and economic changes occurring in Latin America during the past several decades, resulting in strong tensions and deep bitterness, have also invited military intervention. The surge of industrialization, the revolution of rising expectations, and the cry for land have created pressing problems and social crises which the governments have been unable to cope with. Often in the class struggle between the old oligarchy attempting to maintain the status quo and labor and other new social forces attempting to alter it, the armed forces have been called upon to intervene by one group or the other.

10. Finally, in some countries, such as Brazil, the military have established for themselves a recognized role and peculiar responsibility as arbiters in the nation's affairs. "The position of the Brazilian armed forces is in many ways unique," says Edwin Lieuwen. "Politically, they are above partisan politics. As supreme guarantors of constitutional processes, they sit in judgment over presidents, judges, legislators, and all nonuniformed mortals. When it becomes necessary to correct a political situation which they regard as illegal or unconstitutional, they do not descend to the street level, operating with brute force. Rather they quietly issue a dignified ultimatum, from which there is no appeal, and which astute politicians have learned to respect. In other words, a president's policies, especially if they involve significant innovations, are, in practice, subject to veto by the military."[13]

INFLUENCES TENDING TO LESSEN
THE POWER OF THE MILITARY

While many influences in the region have unfortunately tended to stimulate militarism, other influences have served to contain, lessen, or even eliminate it. These counteracting influences are: the constitutional and legal restrictions imposed on members of the military regarding political activity, the increasingly strong democratic civilian groups, and rivalries between the several branches of the armed services.

---

[13] Lieuwen, op. cit., pp. 166–67.

The constitutions of the various countries contain many provisions explicitly designed to restrain the military. One can almost visualize the idealistic constitution makers as they rack their brains, hoping somehow to be able to assure civilian control.

In Colombia the armed forces are specifically declared to be "obedient" and "not deliberative." They are not to assemble except by order of legitimate authority, nor are they to address any petition to the government except upon matters that are related to their efficiency and morale.[14]

In Chile the constitution attempts to protect the president, the Congress, and the judiciary from any direct coercion by the military. "Every decision that the President of the Republic, the Chamber of Deputies, the Senate, or the tribunals of justice may agree to in the presence or on demand of an army, an officer at the head of an armed force, or of any assembly of people, with or without arms, and in disobedience of the authorities, is null in law and cannot produce any effect."[15]

Many other constitutional restrictions commonly adopted are also designed to limit political activities of members of the armed forces. They are not allowed to run for public office, to be active in a political campaign, or to exercise their franchise while on active duty. They may be restricted from even taking part in political discussions. In Nicaragua, so restricted is a member of the armed forces that he may not "collectively or individually express an opinion on matters relating to the service or which in any way attacks or criticizes the laws of the Republic."[16]

Although the constitutional restrictions have usually been just so much verbiage, they nevertheless do serve a useful purpose. Written not only on paper but also in the aspirations of liberty-loving citizens, they serve notice on the military of what their fellow countrymen expect—and for what they will try to exact punishment if the military violate their trust.

Important as these constitutional principles are in attempting to hold the military to account, far more tangible restrictions are represented by the rising civilian groups that are unalterably opposed to any participation by the military in politics.

With the exception of the big landowners, who have managed to maintain themselves in power largely with the support of the military, civilian groups generally are strongly opposed to the military's taking an active part in politics. This participation in the past, they well know, has thwarted social and economic reform, hindered the development of truly democratic government, and saddled the nations with ruinous economic burdens. Three civilian groups in particular are unequivocally antimilitaristic—the political parties, the rising urban middle class, and the labor unions.

Political parties, with their democratic programs and leadership, usually

---

14 Constitution of 1886, Article 168.
15 Constitution of 1925, Article 23.
16 Constitution of 1950, Article 317.

have interests that are quite antithetical to those of the military. They advocate many basic reforms in society—reforms to be achieved by evolution if possible but by revolution if no other course is open. Their main tenet is constitutional, democratic government, a *sine qua non* of their very existence. They also support free elections, freedom of speech, the press, and assembly, and universal suffrage. In short, free political parties advocate that civilians control the government and decide public policy—objectives that toll the knell of arbitrary, irresponsible military rule.

The rising middle class is another large group opposed to the military's taking an active part in politics. This class, mainly responsible for the growth of industrialism and economic development generally, depends on sound economic policies for its prosperity and well-being. Some of its most influential members, the industrialists and businessmen, also need governmental stability as a political climate favorable to their enterprises. The many revolutions instituted by the military, as well as their frequently ruinous economic policies, are harmful to the interests of the industrialists, businessmen, and other members of the middle class.

But the most serious threat of all to the power of the military is that posed by the labor unions, highly organized and often led by fiery leaders capable of inciting mass action and commanding the intense loyalty of great blocs of the underprivileged. While others speak feelingly of liberalism and profess its idealistic tenets, the workers are the one group in society willing to fight, bleed, and die for their liberal principles if necessary. They have a potent weapon too, the general strike, which can paralyze the economic life of the nation and bring its multifarious activities to a standstill. It is a weapon that cannot be countered by the heaviest tanks, the deadliest bazookas, or even bombs dropped by flashing jet planes. It is a weapon as potent as Gandhi's renowned passive resistance in India that brought the mighty British Empire to terms. The military are well aware of the potency of the general strike; it has often triggered the overthrow of an established military regime.

Interservice rivalries have also aided in curbing militarism. When the armed forces are united, they are practically irresistible. But, like our own armed services, they are sometimes as much concerned with cutting each other's throats as with coping with a common enemy. Division within the camp has often proved to be the Achilles' heel of the military. In Argentina the government of General Juan Perón was overthrown largely as a result of the infighting between the army, navy, and air force.

Other influences too are operating to lessen the power of the military and curtail its role in civilian affairs.

Channels for the orderly transfer of government power are beginning to work and . . . will tend to narrow the field of political action for the armed forces. . . . Mass communications will weaken provincialism and tend to strengthen the central authority, which promises reduced opportunities for the armed forces to plunge into politics in order to save the nation. . . . Children of officers, because they have educational advantages not enjoyed by the majority, may be expected to fill an increasing number of the appointive and elective government offices, which means that the interests of officers will be well represented without their forceful intervention in the civilian area. Also, it may be anticipated that the voters will continue to view with caution officers who offer themselves for elective position.[17]

THE MILITARY AS SOCIAL REFORMERS

During the past several decades many members of the military, especially the younger officers, have sided with the new rising groups struggling to change the status quo and initiate programs of reform. This new social alignment is quite different from the army's leanings during the nineteenth century and the first quarter of the present one. Its sympathies then were unmistakably with the oligarchy, whose power and interests it could invariably be counted upon to support and protect.

This earlier military support of the propertied elite came about quite naturally. Only members of the Creole aristocracy could become officers. With their aristocratic background, they naturally sided with the class from which they came. Moreover, the officers, especially the higher ones, often used their positions to amass fortunes. Becoming wealthy from perhaps controlling a state monopoly or acquiring a large landed estate, it was easy for them to become staunch supporters of the prevailing social and economic order in their society.

After World War I, however, many of the officers, especially the younger ones, now gave their loyalty and support to the new groups rising in society and struggling for recognition and power. Various factors account for this changing social attitude. Many of the young officers were now coming from a middle class that included industrialists and managers, bureaucrats and professional men, technicians, proprietors, and others. Representing these new urban elements, the young officers had no ties with the landed oligarchy, and no interest in perpetuating the traditional social order. Rather, they identified themselves with the middle class and accepted its social values.

They also approved of the economic policies of their class, policies which emphasized industrialization as the key to national development.

Under the widening impact of nationalism, both the civilian and military elements have tended increasingly to equate industrial growth with national progress. Officers, thanks to their training in organization, have found employment as directors of state-controlled economic enterprises, and the armed forces look forward to domestic production of war matériel. Thus, despite

---

[17] John J. Johnson, *The Military and Society in Latin America* (Stanford, Calif.: Stanford University Press, 1964), pp. 255–56. But the author envisages that there are contrary forces at work which will unfortunately prolong the dominance of the military for another 10 to 25 years. For these adverse forces, see pp. 258–62.

differences in their approach to politics, the military and the civilian components of the middle sectors tend to agree on their broad social and economic objectives.[18]

The tie between the young officers and the urban middle class they came from was probably the main cause of the junior officer uprisings in the second quarter of the twentieth century. "In general," concludes Edwin Lieuwen, "the ideological conflict was between the old and the new generation, between the generals, on the one hand, and the majors, captains, and lieutenants on the other, with the colonels often pulled in both directions. Such cleavages were nothing new in Latin America; what was new was their origin in social conflict."[19]

In the social conflict of the past several decades, the popular revolutions of Latin America have usually been led by the young officers who sponsored public welfare measures and basic social reforms. It was they who precipitated the break that occurred in Brazil between the old landed aristocracy and the army. In the early 1920s, the *Tenentes* (lieutenants) began to advocate changing the status quo in the nation. Although unsuccessful in two revolutionary attempts, they later succeeded in a third, the revolution of 1930, which brought Getulio Vargas to power.[20]

In Argentina, too, it was the younger officers led by Colonel Juan Perón who instituted the sweeping movement for social and economic development in the nation. Belonging to the middle class himself, Perón was quite contemptuous of the landed aristocracy. Consequently his program was largely aimed at undermining their vested power and benefiting the urban masses of Argentina.

Perón's program in behalf of the workingman had a powerful appeal.

It was not surprising that by October 1945 the majority of workers considered Colonel Perón to be a more important man than their traditional leaders. And, no matter how demagogic his methods, he had accomplished more for them in two years than the Socialist Party had achieved in decades of patient and constantly obstructed legislative effort. . . . 'Social justice' was certainly a worthy ideal; and under Perón—especially in the first phase of his rule—not only did the workers appreciate that the state was mindful of their needs, but they also felt that they themselves were at last being allowed to share in the responsibilities of Government.[21]

---

[18] John J. Johnson, *Political Change in Latin America: The Emergence of the Middle Sectors* (Stanford, Calif.: Stanford University Press, 1958), p. 14.

[19] Lieuwen, *op. cit.*, p. 126.

[20] For the development and program of the *Tenentes* movement, see Robert J. Alexander, "Brazilian Tenentismo," *Hispanic American Historical Review*, Vol. XXXVI, No. 2 (May 1956), pp. 229–42.

[21] George Pendle, *Argentina* (Royal Institute of International Affairs) (3rd ed.; London: Oxford University Press, 1963), pp. 99 and 177.

"For the first time in Argentine history," says John J. Kennedy, "the factory hand, the bus driver, and the packing-house worker could feel that he was participating in public affairs and that his participation was not only accepted, but eagerly solicited." (John J. Kennedy, "Accountable Government in Argentina," *Foreign Affairs*, Vol. VII, No. 3 [April, 1959], pp. 455–56.

In Colombia, another military reformer, General Rojas Pinilla, seized the presidential power in June, 1953, with general popular approval. Rojas was the able and respected head of the nation's armed services. His country had been ravaged for five long years by internecine civil war, and he appeared to be the only one who could end the fratricidal strife and bring order out of chaos.

The program of reform which he initiated was popular with the mass of citizens. Under it, the workers were to accept discipline, and the struggle between the classes was to cease. Labor unions were to devote their efforts to protecting the workers' rights rather than to supporting any political party. Small businesses were to be encouraged and aided to survive amid the flourishing monopolies. Land was to be provided for the landless farmers who would be trained in modern farming methods. In short, the goal of Rojas' program was social justice that would benefit all classes of society. "The ideal is not that there be fewer rich men," said Rojas, "but rather, fewer poor people."[22]

But however sincere the officers might be in their espousal of reform, they faced almost insuperable odds in attaining their objectives. In Colombia the reforms proposed by Rojas for correcting basic weaknesses in the nation would perforce be very costly. To pay for these extensive social benefits for the underprivileged, he proposed that the tax structure be reformed to impose most of the costs of his program on the wealthy, who were best able to bear them. But the oligarchs bitterly resented being called upon to shoulder this burden and fought Rojas with every weapon at their command.[23]

Yet their opposition was by no means solely responsible for the failure of Rojas' program and his removal from office by the military in 1957. Like many another reform-minded general, especially Juan Perón, he had but little competence in the realm of economics. Consequently his ambitious programs of social security, public works, and economic development, laudable though they were, threatened to plunge the country into bankruptcy.[24]

Even though military reformers with their programs were generally popular in their nations, they nevertheless had one weakness that invalidated all their good intentions. They were very contemptuous of democracy—"decadent democracy," as they often referred to it. Scorning the ability of the people to govern, they established authoritarian governments which became increasingly oppressive when they encountered difficulties or suffered reverses. An outstanding example of this is the regime of Rojas Pinilla, which began as a blessing to Colombia but ended as a curse.

---

[22] Vernon L. Fluharty, *Dance of the Millions: Military Rule and the Social Revolution in Colombia, 1930–1956* (Pittsburgh, Pa.: University of Pittsburgh Press, 1957), pp. 265–66.

[23] For the opposition of the oligarchy to Rojas' program, see *ibid.*, pp. 237–45.

[24] Lieuwen, *op. cit.*, pp. 146–47.

Among other social reform-minded military presidents who eventually became very unpopular and lost their following because of their authoritarian methods were: Carlos Ibáñez, Chile, 1924–32; Rafael Franco, Paraguay, 1936–37; Germán Busch, Bolivia, 1937–39; Gualberto Villarroel, Bolivia, 1943–46; Juan Perón, Argentina, 1945–55; and Jacobo Arbenz, Guatemala, 1950–54.

Many so-called reformers among the military were not genuinely interested in promoting reform and did not conscientiously concern themselves with the social and economic betterment of their people. In many instances they were mainly interested in bolstering vested interests or perhaps feathering their own nests.

But even when their motives were of the best, military reformers almost invariably turned out to be poor presidents. Eduardo Santos, distinguished statesman and former president of Colombia, eloquently explains the reasons for their notorious incompetence in governing. "The military profession," he says, "is not exactly the best school in which to learn the difficult art of government. If governing were merely commanding, as the military believe, the role they assume would be justified. But to govern means to interpret, to reconcile, to respect the rights of all, to give freedom of expression to every opinion, to abide by the laws and never subordinate them to personal caprice. To govern—to govern well—often means to have the courage to rectify a mistake; to ask for and listen to advice; to have patience; and to realize that one owes one's power to the will of the people and exercise it for the period they have determined and within the limitations they have established. All of this is difficult for the military to understand and accept, accustomed as they are to the blind obedience of their inferiors, the dry voices of command, and the narrow horizon of their profession, which rarely encompasses the element of humanism."[25]

Does the incompetence of the military in governing mean, then, that military reformers have failed completely? Far from it. Although their programs are usually swept away by the counterrevolutions which oust them from office, they nevertheless often leave behind them enduring monuments in the minds and hearts of their underprivileged fellow countrymen—a faint ray of hope of better days to come . . . a glimmer of faith in the eventual triumph of justice . . . a glimpse of the freedom that ignites human aspiration.

"Rojas has turned the clock forward on social achievement for the masses," wrote Vernon L. Fluharty. "He has given them status, and a

---

[25] Eduardo Santos, "Latin American Realities," *Foreign Affairs*, Vol. 34, No. 2 (January, 1956), p. 256.

Since World War II, direct intervention by the military has tended to take the form of government by juntas, representing all branches of the armed forces. The juntas have been just as inept in governing as the single traditional military dictator—perhaps even more so. They have been notoriously incompetent as administrators intrusted with public responsibility, have stifled public debate and thwarted a democratic solution of problems which they inherited from democratic leaders, and have flubbed at promoting industrial development. (Johnson, *The Military and Society in Latin America, op. cit.,* pp. 252–53.)

sense of their importance, if only because his government has emphasized their welfare. That lesson they will never forget, and nothing less will be acceptable from other governments to come. No regime in Colombia's future will be able to ignore successfully the needs of the '95 percent.' "[26]

THE MILITARY IN THE SEVERAL NATIONS TODAY[27]

The striking decrease in the number of military presidents in Latin America during the past decade has often been termed a "democratic revolution." Yet despite the pronounced trend toward civilian government, members of the military continue to exercise a strong influence in most of the countries. Sometimes it is exercised so brazenly through *pronunciamentos*, threatened uprisings, or military takeovers that the rest of society is well aware of what is going on. More often, however, it is done so quietly and in such behind-the-scenes fashion as not to be apparent except to the more perceptive.

The degree of political control exercised by the military varies widely among the 20 republics. Between Paraguay, which maintains the most obvious military dictatorship in Latin America, and Costa Rica, which is so nonmilitaristic that it does not even have an army, there are 18 gradations representing the other nations in the region. However, they may all be classified into three main groups approximately equal in number but varying considerably in importance.

Group I. The nations in which the military dominate politics are: Dominican Republic, El Salvador, Haiti, Honduras, Nicaragua, and Paraguay. These nations, which constitute only about 8 percent of the region's population and 4 percent of its area, are the least important in Latin America. They all have similar social and economic characteristics, including a high rate of illiteracy, low per capita income, primitive agricultural economy, great concentration of wealth, very little industry, little or no middle class, and a weak labor movement.

In the realm of government, too, these nations have a monotonous pattern of dictatorial rule by the military, accompanied by the suspension of private rights, the suppression of civilian political activity, and the elimination of the opposition by incarceration, assassination, or exile.

Sometimes the military do not even bother to disguise their naked dictatorial intent. In Honduras, although accepting a civilian president, they clearly showed their determination to maintain a stranglehold on the nation. In the proclamation which they issued on the eve of the 1957 election, they bluntly stated that they would "assume the irrevocable functions of permanent guarantors and zealous keepers of the integrity of the country's institutions."

---

[26] Fluharty, *op. cit.,* pp. 316–17.

[27] For extensive discussions of this subject see Lieuwen, *op. cit.,* pp. 154–72, and Theodore Wyckoff, "The Role of the Military in Latin American Politics," *Western Political Quarterly*, Vol. XIII, No. 3 (September, 1960), pp. 745–63.

Group II. The nations in which the military are in a state of transition from political to nonpolitical bodies—Argentina, Brazil, Cuba, Ecuador, Guatemala, Panama, Peru, and Venezuela.

Courtesy of Mott Long and the
Minneapolis Tribune

"He sure looks lifelike doesn't he?"

Courtesy of Interlandi and
the *Los Angeles Times*

"It's just an old-fashioned, military, dictatorial, extreme right-wing Latin-American coup. How soon can we expect recognition?"

Courtesy of Berry and The N.E.A.

"Remember, I'm running this show."

Courtesy of Aldor and *El Tiempo,*
Bogotá

*The Peruvian junta: "Why don't they
realize that we follow in the steps of
democracy?"*

This group is especially important because it contains several of the
largest nations in Latin America, as well as more than 60 percent of the
region's population, 70 percent of its area, and the greater part of its natural resources.

Like the states in Group I, these too have certain characteristics in common. They include a social structure that is more complex; wider variety
of crops, occupations, and industry; economic power that is more widely
diffused; stronger political parties; and personal freedoms that are usually
respected.

In these states the armed forces themselves are apt to be torn by dis-
unity regarding the role they should take in resolving social crises. One
group of officers, usually the senior, conservative ones, prefers to maintain the status quo. To this end these officers prefer to have a dominant
role in politics in order to thwart social change if possible, or at least to
tone it down. A second group of officers would remove the military completely from politics. Some of these are dedicated professionals who feel
that the armed forces should eschew politics; others, remembering the
failure of military presidents to resolve economic and social crises, are convinced that government and politics should be left to civilians. Still a third
group consists of young officers imbued with strong social consciences
and sympathy for the masses. They believe the military should take up
the cause of social revolution and actively intervene to better the condition of the underprivileged.[28]

   Group III.   Nations in which the military are nonpolitical are: Bolivia, Chile, Colombia, Costa Rica, Mexico, and Uruguay.

   These six nations are quite important too, containing approximately
one-third the population and one-fourth the area of the region, as well
as many of its important natural resources. With the exception possibly
of Bolivia, they have a number of features in common, including political
and economic stability; a fair degree of social mobility; a high degree of
literacy and culture; effective constitutional government; a meaningful
political opposition; and freedom of speech, religion, and the press, as well
as many other personal rights.

   In these countries the military have a politically neutral, professional
status that removes them from a decisive role in politics.

   In Chile and Colombia, the armed forces have a unique status. They
have long been aloof from politics—in Chile, except for the brief period
1924–32, and in Colombia, for the period 1948–58[29]—and are in effect
autonomous bodies, not really under the direct control of the civilian governments. Rather, under a sort of gentlemen's agreement that exists in
both countries, they are allowed to operate without interference and to
make their own military decisions in return for which they strictly mind
their own business and remain aloof from political activity.

   Easily one of the most nonmilitaristic states of Latin America is Uruguay. "The ministry of national defense," says Russell Fitzgibbon, "does
not call the tunes in Uruguay, as is unhappily often the case in other
Latin American countries."[30] Its demilitarization is primarily the result of

---

   [28] Lieuwen, *op. cit.*, pp. 163–64.
   [29] The Leticia controversy between Colombia and Peru during 1932–33 resulted
in the beefing up of the nation's weak army; and preparedness during World War II
as an ally of the United States served to further strengthen it. During the tragic civil
war which raged from 1948 to 1958, "the army became the rock upon which the
state clung for survival." (J. León Helguera, "The Changing Role of the Military in
Colombia," *Journal of Inter-American Studies,* Vol. III, No. 3 [July, 1961], pp. 353
and 355.)
   [30] Russell H. Fitzgibbon, *Uruguay: Portrait of a Democracy* (New Brunswick,
N.J.: Rutgers University Press, 1954), p. 158.

two influences. The nation is a buffer between two giants and has always been able to depend upon their mutual animosities to guarantee its existence and borders. More specifically, its abolition of militarism was primarily the work of its great national patriot and statesman, José Batlle, who established the framework of most of its contemporary political institutions.

In Bolivia, too, the military have supposedly been shorn of most of their power and relegated to the position of servants of society. In the Chaco War with Paraguay, the nation suffered a humiliating defeat when the Army turned out to be a bumbling and ineffective military machine. Later, after it tried unsuccessfully to stamp out the 1952 revolution, the triumphant new government completely wiped out the old Army and attempted to set up careful procedures to insure a loyal, subservient military force. Thereafter, members of the officer corps were systematically allocated on a 20, 30, and 50 percent basis to the sons of peasants, of city workers and miners, and of middle class MNR (Movimiento Nacional Revolucionario) members of at least six years standing, respectively. The size of the Army was greatly reduced and its budget kept very low. Moreover, 5,000 of the 8,000-man force were kept at a safe distance from the capital, assigned to colonization and road-building projects in the faraway eastern part of the country or to agricultural projects on the altiplano.[31] However, after the successful military-civilian revolt which ousted President Paz in early November, 1964, and resulted in the vice-president, General René Barrientos of the Air Force, taking over the office of president, Bolivia's supposedly nonpolitical Army appears to be back in politics again.

Another country that has been very successful in throttling militarism and firmly establishing the control of civilian authorities is Costa Rica. In fact, the nation does not even have an army. It was abolished shortly after the 1948 revolution was suppressed, and in its place was substituted a small National Police Force equipped only with side arms. Purposely lightly armed, its functions are only to provide ordinary police protection for the inhabitants, and to furnish a corps of officers for the civilian militia charged with defending the nation in case of invasion.

Relieved of the heavy expense of maintaining an army, Costa Rica is using its resources for peaceful development. Less than one-eighth of the national budget is spent on the National Police Force—very low for Latin America. Quite symbolically, the former Bella Vista Barracks have been turned into a museum of fine arts, and the nation in 1959 initiated a program to trade its surplus arms to a United States company in return for farm tractors—a modern version, Costa Rican style, of converting "swords into plowshares."

Perhaps the best expression of the nation's attainment of true constitutional government is the power of the president over the police force. In

31 Robert J. Alexander, *The Bolivian National Revolution* (New Brunswick, N.J.: Rutgers University Press, 1958), pp. 24, 47, and 151–57.

exercising his authority, the president does not mince words or pull punches. In November, 1960, President Echandi, sure of his constitutional prerogatives, did not hesitate to order the arrest of the police force's commanding officer, Colonel Fernandez, on disciplinary charges.

Among the larger nations of Latin America, Mexico is the only one that has managed to throw off the shackles of militarism. Its achievement, historic in the annals of Latin America, affords a provocative case study of militarism.

HOW MEXICO SUCCEEDED IN CURBING MILITARISM[32]

Subjecting the military to civilian control is one of the most dramatic achievements of Mexico's sweeping social revolution that began in 1910. If any nation in Latin America is qualified to write authoritatively on "How to Succeed in Curbing Militarism," it is Mexico. In a region where most of the countries are still plagued with the vicious affliction, this success story should be a best seller—required reading too!

Mexico has probably suffered more from the ravages of rampant militarism than any other country in Latin America. Flourishing lustily there, the weed seed of militarism early extended its tenacious taproot of military control deep down into the political and economic subsoil of the nation. The results were as harmful as noxious weeds in a field of sweet clover.

Responsible democratic government, an ideal embodied in the first constitution, was almost completely stifled after independence because the military refused to demobilize. Instead, the leaders and their ragged armies now fought each other for the prized privilege of controlling the government. As a result, every established government soon found itself confronting military rebellions on every side, instigated by generals who were greedy for power, prestige, and property. During the first century of independence the nation was plagued with more than 1,000 armed uprisings, many of which were successful.

The result was political and economic chaos.

The new head of the nation hardly had an opportunity to unpack in the presidential palace and get acquainted with the problems of government before he was thrown out by a revolution, just as he had seized power only a short while before. The turnover in heads of state was fantastic. According to William Robert Shepherd, during Mexico's first 55 years of independence, it was governed by at least 74 different executives! These included two "emperors," some 36 presidents, 9 "provisional presidents," 10 dictators, 12 "regents," and 5 supreme "counselors."[33]

---

[32] For a comprehensive treatment of this subject, see Lieuwen, *op. cit.*, pp. 101–21, and Virginia Prewett, "The Mexican Army," *Foreign Affairs*, April, 1941, pp. 608–20.

[33] William Robert Shepherd, *The Hispanic Nations of the New World* (New Haven, Conn.: Yale University Press, 1919), p. 123.

The continued rivalry of military chieftains seeking to control the government did far more than prevent any possible political stability; it jeopardized the very survival of the nation.

With every *jefe político*, commander, general, governor, cacique, or other military leader seeking to establish control over his locality, to make and enforce its laws, and to levy and collect its taxes, the country was in danger of imminent dismemberment. For years at a time, large regions controlled by local leaders were completely independent of the federal government. In fact, with the whole country threatened with dismemberment, it is nothing less than miraculous that Texas was the only region that separated itself permanently from the rest of the country.[34]

Besides causing political chaos, the numerous military uprisings kept the nation in a state of continual bankruptcy. An established government was forced to spend most of its revenues in quelling uprisings against it. In addition, vast sums were lavished upon its own troops in the hope, often futile, of holding their loyalty. So extreme were the demands of the military that during Mexico's first quarter century of independence, the military budget was greater than the total government revenue in two out of every three years. In fact, in the 23 years from 1823 to 1846, the total income of the nation was $291,236,796 during which time the Army was allocated $326,506,715.[35]

The greed of the military leaders seemed insatiable.

All wanted to be cavalry colonels, or at least infantry colonels. All wanted to be heads of military expeditions against real or imaginary bandit groups, against peaceful or savage Indians, with unlimited expense accounts. All wanted to have the income from ports or fiscal offices, all wanted gold, either private or public, all wanted concessions, *haciendas*, houses, titles, to establish gambling houses, all wanted their exemptions to cover past, present and future crimes. All wanted everything and the president, instead of being the leader of a government and governor of an army, became the servant and slave of an army of an unstable group of bandits.[36]

Often forced to spend the amount of its annual collected revenue, it is no wonder that Mexico never once achieved a balanced budget until 1894. According to Francisco Bulnes, there was a revolution whenever the deficit exceeded 25 percent.[37] Yet however extravagant the demands of the military were, and however disastrous their effects on the public treasury, they were always satisfied, even by the resort to forced borrowing, if necessary. Although the nation was sadly in need of roads and railroads, schools and hospitals, public utilities and industries, it was bludgeoned into dissipating its limited resources upon the profligate military.

Yet despite the huge public outlays for the nation's "armed might," its

---

[34] Frank Tannenbaum, *Peace by Revolution: An Interpretation of Mexico* (New York: Columbia University Press, 1933), pp. 82, 85, 89–90.

[35] *Ibid.*, p. 85.

[36] *Ibid.*, pp. 84–85.

[37] Parkes, *op. cit.*, p. 179.

military effectiveness was a farce. The Army was ludicrously top-heavy in brass. According to one description of it, "For every two men that carried a gun, there were two commanders that ordered them about, one official who commanded the commanders, one musician who played the tune, and one retired officer who criticized the operations and collected his gratuity."[38]

Despite the great expenditures on the military, the rank and file of the Army were a miserable rabble. Ragged, barefooted, little disciplined, and poorly armed, they were so scantily paid—only three or four pesos a month—that they were often forced to scrounge around and live off the country. The generals, given a daily allowance for troops' rations, often pocketed most of it. Indeed, the general who commanded an army of several thousand engaged in suppressing a Maya rebellion managed within three years to accumulate a private fortune of 10 million pesos at the expense of his men, who were reduced to filth and semistarvation.[39]

Few of the soldiers had entered the military service voluntarily; none of them had received a courteous, ceremonial notification from their local draft board beginning, "Greetings." Rather, the ranks were filled with a motley assortment of agitators and beggars, bandits and criminals, adventurers and vagabonds, many of whom had been thrown into the Army by local political bosses as a convenient way of getting rid of them.

In the decades preceding the 1910 revolution, the president, General Porfirio Díaz, accomplished the seemingly miraculous by providing the nation with sorely needed stability. Imposing tyranny and organized violence—"Díaz-potism," many called it—he maintained peace and order in the land by rigidly controlling the Army.

But when Díaz was overthrown following the revolution of 1910, the nation reverted to its previous state of chaos. Once again, reminiscent of the first half-century of independence, the government was beset with hundreds of ambitious, self-seeking military leaders that sprang up all over the country. Commanding his own private army, each was an irresponsible autocrat in his own state or region. Entirely independent of the central authority, each exercised complete control over the lives, property, and destinies of those who lived within his authority; in brief, he was the law and the government.[40]

Controlling the noxious weed of militarism was in many respects the most difficult part of the revolution, and credit for the achievement belongs to four of the nation's outstanding leaders—presidents Obregón, Calles, and Cárdenas, and General Joaquín Amaro, the able and zealous Indian general of the revolution who was as ardently pro-professional as he was antimilitaristic.

---

[38] Tannenbaum, *op. cit.*, p. 80.

[39] Hubert Herring, *A History of Latin America from the Beginnings to the Present* (2d ed. rev.; New York: Alfred A. Knopf, Inc., 1961), p. 342.

[40] Frank Tannenbaum, *Mexico: The Struggle for Peace and Bread* (New York: Alfred A. Knopf, Inc., 1954), p. 95.

Álvaro Obregón, president from 1920–24, was a civilian—a self-made wealthy farmer who had risen to heroic stature in the revolution. Popular with the army and the masses alike, he capitalized on his popularity and personal prestige in his measures designed to curb the rampant militarism. A shrewd politician as well, he knew when it was advisable to "give." When his minister of war, General Francisco Serrano, lost 80,000 pesos at the gambling table in one sitting, Obregón magnanimously authorized the treasury to pay the debt.

But if he diplomatically knew when to bend, he just as adroitly knew when and how to apply needed pressure too.

As an apparently magnanimous gesture, he had all the revolutionary generals put on the government payroll and incorporated into the national army. This was a shrewd act, for it put under governmental authority the hundreds of irascible generals who had mushroomed during the many years of civil war and internal strife. In deciding who was entitled to what, President Obregón was too smart to quibble about details, holding that "if a man calls himself a general, he must be one."[41]

Meanwhile, professionalism was being adroitly promoted among the lower officers of the Army. The old Colegio Militar at Chapultepec was reopened for new officers who could take a three-year specialized course to prepare them for the infantry, cavalry, or artillery. Also, many of the promising young officers were sent abroad, particularly to Spain or France, Germany or the United States, to study military science and tactics. Another significant sign of demilitarization was Obregón's reducing the size of the Army, and also its share of the federal budget, from 142 million pesos in 1921 to 117 million in 1924.[42]

The number of generals was conveniently reduced, too, especially after the unsuccessful uprising of 1923 led by the military. Some of the leaders were exiled, others were simply shot. This unceremonious treatment of the hitherto sacrosanct generals was no graduated deterrent. Rather, it was a form of massive retaliation that magically diminished the enthusiasm of the military for instituting insurrections against the government.

Plutarco Calles, president from 1924 to 1928 and behind-the-scenes ruler until 1934, continued the work of deemphasizing the military that Obregón had so successfully begun. General Joaquín Amaro, a dedicated professional officer, was made secretary of war, "to transform Mexico's semi-feudal Army into a truly national body."

Initially, General Amaro shrewdly avoided a direct challenge to the powerful revolutionary generals whom he aimed eventually to break. Instead, he concentrated mainly on winning over the other military elements in the Army. More of the younger officers were sent abroad for training, and upon their return to Mexico were used to build up an efficient

---

[41] *Ibid.*, p. 63.
[42] Lieuwen, *op. cit.*, p. 110.

staff. In addition to advanced training, emphasis was placed on loyalty to the military profession and to the nation. For President Calles was convinced that loyalty and national pride were the ultimate cures for the country's persistent militarism.[43]

In addition to bettering the training and career opportunities of the younger officers, President Calles and his able secretary of war were very concerned with the men in the ranks. To win them over, President Calles saw that they were given better uniforms, better food and barracks, as well as better equipment.

With the morale of the rank and file thus greatly improved and the younger officers favorably disposed, President Calles and General Amaro were now ready to tackle the old revolutionary generals. Accordingly, they deliberately launched the policy of shifting military commands, a radical change that was shrewdly calculated to provoke the generals. It had long been customary for a general to regard his troops as his very own, in effect belonging to him. He had recruited, trained, and equipped them; they were as much a part of his military prerogatives as were his title, decorations, and emoluments—so much so that he always expected to move only with his own troops. In fact, it was unthinkable that he be transferred to command a strange new outfit that owed him no personal loyalty whatever.[44]

The administration's intentionally provocative move encountered vehement resistance, just as Calles and Amaro had expected. But they were fully prepared for it. Assured of the loyalty of the younger officers and of the men in the ranks, they effectively crushed the two uprisings that occurred, the first in 1927 and the second in 1929, dismissing the errant generals. This time the civilian leaders were so sure of themselves that they did not bother to shoot the military insurrectionists.

With militarism reeling from these body blows, General Lázaro Cárdenas, president from 1934 to 1940, succeeded in delivering still other telling punches. Realizing that the remaining revolutionary generals had become large landowners and big businessmen who would naturally oppose his radically new land and labor reforms, President Cárdenas determined to build up other forces which could counteract and defeat any pressure that these generals might exert. Confident that the landless peons were sold on his land reform program and that he could count on their loyalty, Cárdenas equipped them with weapons and organized them into powerful army reserves. In like fashion, he organized into an independent labor militia the mass of workers benefiting from his regime's social reforms.[45]

Still other measures were taken to establish the Army as a professional, nonpolitical career. Beginning in 1936, competitive examinations were

---

[43] *Ibid.*, pp. 110–11.
[44] Tannenbaum, *Mexico: The Struggle for Peace and Bread,* op. cit., p. 91.
[45] Lieuwen, *op. cit.,* p. 113.

required for the promotion of all officers, and the following year it became unlawful for them to have a civilian occupation. This emphasis on professionalism was accompanied by rigid restrictions on the political activities of all military personnel. They were prohibited from participating in public political activities of any kind, whether meetings, discussions, or public expressions of their opinion. Moreover, the officers were specifically forbidden to exercise any political influence whatever over their subordinates.[46]

President Cárdenas, in addition to arming the agrarian and labor groups, promoting professionalism, and forbidding political activity, gave another mighty punch to militarism by his reorganization of the Revolutionary Party in December, 1937. The new federated party, as reorganized, was composed of four equal groups; labor, peasant, popular, and military. Under this new arrangement the Army could always be outvoted and its political strength could be nullified by pitting the other three forces against it. When President Cárdenas was soundly criticized by some for allegedly bringing the Army into politics, his retort was shrewdly to the point: "We did not put the army in politics," he said, "it was already there. In fact, it had been dominating the situation, and we did well to reduce its influence to one vote out of four."[47]

In 1940, after less than three years of existence, the military sector was dissolved. This did not mean that the Army was completely divorced from politics but that henceforth its influence, still strong though less obvious, would be exerted through the Popular sector of the party.[48]

Curbing the nation's erstwhile unrestrained militarism has proved to be one of the most beneficial reforms accomplished by the Mexican social revolution. No longer are the military a serious drag on the economy, consuming a disproportionate share of the national budget, as is unfortunately the case in most of the other Latin-American countries. The size of the Army—about 50,000 men—has been purposefully kept small in comparison to the size of the rest of the population. And it is allocated only about 12 percent of the national budget—one of the smallest proportions in all Latin America. Precious national revenues, seemingly always too meager for the nation's burgeoning needs, can now be beneficially used for building roads or hospitals, financing schools or literacy campaigns, rather than squandered on a bloated, parasitic, unneeded military machine.

No longer does the military interfere in politics either, overturning or threatening to overturn the government at will. Instead, civilian officials, now firmly in control, run the government and decide national policy

---

[46] *Ibid.*, p. 118.

[47] *Ibid.*, p. 114.

[48] Robert E. Scott, *Mexican Government in Transition* (Urbana, Ill.: University of Illinois Press, 1959), pp. 133–34; and William P. Tucker, *The Mexican Government Today* (Minneapolis: University of Minnesota Press, 1957), pp. 43 and 193.

without interference from the armed forces, which may be freely over-ridden, even on strictly military issues.[49]

Although the political power of the Army has been effectively curbed, its efficiency and effectiveness have been greatly increased. Its organiza-tion, discipline, and training, all patterned after the armed forces of the United States, have been greatly strengthened, and its leadership now consists of a well-trained, highly professional corps of capable, loyal officers.

Instead of impeding national progress as earlier, the armed forces are now engaged in many constructive activities, including a widespread public works program. They build schools and hospitals, conduct re-forestation and irrigation programs, and help with the maintenance of the nation's road system. All in all, their changed role has been largely responsible for the great progress that Mexico is very proud of.

"For the past generation," says Edwin Lieuwen, "the entire nation, including the armed forces, has been reaping the rewards of this basic political reform and will almost certainly continue to do so. . . . In deal-ing with militarism, Mexico has set an example which other Latin Amer-ican nations might be well advised to follow."[50]

To which conclusion the many friends of Latin America concur in a fervent "Amen."

SUGGESTED READINGS

ALEXANDER, ROBERT J. *The Bolivian National Revolution*, chap. 8. New Bruns-wick, N.J.: Rutgers University Press, 1958.

———. "The Army in Politics," *Government and Politics in Latin America* (ed. HAROLD EUGENE DAVIS), chap. 6. New York: Ronald Press Co., 1958.

———. "Brazilian Tenentismo," *Hispanic American Historical Review*, Vol. XXXVI, No. 2 (May, 1956), pp. 229–42.

ARCINIEGAS, GERMÁN. *The State of Latin America*, chap. xvii. Trans. HARRIET DE ONÍS. New York: Alfred A. Knopf, Inc., 1952.

GRUENING, ERNEST. *Mexico and Its Heritage*, pp. 280–331. New York: D. Ap-pleton-Century Co., Inc., 1934.

HELGUERA, J. LEÓN. "The Changing Role of the Military in Colombia," *Jour-nal of Inter-American Studies*, Vol. III, No. 3 (July, 1961), pp. 351–58.

JOHNSON, JOHN J. *The Military and Society in Latin America*. Stanford, Calif.: Stanford University Press, 1964.

———. (ed.). *The Role of the Military in Underdeveloped Countries*. Princeton, N.J.: Princeton University Press, 1962. Chaps. by VICTOR ALBA, EDWIN LIEUWEN, AND JOHN J. JOHNSON on the Latin American military.

LIEUWEN, EDWIN. *Arms and Politics in Latin America*. Rev. ed. Council on Foreign Relations. New York: Frederick A. Praeger, Inc., 1961.

---

[49] Lieuwen, *op. cit.*, p. 119.
[50] *Ibid.*, p. 121.

————. "The Changing Role of the Military in Latin America," *Journal of Inter-American Studies,* Vol. III, No. 4 (October, 1961), pp. 559–69.

McALISTER, L. N. "Civil-Military Relations in Latin America," *Journal of Inter-American Studies,* Vol. III, No. 3 (July, 1961), pp. 341–50.

POTASH, ROBERT A. "The Changing Role of the Military in Argentina," *Journal of Inter-American Studies,* Vol. III, No. 4 (October, 1961), pp. 571–78.

PREWETT, VIRGINIA. "The Mexican Army," *Foreign Affairs,* April, 1941, pp. 608–20.

SANTOS, EDUARDO. "Latin American Realities," *Foreign Affairs,* Vol. 34, No. 2 (January, 1956), pp. 244–56.

STOKES, WILLIAM S. *Latin American Politics,* chap. 7. New York: Thomas Y. Crowell Co., 1959.

WYCKOFF, THEODORE. "The Role of the Military in Latin American Politics," *Western Political Quarterly,* Vol. XIII, No. 3 (September, 1960), pp. 745–63.

PART III

PROMOTION OF THE
GENERAL WELFARE:
BY EVOLUTION OR REVOLUTION

AGRICULTURE AND LAND REFORM:
The Cry for Land and Its Portent

AGRICULTURE is very important in every nation. In the United States, the farmers like to regard it as the "backbone of the economy." In the 20 Latin American republics, agriculture is of especial significance to the society. It serves primarily, of course, to feed the region's rapidly increasing population, which is leading the field in the world-wide population explosion. Moreover, it provides a livelihood for a large majority of the people, 60 percent or more of whom are engaged in farming for a living,[1] as Figure 8–1 shows by countries. And, as in other underdeveloped nations, it provides most of the capital which the countries must rely on for industrialization. Furthermore, the sale of agricultural products abroad enables the nations to buy the consumer goods which they do not produce themselves and the machines and tools which they must have in order to industrialize.

CONCENTRATION OF OWNERSHIP OF LAND

One of the most distinctive features of agriculture in Latin America is the highly concentrated ownership of land. In fact, a handful of *hacendados*, or large landowners, has controlled a large proportion of the farmland in every one of the nations except Haiti.

The hacienda, known in Argentina as the estancia and in Brazil as the fazenda, was the prevailing pattern of land ownership in most of Latin America until World War I, and in many of the countries it continues today with hardly diminished vigor. According to a United Nations estimate in 1951, only 1.5 percent of the total number of farm properties, averaging more than 15,000 acres each, contained 50 percent of the total agricultural land in the whole region. In Chile, one of the many nations

---

[1] In the United States today, despite its unmanageable agricultural surpluses, only about 12 percent of the population farms for a living.

FIGURE 8-1

PERCENTAGE OF POPULACE ENGAGED IN AGRICULTURE

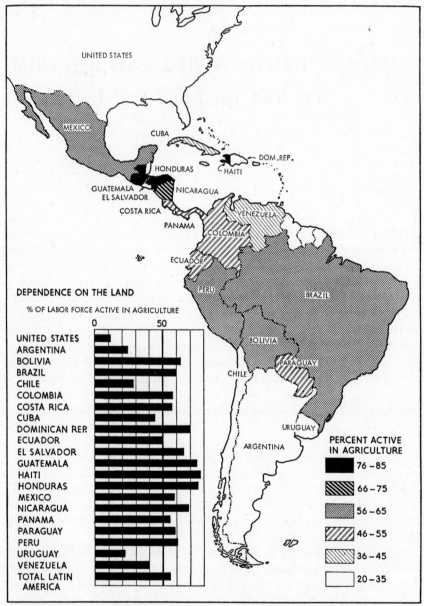

SOURCE: *Center of Intercultural Formation* (CIF) *Study No. 1,* p. 125. Reproduced by permission.

where the *latifundios* still flourish, 1 percent of the landowners control 43 percent of the total farmland. In Bolivia, according to the 1950 census, 4.5 percent of the population owned 70 percent of the total farm acreage.

In Ecuador and Peru, other Andean nations with relatively little developed tillable land, the situation was about the same. Some estimates, however, as Table 8–1 indicates, suggest an even higher degree of concentration.

TABLE 8–1

MINIFUNDIOS AND LATIFUNDIOS

COUNTRY (In order of total area of farmland)	YEAR of census	Percentage of total number of farms		Percentage of total area of farmland	
		less than 5 hectares (12.36 acres)	more than 2,500 hectares (6,177.6 acres)	less than 5 hectares (12.36 acres)	more than 2,500 hectares (6,177.6 acres)
BRAZIL	1960	34.0*	—	1.0*	—
ARGENTINA	1960	15.7	2.6	0.1	59.8
MEXICO	1950	72.6	1.3*	0.9	77.0*
BOLIVIA	1950	59.3	3.8	0.2	81.8
COLOMBIA	1960	62.5	0.1	4.5	20.2
CHILE†	1955	36.9	1.1*	0.3	63.7*
PERU	1961	82.9	0.1	5.2	64.5
URUGUAY†	1961	14.7	1.4	0.2	33.4
CUBA	1952	13.9	—	—	—
ECUADOR	1954	73.1	0.1	7.2	25.9
GUATEMALA	1950	81.0*	0.1	11.0*	27.5
HONDURAS	1952	57.0	0.0	8.1	13.2
NICARAGUA‡	1952	26.0	0.1*	1.5	20.0*
DOMINICAN REPUBLIC	1960	86.3	0.0	—	—
COSTA RICA‡	1955	36.0*	0.1	2.0*	21.0
EL SALVADOR	1961	85.1	0.0	15.0	7.2
PANAMA†	1950	52.0	0.1*	8.3	10.0

— Data not available. 0.0 represents magnitude less than half of the unit employed.
* Estimate.
† Excludes farms of less than 1 hectare.
‡ Excludes farms of less than 0.7 hectare.
SOURCE: *Américas*, November, 1964, p. 47. Reproduced by permission.

Ownership is very concentrated in Argentina, where some 500 or so owners possess 18 percent of the total national farmland. The stranglehold which the small number of *hacendados* exercise over the whole agricultural economy has often been severely criticized. One of its most trenchant critics was Juan Perón. Quite contemptuous of the landed oligarchy, he did not hesitate to castigate it. An attempt had been made, he contended, to mislead the public into believing that the oligarchy, an unruly bunch of demagogues, were the "ruling class in the country, its elite, and as such was made up of wise, rich, and good people. We must observe that 'the wise are seldom rich, and the rich seldom good.' Nor must we forget that neither the wise nor the good found a place among Argentine politicians."[2]

But not even Perón, with his strong dictatorial rule of ten years and his many restrictive measures applying to agriculture, was able to dislodge

---

[2] *Perón Expounds His Doctrine*, trans. Argentine Association of English Culture (Buenos Aires, 1948), p. 49.

the landed oligarchy from their long entrenched position of power. And despite the concern occasionally expressed over large holdings, concentration of ownership of land in the nation is apparently increasing rather than decreasing, squeezing out many of the small farmers.[3]

Concentration of ownership has been especially pronounced in Mexico where, prior to the 1910 revolution, just 1 percent of the population owned 97 percent of the land. Even since the revolution, one of whose major aims was to break up the large landed estates and give land to the landless, a small handful of owners still hold a large proportion of the farmlands. Although the agrarian laws of the nation limit owners to 100 hectares of irrigated land and 200 of nonirrigated land, the agricultural census of 1940 showed that properties of 1,000 hectares or over, constituting only .3 percent of the total number of holdings, comprised 61.9 percent of the whole farmland of the nation. Of these large farms, 301 each had an acreage of more than 40,000 hectares.[4]

TYPES OF LARGE-SCALE AGRICULTURAL ENTERPRISES

Corporate Mechanized Farms

There are two main types of large-scale agricultural enterprises in Latin America. One consists of the relatively new, large mechanized plantations, often referred to as "factories in the field." Usually foreign-owned and foreign-managed, they are models of intensive, scienufic farming, requiring a high decree of managerial and technical skill. Representing a large investment, these efficiency-expert farms use modern methods and machinery, thereby achieving a high level of production.

Relations between management and the labor are on a strictly business basis. On arriving at work, the laborer punches an impersonal time clock, instead of deferentially saying, "Buenos días, patrón," and a scrupulously accurate record of his labor is kept by a timekeeper. The corporation usually provides houses for the workers, also a school, chapel or church, soccer field, clinic for medical assistance, and a system for supplying water and electricity. Many of the workers, migrants from backwoods, rural areas, have grown up under the paternalistic *patrón* system, and have difficulty adjusting to this revolutionary, impersonal economic enterprise.

Haciendas

The old traditional hacienda as it has long existed in Latin America is the very antithesis of this efficient, productive, and impersonal agricultural enterprise. In most cases, the hacienda has been inherited for genera-

---

[3] Felix J. Weil, *Argentine Riddle* (Latin American Economic Institute) (New York: John Day Co., 1944), pp. 93–94.

[4] For statistics regarding the number and size of *latifundios* and *minifundios* in most of the countries, see Joâo Gonçalves de Souza, "Land for the Farmer: Problems of Agrarian Reform in Latin America," *Américas*, Vol. 12, No. 8 (August, 1960), p. 14.

tions, and has long been accustomed to a slow, poky, easygoing way of life. It is never worried about making a return on an investment, since little or no capital has ever been put into it. Its main objective has always been to be as economically self-sufficient as possible, producing on the place everything that is needed there.

The hacienda does not have to worry about labor problems either. The hands on the estate are of a home-grown variety; their ancestors have lived there for generations, sometimes by choice but often because of owing their souls to the plantation store. And quite unlike the businesslike "factory in the field," the hacienda is the essence of paternalism. The *hacendado* is no impersonal labor boss. Rather, he is the *patrón* of all the families who live on his place, giving them help when they need it, chastizing them when he thinks they deserve it, and in general directing their work and life. He is also the godfather to many of the children born on the place, some of whom he may have sired himself while the husband was busy in the field.

Origin of the Haciendas. How did the haciendas originate, you may wonder. We have some large farms in the United States, such as the King Ranch in Texas with its approximately 1 million acres of land; but the great majority of farms in our country are family-sized units, ranging from perhaps a dozen acres or so if the land is to be farmed intensively, such as for growing truck, to several hundred acres if the land is to be used extensively, such as for raising cattle. In Latin America, however, such family-size farms are the exception in most countries.

In Brazil, the fazenda was the result of an ultra generous policy of the Portuguese monarch in making grants of land in the New World. After Portugal's title to the region of what is now Brazil was recognized, the monarch granted all the land from the coast to the line of demarcation to 12 noblemen; but these king-sized grants accomplished very little in the way of encouraging immigration to the area or increasing the revenue which the monarch hoped to receive from the overseas empire. Accordingly, the king later modified the original agreement by designating a viceroy to head the government of Brazil and providing that land would be available to all Portuguese who applied for it, with generous limits to the grants.

As a result of this policy, the fazendas of Brazil tower in size above the other large acreages in Latin America. One *fazendeiro*, or large land-owner, possessed an agrarian domain which was larger than the whole area of the mother country, Portugal. Another huge estate was that owned by the Costa Ferreiras in the vast Amazon region; it was bigger than England, Scotland, and Ireland combined.[5]

Large grants of land were likewise made in Spain's colonial empire,

---

[5] Gilberto Freyre, *The Masters and The Slaves: A Study in the Development of Brazilian Civilization*, trans. Samuel Putnam (2d Eng. ed. rev.; New York: Alfred A. Knopf, Inc., 1956), p. *liv*.

accounting for haciendas which have existed for centuries in most of
the nations. But Argentina's problem of *latifundios* today is of relatively
recent origin, and is the result of a very shortsighted governmental policy.
Latifundismo made a strong beachhead there soon after independence
when the government made large grants of land to individuals and companies in order to add to its short-term income, settle the interior of the
country, and push forward the frontier against the Indians. These large
acreages were granted at very nominal prices, and sometimes without any
charge whatever.

Indeed, the 1826 Act of the Argentine Congress was one of the biggest
giveaways in all the history of Latin America. According to the law,
public lands could be distributed without being put up for sale, with no
restriction at all as to the amount of land any individual could obtain. As a
result of this myopic policy, many speculators were able to grab up huge
acreages, with no thought of farming or developing them, but solely for
holding them for a profit or the personal prestige of the owner. The nation's precious resource of fertile land was further dissipated by Rosas,
who either gave away large acreages of frontier land or sold them for a
ridiculously low price to be paid for in installments and without interest.
Other large tracts were given to military veterans who had participated
in the war of extinction against the Indians. Thanks to these reckless
grants, many an Argentine became a multimillionaire by taking advantage
of shortsighted governmental policies, hogging a large part of the nation's
agricultural wealth, without any work or investment whatever on his
part.

Argentina's policy regarding grants of public land was very different
from that of the United States. Here, the policy was to promote an
agrarian community of small and medium size farmers who owned and
worked their properties; no individual was allowed to bite off more
than he could chew. The Homestead Act of 1862, enacted to reward
veterans who fought in the Union Army, was a milestone in American
history, since free land had long been the ardent goal of many citizens.
But the act was not designed to make agricultural fat cats of speculators
who had no intention of farming. Each veteran was eligible to receive only
up to a quarter section, 160 acres, about enough for a family-sized farm;
and he did not receive full title to it until he had lived on it for five years
and had made certain specified improvements.

In Mexico, the large landed estates began and have continued in quite
a different fashion. As in most of the other Hispanic colonies, large grants
of land were made by the crown. Many such grants were made to the
Church, which by this and other means in time became by far the largest
landowner in Mexico, controlling in some areas an estimated 80 percent
of the land. After independence had been won, many of the secular
latifundistas took advantage of laws or decrees requiring the Church to
sell its vast holdings, often buying valuable properties for a song, properties

which, divided up into small tracts, might well have started the nation on the road to becoming a stable society of small and medium-sized farmers.

Equally as significant were the predatory tactics which the *latifundistas* used against the native Indian communities. Before independence, the Indians were able to look either to the crown or to the Church for protection of the meager ancestral lands which they had somehow managed to preserve. After independence, however, the Indians were completely on their own, without the protection of the clergy or of the government either. In fact, under the guise of liberalism and individual initiative, the *latifundistas* further expanded their holdings by getting possession by one means or another of most of the remaining farmland and woodland which had been recognized for centuries as the propertied heritage of the Indian communities.

In expanding their holdings at the expense of the helpless Indians, they had no scruples against using the most ruthless and savage tactics, when necessary for gaining their ends.

Government and *hacendados* were one. Obstreperous villagers were sentenced to the army by the local judge or *jefe político*, and sent to remote regions as soldier-convicts. Often they never saw their families again. In Hidalgo, when the spokesmen for a pueblo became threatening, they were seized by order of the governing and landowning Cravioto dynasty, and buried to their necks in the center of the *ejido* they were trying to save. Then the *Rurales* [mounted police] galloped over them.[6]

Life at the Hacienda. The *hacendados* and their families, the privileged, aristocratic elite of the society, enjoyed a life of luxury and leisure, as colorful and romantic as that of the ante-bellum plantation owners of the Old South. Lords over all they surveyed, they enjoyed the prestige and fruits of their landed empires.

"Outside the cities," writes Henry Bamford Parkes, "the valleys of central and southern Mexico were dotted with enormous white houses where creole *hacendados* lived in lonely grandeur, owners of estates which might cover hundreds of square miles of mountain and forest and in which grazed herds of oxen which were sometimes numbered by tens of thousands. They spent their days on horseback, hunting and shooting, or supervising the peons who worked in the wheatfields or the sugar plantations; and any traveler who broke in upon their solitude was greeted with a Castilian courtesy and entertained with a bullfight, a picnic with music in the fields, or an exhibition of the skill of the *vaqueros* in throwing their master's cattle."[7]

---

[6] Ernest Gruening, *Mexico and Its Heritage* (New York: D. Appleton-Century Co., Inc., 1934), p. 129. For the "Rape of the Pueblos," as Eyler N. Simpson terms it, see his *The Ejido: Mexico's Way Out* (Chapel Hill, N.C.: University of North Carolina Press, 1937), pp. 29–33.

[7] Henry Bamford Parkes, *A History of Mexico* (3rd ed. rev.: Boston: Houghton Mifflin Co., 1960), p. 117. For colorful accounts of visits to haciendas, see George McCutchen McBride, *Chile: Land and Society* (American Geographical Society Research Series No. 19) (New York, 1936), pp. 3–8 and 47–54.

Separated by many miles of territory from adjoining haciendas, with only rarely used paths connecting them, each hacienda is an isolated, self-sufficient social unit. All of those who live on the place, both the many peons and the residents of the Big House, have to depend on one another for entertainment and pleasure. Sunday is always a big day, when the peons dressed in their Sunday best attend services at the chapel located near the Big House. A christening or wedding or saint's day of the owner or another member of his family is celebrated as a festive holiday that is long remembered. On these occasions, everyone on the place turns out to enjoy the carefree festivities, including dancing to a hot beat and drinking all he can handle, often more.

Such occasions are the highlights the peon likes to remember. But his everyday life is quite different from this; it is a monotonous, humdrum existence of sweat and toil from early sunup to late sundown. He and his family live in a rude hut or shack that usually has only one room, sometimes two, with only the simplest of furnishings: a crude table and several crudely made chairs, a box or trunk for clothing, a chest of drawers, and an iron bedstead or two.

In return for cultivating a small plot of his own and possibly pasturing an animal or two, the peon obligates himself to farm a certain number of hectares, raising such crops as the landlord specifies and on terms which are mutually agreed upon. These agreements vary widely in their terms, as there are many different kinds of land tenure in the whole region.[8] Under the more customary form of agreement, the landowner provides the land, seed, tools, and maybe work animals in return for which the peon raises the crop which is divided between the landlord and himself on a previously agreed upon basis. Usually the peon, as well as members of his family, agree to give a certain number of days of free labor every year, performing such chores as mending fences, rounding up and checking cattle, digging wells, or possibly working in the Big House.

Effects of the Hacienda on Society. The hacienda and the landed aristocracy which it supports have had far-reaching effects on the society, most of them bad. For the most part, the hacienda had been a tremendous obstacle to the economic development of the nations. Because of its agricultural practices, land which is the main natural resource of the region is only partially utilized. Despite the abundance of farm manpower and the need of the region for agricultural products, most of the land is allowed to lie idle. For under the system, there is no incentive—or pressure —for putting all the fertile acres to work. Self-sufficient as the hacienda is, and incurring practically no outside expenses in making a crop, whatever

---

[8] For a summary of the various forms of land tenure in the several nations, see International Labour Office, *The Landless Farmer in Latin America* (Geneva, Switz., 1957), chaps. i–iv. For the forms of tenure in Peru, see Thomas R. Ford, *Man and Land in Peru* (Gainesville, Fla.: University of Florida Press, 1955), chap. 4.

the crop brings when sold on the commercial market is clear profit, which the *hacendado* and his family use to enjoy a very affluent standard of living. In planning his farming program, the *hacendado* is concerned only with this, and not the least bit with the productivity per acre, per worker, or per man-hour employed. Nor does he have any incentive to invest in modern machinery and tools, or to require the workers to use efficient methods for the various farming operations. As a result, the yield of crops raised is usually extremely low per acre or per worker. The absurdly low productivity of the peon compared with that of the worker in other major fields is shown by Figure 8–2.

These poor farming practices are very different from the efficient ones used more than four centuries ago by the Incas. Masters of efficient, productive farming, the Incas used ingenious methods which would put most *hacendados* to shame. Every square foot of tillable soil was cultivated, even the steep slopes by means of the construction of masonry terraces which provided narrow stretches of flat land and kept the soil from eroding. The crops planted there were fertilized by fish and guano and irrigated by an elaborate system of aqueducts which tapped mountain streams far above the agricultural lands and carried their cold, nourishing waters to the intensively cultivated terraces, a sort of staircase system of farming.

In moments of flippancy or exasperation, we sometimes say, "Let's give the country back to the Indians!" In Latin America, a cynic would say that some of the nations might do well to do so.

Besides inefficiency of production and very low yields for the land's potentiality, the hacienda poses another problem because of its concentration on money crops which can be sold on a national or world market. The concentration of effort on such crops has prevented even a semblance of diversified farming. As a result, little or no attempt has been made to raise fruits, vegetables, dairy products, or many other foodstuffs which are sorely needed to feed the population. Consequently, foodstuffs often have to be imported at a heavy cost, although most of the population is engaged in agriculture. Failing to raise the food needed by the populace, the hacienda is mainly responsible for the lack of a balanced diet which plagues most of Latin America and consigns a large part of its populace as expendables to low efficiency, sickness and disease, and an early death.

The hacienda has been a harmful influence on another score. Having helpless and servile labor within its grasp, it has often exploited this labor to the fullest. A low grade of liquor was usually one of the main commodities sold by the store on the hacienda. Sometimes the workers, paid for their labor in wooden or metal tokens good only on the plantation, were required to buy a prescribed minimum amount of the booze, sold at exorbitant prices. Sometimes the workers in the fields were even given a glass of liquor free of charge during their rest period "as a tonic or

FIGURE 8–2

Size of Labor Force and Worker Productivity

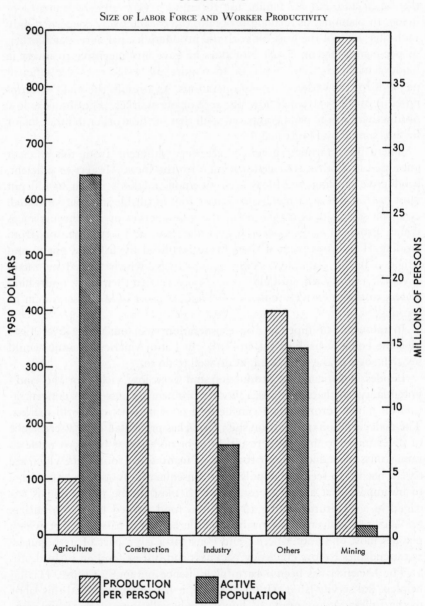

SOURCE: *Center of Intercultural Formation* (CIF) *Study No. 1,* p. 216. Reproduced by permission.

energizer." The coca drug was also sold at plantation stores, part of the wage often being paid in coca leaves. These leaves have a potent effect on the user, anaesthetizing the gustatory and digestive nerves and spurring him to a level of activity that transcends all normal human bounds of endurance. ". . . coca-chewing workers have been found to exert themselves sometimes as much as twenty hours a day over a period of weeks and even months in a state of serious undernourishment."[9]

Sometimes the exploitation of labor was more systematic and complete. In Peru, a descriptive Spanish term, *gamonalismo,* was used to connote the exploitation of Indians. According to Moisés Sáenz, *gamonalismo* was a social attitude and mores which supported

the condition of inequality of the Indian with respect to the other social classes of the country . . . it is colonialism and clericalism projected through a century of independent life; it signifies spoliation . . . the connivance of . . . authorities, clergy, and landholders in exploiting the Indians without conscience and without scruple.[10]

In still another respect, the hacienda has greatly retarded the region's economic development. Although it represents a considerable part of the income and wealth of most of the nations, it contributes very little in the form of taxes for the support of local or national government. As is well known, the tax rates on farm properties are notoriously low throughout Latin America; and sometimes even the ludicrously low taxes which are assessed against the properties are not paid. In Paraguay, 53 percent of the taxes levied on land were delinquent for more than 1 year; 34 percent, for more than 6 years; 14 percent, for more than 11 years; and 8 percent, for more than 21 years. What is especially significant, delinquency in paying taxes on farmland was much more habitual among the large owners than among the small ones.[11]

Furthermore, the hacienda, with its far-flung acres, is a problem for the rest of society because of its very size. Some haciendas would be regarded as inordinately large by any criterion; the Terrazas in the state of Chihuahua, Mexico, owned 30 million acres of land—an estate about the size of the whole state of Mississippi. Of course most *hacendados* own nothing like this much property. But as a group, constituting only 1 or 2 or maybe 3 percent or so of the total landowners, they control most of the cultivable land in the nation. Their tight control handed down from generation to generation has made it impossible for a large number of individuals to own moderately small or medium-sized acreages—a dispersion of ownership which has contributed so importantly to the agricultural economy of many nations.

Indeed one of the worst effects which the *latifundios* have had on the society is the inevitable existence of a great number of *minifundios* or

---

[9] George Soule, David Efron, and Norman T. Ness, *Latin America in the Future World* (National Planning Association) (New York: Farrar & Rinehart, Inc., 1945), p. 27.

For the history of cocaism, its medical and social causes and effects, and legislation on the coca leaf, see International Labour Office, *Indigenous Peoples: Living and Working Conditions of Aboriginal Populations in Independent Countries* (Studies and Reports, New Series, No. 35) (Geneva, Switz., 1953), pp. 153–78.

[10] In Ford, *op. cit.,* p. 111.

[11] Haskell P. Wald, *Taxation of Agricultural Land in Underdeveloped Economies* (Cambridge, Mass.: Harvard University Press, 1959), p. 53.

tiny holdings of land. With a small number of *hacendados* owning most or a disproportionate amount of the land, the relatively small balance had to be shared by a large number of small farmers. The acreage which they possess is absurdly small by comparison—it is but a few acres at most and often far less. In fact, some of these "farms" are so minuscule that they are calculated in terms of so many rows in the field, or maybe just so many square feet of space.

The haciendas with their spacious acreages have done more than corner most of the land—they have also gotten by far the best part of it. As you ride through the countryside, pausing now and then to admire the fertile land and lush crops, you soon realize that the haciendas contain all the rich lands in the valleys, also the acreages on the gentle slopes and low rolling hills, obviously the best land of all. The rest, hardly worth fooling with, usually comprises the *minifundios*, whose owners cling tenaciously to the land. The grade is often so steep that after several seasons of cultivation the topsoil has completely washed away and the owner has to seek a tiny patch elsewhere. As you look at these "farms" high up on the steep mountainside, you wonder how a farmer manages to keep his footing there while growing his crop or harvesting it. He wonders too; sometimes he even has to hold onto a rope in order to keep his balance!

Also on the debit side of the ledger, the hacienda has served to perpetuate servility on the part of a large majority of the populace. In Bolivia, prior to the 1952 social revolution, it was customary and in accordance with the tradition of lordly master and humble servant for the Indians on a hacienda to bend their knees and kiss the hands of the *hacendado*.

The hacienda has done more than perpetuate servility. It has continued to maintain a form of debt slavery which violates the letter and spirit of the constitutions of all the republics. Even within recent years, advertisements have appeared in newspapers telling of a hacienda for sale and specifying how many peons "went along with the place."[12]

Yes, the hacienda is vulnerable on many counts.

Perhaps most serious of all is that it fostered and maintained a social ideal in which the hacendado was the representative type—ideally a superior being possessed of broad acres and numerous servants, dominant, domineering, patronizing, and paternal, with nothing between himself and the peon on the plantation. All other elements in society . . . were looked upon with disdain as a necessary affliction that had at best to be suffered. . . . The hacienda system was thus a major influence in preventing either the democratic or eco-

---

[12] One does not have to go as far away as Latin America to find peonage in recent years. In 1950, the author purchased a plantation in south Georgia, on which he put in a stint of several years of dirt farming. In order to keep some of the tenant families which "went with the place," he had to pay their alleged indebtedness to the seller. When at the end of the first year of farming the tenants not only completely paid up their debts but also had a little money besides, they could hardly believe that for the first time in their lives they were free men—and could really move if they wanted to.

nomic development of Latin America. If Latin America has fallen behind the United States and Western Europe in industrial expansion, politically stable and democratic government and in the growth of an educational system adequate for the present time and present need, much of the fault lies with the hacienda system.[13]

PIECEMEAL ATTEMPTS AT REFORM

Many Latin-American countries, realizing the harm done to their society by the haciendas, have enacted into law a number of changes intended by one means or another to correct the situation. Sometimes a frontal attack was made in an effort to correct the obvious abuses which existed. Thus, in Peru, the Law of Yanaconaje, passed in 1947, provided for written contracts, freedom of the *yanacona* to sell his crop in whichever market he preferred and to trade wherever he chose, and a prohibition against any form of unpaid labor expected to be rendered on the place. If the provisions of the law had been enforced, they would have gone far toward transforming the hacienda in Peru into a modern progressive economic institution. However, only lip service has been given the law, with the result that the hacienda in Peru continues with its four-centuries-old attitude of business as usual.

Another possible means of accomplishing needed reform is the imposition of an adequate and effective tax on land. Such a tax would have many advantages over other forms of revenue[14] and would serve to promote the efficient use of land. "We feel that the most effective method of achieving maximum utilization of land is a system of taxation which would penalize poor use of good land," concluded the World Bank Mission to Colombia. "The important thing is that these evaluations be made and the rate of progression determined in such a way as to provide an immediate and positive incentive to correct a present misuse of the best lands of Colombia, which constitute much of the largest part of the national patrimony."[15] In Colombia, as in many of the other nations, a substantial tax on the lands of rich absentee landowners who now graze cattle on very fertile farmland or simply hold on to it as profitable investment

---

[13] Frank Tannenbaum, "Toward an Appreciation of Latin America," *The United States and Latin America* (ed. Herbert L. Matthews) (The American Assembly) (2d ed.; New York: Columbia University Press, 1963), p. 39.

[14] For these advantages in detail, see Wald, *op. cit.,* pp. 184–85.

Referring to Chile's programs for stimulating subdivision of the land by taxes on farmland, on real income derived from the land, and on inheritance of property, James Becket concludes: "The tax approach sounds better in theory than it works in actuality. The best and simplest measure would be a stiff real-estate tax. This suffers from the same 'political reality' as does the matter of assessments." (James Becket, "Land Reform in Chile," *Journal of Inter-American Studies,* Vol. V, No. 2 [April, 1963], pp. 202–3.)

[15] International Bank for Reconstruction and Development, *The Basis of a Development Program for Colombia: Report of a Mission* (Washington, D.C., 1950), pp. 384–86.

would force them either to utilize their land fully by planting it in crops or to sell the land to farmers or to the government for distribution to peasants.

Such proposals for the effective taxation of land, both to obtain needed governmental revenue and to promote efficient use of the land, have been made so often as to sound like a record with the needle continuing to grind away in the same groove.[16] For the oligarchy with their great power have always been able somehow to thwart the levy of such a tax.

Still another means of at least partially remedying the great concentration of ownership in a few hands is for the government itself to undertake a program of purchasing farmlands from the *hacendados* and reselling them in small parcels to eager would-be owners. Many such programs have been instituted in Latin America, usually without any opposition from the *hacendados*. In fact, from the outcome of the programs, you would suspect that they were the very ones who initiated them. For the land was usually sold to the government at exorbitant prices, which were passed on to the unsuspecting dirt farmers who purchased the small parcels. When they were unable to meet the high payments necessitated by speculative, jacked-up prices, they had to give up their properties, along with all improvements which had been made. The improved property reverted back to the *hacendado*, who gained handsomely by both of the transactions.[17]

Still another method of reform intended to improve agriculture and provide more land for the landless is colonization. Every one of the nations has had at least one colonization scheme of some sort. Sometimes the plan provides for bringing in skilled farmers from abroad to increase the nation's agricultural output and to set up model farms with modern methods and machinery to serve as examples for the rest of the farming populace. Thus, in Bolivia, a colony of Okinawans, established in the fertile Santa Cruz area, operates in effect model experimental farms which can be of great help to native farmers. Another plan for colonizing a part of the national farmland with farmers brought in from abroad is the arrangement made by Paraguay with the Japan Overseas Immigration Promotion Company. Under this plan, the company has purchased several large acreages of land and has brought in many Japanese families to farm it.

Most of the colonization projects, however, were designed for quite a different purpose—to provide land for small native farmers by opening up new areas of farmland. Although often boldly conceived, these projects

---

[16] A conference on fiscal policy which may be very fruitful, however, was held at Santiago, Chile, in December 1962, under the auspices of the Joint Tax Program of the Organization of American States, Inter-American Development Bank, and Economic Commission for Latin America. For a summary of the problems of tax reform considered and the conclusions reached, see *Economic Bulletin for Latin America* (UNESCO), Vol. 8, No. 1 (March, 1963), pp. 89–94.

[17] Soule *et al.*, *op. cit.*, pp. 78–79.

have usually failed to provide land for many new farmers or to increase perceptibly the total agricultural output of the nation. As one studies these projects, the reasons for their failure are soon obvious. Sometimes the projects are merely sops to the vociferous demands of idealistic visionaries. For the most part, however, the projects are simply diversionary tactics promoted by the landed powers that be for taking the heat off the haciendas and appearing to give a sincere solution to the widespread popular demand for land to be distributed among many small farmers. In effect, most colonization projects merely brush off the region-wide problem of the intense yearning for land felt by tens of millions of farm laborers who sweat out their whole lives toiling on the land all for the benefit of the affluent *hacendado*.

As diversionary tactics, the colonization projects have achieved a calculated measure of success in forestalling basic changes, even when they were complete flops. In their real impact on the great landless society, however, they have usually been a mere "spit in the bucket" as far as the big problem of equitable land distribution is concerned.

THE CRY FOR LAND: ITS REVOLUTIONARY SIGNIFICANCE

As a result of the many harmful effects on society of the haciendas and the inflexible determination of their owners to maintain their vested interests at all costs, a revolutionary ferment exists throughout most of Latin America today. This is the "cry for land" whose ominous rumblings of discontent are jarring many nations and threatening to turn their societies upside down. Heedless of these warnings, however, the vested interests appear determined to maintain their long privileged positions, scarcely deigning to yield an inch. They are convinced that "it cannot happen here."

But it has happened in several of the countries whose masses got tired of paper constitutions and laws, empty promises of politicians, and diversionary tactics designed to mislead them. To date, three of the republics have had to resort to social revolution to achieve their democratic ideals and give all citizens an equal opportunity under the law.

Mexico, Bolivia, and Cuba have undergone the excruciating ordeal of social revolution in order to achieve a more democratic society. In every one of these nations, and in Guatemala as well, where an abortive social revolution did not succeed, land reform was the primary goal. Agricultural specialists in the United States and elsewhere may differ as to the exact meaning of land reform; does it mean simply providing the peasant with land of his own, or does it mean also furnishing him with many auxiliary services, such as agricultural credit, technical advice, marketing facilities, and many other forms of governmental assistance which would greatly help the new landowner? The concept of land reform may be "a

Courtesy of Yardley and *The Baltimore Sun*

"He's not the biggest threat to this Hemisphere, señor!"

semantically intriguing topic" to the agricultural specialist,[18] but to the simple peasant in Latin America land reform means *just one thing*—a few acres of ground that he can really call his own.

The "cry for land" and need for agrarian reform were largely responsible for the revolutionary ferment which completely destroyed the existing social order and culminated in the radical agrarian reform programs of Mexico, Bolivia, and Cuba. Speaking of Bolivia's social revolution which began in 1952, Robert Alexander says: "Agrarian reform is the cornerstone of the National Revolution. Social justice demanded it. Economic development was impossible without it. Advance toward a democratic society was inconceivable until it had been accomplished. Bolivia would not truly be a modern nation until agrarian reform had been achieved."[19]

---

[18] For the different opinions as to what land reform means, see Roland R. Renne, *Land Economics: Principles, Problems, and Policies in Utilizing Land Resources* (rev. ed.; New York: Harper & Bros., 1958), p. 559; and Thomas F. Carroll, "The Land Reform Issue in Latin America," *Latin American Issues: Essays and Comments* (ed. Albert O. Hirschman) (New York: Twentieth Century Fund, 1961), p. 162.

[19] Robert L. Alexander, *The Bolivian National Revolution* (New Brunswick, N.J.: Rutgers University Press, 1958), p. 57.

MEXICO'S REVOLUTIONARY PROGRAM
OF LAND REFORM

Breaking up the haciendas and distributing their large acreages to many small farmers were two of the major objectives of Mexico's social revolution which began in 1910. Seeking to advance these basic goals, the Constitution of 1917 established radically new norms and concepts regarding land. According to Article 27 of the constitution, the ownership of land is vested originally in the nation, which alone has the power to grant titles to private persons, thereby constituting private property. But in constituting this private property, the nation had the right to impose certain limitations upon it in the public interest. And to serve this interest, the large landed estates might be divided up to provide small holdings for many landless farmers.

The idea that the title to all land was originally vested in the nation, which could freely exercise its power of expropriation in order to promote the public interest, was a radically new concept of property. In establishing this norm, Mexico was blazing the trail for other social revolutions; its own revolution was already seven years old when the more renowned Russian Revolution began.

In Mexico's pioneering venture, most of its program was indeed freewheeling. For the "Mexican Revolution had no prophet and no body of positive theory; it was obliged to formulate its own ideology and its own program as it went along, a halting, fumbling, misdirected series of experiments. . . ."[20]

The lands expropriated from the *hacendados* were utilized in a unique fashion. They were not granted to individuals as private property which they could control and dispose of as they saw fit. Rather, the land was distributed by the government to small agrarian communities known as *ejidos* whose populations might vary from less than 100 inhabitants to several thousand. The land which the *ejido* possesses may be farmed either as a collective enterprise or as small individual plots.

The collective *ejidos*, which constitute only about 5 percent or less of the total number, are located in the fertile cotton land of the La Laguna region, in the rice-growing country of Lombardia and Nueva Italia, and in the henequen plantations on the Yucatán peninsula. The lands given to these collectives are among the most fertile in the entire nation. Most of these lands formerly belonged to the more progressive *hacendados*, who farmed the properties by means of machinery and modern methods, and accounted for much of the commercial production in the nation. In expropriating these properties, the government wisely decided that they should be collectively owned and farmed, in order to retain most of the

---

[20] Carleton Beals, *Mexican Maze* (Philadelphia: J. P. Lippincott Co., 1931), p. 45.

advantages which the units had enjoyed by virtue of their large scale operations.

In these collectives, a careful daily record is kept of the work that each member of the group performs, and he is paid for this at the end of every week in accordance with an established wage scale.[21] This payment is really not a wage or salary, but rather an advance against his total contribution for the year as a member of the cooperative. At the end of the year, when the books are balanced and closed, he may receive another payment as his share of the profits.

The cooperative *ejidos* have certain distinct advantages and disadvantages as compared with the individually owned plots. On the plus side, they use modern farm machinery which would be uneconomical on small tracts; utilize the skills and aptitudes of the *ejidatarios* as managers, mechanics, bookkeepers, or tractor operators, rewarding each individual according to his contribution; make possible the rotation and specialization of crops; temporarily withhold products from the market when advisable to obtain a better price; establish a uniform quality for their products, thereby obtaining a better price; develop supplementary enterprises which can provide employment during slack seasons; and provide various types of social services for their members, including social security for widows and disabled members of the group.

The cooperatives have some recognized disadvantages too, the most important of which are the lack of adequately trained local leaders, the lack of discipline on the part of members, and the longing on the part of many members for a plot of their own to work as they please.[22]

In contrast to these cooperative "one for all and all for one" ventures, approximately 95 percent of the *ejidos* provide for parceling of their total allotment into small plots which the individual farmer or *ejidatario* cultivates and manages pretty much as his own. He does not really own the land, but rather has a "use title" to it. Thus, he can will it to an heir, but he cannot sell, lease, rent, mortgage, or alienate the land in any way. About the only way in which he can lose the title to his land is by not working it for two years.

Each *ejido* is supervised in general by the Ministry of Agriculture, the Agrarian Department, and the National Ejido Bank, and enjoys a large measure of self-government. Its general assembly, which usually meets once a month, comprises all members of the group and is authorized to discuss and decide various matters of interest to them. The day-to-day management of the business of the *ejido* is vested in an executive com-

---

[21] For an explanation of the working arrangements made in the *ejidos* in the La Laguna region, see Clarence Senior, *Land Reform and Democracy* (Gainesville, Fla.: University of Florida Press, 1958), pp. 96–98 and 112–16.

[22] Nathan L. Whetten, *Rural Mexico* (Chicago: University of Chicago Press, 1948), pp. 211–14. For an assessment of how well the collective *ejidos* of La Laguna have accomplished their purposes, see Senior, *op. cit.*, pp. 185–212.

mittee made up of three members and three alternates elected by the assembly for a term of three years. Still another body, the vigilance committee, is charged with the duty of checking on the activities of the executive committee to see that they conform to the regulations of the Agrarian Code and that the decisions of the general assembly are carried out.[23]

A presidential decree of October 6, 1936, established certain procedures and requirements for expropriating land for *ejidos*. In order to obtain a grant of land from the government, at least 20 persons must join together and apply for it. If their application was successful, they would receive a grant amounting to approximately four hectares, or ten acres, per person. In order to be eligible to receive land, a peasant must have worked for at least six months in the region and live within seven kilometers (approximately four and one-third miles) of the property to be expropriated.

The owner of the land to be expropriated was allowed to retain as inalienable private property a minimum of 150 hectares, or approximately 370 acres. Moreover, he had the privilege of deciding exactly which land he chose to retain. As a result of this provision of the law, the land of an *ejido* was the "leavings" and usually was divided into various scattered tracts.[24]

As regards payment, the law provided that any property expropriated would be paid for at its assessed valuation plus 10 percent, with payment to be made in the form of agrarian bonds. In shrewdly deciding upon the assessed valuation of properties as the basis for payment, the government could buy many a hacienda for virtually a song—confiscation, some would regard it.

But a song was all the property was worth according to the self-declared valuation of *hacendados* who had lived off the fat of the land for generations but had contributed very little to society in the form of taxes. In the case of the *ejidos* of La Laguna, the owners of expropriated lands were paid for improvements to their property, such as wells and warehouses, in ten annual installments which totaled 10,566,000 pesos ($2,893,-150). But the owners chose not to take agrarian bonds as payment for the land itself, figuring that by accepting such bonds they would compromise their claims against the government.[25]

Payment for expropriated properties on the basis of assessed valuations was pretty rough on the *hacendados*, but it might have been worse. From the viewpoint of many a peasant the land returned him by the government was simply a matter of restitution, since it had earlier been stolen from him or his ancestors. Indeed, according to one sympathizer, the gentlemanly

---

[23] For a detailed discussion of the organization of the *ejido* and the supervision exercised over it, see Whetten, *op. cit.*, pp. 187–200.

[24] For maps showing how land of some of the *ejidos* is distributed, see Senior, *op. cit.*, p. 92, and Whetten, *op. cit.*, p. 183.

[25] Senior, *op. cit.*, pp. 93–94.

nature of the revolution was proved by the fact that no compensation was demanded from the *hacendados* for their long use of the land![26]

Progress in accomplishing land reform, as well as the other revolutionary goals which the society aspired to achieve, was dearly paid for. The tremendous cost in fratricidal bloodletting and insensate destruction paralyzed the nation for more than a decade.

It was a hard, and often bloody, struggle all through the twenties and early thirties. Landlords were recalcitrant; the peons and their representatives were often hoodwinked; sometimes the peons were patient, but generally they were adamant that they receive land; laws were not clear, and were constantly being changed; the courts often sided with the landowners almost regardless of how the laws were drafted. The struggle shifted from battlefields to government offices and courtrooms. Two systems of social values were locked in a death struggle.[27]

Faced with an intransigent opposition and forced to battle for any gain, however slight, which was made, the government was able to make only slow and laborious progress in land reform during most of two decades, as Table 8–2 shows.

TABLE 8–2

LAND DISTRIBUTION IN MEXICO: 1916–64

Period	Number of Hectares* Distributed (thousands)		Number of Persons Receiving Land (thousands)	
	Total	Average per year	Total	Average per year
1916–34	7,800	410	783	41
1935–40	17,900	2,982	815	136
1941–58	17,800	988	800	44
1959–64	16,000	2,666	760	127
Total	59,500	1,214	3,158	65

* One hectare = 2.47 acres.

SOURCE: Compiled from James G. Maddox, "Mexican Agrarian Reform," *American Universities Field Staff Reports Service* (July, 1957); Howard F. Cline, *Mexico: Revolution to Evolution: 1940–1960* (Royal Institute of International Affairs) (New York: Oxford University Press, 1962), pp. 213–14; and state of the union messages of the presidents. Used by permission.

Until Lázaro Cárdenas became president in 1934, the program of land redistribution merely limped along, doing well to keep going at all. There were many reasons for this. Without question the main reason was the determination of landowners to fight their cases in court to the bitter end, using the writ of *amparo* and every other legal weapon at their disposal. A large majority of the disputes were actually decided in favor of the *hacendados*. But whether the court's action was favorable or unfavorable, it delayed the execution of the law, often for many years.

---

[26] *Ibid.*, p. 25.

[27] James G. Maddox, "Mexican Agrarian Reform," *American Universities Field Staff Reports Service* (July, 1957), p. 22.

In 1929, however, the Supreme Court changed its mind regarding the agrarian disputes. In rapid-fire order, it rendered five decisions which ruled adversely against the *hacendados*, thereby dealing them a severe blow. These five decisions established a precedent in Mexican judicial practice which was as binding on future actions as a decision handed down by the Supreme Court of the United States.[28] In effect, the Mexican Supreme Court established a self-denying principle that cases involving agrarian reform were not to be subject to judicial review, but were to be decided by administrative discretion without right of appeal to the courts, except for issues of evaluation and compensation.

This action by the court, together with President Cárdenas' zeal for stepping up the tempo of land reform, served to increase greatly the number of properties which were expropriated and distributed in small acreages to the peasants. In fact, during Cárdenas' term of six years, more than twice as many hectares of land were distributed to peasants as during the whole preceding 18-year period. After 1940, however, the distribution of land again proceeded at a slow tempo.

Governmental policy was primarily to blame for this, although there were extenuating circumstances. There was hardly enough land to go around. Mexico is one of the most mountainous countries in the world; a large proportion of its area is either too steep to farm or is intensely hot and arid or stifling and humid. Consequently, only about 10 percent of the land is arable, as compared with more than 50 percent in the United States. The tempo of redistribution was again greatly speeded up under the administration of President López Mateos, 1958–64. Most of the land distributed during these years was in new agricultural areas opened up by the government.

During the first two decades of the nation's land reform program, it was a highly controversial issue and constantly under fire.[29] Within the past two decades, however, the *ejidos*, the basis of agrarian reform, have become such a revered part of the revolution as to be politically sacrosanct. In 1954, however, a great debate as to their value erupted when Professor Antonio Díaz Soto y Gama declared that the *ejidal* system of land tenure should be scrapped. All *ejidatarios* except the most primitive Indians should be converted to small landowners with the right to use and dispose of their land individually as they saw fit. The *ejido* was not working well for the whites or mestizos, he charged, and only the isolated, backward Indians who "need state protection against their own irresponsibility" should have to continue under the *ejido* system. Professor Díaz' criticisms of the *ejido* were a bombshell, for he had been very active in promoting

---

[28] Simpson, *op. cit.*, pp. 118–20.

[29] For the many criticisms made of the laws enacted and procedures followed in carrying out the agrarian reform, also the changes made to meet these criticisms, see Frank Tannenbaum, *The Mexican Agrarian Revolution* (Washington, D.C.: The Brookings Institution, 1930), chap. x.

land reform from the early days of the revolution, and had even helped design the *ejidal* system under which the lands distributed were held communally instead of individually.

Among those who sided with Professor Díaz was José Vasconcelos, former minister of education and a renowned philosopher. "The case is as clear as water," he said. "The *ejido* has been effective politically because it organizes farmers behind the government party, but it has been disastrous economically as thousands of *braceros* who left not only their land but their country have shown."[30]

As these and many other critics realized, the *ejidos*, certainly those farmed in individual plots, can hardly be regarded as a success from a strictly economic point of view. The hundreds of thousands of small land units have contributed practically nothing to the nation's economy; in fact, they have not even pulled their own weight by growing sufficient food for the *ejidatarios* themselves. Indeed, many of them have turned out to be simply part-time farmers, depending on work off the place for much of their livelihood. Others migrate annually to the United States for seasonal farm work, entering the country legally or sometimes slipping across the river as wetbacks. Many others have moved to the city, giving up their claims to their parcels.

Proponents of the *ejido* have rushed to its defense. Instead of being abolished, they maintain, it should be strengthened and its deficiencies remedied. The poverty of *ejidatarios* and their low productivity, they contend, are no fault of the system of landholding, but are the result of inadequate credit,[31] the lack of education, and too small acreages to farm.

It is the fervent conviction of its partisans that the *ejido* has contributed greatly to Mexico's progress. The guaranteed possession of even a modest acreage afforded the humblest peons a measure of independence and security which they had never enjoyed before and could not otherwise be sure of. Moreover, their participation in the discussions and decisions of the *ejidal* assemblies, as well as possibly serving on one of the two main committees, was grass-roots training in responsible citizenship—a far cry from their servile days under the *hacendados*.[32]

Whatever decisions are made regarding the future of the *ejidos*, the government has for the past two decades wisely followed the policy of not putting all of its eggs in one basket. It is continuing to distribute land to many landless farmers, but in such a way as to benefit by its past mistakes.

---

[30] *New York Times,* March 10, 1954, p. 11, col. 1.

[31] Some of them are able to obtain loans from official banks at interest rates of 6 to 8 percent per annum; some of them obtain credit from private banks which charge 12 percent. But more than half of them have to depend for credit on private lenders whose rates run from 120 to 240 percent per year. (Senior, *op. cit.,* p. 29.)

[32] For the participation of the *ejidatarios* in the self-government of La Laguna *ejidos*, see *ibid.,* pp. 86–87, 131–32, and 185–87. For an assessment of the Laguna experiment in terms of the goals of democracy, see pp. 185–212.

As a means of preventing future *minifundios*, the size of grants made by the government has been considerably increased. In December, 1949, the Agrarian Code was amended to establish a minimum size of 25 acres of irrigated land or approximately 50 acres of other land.

Besides aiding small farmers, the Mexican government has also been paying particular attention to the individual landowners who constitute the private agricultural sector of the economy. It is this group which produces most of the foodstuffs for market. To assure them of secure ownership of their properties, changes were made in the Agrarian Code in 1949 which provided that private holdings would be given legal protection by being granted certificates of "inaffectibility" which exempted them from future expropriation. In accordance with this policy, most of the land that is now being granted to the landless comes from publicly owned lands instead of expropriated haciendas as formerly. In order to obtain the large amount of land needed for distribution, the government has aggressively promoted colonization in new areas of the nation. As of 1958, there were more than 900 such colonies, farming more than 16 million acres of land. In fact, the nation's program of colonization is unquestionably one of the most successful in Latin America.

Furthermore, while the government has apparently been neglecting the *ejidos* as regards credit and other forms of assistance which certainly would have helped them, it has by no means neglected agriculture generally. Rather, it has been channeling most of its limited resources to aid the large private farms on which the nation so critically depends. These commercial farms have been helped in every way possible: by a greatly expanded governmental program of irrigation, by whatever assistance was needed in obtaining the most modern equipment, adequate fertilizer, and improved varieties of seed. This policy of aiding and encouraging the private sector has paid off well. Between 1945 and 1957, agricultural production more than doubled while the population grew by only 40 percent.[33]

In conclusion, despite its many mistakes and shortcomings, Mexico's revolutionary program of land reform is primarily responsible for the striking progress which the nation has made. As James G. Maddox well expresses it:

. . . most of the available evidence points toward the conclusion that Mexico has made giant strides in becoming a united nation, in speeding up economic, social and political development, and in raising the levels of living of at least 95 per cent of her people, *precisely because* of her Revolution. Moreover, land reform was the single most important ingredient of the Mexican Revolution, and it is quite probable that its other component parts, such as a national pro-

---

[33] For the nation's noteworthy progress in agriculture, see Oscar Lewis, "Mexico Since Cárdenas," *Social Change in Latin America Today* (Council on Foreign Relations) (New York: Harper & Bros., 1960), pp. 312–19.

gram of public education, the building of a national highway system, the
fostering of an organized labor movement, and heavy emphasis on industrializing the country, would not have gone forward with anything like the speed
that they have, if there had not been a redistribution of the land.[34]

BOLIVIA'S REVOLUTIONARY PROGRAM
OF LAND REFORM

Bolivia was the second nation in Latin America to tackle the thorny
problem of land reform as one of the goals in a sweeping social revolution. The experiment was indeed a "bold one," observed John Lindberg.
"Nevertheless . . . it appears to be the least dogmatic and one of the
most flexible attempts so far tried in the solution of basic problems of
economic growth under modern conditions. It should be carefully
watched by all those who are concerned with the development of sub-
standard areas."[35]

The program of land reform adopted by the new revolutionary regime
was a relatively moderate one. The MNR, then in the driver's seat as a
result of the April 1952 revolution, could hardly have undertaken any
other kind of program. For it was no tightly knit, cohesive party, but
rather a loose coalition of groups with the most divergent interests and
goals. Indeed, its various groups with their clashing ideologies made southern and northern Democrats look like bosom pals. The left wing of the
party advocated an extreme program of agrarian reform; the right wing,
on the other hand, opposed any real reform whatever. Caught in the
middle were the moderates, led by such middle of the roaders as President
Victor Paz Estenssoro and Vice-President Hernán Siles. Split wide open
on the issue of what kind of land reform to adopt, the new regime stalled
for time. Meanwhile, landless peasants around Cochabamba took matters
into their own hands, seizing farms by force and keeping the properties,
livestock, and equipment as their own. Goaded into immediate action, the
president hastily appointed the Agrarian Reform Commission, giving it
only 120 days in which to study the land problem and draft a comprehensive program of reform.[36]

The Agrarian Reform Law promulgated on August 2, 1953, was a milestone in the nation's history, and determined much of its later policy and
action. "Law Number 03464," says Eduardo Palomo, referring to the new
agrarian law, ". . . in its magnitude and historic importance can only
compare with the Proclamation of Independence in 1825. Actually it

---

[34] Maddox, op. cit., p. 22.

[35] John Lindberg, "Bolivia: Mines Without Industry," Current History, Vol. 22
(March, 1952), p. 149.

[36] For the decree which created the commission, the general plan for its study of
agrarian reform, the report to the president, the text of Decree Law 03464 and Decree
Law 03471 which created the National Service of Agrarian Reform, see Revista
Juridica (Organo Oficial de la Facultad de Derecho, Universidad de Cochabamba)
Cochabamba, Bolivia: (Imprenta Universitaria, 1953), Año XVII, Nos. 63–66.

represented the liberation of more than 2 million human beings from a state of semi-slavery."[37]

The moderate tone of Bolivia's land reform is also shown by the method used to obtain land from the large landowners to distribute among the landless peons. For obtaining the needed land, the government decided upon a policy of expropriation rather than one of confiscation which the left wing of the party strongly advocated. Any land taken for redistribution would be paid for at its assessed tax valuation by bonds which would mature in 25 years and bear interest at 2 percent per annum. The bonds would have two kinds of collateral: a mortgage on the land which the peasant received, as well as a lien on his cattle, crops, and farming equipment; and the guarantee of the government that the bonds would be honored.

The program of land redistribution was not intended to be a national giveaway. Payment for lands expropriated would not be a burden on the government, but would be borne by those who received the land. This requirement in itself was a radical departure from earlier programs of land reform in Latin America. A peasant who received land expropriated by the government would pay for it over a maximum period of 25 years. He would make his payments semiannually, and if he missed making four payments, his land would automatically revert to the government, which might then grant it to another individual.

The strict requirements for repayment by grantees of land were a matter of serious concern to some who helped formulate the land reform program. In their opinion, 25 years to pay for land was regarded as a very short period, especially in view of the many serious hazards which Bolivian farmers face. Indeed, the stringent provisions for repayment could burden the state with unpaid-for lands, thus defeating the very purpose of the program, since the government might have to decree a moratorium to relieve farmers in distress, thereby setting a potentially dangerous precedent.[38]

The ensuing inflation which engulfed Bolivia benefited all debtors, who could easily pay off their debts in the highly inflated currency. To compensate for this trend, the government decreed in the early days of the land reform program that former owners would be paid on the basis of five times the assessed valuation of their property. But as inflation skyrocketed, no further efforts were made to equate the value of expropriated properties with that of the *boliviano*.

Still another feature of the nation's agrarian reform which shows its essentially moderate character is the status of farmlands after redistribu-

---

[37] "Agrarian Reform," by Eduardo Palomo, Associate Director, Servicio Agrícola Interamericano, in collaboration with Eugene C. Reichard and Clifford Belcher (La Paz, Bolivia, January 20, 1961), p. 2.

[38] Edmundo Flores, "Land Reform in Bolivia," *Land Economics*, Vol. 30, No. 1 (February, 1954), pp. 122–23.

tion. Charting a course different from that of earlier programs of reform, Bolivia distributed land to the peons to be owned as private property, except in the case of communal land which was restored to the Indians under the age-old pattern of common ownership and control.

"Before drawing up this law," said Dr. Ñuflo Chávez, the minister of rural affairs, "we made a careful study with the help of United Nations experts because we wanted to avoid the mistakes made in Mexico and Guatemala. In Mexico, peasants were given the communal use of land, but not the title to it. In Guatemala the government became the landlord. Under our law the peasant becomes the owner, except where groups of Indians preferred communal ownership."[39]

The various safeguards established by the government to protect the rights of landowners and assure that any expropriation would be made in accordance with law further attest to the moderate nature of the reform program. Any landowner who desired to contest the expropriation of his property would have four opportunities to do so: to the topographer who made the survey, and thus possibly have the survey invalidated; to the local agrarian board, as to how much of his land, if any, would be expropriated and how it should be divided; to the National Agrarian Council, to review these same issues; and even to the president himself. Most of the landowners whose properties were affected took full advantage of their right to appeal. As a result, many cases lingered on for years until they were finally disposed of—a painful revolutionary concession to legality.

In its day-to-day operations, the agrarian reform program has shown various weaknesses of administration. Intending to remove the program as far as possible from political pressure, the government early established the *Servicio Agrario*, or Land Reform Organization, and put it under competent professional leadership. Eduardo Arce, who was made head of the body, was a qualified technician and not even a member of the MNR. Moreover, his assistant, Edmundo Flores, was a Mexican and a member of the American Technical Aid Mission.

But as was perhaps inevitable in the revolutionary society, political considerations have influenced the administration of the program. The lands of persons who belonged to the MNR or were sympathetic to it were apt to be regarded as inviolate and exempt from the provisions of the expropriation law, however large their estates might be. But the lands of political opponents of the regime were likely to feel the axe of expropriation.

"The agrarian reform in Bolivia," charged Alberto Ostria Gutierrez, ". . . had as its primary objective the economic ruin of the adversaries of the regime, whatever the size of the property they owned."[40]

---

[39] In "Bolivia's Revolutionary Regime: Political and Economic Development," *The World Today*, Vol. XI, No. 4 (April, 1955), p. 172.

[40] Alberto Ostria Gutierrez, *The Tragedy of Bolivia: A People Crucified* (New York: Devin-Adair Co., 1958), pp. 169–70.

Another hindrance to the effective administration of the program was the severe shortage of trained engineers qualified to delineate accurately the boundaries of acreages to be distributed. And equally as serious was the shortage at both the local and appellate levels of judicial personnel qualified to render competent and impartial decisions on intricate points of law.

Furthermore, local officials were apparently not averse to using their privileged position to engage in petty but profitable boon-doggling. Alleged Fausto Beltran and José Fernandez:

The rural councils, interpreting the law to suit their whims, brought insecurity and anarchy into the country. Their trips for the verification of hearings were virtually expeditions of pillage. Aside from special "gifts," the members of the council collected many *"viaticos"* [provisions for a journey] from the *campesinos*. As for verification of the data, one can say that it was incomplete, superficial, and partisan. The council gathered the data during a visit of a few hours in the house of the *hacienda*, changed it to suit themselves in their offices, and usually slanted it so that *campesinos* and their leaders would be swayed by it.[41]

But despite the many obstacles which agrarian reform has encountered, the program is moving ahead, as shown by Table 8–3.

TABLE 8–3

Increasing Tempo of Land Reform in Bolivia

Calendar Year	Number of Properties Expropriated	Number of Titles Granted	Number of Families Benefiting	Number of Hectares Distributed
1953–54	0	0	0	0
1955	32	3,400	2,809	51,811.33
1956	75	4,463	3,863	47,183.65
1957	281	11,400	8,028	276,395.66
1958	216	9,193	5,709	201,997.71
1959	313	18,380	12,097	320,502.13
1960	904	38,897	22,410	852,770.55
1961	1,186	45,511	28,210	1,167,820.78
1962	1,880	50,129	28,843	1,280,714.59

Source: *RESUMEN GENERAL:* Numero de Títulos Ejecutoriales, Jefes de Familia, Superficies Individuales y Colectivas Entregadas a Campesinos por Años 1953–1962, Servicio Nacional de Reforma Agraria, Departamento de Estadistica, La Paz, 17 de junio de 1963.

During the first several years of the program, when progress was made at a snaillike pace, a nationwide organization was being established to administer the program, and engineering surveys were being made to ascertain boundary lines of parcels to be expropriated and allocated. Since 1957, however, the program has really been rolling. In fact, progress since 1960 has been at such a fast pace that Raul Alfonso García, president of the National Council of Agrarian Reform, confidently predicted on July

[41] Fausto Beltran and José Fernandez, *¿Donde Va La Reforma Agraria Boliviana?* (La Paz, Bolivia: Talleres Graficos Bolivianos, 1960), p. 61.

11, 1963, that the entire program of land redistribution and validation of titles would be accomplished within another ten years.[42]

During most of the first decade of the new revolutionary regime, the total volume of agricultural products sold on the market was considerably less than in prerevolutionary days. The decline in production was attributable to several factors. The slowness in legalizing properties and the uncertainty of owners as to whether their properties would be affected were largely responsible for the decline. Probably even more responsible was the attitude of hundreds of thousands of Indian farm laborers who in the past had worked under the close supervision of *hacendados*, but, having acquired a bit of land of their own, were now for the first time in their lives completely on their own and enjoying it. "No use working so hard," the Indian farmer, now more dignifiedly called *campesino*, thought as he luxuriated in his new-found freedom.

For the past several years, however, agricultural production has been climbing upward at a rapid pace, each year setting new records for the nation. "The Agrarian Reform," says Abelardo Villalpando, "accomplished without question the function of freeing prodigious productive forces that were stifled by the feudal system of the *latifundios*."[43]

The production of rice, for example, increased from 28,176 metric tons in 1960 to an estimated 33,500 tons in 1963. The sharp increase is very significant; although the 1960 output was considerably short of the nation's consumption needs, the 1963 crop represented an estimated surplus of approximately 1400 tons available for export. A major stimulus to the sharply increasing production is the Cooperative for Marketing Rice, popularly known as CONCA, an alphabetization that is in itself indicative of the nation's progress. The considerable increase in production plus the better prices received under CONCA's marketing system were responsible for the more than 40 percent increase in prices paid to growers—almost doubling their income.[44]

The upsurge in agricultural production and improved marketing practices which have been established are providing a solid foundation for the national economy. No longer does agriculture have to be a drag on the economy, necessitating the importation of foodstuffs—an absurdity for a society that is more than 80 percent agrarian—thereby taxing the nation's already short supply of much-needed foreign exchange. With the em-

---

[42] Interview with the author in La Paz, July 11, 1963.

[43] Abelardo Villalpando R., *El Problema del Indio y la Reforma Agraria* (Publicación del Departamento de Cultura de la Universidad Tomas Frias, Potosí, Bolivia, 1960), p. 126.

[44] For a detailed account of CONCA's work and accomplishments, see *Annual Report; 1962* (Marketing and Co-operatives Division, Servicio Agrícola Interamericano) (La Paz, Bolivia: Ministerio de Agricultura), pp. 43–44. For the increase in crops since the institution of agrarian reform, see *Breve Informe Sobre La Reforma Agraria en Bolivia, Su Ejecución* (La Paz, Bolivia: Consejo Nacional de Reforma Agraria, March 12, 1963), pp. 13–14.

phasis put on agriculture by the new regime, this sector of the economy is showing a healthy rise of agrarian prosperity.

Expropriating the properties of the *latifundios* outlawed under the 1953 Agrarian Reform Law provided small tracts of land for many new farmers throughout the nation. But the government realized from the beginning of its land reform program that merely breaking up the *latifundios* would fall far short of satisfying the hunger for land felt by the large mass of citizens. Fortunately, the nation's eastern area, the *Oriente*, is a large virginal, fertile expanse which eventually, with considerable labor and expense, can be developed into highly productive farmland. This area is large enough to provide sufficient land for all the *campesinos*, in fact, to support a population several times that of Bolivia's today. Colonization of the area by *campesinos* from the crowded altiplano and upland valleys is recognized to be the real solution to the problem of providing land for all who desire it.

In Alto Beni and Chaparé, two of the main colonization projects, as well as in the *Oriente* generally, Bolivia is boldly pioneering in a program of extensive colonization. "Its experiments in colonization are among the most significant in all Latin America and give probably the best promise of a sound, workable solution to basic agricultural problems."[45]

In Alto Beni, the government plans, finances, and supervises the whole project, and maintains considerable control over all phases of its development. It carefully screens and selects the colonist; provides him with 12 hectares of land, one of which is cleared before his arrival and planted in bananas, rice, corn, and yucca; builds for him a home suitable for his temporary needs; provides a small amount of needed credit; and builds at government expense a school and a hospital to provide education and medical services free of charge.

In return for these generous measures of assistance, practically all of which, except the cost of the school and hospital, have to be repaid by the colonists, the government exercises not only general supervision over the project, but also specifies what crops are to be raised on 10 of the 12 hectares. The crops specified are those which are well adapted to the area, can usually be grown successfully, and are reasonably sure of a market, especially a foreign one.[46]

In striking contrast to Alto Beni, the colonization of Chaparé is an unplanned, uncontrolled, unsubsidized, haphazard type of resettlement—a sort of wildcat operation. In this do-it-yourself resettlement program, the colonists have cleared every hectare of their land, built their homes by their own labor, and completely supported themselves while getting a toehold in farming. They have even built their own schools, as well as

---

[45] "Bolivia's Revolutionary Regime . . ." *op. cit.*, p. 182.

[46] The information regarding Alto Beni was given the author by Fadrique Muños Reyes, Director of Special Projects of USAID, Bolivia, in an interview in La Paz, July 24, 1963.

most of the roads. The national government does not have an office or even a representative in the area. Local self-government is exercised through the half dozen *sindicatos* or locally organized groups of citizens in the area. Each *sindicato*, at a meeting of all the men who belong to the group, elects a council of from 6 to 8 members, also a secretary-general who is recognized to be the group leader. In the absence of national governmental authority, the *sindicato* exercises extensive control, allocating to each family who moves to Chaparé, as well as to each person who is capable of working the land, a plot of 10 hectares of ground. All the national government does is to send out a technician later from La Paz to see that the requirements of two years' residence and clearing at least a third of the land have been complied with; if so, it grants the individual a title to the property.[47]

With its large area of unused fertile land which can be cleared and put into crops, Bolivia is stressing colonization as a means of providing land for all who desire it. Taking advantage of this opportunity, *campesinos* by the thousands are pulling up stakes and heading for the greener pastures of the areas open for colonization. This is a movement which has great promise not only of enabling the nation to accomplish a comprehensive program of land reform, but also of integrating the Indians into the national life, thereby transforming both agriculture and the society.

"Within perhaps a generation," says Richard Patch, describing the migration into the new areas of colonization, "Bolivia will be thought of not as a nation characterized by the poverty of the windswept reaches of the Andes and the marginal mines of the sierra but as the land of the lush tropics and limitless agricultural potential of the northeast. It only requires roads, and slowly, often by hand, the roads are being built."[48]

CUBA'S REVOLUTIONARY PROGRAM OF LAND REFORM

Cuba is the third nation in Latin America to institute and apparently accomplish a comprehensive revolutionary program of land reform.[49]

---

[47] The information regarding Chaparé was given the author by Lucio Arce, of Servicio Agrícola Interamericano, in La Paz on August 7 and 8, 1963.

[48] Richard W. Patch, "Bolivia's Developing Interior," *American Universities Field Staff Reports Service,* West Coast South American Series, Vol. IX, No. 3, Bolivia (March, 1962), p. 1.

[49] Guatemala also attempted a broad program of land reform in 1952 under President Jacobo Arbenz. Its chief aim was to expropriate lands not actually used for farming and distribute them among many small holders. A principal target of its reform was the United Fruit Company, from which the government expropriated 160,000 hectares of uncultivated land. When President Arbenz and his communist backers were ousted in June, 1954, very largely by American backing, Guatemala's short-lived land reform went down the drain. For an account of this abortive land reform, see Richard N. Adams, "Social Change in Guatemala and U.S. Policy," *Social Change in Latin America Today, op. cit.,* pp. 266–73.

Land ownership and agriculture generally in the small island republic were sadly in need of reform. Approximately half of the total cultivable area was owned by sugar plantations, the largest of which belonged to American companies. Atlantica del Golfo and the Riondo group each owned 500,000 acres; the Cuban-American Sugar Company, 330,000 acres; and the United Fruit Company, 266,000 acres. In addition to owning half of the total cultivable area, the sugar plantations rented another 800,000 acres, thereby giving them control over three-fourths of the total farmland of the country.

This top-heavy ownership by large corporations and emphasis on the production of a single crop had many adverse effects on the nation. Only about one-half of the total farmland was cultivated, despite the fact that farm laborers were unemployed for most of the year and subsisted on a very poor diet mainly of beans and other starchy foods, with little meat, fruits, vegetables, and dairy products. Indeed, so little attention was given to the production of adequate foodstuffs that the nation had to import a large part of what it consumed—almost $100 million worth a year.

A sweeping program of land reform was one of the first goals of the new revolutionary regime. As promulgated in May, 1959, the Agrarian Reform Law made radical changes in the ownership and tenure of farmland. According to the provisions of the law, only citizens are permitted to purchase such land, and no foreigners are allowed to inherit it. No cane plantation can be operated by a corporation unless every stockholder is a Cuban citizen, and, even then, the plantation cannot be connected in any way with the sugar refineries.

The law also restricted the amount of land which any single individual or corporation may own for general farming. The maximum is 393 hectares, approximately 980 acres. A more generous limit was set for cane and rice plantations, also cattle ranches. If the government approves their operation, these specialized farms may be allowed to have up to 3,333 acres. But there is a joker in these maximum limits. Any farm, whatever its size, may be expropriated if it is cultivated by tenants or squatters. Under this sleeper provision, the government can legally take almost any of the farms in the nation, as the many tobacco growers in Pinar del Rio Province soon realized. Their holdings, although small, were the first to be expropriated, since they were cultivated by sharecroppers.

The law also establishes a certain "vital minimum" of land which a farm family shall own in order to have a reasonable level of living. This minimum is 67 acres, which is given to a tenant or squatter without cost. The land which he receives is often part of the very acreage which he cultivated for one of the large corporations or absentee landowners.

Lands distributed under the Agrarian Reform Law cannot be sold or mortgaged and can be inherited by only one member of a family. By setting a generous minimum of 67 acres for a farm holding and stipulating that this cannot be subdivided among heirs, the government intends to avoid the creation of *minifundios,* which in the past have hampered both Mexico and Bolivia in accomplishing their programs of reform.

According to the constitution of 1940, any private property expropriated by the government must be paid for in cash before it is taken over. Although the Castro regime is supposedly operating under this constitution, lands expropriated under the Agrarian Reform Law have been paid for by government bonds which mature in 20 years and pay interest at 4.5 percent per annum. "We do not wish to damage anyone," said the bearded prime minister, attempting to justify the payment in agrarian bonds instead of cash on the barrel head, "but these are dollars in the future. They are not dollars in the present because our present dollars are in the United States Bank." They had been put there, he went on to explain, by ousted President Batista and his officials who had swiped and carried away the contents of the national treasury. If the United States government returned these funds, Cuba would be able to pay in cash for land expropriated, as the constitution specifies.[50]

To administer the new program, the government set up the National Institute for Land Reform, giving it almost unlimited powers for planning and carrying out the reform. Headed by Castro himself, the super agency has had no trouble in carrying out its edicts, often using the raw power of the military for taking over properties which it decides to expropriate.

In carrying out the program, the government has apparently been guilty of numerous acts which were highly irregular and even illegal. In many cases, civilian or military authorities, supposedly acting in the name of the government, have taken over a property without a court order or any written authorization whatever. Moreover, they have not bothered to take an inventory of farm machinery, cattle, timber, or other things of value on the place. Without an authentic receipt for property taken, the owner has no chance of ever being paid for it, even in agrarian bonds which will supposedly mature in 20 years.

In utilizing the lands expropriated, the revolutionary regime has evolved its own distinctive pattern of land ownership. Some of the properties taken over have been divided and distributed as small individual holdings, thereby creating a large number of new small landowners. But other properties expropriated, particularly the large sugar plantations, have been maintained intact, and are being operated by the government as cooperatives. Splitting up these large efficient enterprises into small individual units would be disastrous to the economy, the government realized; consequently, the plantations continue to operate pretty much as before, except that the government now supervises all their activities and has the final word. In a few cases, large acreages have become state farms, directly owned and operated by the government as enterprises of the state.

---

[50] *New York Times,* July 28, 1951, p. 2, col. 4.

Contrary to the hopes of many Americans, the economy of Cuba did not collapse after Castro's expropriation of the large private holdings. In fact, just as Egyptians proved in 1956 that they too could operate the Suez Canal, quite efficiently too, so have the Cubans shown that they can produce sugar without American help and sell it on the world market, thanks mainly to an assist from Moscow.

THE PROSPECTS FOR LAND REFORM
BY PEACEFUL MEANS

To date, only one nation in Latin America has been able successfully to institute and carry out an extensive program of land reform by legal, peaceable methods. Venezuela is the nation that enjoys this distinction.

The Agrarian Reform Law promulgated by the Venezuelan government in March, 1960, was the result of long and painstaking deliberation. The nonpartisan commission which spent seven months carefully drafting the law was so chosen as to reflect all shades of public opinion. The Archbishop of Caracas was one of the members, and several well-known Communists were members too. Dividing itself into four subcommittees, charged with studying the legal, economic, social, and agro-technical aspects of land reform, the nonpartisan group reflected, so far as could be determined, the thinking of the entire nation. Thus the extensive program of land reform which the commission proposed was approved by the Congress with only a few modifications.[51]

The new law recognizes the concept of the "social function of landed property." Under this concept, all property must be held and used in such a way as to benefit the whole society. If it is not so owned and used, it may be expropriated, but only under such conditions and in accordance with such procedures as are prescribed by law. Only three kinds of land many be expropriated by the government: lands which are not being cultivated; farms that are cultivated by renters, sharecroppers, or day laborers; and lands which are being used to graze livestock, although they are fertile enough to grow crops.

From almost any angle, Venezuela's democratically inaugurated land reform is a moderate program. The law does not contain any provisions limiting the size of farms, discriminating against foreign owners, or breaking up the large estates unless they are unproductive. Moreover, no land can be expropriated except in accordance with due process of law, with the courts passing on the legality of the procedure. Also, any lands taken over are paid for in cash up to a value of $30,000; in the case of properties valued above this amount, payment is made partly in cash and the rest in bonds.

---

[51] For a full account of the deliberations of the four subcommittees, see Venezuela, Ministerio de Agricultura y Cria; Comisión de Reforma Agraria, *Reforma agraria,* Vols. I–IV (Caracas, 1959).

What most of all sold the government's program to the large, power-ful landowners was the provision that any lands which are expropriated will be paid for at their current market value. Approximately 2500 large farms, totaling some 45 million acres, contain more than half of the farm-land in the nation. The unique provision of the law enabling these large owners to sell their surplus properties to the government at current market value has made the land reform program quite acceptable to them, and many have availed themselves of the opportunity for selling their excess lands, which the government is buying and distributing to make many new small landholders.

The reform law also established a scale of graduated land taxes which in effect tells landowners, "you must either cultivate your properties intensively and efficiently or sell them to the government."

Venezuela has just cause to be proud of its unique, peacefully instituted program of land reform. The reform law was "made for Venezuela," said Dr. Victor Jimínes Landinez, minister of agriculture. "The agrarian prob-lems of Venezuela should not be guided by norms in other countries. The Law is neither leftist nor rightist—it is simply just. The only limit to property is the limit of social function; nobody will be permitted to maintain land idle or uncultivated when others need it." The aim of the bill was "to put land in the hands of those who work it."[52]

Adequately financed by revenues from its rich oil properties, Vene-zuela's ambitious program of land reform was originally calculated to benefit approximately 300,000 rural families within ten years. Since this figure included practically all the landless families in Venezuela, the government, by carrying out its scheduled program of dispersed owner-ship, would be able to provide land to all farmers who desire it.

During 1960 the government came close to achieving its ambitious goal, as Table 8–4 shows.

TABLE 8–4

DISTRIBUTION OF LAND IN VENEZUELA: 1959–62

Year	Number of Properties Acquired	Number of Families Benefited	Number of Hectares Granted
1959	53	5,874	460,769
1960	308	25,221	748,933
1961	141	11,074	156,089
1962	135	14,603	167,283
Total	637	56,772	1,533,074

SOURCES: *Reforma Agraria y Desarrollo Agropecuario en Venezuela: 1959–63* (Ministerio de Agricultura y Cría) (Caracas, 10 al 14 de junio de 1963), p. 7; and *Instituto Agrario Nacional: Informe Anual, 1962* (Caracas, 1963), p. 3.

In 1961 and 1962, as the above figures show, the government fell con-siderably short of its planned pace, thanks largely to the violence and

---

[52] *New York Times*, July 24, 1959, p. 7, col. 1.

subversion which convulsed the nation prior to the December, 1963, election, a calculated Castroite campaign of destruction and terror intended to paralyze the nation and prevent by whatever means necessary the democratic, constitutional transfer of authority from one popularly elected administration to another.[53]

While Venezuela deserves much credit for conceiving and effectuating its land reform law by peaceful, constitutional means, its reform can hardly be regarded as a pilot program which will set an example for other Latin-American nations, as some tend to regard it.[54] For with its fabulously productive oil lands, Venezuela is "filthy rich" compared with the other nations of Latin America. With that sort of bankroll to rely upon, just about any nation, if it chose, could institute a peaceful, "acceptable," constitutional program of reform.

Surveying the whole Latin American situation realistically, just what are the chances of accomplishing much-needed reforms by peaceful methods? Frankly, they are very slim, one studying the problem is forced to conclude.

"The hacienda system has in fact reached an impasse from which it cannot escape," reasons Frank Tannenbaum. "The pressure for economic, political, and social change is building up so rapidly that the system cannot avoid the challenge to its traditional ways, and it cannot meet it. *The hacienda has no built-in device that will allow for reform of the system*, that will enable it to transform itself so as to survive and propitiate the new ways that are undermining a traditional and age-old form of social organization."[55]

Despite the gravity of the situation and the widely recognized need for reform, the *hacendados* have been so inflexible in their thinking and in their unwillingness to concede even an inch that there has been scarcely a semblance of a meeting of minds between them and the landless mass. Today, just as centuries ago, the basic problem still is, "men without land and land without men."

Instead of facing the problem squarely and attempting to arrive at genuine solutions, the *hacendados* continue to fiddle while peasant resentment burns fiercely. Either unaware of the intensity of this resentment, or determined, as we noted earlier, to hold down the safety valve of the boiler and take a chance on its bursting, the big landowners continue to

---

[53] For the organization of the nation's National Agrarian Institute, see *El Instituto Agrario Nacional y Su Organización* (Caracas: Febrero, 1962).

And for its well-heeled budget and accounting of expenditures, see *Instituto Agrario Nacional: Balance General*, 31 de Diciembre de 1962 (Caracas, 1963).

A good background account of the nation's hangover from dictatorship, the critical need of land reform, and the bold program advocated by Democratic Action is given by Ramón Quijada, *Reforma Agraria en Venezuela* (Caracas: Editorial Arte, Mayo de 1963).

[54] Carroll, *op. cit.*, p. 188.

[55] Frank Tannenbaum, "Toward an Appreciation of Latin America," *The United States and Latin America, op. cit.*, p. 40.

rely upon diversionary tactics. While peons cry for land, politicians appoint still more committees "to study the problem" and dangle the bait of tax reform or colonization before the peons as adequate to solve the agrarian ills of the society.

In Latin America, as elsewhere, "undoubtedly everyone would be happier," says Clarence Senior, "if land could be distributed on a Sunday afternoon with the ceremonies followed by pretzels and beer, or hot dogs and soda pop, or *tortillas* and *pulque*, or rice cakes and *sake*."[56] The *hacendados* with their recalcitrant attitude may have some such idealized concept as to how land reform may operate. But the numerous members of the poverty-stricken, landless mass have no such illusions. From one end of Latin America to the other, they are showing their determination to take matters into their own hands.

In country after country, masses of peasants led by fiery leaders have moved onto the large estates to take them over for their own use. These tactics have become so prevalent in the whole region that members of the invading horde are popularly known as "parachuters," since they seemingly swarm out of nowhere by the hundreds, sometimes thousands.

Sometimes such a peasant invasion is so serious that the government hastily purchases the property and distributes it among the invaders, hoping thereby to relieve temporarily the explosive situation. Far more often, however, determined to dislodge the would-be landowners, the government uses whatever force is necessary for this purpose, whether heavily armed members of the civilian police or units of the nation's armed forces. The frequent invasions of private property often involve bloodshed and sometimes heavy loss of life. Any one of them could easily trigger another revolutionary program of land reform, even another social revolution—such as the Mexican, Bolivian, or Cuban—which completely remakes the society.

For an increasing number of the desperate landless mass are becoming convinced, as one of Zapata's followers stirringly expressed it, that *it is better to die on your feet than to live on your knees.*

SUGGESTED READINGS

ALEXANDER, ROBERT J. *The Bolivian National Revolution*, chaps. 4 and 5. New Brunswick, N.J.: Rutgers University Press, 1958.

BECKET, JAMES. "Land Reform in Chile," *Journal of Inter-American Studies*, Vol. V, No. 2 (April, 1963), pp. 177–211.

BIESANZ, JOHN, AND BIESANZ, MAVIS. *The People of Panama*, pp. 119–36. New York: Columbia University Press, 1955.

CARROLL, THOMAS F. "The Land Reform Issue in Latin America," *Latin American Issues: Essays and Comments* (ed. ALBERT O. HIRSCHMAN), pp. 161–96. New York: Twentieth Century Fund, 1961.

---

[56] Senior, *op. cit.*, p. 6.

CLINE, HOWARD F. *Mexico: Revolution to Evolution: 1940–1960*, chaps. xxii and xxviii. Royal Institute of International Affairs. New York: Oxford University Press, 1962.

FALS-BORDA, ORLANDO. *Peasant Society in the Colombian Andes: A Sociological Study of Saucío*, pp. 64–82, 114–31, and 172–73. Gainesville, Fla.: University of Florida Press, 1957.

FORD, THOMAS R. *Man and Land in Peru*. Gainesville, Fla.: University of Florida Press, 1955.

GRUENING, ERNEST. *Mexico and Its Heritage*, pp. 111–67. New York: D. Appleton-Century Co., Inc., 1934.

GUTIERREZ, ALBERTO OSTRIA. *The Tragedy of Bolivia: A People Crucified*, pp. 158–73. New York: Devin-Adair Co., 1958.

HOLLY, MARC AURELE. *Agriculture in Haiti*, with Special Reference to Rural Economy and Agricultural Education. New York: Vantage Press, Inc., 1955.

HOLMBERG, ALLAN R. "Changing Community Attitudes and Values in Peru: A Case Study in Guided Change," *Social Change in Latin America Today*, pp. 63–105. Council on Foreign Relations. New York: Harper & Bros., 1960.

HOLMBERG, ALLAN R., AND DOBYNS, HENRY F. "The Process of Accelerating Community Change," *Human Organization*, Vol. 21, No. 2 (Summer, 1962), pp. 107–9.

INTERNATIONAL BANK FOR RECONSTRUCTION AND DEVELOPMENT. *The Agricultural Development of Colombia*. Washington, D.C., May, 1956.

———. *The Basis of a Development Program for Colombia*, chaps. v and xviii. Washington, D.C., 1950.

INTERNATIONAL LABOUR OFFICE. *Indigenous Peoples: Living and Working Conditions of Aboriginal Populations in Independent Countries*, chap. vi. Studies and Reports, New Series, No. 35. Geneva, Switz., 1953.

———. *The Landless Farmer in Latin America*. Studies and Reports, New Series, No. 47. Geneva, Switz., 1957.

LEONARD, OLEN E. *Bolivia: Land, People and Institutions*, chaps. vii and viii. Washington, D.C.: The Scarecrow Press, Inc., 1952.

MADDOX, JAMES G. "Mexican Agrarian Reform," *American Universities Field Staff Reports Service* (July, 1957).

MAY, STACY (dir.), *et al. Costa Rica: A Study in Economic Development*, chaps. 3 and 4. New York: Twentieth Century Fund, 1952.

MCBRIDE, GEORGE MCCUTCHEN. *Chile: Land and Society*. American Geographical Society Research Series, No. 19. New York, 1936.

NELSON, LOWRY. *Rural Cuba*, chaps. v–vii and xiii. Minneapolis: University of Minnesota Press, 1950.

PARSONS, KENNETH H., PENN, RAYMOND J., AND RAUP, PHILLIP M. (eds.). *Proceedings of the International Conference on Land Tenure and Related Problems in World Agriculture*, Madison, Wis., 1951. Madison, Wis.: University of Wisconsin Press, 1956.

PATCH, RICHARD W. "Bolivia's Developing Interior," *American Universities Field Staff Reports Service*. West Coast South American Series, Vol. IX, No. 3, Bolivia (March, 1962).

SENIOR, CLARENCE. *Land Reform and Democracy*. Gainesville, Fla.: University of Florida Press, 1958.

SIMPSON, EYLER N. *The Ejido: Mexico's Way Out*. Chapel Hill, N.C.: University of North Carolina Press, 1937.

SMITH, T. LYNN. *Brazil: People and Institutions*, Part IV. Rev. ed. Baton Rouge, La.: Louisiana State University Press, 1963.

SOULE, GEORGE; EFRON, DAVID; AND NESS, NORMAN T. *Latin America in the Future World*, chaps. 6 and 14. National Planning Association. New York: Farrar & Rinehart, Inc., 1945.

STOKES, WILLIAM S. *Latin American Politics*, chap. 9. New York: Thomas Y. Crowell Co., 1959.

TANNENBAUM, FRANK. *The Mexican Agrarian Revolution*. Washington, D.C.: The Brookings Institution, 1930.

———. *Mexico: The Struggle for Peace and Bread*, chaps. 6 and 9. New York: Alfred A. Knopf, Inc., 1954.

———. *Peace by Revolution: An Interpretation of Mexico*, chap. 14. New York: Columbia University Press, 1933.

TUCKER, WILLIAM P. *The Mexican Government Today*, Part V. Minneapolis: University of Minnesota Press, 1957.

WEIL, FELIX J. *Argentine Riddle*, chap. iii and Appendix A. Latin American Economic Institute. New York: John Day Co., 1944.

WHETTEN, NATHAN L. *Guatemala: The Land and the People*, chaps. 7 and 8. Caribbean Series, 4. New Haven, Conn.: Yale University Press, 1961.

———. *Rural Mexico*, Part II, chaps. iv–xi. Chicago: University of Chicago Press, 1948.

WILGUS, A. CURTIS (ed.) *The Caribbean: Venezuelan Development, A Case History*, Part V. Caribbean Conference Series, One, Vol. XIII. Gainesville, Fla.: University of Florida Press, 1963.

WOLF, ERIC R. *Sons of the Shaking Earth*, chap. x. Chicago: University of Chicago Press, 1959.

YOUNG, MAURICE DE. *Man and Land in the Haitian Economy*. Inter-American Studies, Monograph Series No. 3. Gainesville, Fla.: University of Florida Press, 1958.

CHAPTER 9

INDUSTRY:
The Revolution of Rising Expectations

INDUSTRIALIZATION and technological progress have been characteristic features of the "Western way of life" for more than a century and a half. But not all of the nations in the region have enjoyed the benefits—or suffered the afflictions—of the industrial revolution. Indeed, the revolution was quite late in coming to Latin America. Since its arrival, however, its influence has been momentous; there, as elsewhere, it is reshaping the society and reorienting its values and goals.

THE DRIVE FOR INDUSTRIAL DEVELOPMENT: BACKGROUND AND MOTIVATIONS

It was not until the last quarter of the nineteenth century that Latin America really felt the impact of the industrial revolution. But as immigrants poured in, together with foreign investors and traders, technological advances and new ways of thinking in manufacturing, transportation, and communications were brought into the region. During this first period of industrialization, many enterprises were established to manufacture or process commodities. There were cotton gins and cottonseed oil mills, flour mills and grain elevators, sugar mills and refineries, canneries for fruits and vegetables, laboratories for producing pharmaceuticals, plants for bottling carbonated soft drinks, and breweries that utilized the potent grain and fruit of the vine. The large hat and shoe factories of São Paulo, Brazil, made it renowned as the "Pittsburgh of South America." There were even some small iron foundries and steel fabricating plants.[1]

Although Latin America was not directly involved in World War I, the war had a decided impact there as on the rest of the international econ-

---

[1] Harry Stark, *Social and Economic Frontiers in Latin America* (2d ed.; Dubuque, Ia.: Wm. C. Brown Co., 1963), p. 250.

omy. The war and its aftermath disrupted international trade and changed the whole complexion of international investment. As a result of the war, Latin America, which had long been closely tied to Europe by friendly bonds of trade and investment, was pretty much on its own. "In a very real sense Latin America had lost its moorings," concluded Miron Burgin. "It could no longer count upon Europe to maintain intact the order in which Latin America had grown and prospered, and had felt secure. In the aftermath of World War I Latin America was forced to mobilize all its moral and material resources in order to adjust itself to a new, tortuously emerging world environment."[2] The deprivation of needed imports during the four years of conflict and the necessity later of having to adjust to alien patterns of trade were great stimuli to the development of a variety of industries throughout the region.

The depression of the 1930s was another big stimulus to industrialization. As nation after nation in the region felt its blighting effects and futilely tried to cope with it by restricting imports by such devices as quotas, licenses, clearing agreements, and higher tariffs, international trade, which was the economic lifeblood of Latin America, shrank to a fraction of its former volume. In some of the nations the drop in exports was of fantastic proportions. From 1929 to 1932, Chile's exports dropped 88 percent; her foreign trade suffered more during those years than that of any other nation in the world. During the same period, Bolivia's exports fell 80 percent; Cuba's, 70 percent; and those of the 20 republics as a whole, 65 percent.[3]

The nations suffered acutely from the inability to export their products and import the goods which they needed. Indeed, the depression confirmed and strengthened the conviction of many Latin Americans that their economic salvation lay in self-sufficiency, which could be achieved only by the establishment of new industries and the diversification of production to take care of the needs of the domestic market. In the United States too, whose high Smoot-Hawley tariff greatly aggravated and probably prolonged the depression, there were many who advocated a similar course of action.[4]

World War II and the ensuing "cold war" were other strong incentives to the development of industrialization in the region. During the war the manufacturer or would-be manufacturer of any commodity from diapers to doughnuts could operate freely without fear of foreign competition. For the United States, one of Latin America's main markets and also the

---

[2] Miron Burgin, "New Fields of Research in Latin American Studies," *Responsible Freedom in the Americas* (ed. Angel del Rio) (Garden City, N.Y.: Doubleday & Co., Inc., 1955), p. 189.

[3] Sanford A. Mosk, *Industrial Revolution in Mexico* (Berkeley: University of California Press, 1954), p. 11.

[4] One of these was Charles Beard, whose *Open Door at Home* would make the United States economically self-sufficient, and let the rest of the world go by.

source of most of its imports, was now devoting its productive capacity to manufacturing weapons of war and taking care of the needs of its own civilian population. Engaged in a titantic struggle on two fronts, the nation had very little in the way of manufactured goods that could be spared for Latin America. England and the other European nations were in the same boat. Moreover, much of the small part which could be diverted from the war effort to the needs of the region was sunk by Hitler's submarines, which prowled the eastern seaboard, sinking merchant ships at will.

In addition to affording the industrialist a heyday for establishing or expanding an enterprise, the war favored him in other ways too. Whatever surplus the region produced during the conflict and for several years later and could sell abroad was worth its weight in gold; the high price that it brought on the world market afforded a measure of prosperity which some of the nations had never enjoyed before.

World War I, the depression, and World War II were strong environmental influences prodding the nations to industrialize. The deeply felt aspirations of the population have also been spurs in the same direction. The industrialized nations enjoy a much higher standard of living, Latin Americans are convinced, after seeing movies from Hollywood, watching television, or seeing tourists from the United States with their obvious affluence. They too would like to enjoy the same advantages. In fact, the revolution of rising expectations is as strongly felt in Latin America as in any other part of the world.

Another strong motivation for industrialization is the determination of ✓ the nations to free themselves from economic colonialism. Every one of them has the essential attributes of a colonial economy and is quite dependent upon foreign trade and investment. In most of them the economy is largely based on the production of one or two staple commodities, such as bananas in Honduras, coffee in Brazil and Colombia, copper and nitrates in Chile, and oil in Venezuela.

Such reliance upon one or several commodities, most of which are exported rather than consumed at home, places the nations in a very disadvantageous position. The prices of the commodities fluctuate widely and are often severely depressed by factors in the international market completely beyond the control of the producing states. The dumping of tin on the market by Russia in 1958, causing a sharp decline in its price, was a severe blow to Bolivia, whose economy is dependent upon foreign exchange derived from the sale of the metal.

The Latin American, producing for a foreign market which determines the price it will pay him, sometimes pretty arbitrarily, often feels as frustrated and cheated as does the farmer in the United States, who helplessly sees his choice cattle sold at a depressed price of 25¢ a pound in the stockyard but appear as choice steaks in the meat counter at $1.75 a pound. To compound the Latin American's grievances, the prices he receives for his products may hit rock bottom, yet the prices he has to pay for the machines, tools, and consumer goods which he imports remain the same, or, if they change, climb higher.

Still another motivation for industrializing is the impact on the region of the population explosion. The population is increasing at an annual rate of 2.7 percent (nearer 3 percent, according to some estimates)—the highest of any major region in the world. Every year there are millions of new mouths to feed, taxing to the fullest the ability of the agricultural sector to produce the food needed by the proliferating population. Every year there are millions of new jobs which have to be created for the region's rapidly increasing number of young men and women, challenging to the fullest the ability of industry and other parts of the society to measure up to their responsibilities.

Yet another incentive for industrializing is the intense feeling of nationalism which pervades Latin America. Whether in Argentina or Chile, Panama or Guatemala, there is an increasing sense of pride in the nation and confidence in what it stands for and hopes to achieve. "Made in the U.S.A." stamped on the bottom of a percolator or rear of a washing machine may indicate high quality, as well as where it was produced. However, it suggests to the Latin American his inability to produce this product and reminds him of his condition of economic colonialism. What warms his heart is to see "Made in Argentina" or whatever his nation is. The growing feeling of national pride has played a part in the establishment of many an industry.

Industrialization is an accepted goal in most of the nations, and is strongly supported there. The new moneyed elite consisting of industrialists, entrepreneurs, businessmen, and bankers, many of whom have made fortunes and are recognized as belonging to the upper class, are staunch supporters, believing that industrialization will advance the nation's interests and their own. Members of the middle class for the most part have the same attitude; the realization of their ambitions for an education and a higher standard of living depend mainly on progressive economic development. Labor leaders and their many union members are another large group which heartily favors industrialization, realizing how much they gain from each new industry that is established.

But other groups have been far from enthusiastic about industrialization and its effects upon society; in fact, for one reason or another, they are covertly or openly opposed to it. The large landowners, primarily interested in a plentiful supply of cheap labor, are wary of industrialization, fearing that it may siphon off their labor and force them to pay higher wages. In Venezuela landowners complained bitterly about the many effects of the petroleum industry on their labor. One complaint was that instead of paying their farmhands once a month as formerly, they now had to pay them every week, as the oil companies did their labor. As a result, their hands now went on a binge once a week instead of just once a month.[5]

The large landowners have another gripe against industrialization. The social infrastructure of an industrial society means more schools, libraries, hospitals, and roads, all of which represent a considerable cost, and much of which they would have to bear as wealthy members of society.

While the landed oligarchy does not usually openly oppose industrialization and technological progress, intellectuals do not hesitate to do so. In most underdeveloped nations, these individuals have played a major role in promoting the industrial revolution and winning popular acceptance for it.[6] But not in Latin America. There, values of Hispanic culture are basically antagonistic to technology, which is the very foundation of industrialization. Indeed, the *pensadores* look down their long Spanish noses at technology and all the values and activities related to it. They decry the very thought of a technical education, necessary for training the many administrators, engineers, scientists, and specialized experts which are needed in an industrial society. Moreover, they are very critical of mechanization, specialization, and concern with profits, all of which in their opinion destroy artistic appreciation and creativity, dehumanize the individual, and make him a money-minded member of a materialistic society.

PROGRESS MADE IN INDUSTRIAL DEVELOPMENT

The economic development of Latin America has been one of the most colorful aspects of its colorful history. In Brazil:

. . . the history of [the] economy is a sensational record with amazing fluctuations. It is a history of the appearance and disappearance of entire industries. Its leitmotif is the perpetual change of the "kings." Sugar, cacao, gold, tobacco, cotton, rubber, coffee—each of these products has its place in the history of the country and was at one time the axis of the national (or state) economy, lending to Brazil a temporary world supremacy.[7]

In measuring economic development in Latin America, as elsewhere, three of the indexes frequently used are the GNP (gross national product) per capita, consumption of electricity per capita, and amount of steel pro-

---

[5] Rodolfo Luzardo, "Farming and Ranching vs. Petroleum," *Venezuela: Business and Finances* (Englewood Cliffs, N.J.: Prentice-Hall, Inc., 1957), chap. 15.

[6] John H. Kautsky (ed.), *Political Change in Underdeveloped Countries: Nationalism and Communism* (New York: John Wiley & Sons, Inc., 1962), pp. 24 and 44–49.

[7] J. F. Normano, *Brazil: A Study of Economic Types* (Chapel Hill, N.C.: University of North Carolina Press, 1935), p. 18. In Chapter 2, "The Perpetual Change of Leading Products," the author gives a graphic account of the ups and downs—mostly downs—of the products which have been virtually a history of Brazil.

duced.[8] On the basis of these indexes, how fast is Latin America progressing economically?

In the years immediately following World War II, the prosperity enjoyed by many of the nations was very favorable for economic development. In fact, the GNP increased 4.5 percent a year from 1950 to 1957, during which time the population increased 2.5 percent a year. Thus the region realized a yearly per capita growth increase of 2 percent in the value of its total goods and services. With production increasing considerably faster than population, the region confidently looked forward to a rise in the standard of living.

Since 1958, however, the economic progress of the region as a whole has been disappointing. The rate of economic growth has slowed down until it is barely keeping ahead of the increase in population. From 1958 to 1961, the average annual rise in income was less than 1 percent per capita—particularly serious because of the very low incomes of the region. This slowdown in the rate of economic growth in the face of the low standard of living and the high increase in population is the number one problem in Latin America, in the opinion of Dr. Raúl Prebisch, one of its leading economists.[9]

The situation has improved somewhat since the institution of the Alliance for Progress. According to its annual report for 1962, 10 of the 19 republics exceeded the goal of a 2.5 percent annual increase in per capita income for the year. But the average for the hemisphere showed but little improvement over earlier years because of the poor performance of Argentina, Brazil, and Chile, which account for over half of the region's population and agricultural and industrial production. Brazil and Chile failed to show any economic growth; the increase in output was about the same as the increase in population. Argentina's performance was the most disappointing of all; its gross national product actually declined by more than 3 percent in 1962.

In the production of electrical energy,[10] another index of economic development, the region is rapidly moving ahead. In 1959 it generated more than 62 billion kilowatt hours of electric energy, a tremendous jump from the 8 billion generated in 1929. According to those figures, production in the three decades increased by approximately 660 percent. Experts

---

8 Other indexes besides these are: the number of doctors per 1,000 inhabitants; newspaper circulation, also number of radios, telephones, and vehicles in proportion to population; percent of total population in cities over a certain size; and percent of literacy and ratio of enrollment in primary schools to population of school age. (Everett E. Hagen, "A Framework for Analyzing Economic and Political Change," *Development of the Emerging Countries: An Agenda for Research* [Washington, D.C.: The Brookings Institution, 1962], p. 5.)

9 *U.S. News and World Report*, August 14, 1961, p. 62.

10 For a history of the development of electric power in Latin America by nations, see Lloyd Hughlett (ed.), *Industrialization of Latin America* (New York: McGraw-Hill Book Co., Inc., 1946), pp. 319–45. This work also contains histories of the other important industries in Latin America.

predict that by 1970 the region will need 200 billion KWTs, more than triple the production of 1959. The necessary expansion would require a gross investment of $13 billion.[11]

The increase in production in recent years is shown by Table 9–1 which gives statistics for representative states.

TABLE 9–1

PRODUCTION OF ELECTRIC ENERGY
(Millions of Kilowatt Hours)

Country	1954	1960	1961	1962
Brazil	11,871	22,865	24,405	26,890
Chile	3,567	4,523	4,829	5,193
Haiti	20.8	60.0	60.3	64.2
Mexico	6,282	10,728	11,746	12,506
Nicaragua	104.7	183.2	194.7	212.3
United States	544,645	841,616	878,712	943,053

SOURCE: United Nations, *Statistical Yearbook, 1963*, pp. 339–41. Reproduced by permission.

The production of electric power per capita is considerably lower than in Canada or in the United States, as Fig. 9–1 shows. Furthermore, production varies from a high of approximately 600 kilowatt hours per capita for Venezuelans to 20 for the Haitians, who wash their clothes by hand and go to bed with the chickens.

Most of the nations have a hydroelectric potential which is vast and untapped. Brazil, the most favored in this respect, has a potential of more than 16 million kilowatts, but its installed capacity is less than 2 million kilowatts.[12] To take advantage of this enormous power potential, many hydroelectric plants are being built throughout the region. In July, 1962, Brazil inaugurated two new electric power units of the huge Três Marias hydroelectric project on the Upper São Francisco River, about 200 miles north of Belo Horizonte, Minas Gerais. Três Marias is the fifth largest hydroelectric project in the world and will greatly aid in the development of Minas Gerais and the rest of the northeast territory.

In late 1963, Brazil began the construction of another huge hydroelectric project. The Jupiá, as it is called, is located on the Paraná River near the Urubupungá Falls, will cost more than $200 million, and will have a generating capacity of 1.2 million kw. Easily the most ambitious hydroelectric project of all is the one contemplated at Salto Grande on the Uruguay River. Its cost of $407 million would be jointly borne by Argentina and Uruguay, who would pay $225 million and $182 million, respectively. The agreement signed by the two nations for the construc-

---

[11] United Nations Economic Commission for Latin America, *Report of the Latin American Electric Power Seminar in Mexico City* (Santiago, Chile, February, 1962), p. 12.

[12] The power potentials of the various nations are given in Stark, *op. cit.*, p. 261.

FIGURE 9-1

ELECTRIC POWER PRODUCTION: 1960
(Total for Public and Private Generating Plants)

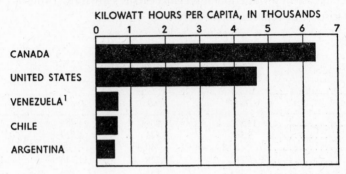

KILOWATT HOURS PER CAPITA, IN THOUSANDS

CANADA
UNITED STATES
VENEZUELA[1]
CHILE
ARGENTINA

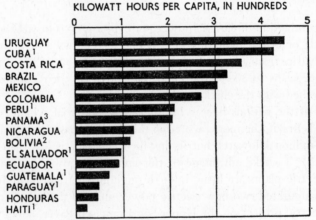

KILOWATT HOURS PER CAPITA, IN HUNDREDS

URUGUAY
CUBA[1]
COSTA RICA
BRAZIL
MEXICO
COLOMBIA
PERU[1]
PANAMA[3]
NICARAGUA
BOLIVIA[2]
EL SALVADOR[1]
ECUADOR
GUATEMALA[1]
PARAGUAY[1]
HONDURAS
HAITI[1]

NOTE: Figures for the Dominican Republic not available.
1. 1959.
2. 1958.
3. For public generators only.
SOURCE: *Américas*, Vol. 15, No. 8 (August, 1963), p. 43. Reproduced by permission.

tion of the international project is as audacious in scope as a power project long contemplated in the United States—harnessing the tides at Passamaquoddy Bay.

In addition to hydroelectric power, nuclear reactors may be feasible in large interconnected systems, such as the São Paulo—Rio de Janeiro region in Brazil or the Buenos Aires seaboard area in Argentina, or in smaller systems serving industrial complexes situated in areas devoid of hydroelectric resources and depending on coal with its high transportation costs, such as in the northern part of Chile.[13]

---

[13] *Report of the Latin American Electric Power Seminar in Mexico City, op. cit.,* p. 112.

In the production of steel, still another index of industrial development, the region is forging ahead, as the following statistics of the main producing nations indicate.

TABLE 9–2

PRODUCTION OF CRUDE STEEL
(Thousands of Metric Tons)

Country	1948	1960	1961	1962
Argentina	122	277	441	644
Brazil	483	1,843	1,995	—
Chile	30	422	363	495
Colombia	157	176	137	—
Mexico	270	1,500	1,725	1,851
United States	80,413	90,067	88,917	89,202

SOURCE: United Nations, *Statistical Yearbook*, 1963, p. 283. Reproduced by permission.

A plant for producing steel is regarded as the hallmark of an industrialized society.[14] The Chileans take great pride in Compañia de Acero del Pacifico, the steel plant at Huachipato which began production in 1950, and the Brazilians are equally proud of the Volta Redonda Iron and Steel Plant, which began production in 1946. But the production in these and other more recently built plants has been unable to keep pace with the increasing requirements of the secondary transforming industries engaged in the manufacture of automobiles and trucks, the construction of skyscrapers and bridges, and the shipbuilding programs and modernization of railways.

In 1958 the first semi-integrated steel mills began operation in El Salvador and Panama; since then, the production of steel has had an even higher priority in every one of the more industrialized nations. Mexico, which is second only to Brazil in the output of steel ingots, produced 1,851,000 tons in 1962—an increase of almost 600 percent over its production of 1948.[15]

Industrialization and economic independence are goals which most of the nations of Latin America are striving hard to attain. Their measure of success is reflected by the percentage of the gross domestic product ac-

[14] Economists maintain, however, that developing or underdeveloped countries should not try to develop heavy industries, such as integrated steel mills, because these require large capital outlays and a big supply of highly skilled workers. For this viewpoint, see Eugene Staley, *The Future of Underdeveloped Countries* (Council on Foreign Relations) (New York: Harper & Bros., 1961), p. 305; Committee for Economic Development, *Economic Development Abroad and the Role of American Foreign Investment* (A statement by the Research and Policy Committee) (New York: February, 1956), p. 13; and DeVere E. Pentony (ed.), *The Underdeveloped Lands: A Dilemma of the International Economy* (San Francisco: Chandler Publishing Co., 1960), p. 13.

[15] For a brief but graphic account of the Mexican steel industry, see Dennis J. Cipnic, "More Mexican Steel: Monterrey Plan Develops New Process," *Américas*, Vol. 14, No. 10 (October, 1962), pp. 13–16.

counted for by manufacturing compared with that of agriculture, trade, services, and public administration and defense, as given in Figure 9–2. But while some of the nations have made much progress in industrialization, as shown by their hydroelectric projects, steel mills, aluminum plants, automotive factories, and oil refineries, other nations in the region have only elementary industries, such as breweries for making *cerveza* (beer) or bottling companies for turning out soft drinks, small canning plants, home industries for making clothing, and various other small enterprises for manufacturing or processing simple products for the consumer market.

These nations which are lagging so in industrializing have certain characteristics in common: a very low annual income, a high rate of illiteracy, political instability, strong military influence or control, and social immobility. Unevenness of economic development, even within a nation, can be a serious problem too. In Brazil, the concentration of industry and income in São Paulo, with a consequent reduction in industry and income elsewhere, especially in the northeast, has been one of the nation's serious problems.[16]

TRADITIONAL METHODS FOR PROMOTING INDUSTRY[17]

Mercantilism during colonial days was a far more potent force in the New World possessions of Spain and Portugal than in the British colonies. The crowns of Spain and Portugal were omnipresent, closely supervising the trade of the colonies to make sure that it would accrue to the benefit of the mother country.

Mercantilism has never died in Latin America. To protect their infant home industries and encourage industrialization, the nations have adopted many measures designed to this end, including customs duties, import quotas, exchange controls, licensing, embargoes, loans, subsidies, and tax exemptions.

The protective tariff has been the most widely used method of promoting domestic industries; in fact, the young manufacturing enterprises in Latin America grew up behind the sheltering barriers of high tariff walls, just as industries developed in the United States. The more industrially advanced nations were the first to adopt a protectionist trade policy —Argentina in 1876, Brazil in 1889, and Chile in 1897. The other nations in time followed a similar policy.

Venezuela's import duties, for example, were originally designed solely to obtain revenue, but were stiffly adjusted upward in order to promote

---

16 Celso Furtado, *The Economic Growth of Brazil: A Survey from Colonial to Modern Times*, trans. Ricardo W. de Aguiar and Eric Charles Drysdale (Berkeley: University of California Press, 1963), pp. 264–66.

17 Much of the following information and treatment is from George Wythe, *Industry in Latin America* (2d ed.; New York: Columbia University Press, 1949), pp. 65–76.

FIGURE 9-2. GROSS DOMESTIC PRODUCT, PERCENTAGE BY AREA OF ACTIVITY

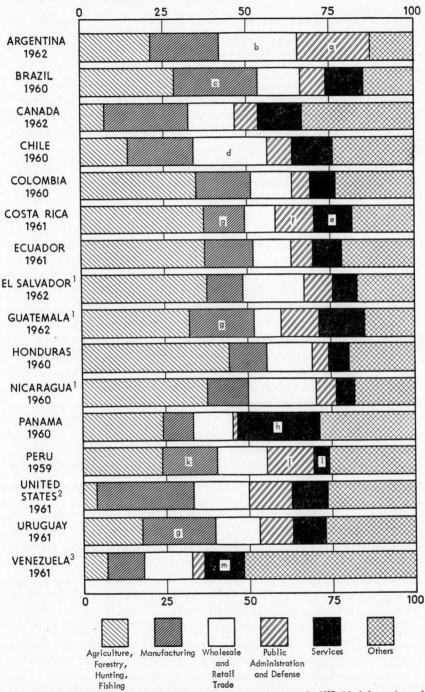

[1] At market prices. [2] Net domestic product. [3] At market prices, and constant for 1957. [a] Includes services and electricity, gas, water and sanitary services. [b] Includes transportation, storage, and communication. [c] Includes mining and quarrying, construction and electricity, gas, water and sanitary services. [d] Includes all services of general government. [e] Includes electricity. [f] Includes water and sanitary services and all services of general government. [g] Includes mining and quarrying. [h] Includes services provided to the Canal Zone. [i] Includes rental income, ownership of dwellings, real estate, and miscellaneous services. [j] Represents total expenditure of general government, including consumption expenditure and fixed capital formation. [k] Includes construction. [m] Includes banking, insurance, and real estate.

SOURCE: Américas, January, 1964, pp. 42, 43. Reproduced by permission.

industrialization. From the standpoint of their policy objective, the nation's customs duties and commodities can be classified into three main categories: (1) furniture, apparel, and processed foods, protected by a tariff so high as to make it impossible for foreign imports to compete with them; (2) vegetables, lard, beer, and many other items protected by a tariff of from 50 to 100 percent of the domestic wholesale price, which protected the home industry but did not preclude foreign competition; and (3) capital equipment, tools, and semifabricated products which the nation did not produce, admitted at a low rate.

The survey of Venezuela's tariff policy concludes: "Venezuelan protective policy has in general been successful in creating the basic socioeconomic framework within which domestic manufacture could develop and experience be gained in management and skills."[18]

In Latin America generally, a tariff schedule usually contains four levels of duties: protective duties on agricultural commodities and manufactures produced or suitable for production in the nation concerned; high duties on luxuries; revenue duties on articles which cannot be feasibly produced in the country; and nominal duties on machinery, raw materials, and semimanufactures which are not produced in the nation concerned.

As a rule tariff rates are not fixed by congress and embodied in legislative enactment; rather, they are determined by the executive who has broad authority to raise or lower them by executive decree. Consequently, rates are changed more frequently than in countries such as the United States where tariff making is primarily a legislative function, with certain discretion delegated to the president.

The duties levied were high enough to protect the sprouting home industries until 1930, when the depression seemingly forced all nations to adopt many new restrictionist trade measures to keep afloat at the expense of their neighbors. The nations of Latin America fell into line. Brazil, for example, required all importers of wheat and wheat flour to mix with their products a certain proportion of native mandioca flour.

The nations during this time also adopted many positive measures to promote economic development. They made loans at a low rate of interest, gave guarantees of a minimum rate of return, and granted subsidies without any obligation of repayment.

Another inducement which was often successful was special tax treatment given to an industry. In Brazil, a decree of 1932 granting a ten-year exemption from import duties on machinery required in the construction and expansion of plants was designed to promote the development of the cement industry. The tax concession accomplished its purpose, resulting in the establishment of some of the nation's largest cement plants. Tax concessions are still effective inducements for encouraging industry. When Costa Rica, to encourage light industry, enacted in 1963 a Protection of

Industries Law which offers virtually a ten-year tax holiday to manufacturers of products not previously produced there, the law produced a spate of widely diversified small enterprises, which produced such products as fiber glass, toothpaste, shoe polish, detergents, corrugated roofing, collapsible plastics, wrapping paper, and hairpins.

OBSTACLES TO INDUSTRIAL DEVELOPMENT

There are many obstacles to industrial development in Latin America. The main ones which we will consider are: lack of capital, shortage of engineers and skilled labor, high cost of production, politicial instability and governmental bureaucracy, and antipathetic mores and cultural values.

Lack of Capital

Lack of capital which industrialists or would-be industrialists need in order to establish, expand, or modernize an enterprise is unquestionably one of the main hindrances to industrialization. This shortage, which is felt by governments and individuals alike, is apparent in many ways. Hardly a week passes that one of the nations, maybe several of them, does not apply to the World Bank or some other international agency to borrow money needed for its economy. As one travels through Latin America, he sees many tangible evidences of the great need for capital. In city after city, even in the capitals of Bogotá, La Paz, and Buenos Aires, showplaces for the nation and the world, he is impressed by the skeletons of tall buildings whose construction began years ago but which could not be completed because of lack of funds.

The scarcity of capital available to the entrepreneur[19] is the result of many significant factors. The disadvantageous terms of trade whereby the region sells its agricultural and other exports at a cheap price but pays dearly for the manufactured products it imports have severely limited its financial resources.

Equally as serious has been the flight of capital from the region. The fantastic wealth which dictators—occasionally constitutional presidents too —manage to smuggle out of the nations and deposit to their personal accounts in Swiss, American, or other foreign banks and enterprises is well publicized by the press. Indeed, when a dictator and his entourage have to go into exile after a successful revolution, it is rather assumed that the suitcases, trunks, and other luggage loaded onto departing planes contain the receipts of the national treasury. But even more serious from the standpoint of a nation's economic development is the quiet, little publicized, insidious flight of capital from where it was produced and is greatly

---

[19] For a breakdown by countries of the sources of savings for gross capital formation, with the relative importance of each source, see William I. Abraham, "Saving Patterns in Latin America," *Economic Development and Cultural Change,* Vol. 12, No. 4 (July, 1964), pp. 380–81.

needed to areas which have money to spare. In short, many of Latin America's wealthiest citizens have so little confidence in their nations that while they do not mind bleeding them for all they can get, they surreptitiously take their profits elsewhere for investment and safekeeping.

The very threat of the flight of capital is so serious that it can hamstring a government, preventing it from making much-needed reforms, in taxation for instance. "The capacity and willingness to tax are limited by many circumstances," concludes Raymond Vernon, referring to Mexico, "by a long tradition of tax evasion and corruption, by technical limitations in the tax-collecting apparatus, and by a justifiable fear that high taxes will either induce capital flight or generate widespread public unrest, depending on their form. As a result . . . the government seems incapable for the present of collecting more than 10 or 11 per cent of its gross national product in the form of tax revenues."[20]

Elsewhere, capital is fleeing from some of the nations which need it most. In Argentina an estimated $1 or $2 billion has left the country during the last several years. In Peru the situation is apparently far worse; an estimated $1 billion in profits leaves the country every year for safekeeping abroad, according to the confidential estimate of a top government official.[21]

Capital tiptoes out of the countries so stealthily that even the approximate amount kept in foreign banks or invested in foreign enterprises is unknown. It may be from $5 billion to $25 billion—perhaps as much as the United States plans to invest in Latin America during the ten-year program of the Alliance for Progress. "This is money that could be used to build roads, finance land reforms, and perhaps even to hold back a violent social revolution," deplores Tad Szulc. "But the vicious circle of greed still holds Latin America in its grip."[22]

A prominent Latin American is equally as frank in contemplating the problem. "Native capital flees from Latin America," writes Germán Arciniegas. "Only in Montevideo and Mexico City have large fortunes found refuge. *If the amount of Latin American funds on deposit today in the banks of New York and Switzerland were accurately known one would conclude that Latin America possesses all the capital it needs.*"[23]

The shortage of domestic capital available for the entreprenuer is further complicated in many of the countries by the unfavorable climate for foreign investment. Nationalization of foreign properties and disregard

---

[20] Raymond Vernon, *The Dilemma of Mexico's Development: The Roles of the Private and Public Sectors* (Cambridge, Mass.: Harvard University Press, 1963), p. 185.

[21] Interview with the author in Lima, June 27, 1963.

[22] Tad Szulc, *The Winds of Revolution: Latin America Today—And Tomorrow* (New York: Frederick A. Praeger, Inc., 1964), p. 70.

[23] Germán Arciniegas, *The State of Latin America*, trans. Harriet de Onís (New York: Alfred A. Knopf, Inc., 1952), p. 391. Italics in the cited material have been supplied by this author.

of contracts with foreign companies have scared away investment funds from abroad which Latin America greatly needs. Investors, already leery of Argentina because of its political and economic instability, shied away even further after President Illía, carrying out a campaign pledge, in November, 1963, canceled the contracts under which foreign companies had been producing oil or drilling wells in Argentina for the State Petroleum Authority, investing more than $250 million in the operations. Repudiation of the contracts signed with the former Frondizi regime, together with the nationalization of foreign properties in many of the countries, has deprived the nations of much private capital which they might otherwise have had.

The lack of capital in the nations is also due to the traditional neglect of agriculture and the resulting inability of this important segment to play its role in materially aiding the economy. The concentration of landownership in relatively few hands, failure to use modern methods or machinery, letting large acreages lie idle, and concentrating on money crops have prevented agriculture from feeding the populace properly or making the contribution which it might to the formation of capital.

The priority given by Mexico to land reform should be heeded by the other nations of Latin America. For about 20 years after the civil strife ended, agrarian reform and agrarian policy were the main interests of the Mexican government. Getting land into the hands of the peasants and carrying out the agrarian revolution were the priority tasks to which the government devoted itself. It was not until after 1940 that its attention shifted sharply from agriculture to industry and the nation began to make great headway in establishing a base for full-scale industrial development.[24]

Genuine land reform is a *sine qua non* of sound economic development and should be given top priority in every state where it is needed. "The future of Brazil," says T. Lynn Smith, "is dependent on the land system it adopts or fails to adopt more than upon any other factor."[25]

Shortage of Engineers and Skilled Labor

Another obstacle which industrialists in Latin America often encounter is the shortage of engineers and skilled labor. Since engineering is not regarded as one of the professions of high status, college students have passed it by in preference for law, medicine, or other fields which have more *dignidad*. Consequently, the region is very short of capable, trained engineering talent. The dilemma of Brazil is common to many other nations in the region. Although Brazil is staking its future very largely on its ability to industrialize rapidly, it needs many more engineers to accomplish this; it has only about one-quarter as many proportionately as does the United States. One year a single factory in São Paulo proposed to hire

---

[24] Mosk, *op. cit.*, p. vii.
[25] T. Lynn Smith, *Brazil: People and Institutions* (rev. ed.; Baton Rouge, La.: Louisiana State University Press, 1963), p. 621.

the entire graduating class of the Polytechnic School, which supplied a large proportion of the nation's engineering graduates.[26]

Eschewing dirty hands or manual labor, even those students who study engineering get a better theoretical than practical education. They balk at putting on coveralls, getting down to earth with machinery, and applying the principles and knowledge which they have learned. As a result of this attitude and the emphasis on theoretical rather than practical training, the factories are often far from models of progressive industrial enterprises. In Brazil a study by the United Nations pointed out many weaknesses in the important textile industry. Overage machines were one problem, but more important were the inadequately specialized techniques of production and improper conditions of manufacture, such as uncleanliness, sloppy maintenance of machines, and lack of other sound engineering practices.[27]

The shortage of engineers in the region has been greatly aggravated by their desire to immigrate to other nations, particularly the United States, where engineering is not only a very respected profession but also one which pays relatively well. During the period 1951–61 some 3,284 Argentine technicians immigrated to the United States.[28]

An inadequate supply of skilled labor has also been a problem for industrialists. Uneducated as most workers are and unfamiliar with machinery of any sort, training them for the many skilled operations of modern production has been a burden on industry. Yet illiteracy and the lack of experience have not prevented the natives from becoming skilled productive workers in a short time when they were interested. Indeed, Indians fresh from the *communidades* in the hinterlands and with no training at all for skilled industrial jobs rapidly become proficient in operating machines or performing manual operations which require fast handwork and good coordination. "Moreover, they are artistic perfectionists," a textile engineer explained to the author, "and create beautiful, creative designs when they have the opportunity."

High Costs of Production and Distribution

The high costs of production in Latin America are facts of life which must be reckoned with. They are very frustrating to the entrepreneur—to the Argentine automobile manufacturer, for example, who has to charge $4,800 for a Rambler which sells for $2,400 in the United States. The price is so high as to greatly reduce the demand, further depressing an industry which is finding it difficult to keep going. The high costs of production are also a matter of serious concern to policy makers. In Chile the decision by the Kennecott Copper Corporation which controls El Teniente to invest $100 million to boost the production of its mine in

---

[26] Richard M. Morse, *From Community to Metropolis: A Biography of São Paulo, Brazil* (Gainesville, Fla.: University of Florida Press, 1958), p. 231.

[27] *Ibid.*

[28] *Hispanic American Report,* Vol. XVI, No. 8 (October, 1963), p. 810.

Utah , rather than in Chile largely because of the high costs of operating there was almost as bad news to the nation as a destructive earthquake.

The great expense of distribution is also a serious problem of the entrepreneur. The cost of shipping a product is so high that relatively inefficient plants can sell to local markets from which the goods manufactured at lower cost elsewhere are excluded; the difficulties and costs of transportation have been among the most adverse factors hindering the development of a national market.

The high rate of interest which entrepreneurs must expect to pay is another restricting factor on production. While some of the nations have regulations which supposedly set limits to the rate of interest which can be charged, in practice the going rate is whatever the traffic will bear— 15 percent, 25 percent, or maybe much more. In the fast growing metropolis of São Paulo, the industrialist who seeks capital to establish or expand his enterprise may have to pay annual interest rates of 50 to 70 percent. Indeed, competition for working capital and commercial credit has reached such a point in the nation that finance companies flourish by making short-term loans at 45 to 60 percent interest.

The limited market which is characteristic of the region is also largely responsible for the high cost of production. Although Latin America's population is approximately 200 million—about the same size as that of the United States—this group does not constitute a market as we think of it in the United States. In Latin America, production goals are usually established for what by our standards would be a very small market—10 percent of the population, 5 percent, or possibly much less. There is no thought of mass production for a mass market.

The limited market is the result of the interplay of many social and economic conditions. The income of a large part of the population is pathetically low—less than $100 per year in several of the countries. The difficulty of even subsisting on the low incomes has been greatly aggravated by inflation, which is rampant in some of the nations, as shown by the consumer goods and food indexes. Taking 1958 as the base year, the cost of food in 1964 in São Paulo is ten times higher. In Buenos Aires all consumer goods are almost six times the 1958 price; Chile and Uruguay have also experienced serious inflation with all goods three times their 1958 price.[29]

The spiraling increase in the cost of living greatly outstrips the increase in wages and works a severe hardship on the low income members of society. The unbridled inflation may be fundamentally, as some believe, a struggle among groups for the redistribution of real income, with the rise in the price level merely the external expression of that struggle.[30] This interpretation takes cognizance of the government's use of the printing press to stimulate the economy and its ability to establish a firm

---

[29] *International Labour Review*, Statistical Supplement, Vol. XC, No. 1 (July, 1964), pp. 9–12.

[30] Furtado, *op. cit.*, p. 253.

effective policy which can quickly curb inflation. Colombia was singularly successful in 1963 in curbing inflation. The nation's able, tough-minded minister of finance, Carlos Sanz de Santamaria, inaugurated a stern program of austerity and drastic fiscal reforms which were vigorously opposed by the bankers, the congress, the coffee growers, and other powerful interests. But sticking to his guns, Señor Sanz made his program stick —and curbed the rise in prices.[31]

While inflation aggravates the maldistribution of income within the society, the tax structure is largely to blame for this maldistribution. The tax systems of 14 nations for which statistics are available are regressive, based in large part on indirect taxes which bear heavily upon the many low-income wage earners. Half of these nations obtain more than 50 percent of their revenue from indirect taxes; in two of them, the percentage reaches 70 and 85 percent. In the other half of the 14 nations, indirect taxes provide more than one-third of the revenue, except in Venezuela, which receives a high proportion of its income from direct taxes on petroleum.[32] Even the low income taxes which were levied according to law on the larger incomes in the nation were often successfully evaded. In Argentina the government in late 1963 instituted a substantial revision of the income tax scale which was calculated to cut down on evasion, officially estimated at 55 percent. A total of 8,600 cases of evasion were pending in the tax courts.[33]

Change in the tax structure to place more of the financial burden on those most able to carry it is generally recognized as one of the most urgently needed reforms in the region. "Taxes fall too heavily upon the shoulders of low-income groups while those in the higher brackets do not pay their share," complained Raúl Prebisch. "The tax system has not been used, as it has in the United States and other advanced countries to diminish greatly the wide differences in distribution of income."[34]

Reform of the nations' tax laws in order to achieve a more just distribution of the taxpayers' load would accomplish two important results, asserted Galo Plaza: "that those who are most able to pay, do pay; and a reduction, insofar as possible, in the indirect taxes that unjustly weigh most heavily on those least able to pay."[35]

Certain aspects of government have also served to hinder the advance of industrialization. The well-known governmental instability of nations in the Caribbean and Central America has discouraged foreign investors. Too, the many dictatorial military regimes have prevented the development of a healthy, competitive economic order, and dissipated much of the nations' limited income on large military establishments.

---

[31] *New York Times*, "Hemisphere Business Review," January 17, 1964, p. 62, col. 1.
[32] Elba Kybal, "Why More Taxes?" *Américas*, Vol. 14, No. 4 (April, 1962), p. 12.
[33] *Hispanic American Report, op. cit.*, p. 810.
[34] *U.S. News and World Report, op. cit.*, p. 62.
[35] Galo Plaza on "The Obstacles to the Alliance," *Américas*, Vol. 14, No. 3 (March, 1962), p. 9.

Moreover, with governments assuming a larger role in promoting economic development, an increasingly large number of trained, efficient administrators and specialists is needed. Such personnel, however, are in as short supply as engineers.

The very top-heaviness of government is a great burden on economic and social development. In Uruguay, padded personnel rolls are a serious financial drain on the nation. Twenty percent or more of the total population depend for their livelihood on wages, salaries, and other income from the government, and three-fourths or more of the budget is normally allocated for the payment of personnel.[36] Argentina has a similar problem: according to President Arturo Frondizi, 7 million inhabitants [more than one-third of the total population] are dependent upon employment by the national, provincial, or municipal government. "More than 30 percent of the state's income is spent on wages," said Frondizi, "and this explains why there is no money to build houses, roads, schools, or even to repair pavements or give more light to our dark streets."[37]

Cultural Values and Mores

The cultural values and the mores of Latin America have also served in many ways to obstruct the progress of industrialization. The upper class which might logically be expected to provide entrepreneurial talent is contemptuous of such mundane economic pursuits. But even when a member of this class does enter private business—in a "respectable" position, of course, as president of the company or chairman of its board of directors—his cultural background is a hindrance rather than a help. Accustomed to giving orders to peons and others who are inferior to him, he cannot help but be authoritarian in his conduct of a modern business enterprise. He may agree with the principle of delegating duties, but the very idea of delegating to inferiors the authority necessary to operate effectively is culturally repugnant to him. Even more repugnant is sitting in a staff meeting and listening to the opinions and recommendations of subordinates.

Also obstructing industrialization are the deeply ingrained investment habits which are antithetical to the widespread mobilization of large capital upon which modern industry depends. Most persons with money to invest prefer to put it into farms, office buildings, or apartment buildings, all of which are socially respectable as well as tangible types of property. They are loath to use their money to buy stocks and bonds or any other "mere pieces of paper." In fact, unless they personally know the individuals or group they are dealing with, they have no confidence in them. As a result of this suspicious attitude, it is most difficult for corporations to float large

---

[36] Russell H. Fitzgibbon, "Uruguay: A Model for Freedom and Reform in Latin America," *Freedom and Reform in Latin America* (ed. Fredrick B. Pike) (Notre Dame, Ind.: University of Notre Dame Press, 1959), pp. 249–50.

[37] In Lewis Hanke, *South America* (New York: D. Van Nostrand Co., Inc., 1959), p. 163.

issues of stocks and bonds, or for banks and insurance companies to develop. Many family businesses have been converted into corporations for tax advantages and other purposes, but their stocks are tightly held by members of the family and are not open to the public.[38]

Certain other cultural habits are in contradiction to the regimentation found necessary by modern industry, such as getting to work on time and leaving on time, and putting in eight hours of work a day for five days a week, with reasonable time off for lunch. In "siesta land," it is the almost universal custom to take a three-hour break in the middle of the day for a leisurely meal and lengthy nap. Neither the pressure of business nor noisy, crawly traffic jams have been able to change this hallowed custom, desecrated only by the American Embassy and AID staffs, and American companies whose personnel bring their lunches with them or eat in the company cafeteria.

Even more frustrating to the production schedules of modern industry are the many days taken off for *fiestas*, celebrations of religious or national holidays or of births, weddings, and burials. The celebrations were marked by "untiring dancing and drinking. . . . The expense . . . (when combined with the purchase of coca leaves) tends to absorb available surplus income and also to reduce working time and labor efficiency. As long as this primitive pattern of habits prevails, it is almost impossible to achieve improvements in standards of living."[39] The Bolivian pueblo of Mairana in the province of Florida had a total of 107 days off from work in 1960 for such *fiestas*.[40]

THE EXPANDED ROLE OF GOVERNMENT IN ECONOMIC DEVELOPMENT

In every one of the Latin American nations, the government plays a very active role in promoting economic development. It performs or directly controls many services which in capitalistic nations are customarily regarded as being within the province of individual enterpreneurs. Even as early as the 1920s, several of the governments, particularly those of Uruguay and Chile, adopted programs of social welfare which were quite advanced for the time—the United States adopted them years later as part of the New Deal.

The greatly expanded activity of government in promoting economic

---

[38] The effects of personalism and family ties on industrial development are discussed by John P. Gillin in "Some Signposts for Policy," *Social Change in Latin America Today* (Council on Foreign Relations) (New York: Harper & Bros., 1960), pp. 29–40.

[39] John Lindberg, "Bolivia: Mines Without Industry," *Current History*, Vol. 22 (March, 1952), pp. 145–46.

[40] Alfredo Chavarria Frias, "Estudio Socio-Económica de la Provincia Florida Realisado por la Agencia de a Extensión," (Unpublished Report, Santa Cruz, Bolivia, 1961).

development and utilizing tax funds and public credit was the result of an accident of history—or, as some would say, a dispensation of divine providence. The awesome earthquake of January 24, 1939, in Chile, which killed more than 30,000 people, injured 50,000 others, and destroyed most of the large cities of Concepción and Chillan, as well as many smaller towns and villages, was one of the most destructive in history. However, it provided the needed stimulus for a program of action which greatly benefited the nation, and the other countries of Latin America too. A temporary emergency program of reconstruction was adopted to provide all aid possible to the stricken areas. Of greater social significance, however, was the companion governmental program for promoting long-range economic development in the whole nation—a program not only ambitiously wide in scope but also so challenging as to bring out the latent possibilities of every segment of the economy.

The resulting Chilean Fomento, or Development Corporation, unique in the annals of Latin America, was the prototype of other similar government authorities which have greatly influenced public policy and the course of economic development throughout the region.

Chile's Fomento, designed both to rehabilitate the earthquake-stricken regions as well as to promote economic progress in general, was endowed with wide authority and charged with weighty responsibilities. These included: drawing up a comprehensive plan for stimulating production so as to raise the standard of living; making studies to discover the most effective means of increasing production; conducting experiments in producing and selling goods; and aiding domestic producers to gain a larger share in the nation's industrial and commercial activities.

The Fomento, regarded by some as the epitome of governmental interference in the economic realm, had as a primary aim stimulating production by assisting private efforts. It invested its funds in carefully selected enterprises that needed help, often running the risk of a loss, and later pulled out, turning the operations over to private ownership when they became going concerns.

The funds needed by the Fomento for its activities were derived from certain allocated taxes, mainly a special tax on copper; loans from the Export-Import Bank of the United States; and revenues derived from government enterprises. To protect the interests of the public when tax monies were invested either in mixed public-private or completely private undertakings, the government usually had several representatives on the board of directors but did not presume to dictate policy. Rather, in the contractual agreements with the enterprises, it established the terms and conditions deemed to be in the public interest and had inspectors for checking to see that the agreements were observed.

In promoting economic development, the Fomento gave needed assistance to just about every phase of the economy: sources of energy and fuel, such as hydroelectric projects, coal mines, or oil wells; industries of every sort, including metallurgical, chemical, textile, cement, and timber and forestry; mines producing a wide variety of minerals, including manganese, cobalt, zinc, lead, tungsten, gold, talc, kaolin, graphite, and aluminum sulphate; land, sea, and air transportation; and agriculture and ranching.

In short, to promote Chile's economic development, the Fomento could undertake any project from constructing a modern steel mill or building a huge hydroelectric dam to erecting a silo for a rancher and aiding him to get started in producing purebred cattle.

Exercising a wide authority, Chile's Fomento has played a most important role in the economic development of the nation. "The initiative, the forethought, the spirit of going out after business and the ability to do so successfully, are evident from first-hand observation of the Corporation's methods and personnel, and show clearly that there is a large fund of ability and public spirit at work," wrote Herman Finer. "The feeling that Chile is being rebuilt or built for the first time causes a remarkable release of devotion and thinking. Capable young men are being interested and introduced into economic administration at a stage which is both creative and adventurous. This is a most important factor for the future of Chilean development."[41]

Following Chile's lead, the other nations have adopted development corporations of one sort or another, and their governments have been taking a very active part in promoting and participating in economic development. As evidence of this, public investment constitutes a much larger proportion of the total investment than in the United States. In Latin America new public investment during the period 1950–56 averaged approximately 25 percent of the total amount. This was more than ten times the figure in the United States for the same period.

The extensive intervention of government in Latin America to promote economic development is due to many deeply rooted causes. Capital is in short supply, and domestic capital, which should carry most of the load, often is not interested in investing in local enterprises, as we have noted. Hoping to change this attitude, the International Bank has sometimes recommended that a nation establish a *fomento*, whose main purpose would be to encourage individuals to invest their capital in productive domestic undertakings.[42]

---

[41] Herman Finer, "The Chilean Development Corporation: A Study in National Planning to Raise Living Standards," *International Labour Office, Studies and Reports* (New Series No. 5) (Montreal, 1947), p. 80. A more recent, brief account of Fomento's activities may be found in Alvin Cohen, *Economic Change in Chile, 1929–1959* (Latin American Monograph Series) (Gainesville, Fla.: University of Florida Press, 1960), pp. 31–36.

[42] In Nicaragua, the International Bank figured that if the upper 1 percent of the income recipients invested just 10 percent of their incomes in such enterprises, the existing current rate of investment would increase by 50 percent. (International Bank for Reconstruction and Development, *The Economic Development of Nicaragua*, 1953, p. 12.)

Government intervention is also largely the result of a frequently expressed prejudice against reliance upon foreign capital as a possible alternative for financing economic development. The region has long been dependent upon outside capital for underwriting its economic growth; investment from the United States alone amounts to more than $7 billion. Objections to foreign capital from the United States and elsewhere have come from many sources. Military leaders, motivated by considerations of national security, are opposed to foreign control of such sensitive operations as communications systems, which explains why most Latin American governments own the telephone companies.[43]

Besides military leaders, many others are opposed to the entry and influence of foreign capital if it can possibly be avoided. Rising local entrepreneurs are convinced that it puts them at a distinct competitive disadvantage, even when their competitors are large native operators financed by foreign capital.[44] Ardent nationalists too have often been resentful at what they regard as the intrusion of foreign capital. Some have drawn the line at foreign exploitation of petroleum. To maintain the national *dignidad* and derive what they regard as full advantage from the resource, they prefer to let it lie underground where it has been for a million years or so and can remain for awhile longer until they are in a position to exploit it.

Other ardent nationalists have been opposed to foreign investment in general. In Uruguay, the government's extensive participation in the economic realm began with the vigorous nationalistic doctrine which José Batlle directed against the foreign businessman.

This antiforeignism combined with the conviction that domestic private enterprise lacked the capacity to replace foreign capital led to State intervention in the economy. Subsequently the preference for State enterprises has stemmed more from the failure of private initiative to make the expected contribution to output and services and less from any strong belief in fundamental social theories.[45]

In intervening to promote economic development, governments have been motivated by still other considerations. Besides finding useful the revenues produced by publicly owned projects, they can speed up the tempo of economic development by vigorous, intelligent intervention. Moreover, they can promote balanced and diversified development, with which private initiative is not concerned. In Venezuela, foreign and domestic private capital has been lopsidedly concentrated in one area alone, the exploitation of oil; consequently, governmental activity has been

---

[43] If many of these companies operated as the one in Managua, the capital of Nicaragua, control of the system even by the enemy would only serve to confuse and frustrate him. For it often takes so long to make a phone call there that the caller gives up in disgust and sends a telegram or a message by a runner. (*Ibid.*, p. 250.)

[44] Mosk, *op. cit.*, p. 26.

[45] John J. Johnson, *Political Change in Latin America: The Emergence of the Middle Sectors* (Stanford, Calif.: Stanford University Press, 1958), p. 56.

necessary to take care of the many neglected aspects of the economy.

Government's intervention to further economic development has also been strongly motivated by the need for comprehensive planning. For want of vision, a people perish, goes a familiar adage. Latin Americans prefer to exercise vision, and plan as best they can for their future.

"What is the need for planning?" Raúl Prebisch was asked in an interview.

"Because we do not believe that under present circumstances, the mere play of economic forces alone will solve the problems of growth fast enough or decisively enough," he answered. "There must be conscious and deliberate action to influence growth and further the system of individual initiative."[46]

Planning is unfortunately sometimes not as sound as it should be. In Uruguay, long an ardent exponent of the planned economy, planning in recent years appears to be "jerry-built and in some instances the product of emergency and erratic response to exigencies as they developed one by one."[47]

Yet planning is urgently needed on both the national and regional levels. Upon its wisdom and effectiveness depend the realization of Latin America's aspirations for a better tomorrow.

SUGGESTED READINGS

ALEXANDER, ROBERT J. *The Bolivian National Revolution*, chaps. 6, 9, 11. New Brunswick, N.J.: Rutgers University Press, 1958.

BENHAM, F., AND HOLLEY, H. A. *A Short Introduction to the Economy of Latin America*. Royal Institute of International Affairs. New York: Oxford University Press, 1960.

BURGESS, EUGENE W., AND HARBISON, FREDERICK H. *Casa Grace in Peru*. Second Case Study, United States Business Performance Abroad. National Planning Association, 1954.

CLINE, HOWARD F. *Mexico: Revolution to Evolution: 1940–1960*, chaps. xxix and xxx. Royal Institute of International Affairs. New York: Oxford University Press, 1962.

————. *The United States and Mexico*, chaps. 16 and 17, rev. ed.; Cambridge, Mass.: Harvard University Press, 1963.

COHEN, ALVIN. *Economic Change in Chile, 1929–1959*. Latin American Monograph Series. Gainesville, Fla.: University of Florida Press, 1960.

ELLSWORTH, P. T. *Chile: An Economy in Transition*. New York: The Macmillan Co., 1945.

FINER, HERMAN. *The Chilean Development Corporation*. Montreal: International Labour Office, 1947.

FITZGIBBON, RUSSELL H. *Uruguay: Portrait of a Democracy*, chap. vii. New Brunswick, N.J.: Rutgers University Press, 1954.

---

[46] *U.S. News and World Report, op. cit.,* p. 64.
[47] Fitzgibbon, *op. cit.,* p. 248.

FURTADO, CELSO. *The Economic Growth of Brazil: A Survey from Colonial to Modern Times.* Trans. RICARDO W. DE AGUIAR AND ERIC CHARLES DRYSDALE. Berkeley: University of California Press, 1963.

✳GORDON, WENDELL C. "Freedom and Reform in Urban and Industrializing Latin America," *Freedom and Reform in Latin America* (ed. FREDRICK B. PIKE), pp. 177–202. Notre Dame, Ind.: Notre Dame Press, 1959.

HANSON, SIMON H. *Economic Development in Latin America,* chaps. 6, 7, 10, and 14. Washington, D.C.: Inter-American Affairs Press, 1951.

HUGHLETT, LLOYD (ed.). *Industrialization of Latin America.* New York: McGraw-Hill Book Co., Inc., 1946.

INTERNATIONAL BANK FOR RECONSTRUCTION AND DEVELOPMENT. *The Economic Development of Venezuela,* chaps. 2, 4, 7, 10, and Annex I. Baltimore: Johns Hopkins Press, 1961.

KALIJARVI, THORSTEN V. *Central America: Land of lords and lizards,* chap. 7. Princeton, N.J.: D. Van Nostrand Co., Inc., 1962.

LIEUWEN, EDWIN. *Venezuela,* chap. iv. Royal Institute of International Affairs. New York: Oxford University Press, 1961.

MACGAFFEY, WYATT, AND BARNETT, CLIFFORD R. *Cuba.* Survey of World Cultures, chaps. 3 and 16. New Haven, Conn.: HRAF Press, 1962.

MAY, STACY (dir.), *et al.* *Costa Rica: A Study in Economic Development,* chaps. 2, 6, 9 and 10. New York: Twentieth Century Fund, 1952.

MAY, STACY, AND PLAZA, GALO. *The United Fruit Company in Latin America.* Seventh Case Study, United States Business Performance Abroad. National Planning Association, 1958.

MOORE, WILBERT. *Industrialization and Labor: Social Aspects of Economic Development,* Part 1. Institute of World Affairs. Ithaca: Cornell University Press, 1951.

MORSE, RICHARD M. *From Community to Metropolis: A Biography of São Paulo, Brazil,* chaps. 14–18. Gainesville, Fla.: University of Florida Press, 1958.

MOSK, SANFORD A. *Industrial Revolution in Mexico.* Berkeley: University of California Press, 1954.

NORMANO, J. F. *Brazil: A Study of Economic Types.* Chapel Hill, N.C.: University of North Carolina Press, 1935.

OSBORNE, HAROLD. *Bolivia: A Land Divided,* pp. 106–34. Royal Institute of International Affairs. London: Oxford University Press, 1954.

PIERSON, WILLIAM W., AND GIL, FEDERICO G. *Governments of Latin America,* chap. 15. New York: McGraw-Hill Book Co., Inc., 1957.

RIPPY, J. FRED. *The Capitalists and Colombia.* Studies in American Imperialism. New York: Vanguard Press, 1931.

———. *Latin America and the Industrial Age.* New York: G. P. Putnam's Sons, 1944.

SALERA, VIRGIL. "Government and the Economic Order," *Government and Politics in Latin America* (ed. HAROLD EUGENE DAVIS), chap. 15. New York: Ronald Press Co., 1958.

STARK, HARRY. *Social and Economic Frontiers in Latin America,* chaps. 1, 4, 9, 12–14, 18–28. 2d ed. Dubuque, Ia.: W. C. Brown Co., 1963.

STOKES, WILLIAM S. *Latin American Politics,* chap. 10. New York: Thomas Y. Crowell Co., 1959.

TANNENBAUM, FRANK. *Mexico: The Struggle for Peace and Bread*, chaps. 11-13. New York: Alfred A. Knopf, Inc., 1954.

TAYLOR, WAYNE C., AND LINDEMAN, JOHN, with the collaboration of VICTOR LÓPEZ R. *The Creole Petroleum Corporation in Venezuela*. Fourth Case Study, United States Business Performance Abroad. National Planning Association, 1955.

VERNON, RAYMOND. *The Dilemma of Mexico's Development: The Role of the Private and Public Sectors*. Cambridge, Mass.: Harvard University Press, 1963.

WEYL, NATHANIEL, AND WEYL, SYLVIA. *The Reconquest of Mexico: The Years of Lázaro Cárdenas*, chap. x. New York: Oxford University Press, 1939.

WILGUS, A. CURTIS (ed.). *The Caribbean: Venezuelan Development; A Case History*, Parts III and IV. The Caribbean Conference Series, One, Vol. XIII. Gainesville, Fla.: University of Florida Press, 1963.

WOOD, RICHARDSON, AND KEYSER, VIRGINIA. *Sears, Roebuck de Mexico, S.A.* First Case Study, United States Business Performance Abroad. National Planning Association, 1953.

WYTHE, GEORGE. *Industry in Latin America*. 2d ed. New York: Columbia University Press, 1949.

CHAPTER 10

LABOR:
A Fair Share or Else

LABOR is a third member of the economic triumvirate, along with agriculture and industry. It was late to organize and exert the weight of its organized influence in Latin America. Yet it plays a strong role in the political dynamics of the region today and is a force to be increasingly reckoned with. Large landowners, military leaders, and high officials of the Church—traditional representatives of established power and influence—all recognize and respect the power of this new revolutionary force which has an important role in shaping the region's development.

ORIGIN AND DEVELOPMENT OF TRADE UNIONISM[1]

Trade unionism was relatively late in coming to Latin America. In some countries the stirrings of the labor movement can be traced as far back as the 1860s and 1870s to the workers in the cotton gins and cottonseed oil mills, flour mills and grain elevators, sugar mills and refineries, and many other local enterprises, including the hat and shoe factories of the "Pittsburgh of South America." Up until World War I, organized labor, like its counterpart, industry, was struggling to establish itself and make its influence felt in the society.

Just as World War I gave industrial development a potent shot in the arm, it gave a strong stimulus to the organization of labor. As new industries were established and expanded during and after the war, often enabling their owners to reap great fortunes, they also redounded to the good fortune of the workers, who made higher wages and joined labor unions in increasing numbers.

---

[1] Much of this background is from Moises Poblete-Troncoso and Ben G. Burnett, *The Rise of the Latin American Labor Movement* (New Haven, Conn.: College and University Press, 1960), pp. 13–19.

Later, during the 1930s and '40s, just as industry developed during the depression and particularly during and after World War II, so did the labor movement expand and increase in stature. The total number of organized workers increased enormously. In many of the countries, especially Argentina and Mexico, practically all the presently organizable workers belong to a union.

In their evolution, labor unions have passed through three stages of development. In the early days of the movement, they were mutual benefit societies which in return for small contributions from members provided them with night schools and libraries to enable them to get ahead and also paid for their medical treatment, drugs, and funeral expenses.

In the second stage, labor groups became societies of resistance. No longer content with being merely mutualist associations whose main purpose was to pass the hat around for the mutual protection of one another, they now felt ready to stand up to employers and assert what they believed their rights should be as partners in the enterprises. This new posture of labor resulted in long and bitter conflict with capital—a strike against a mine, a factory, or a workshop, or sometimes against an entire industry. Almost every gain which labor made, however small, was accomplished at the price of violence, bloodshed, and often loss of life.

Finally, organized labor graduated into its third and current stage of development, when as a modern, strong trade union movement, it has become recognized as one of the powerful pressure groups in society, representing the interests of a very large part of the citizenry.

In achieving their present status, the unions have had to surmount or circumvent many a formidable obstacle. Employers were very hostile to the growing power of their laborers and did their best to stifle it by means of lockouts, blacklists, and various other methods of coercion. The government was an even more formidable adversary. Representing the interests of the large landowners and other wealthy members of society, it usually did not hesitate to put labor in its place, which normally meant beating it to its knees. Controlling the armed might of the civilian police and the army, the government was virtually in a position to break a strike at will by summarily putting recalcitrant workers into uniform and shipping them to distant parts of the country for months and even years, and by dealing even more summarily with labor "agitators," simply shooting them on the spot or putting them before a firing squad.

Other obstacles have stood in the way of labor's determined efforts to organize and achieve recognition. Ideological differences of anarcho-syndicalism, socialism, and communism have often divided workers into hostile factions which fought one another even more bitterly than they fought any outside adversary.[2] Moreover, the lack of able, honest leader-

---

[2] Syndicalism, similar in some respects to *corporatismo* (trade unionism), democratic socialism, anarchism, and Marxism, is essentially different from them. (Hubert Lagardelle, "Características del Sindicalismo," *Teoría y Práctica del Sindicalismo* [ed. Guillermo Davalos] [Buenos Aires, 1958], pp. 67–89.)

ship was a great disadvantage in dealing with competent, sophisticated employers, who often resolved a labor dispute by the simple expedient of buying off the labor representatives. The illiteracy of workers, too, together with their lack of information and experience, also impeded the growth of trade unionism; workers with such handicaps could hardly comprehend the goals they were collectively striving for, much less the responsibilities which they as members of the union should assume.

DISTINCTIVE FEATURES OF THE LABOR FORCE

There are several distinctive features of the labor force in Latin America. Much of it is either underemployed or unemployed, a condition which reduces the region's productivity and constitutes quite a problem for anyone in need of a job. A large proportion of the women are employed, mainly in the lower and middle classes; and many legal safeguards have been adopted for their protection. Child labor too is common throughout the region; laws adopted in behalf of minors seek to minimize the dangers to them and also to assure that work will not interfere with their education.[3]

Underemployment and Unemployment

Underemployment, which is characteristic of the economies of underdeveloped nations, may be either visible or invisible. In the case of the former, workers are employed only part time or less than normal periods of work, although they could work full time and prefer to do so. In the case of the latter, productivity or earnings are abnormally low, and jobs do not permit workers to use fully their capacities or skills.[4]

In Latin America underemployment exists at practically all levels in the society. The shortage of well-paying positions in the private sector forces many young men and women with college educations to seek employment in government. The fact of too little work to go around mainly accounts for the top-heavy government bureaucracies, especially those in Argentina and Uruguay which we noted earlier. The clamor to squeeze into the bureaucracy, already absurdly overcrowded, reminds one who has visited Latin America of the determination of many to ride an overcrowded streetcar, even if it means hanging outside on the rear bumper, holding on for dear life as the motorman guns his vehicle.

Another evidence of underemployment among urban workers is the relatively large percentage of them engaged in services of various kinds, as

---

[3] Still another distinctive feature, forced labor, was discussed in Chapter 2. Peonage in the form of *concertaje, yanaconazco, shirongaje, acasillaje,* and *mita* has long been a problem in Latin America, despite the many legal measures which the nations have adopted aimed at abolishing it. (Miguel Mejía Fernandez, *El Problema del Trabajo Forzado en América Latina* [Mexico, D.F.: Instituto de Investigaciones Sociales, Universidad Nacional, n.d.], pp. 7–30.)

[4] International Labour Office, *Employment and Economic Growth* (Studies and Reports, New Series, No. 67) (Geneva, Switz.: 1964), p. 25.

compared with the other major areas of work, shown in Table 10–1. The proportion of persons so employed is increasing, too. In 1948, 54 percent of the total labor force was engaged in agriculture; by 1955, however, only 50 percent were so employed. During the same period a constant 18 percent were engaged in manufacturing and construction. However,

TABLE 10–1

DISTRIBUTION OF THE LABOR FORCE BY MAJOR SECTORS
(Percentage)

Country	Total	Raw Material Production Agric.	Mines	Total	Industry Manu-facturers	Con-struc-tion	Serv-ices	Activi-ties Not Specif.
Venezuela	43.8	41.2	2.6	15.5	10.1	5.4	32.3	8.4
Argentina	25.2	24.7	0.5	29.0	22.9	6.1	43.7	2.3
Uruguay*	21.8	21.7	0.1	28.1	23.8	4.3	46.4	3.7
Cuba	44.2	43.8	0.4	18.3	15.6	2.7	36.6	0.9
Chile	34.6	29.8	4.8	24.0	18.5	5.5	37.6	3.8
Costa Rica	56.7	56.4	0.3	14.7	10.6	4.1	25.7	2.9
Panama	55.0	54.9	0.1	9.7	7.1	2.6	25.7	9.6
Mexico	59.0	57.8	1.2	14.8	12.0	2.8	21.8	4.4
Colombia	57.9	56.4	1.5	17.5	14.4	3.1	21.1	3.5
Brazil	61.8	61.1	0.7	16.7	12.8	3.9	21.2	0.3
Guatemala	74.9	74.8	0.1	10.3	8.3	2.0	11.6	3.2
Dominican R.	69.7	69.7	0.0	10.8	8.1	2.7	17.5	2.0
Honduras	76.4	75.7	0.7	9.3	7.4	1.9	11.0	3.3
El Salvador	64.4	64.2	0.2	13.9	11.1	2.8	18.5	3.2
Nicaragua	70.6	69.7	0.9	13.2	10.7	2.5	16.2	–
Peru*	60.2	59.8	1.4	18.4	15.5	2.9	19.6	1.8
Ecuador	51.3	50.9	0.4	25.3	23.1	2.2	19.1	4.3
Paraguay	59.1	58.3	0.8	17.5	14.8	2.7	20.8	2.6
Bolivia	67.5	63.3	4.2	13.2	10.7	2.5	18.4	0.9
Haiti	77.4	77.4	0.0	7.4	6.6	0.8	11.5	3.7
Latin America	54.1	53.1	1.1	18.2	14.5	3.7	25.3	2.4

* Estimate.
SOURCE: Federico Debuyst, *La Población en América Latina* (Madrid: FERES, 1961), p. 174, as given in CIF *Study No. 1*, p. 126. Reproduced by permission.

during this time those engaged in the many service occupations increased from 25 to 30 percent. The increase in the number of service and white-collar employees, who are paid lower than average wages, reflects the fact that the population of working age is increasing more rapidly than are job opportunities in industries producing physical goods.[5]

Underemployment is especially prevalent in agriculture where for many reasons, such as poor farming practices, failure to use machinery, or concentration on one or two crops, the ability and potential productivity of the farm laborer is barely tapped. Probably the most serious aspect

---

[5] A. J. Jaffe, *People, Jobs, and Economic Development* (A Case History of Puerto Rico, Supplemented by Recent Mexican Experiences) (Glencoe, Ill.: Bureau of Applied Social Research of Columbia University, 1959), pp. 264–65.

of underemployment in agriculture is the farm laborer's being employed only part time. A rural worker works an average of 218 days a year in Argentina, 210 in Chile, about 200 in Colombia, and barely 180 in El Salvador. In areas where a single main crop is grown for export, usually coffee, sugar cane, and cotton, the situation is far worse than any national average can portray. In such areas, the rural worker actually works only from 80 to 100 days a year and often has to travel a long way to obtain employment.[6]

Many measures have been proposed for remedying underemployment. In the agrarian sector, they range from providing the farm laborer with an ox or tractor to pull his plow to instituting a nationwide program of land reform where the multitude of landless farmers would have parcels of their own. In industry they range from instituting programs to train workers for skilled, technical operations to establishing whole new industries which will not only provide needed products but also employ more of the labor force.[7]

Employment of Women

Since a large proportion of the women, mainly in the lower class but also in the middle, are gainfully employed, governments have found it advisable to adopt many laws designed to protect them. According to most constitutions and labor codes, women are not allowed to do unhealthy or dangerous work, sometimes spelled out as working in quarries or underground in mines. Nor may they be employed to do very strenuous tasks, such as lifting weights above a specified amount. With the exception of certain occupations such as those of nurses, telephone operators, and entertainers, they are not allowed to work during the night hours.

Pregnancy and maternity are given especial consideration. An expectant mother is given a prescribed time off both before and after the birth of her child, with pay and without any prejudice to her job. During the period of lactation, she is given time off both in the morning and afternoon for nursing the baby.

Brazil affords what is perhaps the most chivalrous protection of all; it exempts women from military service, letting them perform such duties as the law may establish.[8]

---

[6] United Nations Economic Commission for Latin America, "An Agricultural Policy to Expedite the Economic Development of Latin America," *Economic Bulletin for Latin America*, Vol. VI, No. 2 (October, 1961), p. 4.

In Cuba during the *zafra* (the cane harvest), there has been such a great demand for labor that workers have been imported from Jamaica and Haiti to help harvest the crop. Yet during the seven months of the "dead season" between harvests, about 20 percent of the farm labor was unemployed. (Wyatt MacGaffey and Clifford R. Barnett, *Cuba* [Survey of World Cultures] [New Haven: HRAF Press, 1962], pp. 139–40.)

[7] International Labour Office, *op. cit.*, pp. 123–72, and E. H. Phelps Brown, *The Economics of Labor* (New Haven, Conn.: Yale University Press, 1962), pp. 107–9.

[8] Constitution of 1946, Article 181, Section 1.

Employment of Minors[9]

In the more economically advanced nations, which have a higher standard of living, child labor has been almost eliminated. In the United States and Canada, the percentage of minors under age 15 and gainfully employed is 0.4 boys and 0.3 girls; in Switzerland, the figure is even lower —0.1 per cent. In Latin America, however, a large proportion of whose children are under age 15, as Table 10–2 and Figure 10–1 portray, many in

TABLE 10–2

PERCENTAGES IN THREE MAJOR AGE GROUPS IN LATIN AMERICA

Country	Year	0–14	15–64	65 and Over
Mexico	1950	41.8	54.8	3.3
Guatemala	1950	42.3	55.3	2.5
Honduras	1950	40.6	55.4	4.0
El Salvador	1950	41.1	55.9	3.0
Nicaragua	1950	43.3	53.9	2.8
Costa Rica	1950	42.9	54.2	2.9
Panama	1950	41.6	55.1	3.3
Cuba	1953	36.4	59.4	4.2
Haiti	1950	38.0	57.8	4.0
Dominican Rep.	1950	44.5	52.6	2.9
Venezuela	1950	42.0	55.3	2.6
Colombia	1951	42.9	55.1	3.1
Ecuador	1950	42.5	54.0	3.5
Peru	1956	44.1	53.6	3.0
Bolivia	1950	39.6	56.1	4.3
Brazil	1950	41.9	55.6	2.4
Argentina	1947	30.9	65.0	3.9
Chile	1952	37.4	58.4	4.0
Uruguay	–	26.6	64.5	5.3
Paraguay	1950	43.8	52.5	3.7

SOURCE: Federico Debuyst, *La Población en América Latina* (Madrid: FERES, 1961), p. 16 as given in CIF *Study No. 1*, p. 78. Reproduced by permission.

this age group are gainfully employed, ranging from a low in Chile of 1.6 percent for boys and 2.0 percent for girls to 11.4 percent for both sexes in Honduras. The percentage in certain other countries is: Colombia, 3.8 and 5.8 for boys and girls, respectively, excluding the indigenous population; Peru, 5.6 and 9.1; and Brazil, 6.7 and 10.8.

Most of the young workers are found in agriculture, where it is customary for children of the many peon or sharecropper families to help with such farming operations as planting, cultivating, and harvesting the crops. In Brazil according to the 1950 census, 20.1 percent of the children between ages 10 and 14 were employed in agriculture. Many young workers are found in the cities too. The percentage of those who work is known to be high; no reliable figures are available, however, because a large

---

[9] This information is mainly from "Youth and Work in Latin America," *International Labour Review*, Vol. XC, No. 1 (July, 1964), pp. 1–23.

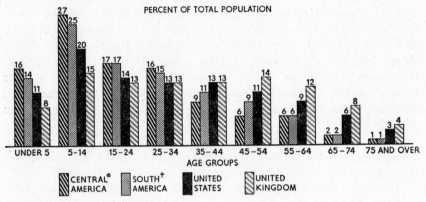

FIGURE 10-1

PERCENTAGES IN AGE GROUPS IN LATIN AMERICA, UNITED STATES, AND BRITAIN

PERCENT OF TOTAL POPULATION

CENTRAL* AMERICA SOUTH† AMERICA UNITED STATES UNITED KINGDOM

* Excluding Cuba, Guatemala, Haiti.
† Comprising Argentina, Chile, Ecuador, Paraguay, Peru, Venezuela.
SOURCE: *UN Demographic Yearbook* as given in Chase National Bank, *Latin American Business Highlights,* 3rd Quarter, 1964, p. 7. Reproduced by permission.

number are secretly employed in many small workshops or independently carry on minor street trades.

As in the case of women, the law tries to protect the minor worker in many ways, such as prohibiting his being employed at night or doing certain heavy or dangerous work and requiring that he be given a minimum number of hours rest. Moreover, he cannot be employed unless permission is given by official authorities. To obtain this permission, certain documents have to be submitted, such as the father's or guardian's consent, proof of age, state of health, and amount of schooling. If the authorities are satisfied, permission to work is given in the form of a card or employment book which specifies the conditions of employment. Such permission is not necessary, however, for employment in agriculture and domestic service, two sectors which employ a large percentage of children.

The many laws adopted for the benefit of minors have no doubt afforded a measure of protection which they would not otherwise have enjoyed. However, the basic problem of eliminating child labor cannot be resolved until two fundamental conditions are met—a high enough income for adult workers to take care of all young members of the family and a school system that can provide an education for all pupils.

GOALS AND GAINS

The Right to Organize and Strike

In every one of the republics, labor is recognized in the constitution, labor code, or both, as having the right to organize and strike.

This right, accepted as matter of fact today, represents for the working man a revolutionary gain which has been achieved only within the last several decades. In Mexico the Penal Code of 1872 prevented any effective attempts on the part of workers to improve their conditions, punishing by arrest and fine "those who make a tumult or riot, or employ any other method of physical or moral violence for the purpose of raising or lowering the wages of the workers, or who impede the free exercise of industry and labor." In 1907, when textile workers toiling for 13 hours a day in damp, hot, lint-filled rooms, humbly petitioned for better conditions, they were "locked out," to be starved into submission. When another group, maddened by hunger, raided the company store, troops massacred 200 men, women, and children, sending others to the dungeons of San Juan de Ulloa.[10]

Such atrocities, commonplace in most of the countries until only a few decades ago, are hardly conceivable today, thanks to the recognition and status which organized labor now enjoys.

The large mass of labor laws and codes which confer many rights on labor also impose certain restrictions too. Most of the countries specify that the objectives of the union must be economic and social, not political. Moreover, no one can be coerced into joining the union against his will. Furthermore, certain groups are specifically forbidden to organize. In Brazil there are four categories of such workers: domestic help, farm laborers, government employees at all levels, and employees of semistate autonomous bodies.[11]

Higher Wages

One of the main objectives of organized labor has been to obtain higher wages for its members. Consequently, either as a result of bargaining with employers or of direct governmental action, members of the union frequently obtain increases in wages. Indeed, from the tenor of press accounts from these nations, one may understandably conclude that extravagant wage demands have been mainly responsible for the soaring inflation in many of the nations.

Unquestionably, wage increases have often proved to be illusory gains in terms of real income—the amount of bread or potatoes or medicine that it would purchase. For often when granting a wage increase with its right hand, government was taking action with its left which completely nullified the supposed gain. Thus when Chile in 1937 adopted a minimum wage law tied to the cost of living index, the intent of the law and any possible advantage to be derived from it by the intended recipients was nullified by the printing presses flooding the country with new bills.

Another tactic which frequently nullifies any possible gain to be derived from a wage increase is the delay of the government, intentional

---

or otherwise, in taking action to put it into effect. In Brazil, several months pass from the time a minimum wage board is named until new wage levels are decreed; during this time the businessmen boost prices even more than the normal increase. As a result, the anticipatory price rise has already more than offset the increase in wages when the latter finally goes into effect.[12]

Contrary to the belief of many, the worker is far more often the victim of inflation than the cause of it. Indeed, certain other groups in society who actually benefit by inflation welcome or encourage it. Thus in Chile inflation has been favored by those who profited from price increases—landowners, government employees, and advocates of industrialization who believed that capital formation could be increased only by this means.[13]

Many others who do not prefer or promote inflation nevertheless easily learn to live with it, floating on its crest as zestfully as a good swimmer rides the breakers in a strong surf, coasting on top to the very edge of the seashore. In Brazil a large nationally known clothing manufacturer who has many retail outlets did not have any trouble doing business, or even offering easy credit terms, in the midst of the nation's wild inflation, which amounted to 80 percent in 1963. "We simply owe the textile suppliers about the same amount the retail public owes us," he explained.[14]

Though others may benefit from inflation, or at least learn to live with it comfortably, this is not so of the great majority of workers. In fact, they suffer severely from inflation. Wage increases cannot and do not keep up with the inflationary price spiral which benefits some others in the society. In both Brazil and Chile, the industrial worker apparently had a lower real income in 1956 than in 1940.[15] This is probably true in 1964 too.

In wondering what is going on, the worker might feel better—or perhaps worse—if he could read and understand some of the economic explanations for his problems. For one thing, his developing society is basically different from the earlier ones in that there are many more goods and services for which he can beneficially spend his income today than there were a century or so ago. The conveniences and necessities which he knows about and aspires to possess are far more numerous than they were in the wealthy nations when these had the income levels now common to Latin America.[16]

---

[12] *Ibid.*, p. 125.

[13] W. Brand, *The Struggle for a Higher Standard of Living: The Problem of the Underdeveloped Countries* (The Hague and Bandung: W. Van Hoeve Ltd., 1958), p. 245.

[14] *New York Times*, January 17, 1964, Hemisphere Business Review, p. 72, col. 5.

[15] Alexander, *op. cit.*, p. 6.

[16] Wilbert E. Moore and Arnold S. Feldman, *Labor Commitment and Social Change in Developing Areas* (New York: Social Science Research Council, 1960), p. 214.

Another thing which might make the worker unhappy, even antisocial, is to realize that by virtue of his low real wages in a time of rising prosperity he is being called on to pay for the cost of industrialization. He is doing just this in Brazil, where his "real wages are kept down to provide the large profits characteristic of the Brazilian economy, most of which are to a large degree ploughed back into its further development."[17] He is doing the same thing in Mexico too, where it may "correctly be said that the true hero of the Mexican investment boom is the ordinary Mexican worker, whose acceptance of a declining real income has in effect 'subsidized' much of the nation's building."[18]

The plight of the mass of workers whose wages are pathetically low while much of the rest of society enjoys affluence, some even sending their profits abroad for safe investment, is at least widely recognized, although little to date has been done about it. In Argentina, President Illia in his inaugural address of October, 1963, stressed the hardships of the workers, and promised that a major goal of his administration would be to see that they got "just wages with real purchasing power."[19]

The plight of the Chilean worker who has suffered from inflation while many others in the nation have benefited from it is also well recognized.

Although labor's voice was hardly heard despite its remuneration's lagging behind, noted W. Brand, ". . . it might be mainly the increased power of wage earners that will lead, even in the undeveloped countries, to resistance against inflation as a means of capital formation, and to the insistence that increased investment shall lead to increased consumption for the masses with only a modest lag."[20]

A Shorter Working Day

Another of the primary objectives of organized labor has been to reduce the hours of labor and establish a workday and workweek of reasonable length. Before labor became organized, there were no effective ground rules whatever for governing the length of time which laborers were required to be on the job. In Mexico's textile plants, the workers were required to put in 13 hours a day. In the bakeries, they were not even allowed to leave the shop except to hear Mass on feast days and then always accomplished by an overseer who never let them out of sight.[21]

Within recent decades and due mainly to the power of organized labor, the hours of work have been reduced to humane and reasonable limits. Today the eight-hour day and five-and-a-half- or six-day week exist throughout the region. About the only ones now who do not enjoy this

17 Alexander, op. cit., p. 134.
18 Oscar Lewis, "Mexico Since Cárdenas," Social Change in Latin America Today (Council on Foreign Relations) (New York: Harper & Bros., 1960), p. 326.
19 Hispanic American Report, Vol. XVII, No. 5 (July, 1964), p. 447.
20 Brand, op. cit., p. 245.
21 Gruening, op. cit., p. 335.

privilege are the groups, mainly domestic help and farm laborers, that are forbidden by law to organize or belong to labor unions. As recently as 1962, Nicaragua adopted certain "labor reforms" applying to domestic servants. One of the main "reforms" was limiting their working day to 14 hours!

Better Working Conditions

One of the high priority goals from the first days of organized labor was to obtain better working conditions for the laborer. Until labor became organized and had a voice which was at least respectfully listened to, the worker performed his tasks in deplorably unhealthy, even dangerous surroundings. Ill-lighted, poorly ventilated, and with no regard whatever for safety, the factories and workshops, quarries and mines debilitated and slaughtered workers, who were in effect just so many expendables. The advent of unions with their demands for better working conditions did not bring about the millennium but did serve to ameliorate some of the harsher conditions.

Said an official of Las Camelias Mine, referring to the improved condition of workers in Mexico after the 1910 revolution:

Formerly when a man was killed in the mine we bought a wooden box to bury him in. Now we have to pay his family a fine of $3,000 pesos and half-pay for three or four years according to the number of dependents he leaves. So we have to be very careful now. We spend a great deal in safety appliances, and both our inspectors and the Government's are going through the mines at all times. We are glad of it. It saves us a lot of money. We also have a system of paying each of our foremen 5 pesos every time 1,000 men have passed through their shifts without getting hurt. This has also proved a great money saver, for accident indemnity runs high.[22]

The efforts of the unions, as well as other influences, have made employers more conscious of their responsibilities. Yet a great deal still remains to be done to afford workers the healthy and safe conditions of employment which they should have. There are still many dangerous hazards in their working environment which need to be and can be corrected. Accidents occur at least six times as frequently in the mines and industries in Latin American nations as in the older industrialized countries. Moreover, occupational diseases are still very prevalent in Latin America, although in other countries many of them have practically disappeared. Silicosis remains a serious problem; another is poisoning from toxic metals, gases, vapors, or smoke. "The application of preventive measures to control occupational accidents and diseases is practically unknown in some countries and is only in its beginning stages in others. Social legislation has placed greater emphasis on compensation than on prevention."[23]

[22] *Ibid.*, p. 345.
[23] "Report from the Outposts," *Américas*, Vol. 14, No. 7 (July, 1962), p. 35.

Lack of regard for the safety of workers, besides causing untold misery and suffering, imposes a terrific economic burden on the whole society. Economic losses caused by the high rate of worker disability amount to approximately 15 percent of the total national income, and equal from 50 to 100 percent of the countries' national budgets.[24]

Security of Tenure

Workers in Latin America, like those in the United States, enjoy eating regularly and have a dread of losing their jobs. Responsive to the unions' influence and concern, the labor laws contain many provisions designed to afford the worker security of tenure and to protect him from being fired summarily. Sometimes the safeguards have been carried so far as to make it virtually impossible for an employer to fire a worker, however much he deserves to be dismissed. In Cuba, the laws were so rigid that the inability to fire workers was known as *inamoviladad* (immobility). Even though workers had stolen from the company, beaten up other employees, sexually molested female workers, committed acts of sabotage, or refused to perform the duties which they were assigned, they still could not be fired.[25]

"The inability to fire workers, even for cause, was perhaps the most acute problem faced by employers," say Wyatt MacGaffey and Clifford R. Barnett. "It was commonly said that it was more difficult to fire a worker than to divorce a wife (although it was often easier to find a new wife than a new job)."[26]

The overconcern for job security and the excessive safeguards for providing it have sometimes provoked backlashes which largely defeated the purpose of the measures. In Brazil although the labor law was intended to give workers greater stability of employment and protect their jobs, in many instances it has had exactly the opposite effect. An employer who wants to dismiss a worker who has *estabilidade* (tenure) finds that it is very difficult to get the necessary permission from the labor court; the only way he can get rid of him is to buy him off, at a high price of course. As a result, many employers refuse to allow their workers to acquire ten years' tenure, which gives them a claim to their jobs by virtue of which they cannot be dismissed except for grave misbehavior or *force majeure*, adequately proved. Determined to maintain a free hand over employees, employers have dismissed their workers after nine years so as not to be bound by the law. However, labor courts, noting this practice, held that it amounted to an attempt to circumvent the laws; accordingly, they ruled that workers with nine years' standing were regarded as having tenure. But employers were by no means ready to give up on the issue—to keep

---

[24] *Ibid.*
[25] International Bank for Reconstruction and Development, *Report on Cuba* (Baltimore: Johns Hopkins University Press, 1951).
[26] MacGaffey and Barnett, *op. cit.*, p. 148.

from being bound by the law, they often fire employees after seven and a half or eight years, regardless of ability.[27]

Other Goals

Organized labor has had many other goals besides those discussed. Profit sharing is one of these. Foreign enterprises, domestic ones too, have often boasted of making large profits—50 percent a year, sometimes 75, 100, or more. To workers hardly paid enough to keep body and soul together, a larger share of the take has seemed quite a legitimate goal. Getting this incorporated into the labor laws was a relatively easy matter, for the Latin American will pass a law on anything as the easy way out just so long as he does not have to enforce it. But like many another law, one requiring profit sharing has been easier to enact than to enforce. For the governments in time proceeded to tax away a large part of the profits of foreign enterprises; much of the governments' revenues come from this source. Moreover, companies often had bad years when there were no profits to tax, much less to share. Yet wedded to the concept of profit sharing, organized labor clings to it as a possible means of raising the income of its members. To date the legal requirements upon industry to share profits with labor have been just so much verbiage, yet nations continue to adopt such social measures.

One of the most recent to adopt profit sharing is Mexico. An amendment was added to its constitution on November 20, 1962, which gives the government power to force both Mexican and foreign concerns to share their profits with workers. A special committee representing government, management, and labor are to rule on how much of a company's profits shall go to the stockholders and how much to the workers.[28]

Having some say-so in policy is another goal to which unions aspire. In most of the countries, however, they have not had much success with this. Even in Argentina, Brazil, and Chile, which are three of the most industrially advanced nations and have some of the most progressive labor policies, employers are still very jealous of the "prerogatives of management" and are loath to share these with either the unions or the government. They are determined as far as possible to keep under their control the important powers of making rules and enforcing them.[29]

In Mexico, however, the unions have become so strong and so favored by government that they have a voice in rule making and enforcement.

The power of the *sindicatos* has so increased that in addition to having established the common closed-shop and seniority principles, the labor organization in some instances has taken over many functions of management and even of the community. . . . The *sindicato* not only determines most policies at levels below that of the general manager (representing the owner), with whom the

---

[27] Alexander, *op. cit.*, p. 121–22.
[28] *Hispanic American Report*, Vol. XVI, No. 11 (January, 1963), p. 994.
[29] Alexander, *op. cit.*, p. 19.

labor organization works in friendly cooperation, but acts also as the disciplinary agent in the factory and in the town.[30]

A comprehensive program of social security is still another goal of the unions. Mainly as a result of labor's prodding, the nations have all adopted such programs. Usually they consist only of health insurance, occasionally including pensions for the aged, and, only rarely, unemployment benefits. In most of the countries, however, these programs exist more on paper than in reality. Even in the several nations where they are most active, some persons are convinced that their impact on society is more harmful than beneficial. Argentina, Brazil, and Chile all have systems of social security which afford extensive protection for the ill, the aged, and the disabled. They were passed, according to Robert J. Alexander, to gain political support from the workers, with little or no consideration of their heavy costs and the ability of the nations to sustain such programs, however desirable.[31]

Other scholars too are very critical of the programs:

. . . Latin American policy makers [would] do well to re-examine social security and labor legislation passed during the past two decades. They have attempted to impose upon their economies some of the most extreme social security programs seen in the world and, by doing so, have injured the class they intended to benefit, have hampered their own programs of internal economic development, and have made more difficult a profitable participation in international economic relationships.[32]

Organized labor has also been hurt by many unscrupulous leaders who did not hesitate to betray the trust and interests of their followers for their own personal advantage. Sometimes they played one union against another in order to increase their personal power; sometimes they used collective bargaining to enrich themselves instead of to promote the welfare of the workers. Just such a reprehensible character was Luis N. Morones, head of the Mexican labor movement during the 1920s and '30s. Unscrupulously profiting from his position, he amassed a large fortune and lived lavishly, sporting at least a half dozen automobiles, a swank "retreat" for entertaining guests, and diamonds which were the talk of the nation.[33]

On the plus side, the very formation of a union and the transaction of its business are novel and educational experiences for most of the member-

---

[30] Wilbert E. Moore, *Industrialization and Labor: Social Aspects of Economic Development* (Institute of World Affairs) (Ithaca, N.Y.: Cornell University Press, 1951), pp. 283–84.

[31] Alexander, *op. cit.,* p. 17.

[32] Harry Stark, *Social and Economic Frontiers in Latin America* (2d ed.; Dubuque, Ia.: Wm. C. Brown Co., 1963), p. 398. Wilbert Moore terms Latin America's program as "overly advanced labor legislation" and concludes: "It is doubtful if all existing legislative standards in . . . Latin America could be immediately enforced without a greater economic disruption than the good accomplished for the workers." (Moore, *op. cit.,* p. 144.)

[33] Gruening, *op. cit.,* p. 390.

ship. The adoption of a constitution and bylaws, the parliamentary conduct of a meeting, the debate as to whether or not to strike, and the election of officers and selection of delegates to regional and national conclaves are all exercises in democratic responsible citizenship, albeit elementary, even though control is often exercised by an inner clique or boss.

In addition to affording training in citizenship, the labor union, like the army, is an important avenue of social mobility, providing an outlet for leadership and an opportunity for advancement to persons who would otherwise be barred by their social status from exercising political and economic influence. In Cuba Negroes were active in both agricultural and industrial unions. Lázaro Peña, powerful leader of the national labor confederation, is a Negro, and until 1960 most labor federations had special committees to deal with the problems of Negro members.[34]

LABOR-MANAGEMENT RELATIONS AND COLLECTIVE BARGAINING

Labor-Management Relations

In the realm of labor-management relations, employers have had certain advantages which they exploited in dealing with labor. The industrialists, for example, were a closely knit group who had long had their local and national associations of manufacturers. The Sociedad de Fomento of Chile was organized in 1883; the Unión Industrial Argentina, in 1887; and the Sociedad National de Industrias of Peru, in 1896. Well established, tightly organized, and having a close community of interests, the industrialists were in a good position to influence government by presenting their point of view.[35]

Moreover, with their large financial resources, the corporations do not hesitate to vie with the unions for the allegiance of their employees. In Chile many employers have formed company unions which are subject to the influence or control of the employers. These unions are especially numerous in the textile industry. In Brazil some employers provide extensive fringe benefits for their employees. The Varig Aviation Company, through a related foundation, gives the following benefits to its personnel: a loan fund from which employees can borrow money interest-free to build homes; big low-priced stores located in the airports of Porto Alegre, São Paulo, and Rio where employees only can trade; vacation spots be-

---

[34] MacGaffey and Barnett, *op. cit.*, p. 151.

[35] George Wythe, *Industry in Latin America* (2d ed.; New York: Columbia University Press, 1949), p. 74. In some of the presently developing nations, a labor movement may become a political force before the native capitalists do, reversing the historical experience of the West, including Latin America. (John H. Kautsky [ed.], *Political Change in Underdeveloped Countries: Nationalism and Communism* [New York: John Wiley & Sons, Inc., 1962], p. 23.)

longing to the company, with transportation provided gratis for employees and their families; and pensions to superannuated personnel.[36]

While individual companies may have their own benefits, Brazilian employers as a group have a unique program for wooing their employees and winning their allegiance. Many paternalistic services are provided for them by SESI (Serviço Social de Industria) and SESCI (Serviço Social de Commercio), nationwide institutions which perform a wide variety of social services for employees on behalf of employers. Financed by compulsory contributions from all employers on the basis of 2 percent of their payrolls, SESI and SESCI render about every social service that a union could hope to provide—and more. Commissaries with a wide variety of low-priced goods, company dining rooms with cheap meals, and medical and dental service at cost are all soothing to the employee pocketbook. In addition, some 1,800 schools provided by SESI have afforded an education for many thousands of students, have also taught many adult illiterates how to read and write. A corps of lawyers is available to handle family legal problems and give advice to workers on employment problems— advice that is probably not antagonistic to the interests of employers. In São Paulo SESI is even engaged in a social orientation program designed to develop future union leaders. The purpose is not to develop leaders who will be subservient to the wishes of employers, SESI asserts, surely tongue in cheek, but to develop leaders who will counteract the union activities of the Communist Party.[37]

But when it comes to sitting down at the bargaining table and dealing directly with employees, most employers find it a very trying task. In Mexico the older industrialists were decidedly hostile to the unions, regarding themselves as the victims of laws which tipped the scales in favor of labor leaders in the settlement of industrial disputes. However, the new small manufacturers, sometimes referred to as the New Group, were more favorably inclined to the unions; often having risen recently from the ranks of labor to owning their small businesses, they welcomed negotiations with the unions.[38]

Collective Bargaining

The process of collective bargaining in Latin America is very different from the process as we know it in the United States. It is neither free, nor collective, nor really bargaining. Special labor courts often hear the disputes and decide them. In actuality government usually has the whip hand and exercises it to bring about an "agreement." The process, as meticulously prescribed in the labor codes, is usually quite different from what

---

[36] Alexander, *op. cit.*, pp. 18 and 105–6.

[37] *Ibid.*, pp. 106–9.

[38] Sanford A. Mosk, *Industrial Revolution in Mexico* (Berkeley: University of California Press, 1954), pp. 27–31.

actually takes place to resolve a dispute, as is shown in the case of Mexico.

According to Mexico's Federal Labor Law of 1931, if the employer and the union are not able to reach an agreement, the union may call a strike after complying with certain conditions. It must give the employer written notice of the proposed strike at least six days before it is to take place, or ten days in the case of public services such as transportation, communications, light, gas, water, and hospitals. It also notifies a board of conciliation and arbitration, which in turn notifies the employer, giving him 48 hours to reply to the union's statement. At the end of this time, the board tries to get the parties to reach an agreement. If this fails, it then declares the strike to be legal, and the walkout takes place. The strike is ended in time by an agreement reached between the employer and the union, by a decision of an arbitral body chosen by the parties, or by a decision of the board of conciliation and arbitration.[39]

In practice, however, labor disputes in Mexico are settled quite differently from the procedure described in the labor law. While they are almost always settled by arbitration or conciliation, more frequently by the latter, the minister of labor plays a key role in bringing about a settlement. He:

. . . opens and shuts the valves of labour militancy. He largely determines whether the publicly demanded changes will be made in wages or conditions. The wage policy he imposes must be accepted by labour; any changes must come through peaceful means. . . . When strikes persist beyond acceptable limits [he] can and will invoke all necessary party and government apparatus to bring the situation back into line.[40]

However desirable real collective bargaining might be, it has not been practicable in Latin America, for the process has almost invariably lacked three essential conditions: accurate information as to wages, earnings, and other relevant factors; mutual confidence and good will; and genuine freedom of the parties to reach an agreement between themselves.

Regarding information needed, since unions cannot afford to employ economists, statisticians, engineers, and lawyers, they really have no expert opinion upon which to base their wage demands; consequently the raise they seek is determined arbitrarily and may be 25 percent, 50 percent, or 200 percent.

Moreover, with class lines drawn as rigidly as they are and with the authoritarian attitudes of those who wield power, it is not surprising that a patrician industrialist and a plebeian union leader can hardly sit down together at the same bargaining table. In fact employers have often refused to deal with unions at all except through their lawyers, and labor

---

[39] William P. Tucker, *The Mexican Government Today* (Minneapolis: University of Minnesota Press, 1957), pp. 316–28.

[40] Howard F. Cline, *Mexico: Revolution to Evolution: 1940–1960* (Royal Institute of International Affairs) (New York: Oxford University Press, 1962), p. 226.

leaders have frequently viewed the differences between them as a "class struggle." Even attempts to negotiate a working arrangement directly with management are often viewed with disdain by union members, as though such attempts were collaboration with an enemy.[41]

Finally, the large role played by government in determining the labor contract is fatal to genuine bargaining. In Cuba:

> . . . the machinery provided by law for the settlement of disputes often failed to function. There was no effective civil service system to promote the development of a body of trained conciliators in the Ministry of Labor, and since most officials were political appointees, both labor leaders and employers distrusted their impartiality. During the 1940s the strongest unions were able to pack the Ministry of Labor with friendly officials.[42]

INVOLVEMENT IN POLITICS

Before World War I many of the trade unions inserted in their bylaws provisions that they would remain aloof from politics and that none of their leaders could hold public office. Nevertheless, some of the leaders took an active part in politics to promote the interest of the union, or sometimes, as in the case of Luis Morones of Mexico, to promote the cause of labor and also the cause of Morones.

Abstaining from participating actively in politics or from pledging themselves to support a certain party or faction was good strategy; labor could thereby play off one group against another and give its support to the one which best served its interests.

Abstention from participation in politics, however, proved to be better in theory than in practice. In Mexico, for example, the small but influential labor movement in 1928 made a well-nigh fatal decision. It decided not to support either Calles or Obregón, believing that it should be an independent labor movement and was strong enough to "go it alone." On its own however, it almost disintegrated. "It has not made that error again, nor is it likely to."[43]

Dependence Upon Government

As the trade union in Mexico and the other nations well realizes, it is dependent upon government in many ways. In order even to exist and carry on its many activities, it must first be recognized by government as a legitimate legal entity—the failure of government to grant a birth certificate has snuffed out the life of many a would-be young union. Even if it is recognized and becomes a dynamic, going concern, government can still destroy it by the mere stroke of a pen. In Chile when unions conducted strikes against the railroads and mining operations in 1936, Presi-

---

[41] MacGaffey and Barnett, op. cit., p. 153, and Poblete and Burnett, op. cit., p. 149.
[42] MacGaffey and Barnett, op. cit., p. 154.
[43] Cline, op. cit., p. 223.

dent Arturo Alessandri resolved the dispute by the most direct executive action—a presidential decree which forthwith dissolved the unions.

Unions are also very dependent upon government and politicians for funds which they need in order to operate. The dues of members are very low, as one would expect from their pitifully low incomes. But unions need money for many purposes, from paying the expenses of the organization to rendering various services to members. In Latin America unions operate on a shoestring—a short one at that. They probably would not believe that such welfare funds and war chests as those of the AFL-CIO and Teamsters in the United States exist.

Brazil has solved the problem of the need for union funds by a very simple expedient. The *imposto sindical,* or trade union tax, is levied upon all workers who belong to unions and is collected by the government. Sixty percent of the tax collected goes back to the individual unions; 15 percent is paid to the federation to which the union belongs; and 5 percent goes to the confederation to which the federation belongs. The remainder, as well as any other funds not used by the unions, federation, or confederation, goes into the Fundo Social Sindical, which provides theater and other recreational facilities, educational activities, and special social services, all of which benefit the workers in an area regardless of whether they belong to a union.[44]

Moreover, however independent labor might like to be, it is also very dependent upon government for aid in collective bargaining. The worker who leaves his job to join in a strike is taking a risk which few of us in the United States would dare to take. He probably has enough beans and bread at the house to last the family for a day or two, maybe several pesos too. But the very idea of being able to hold out for 60 days, 90 days, 120 days, or sometimes much longer, as our unions often do, is to him inconceivable. With the far greater resources which management in Latin America has, some of it a part of his own wages which is helping to finance industrialization, the worker on strike is in no position to hold out for more than a few days. It is thus critical that a decision be made promptly to resolve the dispute, whether in his favor or against him. Obviously the only one in a position to require this is government.

Supervision by Government

The benefits obtained from reliance upon government have a price tag, of course. In return for its help to labor, government exacts the price of submission to governmental control in certain key areas: mainly in supervision of union funds, general control over union elections, and having the final word in collective bargaining.

Regarding supervision of funds, unions in Mexico can acquire only those assets which are absolutely necessary to carry out their legitimate objectives. They cannot engage in any kinds of commercial activities with

---

[44] Alexander, *op. cit.,* pp. 85–86.

the view of making a profit. Moreover, union leaders must render a semi-annual accounting for all revenues. In Chile, union funds do not belong to the workers but to the organization. They must be deposited in an account in the National Savings Bank in the name of the union, and the manager of the bank and the government inspector will determine how they are to be invested. In Brazil every union is required to submit its next year's budget for the approval of the Ministry of Labor, Industry, and Commerce. The regional labor delegate representing the government also checks the union's books when they are submitted.[45]

In return for supporting labor, government also insists upon the power to supervise union elections and important union decisions. Thus when leaders are to be elected or a strike is to be voted upon, an inspector from the department of labor is apt to be on hand, in accordance with the labor law in the nation. This law also prescribes the conditions for voting. A secret ballot is usually required. In Brazil members who have belonged to the union for more than six months may vote provided they are at least 18 years of age. In Chile anyone who has belonged to the union more than three years has the right to cast two ballots.[46]

Government also insists on having the final word in collective bargaining. Unions come to expect this as the *quid pro quo*.

In return for recognition—a place at the council tables of party and Government [in Mexico], labour has tacitly accepted certain limitations, as full co-partners in the Revolution. It cannot engage in all-out warfare against industry, nor exert full economic pressure against the Government to obtain more desirable wages and conditions. In the total system, the claims of labour for more wages, for example, must be weighed by the Government against such national considerations as trade balances, export prices, the level of domestic prices, the preservation of an attractive climate for domestic and foreign investment, and other elements producing general economic development, now a major goal of the Revolution.[47]

In most of the nations, governmental supervision is extensive in normal times; it is far more so during dictatorships, even those which profess to be labor governments. During the Vargas regime in Brazil, labor as a group had no political rights. Strikes and lockouts were forbidden as "antisocial, harmful to labor and capital, and incompatible with the supreme interests of national production." Only those unions which were thoroughly under government's thumb were allowed to continue in existence.[48] In Argentina, Perón's ten years or so of *justicialismo* provided many benefits for the urban workers but also exacted strict subservience to the state.[49]

---

[45] Poblete and Burnett, *op. cit.*, p. 30; Alexander, *op. cit.*, p. 84.

[46] Poblete and Burnett, *op. cit.*, p. 30.

[47] Cline, *op. cit.*, pp. 225–26.

[48] Lowenstein, *op. cit.*, p. 342.

[49] George I. Blanksten, *Perón's Argentina* (Chicago: University of Chicago Press, 1953), pp. 257–75.

Labor's Weapons

The Ballot. Deeply involved as it is in politics, whether labor would prefer it that way or not, it has a varied arsenal of weapons for slugging it out if necessary to survive or further its goals. The ballot, the general strike, and even armed might are potent weapons which even labor's most powerful adversaries have learned to respect.

Where workers are allowed under law to vote freely and are not barred by literacy requirements, the ballot is an effective means of their expressing approval or disapproval of an administration. When it is one which has won their approval and support, it is almost sure to receive a strong vote of confidence from the labor sector. In Bolivia only 126,125 persons voted in the 1951 presidential election. But following the 1952 revolution which practically remade the society and established universal suffrage without literacy requirements, the workers gave their massive, unqualified support to the new regime. Of the 955,412 votes cast, the MNR, the party which was responsible for the revolution and the workers' improved status, received 786,792.[50]

Knowing which side its bread is buttered on—one does not have to be able to read and write to know this—organized labor has thrown the weight of its support solidly behind the party regarded as most favorably disposed toward its interests.

The socialist parties of the several nations, which have championed the cause of the workers, have traditionally received labor's support. However, the communist parties in recent decades have managed to chisel in, directing their appeal mainly to the workers, especially members of the urban working class. The Aprista parties have also drawn much labor support, although they are not avowedly labor parties. Other parties, too, such as the Christian Democrats, Liberals, and Argentine Radicals have appealed to and received much support from labor.

The General Strike. While the ballot is the usual means whereby labor expresses its preference for an administration, the general strike is much more formidable. Its use—or even threatened use—represents in effect throwing down the gauntlet and squaring off for a bitter struggle if necessary. The strike is of course more effective in the more highly industrialized nations, a large proportion of whose citizens are dependent upon a regular supply of needed goods and services for their comfort and even daily existence. It is apt to fail when the government is determined to have a showdown and is willing to risk heavy loss of life to maintain its point of view. But it often succeeds in toppling or helping to topple a regime, or putting one in power.

In Argentina labor stepped into the picture at a critical moment to throw its support behind Juan Perón. The idol and boss of the trade union movement, he appeared to be washed out when he was shunted aside by

---

[50] *Political Handbook of the World, 1957*, p. 14.

a faction of the army opposed to his personal ambitions and sent to the prison island of Martín García. But the myriad of workers loyal to him staged a virtually spontaneous general strike throughout the country. In Buenos Aires and the suburbs, the packinghouse workers from nearby La Plata and Avellaneda filled the streets, taking over the city. Bowing to the will of this unprecedented display of popular support, the army permitted Perón to return from Martín García. From October 17, 1945, when he returned to power, until June 16, 1955, Perón exercised strong control with the support of organized labor and the armed forces.

Armed Might. Besides customarily using the ballot and occasionally the general strike for putting its program over, labor has sometimes even supplied armed might to support a regime which has been favorable to its interests.

In Mexico, Venustiano Carranza, engaged in a civil war with the forces of Pancho Villa and Emiliano Zapata in 1915, made a deal with the weak Mexican labor movement in return for its support of Carranza's bid for power. The unions were promised the support of his government in unionization and in trade disputes in return for six 'red' battalions of workers who enlisted in Carranza's army.[51]

Years later, President Lázaro Cárdenas, 1934–40, was determined to complete his program of land reform and nationalization of certain industries, especially oil. Doubting the political dependability of the army, he fell back on the organized unions and provided arms to his labor supporters, who organized a labor militia. In return for this support, they received many benefits, among which were wage increases and better working conditions.

Labor also took up its cudgels to support the new revolutionary movement in Bolivia in April, 1952. When the national police who led the revolt appeared to be beaten after two days of fighting, the tide was turned by the determined support of the organized workers of La Paz and the tin mines. The workers could claim most of the credit. According to popular accounts, the organized Indian women who had their established places for selling in the marketplace did their bit too in turning the tide of battle. Many a woman offered herself to one of the raw army recruits fighting for the government, then disarmed him and turned him over to the rebel forces.[52]

Any participation in politics, especially such all-out support, is risky business. When labor hitches its star to the wrong party or cause, the consequences can be disastrous. But when the gamble is successful, it pays off handsomely, as Mexico's labor movement can attest. "As a favourite

---

[51] Henry Bamford Parkes, *A History of Mexico* (3rd ed. rev.; Boston: Houghton Mifflin Co., 1960), p. 352.

[52] Labor's support is given in detail by Robert J. Alexander, "Organized Labor's Role in the National Revolution," *Bolivian National Revolution* (New Brunswick, N.J.: Rutgers University Press, 1958), chap. 7.

child of the Revolution," observed Howard F. Cline, "Mexican labour has had a somewhat unique experience. It has never faced some of the other issues that inevitably trouble organized labour seeking to establish a partnership in an economy: survival and permanence, ideology, appropriate structure, discipline, and programmes. These are all provided by the Revolution."[53]

Regarding its future, organized labor in Latin America should feel optimistic. It has won many benefits for its members which they would never otherwise have had; union members realize this and strongly support their organization. Moreover, organized labor represents the largest single block of voters in many of the nations; their weight in elections is bound to increase as industrialization advances and more workers become organized, or as the less progressive nations relax their voting requirements to permit illiterates to vote. Furthermore, the labor unions constitute the only organized group in the society which is (sufficiently) strong enough to counterbalance or possibly curb the long entrenched power of the armed forces.

As organized labor becomes stronger, as it almost surely will, it can be expected to participate less directly in politics and devote more of its efforts to the economic objectives for which unions were founded. But the battle is a long way from being won. No one realizes this better than the maid in Nicaragua, who still has to work 14 hours a day!

SUGGESTED READINGS

ALEXANDER, ROBERT J. *The Bolivian National Revolution,* chap. 7. New Brunswick, N.J.: Rutgers University Press, 1958.

————. *Labor Relations In Argentina, Brazil, and Chile.* New York: McGraw-Hill Book Co., Inc., 1962.

————. "Organized Labor and Politics," *Government and Politics in Latin America* (ed. HAROLD E. DAVIS), chap. 7. New York: Ronald Press Co., 1958.

CLINE, HOWARD F. *Mexico: Revolution to Evolution: 1940–1960,* chap. xxiii. Royal Institute of International Affairs. New York: Oxford University Press, 1962.

FURTADO, CELSO. *The Economic Growth of Brazil: A Survey from Colonial to Modern Times,* pp. 127–54. Trans. RICARDO W. DE AGUIAR AND ERIC CHARLES DRYSDALE. Berkeley: University of California Press, 1963.

GRUENING, ERNEST. *Mexico and Its Heritage,* pp. 335–90. New York: D. Appleton-Century Co., Inc., 1934.

HANSON, SIMON G. *Economic Development of Latin America,* chap. 15. Washington, D.C.: Inter-American Affairs Press, 1951.

INTERNATIONAL LABOUR OFFICE. *Indigenous Peoples: Living and Working Conditions of Aboriginal Populations in Independent Countries,* Studies and Reports, New Series, No. 35, pp. 199–264. Geneva, Switz., 1953.

---

[53] Cline, *op. cit.,* p. 222.

——— . "Youth and Work in Latin America," *International Labour Review,* Vol. XC, No. 1 (July, 1964), pp. 1–23.

JAFFE, A. J. *People, Jobs, and Economic Development.* A Case History of Puerto Rico, Supplemented by Recent Mexican Experiences. Glencoe, Ill.: Bureau of Applied Social Research of Columbia University, 1959.

MACGAFFEY, WYATT, AND BARNETT, CLIFFORD R. *Cuba,* chap. 7. Survey of World Cultures. New Haven, Conn.: HRAF Press, 1962.

MOORE, WILBERT. *Industrialization and Labor: Social Aspects of Economic Development,* Part II, chaps. ix–xii. Institute of World Affairs. Ithaca, N.Y.: Cornell University Press, 1951.

MOSK, SANFORD A. *Industrial Revolution in Mexico,* chaps. vi and xiii. Berkeley: University of California Press, 1954.

PIERSON, WILLIAM W., AND GIL, FEDERICO G. *Governments of Latin America,* chap. 14. New York: McGraw-Hill Book Co., Inc., 1957.

POBLETE-TRONCOSO, MOISES, AND BURNETT, BEN G. *The Rise of the Latin American Labor Movement.* New Haven, Conn.: College and University Press, 1960.

SOULE, GEORGE; EFRON, DAVID; AND NESS, NORMAN T. *Latin America in the Future World,* chaps. 7 and 13. National Planning Association. New York: Farrar & Rinehart, Inc., 1945.

STARK, HARRY. *Social and Economic Frontiers in Latin America,* chap. 11. Dubuque, Ia.: Wm. C. Brown Co., 1963.

STOKES, WILLIAM S. *Latin American Politics,* chap. 11. New York: Thomas Y. Crowell Co., 1959.

TANNENBAUM, FRANK. *Mexico: The Struggle for Peace and Bread,* chap. 7. New York: Alfred A. Knopf, Inc., 1954.

——— . *Peace by Revolution: An Interpretation of Mexico,* chaps. 19–23. New York: Columbia University Press, 1933.

TUCKER, WILLIAM P. *The Mexican Government Today,* chap. 22. Minneapolis: University of Minnesota Press, 1957.

WEYL, NATHANIEL, AND WEYL, SYLVIA. *The Reconquest of Mexico: The Years of Lázaro Cárdenas,* chaps. ix and x. New York: Oxford University Press, 1939.

PART IV

DYNAMICS OF POLITICAL CHANGE:
BULLETS OR BALLOTS

CHAPTER 11

CAUDILLOS AND
REVOLUTIONS:
Bullets, if Necessary

LATIN AMERICA is often referred to as one of the largest areas in the world embracing democratic government. In reality, however, only a few of the nations have developed genuinely democratic governments. Most of them have been plagued by dictatorships during much of their history. "They have been so numerous," concludes J. Fred Rippy, "their sway has been so constant, that the national history of most of the countries of the area is to a large extent the biography of these imperious personalities."[1]

CAUDILLOS

Origin and Duration

The *caudillos*, Latin America's home-grown variety of dictators, first rose to power during the wars of independence as leaders of the armies fighting the Spanish forces. Commanding what was often a fanatical devotion from their personal armies, these men on horseback were not only to throw off the Spanish yoke but also to be the future rulers of their countries. So strong was their influence that the early decades of independence are often referred to as the "era of the *caudillos*."

It is easy to ascertain when the dictators first appeared on the national scene, with their heroic exploits in battle and later strong-man rule of their countries. But what is more difficult to be sure of is how long *caudillismo* or dictatorship has continued in the various countries. Several

---

[1] J. Fred Rippy, "Dictatorships in Spanish America," in Guy Stanton Ford (ed.), *Dictatorship in the Modern World* (Minneapolis: University of Minnesota Press, 1935), p. 51.

of them managed to escape fairly early from its grip; by the middle of the nineteenth century four of them were able to rid themselves of at least its more violent aspects. Chile, which shook off *caudillismo* about 1830, was followed later by Uruguay, Brazil, and Argentina. In succeeding decades, other nations too have been largely able to throw off the yoke of these dictatorial rulers.

But, unfortunately, *caudillismo* is far from dead in Latin America; quite to the contrary, it shows a surprising vitality. Indeed, several of the nations, including the Dominican Republic, Haiti, Nicaragua, and Paraguay, have made little, if any, progress in freeing themselves from its clutches. Their strong-man rulers, although they have more *savoir-faire* and probably a crease in their pants, are every bit as much *caudillos* as their predecessors of a century and a half ago.

In addition to these four states, there are many others—a majority of the total number—which vacillate between absolutism and constitutionalism, bogging down much of the time in the former. Indeed, the recent history of even some of the most democratic states, such as Getulio Vargas' regime in Brazil and Juan Perón's in Argentina, shows that there is always the danger of slipping back into its insidious grip.

In fact, judged by the record of the last several decades, there are apparently only four states—Chile, Costa Rica, Uruguay, and Mexico—that are not in danger of a serious relapse. These states have developed "the capacity to make the transition from one administration to another of opposing political views without resort to arms," which is the acid test for determining whether a nation has emerged from *caudillismo*.[2] One of the four states, Mexico, is governed by a single political party, Partido Revolucionario Institucional, known as PRI, which easily wins every election and is hardly representative of the best democratic practice.

Background and Personal Qualifications for Governing[3]

The many *caudillos* who have dominated the destiny of Latin American nations since independence have differed widely in their background and personal qualifications for governing. Indeed, they present a frustrating record for any student of political leadership who hopes to be able to classify his specimens and reach some definite, irrefutable conclusions. For the *caudillos* have been a most heterogeneous lot, possessing many contrasting characteristics of all shades and colors.

The Many Differences Between Them

Military or Civilian Status and Scope of Authority. Most of the dictators have been military leaders, literally men on horseback, who became

---

[2] J. Fred Rippy, *Historical Evolution of Hispanic America* (3rd ed.; New York: Appleton-Century-Crofts, Inc., 1945), p. 166.

[3] For a list of the more prominent *caudillos*, classified according to their character and merit, see Charles Edward Chapman, *Republican Hispanic America: A History* (New York: The Macmillan Company, 1937), pp. 119–20.

political bosses and absolute rulers in the country. On the other hand, some of them were civilians, as were Carlos Antonio López of Paraguay, García Moreno of Ecuador, Estrada Cabrera of Guatemala, and others. But whether a military man or a civilian, it was absolutely necessary for the dictator to have control of the armed forces, and to be able to count on their loyalty and support. Because of this recognized dependence, *caudillismo* has a symbiotic relationship to militarism, the armed forces being the most important single power group in most of the nations.

Although many of the *caudillos* governed an entire nation, most of them controlled only a region or perhaps an isolated district in their country. One of the most powerful and colorful of the many regional bosses was Pancho Villa of Mexico, who led a private army of 40,000 and controlled a large part of northern Mexico. In the various nations, these regional and local *caudillos* spent much of their time and energy fighting one another to achieve hegemony. Usually one of them managed to emerge supreme, and the nation then had a dictator as its chief of state.

Family. Some of the dictators were born with silver spoons in their mouths; they came from the small elite whose families had prestige, privilege, wealth, and power. Others, however, were of very humble origin— from a log cabin, so to speak—and came up the hard way, triumphing over the most adverse circumstances. Those from the elite bore proud family names. Many of the others, however, were unrecognized *naturales* who resented the stigma attached to bastardy and were themselves resented by the society which they controlled. Bernardo O'Higgins was the illegitimate son of a Creole mother and the Irish Ambrosio O'Higgins, who served as governor of Chile and later as viceroy of Peru. Bernardo, sometimes called the George Washington of Chile, was dictator from 1818 to 1823 and instituted a number of reforms which gave the young nation a good start toward democracy. But the blue bloods of Santiago opposed his reforms and finally managed to throw him out; they "could not stomach a bastard son of an Irishman as the standard-bearer for their new nation."[4]

Race. The racial backgrounds of the *caudillos* were as varied as their family origins and environments. Some of them were whites; a few were Negroes or mulattoes; but the large majority were mestizos. But whether Negro or mulatto, Indian or mestizo, "no sooner did these men reach power," says Tad Szulc, "than they made themselves the hubs of hero elites, even if it was in the crudest sense of the word, and provided a monotonous repetition of the old story of how power corrupts."[5]

Education. Their educational backgrounds differed widely too. Some of the *caudillos* were among the most cultured and talented persons in the country. Doctor Francia of Paraguay, president from 1811 to 1840, was such an individual. With his degrees of master of philosophy and doctor

[4] Hubert Herring, *A History of Latin America from the Beginnings to the Present* (2d ed. rev.; New York: Alfred A. Knopf, Inc., 1961), p. 576.
[5] Tad Szulc, *Twilight of the Tyrants* (New York: Henry Holt & Co., 1959), p. 16.

of sacred theology, he was for several years professor of Latin at the
Royal College of San Carlos. Moreover, he had the distinction of owning
the largest library in all Paraguay. Many other dictators, however, had
little if any formal education; some were practically illiterate. Their
meager background was sometimes quite apparent, as when Mariano Melgarejo, the hated ruler of Bolivia from 1864 to 1871, spiritedly debated
with his advisers the issue of which was the greater man, Napoleon or
Bonaparte.

Religion and Morals. In the areas of religion and morals, too, the
caudillos ran the gamut, defying classification. Some, such as García
Moreno of Ecuador, led very upright, pious lives. Moreno, described by his
votaries as a "Christian Hercules," was motivated by a deep religious
fervor and a strong conviction that "civilization is the fruit of Catholicism." Accordingly, he tried to reshape Ecuador into a theocratic state "in
which the church would exercise moral and spiritual authority in the
name of the Almighty." The crowning proof of his devotion to the Roman
Catholic Church came in 1873 when the congress at his urging solemnly
dedicated the nation to "the sacred heart of Jesus."[6]

Most of the *caudillos*, however, represented the opposite extreme; they
were gamblers, drunkards, gluttons, and unrestrained libertines. Often
they neglected their governmental responsibilities and devoted so much
time to wine, women, and song—mainly the first two—that they completely burned themselves out. Broken in health, they would leave the
country to seek needed medical treatment abroad. Just such a dissolute
reprobate was Cipriano Castro, ruler of Venezuela from 1899 until he left
the country in 1908 for medical care in Paris.

Some of the *caudillos* had their own peculiar brand of morality, as in
the case of Juan Vicente Gómez, undisputed boss of Venezuela from 1908
to 1935. Gómez never smoked, drank, or got married. But he had a roving
eye for feminine pulchritude and apparently aspired quite literally to be
"the father of his country." He managed to possess almost any lady in
the nation that he desired and is said to have sired 200 or so illegitimate
children in these unions.[7]

Personality. Personality is still another realm in which the dictators
have differed widely. Some have preferred to remain quietly in the background, shunning any publicity whatever. Others have been bombastic
demagogues, seeking to attract attention by any means possible. Fidel
Castro's heavy beard, fatigue clothes, and long harangues are vivid symbols of his blatant appeal. Santa Anna of Mexico, who dominated the nation's history from 1823 to 1855, holding the presidency a number of times,
was a master of demagoguery. Suffering a leg wound which necessitated

---

[6] Herring, *op. cit.*, pp. 529–31.
[7] The amorous interests of Gómez are given in Thomas Rourke, *Gómez: Tyrant
of the Andes* (New York: William Morrow & Co., 1936), pp. 140–46; and in John
Lavin, *A Halo for Gómez* (New York: Pageant Press, 1954), pp. 157–66.

amputation when the French seized Vera Cruz in 1838, he made a bombastic farewell address, as one who was about to die, and when he did not do so, he held a funeral for his leg, which he replaced with a wooden one.

Verdict of History. The *caudillos* differ in still another significant aspect—the regard in which later generations of their fellow countrymen and others hold them. Some of them are deeply revered for their heroic exploits and selfless, worthwhile contributions to their nations' welfare. José Gervasio Artigas, who doggedly led his guerrilla bands against the Spanish armies and raised the flag of a free Uruguay, is affectionately remembered by his fellow countrymen as "the father of Uruguayan independence."[8]

At the other extreme are *caudillos* who are remembered as vicious, unqualified miscreants or "crackpots" whose names, like their misdeeds, live in infamy. Melgarejo of Bolivia was an eccentric of the first order.

He taught his favorite charger to drink beer, ordered his army officers to lie down and roll over like poodles, commanded his soldiers to march through a second-story window and fall to the ground, decreed that his birthday should be celebrated along with the resurrection of Jesus, threatened to shoot the members of his cabinet when they talked of resigning, and had them march with him from city to city at the head of his army, compelling them to travel hundreds of miles over mountain trails and through torrid jungle.[9]

El Salvador was another nation that suffered greatly from the rule of a "crackpot" dictator. Maximiliano Hernández Martínez, president from 1930 to 1944, was regarded by many of his fellow countrymen as a madman who attempted to bewitch the peons by prescribing magic drinks for curing their illnesses and for increasing their harvests. A theosophist, he is remembered for saying: "It is a greater crime to kill an ant than a man, because when a man dies, he is reincarnated, but the ant dies forever." Martínez never killed an ant, but in 1932 alone he killed more than 20,000 peasants who had rebelled because of hunger.[10]

The Three Basic Similarities. By almost any criteria the *caudillos* have been a very heterogeneous lot. But however much they may differ in other respects, there are three basic characteristics which they have in common.

Ambition. First, they are inordinately ambitious, with little or no sense of their personal limitations and with complete self-confidence in their ability to rule the nation. The erstwhile dictator of the Dominican Republic from 1930 to 1961, Generalissimo Rafael Leonidas Trujillo

---

[8] The epic of Uruguayan independence and the influential role of Artigas are graphically portrayed in John Street's *Artigas and the Emancipation of Uruguay* (London: Cambridge University Press, 1959).

[9] J. Fred Rippy, "Dictatorships in Latin America," in Guy Stanton Ford (ed.), *Dictatorship in the Modern World* (2d ed.; Minneapolis: University of Minnesota Press, 1939), pp. 198–99.

[10] Alfredo Pareja Diezcanseco, "Thinkers of the Americas: Alberto Masferrer," *Américas*, Vol. 14, No. 4 (April, 1962), p. 10.

Molina, was not one to hide his candle under a bushel. According to Abelardo R. Nanita, he rose to the top because of his physical stamina, mental acumen, dynamism, discipline, persevering effort, and unswerving pursuit of a goal. "Trujillo is a man who never loses sight of his main objective," effuses Nanita. "He knows what he wants and how to obtain it. He leaves nothing to chance and all his plans include alternate courses to meet any contingencies that may arise. It is difficult to catch him unaware; . . ."[11]

Ability. Another characteristic common to the *caudillos* is their unusual ability. In the fiercely competitive milieu of Latin American politics, they had to be very able individuals in order to rise to the top and to rule their countries, with the many pressing problems they presented. Juan José Flores, twice dictator of Ecuador and for almost 40 years one of the most powerful individuals in the country, was one of many whose ability proved outstanding and was well recognized. "His measures were generally chosen with an astonishing degree of ingenuity and skill," wrote Van Allan, our diplomatic agent in Ecuador, "and he had a profound knowledge of men, and of motives. His persuasion was irresistible, and the fascination of his presence and manners was great. . . . His mind is one of surprising acuteness and readiness of apprehension. He is a constant observer and quick thinker."[12]

Vanity. Still another characteristic common to the *caudillos* is their extreme vanity. Their self-appreciation is boundless and is well reflected by the honors which they so generously bestow on themselves. Among the many titles which they have freely assumed are: Benefactor of the Fatherland, Liberator, Restorer of Liberty, The Only Man Capable of Saving the Country, National Regenerator, Illustrious American, Deliverer of the People from Chains, Voice of the People, and Restorer of Financial Independence.

Basking in their many self-bestowed honors, the *caudillos* delight in pompous ceremonies and parades, in the ostentatious display of medals and ribbons, and in flamboyant uniforms. When Francisco Solano López, dictator of Paraguay from 1862 to 1870, was told that he resembled the great Napoleon, he promptly ordered uniforms resembling those the Corsican had worn, as well as a replica of his crown.

Nothing pleases the dictator more than the ubiquitous signs of his benign being. In this respect, Rafael Leonidas Trujillo of the Dominican Republic was one of the vainest of the lot. The name of the national capital was changed from Santo Domingo to Ciudad Trujillo, or Trujillo City, and along its main street were huge neon signs reading, "Trujillo Forever" and "God and Trujillo." Every automobile license plate in the nation

---

[11] Abelardo R. Nanita, *Trujillo* (5th ed. rev.; Cuidad Trujillo, D.R.: Editora del Caribe, C. por A., 1954), pp. 100 and 114–15.

[12] A. Curtis Wilgus (ed.), *South American Dictators During the First Century of Independence* (Washington, D.C.: George Washington University Press, 1937), pp. 359–60.

shouted, "Viva Trujillo," and every school and other public building proclaimed in bold bronze letters, "Era of Trujillo." On all four walls of every government office were photographs of the nation's ruler. The drinking fountains along the highway long carried the inscription, "God and Trujillo supply you with water." But Trujillo, like other dictators, disliked sharing the credit with anyone; in time the inscription was changed to read, "Trujillo is the only one who gives you water."

Generalissmo Trujillo has been accused of many things but never of modesty. He is "undoubtedly . . . among the most decorated men in the world," gushes Ernesto Vega y Pagan. "At present he has over sixty-five decorations and countless medals bestowed upon him during his brilliant career."[13]

The Caudillo's Rise to Power and Exercise of Governmental Authority

How He Attains Power: Revolution or Election. The *caudillo* may obtain supreme power in the nation by one of several means. The one most frequently used is revolution against the established government, with the *caudillo* taking over the presidential office if the revolution is successful. The first revolution may not succeed, nor the second. But if an ambitious would-be leader is able, persistent, and determined, he has a good chance of eventually toppling the government.

A number of dictators, however, became heads of nations with popular approval and in conformity with constitutional and legal requirements. Thus, Francia of Paraguay rose to power when he was elected one of a five-man junta to govern the new nation in 1811; and in 1814 Congress made him the sole ruler of the country, giving him dictatorial powers. To assure his selection, Francia apparently out-maneuvered his opponent, Don Fulgencio Yegros, who was preferred by most of the Congress. Using shrewd parliamentary tactics, Francia managed to stall the final decision until the deputies ". . . tired of assisting at the Congress, and of living at their expense in the capital . . . voted with a great majority for Doctor Francia."[14]

Juan Manuel de Rosas, who dominated Argentine politics from 1829 to 1852, did not assume supreme authority until the ruling junta had repeatedly begged him to, even finally offering him "total power . . . for as long as he thinks necessary." Rosas, however, in a further gesture toward legality, refused to accept this endowment of complete power until a popular plebiscite assured him that it was the will of the people. The vote

---

[13] Ernesto Vega y Pagan, *Military Biography of Generalissimo Rafael Leonidas Trujillo Molina*, trans. Ida Espaillat (Cuidad Trujillo, D.R., 1956), p. 132. A list of his foreign honors and decorations is given on pp. 195–99.

[14] Rengger and Longchamps, *The Reign of Doctor Joseph Gaspard Roderick de Francia, In Paraguay: An Account of a Six Years' Residence in that Republic, from July, 1819 to May, 1825*, trans. J. R. Rengger (London: Thomas Hurst, Edward Chance & Co., 1827), pp. 19–20.

was overwhelmingly in his favor—9,315 ayes and 5 noes.[15] More recently, in Argentina, the most renowned *caudillo* of the twentieth century, Juan Perón, was elected president in 1946 and reelected in 1951.[16]

Sometimes the "election" whereby a dictator attains the presidency is a mere sham, with only the barest semblance of legality. When President Horacio Vásquez of the Dominican Republic was overthrown by a revolution in 1930, Leonidas Trujillo, head of the well-equipped, American-trained constabulary, managed to win presidential office through the façade of legal election, after his henchmen had beaten, terrorized, and killed many of his opponents. With the opposition so mauled that it finally withdrew from the campaign, Trujillo's "election" was proclaimed to be "virtually unanimous."[17]

How He Exercises Power: Directly or Indirectly. In exercising power once he gets it, the *caudillo*, although unquestionably the most powerful man in the nation, may prefer not to become president at all but rather to remain behind the scenes where he can exercise control through his puppet president. Thus Fulgencio Batista, who became Cuba's strong man in August 1933 after throwing out Gerardo Machado, did not assume the presidency in his own name until 1940. In the intervening seven years, he ruled through puppets, seven of them in seven years. Such indirect exercise of power is unusual, however; ordinarily a dictator prefers to govern in his own name.

The Absolute Power He Wields. However the dictator chooses to exercise power, whether through puppets or by becoming president himself, one thing is certain: there is no doubt whatever in the nation as to where plenary power really lies. The *caudillo* is a "monarch in republican dress," and an absolute monarch at that. In effect, he is the constitution, the government, and the law. Whatever he says goes; regardless of the nation's forms and trappings of democracy, he rules the country with as wide a latitude as he chooses.

"Power for its own sake is the ideal of such men," concludes F. García Calderón.[18] "The less important chieftains are satisfied by the government of a province; the great leader aspires to rule a republic." More-

---

[15] Herring, *op. cit.*, p. 633.

[16] For an excellent account of both elections, see George I. Blanksten's *Perón's Argentina* (Chicago: University of Chicago Press, 1953), pp. 63–86.

[17] For a very different account, portraying Trujillo as fairly and democratically elected, see a typical sycophant's version, Lawrence de Besault, "Rise to the Presidency," *President Trujillo: His Work and the Dominican Republic* (2d ed.; Washington Publishing Co., 1936), chap. iii.

[18] F. García Calderón, *Latin America: Its Rise and Progress*, trans. Bernard Miall (London: T. Fisher Unwin, 1913), pp. 366–67. Pérez Jiménez was such a *caudillo*, "thoroughly obsessed with the idea of power. . . . Venezuelan psychiatrists, who studied Pérez Jiménez' record as a clinical case after the revolution that ousted him in 1958 . . . found him to be a 'paranoiac, megalomaniac, neurotic.'" (Szulc, *op. cit.*, pp. 254–55.)

over, in exercising his virtually unlimited power, the "great leader" may be governed either by reason and seasoned judgment or, perhaps, by emotion, ignorance, prejudice, and whim.

His Preference for Legitimacy and Constitutional Sanction. Almost no ruler in Latin America likes to be regarded by his fellow countrymen or the rest of the world as an interloper. Accordingly, he makes every effort to give his regime the appearance of legitimacy and constitutionality. To this end, one of the first things that he does after becoming head of the nation is to promulgate a new constitution, tailored to legitimize his accession to power and his exercise of governmental authority.

"Of necessity their governments must have constitutions," observed A. Curtis Wilgus, speaking of *caudillos*, "for national policies demand them and international opinion requires them, but their predecessors' constitutions are 'outgrown', 'past history', or 'incompatible with the public good'; and besides, to the Hispanic American, change means progress."[19]

Sometimes the *caudillo*'s determination to have his regime legitimized by a constitution and to present a democratic front to the world tends to run riot. During the 27 years in which Vicente Gómez exercised dictatorial control over Venezuela, he promulgated a total of six constitutions. Each succeeding constitution professed to establish democracy more firmly in the nation and to guarantee the basic liberties of citizens, while at the same time concentrating more and more absolute power in Gómez' hands.

Besides showing respect for a constitution, however much it has been perverted to serve his own ends, the *caudillo* also prefers to govern through the regular, constitutionally established organs of government, since they give his regime the appearance of democracy. But the legislative and judicial branches had better resign themselves to being merely subservient rubber stamps, ready, willing, even eager to carry out his wishes. In Peronist Argentina, after the Supreme Court of Justice presumed to exercise its independent authority and to declare a number of executive decrees unconstitutional, Perón instigated a purge of the entire court, a purge that extended throughout the nation's judicial system.[20]

The Argentine Congress was likewise reduced to a bootlicking body, with little semblance of any independent exercise of authority. The 1948 session mirrored the complete control that Perón exercised over the body. The members of the Chamber of Deputies, consisting mainly of Peronistas, adopted an 8.6 billion peso ($1.8 billion) budget, hardly bothering to look at the mimeographed budget report on their desks. And in just four hours they passed a total of 28 bills, including one which gave Perón dictatorial powers by authorizing him to mobilize men and resources by decree whenever he thought the nation's welfare demanded it.

---

[19] Wilgus, *op. cit.*, p. 9.
[20] Blanksten, *op. cit.*, pp. 122–32.

How the Caudillo Maintains His Power Over the Nation

Satisfying His Henchmen and Supporters. In maintaining dictatorial control over the nation, the *caudillo* shows consummate skill. The accepted rule of thumb is to spare no effort to satisfy his henchmen and supporters, especially the members of the armed forces whose unswerving allegiance is essential to his continuance in office. To assure the support of them all and keep them happy, he gladly shares with them the spoils of office, tapping every possible source of wealth. Funds in the public treasury, customs duties and taxes, land comprising the national domain, and the confiscated property of his opponents are all utilized to keep his following in line.

Keeping the Opposition under Control. Also critically important to the dictator is keeping the opposition under control. The policies and techniques for accomplishing this vary widely. Sometimes a *caudillo* is very indulgent with members of the opposition, permitting them to exercise their constitutional rights, possibly to criticize him publicly, even to campaign against him politically. And sometimes even when he catches them red-handedly conspiring to overthrow his regime, he metes out only mild punishment, such as sending them into exile. But this kind of treatment of adversaries is not subscribed to by most dictators, and for good reason. Many a conspirator released to go into exile has later returned to institute a successful revolution against the regime in power—possibly, too, to execute the deposed head of state whose brand of *Realpolitik* did not work.

Much more often, the *caudillo* instinctively realizes that any opposition, however small, is a challenge to his power and may eventually undermine him. With this in mind, he is apt to be ruthless in ferreting out opposition and brutal in suppressing it. An example of this type of brutality is furnished by Melgarejo, who on December 6, 1865, decreed that all who opposed his government would be regarded as traitors to the nation, given an oral trial, and condemned to be shot.[21]

The most sadistic tortures are often inflicted on the regime's opponents. In Cuba the security police of Batista did not hesitate to extract information by any means they chose, whether by yanking out fingernails with pliers, or carbonizing hands and feet in red hot vises. Castrating males was another technique often employed. In Venezuela the 27-year regime of Vicente Gómez was also characterized by the most sadistic brutalities.[22]

In view of the awful brutalities inflicted upon opponents, it is no wonder that they often describe the *caudillo* as they do. Henri Christophe, who ruled the northern part of Haiti from 1806 until he committed suicide in 1820 to keep from being captured alive by the opposition, was one

---

[21] Wilgus, *op. cit.*, p. 337.
[22] For the many cruel means of torturous punishment used, see Lavin, *op. cit.*, pp. 208–20, and Rourke, *op. cit.*, pp. 147–54 and 231–37.

of the most feared and hated rulers in all Latin America. According to his enemies, he was a "rude, indigested mass of matter; his laugh, the grimace of a tiger; and when he opened his mouth in rage it extended from ear to ear, disclosing a double row of long, pointed, cannibal teeth. 'He was without honor, without faith, without law, and without religion—in obscenities surpassing all the sacrilegious and filthy horrors with which Sardanapalus and Nebuchadnezzar were formerly reproached—a slave to his passions, an enemy of justice, cruel, arbitrary, avaricious, proud, selfish, blood-thirsty, incapable of the least sentiment of gratitude.' "[23]

Keeping the Mass in Tow. Dealing with known members of the opposition is a primary concern of the *caudillo;* keeping the mass of people in line is another. An effective means which he uses for this purpose, in addition to rumors of torture that spread among the people, is fear—a paralyzing fear of what will happen to them if they dare to oppose him. To impress this upon them, as well as to seek out any incipient opposition, he usually has an elaborate system of espionage, as did Gómez in Venezuela. Relying heavily on his secret police, Gómez is said to have spent two and a half times more for this suppressive force than for public education![24]

The Caudillo's Concern for His Safety

Maintaining his power by violence and terror, the *caudillo* is himself infected with the very fear that he disseminates among the populace. Feared by his subjects and bitterly hated by his enemies, he knows that he can trust no one. Lurking in any shadow or mixed in any group may be a victim or a relative determined to inflict revenge. Many a fellow countryman would gladly give his life for the privilege of assassinating him. Not even the closest associate can be completely trusted, for he may be jealous of the chief's authority and have ambitions of his own. Since the *caudillo* owes his success to violence, he well realizes that he will probably meet his end by violence too. One *caudillo* is even said to have erected in front of his quarters a scaffold with an inscription on it reading, "For them or for me."

Francia of Paraguay was so obsessed with his safety that he had all the trees cut down around the presidential mansion, removing vantage points where an assassin might lurk. Hoping to thwart a potential assassin, Francia slept in a different room in the presidential mansion every night and even personally doled out the cartridges to the supervisors of prisons and powder magazines to insure as far as possible that the bullets would be used against his enemies and not against him.[25]

---

[23] Wilgus, *op. cit.,* p. 11, and *The New York Advertiser,* February 5, 1821.

[24] For Gómez' all-seeing, all-hearing, and omnipresent spy system, see Lavin, *op. cit.,* pp. 313–21.

[25] Rengger and Longchamps, *op. cit.,* p. 44.

The *caudillo*, realizing that his hated regime will probably fall by the sword, just as it was established by the sword, usually makes elaborate preparations for a hurried departure from the nation should a turn of fortune make this necessary. Anticipating this possibility, he smuggles his vast loot out of the country and stores it safely in banks in the United States, Switzerland, and elsewhere. In times of unusual tension, his suitcase is packed and a plane is warming up at the airport to whisk him away on short notice. If all these meticulously made plans fail, he may even use a carefully kept silver bullet to end it all, as did Christophe of Haiti when he was about to be captured by his opponents.

But however great are the risks inherent in exercising dictatorial power, the *caudillo* is quite willing to gamble with his safety and even with his life. For "in his own view, the *caudillo* is an indispensable man," says George I. Blanksten, ". . . the only figure on the national scene who can 'save the country.' He . . . bears a striking resemblance to Max Weber's 'charismatic' leader, who feels an 'inner call.' "[26] When Doctor François Duvalier of Haiti—"Papa Doc," his admiring followers call him—had himself installed as president for life in April 1964, he told his crowd of well-wishers that he considered himself an exceptional man—the kind of man that Haiti can produce only once every 50 or 75 years.[27]

Regarding himself as indispensable and determined to remain in office as long as possible, the dictator often enjoys a long tenure. Porfirio Díaz, president of Mexico from 1876 to 1911, had the longest tenure of all—a total of 35 years. (During the four years from 1880 to 1884, Manuel Gonzáles, put in office by Díaz, was president, faithfully carrying out Díaz' policies.)

Despite the bitter hatred felt against *caudillos* and the great risks which they run, many of them do die in bed at a ripe old age. This was true of Francia of Paraguay (who died at 74), Gómez of Venezuela (78), Rosas of Argentina (84), and Díaz of Mexico (85).

But whether the dictator dies in bed of old age (usually outside the country, enjoying his hidden-away wealth) or whether he is cut down by an assassin's bullet, his passing is an occasion for riotous celebration, expressing the people's pent-up frustration and bitterness. Crowds surge through the streets, sacking and destroying any remaining possessions of the dictator or his family.

Why Dictatorship Has Continued to Flourish

The persistence and frequency of dictatorships have provoked much soul-searching on the part of Latin Americans and analytical thought on

---

[26] George I. Blanksten, *Ecuador: Constitutions and Caudillos* (Berkeley: University of California Press, 1951), p. 35.

[27] *New York Times*, April 2, 1964, p. 1, col. 6.

the part of others. The explanations that have been offered are many and varied.[28]

Geography has had a very important effect. Much of the area is covered by lofty mountains or tropical jungles, tremendous obstacles to easy intercourse between the different regions of a nation. There are few roads —usually poor ones—for reaching regions isolated from the seat of government. As a result, there is a strong feeling of regional loyalty, which makes it easy for a local *caudillo* to rise to power and difficult for the central government to suppress an insurrection once it has begun. Pancho Villa, notorious regional *caudillo* in Mexico, managed to avoid capture by the Mexican government and even by the United States Army under General Pershing, sent across the border to apprehend him.

Another factor that has made for *caudillismo* is the tradition of strongman rule in the history of the several races of Latin America; this is true of the Spanish and Portuguese, as well as of the Indian and Negro. Each of these races has long been accustomed to the dictatorial rule of a monarch or cacique. The Inca, for example, was one of the most absolute rulers to be found anywhere. He was the Supreme Chief of the nation, the leader of the army, the High Priest of the religion, and the Supreme Law Giver. Owing him blind obedience, the mass of Indians were accustomed to forced labor without pay and were not even permitted to choose their occupations. In fact, every aspect of their life conditioned them to absolute rule.

The heterogeneous racial composition of the region has also been a very influential factor. In most of the nations, a large part of the population is Indian or mestizo, with culture, mores, and interests quite different from those of the whites and Negroes. Strong animosities are generated by these differences, and the resulting tensions in society are tempting targets for demagogues, who often rise to power by playing off one racial group against another.

"Our political backwardness," wrote Lucas Awarragaray about anarchy and *caudillismo* in Argentina, "is and always has been simply a phenomenon of the psychology of race; a hybrid mind has been the source of Creole, that is, hybrid anarchy. The mestizo element has been the cause of the most fundamental defects in our character."[29]

Another influence often regarded in Latin America as encouraging to dictatorship is the Spanish temperament, certain aspects of which are con-

---

[28] For some provocative explanations, see W. W. Pierson (ed.), "Pathology of Democracy in Latin America: A Symposium" (Arthur P. Whitaker, "A Historian's Point of View"; Russell Fitzgibbon, "A Political Scientist's Point of View"; Sanford A. Mosk, "An Economist's Point of View"; and J. Rex Crawford, "Discussion: A Sociologist's Point of View"), *American Political Science Review*, Vol. 44, No. 1 (March, 1950), pp. 100–49; also Rippy, "Dictatorships in Latin America" (2d ed.), *op. cit.*, pp. 179–85; and Chapman, *op. cit.*, "The Age of the Caudillos," chap. vii.

[29] In Pierson, *op. cit.*, p. 106.

ducive to violence and strong rule. Among the traits regarded as typically
Spanish are arrogance, conceit, selfishness, impulsiveness, verbosity, an
exaggerated sense of dignity, and a theatrical sense of the heroic. "To
die for a principle, how glorious!" thinks the Latin American, a born
revolutionary. "But to live for a principle, how dull." Moreover, the
Spaniards coming to the New World were intensely individualistic, impatient with authority, and unwilling to regard themselves as subject to
law, as Anglo-Americans do. With few restraining influences on them in
the new society, their tendencies toward aggrandizement and turbulence
were given free rein. Strong government was necessary to hold them in
check.

The high rate of illiteracy prevailing in Latin America has been another factor conducive to dictatorship. Man's political history has shown
that where a large part of the citizenry is illiterate, this uneducated group
cannot adequately assume its responsibilities in a democracy. Latin
America has proved no exception to the rule. There, the ignorant masses
have often been the easy prey of demagogues who prated about the
rights of man, harangued them into an emotional frenzy, and enlisted
their enthusiastic support for a revolution. Yet the demagogues promptly
forgot about the rights of man after they managed to get control of the
government, and set up just another dictatorship in the long, monotonous
pattern of the region.

Still another factor conducive to dictatorships was the lack of appren-
ticeship in self-government during the more than 300 years of colonial
status..[30] The only self-government enjoyed then was participation in the
cabildos or town councils. Consequently, the citizens of the new independent nations, denied wider political experience, lacked the habits of
independent judgment, self-direction, and self-restraint which citizens of
a truly democratic nation must have.

In short, the people really were not ready for self-government. Simón
Bolívar was fully convinced of this, and was very pessimistic about
Latin America's future. "For centuries we were political ciphers [under
Spanish rule]," he declared in his famous Jamaica letter of 1815. "That is
why it is so hard for us to rise to the enjoyment of freedom. . . . Events
have already shown that completely representative institutions are not
suited to our present character, habits, and educational background."

The economic conditions and problems of the region have also done
much to further dictatorship. The extremes of great wealth for the few
and blighting poverty for the mass are mainly responsible for the sharp
cleavage between social classes and the bitter social conflicts that often
result. Members of the mass, who eke out a bare subsistence and live in

---

[30] The *caudillo* is "the receiver of the bankrupt colonial regime of Latin America.
In a few of these countries his function has already been fulfilled." (George S. Wise,
Caudillo: A Portrait of Antonio Guzmán Blanco [New York: Columbia University
Press, 1951]), p. x.

miserable squalor, are receptive to almost any appeal which promises somehow to improve their condition.

Still another factor that has played a part in the continuance of *caudillismo* is the role of foreign capital in the society. Lacking the means to develop their own economic resources, the countries have had to rely heavily on the investments of foreign companies, particularly those of the United States, Britain, Germany, and Japan. Foreign capital has been invested in a variety of enterprises, including mines and petroleum, railroads and rapid transit companies, and banks and public utilities. Although capital from abroad was badly needed and usually eagerly welcomed, its presence was often a disturbing influence that could easily be exploited for political purposes. Ofttimes the foreign companies were bitterly criticized and charged with making excessive profits, wasting irreplaceable natural resources, exploiting native labor, paying inadequate taxes to the government, enjoying undeserved privileges through concessions, favors, and exemptions, and intervening in local politics to protect their privileges and interests. Aroused by these criticisms, public opinion in Latin America has been decidedly antiforeign and strongly nationalistic. Charges of economic imperialism, whether solidly or superficially supported, have often proved to be an effective technique that enabled an ambitious demagogue and incipient *caudillo* to rise to power.

Still another factor that has figured prominently in the persistence of dictatorships is personalism, the tendency of citizens to support or oppose a leader for such purely personal reasons as his personal appeal or family background, rather than the program he espouses or party he represents. Taking advantage of this tendency, the *caudillos* with their dynamic personalities and flair for the dramatic are easily able to capture the attention and support of a following by their personal magnetism.[31] But Latin America pays a high price for personalism, because it results in the rule of men, which is often capricious, arbitrary, and absolute, rather than the rule of law, which is uniform, impartial, and fair.

Effects of Dictatorship[32]

Contributions Made. Although the *caudillos* are absolute rulers and represent the very antithesis of democratic government, they have nevertheless helped their nations in many important ways. Seeking to improve communication and transportation, if only to strengthen and consolidate their power, they built telegraph lines and roads which tied the various sections of the nations together. And usually concerned with economic

---

[31] Sometimes a *caudillo* resorts to personalism as his sole claim to leadership. ". . . Guzmán Blanco has no background to relieve his sheer insistence on his personal glory. There is no assurance behind his claims. He must assert his lone self because he has nothing else to assert." (*Ibid.*, p. 172.)

[32] For a detailed appraisal of the balance sheet of the Vargas regime in Brazil, see Karl Lowenstein, *Brazil Under Vargas* (New York: The Macmillan Company, 1942), pp. 317–62.

development, if only to increase their personal revenues, they stimulated agriculture and industry, developed local resources, and increased foreign trade. Sometimes they supported public education, building schools and public libraries, thereby adding to their long list of titles that of Patron of Arts and Learning. But education of the mass was a recognized hazard, so concern for public education was apt to be mere talk; a citizenry that was educated might catch on to their machinations and "turn the rascals out."

Another contribution of the *caudillos* was the intense nationalism they fostered. During the critical early years of independence, when the young nations were threatened with fragmentation by internal anarchy or dismemberment by foreign invasion, a strong national leader and his stress on patriotism was sometimes the only force that held the nation together. Thus Argentina owes its very existence as a nation today largely to Juan Manuel de Rosas, whose 23 years of dictatorial rule held the nation together during the turbulent early period when it was threatened with dissolution.

Still another noteworthy contribution of the dictators was the order and stability which they were able to maintain. Although their methods were ruthless and violent, they nevertheless managed to curb the turbulence and anarchy which all but swamped the young nations. In the Buenos Aires area alone, there were 12 revolutions in a single year (1820), and other parts of Latin America were almost as chaotic. The rule of the *caudillos* might be strong, even tyrannical, but it afforded the young republics still struggling to maintain themselves a measure of law and order which they sorely needed.

However much a dictator might be disliked or even hated because of his strong rule while in power, he was often sorely missed the moment he was overthrown. Thus, when Bernardo O'Higgins of Chile was forced out in 1823 after five years of firm but enlightened rule, there followed seven years of ruinous disorder. During this period, there were at least ten governments and three different constitutions. Presidents came and went so fast it was almost impossible to keep track of them. "National life reached a very bad state," says J. Fred Rippy, with " 'vandalism in the country, commerce paralyzed, industry at a standstill, finance in disorder, credit vanished, and politics revolutionary.' The Chilean people passed 'from liberty to license, and from license to barbarism.' "[33]

Still another contribution made by many of the *caudillos* was their emphasis on efficiency in government. Often, they reorganized the governmental structure to make the operating agencies more effective and streamlined their procedures to enable them to operate more expeditiously. The dictator sometimes even demanded scrupulous honesty on the part of his officials and personnel—a yardstick he seldom applied to himself or to his cronies.

---

[33] Rippy, *Historical Evolution of Hispanic America, op. cit.,* p. 197.

Harm Done. But whatever the *caudillos* contributed to the welfare of their nations, these contributions were usually very dearly paid for, as the debit side of the ledger clearly shows. Some of the dictators, such as Rosas of Argentina, were quite honest. A wealthy man when he came to power, Rosas carried almost nothing away with him when he went into exile, and he died in England in 1877 virtually a pauper.

But such honesty was quite the exception. Usually, at the same time as the *caudillo* was demanding scrupulous honesty on the part of his officials, he had his hand deep in the national till, taking everything he wanted—including land, money, and lucrative concessions. Although not many *caudillos* were large landowners before they came into power, they were usually among the largest *hacendados* in the nation afterward.

They enjoy accumulating money as well as land, and have stolen public funds in fantastic amounts. Dictators who have been overthrown within the last decade have set quite a record for peculation. Juan Perón is believed to have left Argentina after his overthrow in 1955 with an estimated $700 million, enough to enable him to live comfortably in his old age. Pérez Jiménez of Venezuela and Fulgencio Batista of Cuba, both of whom were overthrown in 1958, were bush leaguers by comparison; yet each is supposed to have taken more than $250 million with him to ease the pangs of exile.

Besides helping himself to all funds in the national treasury, the *caudillo* often regards the nation as his private preserve, and bleeds it as much as he can. In the Dominican Republic, Rafael Trujillo and members of his family had a monopoly on practically every commodity that the people needed—including meat, milk, rice, coffee, vegetable oils, cacao, tobacco, and salt—as well as on lumber and furniture. But the Trujillos were not satisfied with just the profit from commodities, which amounted to millions of dollars a year, thanks to high fixed prices that were charged. They also set up for themselves monopolies on such profitable services as sea and land transportation; the sale of accident insurance; iron and steel used by the government for construction purposes; and even the laundry concession for all the nation. No source of easy money was overlooked. One of the brothers even had a monopoly on houses of prostitution![34]

Sometimes even more harmful to a nation than the graft and corruption of a *caudillo* and his gang are his economic policies. Those of Rojas Pinilla, who guided Colombia's destiny with a firm hand from 1953 to 1957, provided needed benefits for the mass but were very expensive to the nation.[35] Perón's economic program left Argentina with a legacy of internal stagnation and in virtual economic collapse. Indeed, the nation's instability, which has continued since his overthrow in 1955, is largely due to his

---

[34] Albert C. Hicks, *Blood in the Streets: The Life and Rule of Trujillo* (New York: Creative Age Press, Inc., 1946), pp. 65–74.

[35] Vernon Lee Fluharty, *Dance of the Millions: Military Rule and the Social Revolution in Colombia, 1930–1956* (Pittsburgh, Pa.: University of Pittsburgh Press, 1957), pp. 237–58.

economic policies; he left virtually bankrupt a country which had enjoyed prosperity until he came into power.[36] The eminent Argentine economist, Raúl Prebisch, has estimated that Perón's rule cost the nation more than $3 billion—a tremendous sum for the country—which spelled the difference between enjoying economic stability and prosperity or teetering on the brink of economic chaos. But while Argentines sweat it out today at home, Perón manages to live comfortably on the $700 million or so which he took with him into exile.

REVOLUTIONS AND VIOLENCE

One of the most characteristic features of the political process in Latin America is the resort to revolution to bring about changes in political power. So frequently has violence been used for this purpose in the past that change of administration by revolution is regarded as the normal pattern in many of the countries. While such revolutions were more frequent during the nineteenth century, they have continued to thwart the orderly, constitutional processes of government and constitute an accepted means of transfer of political power from one administration to another.

Types of Revolutions

The term "revolution" is used quite loosely in referring to changes in political power brought about by violence. In fact, the term has come to connote three very different political phenomena: 1) the wars for independence during the first quarter of the nineteenth century; 2) changes by force in the apex of political power; and 3) fundamental change in the political structure, accompanied by basic changes in social institutions.

The Wars of Independence. Regarding the wars for independence in the various nations, the successful struggles for freedom resulting in transfer of sovereignty from the mother country to the colonies are usually referred to as "revolutions," in the same sense that we refer to the revolution of the 13 original colonies as the American Revolution. And, just as the American Revolution made very little change in the new nation's social structure and institutions, the Latin American revolutions made few, if any, such basic changes.

The wars for independence, as was the case in the American Revolution, were led for the most part by conservatives who were determined to maintain their vested interests in the new nations. They had no intention whatever of overturning the existing political, economic, and social structure and remolding it into a true democracy. Consequently, although

---

[36] For Argentina's disastrous economic situation in 1955, see Arthur P. Whitaker, *Argentine Upheaval: Perón's Fall and the New Regime* (New York: Frederick A. Praeger, Inc., 1956), pp. 37–38 and 161–64.

Esquire, January, 1961, p. 69. Reproduced by permission.

"Congratulations! We've changed our minds—you're the new President!"

the masses had contributed mightily to the success of the national revolts, supplying most of the soldiers that eventually humbled the military might of Spain, they were to benefit but little from the newly won independence. "The heroic struggle for Bolivian independence did nothing to relieve the Indian of his miserable state," concludes Eduardo Palomo, "although . . . the majority of those who fought and died for independence were Indians. . . . As far as the Indian was concerned, one feudal master had been substituted for another."[37]

In the political realm, the Creole elite, who were now in the saddle after displacing their envied superiors, the *peninsulares*, preempted all political offices and political rights for themselves. In the social realm, they

---

[37] Eduardo Palomo, "Agrarian Reform," (in collaboration with Eugene C. Reichard and Clifford Belcher) (La Paz, Bolivia: Servicio Agrícola Interamericano, January 20, 1961), p. 1.

continued the rigid class system that had existed from the early days of the colonial era. In the economic realm too, they condoned and accepted the great extremes of wealth that had so long burdened the society. These basic disparities—political, social, and economic—were to be veritable mill-stones around the necks of the struggling young nations—millstones which still threaten to submerge them almost a century and a half after independence.

Thus the wars for independence, which made no basic changes in the semifeudal society, can hardly be said to have been revolutions in the true sense of the term. Indeed, the very fact that such changes were not made earlier and have not been made even to date is the main reason for the unrest and instability which prevails throughout most of the region. In fact, many who are very interested in Latin America are quite convinced that the nations will still have to undergo a true revolution in order to achieve the democratic society they profess to aspire to. The liberal leaders of Latin America "know that their own countries must go through a social as well as a political reorganization. . . . ," says A. A. Berle, Jr. "The outstanding necessity is to put an end to the division between age-old oligarchic, irresponsible power cliques and a proletariat living out its life in hunger and disease, without hope of improvement."[38]

Changes in Government at the Top,

How Changes Are Made by Violence. Besides designating the wars for independence, the term "revolution" is also used to denote any change in government at the top brought about by means of force. In such cases, only the presidency, cabinet positions, and other high executive offices are usually affected. The courts may continue to function as before, along with the congress and the administrative machinery of government. These typically Latin American "revolutions" are of two kinds: the *golpe de estado*, or *coup d'état*, and the *cuartelazo*, or barracks revolt.

1. The *Golpe de Estado.* According to William S. Stokes, "the *golpe de estado* . . . is the fastest and potentially the most dangerous of the forceful methods of establishing and changing governments in Latin America. The *golpe* is a direct assault on power, which means the immobilization of the president either through assassination, detention, or exile."[39]

Speedy and effective, this supraconstitutional means of seizing political power by force is frequently used in Latin America. Sometimes it is quite dramatic. In August 1947, José María Velasco Ibarra, president of Ecuador since June 1944, was forced to relinquish his presidential office and depart in haste when Colonel Carlos Mancheno, minister of defense, managed to get into the presidential mansion and compel him at gunpoint to resign

---

[38] A. A. Berle, Jr., "Latin America: The Hidden Revolution," *The Reporter*, Vol. 20, No. 10 (May 28, 1959), p. 20.

[39] William S. Stokes, *Latin American Politics* (New York: Thomas Y. Crowell Co., 1959), p. 319.

in his favor. Mancheno tried to justify his seizure of the presidential office on the ground that "the members of the Armed Forces see ourselves in the necessity of taking over the government temporarily."

Another novel application of the *golpe* was staged in Paraguay in February 1949 when President Raimundo Rolon and most members of his government were invited to dinner by Felipe Molas López. The host, who had surrounded his home with his own henchmen, summarily announced to the group, "Gentlemen, the jig is up." It was, and López thereupon became president of Paraguay.

The *golpe* as a political instrument has several distinct advantages over other violent methods used in taking over the presidential office. For one thing, it is relatively easy to organize. Only a small number—a single individual, in fact—may be able to accomplish the seizure successfully. And, while a ranking military figure would probably have a better chance of succeeding, even a civilian leader with sufficient daring and finesse might be able to finagle his way into the presidential mansion and successfully accomplish his mission.

The *golpe* also has the advantage of obtaining a prompt, often immediate, decision. No widespread seizure of critical installations, no assault in force on the presidential palace or fighting in the streets by military and police, is necessary. If the *golpe* is adroitly planned and executed, the decision is apt to be speedy and irrevocable. A president can say "uncle" and disappear fast when he sees the menacing barrel of a loaded 38 or 44.

2. The *Cuartelazo.* Another effective means of bringing about a change in government at the top by violence is the *cuartelazo* or barracks revolt, which has its origin in the *cuartel* or barracks. The most extensive and careful planning is necessary for its success—planning that is as painstaking as the architect's for constructing a building sturdy enough to withstand the earthquakes which beset the Andean region. Many critical questions must be answered, and answered correctly. What leaders can be counted on to sympathize with the revolt, throw in their forces to make it successful, and be willing to risk their careers, and perhaps lives, on its outcome? What specific program should be adopted that will appeal to the people and justify the new regime's revolting and taking over? How much force will be necessary to achieve control, and just when, where, and how will it be exercised? In short, a successful *cuartelazo* requires consummate strategy, for in essence it is a form of military statesmanship.

The timing of the revolt is of the utmost importance. It is usually set for a Sunday or a holiday, when the president is apt to be alone or lightly guarded, the security forces relaxed, the government offices closed, and the various facilities for communication either closed or on a standby basis. Moreover, the populace will be at the soccer games or at the races, more concerned at the moment with the fate of a five-peso bet than with the safety of governmental authority.

If everything goes as planned, the *cuartelazo* is executed quickly and precisely. All key military and governmental centers, including armories and supply depots, TV and radio stations, governmental buildings and banks, are speedily seized. Using the seized media of communication, the leader of the *cuartelazo* announces to the people that a revolt has taken place and that his group has taken over governmental authority. The "rascals" of the overthrown regime will be properly dealt with, and all of their abuses, which are many, will be corrected in short order. The people are assured that the nation is now in good hands, and their cooperation is requested in restoring and maintaining order.

There have been many such *cuartelazos* in Latin America, some of them brilliantly planned and executed. In fact, whichever side you are on,

A. B. C. IN LATIN AMERICA

SOURCE: Abel Quezada, *The Best of Impossible Worlds* (Englewood Cliffs, N.J.: Prentice-Hall, Inc.). Reproduced by permission.

you cannot help but admire the skill and finesse that are responsible for their success.

One of the most brilliant *cuartelazos* of all time was that executed by Fulgencio Batista of Cuba on March 10, 1952, which put him back in power. During the preceding two decades, he had been a leader to be reckoned with in Cuban politics. A chief figure in the revolt that forced President Machado to resign in 1933, he had dominated the government from then until 1940, and was president from 1940 to 1944. By 1952, after eight years of democratic government, the nation was thoroughly disillusioned by the widespread corruption and abuse of authority. Sensing that it was time for a change, Batista organized a *cuartelazo* which will long rank as a classic in Latin America's revolutionary history.

Precisely at 2:43 A.M. on March 10, 1952, while the nation was asleep, Batista's forces acted with split-second timing, seizing Air Force, naval, supply, and other critical installations. The skillfully synchronized and coordinated maneuver was so adroitly planned and executed that by 4:00 A.M.—just 1 hour and 17 minutes later—every important military installation was in control of the insurgents. And by 8:30 A.M., President Carlos Prio and members of his cabinet had thrown in the sponge and taken refuge in the Mexican Embassy. In a region that rather prides itself on the skill of its revolts, this was indeed one to remember.

Most *cuartelazos*, however, are not so well planned and executed. Indeed, the slightest slip-up can mean the difference between success and failure. A couple of such flukes in execution doomed to failure a revolt attempted in Colombia in May, 1958. Die-hard military men who were determined to keep Alberto Lleras Camargo from being selected as bipartisan president of the nation concocted a brazen plot to kidnap him and also the five members of the military junta who were temporarily ruling the nation.

But the best-laid schemes of generals, as of mice and men, "gang aft a-gley." The conspirators managed to seize Lleras and were carrying him to the military barracks in a panel truck when they committed the tactical error of driving too fast past the presidential palace. It was as careless a mistake as Al Capone's failing to list all his income with the Internal Revenue Service. Palace guards stopped the truck for speeding, recognized with astonishment the prisoner in the back, and with rifles leveled at the kidnappers escorted Lleras Camargo to safety. Meanwhile the *cuartelazo* was further bungled by the failure to capture a fifth member of the military junta, Vice-Admiral Ruben Piedrahita. Temporarily in charge of the government, he ordered all loyal armed forces to aid in suppressing the insurrection, which they did, thus ending the fiasco.

A frequent cause of bungling a *cuartelazo* is the failure to secure the cooperation of all branches of the armed forces, as was shown by the unsuccessful revolt in Ecuador in November, 1961. When José María Velasco Ibarra resigned as president of the crisis-ridden nation, Carlos

Julio Arosemena, the vice-president, prepared to take over. Because of his leftist leanings, however, the Army refused to recognize him as president, and backed Camilo Gallegos Toledo, chief justice of the Supreme Court and a political moderate. The Air Force, however, refused to acquiesce in this decision, and backed up its conviction with force. Three jet planes firing rockets and machine guns swooped low over the legislative palace where Army men were holding Arosemena virtually prisoner, and within minutes the radio stations announced that Army-backed Gallegos Toledo had dropped his claim to the presidency. Apparently the Air Force was more astute politically than militarily. Its political sights were better than its bombsights, for, despite its low-level attack, dead on target, there was not a single hit.

Causes of Disagreement Within the Ruling Class. With many such revolts taking place, whether *golpes* or *cuartelazos*, the question arises as to why they do not accomplish the reforms so badly needed in the political, social, and economic structure of the society. The answer is simple. The many *golpes* and *cuartelazos*, popularly known as "revolutions," are hardly more than "palace revolts"—a sort of in-fighting among members of the ruling class, who have a virtual monopoly on the domain of politics. Since they all have pretty much the same vested interests to protect, they can hardly be expected to advocate basic changes in society which would adversely affect these interests, possibly seriously jeopardizing them.

Although they usually see eye to eye on fundamental issues, members of the upper class are apt to disagree on three main points.[40] Foremost is *personalismo*, or attraction to a leader because of his personal or family appeal. So widespread is *personalismo* that it inspired the political axiom, "in Latin America, almost every 'ism' is a 'somebodyism.' " Juan Perón of Argentina gave rise to *peronismo*, and José Batlle y Ordóñez of Uruguay, to *batllismo*. If President Lyndon Johnson were head of a Latin American state instead of the United States, his program and doctrines would be known as *johnsonismo*. But whatever the "ism" or "ismo," it is not nearly as important as the dynamic, colorful leader who espouses it.

A second main cause of division within the ruling class is regionalism, which is mainly the result of the area's topography. Loyalties to different regions often conflict, causing serious tension within the nation. In Ecuador, a highly competitive and quite unhealthy rivalry has long existed between Guayaquil, the liberal coastal metropolis, and Quito, the conservative capital located in the sierra. And in Bolivia, the altiplano, with La Paz on its fringe, is almost a foreign country to people living in the tropical Oriente. Fears of the central government that the Oriente might actually try to secede and join neighboring Brazil (fears very well founded, incidentally) were responsible for the construction of the modern paved highway of 310 miles between Cochabamba and Santa Cruz, the only

---

[40] George I. Blanksten, "Revolutions," in Harold Eugene Davis (ed.), *Government and Politics in Latin America* (New York: Ronald Press Co., 1958), p. 144.

paved highway in all Bolivia. These and other regional loyalties were usually expressed and directed by members of the ruling class, so that conflicts between regions inevitably aligned members of this class against one another.

A third cause of disagreement among members of the upper class are the conflicting opinions and convictions on momentous social issues which confront the nations today. Earlier, a very controversial issue which split the society from top to bottom was the status of the Roman Catholic Church and the rights, privileges, and immunities which it would be allowed to enjoy. Today, there are other burning issues that are provoking a great debate in many of the nations. Should the upper class, which owns most of the wealth in the society, be taxed more heavily to finance the social reforms which the great mass of citizens are now demanding? The Latin American plutocracy is notoriously allergic to taxes—as much so as oil tycoons in the United States who may have personal incomes of $26 million a year, yet not pay a dollar in income taxes.

Land reform is another hot issue which the upper class is having to face. It owns most of the land, and millions of landless peons, as we saw earlier, are agitating for some land of their own. What should be done about this? Should the big landowners sit tight and try to ride out the storm by appeasing the landless with promises as they have for a century and a half? Or should they institute a genuine program of land reform before the mass takes by force what it believes it is entitled to?

In the past, such highly controversial social issues have not been as divisive an influence among members of the upper class as either *personalismo* or regionalism. But as Latin America moves into the twentieth century, with its old semifeudal institutions frustrating the revolution of rising expectations, such issues may well be the main divisive factor in the upper class in the future. For some of its members have already come out staunchly in favor of reform, hoping thereby to direct the course of change while they are still in a position to do so.

Purposes Served by Such Revolutions. Since the many "revolutions" occurring in Latin America have resulted in very little fundamental change in most of the nations, one may wonder what useful purpose they have served, if any. The very persistence of revolt as an institution indicates that it must have some utilitarian value. It does. Revolt and the resort to violence are often the only possible means of expressing dissent and protest. For an election may be so rigged that it is a farce, and opposition groups may boycott the polls in disgust, hoping thereby to register their disapproval. This is usually a rather futile gesture, however, for the *caudillo* cites the vote in his favor to show his nation and the world that there is little opposition to his regime. And, in a statistically minded world, the election returns are what count most.

The courts of the nation, too, may be frail reeds for members of the opposition to rely on to assure that their constitutional rights will be respected. For the courts of Latin America, as elsewhere, tend to follow the election returns, only more so.

But instituting a revolution is one means of protesting that is bound to be heard and recognized for what it is. The state of siege decreed by the president in effect proclaims to his nation that there is serious opposition within the country. And press dispatches in Washington, Belgrade, and throughout the world carry the news, which is adverse publicity for the government.

Thus, any revolt in Latin America is a significant one, whatever its locale, objectives, or backing. Even one that is unsuccessful, whether crushed by overwhelming force or fizzling out, may accomplish the purpose for which it was intended. For the president ponders the open challenge to his power, dramatically presented for public consideration. And however strongly he is ensconced in power, if he is wise he will consider the demands of the opposition and make some concession toward satisfying them. Thus, revolt sometimes accomplishes a sort of shotgun bipartisanship. It is hardly the best kind, but it is better than none at all.

The Latin Americans themselves well understand that revolution is a valid and efficacious means of protest in their society.

The South American revolutions may be regarded as a necessary form of political activity. In Venezuela fifty-two important revolts have broken out within a century. The victorious party tries to destroy the other groups; revolution thus represents a political weapon to those parties which are deprived of the suffrage. It corresponds to the protest of European minorities, to the anarchical strikes of the proletariat, to the great public meetings of England, in which the opposing parties attack the government. It is [because of] the excessive simplicity of the political system, in which opinion has no other means of expression than the tyranny of oligarchies on the one hand and the rebellion of the vanquished on the other, that the interminable and sanguinary conflicts of Spanish America are due.[41]

In the closed society which is the pattern in most of Latin America, revolutions "at the top" can do more than just register protests and hope to gain concessions, such as having constitutional rights respected. Revolution or even the very prospect of it tends to keep a government on its toes. It is an ever-present opposition, "a social malaria, a fever that strikes almost without warning, subsides, then strikes again."[42]

But it is no loyal opposition, as in Britain. Indeed, its main purpose usually is to overthrow the government and notify the *caudillo* that his "term" of office, probably extended many times by presidential decree, is really up. If it were not for revolutions, most presidents would die in bed (i.. the presidential mansion, of course). Thus, "revolution is also a cure for governmental longevity and self-perpetuation," concludes Harris

---

[41] Calderón, *op. cit.*, pp. 371–72.
[42] Harris Gaylord Warren, *Paraguay: An Informal History* (Norman, Okla.: University of Oklahoma Press, 1949), p. 266.

Gaylord Warren, "since it is an axiom in Latin American politics that the government does not lose an election."[43]

Social Revolutions. The third type of violent revolt against established authority in Latin America is the social revolution. It is quite unlike the *golpe* or *cuartelazo*, whose objectives are to capture control of the government primarily for the privilege of filling government offices, exercising governmental authority, and looting the national treasury as well as the rest of the nation. While the social revolution, too, seeks to get control of the government, this is only a means to an end—a means of accomplishing a fundamental reorganization of the whole society and of setting up completely new rules for the game.

With such a fundamental objective, the social revolution is the only one of the several types of revolts by violence that really deserves to be called a revolution. Compared with it, the *golpe de estado* and *cuartelazo* in their ultimate effects are mere shadowboxing. To date, only two nations in Latin America—Mexico and Bolivia—have undergone the arduous but fruitful ordeal of remaking their society—". . . shatter it to bits—and then remold it nearer to the heart's desire." A third nation, Cuba, is in the process of undergoing such a basic revolution. While only these three so far have dared to take the plunge, many of the other nations of Latin America, burdened with their semifeudal social structure, power cliques, and elite values, teeter on the brink of chaos, either too timid to undergo the needed social surgery or preferring to risk all rather than make fundamental changes in their society.

Painful and costly though it is, the social revolution appears to be the only means of transforming many Latin American nations from nineteenth century, one-cylinder models to 1965 streamlined, chromeplated, 300-horsepower machines, the type of vehicles that upper class Latin Americans profess to want but are unwilling to make the sacrifices for.

While the social revolutions of both Mexico, beginning in 1910, and Bolivia, beginning in 1952, have resulted in many mistakes and found the going exceedingly rough at times, the radical programs undertaken by both nations have accomplished impressive results. Neither nation has achieved all that its visionary idealists hoped to, but the retooling and restyling have obviously taken hold. And although neither nation has accelerated to a 1965 tempo, each is far ahead of the "burro pace" that still characterizes much of Latin America.

Regarding their ideologies, Mexico and Bolivia have accepted as national values the democratic idealism which the United States and most nations of the Western world have long embraced. More specifically, both nations are striving to apply to their new societies the democratic principles professed since the first day of independence. Every individual, regardless of his race, class, educational attainment, or economic worth is recognized to be a full member of society, entitled to all its rights and

---

[43] *Ibid.*, p. 266.

privileges. There is no longer a first-class citizenship, enjoyed by only a very small elite. Quite to the contrary, the centuries-old barriers to individual achievement have been or are being eliminated; no individual is now fettered to a lowly status merely by being born a member of the large lower class. Indeed, in the evolving new egalitarian society, the only limits to achievement will be the individual's own ability and drive.

The application of these democratic, egalitarian principles has been a severe blow to the deeply entrenched groups that long enjoyed a privileged status in these nations. Thus, in Mexico the Roman Catholic Church was stripped of most of its vast wealth, and severely limited in its activities. (In Bolivia the Catholic Church was not nearly so strong, and hence has not been a major concern of the revolutionary regime.) The armed forces too, have felt the mighty impact of the social reform: in Mexico, their power has been greatly curbed, as was described in Chapter 7; in Bolivia, the old Army, which tried to suppress the revolution, was disbanded and a new one was established, much smaller in size and believed to be loyal to the regime. In both countries, the small, aristocratic, and wealthy elite has also been adversely affected, losing its privileged status and much of its wealth, too.

Although these formerly privileged groups have suffered, the mass of citizens of both Mexico and Bolivia have greatly benefited by the many changes instituted in their behalf. In the political realm, the suffrage requirements have been so broadened as to enable almost every adult to vote in elections and thereby express his opinion as to how he should be governed. The extension of the suffrage has greatly increased the size of the electorate. In Bolivia's 1951 presidential election, held the year before the revolution, only 126,125 persons voted out of a population of approximately 3 million. However, in the 1956 election, the first one held under the new revolutionary government, a total of 955,412 ballots were cast in electing the president and members of Congress. (These elections are treated in more detail in the next chapter.)

In the economic realm too, the social revolutions of Mexico and Bolivia have resulted in many changes designed to give the former underdogs a chance. In both nations an extensive program of land reform has been undertaken—a program basically designed to break up the large landed estates whose land was unused or underutilized and to give at least a few acres to the rural farm worker who lives on the land, makes his living from it, and craves a few acres of his own. The extensive programs of land redistribution have made both Mexico and Bolivia primarily societies of many small farmers who work their own private acreages.

In fact the common man in both nations eats better, dresses better, and in general lives better than he ever did before. He may even be able to get an education now—something that was denied to members of his class under the old regime. Now he is a respected citizen of society just like anyone else. He can select any seat on the bus that he desires, buy a home in any neighborhood if he has the money, and be sure that in his socially mobile society neither his race nor color nor religion will prevent him from getting ahead.

In short, he does not worry about the passage or enforcement of controversial civil rights legislation in order to be able to enjoy his constitutional rights. For *his* social revolution is behind him.

SUGGESTED READINGS

BLANKSTEN, GEORGE I. *Ecuador: Constitutions and Caudillos,* chaps. iii and ix. Berkeley: University of California Press, 1951.

————. *Perón's Argentina.* Chicago: University of Chicago Press, 1953.

————. "Revolutions," *Government and Politics in Latin America* (ed. HAROLD EUGENE DAVIS), chap. 5. New York: Ronald Press Co., 1958.

CALDERÓN, F. GARCÍA. "The Political Problem," *Latin America: Its Rise and Progress,* pp. 365–77. Trans. BERNARD MIALL. London: T. Fisher Unwin, 1913.

CHAPMAN, CHARLES EDWARD. "The Age of the Caudillos," *Republican Hispanic America: A History,* chap. vii. New York: The Macmillan Company, 1937.

DRAPER, THEODORE. *Castro's Revolution: Myths and Realities.* New York: Frederick A. Praeger, Inc., 1963.

DUBOIS, JULES. *Fidel Castro: Rebel—Liberator or Dictator?* Indianapolis, Ind.: Bobbs-Merrill Co., Inc., 1959.

FLUHARTY, VERNON LEE. *Dance of the Millions: Military Rule and the Social Revolution in Colombia, 1930–1956.* Pittsburgh, Pa.: University of Pittsburgh Press, 1957.

GRUENING, ERNEST. *Mexico and Its Heritage,* pp. 91–108. New York: D. Appleton-Century Co., Inc., 1934.

GUTIERREZ, ALBERTO OSTRIA. *The Tragedy of Bolivia: A People Crucified.* New York: Devin-Adair Co., 1958.

HAIGN, ROGER M. "The Creation and Control of a Caudillo," *Hispanic American Historical Review,* Vol. XLIV, No. 4 (November, 1964), pp. 481–90.

HICKS, ALBERT C. *Blood in the Streets: The Life and Rule of Trujillo.* New York: Creative Age Press, Inc., 1946.

KOEBEL, W. H. *Paraguay,* chaps. x and xi. London: T. Fisher Unwin, Ltd., 1917.

LAVIN, JOHN. *A Halo for Gómez.* New York: Pageant Press, 1954.

LIEUWEN, EDWIN. *Venezuela,* chaps. 2 and 3. Royal Institute of International Affairs. New York: Oxford University Press, 1961.

LOWENSTEIN, KARL. *Brazil Under Vargas.* New York: The Macmillan Company, 1942.

MACGAFFEY, WYATT, AND BARNETT, CLIFFORD R. *Cuba.* chap. 13. Survey of World Cultures. New Haven, Conn.: HRAF Press, 1962.

NANITA, ABELARDO R. *Trujillo.* 5th ed. rev. Cuidad Trujillo, D.R.: Editora de Caribe, 1954.

PENDLE, GEORGE. *A History of Latin America*, chap. 10. Baltimore: Penguin Books, 1963.

Perón Expounds His Doctrine. Trans. ARGENTINE ASSOCIATION OF ENGLISH CULTURE. Buenos Aires, 1948.

PIERSON, WILLIAM W., AND GIL, FEDERICO G. "Dictators and Revolutions," *Governments of Latin America*, chap. 6. New York: McGraw-Hill Book Co., Inc., 1957.

PIERSON, W. W. (ed.). "Pathology of Democracy in Latin America: A Symposium," (WHITAKER, ARTHUR P. "A Historian's Point of View"; FITZGIBBON, RUSSELL. "A Political Scientist's Point of View"; MOSK, SANFORD A. "An Economist's Point of View"; and CRAWFORD, W. REX. "Discussion: A Sociologist's Point of View"), *American Political Science Review*, Vol. 44, No. 1 (March, 1950), pp. 100–49.

RENGGER AND LONGCHAMPS. *The Reign of Doctor Joseph Roderick de Francia, in Paraguay; An Account of a Six Years' Residence in that Republic, from July, 1819 to May, 1825.* Trans. J. R. RENGGER. London: Thomas Hurst, Edward Chance & Co., 1827.

RIPPY, J. FRED. "Dictatorships in Latin America," *Dictatorship in the Modern World* (ed. GUY STANTON FORD), pp. 178–214. 2d ed. London: University of Oxford Press, 1939.

———. *Historical Evolution of Hispanic America*, chap. x. 3rd ed. New York: Appleton-Century-Crofts, Inc., 1945.

ROURKE, THOMAS (pseud.), CLINTON, DANIEL JOSEPH. *Gómez: Tyrant of the Andes.* New York: William Morrow & Co., 1936.

STOKES, WILLIAM S. "Violence," *Latin American Politics*, chap. 13. New York: Thomas Y. Crowell Co., 1959.

STREET, JOHN. *Artigas and the Emancipation of Uruguay.* London: Cambridge University Press, 1959.

SZULC, TAD. *Twilight of the Tyrants.* New York: Henry Holt & Co., 1959.
———. *The Winds of Revolution: Latin America Today and Tomorrow.* New York: Frederick A. Praeger, Inc., 1963.

TANNENBAUM, FRANK. *Mexico: The Struggle for Peace and Bread*, chap. 4. New York: Alfred A. Knopf, Inc., 1954.

VANDERCOOK, JOHN WOMACK. *Black Majesty: The Life of Christophe: King of Haiti.* New York: Harper & Bros., 1928.

WARREN, HARRIS GAYLORD. *Paraguay: An Informal History*, chaps. xi, xii, xiii. Norman, Okla.: University of Oklahoma Press, 1949.

WHITAKER, ARTHUR P. *Argentine Upheaval: Perón's Fall and the New Regime*, pp. 1–54. New York: Frederick A. Praeger, Inc., 1956.

WILGUS, A. CURTIS (ed.). *South American Dictators During the First Century of Independence.* Washington, D.C.: George Washington University Press, 1937.

WISE, GEORGE S. *Caudillo: A Portrait of Antonio Guzmán Blanco.* New York: Columbia University Press, 1951.

CHAPTER 12

POLITICAL PARTIES AND ELECTIONS:
Ballots, Preferably Honest

IN NATIONS which have achieved political democracy, political parties play an important role in the formulation and expression of public opinion and the election of candidates to public office. Parties play such an important role, in fact, that the vitality of democracy may be gauged by the freedom and effectiveness of party activities.

In the 20 republics of Latin America, where there is a great variation in per capita income and national wealth, literacy, and degree of political sophistication and stability, the operation of political parties has been very uneven, generally successful in some of the nations but undeniably ineffectual in others.

GENERAL ATTRIBUTES OF PARTIES

Personalism

The primary basis for most political parties in the nations has been personalism, the intense, unswerving allegiance to a dynamic leader. So strong has been the influence of leaders that most parties are identified by their names rather than by the official names of the parties. In Mexico, although the Institutional Revolutionary Party has long been dominant, even factions within it take their names from certain of the leaders. The *alemanistas* were followers of former President Miguel Alemán; the *callistas, cardenistas,* and *ruizcortinistas* are the names of other factions that supported particular presidents. In Uruguay, the two major parties, or at least leading wings of them, have been known as *batllistas* and *herreristas* as commonly as by the official names, Colorados and Blancos.

Whether known by its leader's name or not, a party often exists for one reason alone, to promote his political career. In Venezuela one of the minor parties in the 1950s was *Movimiento Electoral Nacional Indepen-*

diente, known as MENI. This small party of apparently only about 15,000 members was the personal vehicle of Vice-Admiral Wolfgang Larrazabal to support his candidacy for the presidency. Soon after he was defeated in the 1958 election, the party disbanded.

Although long a main influence on political parties, personalism is unmistakably on the wane.

A reasonable hypothesis is that the more national a country the less personalistic will be the parties, the more they will adjust conflicting interests within their own mechanisms, the greater will be their concern for institutional self-preservation and the winning of elections as a good in itself. As is to be expected, then, Argentina, Chile, Uruguay, and Costa Rica all have long histories of impersonal party politics. . . .[1]

Charismatic Appeal of the *Caudillo*

The dynamic leader is often an undisguised *caudillo* who unabashedly exalts himself to the role of sole savior of the nation, appealing to Sigmund Neumann's "emotional, rootless, and amorphous masses seeking mystery, devotion, and the miraculous." Whether in the bemedaled and beribboned uniform of a *generalissimo* or in the unpretentious dress of a civilian, a spellbinding leader is easily able to exert his mesmerism over his receptive, dedicated followers.

Sometimes his spellbinding seed falls upon thorny ground yet manages to produce fruit, as an Ecuadorian opponent of José María Velasco Ibarra once lamented:

I was violently opposed to his policies and uniformly voted aganst them. One day, however, President Velasco Ibarra came to congress to deliver personally a message urging passage of one of his projects. . . . Never before had I heard such a speech! When it was finished, the president and congress were unashamedly in tears, and we stood up and voted unanimously for his bill. . . . On my way home, I scolded myself many times, for I had been a fool, such a fool, to vote for his insane measure![2]

Party and Membership Instability

The political parties are also notorious for their transient, precarious existence and high rate of mortality, sometimes with reincarnation under a slightly different format or name. The main exception to this instability is the Communist Party, whether operating under its own name or under some other label and whether in the open or underground. Following an ideological line, this party offers a program from which it rarely deviates in principle, showing cohesion and discipline which are rare for parties in Latin America.

---

[1] K. H. Silvert, "Political Change in Latin America," *The United States and Latin America* (ed. Herbert L. Matthews) (American Assembly) (2d ed.; New York: Columbia University Press, 1963), p. 78.

[2] In George I. Blanksten, *Ecuador: Constitutions and Caudillos* (Berkeley: University of California Press, 1951), p. 50.

Although obviously more stable than others, the Communists and other ideology-based parties operate under disadvantages which are inherent in the region. However capable and respected leaders they may develop, the socioeconomic structure of most of the nations is so lacking in integration, cohesion, and maturity that the parties find it almost impossible to enforce effective internal discipline, as even the Communist parties have shown by their many schisms and dissensions.[3]

Very few of the parties, however, have such a strong ideology, or even what may be regarded as a firm party platform. The lack of an ideological basis and the relative ease of obtaining recognition as a party are mainly responsible for the existence of the large, complicating number of parties. Mexico is an exception to this rule, however. Different from those in most countries, the requirements in Mexico for recognition as a party are stringent. To qualify as a national party, a political group must have at least 75,000 qualified voters; of these, a minimum of 2,500 must reside in each of two-thirds of the nation's 29 states, 2 territories, and the Federal District. The group is required also to present a comprehensive party program for the solution of national problems. In most of the other nations, forming a political party and obtaining recognition as such are quite simple. In Uruguay, for example, a legal minimum of only 50 citizens is all that is necessary in order to register a group as a certified political party.

Apparently it has been even easier to form political parties in Bolivia, Ecuador, and Peru. According to Luis Terán Gómez:

In these times, nothing is simpler than to found a political party. To form a political party, only three people and one object are necessary: a president, a vice-president, a secretary, and a rubber stamp. The party can get along even without the vice-president and the secretary. . . . There have been cases in which the existence of only the rubber stamp has been sufficient.[4]

Identification of Government with a Political Party

In the United States, whichever party wins the national election immediately undertakes to "bind up the national wounds" and disassociate itself from a partisan victory. It commits itself to represent faithfully the interests of all citizens, not just those of its own members.

In Latin America, however, a newly elected regime has no qualms about showing undisguised favoritism to its party, responsible for its victory. It appoints to high office or favors with lush government contracts only party stalwarts, usually meaning close friends. In the political jargon of the region, the practice is known as *amiguismo*, meaning "government by cronies."

---

[3] Russell H. Fitzgibbon, "The Party Potpourri in Latin America," *Western Political Quarterly*, Vol. X, No. 1 (March, 1957), p. 13.

[4] In George I. Blanksten, "The Politics of Latin America," *The Politics of the Developing Areas* (eds. Gabriel A. Almond and James S. Coleman) (Princeton, N.J.: Princeton University Press, 1960), p. 483.

Blatant favoritism is also shown in the lower echelons of government. While most governments permit their civil servants to affiliate with political organizations, it is understood that this permission applies only to joining a political group which supports the administration. Joining any other group is practically asking for dismissal. In fact, government employees are expected to be not only public servants but also party faithfuls who can always be depended upon to promote the interests of the party along with carrying out their governmental duties.

Staffing the government with political supporters who change with each new administration has been a great deterrent to the development of a qualified, professional, nonpartisan civil service.

Intolerance of the Opposition

Victorious parties have usually shown a fierce intolerance of their political opponents. Often mere allegiance to the regime is not enough; it must be publicly displayed for all others to see. During the long dictatorial rule of Juan Manuel Rosas in Argentina, 1829–52, everyone in Buenos Aires was required to wear as a sign of his loyalty a red ribbon inscribed, "Death to the Savage Unitarians," Rosas' political opponents. "Even the ladies of the aristocracy did not dare to be seen in the street without their red ribbon or sash. Doña Encarnación, Rosas' wife and ardent assistant, wore evening dresses of scarlet satin."[5]

More than a century later, colors sometimes still had to be openly worn as an outward manisfestation of political loyalty. In Colombia after the outbreak of civil war in 1948, coloration was not so much protective as to indicate the wearer's political allegiance. Red was the distinctive color of the liberal party, and blue, of the conservative. In the conservative communities the women wore blue skirts; in the liberal, they wore red. Even the containers for beer were red or blue, depending on the community. Wearing the wrong color was interpreted as an insult to the rest of the community; its wearer was very apt to be vilified and beaten up.[6]

THE TRADITIONAL PARTIES

From the time of independence, there were traditionally two main political parties, the conservatives and the liberals. The conservatives, having something to conserve, championed the vested interests of the landowners and the Church. The liberals, representing mainly the new professional, business, and commercial groups, were professedly interested in liberating the society from its semifeudal stodginess by providing free

---

[5] George Pendle, *Argentina* (Royal Institute of International Affairs) (3rd ed.; New York: Oxford University Press, 1963), p. 38.

[6] Orlando Fals-Borda, *Peasant Society in the Colombian Andes: A Sociological Study of Saucío* (Gainesville, Fla.: University of Florida Press, 1962), p. 210.

secular schools, broadening the suffrage, and encouraging foreign trade and immigration. However, these differences were often more theoretical than real.

As a rule, during the nineteenth century both the liberals and conservatives belonged to the upper class, which had a virtual monopoly on government office and political influence. Ordinarily the scrapping between the two "parties" did not involve the whole community and reflected only superficial differences between them. There were two highly controversial issues, however, upon which they differed sharply: the role which the Catholic Church should be allowed in the new nations, and centralized versus decentralized exercise of governmental authority.

The role of the Church was an explosive issue which split many a nation into two warring camps. In the United Provinces of Central America, when the liberals under the leadership of Francisco Morazán were victorious in 1829 and occupied Guatemala City, they celebrated their triumph by a plethora of anticlerical laws which outlawed the religious orders and ended state support of the Church. But when the conservatives regained control of the government in 1838, led by the illiterate fanatic, Rafael Carrera, it was with the vengeful battle cry and program of "Long Live Religion and Death to the Foreigners."[7] Morazán's forces were destroyed and their leader exiled. Elsewhere, too, virulence and violence invariably marked the contests to determine the status and role of the Church.

Another bitter issue between the liberals and conservatives was whether the nation should adopt political centralism or federalism. The centralists, advocating a tightly knit unitary government, wanted all power to be vested in the national government; the federalists, on the other hand, insisted upon a large measure of autonomy for the states, provinces, departments, or other component political units. The centralist-federalist debate resulted in many bloody struggles, especially in Argentina, Brazil, Colombia, Mexico, and Venezuela.

Local autonomy was often championed so strongly that it was almost impossible to govern the nation as a whole. This played into the hands of local *caudillos*, who had to be either suppressed or paid off again and again. The doctrine of "states' rights" in Latin America was a fetish which greatly impeded the political and economic development of the region.[8]

Especially stultifying to the region was the dangerous, almost ludicrous, oversimplification of issues in the conservative-liberal division. As René León Echaíz of Chile perceptively observed, there were "two parties which contested for political supremacy during the early years of Latin

---

[7] Hubert Herring, *A History of Latin America from the Beginnings to the Present* (2d ed. rev.; New York: Alfred A. Knopf, Inc., 1961), pp. 450–51.

[8] J. Fred Rippy, *Latin America: A Modern History* (Ann Arbor: University of Michigan Press, 1958), pp. 180–82.

America's independence. The banner of one party carried a slogan, 'Liberty Even If It Results in Anarchy'; the banner of the other read, 'Order Even It It Means Despotism.' In the case of both groups, the slogans were sometimes inscribed in bloody letters."[9]

Even today nations sometimes show the lingering effects of the earlier liberal-conservative controversy. Ask most knowledgeable persons what is the capital of Bolivia, and the great majority of them will answer, La Paz. While they are technically wrong, they are in reality right, since most of the government operates in La Paz, and operation, like possession, is nine-tenths of the law. Nevertheless the legal capital is still the inaccessible Sucre, where the Supreme Court, faithful to the constitution, continues to hold its sessions. The existence of two capitals is the result of a liberal-conservative controversy; one of the main liberal demands was for the seat of government to be transferred from remote Sucre to the more populous and central La Paz. After liberal José Manuel Pando became president in 1899, La Paz became the *de facto* capital.

THE ONE, TWO, AND MULTIPARTY SYSTEMS

One-Party Systems

Regarding their political parties, the nations of Latin America may be classified on the basis of having a one-party, two-party, or multiparty system.[10]

As a rule, the effective existence of only one political party has been almost prima facie evidence that the government was dictatorial and suppressed all opposition, probably by very ruthless means. For many a dictator in the past has asserted his unquestioned control over the nation by allowing only one party, the official one, to exist.

The Dominican Republic during the long tyrannical rule of Rafael Leonidas Trujillo exemplifies one type of one-party government at its worst. With an amazing display of *caudillo* temerity, Trujillo aspired to erase any effective opposition to his regime not only at home but also in the United States, its main ally. The drugging and kidnapping of Dr. Jesús Galíndez, a member of the staff of Columbia University and an unsparing critic of Trujillo, was a flagrantly presumptuous extension of dictatorial one-party rule. Trujillo stretched his tyrannical power even further by disposing of the incriminating evidence—Gerald Murphy, the

---

[9] René León Echaíz, *Evolución histórica de los partidos políticos chilenos* (Santiago, Chile, 1939), pp. 26–27.

[10] In the opinion of some scholars this categorization is too general and does not provide an adequate basis for classifying political parties. (J. Austin Ranney and Willmore Kendall, "The American Party Systems," *American Political Science Review*, Vol. XLVIII, 1954, pp. 480–81.) However, if the basic differences within a category are properly noted, this classification can afford a realistic and manageable consideration of parties.

American pilot who apparently flew the private plane containing drugged Galíndez to the Dominican Republic.[11]

Recalling the brutally oppressive nature of Trujillo's regime—there have been others like it too—one may jump to the conclusion that the one-party system per se connotes dictatorial rule. This is not true, however, as the experience of both Mexico and Bolivia well shows. In those new revolutionary societies, the new order has been so widely popular that one party has all but cornered popular support.

In Mexico the Partido Revolucionario Institucional, freely translated as the "Party of Revolutionary Institutions" and better known as PRI, is unquestionably the dominant party in the nation. Its revolutionary program, which virtually remade the formerly semifeudal nation, was designed to better the condition of the great mass of citizens, especially by land reform and benefits to the urban workers. As a result, on election day the citizens turn out en masse to give their support to the party which has helped them.[12]

Being able to count on this widespread popular appeal and determined to carry out the revolutionary goals, PRI's governmental practices often reflect its assured position. The new president has usually been selected months, maybe years, before by the incumbent president and given a position of such responsibility as to indicate clearly that he will inherit the mantle. Mexican practice appears to be at first glance *imposición*, or an arbitrary determining of the presidential successor. But it must be remembered that Mexico has no vice-president whom the party has previously endorsed, as in the United States, and who would be the logical successor, receiving the outgoing president's support. Mexico apparently has not suffered from not having a vice-presidency, an office which in most of the Latin American nations has not furthered constitutionalism but has complicated it by jealousy and intrigue.

Long recognized as the groomed successor, the designee accepts the nomination in a national convention as matter-of-factly as would a vice-

---

[11] For an extensive account of the drugging and abduction of Dr. Galíndez, and the role that Murphy unwittingly played in it, see *Life*, February 25, 1957, pp. 24–30. For later revealing his role, Murphy, knowing too much, was apparently thrown over the cliff to the sharks.

[12] For an organizational breakdown of the party into its labor, agrarian, and popular sectors see Frank R. Brandenburg, "Political Parties and Elections," *Government and Politics in Latin America* (ed. Harold E. Davis) (New York: Ronald Press, Co., 1958), pp. 208–9.

Why does PRI win every election, often by overwhelming majorities, as receiving 89 percent of the total votes cast in the 1964 presidential election? There are many reasons for this, including: the saturation campaign of propaganda conducted by the party for a full year before an election, the identification of the party on the part of many voters with the revolution of 1910 and the social goals which it established, the great patronage of the administration, and the party's policies which are skillfully designed to appeal to an extremely wide range of voters, from conservative businessmen to urban workers and landless peasants. (Martin C. Needler, "Changing the Guard in Mexico," *Current History*, Vol. 48, No. 281 [January, 1965], p. 27.)

president in the United States who has been long groomed for the office. PRI's candidate is selected by acclamation, a practice not exactly alien to either our Democratic or Republican conventions.

Although PRI operates with the confidence of a champion (as when the Mexican Tourist Bureau gave the *New York Herald Tribune* a photograph of Díaz Ordaz captioned "Mexico's president-elect" a week before the election), it is by no means the only political party in the nation. In 1963 there were four other registered parties: Partido Acción Nacional (PAN); Partido Popular Socialista (PPS); Partido Nacionalista de México (PNM); and Partido Auténtico de la Revolución Mexicana (PARM). Any other groups may obtain recognition as parties by fulfilling the requirements laid down by law.

The other registered parties, which operate freely, have paradoxically not been the main threat to PRI in presidential elections. Rather, the main opposition in the past has been an *ad hoc* party headed by a prominent member of the regime who was disappointed at not receiving the nomination. After the election, the leader of this opposition was expected to disband his organization and pledge his allegiance to the new president. Party and national unity, we would call it in the United States.[13] In the 1964 election, however, when the several splinter parties received a negligible number of votes, PAN emerged as the main opposition party, receiving just over 10 percent of the total number of votes cast.

PRI's choice for president, selected six months or so before the scheduled date of the election, is as sure of winning as is the Democratic gubernatorial candidate in Mississippi. Nevertheless he conducts a vigorous campaign in all parts of the nation. Why bother to do so? one is prone to ask. To PRI's presidential designate, campaigning as he does provides an opportunity to visit all parts of the nation and learn firsthand the grassroots sentiments and gripes. Visiting these areas serves another purpose too. Many an obscure citizen who has probably never even heard of the candidate before thereby has the opportunity of seeing or meeting the new *jefe*.

After his inauguration, the president must cater to the power groups within PRI and also to the major interests of the country, which are organized into large and influential pressure groups. To keep them loyal to the official party, he must be responsive to their demands.[14]

---

[13] The *Realpolitik* of conflicting political philosophies is confined to PRI itself, where left, middle, and right battle it out for supremacy. Recent years have seen the rise of the right, according to David L. Graham. "The real struggle between the right and the left in the nation goes on silently but firmly inside PRI, not at the polls." (David L. Graham, "The Rise of the Mexican Right," *Yale Review*, Vol. LII, No. 1 [Autumn, 1962], pp. 104 and 110.)

[14] Karl M. Schmitt and David D. Burks, *Evolution or Chaos: Dynamics of Latin American Government and Politics* (New York: Frederick A. Praeger, Inc., 1963), p. 221. One of the most interesting of these pressure groups is the Instituto de Investigaciones Sociales y Económicas (Institute of Social and Economic Research), a non-

In seeking to please them all, the president may thereby have relinquished much or even most of his presidential authority. As Raymond Vernon concludes:

The presidents of Mexico have gradually been eased—or have eased themselves —into a political straitjacket. Eschewing techniques of repression or terror, they have striven to retain the appearance of unanimity. Fearful of the risk of losing touch with any significant element of opposition, they have tried against mounting odds to enlist the loyalty of every source of power in the country. Whereas the leaders of many other nations might feel easy even if a quarter of the national elite were disaffected with their policies and were out of communication with the government, the president of Mexico would be acutely uncomfortable in such a situation.

In a real sense, therefore, the strength of the Mexican president is a mirage. . . . In his ceaseless efforts to achieve unanimity, in his concern to extend the reach of the PRI the full distance to both the right and the left, he is held to a course of action which is zigzagging and vacillating when it is not blandly neutral.[15]

In Bolivia as in Mexico, one political party is unquestionably dominant. The Movimiento Nacional Revolucionario, the Nationalist Revolutionary Movement usually known as the MNR, which led the successful social revolution of April, 1952, has been in control of the government ever since.

Like PRI in Mexico, the MNR is a very heterogeneous political conglomeration. Its membership represents all shades of the political spectrum, ranging from the far left to the far right. These widely differing political groups would hardly have become political bedfellows had it not been necessary for them to join together to overthrow the old regime and institute the nation's social revolution. The program of land reform shows how widely divergent were their social philosophies. The leftists would have divided all the land where Indians were predominant into *minifundios*, thereby converting the nation's entire system of agriculture into subsistence farming, leaving little or no marketable surplus to feed the cities. The rightists, on the other hand, advocated the preservation of productive and efficient agricultural units, however large they might be. The land reform program which was adopted was a compromise between these conflicting views.[16]

---

profit organization which aims at the long range molding of public opinion rather than influencing the passage or defeat of any particular governmental measure. (Merle Kling, *A Mexican Interest Group in Action* [Englewood Cliffs, N.J.: Prentice-Hall, Inc., 1961], pp. 1 and 4.)

[15] Raymond Vernon, *The Dilemma of Mexico's Development: The Role of the Private and Public Sectors* (Cambridge, Mass.: Harvard University Press, 1963), pp. 188–89.

[16] Richard W. Patch, "Bolivia: U.S. Assistance in a Revolutionary Setting," *Social Change in Latin America Today* (Council on Foreign Relations) (New York: Harper & Bros., 1960), pp. 123–26. For vivid profiles of the leaders and their widely divergent social philosophies, see Richard W. Patch, "Personalities and Politics in Bolivia," *American Universities Field Staff Reports Service,* West Coast South American Series, Vol. IX, No. 5, Bolivia (May, 1962).

The political spectrum in Bolivia appears to be too broad for the MNR to encompass, especially in view of the nation's serious economic difficulties and the obvious impossibility of satisfying the demands of all groups. But what threatens completely to shatter the party is the bitter issue of party leadership and presidential succession. When Walter Guevara Arze, one of the rightist leaders of the party, had his presidential aspirations thwarted in both 1956 and 1960, he broke with the party in the latter year and formed the Authentic Revolutionary Party, known as PRA. But the really shattering blow to MNR was the decision of Víctor Paz, president from 1952 to 1956 and 1960 to 1964, to seek reelection in 1964 and even to change the constitution to enable him to do this. This decision alienated Juan Lechín, leftist leader of the miners and other workers and vice-president from 1960 to 1964. In fact, Lechín was expelled from the party after apparently trumped up charges of smuggling cocaine were levied against him by the government. Perhaps the most serious blow to party unity was the expulsion from the party of former President Hernán Siles Zuazo (1956–60), highly respected moderate leader of the nation and party. The ouster of newly elected President Paz in the November, 1964, revolt has further compounded the confusion of the MNR and could be the body blow to its continued existence.[17]

According to some opinion, if the MNR had not in the past resorted to manipulating elections, it would possibly have lost power or even have disintegrated.[18] This conclusion is hardly borne out, however, by the returns of every election since 1956 when the first one was held, the broad range of appeal to the nation's huge underprivileged mass, or even the reactions of some who are admittedly not sympathetic to the regime.

Given the privilege to vote, even though illiterate, the *campesinos* or small farmers have flocked to the voting places in droves and overwhelmingly expressed their preference for the MNR in every election, as Table 12–1 shows.

With its goal of enabling everyone who works the land to own his own acreage if he so desires, the party has won the unqualified loyalty of the *campesinos*, who constitute the great majority of citizens. But with the serious defections from its membership and the divisive expulsions from the party, the MNR as of early 1965 is in a very precarious condition.

"Does the MNR really represent the great mass of voters in the country, as election returns indicate?" the author asked a prominent citizen who was very critical of the regime.

He took a deep drag on his cigarette and gazed reflectively out the window. "I think it does," he replied. "Most of those who were basically

---

[17] Richard W. Patch, "The Last of Bolivia's MNR?" *American Universities Field Staff Reports Service*, West Coast South American Series, Vol. IX, No. 5, Bolivia (April, 1964), pp. 717–41.

[18] Schmitt and Burks, *op. cit.*, p. 177.

TABLE 12-1

ELECTION RESULTS IN BOLIVIA: 1956–62

Year of Election	Kind of Election	Total No. Ballots Cast	MNR	MNRA	FSB	PCB	POR	PSC
1956	Pres. & Congr.	955,412	786,792	—	130,494	12,273	2,329	—
1958	Congr. Only	478,366	391,437	—	56,950	6,913	1,994	2,937
1960	Pres. & Congr.	987,730	735,619	139,713	78,963	10,934	1,420	—
1962	Congr. Only	1,066,480	886,572	44,296	74,148	20,352	—	19,825

MNR — Movimiento Nacionalista Revolucionario
MNRA — Movimiento Nacionalista Revolucionario Auténtico
FSB — Falange Socialista Boliviana
PCB — Partido Comunista de Bolivia
POR — Partido Obrero Revolucionario
PSC — Partido Social Cristiano

SOURCE: *Political Handbook of the World*, 1957, p. 14; 1959, p. 15; 1961, p. 15; and *Political Handbook and Atlas of the World*, 1963, p. 17.

opposed to the Revolution left the country a decade ago, and are hardly interested in what is happening now. The program doesn't help me, or most of us in the middle class—in fact we are being taxed more heavily to pay for it. But," he added, "if I were a *campesino* or a miner, I'd vote for the MNR, wouldn't you?"[19]

Two-Party Systems

Under the two-party system as it operates in the United States, two major parties rather evenly matched in strength compete with each other for control of the government and alternate in running it. Various minor parties may have candidates too, but they are not really serious competitors at the polls. The two-party system or something even closely resembling it is found in only two or three of the nations. Tables 12–2 and 12–3 which give the percentages of votes received, and of legislative seats won, by the three main political parties in recent elections, afford a good insight into the possibility of two-party government in each of the countries.

Uruguay has traditionally had only two main parties, the Colorados and Blancos. They were obviously not very evenly matched, however. Up to 1958 the Colorados, or liberals, had governed the country for the preceding 90 years, although the Blancos, or conservatives, representing

[19] This frank expression of opinion given the author in the summer of 1963 was representative of many which came from persons unsympathetic with or even hostile to the MNR. It is not difficult to find such persons in La Paz, where the MNR's strength is weakest, as a breakdown of election results shows.

TABLE 12-2
LEADING PARTIES AND THEIR STRENGTH IN RECENT ELECTIONS

Country	Voting Participation General Election			Leading Party	Date	Percent of Votes Cast	Percent of Seats in Lower House
	Date	Number of Votes Cast	Percent of Population Voting				
United States	1960	68,412,709	37.9	Democratic Party	1960	54.7	60.09
Canada	1962	7,768,162	42.6	Progressive Conservative	1958	53.7	78.5
Mexico	1958	7,483,403	23.0	Revolutionary Institutional Party (PRI)	1958	90.4	96.6
Costa Rica	1962	350,101	28.6	National Liberal Party (P.L.N.)	1962	50.29	50.88
El Salvador	1962	400,118	16.0	National Conciliation Party (P.C.N.)	1962	100.0	100.0
Guatemala	1958	492,274	13.9	National Demo. Reconciliation Party	1959	.	48.5
Honduras	1957	339,872	19.2	Liberal Party	1957	61.3	62.0
Nicaragua	1957	489,108	36.7	National Liberal Party (P.L.N.)	1957	.	66.67
Panama	1960	241,957	23.0	National Opposition Union (U.N.O.)	1960	41.39	52.83
Cuba	1958	.	.	Integrated Revolutionary Orgs. (P.R.L.)	1958	.	.
Dominican Republic	1957	1,265,681	46.8	Partido Revolucionario Dominicano (PRD)	1962	.	66.2
Haiti	1957	956,856	28.3	National Unity Party	1961	.	100.0
Argentina	1958	9,063,498	44.8	Intransigent Radical Civic Union (UCRI)	1960	24.4	39.6
Bolivia	1960	970,635	28.0	National Revolutionary Movement	1960	74.5	75.0
Brazil	1960	12,586,354	19.1	Social Democratic Party (P.S.D.)	1958	32.3	35.0
Chile	1958	1,245,526	17.1	Radical Party	1961	22.0	27.6
Colombia	1962	2,244,302	15.5	National Front	1962	59.22	62.77
Ecuador	1960	620,469	14.4	National Velasquista Movement	1960	.	48.3
Paraguay	1958	303,476	18.0	National Republican Party (P.N.R.)	1960	94.0	100.0
Peru	1963	1,814,568	12.3	Acción Popular-Democracia Cristiano (AP-PDC)	1963	.	.
Uruguay	1958	1,005,362	36.4	National Party (Blanco)	1958	49.7	52.0
Venezuela	1958	2,722,053	43.1	Democratic Action (A.D.)	1958	49.4	48.3

SOURCES: CIF *Study No. 1*, p. 230; Center of Latin American Studies, University of California; *Statistical Abstract of Latin America 1962*, p. 36; and *Hispanic American Report*, Vol. XVI, No. 6 (August, 1963), p. 597. Reproduced by permission.

TABLE 12-3

SECOND AND THIRD PARTIES AND THEIR STRENGTH IN RECENT ELECTIONS

Country	Second Party	Percent of Votes Cast	Percent of Seats in Lower House	Third Party	Percent of Votes Cast	Percent of Seats in Lower House
United States	Republican Party	44.8	39.91			
Canada	Liberal Party	33.5	18.5	Co-op. Commonwealth Federation	9.7	3.0
Mexico	National Action Party (P.A.N.)	9.4	2.8	Authentic Party of Mex. Rev. (PARM)		0.9
Costa Rica	National Republican Party	35.34	31.58	National Union Party	13.49	15.79
El Salvador	Renovating Action Party (P.A.R.)	0.0	0.0	Social Democratic Party (P.S.D.)	0.0	0.0
Guatemala	National Democratic Movement		20.0	Democratic Union Party		
Honduras	National Party (P.N.H.)	30.0	31.0	Reformist Party (M.N.R.)	8.7	0.7
Nicaragua	Nicaraguan Conservative Party		33.3			
Panama	National Patriotic Coalition	35.62	33.96	Popular Alliance (A.P.)	22.98	13.20
Cuba	none			none		
Dominican R.	Unión Cívica Nacional (U.C.N.)		27.0	P. Nacionalista Revolucionario Demo.		5.4
Haiti	none			none		
Argentina	People's Radical Civic Union (UCRP)	24.4	39.6	Socialist Party		
Bolivia	Authentic Revolutionary Party (P.R.A.)	14.3	20.6	Bolivian Socialist Falange (F.S.B.)	8.0	4.4
Brazil	National Demo. Union (U.D.N.)	19.9	23.4	Brazilian Labor Party (P.T.B.)	19.8	20.8
Chile	Liberal Party	16.5	18.0	Christian Democratic Party		14.6
Colombia	Liberal Revolutionary Movement	18.89	15.96	Conservative Party		18.44
Ecuador	Conservative Party		27.5	Liberal Party		16.6
Paraguay	Liberal Party	0.0	0.0	Febrerista Party	0.0	0.0
Peru	APRA or Peoples Party			Union Nacional Odriista		
Uruguay	Colorado Party	37.7	38.0	Civic Union Party	3.7	3.1
Venezuela	Republican Democratic Union (U.R.D.)	26.8	24.5	Social Christian Party (COPEI)	15.0	13.6

SOURCES: CIF *Study No. 1*, p. 231, and *Hispanic American Report*, Vol. XVI, No. 6 (August, 1963), p. 597. Reproduced by permission.

mainly the large landholders, strongly contested every election. In view of this very one-sided score, Uruguay was hardly regarded by most thoughtful observers as possessing a two-party system. However, in the elections of both 1958 and 1962, the Blancos were victorious, mainly because of the nation's deepening economic crisis and the Colorados' neglect of rural development. In view of the Blancos' two successive victories, "Uruguay has laid to rest any doubts about her two-party system."[20]

In two of the other nations, Panama and Colombia, laws have been passed for the purpose of establishing two-party systems. In Panama, as in most other Latin American nations, political parties have been quite fluid and transitory. José Antonio Remón, who was elected president in 1952, was backed by a coalition of five parties. Convinced, however, that the two-party system works better than the system of many small and ephemeral parties which exist mainly to promote the political fortunes of certain leaders, his administration passed a law that in order to participate in any election a party must have 40,000 registered voters, and in order to continue as a party must poll 40 percent or more of the vote in the preceding election. While the law may have been intended to promote the two-party system, it was widely regarded as primarily a maneuver to wipe out the opposition, since the anti-Remón coalition was officially credited with receiving only 35 percent of the votes in the 1952 election.[21]

A far more significant experiment with a planned and legally instituted two-party system was the one undertaken by Colombia in 1957 for restoring orderly, constitutional government after nine years of internecine civil war and dictatorship. Under the bipartisan agreement reached between the conservatives and the liberals, a National Front government would be established which would last until 1974. The presidency would alternate between the two parties, offices at all levels and branches would be equally divided between them, and certain types of legislation would require a two-thirds majority vote for approval. But while the two parties would jointly participate in governing the nation, each would still be free to criticize and oppose the administration. The unusual pact has worked out well in some ways but fallen short in others.

It performed most satisfactorily the initial task of returning the country to constitutional government with a modicum of party cooperation, the reestablishment of civil liberties and democratic processes, and the stabilization of the financial and economic situation. However, as a means of progress in economic and social reform, and as a political mechanism, it has not been notably successful.[22]

---

20 Schmitt and Burks, *op. cit.*, p. 207.

21 John and Mavis Biesanz, *The People of Panama* (New York: Columbia University Press, 1955), p. 157.

22 Schmitt and Burks, *op. cit.*, p. 230. For a detailed account of this bipartisan political agreement, see John D. Martz, "The Transition to Democracy," *Colombia: A Contemporary Political Survey* (Chapel Hill, N.C.: University of North Carolina Press, 1962), chap. 15.

The Multiparty System

Most of the Latin American states have multiparty systems, each party usually representing a narrow range of interests. In Brazil there are 13 parties, of which only 4 can be considered major national parties. In Panama, where Remón before his assassination envisaged establishing a two-party system by law, at least 15 duly registered parties qualified for the 1964 presidential race; it was even problematical whether enough partisans (approximately 18,000) could be found to man the voting stations, since according to law each station must have a representative of each party, and no electoral official can be related to any candidate.[23] Even in Paraguay, approximately one-third of whose citizens live abroad as political exiles or emigrés from the nation's economic stagnation, there are four minor opposition parties in addition to the predominant and apparently dictatorial Colorado Party of President General Alfredo Stroessner.

While most of the nations have a multiplicity of parties, Chile is the only nation where the parties fall into a left-center-right framework, resembling the traditional pattern of multiparty systems. The political spectrum from left to right consists of four leftist parties: Communist, Socialist, National Democratic, and National Vanguard of the People; two of the center—the Christian Democratic and Radical; and three of the right—Liberal, United Conservative, and Democratic Front. In addition, there are a number of minor parties.[24]

Chile has had a multiparty system for the past 100 years, and the number of parties has varied greatly from time to time. It reached a maximum in 1953, when 24 new parties, in addition to the 12 already represented in Congress, registered to run candidates in the municipal and congressional elections. Since then, the number of parties has decreased considerably. Only 11 parties sponsored candidates for national office in 1961, of which only 8 managed to win representation.[25]

There are several explanations for Chile's complex system of political parties. Foremost is the nation's unfortunate experience from 1891 to 1925 with parliamentary government.

. . . if the liberal democratic party [which instituted it] had deliberately set about the work of undermining the credit and authority of parliament it could not have succeeded better than it actually has, through forcing upon the various groups and parties of parliament the necessity of making shifting and temporary alliances and coalitions. . . . It has gained this success not by con-

---

[23] *Hispanic American Report*, Vol. XV, No. 5 (July, 1962), p. 410.
[24] For a brief history of each of these parties, together with its strength as shown in elections of the past two decades, see *Chile: Election Factbook*, September 4, 1964 (Institute for the Comparative Study of Political Systems) (Washington, D.C.: Operations and Policy Research, Inc., 1963), pp. 22–29 and 32–41.
[25] *Ibid.*, pp. 13, 22, and 23.

sistently following any definite policy of government, but rather by making opportune arrangements with this or that party or faction.[26]

The d'Hondt system of proportional representation in Chile has also tended to encourage the formation of many minor political groups. Moreover, the ease of registering as a political party, by presenting its statutes, the composition of its executive committee, and the signatures of 10,000 registered voters, is also greatly responsible for the large number of parties. [27]

As a result of the nation's multiparty system, no single party received more than one-fourth of the total popular vote cast in a national election during the 20 years preceding 1964. Moreover, since no candidate received an absolute majority of the total votes, as required by Article 64 of the constitution, it became the responsibility of congress to select the president in the elections of 1946, 1952, and 1958. The constitution merely specifies that the choice must be between the two high candidates. In every case, however, the congress has overwhelmingly endorsed the voters' first choice.

In the crucial September, 1964, election, however, the Christian Democrats supporting the moderate leftist Eduardo Frei scored a smashing victory over the Socialist-Communist combination supporting the far leftist, Salvador Allende, leader of the Socialist-Communist Coalition. The Christian Democrats won 56 percent of the total vote, proving that even in the multiparty system, a presidential candidate may receive an absolute majority of the votes.

THE MAJOR PARTIES TODAY

Native Liberal Parties

In many of the nations, native liberal parties have arisen within the last few decades to challenge the old order and advocate strenuously a wide range of social reforms. One of the best known and most influential of these parties is the Aprista or Peoples Party of Peru, led by the long-time liberal crusader and several times candidate for public office, Victor Haya de la Torre. Other new native liberal parties are Democratic Action of Venezuela, National Liberation of Costa Rica, the Cuban Revolutionary (Auténticos) and the Cuban People's (Ortodoxos) parties, the Febrerista of Paraguay, the Nationalist Revolutionary Movement of Bolivia, the Peronista of Argentina, and the Trabalhista of Brazil.

"Although all these parties have risen independently in their respective nations," wrote William W. Pierson and Federico G. Gil, "with little or

---

26 Paul S. Reinsch, "Parliamentary Government in Chile," *American Political Science Review*, Vol. III (1909), p. 521.

27 For the operation of proportional representation in Chile, see *Chile: Election Factbook, op. cit.*, pp. 30–31; and for the registration of political parties and candidates, pp. 42–43.

no contact with one another, and their programs developed in response to peculiar domestic conditions, they are nevertheless strikingly similar in development and in ideology. The similarities could well result from the fact that conflicts of social and economic interests are slowly replacing political or religious issues as a basis of politics in these countries."[28]

APRA's idealistic and comprehensive program consists basicly of two parts, a maximum program for all Latin America and a minimum program for Peru.[29]

The maximum program, intended to benefit all the nations of Latin America, consists of five main objectives:

1. Stemming imperialistic penetration of the region, regarded as the most important problem facing Latin America. During the early days of the movement, the leaders aimed their fire mainly at the United States, but they soon extended it to embrace imperialism from any source.
2. Unifying Latin America, also of the greatest importance. Alike as the nations were in so many ways, it did not make sense that they should exist as 20 entities. Unification would greatly strengthen them politically and economically; continued division, on the other hand, would only perpetuate an unnatural situation. As Haya de la Torre put it, "While we live 'Balkanized,' we will be the Rumanias and Bulgarias, the Serbias and Albanias of this part of the world."
3. Nationalizing land and industry by some type of state ownership of the wealth-producing factors, to promote a just organization of society and create a "Latin America for the Latin Americans."
4. Placing the Panama Canal under the joint ownership and control of all the nations of America, which would be to their mutual advantage. Under such joint direction, the canal could not be used by the United States to discriminate against any Latin American nation, even if the United States should wish to do so. The United States would gain too from the change, as inter-American control of the waterway would strengthen its defense, since all the nations would have a stake in it.
5. Promoting solidarity with the rest of the world, especially with the colonial peoples and the working classes of the capitalist countries, with whom the Apristas feel a kinship.

The minimum program of the party, intended for Peru alone, was also very extensive, consisting of:

1. Broadening the freedom of the people by forbidding censorship of any kind and guaranteeing complete freedom of the press, of speech, and of assembly.
2. Establishing a form of federalism whereby the government would be decentralized and local authorities given greater political, economic, and administrative power. The city would thus become a practical school of government.
3. Improving public administration by establishing a merit system and

---

[28] William W. Pierson and Federico G. Gil, *Governments of Latin America* (New York: McGraw-Hill Book Co., Inc., 1957), pp. 319–20.

[29] Harry Kantor, *The Ideology and Program of the Peruvian Aprista Movement* (Berkeley: University of California Press, 1953), pp. 1–163. Most of the comments regarding APRA are based upon this work.

selecting public employees on the basis of merit alone. This would lessen
nepotism and promote efficiency and honesty in the public service.

4. Reforming the judicial system by reducing the cost of litigation and
speeding up the judicial process, which would further the cause of justice. A
commission of legal specialists would be appointed to study the judiciary and
the legal codes.

5. Developing the economy generally to further the economic independence
of Peru. New wealth which would benefit the entire society should be created,
rather than having the small amount of wealth in the nation redistributed.

6. Developing agriculture by a variety of means to aid small farmers, especially those in the Indian communities. Colonization of the eastern area should
be promoted to enable all who desire land to obtain it.

7. Redeeming the Indian by making him a literate, self-sustaining, integrated
member of society, which would benefit not only the Indian himself but the
entire nation.

8. Reorganizing the educational system to provide free education by the
state to each individual to the limit of his capability. Education would be a
monopoly of the state, separated from all church control.

9. Helping the workers by establishing minimum wages, maximum hours,
safer working conditions, and a broad program of social security to protect the
working population from the many vicissitudes of life.

10. Controlling the armed forces by removing them from politics and
making them subject to civilian control. Socially reoriented, they could be a
constructive influence by educating the raw Indian recruits and teaching them
modern methods of farming.

11. Separating church and state and making the state neutral in religious
matters. The Church would be relegated to a position where it could not be
involved in any activities not purely religious.

APRA has never managed to gain control of the government. Indeed,
the party has been outlawed much of the time and its leader, Victor Haya,
forced to spend much of his life in hiding, in exile abroad, or in the
Colombian embassy in Lima (more than five years there, from January,
1949, to early 1954!). Even when he was allowed to run for the presidency, he was in the opinion of many counted out in the tabulation of
votes. Consequently, while certain reforms envisioned by APRA have
been put into effect by the opposition, the party program as a whole has
never been realized.[30]

Other native liberal parties which advocate social reform have been

---

[30] After a recent study of APRA, Fredrick B. Pike concludes, surveying developments, that the party is by no means defunct; its leaders and programs, he asserts,
have been mainly a hoax and a fraud. The "myths" of the old APRA, in his opinion,
are: its claim as a unique and necessary voice of reform; its professed objective of
protecting and redeeming the downtrodden, proletariat classes; its advocacy of non-
violence and democratic processes for bringing reform to Peru; and the charge of
overwhelming communist influence on its ideology. The "myths" of the new APRA,
as Pike views the party, include: Peru's APRA remaining a vital force for social
progress through revolutionary change; the party's being dead as a major political
force in the nation; and its constituting one of the most effective forces in the nation
against communism. (Fredrick B. Pike, "The Old and the New APRA in Peru: Myth
and Reality," *Inter-American Economic Affairs*, Vol. 18, No. 2 [Autumn, 1964], pp.
3–45.)

more successful in getting their programs adopted. The National Liberation Party in Costa Rica under José Figueres, Democratic Action in Venezuela under Rómulo Betancourt, and the Nationalist Revolutionary Movement in Bolivia under Paz Estenssoro have all managed to gain control of the government and make extensive reforms in their nations, such as broadening the suffrage, establishing social security and many other benefits for workers, and undertaking a genuine program of land reform.

In Venezuela Democratic Action has twice been able to win control of the government, from 1945 to 1948 and from 1958 to the date of this writing, and has thus been in a position to put its program into effect.[31] The reforms made by Democratic Action may be broadly classified as electoral and political, economic, and social. Although a concerted program was pushed on all of these fronts, priority was given in about the order named.

The electoral process was reformed so as to eliminate as far as possible the perpetration of fraud to thwart the desires of the voters. By the simple process of electoral manipulation, the reactionary and oligarchic Democratic Party had been able in the municipal, state, and congressional elections of 1942, 1943, and 1944 to win overwhelming victories, despite the fact that the large majority of citizens favored Democratic Action. Besides setting up procedures to guarantee honest elections, the new regime removed the many restrictions on freedom of speech, press, assembly, and other constitutional rights and greatly increased the electorate by giving the right to vote to women and illiterates.

In the economic realm, too, the new broom swept clean to put Venezuela's house into better order. With a view to balancing the economy, regarded by the new administration as "shamefully lopsided and deformed," it established the Venezuelan Development Corporation to plan and support a wide range of needed economic enterprises. Labor for the first time was genuinely given the right to organize, and many benefits were provided for it by law. An extensive program of land reform was instituted, one of the most dynamic and successful of the several programs adopted in Latin America to date, as we saw in Chapter 8. Pending their being able to own land under the government's redistribution program, farm laborers were allowed, even encouraged, to organize to protect their interests—a right which exists in very few of the nations in the region. To obtain greater benefit from its petroleum deposits, the government required that the agreed-upon 50-50 split of profits should be determined currently, instead of on the basis of an earlier, lower-priced period which greatly benefited the companies.

In the social realm, too, the new broom in Venezuela has been sweeping

---

[31] For a comparison of Democratic Action's strength with that of the other three major parties, COPEI, URD, and PCV, in the three elections of 1946, 1947, and 1958, see *Venezuela: Election Factbook; Elections: December, 1963* (Institute for the Comparative Study of Political Systems) (Operations and Policy Research, Inc., 1963), p. 17. Although Democratic Action won the December, 1963, election too, its strength declined further to only 33 percent of the total vote.

vigorously. Education for the mass of boys and girls is becoming a reality instead of a campaign slogan, as under earlier regimes. In addition to building many new schools all over the nation, the government has instituted a nationwide program of personal and public health. By its concentrated attack against malaria, this age-old scourge which was such a drag on national energy and productivity has been conquered. By its stimulus to the production of meat, fish, and milk, the dietary deficiencies of the people are being remedied, lessening their susceptibility to disease and increasing their mental and physical vigor.[32]

Another native liberal party is the Peronista Party of Argentina through which Juan Perón controlled the nation from 1946 to 1955. Although many years have passed since he was chief of state, he remains a very controversial figure. It can hardly be denied that he is vulnerable to condemnation on various counts. He unquestionably reflected many pro-fascist tendencies, especially in his military career and in Argentina's foreign policy during World War II. Moreover, as a result of his flamboyant and *caudillo*-type rule for a decade, he left the nation's economy in a shambles; by his methods of government and unparalleled corruption, he lowered the nation's moral standards.[33]

Yet despite his regime's dictatorial rule, its corruption, and its eventual economic collapse, Perón's program of social justice had a tremendous appeal to the great mass of workers who lived in ignorance and poverty. Non-men, they have been called, with even their minimum wants and needs ignored by the privileged members of society. To them, Perón's program of social justice was the millennium of which they had dreamed.

Justicialismo, vaguely and variously interpreted as the concept of social justice, was the regime's comprehensive social objective.

The more discerning might be more interested in the interpretation of *justicialismo* as the "third position," still another alternative to Hegel's worship of the concept of the state and Marx's "insectification of the individual." They would probably also be interested in *justicialismo*'s breakdown of society into four basically conflicting forces—idealism, materialism, individualism, and collectivism—and *justicialismo*'s claim that it alone could provide individual and social harmony by enabling each of these basic forces to exercise its proper role in society yet prevent any one or two of them from dominating the others.[34]

But to the great underprivileged mass, *justicialismo* meant just one thing —the opportunity to live like human beings. Social justice in any society is

---

[32] Most of this information regarding Democratic Action's programs and accomplishments is from Edwin Lieuwin, *Venezuela* (Royal Institute of International Affairs) (New York: Oxford University Press, 1961), pp. 64–85 and 105–9.

[33] For the disastrous effects of Perón's economic policies, see Arthur P. Whitaker, *Argentine Upheaval: Perón's Fall and the New Regime* (New York: Frederick A. Praeger, Inc., 1956), pp. 37–38 and 161–64.

[34] This interpretation is mainly from George I. Blanksten, *Perón's Argentina* (Chicago: University of Chicago Press, 1953), pp. 276–93.

a worthy ideal. Under Perón's regime, especially the first phase of it, the large mass of workers appreciated not only that the state was at last mindful of their needs, but also that it at last allowed them to share in the responsibilities of government.[35]

When on September 19, 1955, Perón resigned amid the wreckage of his program and fled for safety to a Paraguayan gunboat lying in the Río de la Plata, many a joyous cocktail party was held to celebrate the downfall of the dictator. But the large mass of citizens were grief-stricken; they had lost their only champion.

Ernesto Sabato, a well-known anti-Peronista, poignantly described the deep emotional rift in Argentine society. When the doctors, landowners, and writers were in the parlor, noisily celebrating the downfall of the tyrant Perón, Sabato "noticed how two of the Indian women in a corner of the kitchen were working there with their eyes full of tears. . . . Great multitudes of humble compatriots were symbolized in those two Indian girls crying in a kitchen . . ."[36]

Christian Democrats

Another political party which is fast moving to the forefront in a number of Latin American nations is the Christian Democratic Party. Since the first one was established in Uruguay in 1910, similar parties have been established in all but four of the nations—Cuba, Haiti, Honduras, and Paraguay.

The Christian Democrats base their program mainly on the Rerum Novarum encyclical of Pope Leo XIII, issued in 1891. Often called the "Magna Charta of labor," the encyclical in an effort to improve the condition of the working man advocated among other things his right to organize and the obligation of the employer to pay him a fair wage, sufficient for his decent support. The Social Democrats, as the party is known in some countries, are reformists, often leftists; recognizing the many social changes which need to be made, they are bent on bringing about a social revolution, but through evolutionary means. Their ideology is based not so much on the tenets of Roman Catholicism as on the Christian ethic itself. "Christian Democracy believes that the modern world is in crisis," asserted Eduardo Frei, the successful candidate in Chile's 1964 presidential campaign, "and that only a complete readjustment of society can save man from materialism and collectivism."[37]

The party is strongest in Chile, where its strength has soared from 3.4 percent of the vote cast in 1941 to 56 percent of the vote in 1964. Social Democrats are quite strong in Venezuela too, where they are known as COPEI. One of the three major parties, it ranks next to Democratic Action and in each national election has shown a sizable increase in its proportion-

---

[35] Pendle, *op. cit.*, p. 177.

[36] Lewis Hanke, *South America* (New York: D. Van Nostrand Co., Inc., 1959), p. 75.

[37] *Time*, Vol. 84, No. 12 (September 18, 1964), pp. 52–53.

ate voting strength. In 1958 COPEI received 16 percent of the total presidential vote and had considerable influence in the coalition government formed by Democratic Action, which received 49 percent. In the December, 1963, election, the gap between the two parties narrowed further; COPEI increased its strength to 20 percent of the total vote, while Democratic Action slipped to 33 percent. In Peru the party was largely responsible for the victory of President Fernando Beláunde in 1963, as a result of which Christian Democrats were given three cabinet posts.

The Communist Party

The Communist Party is legal in only seven of the republics—Bolivia, Chile, Colombia, Cuba, Ecuador, Mexico, and Uruguay. In some of the others it nevertheless continues to operate underground or under another name. In Guatemala where it is illegal, it operates anyway under the name of Partido Guatemalteco del Trabajo. In Peru where it is also illegal, it functions under the name Frente Liberación Nacional. Since the party cannot operate openly in most of the nations, any appraisal of its strength must be only speculative.

An appraisal is also complicated by the tendency to label as Communists any persons or groups who oppose the government in power or criticize the status quo. "The most audacious political-philological tactic of the Police Ruler," contends Juan José Arévalo, former president of Guatemala, "is to call Kommunist every person—especially every politician—who expresses sympathy for the poor, the disinherited, for those who do not belong to any social establishment, for the proletariat whatever its origin, for workers in general."[38]

According to a Senate investigating subcommittee report released in 1959, Communist Party membership in the various Latin American countries during 1958 was as follows:[39]

Argentina	70,000 to 80,000	Guatemala	1,000
Bolivia	4,000	Haiti	Negligible
Brazil	50,000	Honduras	500
Chile	20,000 to 25,000	Mexico	5,000
Colombia	5,000	Nicaragua	200
Costa Rica	300	Panama	500
Cuba	12,000	Paraguay	500
Dominican Republic	Negligible	Peru	6,000
Ecuador	1,000	Uruguay	3,000
El Salvador	500	Venezuela	30,000 to 35,000

---

[38] Juan José Arévalo, *Anti-Kommunism in Latin America*, trans. Carleton Beals (New York: Lyle Stuart, Inc., 1963), p. 68. Arévalo criticizes three main groups for having such a narrow interpretation of Communists—the military regimes of Latin America, the United States Department of State, and the Catholic Church of Guatemala.

[39] For the strength and activities of the Communist Party in the several nations, and steps being taken to combat subversion by the United States, the Organization of American States, and the Alliance for Progress, see Edwin M. Martin, Assistant Secretary of State for Inter-American Affairs, "Communist Subversion in the Western Hemisphere," Bureau of Public Affairs, Department of State (March, 1963), No. 2.

In terms of simple numerical strength, the Communists do not seem impressive in this area. There are apparently only about 200,000 or so Communists in Latin America. This is only about one-tenth of one percent of the total population, far less than the 1.4 percent in France, and the 3.6 percent in Italy. But numerical strength alone is not a true measure of communism's strength and influence in Latin America.

For Communists have managed to worm their way into key positions where they can exert considerable influence. Over many decades they have made a strong bid for leadership of the labor unions, often succeeding.[40] In Mexico, Vicente Lombardo Toledano, a former university professor specializing in labor law, and later governor, congressman, and senator, organized the Confederación General de Obreros y Campesinos de México (CGOCM). Although avowedly not a Communist, Toledano was an ardent admirer of the communist system, and the union was dominated by Marxist leaders. Other influential labor leaders, such as Juan Lechín, twice vice president of Bolivia, have hardly bothered to disguise their communist affiliations or sympathies.

In Guatemala control of labor was the key to the Communists' success in their take-over of the nation.

Organized labor played a crucial role. . . . Without control of the labor movement the Communists could hardly have become a major political force; with it they automatically were. In the early days of the revolution the Communists' home and chief base of operations was among the labor unions. Even after they became a legal party the labor movement provided their main source of mass support.[41]

Communism, whether sneaking in from the outside as an intruder or openly embraced by local radicals who find it an effective medium of rebellion, has managed to penetrate into other important areas of national life. In northeastern Brazil, plagued by drought and poverty, Francisco Julião, a dedicated and avowed Communist, has organized thousands of the desperate farm laborers into militant peasant leagues.

Communists have managed to penetrate the government, too. Although they have long been known as tricky customers to deal with, some administrations have shown a naïve willingness to take the risk. In fact, even the most reactionary dictators have sometimes found it expedient to utilize their support.

---

[40] For a survey of communist activities in the labor movement, see Robert J. Alexander, *Communism in Latin America* (New Brunswick, N.J.: Rutgers University Press, 1957), chap. iv.

[41] Ronald M. Schneider, *Communism in Guatemala: 1944–1954* (New York: Frederick A. Praeger, Inc., 1958), p. 123. During the days of Chile's Popular Front, communist tactics were not to impose their own leaders but to attract those already selected by the unions, then to corrupt them and make them subservient to communist dictation. (Eudocio Ravines, *The Yenan Way* [New York: Charles Scribner's Sons, 1951], pp. 175–76.)

For the devious course which the Communist Party in Argentina has pursued, utilizing labor and other support, see Jorge Abelardo Ramos, *El Partido Comunista en la Política Argentina: Su Historia y Su Crítica* (Buenos Aires, 1962).

Anastasio Somoza of Nicaragua and Rafael Leonidas Trujillo of the Dominican Republic both found it very much to their advantage to work with the Communists during the middle 1940s, using them as a prop to bolster their tottering dictatorships. In Cuba Batista also flirted with the Communists, courting their support for his dictatorial regime.

Chile went even further. In the 1946 presidential election, Gabriel Gonzales-Videla of the Radical Party was elected by the slim majority of only 48,000 votes. Since the Communist Party, which polled 50,000 votes, supplied him with the margin of victory, he promptly recognized his political debt by giving three cabinet posts to Communists. Six months later, however, he dismissed them, publicly accusing them of instigating unrest and subversion through the Chilean Confederation of Labor.[42]

Guatemala, of course, is the classic example of the Communists' managing to infiltrate and control a government. Preferring to remain in the background, they did not become cabinet officers, and only four of them were members of congress. Rather, their strategy was to exercise control indirectly by holding key positions in certain agencies which administered vital governmental programs and shaped public opinion.[43] Even in Ydígoras Fuentes' administration, 1958–63, Communists, according to the ex-president, managed to control the lower courts through subversive students who, as clerks of the courts, had many opportunities to influence the course of justice. From their vantage point, the students were in a position either to expedite or obstruct the administration of justice. Magistrates of the lower courts, usually members of the law faculty, were afraid to contradict the students because they might lose their faculty seats if the students turned against them.[44]

To date the Communists have not been able to gain control of a single country in a popular election. Certainly the most strenuous bid which they have made to win control by constitutional means was in the 1964 election in Chile, where they suffered a smashing defeat.

In Mexico, as in most of the other nations, they seem to have a limited but specific objective. The communist organizations in Mexico, in the opinion of Karl M. Schmitt, do not aspire to build political parties for the purpose of gaining control of the government by constitutional means, nor are they apparently hoping to seize power by force. Rather they exist mainly as propaganda organs to enhance the prestige of the Soviet world and to denigrate the West. Although the Communists have great freedom of action in the nation, they have not been able to capture the imagination of the masses, poor and underprivileged as they are, an ineffectiveness

---

[42] For Videla's methodical campaign to destroy the bridgehead of communism on the Pacific coast of Latin America, also the Communists' retaliation, see Jules Dubois, *Operation America: The Communist Conspiracy in Latin America* (New York: Walker & Co., 1963), pp. 257–58.

[43] Schneider, *op. cit.*, p. 185.

[44] Miguel Ydígoras Fuentes, *My War With Communism*, as told to Mario Rosenthal (Englewood Cliffs, N.J.: Prentice-Hall, Inc., 1963), p. 195.

which has led to factionalism which has further weakened the communist movement. "The Mexican masses will continue to ignore the blandishments of the communists," says Schmitt, "as long as government leaders adhere sufficiently to the revolutionary goals of social and economic justice."[45]

CAMPAIGNS AND ELECTIONS

Qualifications for Voting

Consistent with democratic practice, universal suffrage is increasingly becoming the rule in Latin America. Indeed, many of the nations have not only gone about as far as they can to extend the suffrage but have also made it obligatory.

There are three main requirements today which determine whether or not one is eligible to vote: age, literacy, and citizenship. In a majority of the nations the minimum age for voting is 21; and with the exception of Cuba, which has set a minimum of age 20, the others permit 18-year-olds to vote. In several of the countries the voting age for married persons is lowered to 18, or no minimum age is required.

Literacy continues to be a requirement in five of the nations, four of which—Chile, Colombia, Ecuador, and Peru—are located in the Andean region and have a large number of illiterate Indians. In the fifth, Brazil, the literacy requirement is aimed at disqualifying the large number of illiterate Negroes. In the nations where illiteracy is high but illiterates are allowed to vote, rapport is established by the simple expedient of printing the ballots—election posters, too—of candidates in different colors. *VOTO ROJO!* some posters shriek in living color, urging the voters to "Vote Red!" while others urge them to vote *negro, blanco, amarillo,* or whatever is the distinctive color of their party and candidates.

Citizenship is ordinarily a qualification too. Several of the nations, however, permit foreigners to vote in municipal elections after a certain minimum period of residence, usually five years. Sometimes a *caudillo,* anxious to prove that his regime is really democratic and to roll up a larger majority in his favor, relaxes the requirements. In Venezuela's 1958 election, where dictator Pérez Jiménez was the only candidate on the ballot, he gave all foreigners the right to vote, and urged them to cast a ballot. Americans, who constituted the largest number of foreigners, were warned by the State Department that they ran the risk of losing their American citizenship if they voted in the election.

Women, now allowed to vote in every one of the nations, have raised some peculiar problems with regard to the suffrage. A main reason why they were for so long denied the privilege of voting was the fear that their

---

[45] Karl M. Schmitt, "Communism in Mexico Today," *Western Political Quarterly,* Vol. 15, No. 1 (March, 1962), pp. 123–24.

votes might be influenced by the clergy; it is the women in the family who attend church more regularly and are more heedful of the admonitions of the priests. Another male fear has been that, if allowed to vote, the women might gang up—bloc-voting as we call it—take over, and possibly institute such absurd reforms as requiring husbands to stay home at night. Obviously reflecting masculine misgivings, the Panamanian constitution in giving women the right to vote seeks to avoid open conflict between the sexes by specifying that no political party shall be based upon sex alone. Woman's suffrage, supposedly based upon the premise of equality, is nevertheless slightly tipped in favor of femininity. Since women are so averse to revealing their age, many of the election laws, in deference to such top secrecy, chivalrously exempt them from the requirement of giving their exact age when registering to vote or when voting; they are allowed to state merely that they are over 21 years of age.

Masculine fears about feminine voters possibly deciding the outcome of elections have a fairly substantial basis, as the crucial September, 1964, election in Chile clearly showed. It was the women who elected Eduardo Frei president, giving him his large majority. Since Chilean women use separate ballot boxes, their preference could easily be ascertained. While the masculine vote was split about evenly between Allende and Frei, the women gave Frei almost 63 percent of their vote, enough to assure his election.

Registration of Voters

To enable all to vote who are qualified, yet eliminate the possibility of election frauds, the nations all require registration as a prerequisite for voting. In Venezuela, to make it easier for voters to register, municipal electoral boards are open all working days from six to nine in the evening; in rural areas they are also open on Sundays and holidays from seven in the morning to one in the afternoon. Citizens are registered in the order in which they appear.[46] In Chile registration is compulsory for everyone who is eligible to vote. Any eligible voter who fails to register is subject to a prison term of up to 60 days, commutable to one-half an escudo a day.[47]

The Campaign

In the political campaign, just about anything goes, as in the United States. With the hope of getting elected, the candidates promise anything and everything to the voters. In Uruguay's 1946 presidential campaign, Domingo Tortorelli, a prosperous vegetable salesman and candidate, set a fast pace for the other aspirants. He promised that if he was elected, there would be two fountains on every Montevideo street corner, one with milk for the children, the other with wine for adults. The capital would have a

---

[46] *Venezuela: Election Factbook, op. cit.,* p. 31.
[47] *Chile: Election Factbook, op. cit.,* p. 14.

roof built over it to protect its residents in inclement weather. And since gasoline was in very short supply at the time, a superhighway would be built from Montevideo to Colonia which would run downhill both ways in order to save gas! Tortorelli's nightly speeches sometimes drew crowds estimated as high as 150,000. They often pelted him with vegetables, which of course helped his business. In fact they gave him more vegetables than votes; despite all his promises, he ended up another also-ran.[48]

According to the constitutions and laws, the political opposition has the rights of freedom of speech, press, and assembly. In those nations where constitutional government is more firmly established, the opposition can wage a vigorous and highly critical campaign. In the nations less accustomed to democratic procedures, however, the rub comes when in a heated campaign the opposition takes these rights seriously and criticizes the government. Sensitive of his *dignidad,* many a president effectively copes with a bothersome opponent by the simple expedient of declaring him a traitor to the homeland, giving him a choice of exile or jail. When President Ydígoras of Guatemala was advised that ex-president Arévalo contemplated returning to Guatemala, he laid down the law that his political opponent would not be allowed to return under any circumstances. "There would be only two doors open for him—one at the border and another at the penitentiary."[49]

Another means of effectively disposing of political opposition is to brand it as communistic. Guatemala's 1956 constitution in Article 62 specifies that any individual or joint communist action may be punished. But since no definition is given as to what constitutes communist activity, the executive is free to formulate his own definition; it often means more liberal tendencies than he deems expedient.[50]

Still another means of throttling the opposition is to proclaim a state of siege. The proclamation, whether justified or not, keeps the opposition within close bounds as effectively as a yoke placed around the neck of a fence-jumping maverick. For during a state of siege the opposition cannot campaign freely in the countryside because travel is restricted; it cannot even gets its message across via TV, radio, or the press because all news is censored—in the national interest, of course.

Yet in most elections the opposition does have the opportunity, after a fashion, to present its case to the electorate. But the "ins" who are determined to remain in, and the "outs" who want in are very wary of one another. Indeed, any election is apt to be a no-holds-barred contest, where chicanery may well determine the outcome. One of the various chicane practices is stealing the ballots of the opposition party. In many of the

[48] Russell H. Fitzgibbon, *Uruguay: Portrait of a Democracy* (New Brunswick, N.J.: Rutgers University Press, 1954), p. 152.

[49] *New York Times,* October 24, 1959, p. 7, col. 3.

[50] Nathan L. Whetten, *Guatemala: The Land and the People* (Caribbean Series, 4) New Haven, Conn.: Yale University Press, 1961), p. 399.

nations there is no official ballot, but each party is allowed by law to print and distribute its own ballots. If for any reason these are not available, its partisans of course are deprived of their vote. Thus stealing ballots before elections has become a widespread practice in some of the nations.

In Bolivia, on the eve of the 1960 presidential election, Guevara Arze charged that more than 200,000 ballots which were to have been used by his supporters had been seized by an armed militia. The seizures, he alleged, could cost him the election. In the hotly contested campaign, it was apparently open season for swiping the ballots of political opponents. Paz Estenssoro's ballots had allegedly been stolen by Guevara supporters in Oruro, Bolivia's third largest city, and Paz' henchmen apparently were retaliating in similar fashion. Horacio Ortiz, a supporter of Guevara, gave a dramatic description of what happened when he and five companions arrived by bus in Copacaban on Lake Titicaca with a supply of Guevara ballots.

"We checked into the hotel and five minutes later the head of the local command of Paz's party entered with an armed group," Ortiz recounted. "They seized ballots that we had hidden under mattresses. They told us to come around to command headquarters at 9:00 P.M. and they would return the ballots. When we got there Captain Villamor of the police was there with a group of armed peasants. They started shooting in the air and we ran into the police station. There in the patio they beat us. Afterwards I was forced at gunpoint to march around the town shouting 'Viva Paz!' " Ortiz escaped in the early morning hours, he added, when everyone was drunk.[51]

The Election

When election day comes, members of the armed forces are on duty at all polling places. Their very presence supposedly symbolizes law and order; moreover, by being on hand, they can cope with any disorders which take place and make sure that the loser acquiesces in the results. But sometimes the opposition is as distrustful of the military supervision as it is of the political regime it is fighting. In 1961 opposition leaders in Nicaragua urged the OAS to supervise the election, alleging that if the national guard under Anastasio Somoza, chief of staff, was in charge, fraud and terrorism would prevail. In 1962 United States and Mexican journalists toured El Salvador at the invitation of the ruling junta so they could see for themselves that the armed forces were not used to influence the outcome of the presidential election.

In the nations which have universal suffrage, the voter turnout is usually heavy. To the millions of underprivileged but enfranchised citizens, the opportunity of casting a ballot for electing the president, members of congress, or even local officials is substantial proof that they are full citizens of the republic. The laws which make voting compulsory are also

---

[51] *New York Times,* June 5, 1960, p. 4, col. 1.

largely responsible for the heavy turnout. In Chile the failure of an eligible voter to vote makes him subject to a prison term of up to 60 days, commutable to one-half escudo a day, and the loss of his citizenship for a period up to ten times as long as the prison term.

When the voters are strongly moved to register their disapproval or protest, they resort to one of several means for venting their feelings. Sometimes they stage a mass boycott of the election, a form of political passive resistance intended to discredit the election in the eyes of the country and the rest of the world. Sometimes they cast blank ballots to express disapproval of the alternatives open to them. In Argentina, where the Peronista Party or candidates have been outlawed for most of the past decade, millions of Peronistas have taken the trouble to go to the polls and cast blank ballots. In some nations, instead of turning in their ballots, voters sometimes turn in only the envelopes, filled with black beans, as a protest against the high cost of living and the shortages of such staples as beans and meat.

In Brazil dissidents have their own unique way of registering their disapproval. In São Paulo's 1959 municipal election, there was a popular revolt against politics and politicians. The largest number of votes for city councilman, easily leading all other candidates, was received by Cacareco, who was not even a registered candidate. In fact Cacareco was a 2,400 pound rhinoceros, the third to be born in captivity and the first to be elected city councilman in São Paulo. Cacareco was never sworn into office, however; she was disqualified on the technicality of having her legal residence in Rio, from whose zoo she was temporarily on loan to São Paulo.[52]

Irregularities in voting or tabulating the ballots often vitiate the whole electoral process. Indeed, more elections have been won or lost there than in all the hustings of Latin America.

A common tale in El Salvador is the boast of a citizen of the United States about the efficiency of his voting machines. "Our polls close at 6:00 P.M.," he brags, "and by 10 o'clock we know who is going to be our next President."

"So what?" replies the Salvadorean, "We know that three months in advance."

There are many techniques for stealing elections. Stuffing the ballot box is of course a favorite method. It is sometimes so blatant that it backfires. The heated 1958 contest in the Iguala district of Guerrero, Mexico, was just such an occasion. Profesora María López Díaz, running as a candidate for PRI, received 54,852 votes as opposed to only 2,542 for her opponent, a feminine labor leader, Macrina Rabadán. The plurality was most impressive—so impressive in fact that it completely discredited itself. For accord-

---

[52] *Ibid.*, October 8, 1959, p. 1, col. 8; and October 9, 1959, p. 2, col. 2. Cacareco, it should be noted, is not the first animal to win an election in Brazil. In 1954 a goat named Smelly was chosen city councilman in Jaboatão, Pernambuco.

ing to official records, there were only 42,000 registered voters in the district. Although Macrina received only 2,542 votes out of a possible 42,000, she was declared the winner in the contested election.[53]

Another election which was obviously won by falsification of the returns was the Venezuelan election of 1952. The military junta, having earlier declared Democratic Action, the largest party, to be illegal and ineligible to run, was so confident the junta's candidates could win in a fair election that it permitted Democratic Action and other parties to enter candidates. However, when the early returns indicated that the junta was about to suffer a resounding defeat, it declared a state of siege, and gave out no further news regarding the election until the official announcement two days later that the government's candidates had won.

To guarantee the fairness of elections, 13 of the nations have established electoral courts, either by constitutional provision or by statute. One of the most effective of these is the *Corte Electoral* of Uruguay, established in January, 1924, and composed of four members elected by the national assembly as partisan representatives and five members who are elected as "guarantors of impartiality."[54] The effectiveness of the court, which has gone far toward assuring the fairness of elections, is largely responsible for the reputation which Uruguay enjoys as one of the most democratic nations in the world.[55]

Electoral reform is badly needed in many of the nations. In Argentina the famous Sáenz Peña election law of 1912 provided for universal and compulsory male suffrage, the secret ballot, and a strict system of registration of voters. Designed to put an end to electoral fraud, the law enabled the Argentine people freely to elect a president for the first time in 1916. Thanks to President Sáenz Peña who sponsored the law, Argentine elections have been among the fairest in Latin America. Many other nations would do well to emulate Argentina's practices.

---

[53] Ward M. Morton, *Woman Suffrage in Mexico* (Gainesville, Fla.: University of Florida Press, 1962), pp. 119–21.

Justice has not always triumphed, however. During the wasteful, profligate dictatorship of Antonio Guzmán Blanco, 1870–88, the results of one election were: Blanco, 239,691; General Pulido, 9; General Colina, 6; and one each for three other candidates. (George S. Wise, *Caudillo: A Portrait of Antonio Guzmán Blanco* [New York: Columbia University Press, 1951], p. 91.)

[54] For the operation of the electoral court in Uruguay, see Phillip B. Taylor, "The Electoral System in Uruguay," *Journal of Politics*, Vol. 17, No. 1 (February, 1955), pp. 19–42.

For the electoral courts in the 13 nations, see Helen L. Clagett, *Administration of Justice in Latin America* (New York: Oceana Publications, 1952), pp. 98–108.

[55] In the four studies conducted to date (1945, 1950, 1955, and 1960) by Russell H. Fitzgibbon on the status of democracy in Latin America, polling academicians, journalists, and specialists in regard to certain selected criteria, Uruguay has won the highest rating for democracy in each of the surveys. For the fourth study, which also summarizes the findings of the earlier three, see Russell H. Fitzgibbon, "Measurement of Latin American Political Change," *American Political Science Review*, Vol. 55, No. 4 (September, 1961), pp. 515–26.

SUGGESTED READINGS

ALEXANDER, ROBERT J. *The Bolivian National Revolution*, chaps. 3 and 12. New Brunswick, N.J.: Rutgers University Press, 1958.

————. *Communism in Latin America.* New Brunswick, N.J.: Rutgers University Press, 1957.

————. "The Latin American Aprista Parties," *Political Quarterly*, Vol. XX, No. 1 (January–March, 1949), pp. 236–47.

ANDERSON, CHARLES W. "Politics and Development Policy in Central America," *Mid-West Journal of Politics*, November, 1961, pp. 332–50.

ARÉVALO, JUAN JOSÉ. *Anti-Kommunism in Latin America.* Trans. CARLETON BEALS. New York: Lyle Stuart, Inc., 1963.

BLANKSTEN, GEORGE I. *Ecuador: Constitutions and Caudillos*, chaps. iii and iv. Berkeley: University of California Press, 1951.

————. *Perón's Argentina*, chaps. 14–16. Chicago: University of Chicago Press, 1953.

————. "The Politics of Latin America," *The Politics of the Developing Areas* (ed. GABRIEL A. ALMOND AND JAMES S. COLEMAN), Part 5. Princeton, N.J.: Princeton University Press, 1960.

————. "Political Groups in Latin America," *Political Change in Under-developed Countries: Nationalism and Communism* (ed. JOHN H. KAUTSKY), pp. 140–66. New York: John Wiley & Sons, Inc., 1962.

BRANDENBURG, FRANK R. "Political Parties and Elections," *Government and Politics in Latin America* (ed. HAROLD E. DAVIS), chap. 8. New York: Ronald Press Co., 1958.

CLAGETT, HELEN L. *Administration of Justice in Latin America* (New York: Oceana Publications, Inc., 1952), pp. 98–108.

CLINE, HOWARD F. *Mexico: Revolution to Evolution: 1940–1960*, chaps. xv and xvii. Royal Institute of International Affairs. New York: Oxford University Press, 1962.

DUBOIS, JULES. *Operation America: The Communist Conspiracy in Latin America.* New York: Walker and Co., 1963.

FITZGIBBON, RUSSELL H. "The Party Potpourri in Latin America," *Western Political Quarterly*, Vol. X, No. 1 (March, 1957), pp. 3–22.

————. *Uruguay: Portrait of a Democracy*, chap. x. New Brunswick, N.J.: Rutgers University Press, 1954.

————. "A Statistical Evaluation of Latin American Democracy," *Political Quarterly*, Vol. IX, No. 3 (September, 1956), pp. 607–19.

GIL, FEDERICO G. *Genesis and Modernization of Political Parties in Chile.* Gainesville, Fla.: University of Florida Press, 1962.

————. "Central American Political Parties: A Functional Approach," *Western Political Quarterly*, Vol. 15, No. 1 (March, 1962), pp. 125–39.

GÓMEZ, R. A. *Government and Politics in Latin America*, chap. 3. Rev. ed. New York: Random House, 1964.

GRAHAM, DAVID L. "The Rise of the Mexican Right," *Yale Review*, Vol. LII, No. 1 (Autumn, 1962), pp. 102–11.

INSTITUTE FOR THE COMPARATIVE STUDY OF POLITICAL SYSTEMS. *Argentina: Election Factbook, July 7, 1963.* Washington, D.C., 1963.

————. *Chile: Election Factbook, September 4, 1964*. Washington, D.C.

————. *Peru: Election Factbook; Part II—The Electoral Process*. Washington, D.C. N.D. (1964?).

————. *Venezuela: Election Factbook; Elections, December, 1963*. Washington, D.C., 1963.

JOHNSON, JOHN J. *The Military and Society in Latin America*, chaps. v and vii. Stanford, Calif.: Stanford University Press, 1964.

KALIJARVI, THORSTEN V. *Central America: Land of Lords and Lizards*, chap. vi. Princeton, N.J.: D. Van Nostrand Co., Inc., 1962.

KANTOR, HARRY. *The Costa Rican Election of 1953*. Gainesville, Fla.: University of Florida Press, 1958.

————. *The Ideology and Program of the Peruvian Aprista Movement*. Berkeley: University of California Press, 1953.

KLING, MERLE. *A Mexican Interest Group in Action*. Englewood Cliffs, N.J.: Prentice-Hall, Inc., 1961.

MADARIAGA, SALVADOR DE. *Latin America Between the Eagle and the Bear*, pp. 26–41. New York: Frederick A. Praeger, Inc., 1962.

MARTIN, EDWIN M. "Communist Subversion in the Western Hemisphere," Bureau of Public Affairs, Department of State (March, 1963), No. 2.

MORTON, WARD M. *Woman Suffrage in Mexico*. Gainesville, Fla.: University of Florida Press, 1962.

NEEDLER, MARTIN C. "Changing the Guard in Mexico," *Current History*, Vol. 48, No. 281 (January, 1965), pp. 26–31 and 52.

PATCH, RICHARD W. "The Last of Bolivia's MNR?" *American Universities Field Staff Reports Service*, pp. 717–41. West Coast South American Series, Vol. XI, No. 5, Bolivia (April, 1964).

PIERSON, WILLIAM W., AND GIL, FEDERICO G. *Governments of Latin America*, chap. 13. New York: McGraw-Hill Book Co., Inc., 1957.

PIKE, FREDRICK B. *Chile and the United States: 1880–1962*, chaps. 8 and 9. Notre Dame, Ind.: University of Notre Dame Press, 1963.

————. "The Old and the New APRA in Peru," *Inter-American Economic Affairs*, Vol. 18, No. 2 (Autumn, 1964), pp. 3–45.

RAVINES, EUDOCIO. *The Yenan Way*. New York: Charles Scribner's Sons, 1951.

ROWE, JAMES W. *The Argentine Elections of 1963: An Analysis*. Washington, D.C.: Institute for the Comparative Study of Political Systems, 1963.

SCHMITT, KARL M. "Communism in Mexico Today," *Western Political Quarterly*, Vol. 15, No. 1 (March, 1962), pp. 111–24.

————, AND BURKS, DAVID D. *Evolution or Chaos: Dynamics of Latin American Government and Politics*, chaps. 5 and 6. New York: Frederick A. Praeger, Inc., 1963.

SCHNEIDER, RONALD M. *Communism in Guatemala: 1944–1954*, chaps. 4, 5, and 9. New York: Frederick A. Praeger, Inc., 1959.

SCOTT, ROBERT E. *Mexican Government in Transition*, chaps. 5–7. Urbana, Ill.: University of Illinois Press, 1959.

SNOW, PETER G. "Argentine Radicalism: 1957–1963," *Journal of Inter-American Studies*. Vol. V, No. 4 (October, 1963), pp. 507–31.

STEVENSON, JOHN REESE. *The Chilean Popular Front*. Philadelphia: University of Pennsylvania Press, 1942.

STOKES, WILLIAM S. *Honduras: An Area Study in Government*, pp. 206–64. Madison, Wis.: University of Wisconsin Press, 1950.

————. *Latin American Politics*, chaps. 14 and 15. New York: Thomas Y. Crowell Co., 1959.

TANNENBAUM, FRANK. *Ten Keys to Latin America*, pp. 136–72. New York: Alfred A. Knopf, Inc., 1962.

TAYLOR, PHILLIP B. "The Electoral System in Uruguay," *Journal of Politics*, Vol. 17, No. 1 (February, 1955), pp. 19–42.

WHITAKER, ARTHUR P. *Nationalism in Latin America*. Gainesville, Fla.: University of Florida Press, 1962.

YDÍGORAS FUENTES, MIGUEL (with MARIO ROSENTHAL). *My War with Communism*. Englewood Cliffs, N.J.: Prentice-Hall, Inc., 1963.

STRUCTURE AND OPERATION OF GOVERNMENT IN A DEVELOPING SOCIETY

CHAPTER 13

CONSTITUTIONS, FEDERALISM, AND PRIVATE RIGHTS:
In Theory and in Practice

CONSTITUTIONS

General Characteristics

Newness. Many of the constitutions are quite youthful as constitutions go. In fact, five of them, one-fourth of the total number, were adopted during the years 1960–64 and are still "wet behind the ears." These most recent ones are Bolivia's and Venezuela's, 1961; El Salvador's, 1962; the Dominican Republic's, 1963; and Haiti's, 1964.

A few of the constitutions are notable for their longevity, especially the following: Mexico, 1857–1917 or 60 years; Costa Rica, 1871–1940, 69 years; Colombia, 1886–1965, to the date of writing, 79 years; Uruguay, 1830–1919, 89 years; and Chile, 1833–1925, 92 years. The top honor for longevity goes to Argentina's 1853 constitution which was 96 years old when it was abrogated by Perón in 1949 (it was reinstated in 1957).

The life expectancy of a constitution is very short in Latin America. The mortality rate is high during constitutional infancy, and even higher during adolescence. Only a small percentage of them live to a ripe old age. Among the many cases of short-lived constitutions are the two which Colombia had in a single year, 1811, and the two which Bolivia had in 1839. The Dominican Republic set a record for the region that will probably stand for quite a while. In the eight-year period, 1874–81, the nation had seven new constitutions—one for each year of the period except 1876.

Not a single one of the 20 republics has the constitution that was originally adopted after independence was won.

Length. Compared with the Constitution of the United States, which fills nine pages or so and, with its amendments, another half dozen pages, the constitutions of Latin America are quite lengthy. There are several reasons for this. Sometimes they go into excessive detail to spell out minutely the functions of government, the organization of governmental departments, and the powers which the several branches of government will exercise. Thus, in the Mexican constitution, adopted in 1917 and about 60 pages long, the Congress is authorized to levy taxes on, among other things, matches and *aguamiel*, the unfermented juice of the maguey plant—which ferments quickly in the warm climate.

Another reason for the length of the constitutions is the inclusion of many provisions which are strictly temporary. Sometimes a new constitution will specify by name who the new president is to be and the conditions under which he will hold office. The constitution of Colombia in particular has many such transitory provisions, all hopefully designed to promote respect for constitutional government and end civil strife.

Still another reason for the length of Latin American constitutions is their inclusion of many new functions and responsibilities vested in the government. Mexico's 1917 constitution, embodying the concepts and goals of its social revolution, set a pattern for many later constitutions in Latin America. Thereafter, the organic laws were to contain articles and even whole chapters which embodied a new philosophy of government and new governmental responsibilities. Under these new constitutions, the government was to concern itself with such matters as ownership of lands and waters within the national boundaries and the government's right to expropriate them, the permissible role and activities of religious institutions, distribution of land to the landless, education and culture, labor and social security, and public health and social assistance.

The "Real" Very Different from the "Paper." Also among the distinctive characteristics of Latin American constitutions are the many discrepancies between how government is described in the constitution and how it actually functions. Some such inconsistencies exist in every nation, but in Latin American nations they are quite pronounced. There, constitutions all declare that the people are sovereign, yet dictators exercise control much of the time; constitutions lay down the principle of separation of powers and checks and balances, yet in most nations the executive dominates the government; they enumerate private rights in great detail, yet genuine civil liberty as we think of it is the exception.

Since the written constitutions are so different from the actual operation of government, one may well wonder why the nations bother to have a constitution anyway. For one thing, in the more advanced nations the constitutions do prescribe the organization, structure, and powers of government and pretty well chart the course that it will follow. And in the nations generally, constitutions usually contain the programs government will follow and the goals it will strive for. Thus, Brasilia, Brazil's brave new capital imaginatively located well inward so as to develop the large interior, was more than a campaign slogan or promise of President

Juscelino Kubitschek. The visionary goal of moving the capital inward— as radical a step as moving our capital from Washington to Chicago or Omaha—was written indelibly into the constitution of 1946, which probably largely accounted for the realization of Kubitschek's dream.

Even in those countries often dominated by dictators, constitutions have a purpose. They serve to legitimize the existing regime and to give it at least a façade of respectability in the eyes of the populace.

But whatever the country and whatever its government or degree of development, the constitution expresses the ideals which the society—at least certain influential articulate members of it—aspires to.[1] The aspirations, however, have often led nowhere. "In brief hours of ecstasy," wrote J. Fred Rippy, referring to the earlier days of the republics, "fledgling political philosophers had written into virgin constitutions all the idealism of their time, but it was as if they had attached wings to lead. The constitutions served as a mighty stimulus to individualism, but they were without power to impose restraints."[2]

Formulation and Adoption

In formulating and adopting their constitutions, the Latin American republics have utilized three main instrumentalities: the constitutional convention, whose members were elected specifically to draft new constitutions; the congress, either reconvening in extraordinary session or with its members elected after the president announced the purpose of drafting a new organic law; and the president, acting solely on his own responsibility.

Constitutional conventions can claim the credit for having drawn up many of the present constitutions. The 1917 constitution of Mexico, under which the nation is governed today, was drawn up by a constituent convention which met in Querétaro in December, 1916, and completed its gigantic task in two months. Brazil's constitution of 1946, the most democratic in the nation's history, was also drawn up by a popularly elected constitutional convention. Such a specially elected body also drew up El Salvador's constitution of 1962 and the Dominican Republic's constitution of 1963. The Dominican Republic, for some years in the "doghouse" after three decades of tyrannical government under *caudillo* Rafael Leonidas

---

[1] ". . . although the spirit of the written constitutions may be violated, the very fact that it is preserved in a written document is indeed a 'homage paid by vice to virtue,' proof of the vitality of the ideals of the people." (Vincente Herrero, *La organización constitucional de Iberoamérica* [México, 1944], p. 15.)

However, unless the discrepancy between the real and paper constitutions is adjusted in realistic fashion, unrest and even active resistance will result in reform or abolition of the constitution. (Aurelio García, *Ciencia del estado* [Quito, Ecuador: Imprenta de la Universidad Central, 1947], pp. 259–60.)

[2] J. Fred Rippy, "Dictatorships in Spanish America," *Dictatorship in the Modern World* (ed. Guy Stanton Ford) (Minneapolis: University of Minnesota Press, 1935), pp. 55–56.

Trujillo, made a special bid to adopt a constitution recognized as legal and aboveboard. Justice William O. Douglas of the United States Supreme Court, long a friend of President Bosch, was invited to advise the constituent assembly, which he did.

While the constitutional convention is generally considered to be the most democratic means of formulating and adopting a new constitution, it is by no means immune to political shenanigans. The selection of delegates to Mexico's constituent convention of 1916 was tainted by fraud; only "constitutionalists" (those who followed President Carranza) were eligible to be elected, which automatically excluded representatives of many opposition groups.[3] The constituent convention of El Salvador which drew up its 1962 constitution is vulnerable for the same reason. Politically it was a monolithic body, since all of its 54 delegates were members of the Party of National Conciliation, the party backed by the civil-military directorate.

But however desirable it may be to observe legality and fair play in the selection and functioning of the constituent assembly, they afford no assurance of success. Indeed, they may completely stymie the convention and prove to be its undoing. Thus, in Argentina, Provisional President Aramburu, who headed the caretaker government that liquidated the Perón regime, was so anxious to enforce fair play in the 1957 Constituent Assembly that its efforts came to naught. In the elections of members held on July 28, 1957, which Aramburu decreed should be held under proportional representation, there were no less than 16 parties represented in the assembly of 205 members. Although a majority of the members favored reforming the 1949 Peronista constitution, they could not agree on the exact reforms to be made, split as they were into 16 parties. Such a hopeless deadlock immediately developed that President Aramburu remarked shortly after the convention met that the nation was in a state of "paralysis."[4]

New constitutions are sometimes drafted by the Congress, which ordinarily meets for the purpose in special session. Sometimes, to enable congressional membership to reflect public opinion more closely regarding the proposed new fundamental law, a new election will be held. Bolivia's 1961 constitution was formulated by a special session of Congress, with the vice-president presiding. The extraordinary session accomplished its mission, although under considerable difficulties. There was no quorum on the opening day; many senators and deputies were loath to attend because a state of siege was still in force. Members of the leading opposition parties either boycotted the special session or walked out in protest when they could not be heard. Despite these complications, a new consti-

---

[3] For the problems and work of the body see Ward M. Morton, "The Mexican Constitutional Congress of 1916–1917," *Southwestern Social Science Quarterly*, Vol. 33, No. 1 (June, 1952), pp. 7–27.

[4] *New York Times*, July 31, 1957, p. 9, col. 1, and September 1, 1957, p. 4, col. 5.

tution was drawn up, adopted, and printed not only in Spanish but also in three Indian languages—Quechua, Aymara, and Guaraní.[5]

A third means of drawing up and promulgating new constitutions is by executive action alone. This method was frequently used during the first century of independence but is seldom used today. Smacking of dictatorship and absolutism, this direct method is offensive to the democratically inclined nations in Latin America, as elsewhere. A president may wield a big stick, getting almost exactly the sort of document he desires from a subservient congress or constituent assembly, but at least he is careful to observe the prescribed formalities. One of the few instances in recent times of a constitution drafted and put into effect solely by executive action without even a pretense of congressional or constituent assembly participation was the Brazilian constitution of 1937, promulgated by a decree of dictator-president Getulio Vargas.

The Many Constitutions Most Nations Have Had

Latin Americans are undoubtedly the most experienced constitution makers in the world. For a century and a half, they have had a field day in discarding old constitutions and writing new ones. All together, the 20 republics have adopted a total of approximately 200 constitutions, an average of ten apiece, as Table 13–1 shows. Panama with three and Cuba, Paraguay, and Uruguay with four have the best record for writing an organic law and being willing to live with it, "for richer or for poorer, in sickness or in health." But most other nations have taken their constitutional vows more lightly. Nine of them have had from five to ten constitutions. Seven of them have had 11 or more. These include: Honduras with 11 constitutions; El Salvador, 12; Bolivia, Ecuador, and Peru, 17; and the Dominican Republic, 21. The brass ring goes to Venezuela, which heads the list with 22 constitutions; the nation has changed constitutions almost as frequently as it has changed presidents.

Constitutions have sometimes been changed so frequently and under such circumstances that there is a difference of opinion as to just how many constitutions a nation has actually had. For puzzling questions arise which cannot be categorically answered. Was a "new" constitution really a new one or merely the old one altered by a few amendments? Most new constitutions contain relatively little that is really new. Thus, El Salvador's constitution promulgated in January, 1962, represented a bare minimum of retouching, such as shortening the president's term from six years to five and moving the date of his inauguration from September 15 to July 1.

And what about a constitution which has been drawn up and promulgated but never actually went into effect? Honduras has had three such documents, those of 1831, 1898, and 1921. Should they be counted as constitutions too?

Brazil had more than its share of constitutional confusion during the

---

[5] *Hispanic American Report*, Vol. XIV, No. 7 (September, 1961), pp. 633–34.

TABLE 13-1

LATIN AMERICAN CONSTITUTIONS

Country	Number	Dates of Constitutions
Argentina	5	1811, 1819, 1826, 1853, 1949, (1957, back to 1853)
Bolivia	17	1825, 1831, 1834, 1839 (two), 1843, 1851, 1861, 1868, 1871, 1878, 1880, 1931, 1938, 1945, 1947, 1961
Brazil	5	1824, 1891, 1934, 1937, 1946
Chile	9	1811, 1812, 1814, 1818, 1822, 1823, 1826, 1833, 1925
Colombia	6	1821, 1843, 1853, 1858, 1863, 1886
Costa Rica	7	1825, 1844, 1847, 1859, 1869, 1871, 1917, 1949
Cuba	4	1901, 1934, 1935, 1940
Dominican Republic	21	1844, 1854, 1865, 1868, 1872, 1874, 1875, 1877, 1878, 1879, 1880, 1881, 1887, 1896, 1908, 1924, 1927, 1934, 1942, 1947, 1963
Ecuador	16	1820, 1825, 1843, 1845, 1851, 1852, 1861, 1869, 1878, 1884, 1897, 1906, 1929, 1938, 1945, 1946
El Salvador	12	1824, 1841, 1864, 1871, 1872, 1880, 1883, 1886, 1939, 1945 (back to the 1886), 1950, 1962
Guatemala	6	1839, 1851, 1879, 1945, 1954, 1956
Haiti	13	1801, 1805, 1806, 1843, 1849, 1867, 1879, 1889, 1918, 1935, 1946, 1957, 1964
Honduras	11	1825, 1839, 1848, 1865, 1873, 1880, 1894, 1904 (restored 1894), 1924, 1936, 1957
Mexico	6	1824, 1835, 1837, 1843, 1857, 1917
Nicaragua	7	1826, 1838, 1858, 1893, 1905, 1911, 1939, 1950
Panama	3	1904, 1941, 1946
Paraguay	4	1813, 1844, 1870, 1940
Peru	17	1823, 1826, 1827, 1828, 1834, 1836 (two), 1839, 1855, 1856, 1860, 1867, 1868, 1879, 1880, 1920, 1933
Uruguay	4	1830, 1918, 1934, 1951
Venezuela	22	1830, 1857, 1858, 1864, 1874, 1881, 1891, 1893, 1901, 1904, 1909, 1914 (two), 1922, 1925, 1928, 1929, 1931, 1936, 1947, 1953, 1961

SOURCE: Russell H. Fitzgibbon (ed.), *The Constitutions of the Americas* (Chicago: University of Chicago Press, 1948); and *Statesman's Yearbook: Statistical and Historical Annual of the States of the World* (ed. S. H. Steinberg) (New York: The Macmillan Company).

15-year regime of Getulio Vargas. The constitution of 1937 which he formulated on his own responsibility and promulgated by executive decree was, despite its visionary goals and lofty phraseology a "ghost constitution . . . devoid of living reality." It never really went into effect. Indeed the nation was never quite sure whether it was living under the 1937 Constitution or the 1934 Constitution, or whether it was experiencing the phenomenon of being governed simultaneously by two constitutions.[6]

[6] Karl Lowenstein, *Brazil Under Vargas* (New York: The Macmillan Company, 1942), pp. 46–49.

The large number of organic laws which most of the republics have had can be attributed to several causes. In the politically unstable society where revolution before breakfast is almost as popular as bullfighting, a new constitution serves to legitimize the political *naturale* and to emphasize to the nation and the rest of the world that the republic is under new management. Moreover, the foreign practices and institutions so lavishly borrowed by the constitution makers were political quicksand on which to build sound constitutional structures; often unworkable, they have been a ready justification for scrapping old constitutions and writing new ones. The idealistic Latin American constitution makers would have done well to follow the advice of Juan Bautista Alberdi, father of the Argentina Constitution of 1853. A nation's constitution, he strongly believed, should be based on and reflect its history, its customs and habits, and its ideas and values.

Foreign Influences[7]

One of the main sources which the independent young Spanish republics relied upon in formulating their earlier constitutions was the Spanish constitution of 1812. Formulated by idealists who were intoxicated by French republicanism, the document was quite radical for its time. Under its provisions, the king was to be a mere figurehead, subordinate to the congress; many class privileges were to be abolished; and many private rights were to be guaranteed to citizens. The document with its various radical provisions had a considerable impact on the early constitutions of Latin America.

France was another country from which Latin American constitutionalism borrowed heavily. "The finely developed logic of early French constitutions and the artistic symmetry of their political institutions," says Russell Fitzgibbon, "had a strong effect as the Latin Americans essayed their first steps in these directions."[8] Thus, the new Latin American constitutions reflected not only the egalitarian and republican idealism of France but also many of its governmental institutions and practices. These include: the council of state; the system of ministries, especially the ministry of *gobernación;* the requirement of ministerial signatures for authenticating acts of presidents; parliamentary interpellation; decree legislation; separate courts of administrative litigation; municipal administration; police organization; proportional representation; and structure of codes of law.

The political experience of United States was still another source which the constitution makers of Latin America found quite helpful,

---

[7] In Colombia, these influences had the harmful effect of interrupting historical continuity. (Luis Carlos Sáchica, *Constitucionalismo Colombiano: Historia, Teoría y Realidad del Sistema* [Bogotá, Colombia: Universidad de la Gran Colombia, 1962], pp. 23–25.)

[8] Russell H. Fitzgibbon (ed.), *The Constitutions of the Americas* (Chicago: University of Chicago Press, 1948), p. 6.

particularly in the early days of independence. It was natural that the young nations would look to their northern neighbor for help and guidance. For it too had had a long colonial history, and the successful operation of its government during the preceding four decades of independence had given it considerable prestige. Among the Latin American constitutions which were most influenced by the political experience of the United States were Venezuela's constitution of 1811, Mexico's of 1824, Argentina's of 1853, and Brazil's of 1891.

The influence exerted by the United States has been most profound in Argentina, Brazil, Mexico, and Venezuela, all of whom adopted a federal system of government patterned largely after that of the United States.[9] Thus, the principles of tripartite division of government, separation of powers, and checks and balances were woven into the constitutional fabric of these federal republics. The influence of the United States is further shown in the organization of the congress, the extensive list of private rights, and provisions for the admission of new states.

For the last four decades, Mexico has had the most influence on new constitutions adopted in the other Latin American republics. Its landmark constitution of 1917 embodied the new goals and values of a revolutionary society. Article 27 advanced a new concept of private property; it is regarded by the society as having a social function, and rights of private ownership are subordinate to social welfare. Article 123 of the constitution was likewise quite radical. Often referred to as Latin American labor's Magna Charta, its constitutional guarantees afforded Mexican labor a degree of protection and multiplicity of benefits that were far in advance of similar provisions in most other countries, including the United States. Of much significance too, the 1917 constitution was thoroughly Mexican, expressing the strong nationalism and aspiration welling up within the republic. Influenced by Mexico's bold step, other Latin American nations adopting new constitutions have included in them the new concepts of human rights and their precedence over property rights. Adapting these

---

[9] There is considerable difference of opinion, however, as to how much influence was actually exerted. At one extreme, Nicolás A. Calvo held that the Argentine constitution was copied from the United States Constitution; its only defects were in those respects in which it was different. (Nicolás A. Calvo, *John Story, Comentario sobre la Constitución Federal de los Estados Unidos* [1888].)

At the other extreme, Alberdi maintained that despite superficial similarities, the two documents were entirely different; even to compare them was to "misrepresent and bastardize" the Argentine constitution. (Juan Bautista Alberdi, *Bases y Comentarios a la Constitución Argentina* [Buenos Aires, 1929], pp. 335 and 346.)

Yet a comparison of the two documents shows that 44 sections are practically identical, 22 similar, and 41 different, with 60 sections of the Argentine constitution not found in the American. (Segundo V. Linares Quintana, "Comparison of the Constitutional Bases of the United States and Argentine Political Systems," *University of Pennsylvania Law Review*, Vol. 97, No. 5 [April, 1949].)

A detailed comparison of the two documents is given in Viamonte, *Manual de Derecho Constitucional* (1944), pp. 355–80.

concepts to their own situations, the nations are at last following Alberdi's advice by having their constitutions more nearly reflect their own history and practices, customs and habits, and ideas and values.

Amendment

There are three usual methods prescribed in the constitutions for amending them. The one most often specified is by action of the congress alone, with certain variations from the usual requirements for enacting a law. Bolivia which is one of the nations following this method of amendment requires a two-thirds vote of all members of congress who are present. Ecuador specifies that the change must be approved by an absolute majority of the total membership.

A second method of amendment requires approval by the congress, usually with a two-thirds vote, and ratification by a constitutional convention held later. This is the method of amendment followed by Argentina.

In two of the republics, Mexico and Venezuela, the states too play a role in the amending process—a distinctive feature of their federal form of government. In Mexico, a proposed amendment must be approved first by the congress, specifically two-thirds of the members present, then subsequently approved by a majority of the legislatures of the states. In Venezuela, an amendment can be proposed by the legislatures of two-thirds of the states, then adopted by the congress.

The frequency of amendment varies widely among the 20 nations. Mexico has adopted well over 100 amendments, many of which were found necessary to modify or repeal details which were included in the organic law. Quite different from Mexico's experience, Argentina's 1853 constitution was amended only twice in the whole 96 years of its existence prior to 1949, despite the fact that the process of amendment was easier than in the United States. "This difference may be due in part to the fact that Argentine constitutional provisions have always been regarded as somewhat elastic," concludes Austin F. Macdonald. "The president acts in accordance with his own interpretation of the fundamental law, or even in more or less defiance of it. Members of congress and publicists deplore this deviation from the constitutional ideal, but virtually nothing is done to correct the situation."[10]

Regarding the frequency of amendment to constitutions, Honduras enjoys a unique distinction. The nation to date has had 11 constitutions, including the one of 1957 which is in effect. Although each of these documents included a method of amending it, not a single amendment has ever been adopted.

---

[10] Austin F. Macdonald, *Government of the Argentine Republic* (New York: Thomas Y. Crowell Co., 1942), p. 144.

FEDERALISM

Background

A very controversial issue which has often convulsed the nations of Latin America was whether or not to adopt a federal form of government. The unitary type of governmental organization was quite familiar to them; they had lived under it for more than three centuries of colonial rule. Under this form of government, the central authority located in the national capital exercises full and complete power over the whole nation. There is no such thing as state or provincial and local autonomy—"states' rights" as we would think of it. From its vantage point in the capital city, the central government completely dominates the country, making all the laws, local as well as national, and directly or indirectly appointing all officials.

After independence, there was strong sentiment in most of the new nations to discard the old system of highly centralized supervision and control. In its place, a federal system of government would be adopted under which states or provinces would exercise a wide measure of self-government, with their powers and functions guaranteed by the constitution itself.

Federalism and decentralization of governmental authority had a tremendous appeal in the young republics. It apparently was working very successfully in the United States, which only several decades before had thrown off colonial rule. Impressed as they were by this experience, many Latin Americans were convinced that federalism was a political short cut that could advance their nations by one simple step from medieval to modern government.

Arguments For and Against

For most of the first century of independence, the issue of whether to adopt federalism or retain a unitary form of government was a lively one. Whenever federalists and *unitarios* got together, whether in a constitutional convention, session of congress, or bull session, the issue of federalism sooner or later was bound to come up—usually sooner. When it did, "the fur would fly"; rational discussion would shortly give way to invective and often end in physical violence.

Very cogent arguments were advanced by proponents of each of the two systems of government. In Ecuador, for example, authorities on the internal organization of their republic offer five main reasons why the unitary system is better suited to the nation's needs. This system, they claim, insures administrative uniformity throughout the country, strengthens the national government in combating regionalism, makes for a more efficient administration, insures the administration of laws with greater equality and justice, and facilitates the maintenance of order throughout the country.[11]

The partisans of decentralized control were just as convinced that federalism was the political prescription for democratic, efficient government. According to them, it stimulates grass-roots initiative, makes local and provincial government viable and meaningful, recognizes local differences and their contribution to the nation, and encourages a society of free men rather than of robots controlled from the capital by "Big Brother."

Convulsed by the acrimonious controversy over federalism, the largest republics have tried one system and then the other, depending on which faction was in control of the government. Chile briefly adopted federalism in its constitution of 1826, dividing the nation into eight provinces and assigning to each a large measure of autonomy. But after just two years' trial, this incursion into federalism was quickly dropped. Colombia was another of the larger nations which unsuccessfully experimented with federalism. After a federal plan of government was inaugurated under its constitution of 1853, Colombia became less a nation and more a federation of semi-independent states, beset by numerous bloody uprisings and several years of full-scale civil war. The principle of federalism was discarded in the 1886 constitution, and Colombia once more became a unitary nation with a powerful central government.

Federalism has sometimes been a very bitter issue in the smaller states too. In Honduras a battle to the death took place between federalists and *unitarios*, with the former finally winning out. Accordingly, the constitution of 1824 provided for a federal system. After a few years of trial, however, the nation reverted to the unitary system in its constitution of 1831.

A federal union modeled on the American principle of delegated or enumerated powers for the federal government and reserved or inherent powers for the states was unrealistic. Actually, the new states had never enjoyed any inherent powers. As colonies they were part of a unitary system of government in which their functions were outlined and controlled by the central government. They were therefore not prepared by their experience to make this kind of federalism work.[12]

Federalism in Operation

In the states which have the federal system of government today, the principles governing the distribution of power are far from uniform. Argentina follows the same principle as the United States; the national

---

[11] George I. Blanksten, *Ecuador: Constitutions and Caudillos* (Berkeley: University of California Press, 1951), pp. 144–46.

In Peru the reality of geography in the opinion of some made unitary government a necessity. "Without a centralized system of government," says José Pareja Paz-Soldan, "Perú would not be Perú." (*Derecho Constitucional Peruano* [tercera edición; Lima, Perú: Ediciones del Sol, 1963], pp. 381–82.)

[12] William S. Stokes, *Honduras: An Area Study in Government* (Madison, Wis.: University of Wisconsin Press, 1950), p. 66.

government possesses only those powers which are delegated to it expressly or by implication, and all other powers are reserved to the provinces. The reservation at least in theory of large residual powers to the provinces was the logical result of their having been independent entities before the formation of the federal government, just as in the case of the colonies in the United States.

Brazil follows a similar principle of distribution of power. According to Article 18 of the 1946 constitution, "All powers which, implicitly or explicitly, are not forbidden to them by this Constitution are reserved to the States."

But regardless of the principle of distribution which is followed, the power of the national government has usually far overshadowed that of the states or provinces. In Brazil, the national government possesses not only those powers which ours does but also many more. For example, it is authorized to legislate in such broad fields as production and consumption, which in effect makes federal regulation apply to almost all economic activities. Moreover, the congress under its constitutional power has enacted codes of criminal, civil, and commercial law. As a result of this sweeping legislative power, almost every criminal act in the nation is a federal offense, and every dispute arising from the terms of a contract or will is covered by some federal statute.

With the national government exercising such far-reaching powers, federalism as it operates in the four nations is generally regarded as a sham. Speaking of Mexico's federalism, Emilio Portes Gil, former president of the nation, has bluntly called it "a great lie."[13]

A major reason for the federal system's functioning so ineffectually is the preeminent taxing power enjoyed by the national government. In raising revenue, it utilizes customs duties, taxes on incomes, production and consumption, business transactions, and documents. While it is required by the constitution to share a part of these revenues with the states, apportioning the money on the basis of population, area, and other factors, it nevertheless spends most of the money, and the states are greatly handicapped by not having sufficient revenue for their needs.

In Mexico the states have been very adversely affected by the national government's taking a lion's share of the taxes.

The political disequilibrium in Mexico lies in part in the nature of the tax system. Most of the taxes collected go to the federal government. The states receive a pittance and the municipalities an even smaller one. It thus turns out that all other political divisions in the government are dependent upon the

---

[13] August O. Spain, on the other hand, strongly challenges this point of view. Citing many instances of assertion of state power, state nullification of national authority, and successful state resistance to intervention, he maintains that federalism in Mexico, far from being a myth or sham, may well be the nation's peculiar brand of federalism, stemming from its peculiar background. (August O. Spain, "Mexican Federalism Revisited," *Western Political Quarterly*, Vol. 9, No. 3 [September, 1956], pp. 620–32.)

federal government for favors, for they have no resources of their own. . . .
There is really no prospect of giving Mexico a vigorous democratic government resting upon the broad popular base without first redirecting the flow of
income from taxes so that the towns, the municipalities, and the states can enjoy
financial independence.[14]

Still another reason for the federal system's not functioning effectively
in Latin America is intervention in the states or provinces by the national
government. In each of the four federal republics, the president has frequently intervened, with or without congressional approval, to displace
state or provincial authorities and take over their powers.[15] Sometimes he
is requested to intervene by the state or province, usually when the governor and the legislature are feuding with each other, or when the election
for governor is contested by one or several candidates.

In Mexico the question of the legality of a state government frequently
comes before the federal government because two and sometimes three
"governors," each with his own "legislature," claim to have been elected
by a huge majority. The several competing groups establish themselves as
near the state capitol as possible, organize a government, and bombard the
president, secretary of the interior, and senate with telegrams, each seeking to be recognized as the legal government of the state. The Permanent
Committee of the Senate, probably strongly influenced by the president,
makes the decision as to which governor and legislature were elected. If
the national government did not resolve the issue, there would be civil war
in the state.[16]

Of the four republics having a federal system, only in Brazil have the
regional units been able to take courses of action independently of the
national government.[17] Indeed, prior to 1930, each of the states was a little
world of its own, enjoying most of the privileges of self-government, even
raising part of its revenue from levies on interstate commerce. The
wealthy, progressive industrialized state of São Paulo had twice during the
present century revolted against the central government, protesting that it
bore a disproportionate share of the nation's expenses and would be better
off as an independent nation. São Paulo had a large and well-equipped

---

[14] Frank Tannenbaum, *Mexico: The Struggle for Peace and Bread* (New York:
Alfred A. Knopf, Inc., 1954), p. 100.

[15] See Chapter 14.

[16] Tannenbaum, *op. cit.*, p. 87.

[17] This is not true in time of dictatorship, of course. "What has become of the
United States of Brazil?" asked Karl Lowenstein, referring to the Vargas administration. "The state's rights have become completely obliterated by the steamroller of the
centralizing dictatorship," he concluded. "Practically no field of legislative action is
left in which the state can act without approval of the president of the republic."
(Lowenstein, *op. cit.*, p. 70.)

This is not true, either, of the *municipios*, the primary unit of local government,
according to L. Donald Carr, who concludes that local self-government in Brazil has
not really developed to any appreciable degree. (Donald L. Carr, "Brazilian Local
Self-Government: Myth or Reality?" *Western Political Quarterly*, Vol. 13, No. 4
[December, 1960], pp. 1043–55.)

army that was much more than a mere militia. Moreover, the state maintained quasidiplomatic relations with foreign countries, sending its agents abroad to negotiate with foreign governments on questions pertaining to immigration and the all-important coffee trade. When the state flag was displayed in the public schools, it was often above the emblem of the nation.[18]

Today, too, the Brazilian states sometimes follow such an independent course of action as seriously to embarrass the national government. Just such an action was the expropriation of the United States–owned telephone system by Governor Leonel Brizola, head of the state of Rio Grande do Sul. The expropriation was very embarrassing to the national government—the government of the United States too, since the Congress was in the process of passing the foreign aid bill, a perennial bone of contention, and Brazil was the principal Latin American beneficiary. Governor Brizola's action was as embarrassing to the Brazilian government as was the 1906 rule of the San Francisco school board to our own national government—a measure which segregated all Japanese, Chinese, and Korean children into a separate oriental school and created such an international furor that President Theodore Roosevelt himself stepped in and got the board to rescind its action.

In the Brazilian action, the constitution of Rio Grande do Sul permits expropriation "in the public interest," with "prior and adequate compensation in money," and without the approval of the national government. Indeed, the foreign office promptly advised Washington that the expropriation was not carried out with the approval of the national government and did not reflect its policy toward foreign investments in the nation. Moreover, the government would use its good offices to obtain fair payment for the American property which had been taken over.

The Brazilian press praised the reaction of President Kennedy, who forthrightly served notice to Congress that nothing could be more unwise than congressional action to halt aid to Brazil because of the expropriation. Said *O Jornal*, one of the leading newspapers of the nation: "The imposing of a sanction on the Brazilian people for what Governor Brizola did would be the same thing as condemning all the American nation as racist because of Governor Faubus."[19]

PRIVATE RIGHTS

Respect for Rights Generally

In every one of the 20 republics, the constitution contains an imposing list of private rights—usually a half dozen or more pages of them. As you

---

[18] William Lytle Schurz, *Latin America* (rev. ed.; New York: E. P. Dutton & Co., Inc., 1949), p. 110.
[19] *New York Times*, February 18, 1962, p. 1, col. 4, and March 10, 1962, p. 8, col. 3.

read them, they sound as appealing as the nations' travel ads and literature, shrewdly designed to lure tourists with their dollars, pounds, or other currency. The rights set forth in the constitutions are genuinely respected in some of the countries, as much so as in Britain or the United States. But in some of the others which have never really known democracy, the rights are more shadow than substance—paper rights in a paper constitution.

The enjoyment of private rights as set forth in the constitutions may be vitiated in a number of ways. The 1946 constitution of Ecuador contains an impressive list of rights, almost as long in fact as the whole Constitution of the United States. But the many "guarantees" are hedged with numerous qualifications and restrictions, the most common of which is the phrase, "with such exceptions as the law may indicate."

Besides such constitutional loopholes, private rights are often severely limited by the imposition of a state of siege, which all Latin American nations are quite familiar with, both the more democratic ones where it is sometimes imposed as an emergency measure, and the many others where it is practically a way of life. Wherever imposed, the state of siege very adversely affects the enjoyment of private rights. Sometimes the emergency as proclaimed is of a limited nature, and only a few of the citizen's rights will be affected, such as the right to move freely around the country or to join in any large assembly, whether to participate in a political rally or see the matador jab the bull. The Latin American "Marquis of Queensbury rules" may even be politely enforced. These rules specify, among other things, that political opponents arrested during the emergency may not be transferred from one part of the country to the other, for instance from the coast to the sierra or vice versa, and that a political opponent if arrested cannot be thrown into an ordinary prison but must be detained under house surveillance or allowed to go into exile.

But more often a state of siege ignores such gentlemanly amenities and plays havoc with a bill of rights, suspending virtually all its long list of meticulously drafted guarantees. Citizens are arrested by the secret police in the dead of the night and thrown into prison to languish for weeks, months, maybe even years, in flagrant disregard of constitutional provisions relating to rights of persons accused of crimes.

Among the main private rights usually spelled out in much detail in the constitutions are the following: freedom of speech and the press; freedom of religion; rights of persons accused of a crime; social and economic guarantees; and political asylum.

Freedom of Speech and the Press

Freedom of speech and the press exists in all of the nations, at least according to their constitutions. In some of the nations, this freedom is quite genuine and is comparable to what we have in the United States. "The communication of thought by word, written privately, or published in the press, or by any other method, without necessity of previous censorship, is entirely free," states Article 28 of the constitution of Uruguay; "authors and, as the case may be, printers or distributors, remain liable, according to law, for abuses that may be committed." Under Uruguay's "living" constitution, freedom of speech exists as much in reality as on paper.

In most of the nations, however, various restrictions are imposed on the press, many of which are common to other nations but some of which are peculiar to Latin America. For instance, there has been a strong effort to free the national press from undue outside influence, thereby better enabling it to reflect national values and aspirations and to be responsible only to the nation. Thus, according to Article 42 of Colombia's constitution, no newspaper can receive a grant from a foreign government or corporation except with the permission of the Colombian government.

Chile also has acted to make its press independent of direct foreign influence. Under the Press Control Law, passed in January, 1964, the owners of all newspapers, magazines, and periodicals, as well as the concessionaires of all radio and TV stations, are required to be citizens of Chile. The managers of such operations must also be Chileans, and Chilean capital must constitute 85 percent or more of the economic backing.[20]

Restrictions on freedom of the press are usually imposed either by presidential decree or legislative enactment, supposedly under authority of the constitution.

The main threat to the press stems from the president himself. When it comes to taking criticism, he is notably thin-skinned. He can dish it out vehemently and profusely to his political opponents and others, but he does not stand up very well under public scrutiny, especially the critical scrutiny of a free press. As former President Truman would aptly put it, he cannot stand the heat in the kitchen.

In keeping with the cultural emphasis on personal dignity and pride, Latin American presidents are ordinarily exceedingly sensitive to personal affronts that would be considered "part of the game" elsewhere. And, in many cases, the personal affront may be nothing more than just opposition. Thus, there is likely to be legislation to protect the president from "disrespect" (*desacato*). . . . A hard-hitting article in a newspaper or magazine, a speech delivered during a political rally, even actors providing entertainment can sometimes be punished for offending the dignity of the president. Opposition leaders may be jailed for alleged "disrespect" and find themselves still incarcerated at election time.[21]

With *desacato* interpreted so broadly, it is smart not to blame the president directly for anything but to aim all complaints at his subordinates, pointing out that they failed to advise him properly. For the president has many potent weapons with which he can beat the press to its

---

[20] *Hispanic American Report*, Vol. XVII, No. 1 (March, 1964), pp. 69–70.
[21] R. A. Gómez, *Government and Politics in Latin America* (rev. ed.; New York: Random House, Inc., 1964), pp. 79–80.

knees if he so desires. Newspapers which oppose him too strongly may suddenly find themselves beset by labor problems, government-inspired of course, or suddenly short on newsprint, allocated by the government of course. Sometimes the president does not deign to use these indirect methods; preferring to flaunt his authority and teach the press a lesson, he has the editor thrown into jail and the newspaper padlocked.

Journalists, whose stock in trade is freedom of speech, have many causes for complaint, more in some nations than in others. Two of the worst recent abuses did not occur in the insular republics nor those of Central America where, in the warm climate with its low human boiling point, almost anything can happen. Quite to the contrary, the much criticized restrictions on the press were those imposed by two of the most progressive nations of the region, Chile and Mexico.

Chile's very controversial Press Control Law of 1964, passed with strong government backing, was designed to correct, according to the administration, "abuses of publicity." Significantly though, all the nation's major press associations and schools of journalism strenuously opposed the law, alleging among other things that it was merely an attempted cover-up of the scandals of the Alessandri regime. Opposition parties termed the law the *"Ley Mordaza"* (muzzle law). The very first infraction of the law which the Ministry of the Interior seized upon to prosecute went far toward proving the contention of its opponents. The ministry seized a world encyclopedia which is published in Buenos Aires, because the part of Antarctica claimed by Chile appeared as Argentine territory.[22]

But the impact of Chile's Press Control Law was mild compared with that of Mexico's far more controversial Law of Social Dissolution. The Mexican law applies to those persons who obstruct "the path of the legitimate aims of the government." The definitions of crimes under the law are vague and ambiguous; anyone accused of them is virtually at the mercy of the prosecution. Cracking down under the law, the government arrested a world-renowned Marxist artist, David Alfaro Siqueiros, and a newspaperman, Filomeno Mata, allegedly for conspiring against the government. Apparently the real reason for their arrest was their engaging in a demonstration supported by the Teachers Organization in behalf of political prisoners.

After spending a year and a half in prison, the two men had their first public hearing. Siqueiros, who was 65 years old, and Mata, even older, both had to remain standing during the 11½-hour ordeal in a small, dismal courtroom, which observed the judicial formalities prescribed by law. The spirit and even express provisions of the law were flagrantly violated, however; no specific charges had ever been filed against the two defendants, nor had any supporting affidavits been furnished, as are required under Article 16 of the constitution. The lengthy imprisonment of

---

[22] *Hispanic American Report,* Vol. XVII, No. 1 (March, 1964), p. 69, and No. 2 (April, 1964), p. 101.

Siqueiros and Mata, without even the pretense of observing constitutional and legal requirements, has been quite a *cause célèbre* in Mexico, showing how frail a reed freedom of speech and the press really is in the nation.[23]

On July 13, 1964, Siqueiros was given a pardon by President López Mateos after serving almost four years of an eight-year sentence. According to President Mateos, the pardon was granted so that the famous artist could complete his murals, a task regarded as very much in the national interest. In the opinion of some observers, however, the pardon was a gesture to former President Lázaro Cárdenas and other leftists for their support of Díaz Ordaz, or perhaps a gesture by the government to win the support of leftists within PRI.[24]

Freedom of Religion

Compared with the daily and highly combustible issue of freedom of speech and the press, freedom of religion which all the nations profess has been in recent years a relatively mild issue seldom making the headlines. The right of the individual to worship as he pleases is guaranteed in every one of the constitutions.

In times past, the role of the Catholic Church in national life and the measure of freedom which worshipers of other faiths could enjoy were issues so controversial as to divide many a nation into two hostile, vituperative camps. One political regime, such as that of García Moreno of Ecuador, might try to establish a theocratic Roman Catholic state and dedicate the whole nation to the sacred heart of Jesus. But the next regime which came into power would reject the measures of the religious zealots, would divest the Church of its gains under the theocratic administration and much of what it had had before.

During the nineteenth century, religious freedom to most Latin Americans meant freedom within the teachings and precepts of the Catholic Church. The decision of many of the faithful to disregard Church teachings and decide problems on their own was primarily a family affair, with Catholic liberals challenging a Catholic hierarchy.

In the past several decades, however, religious liberty has taken on a wholly new dimension. Many of the Protestant faiths, viewing Latin America as a fertile field for evangelization, have devoted much of their financial and ministerial resources to carrying Protestantism to the region, as we saw in Chapter 5. As a result, the question of freedom of religion in Latin America today refers not so much to the traditional battle of the faithful against Lucifer as to one Christian faith competing with another. In one nation, the competition was so acrimonious as to amount to a direct confrontation. Protestantism versus Catholicism was one of the fiery issues

---

[23] *Ibid.*, Vol. XV, No. 2 (April, 1962), p. 111, and No. 12 (February, 1963), p. 1086.
[24] *Ibid.*, Vol. XVII, No. 7 (September, 1964), p. 592.

in the no-holds-barred, internecine civil war which wracked Colombia for more than a decade. Since then, both Catholic and Protestant faiths have arrived at a sort of informal concordat which recognizes that freedom of religion, regardless of its outcome, will be tolerated in the nation.

Physical Liberty

There are many constitutional provisions and laws aimed to guarantee the physical liberty of the inhabitants. Thus, it is specifically spelled out in the constitutions that slavery is forbidden. Moreover, one cannot be imprisoned because of indebtedness or required to give his personal labor without his free consent and just compensation.

Besides these general provisions, there are many specific ones which guarantee certain rights to anyone accused of having committed a crime. He cannot be tried and convicted under a law which applies retroactively, unless it is in his favor. If he is a civilian, he cannot be tried and convicted by military court or board. Moreover, he cannot be arrested and imprisoned except for offenses specified by law and under a procedure established by law. If imprisoned, he must be advised in writing of the reasons for his detention and must within 48 hours be brought before a judge qualified to pass on the legality of his arrest and detention. He is not to be subjected to psychological pressure or physical brutality, especially during the interrogation.

But these "rights" and many others which sound so impressive on paper are frequently violated with impunity, even in those nations which have a respect for due process of law. In Argentina, as in all the other republics, habeas corpus has long been recognized as a constitutional right, sometimes under the name of *amparo*, a similar judicial weapon. But in Argentina, habeas corpus is regarded as a "legalized farce" because of the excessive delays which destroy its practical value. An application for the writ may not be considered for days or even weeks, despite the explicit wording of the law requiring prompt action. Since no way has been found to compel speedier consideration, most citizens who are imprisoned make no effort whatever to exercise their right to obtain a writ for a prompt hearing.[25]

Political Asylum

The right of political asylum, whereby political offenders may obtain refuge in the embassy of a foreign country, is recognized by every one of the nations. Because of the prevalent political instability and the usual practice of regarding political opponents as enemies of the regime in power, the right of asylum is frequently exercised. Indeed, hardly a month passes when political offenders in one country or another do not flee for their lives to the safety of a foreign embassy, often with the police or

[25] Macdonald, *op. cit.*, pp. 137–38.

military in hot pursuit, firing at them as they frantically clamber over embassy walls or bang in desperation on embassy doors, pleading for admittance.

According to the ground rules of asylum, the seeker is to be given not only refuge but also safe-conduct out of the country. But on rare occasions a nation will obstinately refuse to grant a guarantee of safe-conduct, and a political refugee will be forced to reside for years as a guest of a foreign embassy. In 1948, the previously mentioned leader of the Aprista Party in Peru, Victor Haya de la Torre, sought refuge in the Colombian Embassy in Lima. The Peruvian government, however, insisting that he was not a political refugee but a common criminal, refused to guarantee him safe-conduct out of the nation. The refusal was the subject of bitter and prolonged dispute until 1954 when Peru finally agreed to give Haya the customary guarantee of safe-conduct.

The record for the longest time spent as a political refugee in a foreign embassy is held by two Argentines, Carlos and Luis Amadeo Cardoza, brothers and former Peronista secret police terrorists who fled to the Paraguayan Embassy in Buenos Aires in September, 1955, after Perón was overthrown. For years Argentina adamantly refused to grant safe-conduct. However, it finally yielded in December, 1963, reportedly only on condition that extradition proceedings to return them to Argentina would be begun as soon as they reached Paraguay.[26]

On even rarer occasions, nations have barbarously disregarded the universally recognized immunity to local jurisdiction enjoyed by foreign embassies. In 1915, an irate mob in Haiti's capital, Port-au-Prince, invaded the French legation to drag out and lynch President Guillaume Sam who had fled there for refuge. In April, 1963, Haiti again disregarded international law when authorities entered the chancellery of the Dominican Republic, searching for political refugees being sheltered there. The flagrant violation so incensed the Dominican Republic that it deployed its armed forces so as to be ready to strike. The two nations were perilously close to war when President Duvalier of Haiti withdrew the guard from the Dominican embassy grounds, and gave guarantees of safe-conduct for the 24 refugees and three Dominican diplomats there.[27]

The practice of asylum sometimes has its lighter moments too. One ambassador, roused by shouts from his garden, looked out and saw his butcher clutching two babies and trying to raise his arms over his head in response to the orders of two armed militiamen. When the ambassador opened the door, the butcher appealed frantically for asylum. Why? the diplomat wanted to know.

"It's my wife," the butcher explained. "We've had a terrible fight and I've decided that I must take asylum with my children." Admitting him,

---

[26] *Hispanic American Report*, Vol. XVI, No. 11 (January, 1964), p. 1100, and No. 12 (February, 1964), p. 1194.

[27] *Ibid.*, Vol. XVI, No. 4 (June, 1963), pp. 354–55.

the ambassador let him sleep it off and persuaded him the next morning to go home.[28]

SUGGESTED READINGS

BLANKSTEN, GEORGE I. "Constitutions and the Structure of Power," *Government and Politics in Latin America* (ed. HAROLD E. DAVIS), chap. 9. New York: Ronald Press Co., 1958.

———. *Perón's Argentina*, pp. 161–85. Chicago: University of Chicago Press, 1953.

———. *Ecuador: Constitutions and Caudillos*, pp. 38–42 and 51–54. Berkeley: University of California Press, 1951.

BUSEY, JAMES L. *Latin America: Political Institutions and Processes*, pp. 16–21, 57–60, 100–105, 132–38, New York: Random House, Inc., 1964.

CARR, L. DONALD. "Brazilian Local Self-Government: Myth or Reality?" *Western Political Quarterly*, Vol. 13, No. 4 (December, 1960), pp. 1043–55.

CHRISTENSEN, ASHER N. (ed.). *The Evolution of Latin American Government: A Book of Readings.* New York: Henry Holt & Co., 1951. Readings 2, 15, and 23–26.

CLINE, HOWARD F. *Mexico: Revolution to Evolution: 1940–1960*, chaps. xiii and xix. Royal Institute of International Affairs. New York: Oxford University Press, 1962.

FITZGIBBON, RUSSELL H. (ed.). *The Constitutions of the Americas.* Chicago: University of Chicago Press, 1948.

———. "Constitutional Development in Latin America: A Synthesis," *The American Political Science Review*, Vol. XXXIX, No. 3 (June, 1945), pp. 511–22.

GÓMEZ, R. A. *Government and Politics in Latin America*, chap. 2. Rev. ed. New York: Random House, Inc., 1964.

LOWENSTEIN, KARL. *Brazil Under Vargas*, pp. 3–105; 237–84. New York: The Macmillan Company, 1942.

MACDONALD, AUSTIN F. *Government of the Argentine Republic*, chaps. 7 and 9. New York: Thomas Y. Crowell Co., 1942.

MECHAM, J. LLOYD. "Mexican Federalism—Fact or Fiction?" *Annals of the American Academy of Political and Social Science*, Vol. 208 (March, 1940), pp. 23–38.

MORTON, WARD M. "The Mexican Constitutional Congress of 1916–1917," *Southwestern Social Science Quarterly*, Vol. 33, No. 1 (June, 1952), pp. 7–27.

NEEDLER, MARTIN C. *Latin American Politics in Perspective*, pp. 123–27; 155–59. Princeton, N.J.: D. Van Nostrand Co., Inc., 1963.

PAN AMERICAN UNION. Constitutions of Individual Republics in Latin America. Washington, D.C.

PIERSON, WILLIAM W., AND GIL, FEDERICO G. *Governments of Latin America*, chaps. 5, 7 and pp. 192–95. New York: McGraw-Hill Book Co., Inc., 1957.

SPAIN, AUGUST O. "Mexican Federalism Revisited," *Western Political Quarterly*, Vol. 9, No. 3 (September, 1956), pp. 620–32.

---

[28] *New York Times* (May 23, 1963), p. 24, col. 1.

Stokes, William S. *Honduras: An Area Study in Government,* chaps. iii and iv. Madison, Wis.: University of Wisconsin Press, 1950.

――――. *Latin American Politics,* pp. 457–64. New York: Thomas Y. Crowell Co., 1959.

Tucker, William P. *The Mexican Government Today,* chap. 5. Minneapolis: University of Minnesota Press, 1957.

CHAPTER 14

EXECUTIVES:
Democratic Caesars and Democrats

TYPES OF EXECUTIVES SINCE INDEPENDENCE

DURING the 170-odd years of its existence, the United States has had only the presidential form of executive. Quite in contrast, however, during Latin America's approximately century and a half of independence, the republics have experimented with several very different types of executives. The main ones have been: monarch and emperor, both constitutional and absolute; life president and life co...ul; parliamentary government; and committee or council.

Monarch and Emperor

After becoming independent, Haiti was ruled by an emperor from 1804 to 1806 and from 1847 to 1859, and the northern part of the country was ruled by a monarch from 1806 to 1820. Under both emperor and king (as well as under most of its presidents), the government was oppressive and tyrannical. Its violence and brutality were relieved only by some of its comic opera aspects, as those surrounding the nobility created by Henri Christophe, King Henri I, a nobility that included the "Duke of Marmalade" and the "Count of Lemonade."

Contrasting sharply with Haiti's experience was Brazil's Empire, which lasted from October 12, 1822, when Pedro I was proclaimed constitutional emperor until November 16, 1889, when his son, Pedro II, was deposed by the army and ordered to leave the country. Under the liberal constitution of 1824 which remained in effect until the establishment of the republic in 1889, the emperor had a "moderate power" that gave him an active and significant role within the framework of effective representative government. In reality, if not in form, Brazil under the reign of its two able emperors, especially the second, was a republic, a democracy with a permanent president. When President Rojas Paul of Venezuela heard the news of the empire's collapse in 1889, he declared: "The only republic which existed in America has come to an end: the Empire of Brazil."

Brazil even today is deeply indebted to the Empire, particularly to the enlightened rule of Pedro II. It gave the young nation a long period of political stability and saved it from dangerous contention over the form of government to be adopted or who should exercise authority. Moreover, it enabled the country to maintain its territorial integrity and to enjoy a long era of freedom from serious internal strife. In brief, the Empire greatly aided the nation's development.

Uneasy lies the head that wears a crown, especially in Latin America. For emperors and kings alike usually met a tragic fate. Jacques I, emperor of Haiti, 1804–6; Augustín I (Iturbide), emperor of Mexico, 1822–23; and Maximilian, emperor of Mexico, 1864–67, were all assassinated or executed. And King Henri I of Haiti managed to avoid death at the hands of his enemies by killing himself.

Life President and Life Consul

Haiti's life president, Jean Pierre Boyer, who governed the southern part of the country from 1818 to 1820 and the whole country until he was overthrown by revolution in 1843, was one of the best rulers the nation has had. Perhaps his greatest achievement was maintaining the young nation's independence, and preventing its reabsorption by France, who still had designs on her former colony. More recently, Haiti acquired another self-styled life president when François Duvalier graciously bestowed that title upon himself on April 1, 1964—apparently not as an April fool joke.

Paraguay's life consul was José Gaspar Rodríguez Francia. One of the country's two consuls from 1813 to 1814, he was named sole ruler in 1814 on a temporary basis and consul for life in 1816, his tenure lasting until 1840. During his long dictatorial reign, he instituted various measures for improving the lot of the Indians and mestizos. However, he greatly retarded Paraguay's development generally by completely sealing it off from all contact with the outside world, even refusing to have diplomatic relations with other nations.

Parliamentary Government

A number of nations in Latin America have experimented with the parliamentary system; Chile and Brazil are interesting examples. In Chile, the bases for cabinet government were established by the constitution of 1833, which provided among other things that members of the cabinet could be chosen from the senate or chamber of deputies and that ministers might attend sessions of congress and debate but not vote. By 1891 the practice was firmly established that the president would select the members of his cabinet from among the majority party in congress and that he should not govern without the support of a majority in congress. The parliamentary system, which lasted from 1891 to 1925, was marred by ministerial instability and frequent cabinet changes.

Brazil instituted cabinet government as an emergency measure in September, 1961, in an effort to avert civil war. When President Jânio Quadros unexpectedly resigned on August 25, 1961, after only seven months in office, a military uprising threatened to prevent the vice-president, João Goulart, head of the Brazilian Labor Party and a confirmed leftist, from becoming president. Civil war was averted only by a compromise that permitted Goulart to be inaugurated on condition that his legal power would be sharply curtailed by a constitutional amendment changing the government from a presidential to a parliamentary system. Taking office on these terms, Goulart was at first largely a figurehead, since the prime minister who exercised most of the executive power was responsible solely to Congress. However, as the result of a national plebiscite conducted in January, 1963, presidential government was reestablished, and Goulart exercised the usual executive powers until his overthrow in April, 1964.

Committee or Council

Still another type of executive has been tried in Latin America—the committee or council. The first Venezuelan republic had a committee for its executive; the weakness and indecision of the committee when strong direction was critically needed were largely responsible for the failure of the first republic.

Another form of plural executive, the *colegiado* of Uruguay, is without doubt the most provocative experiment with executive organization and power undertaken in Latin America. The *colegiado* is the brainchild of José Batlle y Ordóñez, president from 1903 to 1907 and from 1911 to 1915, and one of the great Latin American statesmen of all time. Very much concerned about the threat of dictator-presidents to democratic government and individual liberty, Batlle while on an extended tour of Europe studied the Swiss Council of seven members, which deeply impressed him. This was the answer to dictatorship, he was convinced; and on his return to Uruguay, he proposed that the nation adopt the *colegiado* or plural executive. His proposal was adopted, and was in effect from 1917 until 1933 when President Gabriel Terra discarded the system after a successful *golpe de estado*. Adopted a second time in 1951, the *colegiado* is Uruguay's executive authority today.

The *colegiado*, or National Council, is composed of nine members who constitute the executive branch. The nine councilors are elected directly by the people of the entire nation, which constitutes a single electoral district, from lists of candidates submitted by the political parties and their factions for the consideration of the electorate. The party or coalition which receives the largest number of votes is allotted six seats on the

National Council, and the party or coalition with the next largest number of votes is given three seats.

The National Council then appoints nine ministers who serve as heads of the administrative departments. These ministers are responsible to the council, and also to the Congress; they must resign if the Congress in a joint session votes to censure them. Uruguay's weak, plural executive has its critics,[1] but the nation enjoys a democratic government and personal freedom that are the envy of other Latin American states.

THE PRESIDENT TODAY[2]

The constitutions of Latin America, borrowing heavily from the political experience of the United States, established a tripartite division of government, consisting of the executive, legislative, and judicial branches, all equal and coordinate.[3] And under the correlative principle of separation of powers, each branch of government was to exercise the powers it was given under the constitution, but no more.

But constitution making is one thing, and the practice of government is sometimes quite another. In most of the republics, instead of being equal and coordinate, the executive so far overshadows the other two branches of government that for all practical purposes the president *is* the govern-

---

[1] Benito Nardone, one of the nine members of the National Council, assailing the Uruguayan system of government as "inefficient," has been conducting a campaign for a change in the constitution to adopt a presidential system. See *New York Times*, September 18, 1961, p. 15, col. 1.

For an objective treatment of the adoption of the *colegiado* and the likelihood of its success, see, respectively, Russell H. Fitzgibbon, "Adoption of a Collegiate Executive in Uruguay," *Journal of Politics*, Vol. 14, No. 4 (November, 1952), pp. 616–42; Milton I. Vanger, "Uruguay Introduces Government by Committee," *American Political Science Review*, Vol. 48, No. 2 (June, 1954), p. 500.

[2] For an earlier, but still valid, summary of the presidency in each of the republics, see Miguel Jorrín, *Governments of Latin America* (New York: D. Van Nostrand Co., Inc., 1953), pp. 92–96.

For a provocative analysis of the major types of Latin American executives, classified according to constitutional presidents, demagogic *caudillos*, military guardians, or paternalistic *caudillos*, see R. A. Gómez, "Latin American Executives: Essence and Variations," *Journal of Inter-American Studies*, Vol. 3, No. 1 (January, 1961), pp. 81–95.

For a penetrating study of the executive in Venezuela, see Leo B. Lott, "Executive Power in Venezuela," *American Political Science Review*, Vol. L, No. 2 (June, 1956), pp. 422–41.

[3] In Ecuador, however, the traditional doctrine of separation of powers and equality of the three branches of government has been discarded, in theory at least. While the nation's first 13 constitutions referred to the executive, the congress, and the judiciary as "powers," the constitutions adopted in 1945 and 1946 refer to these organs as "functions." The emphasis of the earlier constitutions was on separation of "powers," the emphasis today is on coordination of "functions." Furthermore, while the earlier constitutions stressed that the three branches of government were equal, the 1946 constitution, in effect in 1964, specifies that the executive and the judicial functions are subordinate to the legislative. (George I. Blanksten, *Ecuador: Constitutions and Caudillos* [Berkeley: University of California Press, 1951], p. 85.)

TABLE 14-1
EXECUTIVES—FEBRUARY, 1965

Country	Incumbent	Date Taking Office	Const. Length of Term	Political Party of Incumbent or Party Replaced
Argentina	Arturo Umberto Illia	10-63	6	Unión Civica Radical del Pueblo
Bolivia	Gen. René Barrientos	11-64 coup	4	Nationalist Revolutionary Movement (MNR). Barrientos, vice-president, replaced Paz Estenssoro, elected president
Brazil	Gen. Humberto Castelo Branco	5-64 coup	5	Branco elected by congress to replace João Goulart, overthrown
Chile	Eduardo Frei	9-64	6	Christian Democrat
Colombia	Guillermo León Valencia	8-62	4	Conservative
Costa Rica	Francisco J. Orlich	5-62	4	National Liberation
Cuba	Fidel Castro Ruz (Prime Min.)	7-59	**	*Elections suspended
Dominican Republic	Osvaldo Dorticos Torrado (Pres.) Civilian "triumvirate" of 2, headed by Donald Reid Cabral	9-63 coup	4	The civilian triumverate of 3 civilians—now only 2 —is a front for the military who deposed Juan Bosch
Ecuador	Military junta, headed by Adm. Ramón Castro Jijon	7-63	4	Overthrew President Carlos Julio Arosemena, who had overthrown President Velasco Ibarra in Nov., 1961
El Salvador	Lt. Col. Julio Adelberto Rivera	7-62	5	Party of National Conciliation (PCN)
Guatemala	Col. Enrique Peralta Azurdia	3-63	6	Overthrew Miguel Ydigoras Fuentes
Haiti	François Duvalier, "reelected"	5-61	**	Official Party. *Duvalier in May, 1964, had himself declared president for life
Honduras	Col. Osvaldo López Arellano	10-63 coup	6	The National Party, winning the Feb., 1965, election for members of a const. convention, were committed to continue López as president
Mexico	Díaz Ordaz	12-64	6	Partido Revolucionario Institucional (PRI)
Nicaragua	René Schick Gutierrez	5-63	4	Partido Liberal Nacionalista
Panama	Marco Aurelio Robles	10-64	4	Partido Nacional Liberal and government coalition of 8 parties
Paraguay	Gen. Alfredo Stroessner	8-63	5	Colorado
Peru	Fernando Beláunde Terry	7-63	6	Acción Popular
Uruguay	National council of nine members	3-63	4	Blanco—6 members; Colorado—3 members
Venezuela	Raúl Leoni	3-64	5	Acción Democratica

ment. "L'état c'est moi," boasted Louis XIV of France; in many of the Latin American nations, the president comes close to being a twentieth-century version of the French monarch. We ordinarily think of Mexico as one of the more politically advanced nations in Latin America, yet "the feudal-istic traditions of Mexico, like those of most of Latin America, make *el presidente* the political *patrón* for the entire republic," says James L. Busey. "In a political sense, Mexico is his *hacienda*. He is father-image and boss-image for all the people of the country."[4]

But not all the presidents in Latin America possess and exercise such wide power as is commonly believed. Quite to the contrary, in those nations where democracy is more firmly established, the president is ex-pected to perform the functions and exercise the powers vested in him by the constitution—these and only these. Nations which hold their president to such accountability include Argentina, Brazil, Chile, Costa Rica, and Uruguay.

Chile's President Jorge Alessandri Rodríguez, in his annual state of the nation address on May 21, 1962, sharply criticized the Congress with which he had many bitter disagreements. The nation's economic health was good, he contended, but continued progress was contingent upon reform of the 1925 constitution.[5] On September 18, 1963, he addressed the nation about the need for a drastic revision of the constitution. Deeply concerned with pressing economic problems and with the often unco-operative attitude of congress, he urged that the constitution be changed to provide for a stronger executive. Moreover, whenever disputes oc-curred between the president and congress, they should be resolved by submitting the issues to a plebiscite or by dissolving the congress and holding another election to enable public opinion to express itself. Further-more, congress should be prohibited from initiating legislation in the fields of taxes and public investment.[6]

In Costa Rica, too, the president often feels a sense of diminished im-portance, since his powers and status have been purposely deemphasized. In fact, after submitting his legislative program to congress, he is as much concerned about its passage as is the president of the United States. For in Costa Rica, he has no assurance whatever that his program will be ap-proved by the congress unless his party constitutes a majority of the membership; even then, some members of his party, like southern Demo-crats, or midwestern Republicans, may balk and fail to give him the support he needs.

Congress considers the president as "just one of the boys"; the rest of the nation does too.

---

[4] James L. Busey, *Latin America: Political Institutions and Processes* (New York: Random House, Inc., 1964), p. 29.

[5] *Hispanic American Report*, Vol. XV, No. 5 (July, 1962), pp. 447–48.

[6] *New York Times*, September 19, 1963, p. 12, col. 5.

It has long been customary for Costa Ricans to think of their President as being a humble man of the people, an individual no better and no worse than themselves. The President is likely to drive his own car, pick up friends whom he sees on the streets, and fill his time with interviews with callers who come to praise, plead, or condemn. Though the President is kept busy with the pleas of friends and enemies, he shares none of the *patrón*-like features that are common to many other countries of Latin America. Everyone feels free to criticize the President, and unless his party enjoys a large and unshakable majority in the Legislative Assembly, no one expects much from him.[7]

QUALIFICATIONS FOR THE PRESIDENT

As elsewhere, the constitutions in Latin America have established various qualifications for persons who would be elected president. Three qualifications in particular are found in all of the nations. First is citizenship. The president must be a native-born citizen, born in the national territory and subject to its jurisdiction, or, if born abroad, a child of native-born citizens. However, Nicaragua goes one step further, and requires that the president must not only be the offspring of Nicaraguan parents but also born within the homeland. A second requirement common to all the countries is a minimum age. Seven of the nations set age 30 as the minimum; nine nations, age 35; and two, age 40. A third requirement found in all the constitutions is a minimum period of residence there; this varies all the way from one year in Mexico to ten years in Peru.

Various other qualifications are specified in the several constitutions. In Colombia, for one to qualify for president, he must have held one of the other high offices of the nation, such as member of the cabinet, ambassador or minister, head of a department, or judge of one of the higher courts. He might also qualify by having been a university professor for at least five years or having practiced a "liberal profession with a university degree." Costa Rica requires that the president must own property worth at least 500 *colones* or have an annual income of at least 200 *colones*. Costa Rica also adds a modest requirement that the president should "be able to read and write." The Paraguayan constitution specifies that the president must "meet the moral and intellectual requirements qualifying him to exercise the office," and El Salvador's stipulates that he must be "of known honesty and learning." Several of the states require that he be a Roman Catholic (apparently, not necessarily a practicing one), while others require that he be a member of the laity.

Besides these formal qualifications laid down in black and white in the constitutions, some of the nations have informal, unwritten qualifications which go a long way toward determining one's chances for the presidency. In Argentina, if you aspire to be president, it helps to be a resident of Buenos Aires; since 1860, only two Argentines who did not live there have

---

[7] Busey, *op. cit.*, p. 75.

been elevated to the presidency. Or if you live in Brazil, you have a far better chance of becoming president if you live in either Minas Gerais or São Paulo; it has long been the custom in the nation to choose presidents alternately between these two dominant states, only occasionally selecting a candidate from Rio Grande do Sul or one of the northern states of the nation. And in Mexico, besides measuring up to all of the qualifications specified in the constitution, you had better be the fair-haired boy of the outgoing president or you won't even get to bat, much less to first base.

To discharge all his responsibilities and accomplish all that is expected of him, the president should have the superhuman qualities of Superman himself. As Lleras Camargo, president of Colombia from 1958 to 1962 and one of the great statesmen of Latin America, aptly expressed it, a president of Colombia must be "a magician, prophet, redeemer, savior, and pacifier who can transform a ruined republic into a prosperous one, can make the prices of the things we export rise and the value of the things we consume drop."[8]

In addition to the various qualifications established for the presidency, the constitutions contain a number of disqualifications which automatically rule out persons in certain categories. Those usually disqualified include: a close relative of either the president or vice-president; one who has actively served in the armed forces of the nation during the previous six months, year, or other specified time before taking office; the leader of a *golpe de estado* or one of his relatives; and a member of the priesthood. Mexico also disqualifies anyone who has ever served as president, in whatever capacity and for whatever period of time.

CALIBER OF MEN CHOSEN TO BE PRESIDENT

Just as in the United States, the caliber of those who have filled the presidential office has varied considerably.

Some of the presidents have been persons of quite modest endowment and background. Enrique Peñaranda, who was pushed into the presidency of Bolivia by conservative army elements, was a *cholo* of little education. When the news of his election reached his mother, the old woman supposedly said: "Why, if I had known Enrique would be president, I would have sent him to school."[9]

But Peñaranda by no means typifies the Latin American presidents. Usually, they are well-educated, having prepared for one of the professions. Many of them have been lawyers, since law is regarded as a natural steppingstone to politics. Some of them, such as Lleras Camargo, or Café

---

[8] *Time*, May 5, 1958, p. 33.

[9] Hubert Herring, *A History of Latin America from the Beginnings to the Present* (2d ed. rev.; New York: Alfred A. Knopf, Inc., 1961), p. 559. But perhaps, as Herring adds, any lack of earlier book learning was offset in 1943 when, visiting the United States, Peñaranda was awarded an honorary doctorate of laws by Columbia University.

Filho of Brazil, were journalists, reaching the presidency after a stormy career of advocating reform. Others, among whom were José María Guido of Argentina and François Duvalier of Haiti, were doctors of medicine; and still others, such as Arturo Frondizi of Argentina, were professors at the university. In this respect, Latin America is more broadminded than the United States; there, the egghead is regarded as presidential timber.

Many of the presidents have been relatively young men; they may have climbed fast via the armed forces or have received recognition for their intellectual competence. Among those who were under 40 when they took the oath of office are Arbenz of Guatemala, Batista of Cuba, and Pérez Jiménez of Venezuela.

The presidents as a group are rather widely traveled too, sometimes by their own choice, as visitors or students, but more often as political exiles at the choice of a successful new revolutionary regime. The period of residence specified in the constitution to qualify one for the presidency is aimed largely at these exiles. The length of the period required is quite significant. The rule of thumb is that the shorter the residence requirement, the more democratic a nation is apt to be, and, conversely, that the longer the requirement, the less democratic a nation is likely to be.

TERM OF OFFICE

The presidential term of office ranges from four to six years in all of the nations except one. The four-year term is found in seven countries: Bolivia, Colombia, Costa Rica, Cuba, Ecuador, Panama, and Uruguay. The five-year term exists in five countries: Dominican Republic, Paraguay, Peru, Venezuela, and Brazil. The six-year term—also very popular— is found in seven countries: Argentina, Chile, El Salvador, Guatemala, Honduras, Mexico, and Nicaragua. One nation, Haiti, is in a class by itself; the constitution adopted on June 14, 1964, provided that the president's term would be for life, paving the way for the national assembly's action a week later, declaring François "Papa Doc" Duvalier permanent president of the country.

The average of the terms established in the constitutions, excluding Haiti's, is approximately five years, which is sometimes said to be approximately the same as the average term of presidents in the United States. But this statistical computation can be misleading. The American presidents have actually served an average term of about five years; in Latin America, however, the actual term is far less than this. For example, although the president's term of office in Ecuador has traditionally been four years, only 23 percent of the presidents have been able to serve out the full term for which they were elected. As a result, presidents actually remain in office an average of only 2.47 years.[10] In Honduras, too, the actual term of office

---

[10] Blanksten, *op. cit.*, p. 88.

has been much shorter than the constitutional term. Throughout the nation's history, the presidency has seldom changed hands peacefully; changes in regime, usually the result of revolution, have been swift and frequent. In fact, from 1824 to 1950, a period of 126 years, the presidency changed hands 116 times![11]

Courtesy of Ross Lewis and the *Milwaukee Journal*

. . . and there's where El Presidente lives when we have one!

ELIGIBILITY FOR REELECTION

Eligibility for reelection has been one of the most sensitive problems confronting constitution makers in Latin America. The republics have had so many dictators who served their term of office and then had themselves reelected many times that the history of some of the countries has seemed to consist largely of the interminable rules of several long-lived presidents. With this bitter experience in mind, most of the nations have set up strong constitutional safeguards to try to prevent a president from perpetuating himself in office.[12]

The main safeguard is the provision regarding eligibility for reelection. Only three of the republics permit a president to seek reelection and

---

[11] William S. Stokes, *Honduras: An Area Study in Government* (Madison, Wis.: University of Wisconsin Press, 1950), p. 181. For the list of presidents who held office from 1824 to 1949 and the dates they assumed office, see pp. 329–31.

[12] These safeguards and the countries embracing them are given in José Miranda, *Reformas y Tendencias Constitucionales Recientes de la América Latina* (1945–1956) (Instituto de Derecho Comparado) (México D.F.: Universidad Nacional Autónoma de México, 1957), pp. 278–83.

continue in office for another term or more. Paraguay permits a president to be reelected, but only for one additional term. Brazil and the Dominican Republic have no express prohibitions against immediate reelection; presumably a president in either of these two countries could be reelected any number of times. In Brazil, however, a sort of tradition against immediate reelection has been established. Prior to the regime of Getulio Vargas, no president had served more than one term except Francisco de Paula Rodríques Alves, who was president from 1902 to 1906 and from 1918 until his death less than a year later. In Argentina, the Peronista constitution adopted in 1949 permitted the president to be reelected, a practice that had been forbidden for nearly a century. But in 1957, the 1853 constitution was readopted, prohibiting a president from succeeding himself in office.

In the other republics, provisions written into the constitutions are unequivocal in forbidding a president to succeed himself in office. Guatemala's constitution of 1945 was one of the many which contained such a provision, and it also contained a unique penalty for violating it. According to Articles 132 and 133:

The presidential term is six years and cannot be prorogued, and one who has exercised the presidency may not be reelected except after twelve years from having ceased in the exercise of it. The author or authors of a proposal that tends in any form to vitiate the principle of alternability in the presidency of the Republic, and any person, official, or employee who co-operates, directly or indirectly, for such a purpose, whatever may be the motives that are invoked and the means that are employed, commit the crime of treason to the Fatherland, cease in the discharge of their respective offices, and, as the case may be, remain permanently disqualified for the exercise of any public function and automatically lose, furthermore, all their ranks. Responsibility for acts that violate or restrict or tend to violate or restrict the principle of alternability in the office of President of the Republic is imprescriptible.

Most of the constitutions do not intend to bench a president permanently after he finishes his term of office, but are determined that he shall sit on the sidelines for a term or two. Ten of the nations require the lapse of at least one term before he can be reelected, and five require two terms or more.

The prohibition in most of the constitutions against immediate reelection has by no means terminated the careers of former presidents. Indeed, it is quite common for them to make a comeback and be elected again to the high office. Among the ex-presidents within the last decade who have been elected after skipping a term are: Rómulo Betancourt of Venezuela, Ibáñez del Campo of Chile, Getulio Vargas of Brazil, and Velasco Ibarra of Ecuador. Ibarra has become almost a perennial candidate in Ecuador, having been elected to the presidency four times, but each time he was overthrown before he could complete his term. "Ecuador is a very difficult country to govern," he has said.

Unfortunately, the many constitutional prohibitions against immediate reelection are not self-enforcing. Politically immature as most of the nations are, their governments represent the rule of men rather than of law. Once he is in office, the enjoyment of power is heady wine to many a president. Basking in the adulation and plaudits of his fellow countrymen, toward the end of his term he conveniently forgets the constitutional restrictions against reelection, also the cogent reasons behind them. Or if he remembers them, he is sure that his case is different from that of other presidents. The program that he had hoped to complete during his term is only partly finished, and he is the only one who can be sure of seeing it through. Moreover, the nation is facing many critical problems, as everyone realizes. Thanks to his experience in the presidency, he and he alone understands them and has the answers for their solution.

Determined that his invaluable experience and insight shall not be lost, he decides that by one means or another he must be reelected—for the good of the country, of course. His reelection and that of many other like-minded presidents are flagrantly contrary both to the intent and expressed provisions of the constitution, and are usually accomplished by the adoption of an amendment permitting the incumbent to succeed himself. This practice of reelection, which is widespread throughout Latin America, is known as *continuismo*, which connotes continuance in office beyond the legal term by the use of peaceful constitutional methods. *Continuismo* has been practiced mainly by the republics of Central America and the Caribbean.[13]

In attempts to forestall *continuismo*, the republics have set up many kinds of constitutional roadblocks. Guatemala's 1945 constitution even legalized rebellion as a means of blocking continuation in office after the presidential term of six years had expired. "The principle of alternate succession in the exercise of the office of President of the Republic is imperative for the national political system," asserted Article 2 of the constitution, "and the people may have recourse to rebellion should anyone venture to violate this principle."[14]

But despite legalizing rebellion or other drastic tactics that have been resorted to, *continuismo* continues to be a threat in most of the republics. There are many devious means whereby a shrewd president can circum-

---

13 For the reasons why it has been so successful in these nations, see Russell H. Fitzgibbon, "Continuismo in Central America and the Caribbean," *Inter-American Quarterly* (July, 1940), pp. 442–44.

14 This provision is not in the 1956 constitution. The drafters of that document were much more circumspect. The sanction of rebellion was dropped, and a proper, innocuous provision adopted that could hardly ruffle any feathers. It reads: "Reelection or any other means used to prolong the term of office of a President is punishable in accordance with the law, and the mandate which a person so doing claims to exercise shall be void ipso jure."

The right of rebellion has often been asserted in other Latin American nations besides Guatemala. Regarding the feasibility and possibility of establishing this principle in constitutional form, see Ricardo Gallardo, *Estudios de Derecho Constitucional Americano Comparado* (Madrid: Ediciones Cultura Hispanica, 1961), pp. 118–42.

vent the prohibition in the constitution against immediate reelection and still stay in the good grace of his people. Getulio Vargas of Brazil utilized a tried and true method; after serving as "provisional president" from 1930 to 1934, he convoked a constitutional convention that rewrote the nation's fundamental law, also obligingly elected him as the first "constitutional president" to serve under its provisions.

In El Salvador, Maximiliano Hernández Martínez executed this effective maneuver twice, convoking constituent assemblies which elected him to a new term in 1939 and again in 1944. Bolivia's constitution of 1961 repealed the earlier provision forbidding a president to succeed himself, thereby permitting President Paz Estenssoro to be reelected in 1964.

A novel means of finagling to continue in office was contrived in 1961 by President François Duvalier of Haiti. In the election for members of Congress which occurred midway during the presidential term, Duvalier had his name printed at the top of the ballot giving the names of the candidates, then announced after the election that he had been reelected president for a new term without opposition.

MEANS OF SELECTION

During the nineteenth century, the presidents of most of the republics were chosen by one of several means of indirect election, namely, by national congresses, by electoral congresses, or by state or provincial assemblies. Indirect election by these means continued in some nations until several decades ago. Among the last to provide for direct popular election were Chile, Cuba, and Peru, which discarded their old method of electoral colleges, and Haiti, which changed from election by the national congress.

At present, Argentina is the only one of the nations whose president is indirectly elected. According to the 1853 constitution, citizens do not cast their votes directly for the president but for presidential electors who cast the deciding votes. Each of the 16 provinces is entitled to twice as many electors as the total number of its representatives in both houses of Congress. The federal capital is also represented on the same basis. After their election, the electors meet at a specified time in their respective provincial capitals and in Buenos Aires and cast their ballots for the president—a system of indirect election that closely resembles the election of the president in the United States.

TRANSFER OF THE OFFICE

After a presidential election has been held, the national congress in accordance with most of the constitutions examines the results and declares elected the candidate who has received the specified majority.

Some of the more recent constitutions assign this function to special electoral courts which are regarded as less susceptible to political pressures.

In the event that no candidate receives a legal majority of the votes cast, the usual procedure is for the congress to choose between the several highest candidates. Sometimes the full congress is designated by the constitution to make this choice; sometimes it is the lower house alone, as in the United States. The vote cast by the congress or by the chamber of deputies sometimes results in a tie, in which event there are some unique methods for resolving it. In Costa Rica, the older candidate is declared to be the winner, while in Ecuador the choice is made by lot.

Having been declared by the congress or the special electoral court to be duly elected, the winning candidate takes his oath of office, swearing to uphold the constitution and to discharge faithfully his duties as president. In most of the countries the oath of office is usually taken before the full congress. Some nations specify, however, that it shall be taken before the supreme court, the council of state, or the chamber of deputies. Having taken the oath before one of these bodies, the president is now vested with the great powers of his office.

POWERS OF THE PRESIDENT

The powers which the president should have are as controversial today as they were a century ago. In Argentina Alberdi at that time urged the constitutional convention to endow the executive with very great power. Within recent decades, however, a fellow Argentine, Calderón, is convinced that such a concentration of power is "anachronistic and anti-republican," contrary to the development of a democratic nation.[15] The threat of "democratic caesarism" has prompted Peru to adopt a semiparliamentary system of government[16] and other nations to try other restrictive measures. But regardless of the system or the measures, the power of the executive in most of the nations is great—far greater than in the United States, as the following analysis of his specific powers will show.

Armed Forces

The constitutions vest in the president quite extensive military powers. In every one of the republics, he is specifically designated as commander in chief of the armed forces, in which capacity he is charged with the

---

[15] J. A. González Calderón, *Derecho constitucional* (1931), p. 286.

[16] "The mistake that the partisans of 'democratic caesarism' make is to seek to perpetuate what has been only a historical accident. Our Latin American nations by tradition, environment, and circumstances require a president who is strong and resolute. But this primacy and effectiveness of presidential authority should not degenerate into tyranny, dictatorship, and personalist *caudillismo* or in the absorption by the executive of the other powers of state." (José Pareja Paz-Soldan, *Derecho Constitucional Peruano* [Tercera Edición; Lima, Perú: Ediciones del Sol, 1963], p. 192.)

responsibility for preserving internal order and defending the nation against external aggression. To these ends, he may decree partial or total mobilization to cope with a serious internal or external threat. As a rule, he may declare war only after having been authorized to do so by congress, but if aggression from the outside occurs and congress is not in session, he can declare war on his own authority. In the normal exercise of his military powers, he appoints the officers of the armed forces. Legislative approval is ordinarily necessary in the case of the highest officers, except for appointment on the field of battle. The president may also be authorized to determine the size of the armed forces, as in Venezuela, also their organization and distribution to cope with a particular situation.

The president is usually authorized to take personal command of troops if he believes it advisable. However, he has seldom done so, even if a former officer, because of the pressure of other responsibilities and duties. In Peru, he is specifically forbidden to take personal command without the permission of congress; and if he does assume command, he has only the powers of a commander in chief, subject to the military and other laws of the republic. In Chile, if the president decides to don a uniform, the appropriate minister in the legal order of succession substitutes for him with his regular duties under the title of vice-president.

On several occasions presidents have found it advisable to exercise their constitutional power of taking personal command of the armed forces. Presidents Mitre and Sarmiento of Argentina both did this in the nineteenth century. And more recently, in the turmoil following the Mexican revolution, the presidents of Mexico have several times assumed their constitutional prerogative of exercising direct command, the last time being in the spring of 1938 when President Lázaro Cárdenas took to the field to crush an uprising led by General Cedillo.

The extent to which provisions in the constitutions actually determine a president's power over the armed forces varies greatly among the 20 republics. In those nations which are more advanced politically and where the armed forces are nonpolitical, the president exercises his constitutional prerogatives, and the armed forces are subject to civilian control.[17] But in less advanced countries, where the armed forces dominate politics, the president is often the mere tool of the military powers that be.

Sometimes the rivalry between the civilian president and the military strong man in the nation is undisguised. In Nicaragua, President Luis Somoza apparently wanted to comply with at least the form of democratic procedure by arranging for the election of an "independent" who could be depended on not to endanger the vast Somoza fortune; however, his brother Anastasio, who commanded the National Guard, felt strongly that this course would be disastrous and that the strong-man tradition should be continued to protect the family's interests. President Luis won

---

[17] See Chapter 7.

out; on May 2, 1963, René Schick was sworn in as president for a four-year term.

In Honduras, the rivalry between civilian and military authorities has been especially bitter as a result of Article 318 of the nation's 1957 constitution. It states: "The Armed Forces shall be under the direct command of the Chief of the Armed Forces; through him the President of the Republic will exercise his constitutional function respecting this institution. Merely administrative functions shall be entrusted to the Secretary of State for Defense." The effect of this provision has been to create a duality of authority, making the armed forces autonomous and their chief virtually independent of the president, who controls the Civil Guard. As a result, the president and the chief of the armed forces vie with each other for supremacy, and the jealous rivalry between the armed forces and the Civil Guard have resulted in several fatal clashes.[18]

Administration

In each of the republics the president is also responsible for seeing that the laws are faithfully executed and that the multifarious functions of government, such as delivering the mail or educating the youth, are properly carried out. In discharging this responsibility, the president is the apex and final authority of the national administative machinery that, day in and day out, conducts a great variety of activities and performs countless services for the citizenry.

As head of the national administrative setup, the president usually has a wide measure of authority that would indeed be the envy of the president of the United States. In Mexico, for example, the president has a much wider leeway. Although executive departments are created by law, their number and organization are purposefully left quite elastic to suit the desires of each president. But as in the United States, the coordination and supervision of the many independent and semi-independent agencies has been a frustrating problem.[19]

In Venezuela, the president is given even greater leeway than in Mexico. When a serious emergency arises and congress is not in session, he can create new public services or modify, even abolish, those already in existence, with the authorization of the permanent committee of congress, known as the "Delegated Committee."[20]

Appointment and Removal

In exercising wide control over the many government departments and agencies, the president has virtually unlimited power to appoint adminis-

---

[18] *Hispanic American Report*, Vol. XIV, No. 2 (April, 1961), p. 103, and Vol. XVI, No. 9 (November, 1963), p. 856.

[19] Robert E. Scott, *Mexican Government in Transition* (Urbana, Ill.: University of Illinois Press, 1959), pp. 281–83.

[20] Venezuela's 1961 constitution, Article 190, Section 11. For the composition and functions of the Delegated Committee, see Article 178.

trative officials and the large number of government employees. As the constitutions neatly express it, the president has the power to appoint "freely." With only lip service paid to civil service, the president and his trusted lieutenants also have almost complete control over the tenure of government employees as well as over their salaries, promotions, pensions, leaves of absence, and retirement.

In the appointment of high officials such as ambassadors and ministers, judges of the higher courts, and ranking officers of the armed services, constitutions usually require that the president's choice must be approved by the senate, the council of ministers, or some other body. This approval, however, is more theoretical than real, as Mexico's Senate was to find out when it took its power of approval seriously.

Soon after President Ávila Camacho was inaugurated, he submitted a number of nominees for the Supreme Court of Justice to the Senate for approval. To the great surprise of the capital, apparently of the President too, the Senate, meeting in closed session, turned down three of the President's choices, terming them "reactionaries." (Although politically naïve, the Senate was on sound constitutional ground, for Article 89, section 18 of the Constitution specifically gives it the authority to pass on the president's appointments to the Supreme Court of Justice.) When the President was informed by a committee of senators of the body's action, he apparently "blew a gasket," for the members of the committee hurried back to the chamber to set things right. The next day the Senate backtracked and capitulated, ratifying the entire list. Explained the president of the Senate, earlier press reports on the secret session were erroneous; the Senate had never refused to approve the nominees. It had merely delayed taking action until more information could be gathered about them.[21]

Legislative

Another very important power of the president relates to his participation in the legislative process. One of his many duties in this realm is to preside at the opening of each annual session, when he gives a "state of the nation" address similar to the one our president gives, and advises congress —the nation too indirectly—of significant national conditions and problems, and, especially, his recommendations for dealing with them.

The president also has considerable control over the sessions of congress. Since the constitutions usually specify that he must be present at the opening session, his absence on occasion has delayed congress from officially convening and beginning its legislative duties. This has caused some speculation as to whether by boycotting a session entirely, a president might thereby prevent congress from meeting at all during its constitutionally authorized session. Whether this is so or not, the president unquestionably has other controls over sessions of the legislative body. He is authorized in most of the nations to prorogue the regular session and also

---

[21] For this episode, see Scott, *op. cit.*, pp. 264–65.

to call congress back into extraordinary session if he deems that a matter of great importance requires it.

Besides exercising these powers, the executive has a very imposing role in lawmaking. He is authorized by the constitution to present bills to the congress, and most of the laws which are enacted are measures which he has proposed. In Honduras, during the period from 1896 to 1941, 93 per-cent of the bills drafted by the executive branch were approved by con-gress. In 12 different years, the body approved without change every bill that was submitted by the executive branch. "Certainly during the greater part of the history of Honduras," concludes William S. Stokes, "the Con-gress has acted as a rubber stamp for the legislative proposals of the executive."[22]

Mexico is another of the many nations in Latin America where the president runs the show. There, as in Honduras, he enjoys almost absolute control of the congress. With his party being the only one represented in the Senate and overwhelmingly controlling the Chamber of Deputies, his measures presented to the congress have a monopoly on the green light. Bills initiated by individuals are virtually unknown. Thus, in the three-year term of the forty-first Congress, some 138 bills were passed by both houses and enacted into law. Of these, only seven were initiated by the Congress itself, mainly from the Chamber of Deputies' Comisión de Estudios Legis-lativos.[23]

Controlling the congress lock, stock, and barrel as he does, the president of most countries finds that his power of the veto is a very superfluous weapon. Why should he want to veto a bill that was written in the first place by one of his own ministers, and passed without the slightest altera-tion by congress? Enjoying a legislative field day as he does, it is no wonder that since the Revolution, presidents of Mexico have cast only two vetoes and both of these on minor technical questions.[24]

But in a few of the nations which are proud of a long tradition of democratic government, the president does not enjoy such easy sailing. There, limited to exercising only the powers which he is granted by the constitution and having to deal with a congress which is also zealous in discharging its responsibilities, the president sometimes finds that the veto is a very useful weapon. Thus in Chile, President Alessandri, in his basic disagreements with congress regarding social security for urban workers and other measures which he regarded as inflationary, cast veto after veto to prevent these measures from becoming law—at least 17 vetoes in the period of a few weeks.[25]

As a rule, however, vetoes by the president are rare in Latin America, and still rarer is the item veto. The constitution of Argentina does not

---

[22] Stokes, *op. cit.*, p. 287.
[23] Scott, *op. cit.*, pp. 263–64.
[24] *Ibid.*, p. 263.
[25] *Hispanic American Report*, Vol. XVI, No. 10 (December, 1963), p. 1000.

even refer to the power to veto items in a bill, so presumably the president does not possess it. Several presidents, however, have in fact vetoed certain items in budget bills, then put the remainder into effect. The item veto was exercised by Irigoyen in 1918, by Justo in 1932, and by Ortiz in 1939. Irigoyen even went so far as to strike out objectionable clauses from laws imposing taxes and regulating the exportation of sugar, then promulgated the laws in this partially vetoed form. Strong protests were made in the public press and also in congress, but the legislation stood as promulgated.[26]

Decree

Another very important power of the president is his authority to issue decrees. In democratic states today, it is accepted practice for laws to be formulated in rather general terms, leaving to the executive considerable discretion for implementing them by administrative regulations. In this way laws can be interpreted and applied to all kinds of situations and problems, thereby carrying out their basic intent. But in Latin America, this universally exercised practice of filling in the details of legislation to make it applicable to the innumerable problems of everyday living has been so grossly perverted as to translate it into a usurpation of the powers belonging to congress. Exercising this unbridled, limitless power, the presidents in most of the nations have acted as a supraconstitutional legislative authority, whose far-reaching decrees were as authoritative as those which in earlier times came from Mount Olympus.

While recognizing that the president and the executive branch of government must have the power to issue supplementary regulations, the constitution makers have done their best to direct the purposes and intended boundaries of decrees. The Argentine constitution, after giving the president the power to issue decrees, states that he should be "careful not to modify their spirit with exceptions in the regulations." The Nicaraguan constitution vests in the executive the power to issue regulations to implement the laws, but "without transgressing or emasculating them."

But these and many other constitutional restrictions intended to limit the decree power of the executive have been of little or no avail. Mexico's experience after 1917 shows how far the power of the president can be exercised to supplant the constitutional authority of the congress. Acting under the authority of Article 29 of the constitution of 1917, which provides for the suspension of constitutional guarantees "in case of invasion, of serious disturbance of the public peace, or any other emergency that may place the people in great danger or conflict," the president has stretched the power of issuing decrees to cover any matter of legislation that he chose, regardless of how basic and comprehensive it was. Thus, from 1920 to 1938, most of the important legislation was in the form of

---

[26] Austin F. Macdonald, *Government of the Argentine Republic* (New York: Thomas Y. Crowell Co., 1942), p. 202.

decrees issued by the president under the justification of a supposed state of grave emergency, when in fact there was no emergency at all. But when congress was requested by the president to delegate to him the power to issue decrees, it willingly did so. Among the many fundamental and far-reaching laws enacted during this period solely on the authority of the president were the following: regulations governing the Church; the Commercial Code; Federal Penal Code and Code of Penal Procedure; Agrarian Code; Law of the Nationalization of Property; General Insurance Law; and General Law on Cooperative Societies.

This unwarranted exercise by the president of powers granted to congress by the constitution lasted until 1938 when a constitutional amendment was adopted which ended such blanket decrees unless a grave national emergency existed.[27]

Honduras, like Mexico, has felt the full impact of the president's authority to issue decrees. There too, the president's control over congress was so strong and the body was so subservient that it virtually surrendered its prerogative of lawmaking to the executive. In 1880 and 1889, he congress gave the president carte blanche authority to enact legislation in the important fields of war and police activities, finance, public instruction, court organization, and *fomento*. And in 1899, having again conferred blanket legislative powers on the president, the congress approved without discussion the penal, mining, and commercial codes which he had formulated and submitted for formal adoption.[28]

Finance

The president also has very broad powers over the nation's finance and economy. Under the constitution he is required to propose to the congress a budget for each fiscal year, giving an estimate of the revenues to be received and the expenditures to be made. He is also required to collect the public revenue which he spends through his ministers that head the various departments. In a brave attempt to give the congress some control over the president's tremendous financial power, the constitution usually specifies that he must render an annual accounting of the receipts and expenditures for the preceding year. But this requirement is virtually meaningless, because neither the congress nor any other public body makes an independent audit of public receipts and expenditures, and what information the president supplies can hardly be relied upon.

Even in some of the most democratic countries of Latin America, the president is sometimes delegated by the congress an extremely wide measure of discretion and authority in public finance and related fields. In 1959, the congress of Chile gave its able, industrialist president, Jorge

---

[27] For the evolution and exercise of extraordinary decree powers in Mexico, see Stephen S. Goodspeed, "The Development and Use of *Facultades Extraordinarias in Mexico*," *Southwestern Social Science Quarterly*, Vol. 34, No. 3 (December, 1953), pp. 17–33.

[28] Stokes, *op. cit.*, p. 286.

Alessandri, virtually absolute control over the nation's economy for one year. Under this unusual grant of power, he was authorized to establish a new monetary system, reorganize the tax structure, and modify the nation's system of banking. He was also empowered to reorganize public utilities, consolidate government or semigovernment agencies, control monopolies and practices that restrict free trade, and fire civil servants. These drastic powers, most unusual for one of the democratic nations of Latin America, were granted because of the nation's acute economic problems, particularly the severe budgetary deficit that it incurred in 1959.[29]

Foreign Relations

Still another area in which the president has broad and significant powers is foreign relations. His is the primary responsibility for determining the nation's policies toward other nations, as well as setting the prevailing tone of friendliness and cooperation or possibly bellicosity and antagonism. A president who is amicably inclined and interested in the peaceable development of his country may contribute greatly to its progress. Just such a president was Pedro II of Brazil. With its huge territory, the "colossus of the south," as Brazil is sometimes called, has common borders with all but two of the nations of South America. This propinquity has involved the nation in many boundary and other disputes with its neighbors. But Pedro I and II, as well as the presidents since Brazil became a republic, followed the course of settling these disputes peacefully by arbitration or friendly negotiation. This wise course is largely responsible for the fact that only six major wars have occurred in Latin America; Brazil participated in only three of them.

A president of a very different stripe was Francisco Solano López of Paraguay, who recklessly plunged his nation into a five-year war with Argentina, Brazil, and Uruguay, the most savage and sanguinary war in the whole history of Latin America. The internecine struggle which Paraguay lost was disastrous for the nation. Its economy was wrecked, its population was mowed down from an estimated 525,000 in 1865 to 221,079 in 1871, of whom only 28,746 were men.[30]

In recent years, a matter of particular concern to the United States has been the attitudes and policies of Latin American presidents in the cold war. Some of the presidents, such as José Figueres of Costa Rica and Rómulo Betancourt of Venezuela, have been staunch friends and supporters of the free world ideals and programs. Some of the other presidents, however, such as João Goulart of Brazil, have shown such leftist leanings as to greatly disturb the United States, their own nations, and their immediate neighbors as well. Of course the greatest disturbing leftist

---

[29] *New York Times*, March 23, 1959, p. 10, col. 2.

[30] Harris Gaylord Warren, *Paraguay: An Informal History* (Norman, Okla.: University of Oklahoma Press, 1949), p. 243.

influence in the hemisphere has been a certain bearded prime minister who has openly converted his island nation into a Communist state.

The president, besides being the final voice in determining foreign policy and directing foreign relations, has other related responsibilities. Among these, he concludes and signs treaties of peace, alliance, mutual assistance, neutrality, trade and navigation, and boundaries. In addition, he appoints ambassadors and ministers who represent his country in other nations and receives the envoys which these nations send to him.

Judicial

In the judicial realm, too, the president has extensive authority. In accordance with the constitution, he is required to oversee the general administration of justice in the nation to make sure that it is impartial and fair to all citizens. As the chief executive charged with enforcing the law, he is also required to see that judicial decisions are enforced. He checks too on the operation of the courts to make sure that the official conduct of judges comports with the national dignity and with their official responsibilities.

Among his important judicial powers, the president may also grant pardons, either full or conditional, as well as commute sentences. Often on a national holiday or just before going out of office, he grants pardons freely to friends and political followers. In an effort to prevent abuse of the pardon power, constitutions often limit it in various ways, such as by making persons convicted of electoral frauds or crimes ineligible for pardon until they have served at least a third of their sentence.

A presidential judicial power which one occasionally reads about in the newspapers is amnesty, a blanket pardon extended to large groups, usually political offenders. With its frequent exercise, the amnesty is as thoroughly Latin American as *machismo*, *chicha*, or the siesta. For in most of the nations, the regime in power has incarcerated a large number of political prisoners who may have been in jail for years and have committed such a serious offense as overtly trying to overthrow the government or such a trivial one as speaking disparagingly of the president. Every so often, the president proclaims an amnesty for certain or all political offenders, possibly motivated by the goodness of his heart, or, more than likely, by the assurance of his established power or by a desire to favorably impress foreign opinion.

Intervention

Another power which the president exercises in those states having a federal form of government is intervention in the states or provinces. As envisaged by constitution makers, intervention is a drastic exercise of federal authority, to be used only for the most cogent reasons and in conformity with the requirements laid down in the constitutions. In Argentina, the national government may intervene in a province in order to repel a foreign invasion, guarantee a republican form of government, support provincial authorities if they request federal assistance, or reestablish them if they have been overthrown. In Brazil, besides these justifications, the federal government may also intervene to assure the execution of a judicial order or decision, reorganize the finances of a state under certain conditions, prohibit the immediate reelection of governors and prefects, and assure the autonomy of municipalities.

Practice varies somewhat between the several federal republics as to who will make the decision regarding intervention. In Brazil, the president can intervene on his own discretion or, under certain circumstances, with the concurrence of the federal supreme court. In Argentina, however, it is a moot constitutional question as to which branch of government has the authority to make the decision. On many occasions the congress has assumed this responsibility when it was a powerful force in the affairs of the republic, but the president has made the decision much more often. Of the 129 interventions that occurred between 1860 and 1942, 83 of them were made by presidential decree, the other 46 by law.[31]

Intervention by the national government in the states and provinces has been intended by constitution framers as a strong weapon to be used discreetly and sparingly; it was designed to preserve the authority and dignity of the national government and the autonomy of the states or provinces. In practice, however, it has deviated far from its intended purpose; it has degenerated into a political bludgeon which the president uses at will to keep the states or provinces politically in line. It is not "an occasional practice—a last resort used only for the purpose of averting anarchy," wrote Austin F. Macdonald. "Far from it. In the Argentine constitutional system it has long been accepted as part of the established routine. Sometimes it is justified by extreme circumstances; more commonly it arises from trifles that can scarcely be considered matters of federal concern. But always the result is the same: the federal government assumes control of provincial affairs."[32]

The practice of frequent and widespread intervention in Argentina began with the administration of Hipólito Irigoyen, the leader of the Radical Party who became president in 1916. Thanks to the Sáenz Peña electoral law of 1912, which in effect gave the nation truly universal suffrage, Irigoyen was the first freely elected president in the history of the nation. Taking over the presidential office, Irigoyen began a systematic campaign of interfering in the affairs of the provinces, replacing the con-

---

[31] Macdonald, *op. cit.*, p. 180.
For an analysis of interventions 1860–1930 by administrations, provinces, and duration, see Rosendo A. Gómez, "Intervention in Argentina, 1860–1930," *Inter-American Economic Affairs*, Vol. 1, No. 3 (December, 1947), pp. 55–73.

[32] *Ibid.*, p. 170. Many Argentines have felt strongly that interventions were undermining the federal system. Estrada, however, defended them as a legitimate use of power to maintain order in a society in a state of turbulence. (José M. Estrada, *Curso de derecho constitucional* [2d ed.; Buenos Aires, 1927], Vol. III, pp. 152–53.)

servative governors, legislators, and other officials with federal officials who could be trusted to enforce the liberal policies of his regime. During his term of office, the president intervened 20 times in the provinces. While intervention had been used in previous administrations for political ends, it had never been used on such an extensive scale.

Irigoyen's political opponents showed that they could play the same political game. Back in office in 1930 under José Uriburu, one of the first things they did was to intervene in 12 of the 14 provinces and "toss the rascals out." The two provinces which were spared were already controlled by the conservatives.[33]

In Brazil too, the power of the central government to intervene in the states has been very much twisted from its original constitutional intent. After Getulio Vargas seized power in 1930, he dismissed all governors of the states except Benedeto de Valladares, governor of Minas Gerais, an able and respected administrator who was regarded as loyal. Just as Irigoyen had done in Argentina, Vargas was to set the pattern in Brazil for wholesale intervention in the states for purely political purposes.

The right of intervention [of the Vargas regime], though defined concretely in line with eventual state deficiences and failures, is so wide as to place the states fully at the mercy of the federal government, that is, of the president. . . . As a matter of fact, although the appearances are carefully preserved, the states are reduced to the status of territorial subdivisions under full central control.[34]

In Mexico too, the national government has frequently exercised its power of intervention in the states by the Senate's declaring that the constitutional powers of a state have "disappeared," warranting the appointment of a provisional governor. Senatorial declarations of disappearance of state powers under Article 76 of the constitution were numerous in the chaos of the early years of the revolution but have been infrequent in recent years.[35] When resorted to, however, intervention has been abusively used for political purposes, some observers are strongly convinced.[36]

State of Siege

Easily one of the most important powers of the president is his authority to proclaim an *estado de sitio*, or state of siege, also known as the suspension of constitutional guarantees. This emergency power is authorized by the constitutions to be used if the nation is threatened by foreign invasion or serious internal disturbances. The state of siege is somewhat similar to what we know as martial law in the United States, the main difference being that under the former the civilian police and regular

---

[33] Macdonald, *op. cit.*, pp. 170–71.

[34] Karl Lowenstein, *Brazil Under Vargas* (New York: The Macmillan Company, 1942), p. 51.

[35] Felipe Tena Ramírez, *Derecho constitucional mexicano* (2d ed.; México, 1949), pp. 126–27.

[36] Scott, *op. cit.*, pp. 273–75.

organs of government continue to function, while under martial law civilian control is superseded by military.[37]

The constitutions of the republics invariably provide that the state of siege may be authorized only by the congress—a bold bid for control of this important emergency power. In practice, however, the president usually requests the congress for authority to exercise the power. If the body is not in session, he is empowered to take action on his own authority, or possibly with the concurrence of members of a permanent legislative commission, a sort of congressional watchdog which functions between sessions of congress. In either event, the president is required to call a special session of congress within a specified period of time, ranging from 2 to 60 days.

The emergency recognized by the state of siege vests extraordinary powers in the president and authorizes him to take drastic steps which affect most aspects of national life. He may for example increase the size of the standing army or call up additional reserves that may be needed, possibly putting into uniform many a college student who had hoped to complete his education before having to serve his stint of compulsory military service. The president may also divert national taxes and income to military purposes and even make forced loans if the government critically needs the money. Another measure that affects all citizens is the suspension of certain private rights guaranteed by the constitution, especially those of freedom of speech and the press, peaceable assembly, privacy of one's home and correspondence, and freedom to move about in the country. In some nations, such as the Dominican Republic, virtually all constitutional guarantees are suspended for the duration of the emergency.

The presidents of some nations resort to the state of siege on the least provocation, when, for instance, there is a possibility of political opponents winning in a forthcoming election; other nations, however, use the emergency power quite sparingly. In the nations that are especially politically unstable or that have long been accustomed to the rule of dictators, a state of siege is practically the normal way of life. In Haiti and the Dominican Republic, the nations of Central America, and Paraguay, the citizens have long been inured to the president's cracking the whip through the medium of the *estado de sitio*.

Even in some of the most democratic and stable nations the state of siege may have a long duration. Argentina lived under four and a half years of emergency rule prior to Perón's election on February 24, 1946, when the state of siege was lifted for 48 hours to permit the holding of the election. With this brief respite over, Argentina was to endure emergency rule during much of Perón's long dictatorship. Likewise, in Colombia,

---

[37] While Argentina, like the other nations, does not recognize martial law, it does recognize a state of prevention and alarm, as well as a state of siege. (Pablo A. Ramella, *Derecho Constitucional* [Buenos Aires, 1960], pp. 417–20.)

when the nation was beset by civil war which took a toll of 200,000 lives during the ten years 1948–58, the nation was under a state of siege most of the time.

Sometimes one of the most politically stable nations resorts to this emergency power for dealing with what is commonly regarded as a routine problem of local authorities in maintaining law and order. Taking advantage of the emergency power, Chile declared a state of siege in 1946 to cope with a strike which occurred in the nitrate mines and again in 1947 when a general strike occurred in the coal mines. In addition to being used on other occasions to deal with violence in labor disputes, the state of siege was also used in 1948 to break up a strike led by university students protesting increases in bus fares.

Fully cognizant of possible abuse of the suspension of constitutional guarantees, the constitutions and laws have tried to hold it within bounds by many restrictions. As the Bolivian constitution tersely states in Article 38, the authorization of emergency powers for the president is not intended to "grant the Executive extraordinary powers, the total of the public power, or accord him supremacy by which the life, honor, and property of Bolivians are placed at the mercy of the government or of any person." Other constitutions and national laws likewise aim to restrict the president's use of emergency powers. Thus he is usually limited as to the time he may maintain a state of siege, and in order to extend it he is required to obtain the approval of congress. Moreover, he is usually required to make a detailed report to the congress, explaining specifically what the dangers were that justified the emergency measures and describing the steps taken by the administration for coping with the emergency. If congress is not satisfied with the president's explanation, it can call him to account for abusing his authority.

Costa Rica has done a particularly effective job in guarding against possible abuses of the state of siege. The constitution makes it clear that the suspension is a legislative act and can occur only with the approval of two-thirds of the legislative assembly. Moreover, the suspension is definitely limited in scope and can affect only certain specified provisions of the constitution. Moreover, the suspension can continue for only 30 days, thus precluding its dragging on for months or even years, as is often the case in other nations. Finally, if the assembly is not in session when the emergency arises, the president may order the suspension of constitutional guarantees, but his act serves automatically to convene the assembly within 48 hours to approve or disapprove of his action.[38]

THE CABINET

Next in importance to the president in the national administration are his ministers, who act as his chief advisers and head and supervise the

---

[38] Constitution of 1871 (in effect in 1965 and the second oldest in Latin America), Article 82, Clause 7, and Article 109, Clause 3.

various administrative departments of the government. Collectively they constitute the cabinet, although the constitutions of Latin America, as in the United States, do not recognize its existence.

The number of ministers varies considerably among the 20 republics, ranging from 8 or 9 in the smallest countries to 25 or so in the largest. Certain ministries are regarded as a "must" in every one of the countries—those of war or defense, *gobernación* ("government" or interior), *hacienda* (treasury), agriculture or economy, education, public health and social welfare, labor and social security, and foreign affairs.

In selecting his ministers, the president takes into account many weighty considerations,[39] for the dependability and competence of his ministers may well determine the success of his administration. The main criterion he applies is trustworthiness. His ministers will be his trusted confidants and advisers—his programs, his accomplishments, even possibly his very life, will depend on their loyalty and faithful performance of duty.

A second important consideration in the selection of a cabinet member is his political affiliation and participation in the party rough-and-tumble in the nation. Sometimes the president selects as ministers only members of his own political party, especially when it represents a large majority of voters and elects heavy majorities in the congress. Thus in Mexico, where the *Partido Revolucionario Institucional,* popularly known as PRI, represents the overwhelming majority of voters, any president would be regarded as being loco if he included in his cabinet a member of one of the small opposition parties. But in other nations, such as Chile or Peru, where the president may have to look to the opposition for the additional support he needs, it is common for his cabinet to include members of these parties.

Certain ministerial posts are regarded as political; they are plums given to the most trusted, most influential, and most likely to be tapped by the president to succeed himself. Such a political post is that of secretary of *gobernación,* who is often second only to the president in power and influence. As the number-two man in government, he exercises the sensitive functions of administration of elections, supervision of provincial and local government, and, especially, control of the national police. The minister of war or defense is also regarded as a political member. Frequently he is a ranking officer in the armed forces who has doffed his uniform but not his rank, perquisites, affiliations, and loyalty. Often he is simply a militarist in civilian garb. When he controls the loyalty of the armed forces and manifests political aspirations, the president had better treat him gingerly, for he is a power to be reckoned with.

A third criterion which the president follows in sizing up a prospective minister is his qualification for handling the post. Some of the ministries require a highly professional or technical background and experience to

---

[39] These considerations are given in Blanksten, *op. cit.,* pp. 98–99, and Martin Needler, *Latin American Politics in Perspective* (Princeton, N.J.: D. Van Nostrand Co., Inc., 1963), pp. 147–49.

qualify the individual for effectively discharging his duties. Such ministries are those of agriculture, mining, education, justice, and foreign affairs. The minister of foreign affairs is seldom a practicing politician and is not selected for the high post on the basis of party considerations. Rather, he is selected because he is a distinguished figure in his country—a respected jurist, scholar, or man of letters. Recognition abroad of his scholarly achievement is quite an asset too. However, he is seldom regarded as presidential timber. Indeed, the very fact of his having lived abroad and acquired cosmopolitan tastes and thinking is apt to make him suspect by many of his fellow countrymen.

Sometimes, in selecting a cabinet, a president tosses political considerations to the winds and selects the men who in his honest opinion are most qualified for the important responsibilities. President Jorge Alessandri of Chile was one who chose his cabinet on the basis of ability rather than political considerations. It was a blue ribbon cabinet, and even Alessandri's strongest critics admitted that it was the most able and the most honest that Chile had ever had.

The president frequently makes changes in his cabinet; he can remove any minister at will, and he often does. Sometimes he relieves a single minister of his duties, usually without the courteous amenities that the President of the United States observes in easing out a member of his administration. Indeed, the president in Latin America does not hesitate to throw out his whole cabinet unceremoniously, without apology or compunction. On April 22, 1957, President Carlos Ibáñez of Chile requested his whole cabinet to resign because in his absence from the capital the minister of interior had caused four lawyers representing *Horizonte*, a communist newspaper, to be arrested and exiled to distant provinces.

Why are there so many changes in the cabinet, one may wonder, in view of the president's being so careful in selecting his trusted lieutenants? For one thing, he regards them as expendable. When some political fiasco or snafu occurs which often he himself is directly responsible for, he has to do something to satisfy the cry for blood by his political opponents. To shunt any blame from himself and preserve his *dignidad* unsullied before the nation, he is quite willing to regard his ministers as the goats of the matter and throw them to the wolves.

There is another explanation for the frequent changes in the cabinet, either individual or collective. They have a definite psychological impact on the citizenry, showing them who is unquestionably the boss, thus reinforcing and maintaining the strong centralized power of the executive.

According to most of the constitutions of Latin American republics, the president cannot take any official action whatever without the approval and signature of the appropriate minister. However, this requirement of ministerial responsibility is entirely theoretical and of no practical significance. For the strong president who dominates the government in most of the nations does not need the approval of any subordinate before exercising any of his executive powers. He alone makes the decision as to a policy to be adopted or course of action to be followed. Cabinet members are expected to give their opinions, even possibly to dissuade him if they believe he is making a mistake, but their disagreement with him cannot force him to change his mind. He knows that he is the only one whom the nation holds responsible for discharging the important duties of his office. With this in mind, the president does not take very seriously the constitutional requirement that his ministers must approve and countersign every one of his official acts, especially since he alone selects his ministers and can dismiss them any time he chooses to do so. If conceivably a minister refused to sign one of his official documents, he would be relieved of his duties pronto and another minister who would sign would be appointed.

The requirement in the constitution of ministerial responsibility is "either a dead letter or a redundancy," wrote Austin F. Macdonald, "a dead letter, if it means that the ministers are responsible to Congress or the people, for they are not; or a redundancy, if it indicates that they are responsible to the president, for such a responsibility is already assured through the chief executive's absolute power of appointment and removal."[40]

METHODS OF EXERCISING PRESIDENTIAL CONTROL[41]

In running the government and putting his program into effect, the president resorts to a varied assortment of weapons and methods.

His power over the patronage would be the envy of Tammany Hall. For he has the final word, directly or indirectly, in the selection of the vast number of government officials and employees ranging from the minister of *gobernación* to dogcatcher and garbage collector. In those countries which have unitary systems of government, this is no constitutional problem, since the president by constitutional authorization controls the entire machinery of government, even in the most remote localities of the nation. In those countries which have a federal form of government, his power of appointment is potent, too, for the provincial or state governors are either his trusted friends or they are removed forthwith. Consequently, his influence in appointments is felt by public employees all down the line, even to the outer edges of government.

A judicious exercise of the principle of checks and balances is another technique which presidents apply instinctively. They may not understand all of its theoretical nuances, but they thoroughly appreciate its practical application. Thus, where the army has proved to be a serious threat, the

---

[40] Macdonald, *op. cit.*, p. 196.

[41] For a provocative treatment of this subject, see William W. Pierson and Federico G. Gil, *Governments of Latin America* (New York: McGraw-Hill Book Co., Inc., 1957), pp. 227–31.

president has sometimes counterbalanced or neutralized its power by strengthening the capability of the national police. And where this does not suffice, the president may even organize and arm a peasant and worker militia that his government can rely upon.

Influencing and controlling the news insofar as he can is another method which every president utilizes. The odds are heavily in his favor. Almost every government has its own official newspaper or papers which serve as the official mouthpiece and enjoy the advantage of a "hot line" directly to the presidential office. Any other newspaper which is cooperative and follows the government line is also given favored treatment. Papers or radio stations which oppose him, however, get an official cold shoulder or worse.

There are many other means by which the president asserts control over the government and the nation, such as designating the members of a constituent assembly to draw up a new constitution, influencing the selection of members of congress, creating an official political party, and controlling the dreaded secret police. On occasion, the president has found that the most effective method of dealing with congress is the straightforward, direct approach. In Argentina in 1908, after President Alcorta had had many strong disagreements with Congress, he finally ordered its members to adjourn and go home. When they balked, he used federal troops to enforce his order.

PRESIDENTIAL RESPONSIBILITY

According to the constitutions, the president is responsible to the congress for any of his acts of omission or commission that violate either the constitution or the laws. These acts comprise a wide range of offenses. In Brazil they include any "attempt" against: the federal constitution and in particular against the existence of the Union; the free exercise of the legislative power, judicial power, and constitutional powers of the states; the exercise of social and political rights; the internal security of the country; probity in the administration; the safekeeping and legal use of public funds; and the enforcement of judicial decisions.

If the president is alleged to have violated the constitution or laws of his country, he may be impeached and tried by the congress to determine his innocence or guilt. According to the usual procedure, charges against him are preferred in the lower house, which appoints a committee to investigate the charges; after the committee makes its report, the house debates as to whether or not the charges are sufficiently substantial to warrant putting the president on trial. To recommend this, a two-thirds vote is necessary. If the impeachment charges are adopted, the upper house has no choice but to proceed with the trial, converting itself into a court presided over by the chief justice of the supreme court.

In those republics which have a unicameral congress, this body acts just as the lower house of a bicameral congress, and the president is then tried before the supreme court. In Panama, however, the one-house national assembly not only prefers charges against the president but also conducts the trial.

Whichever procedure is followed for the trial, a two-thirds vote is necessary to convict the president of the charges. If convicted, he is removed from office, as well as disqualified from holding public office indefinitely or for a specified period. If he has also committed an indictable offense, after being removed from office he may be brought before the ordinary courts and tried as any other citizen of the republic.

Dominating the congress as the president does in most of the countries, his impeachment and conviction by that body have been very rare occurrences. In Cuba, President Miguel Mariano Gómez was impeached and removed from office in 1936 when Batista, controlling the government from behind the scenes, brought pressure to bear on the Congress. More recently, the acting president of Panama, José Ramón Guizado, holding office after the assassination on January 2, 1955, of President José Antonio Remón, was tried and convicted of complicity in the assassination of his predecessor. Guizado was removed from office by the national assembly and sentenced to six years' imprisonment.[42]

Regarding charges made against the president of crimes against the state, he is held accountable in some nations only during his term of office; in other nations, however, this accountability lasts for six, maybe twelve, months after he leaves office. Whatever period is specified, the president is required to remain within the country during this time.

A celebrated case in which a former president was tried for having committed offenses against the state during his term of office was that involving Rojas Pinilla, dictator-president of Colombia from 1953 until his overthrow in 1957. Following his overthrow, the government appointed a bipartisan national commission to investigate allegations of corruption and illegal acts on the part of Rojas and his officials. Acting upon the findings of the commission, the Chamber of Deputies voted 107 to 7 in favor of filing criminal charges. As a result, Rojas was tried by the Senate and found guilty of having acted "in violation of the national constitution" and of "abuse of power by improper conduct in the exercise of the office of president." Specifically, he was found guilty of ordering customs officials to admit duty-free the purebred cattle imported by a friend and of forcing banks to lend $7 million to friends, relatives, and himself without collateral. The vote in the Senate for conviction was overwhelming—62 to 4 on the first charge and 65 to 1 on the second, with several senators abstaining. Following conviction, the Senate deprived Rojas of his political rights, thereby barring him from voting, holding

---

[42] A detailed account of the drama of Guizado's impeachment and trial is given in John D. Martz, *Central America: The Crisis and the Challenge* (Chapel Hill, N.C.: University of North Carolina Press, 1959), pp. 293–304.

political office, or serving further in the Army. He was also deprived of his honors and titles, as well as his pension of $3,000 a month, given by the nation to ex-presidents.

The charges against Rojas were then supposed to go automatically to the Supreme Court, which would try him for "common crimes." But after Rojas had been detained under house arrest for nearly two years without any action being taken by the court, he was finally released on the payment of 5,000 pesos (about $750) bond, apparently closing the case.[43]

EXPOSURE TO THE PUBLIC—A RISK OF THE GAME

In Latin America, unless the president is a dictator, it is customary for him to appear freely in public without a bodyguard or other armed protection. He strolls down the boulevard, mingles with the people, and enjoys himself as any other citizen, without any special precautions for his safety—a practice quite different from that in the United States.

Sometimes the risk to his personal safety is especially great, as when a president on occasion has defied danger to perform a dramatic act of heroism. In Chile, when a group of *Nacistas*—Chilean Nazis—opened fire on the presidential palace for the purpose of storming it, mortally wounding a policeman on duty nearby, President Alessandri rushed out to aid the dying man, dragging him to shelter while bullets whizzed around him.[44] And in Bolivia, when an infuriated mob took out its wrath against *Time* magazine by storming the American Embassy and sacking the U.S. Information Office, President Hernán Siles took to the streets in an attempt to calm the mob, even crossing the heavy police lines guarding the embassy, and addressing the throng from the nearby headquarters of the MNR, urging it to obey the law and maintain order.[45]

Running as many risks as they do, it is inevitable that some of the presidents meet with violence. A number of them have been assassinated. In Mexico, during the turbulent early years of the revolution, two of the presidents were assassinated, Madero in 1913 and Carranza in 1920, also president-elect Álvaro Obregón in 1928. In Ecuador, two of the presidents were assassinated—Gabriel García Moreno in 1875 and Eloy Alfaro in 1911. Among other presidents who suffered a similar fate were José Balta in 1872 and Luis Sánchez Cerro in 1933, both of Peru, also Anastasio Somoza of Nicaragua and Carlos Castillo Armas of Guatemala, both in 1957, and most recently Rafael Leonidas Trujillo of the Dominican Republic in 1961. A president of Panama, José Remón, was murdered in

[43] The information regarding Rojas is from the *New York Times* files, May, 1957–October, 1960.

[44] Austin F. Macdonald, *Latin American Politics and Government* (New York: Thomas Y. Crowell Co., 1949), pp. 297–98.

[45] For a vivid account of the mob violence and Siles' role, see *New York Times*, March 3, 1959, p. 8, col. 3.

1955. The list of presidents who have met violent ends would be much longer if many a beleaguered president had not fled to a foreign embassy and been saved by the grant of political asylum.

But sometimes a president is not so fortunate when a bloodthirsty mob overturns his government. When this happened to President Gualberto Villarroel of Bolivia in 1946, the vengeful mob dragged him out of an upstairs closet in the presidential palace where he was hiding, beat him up, shot him, then threw him out of the window where those on the street below lynched him, stringing him up to a lamp post that stands in front of the building. President Vilbrun Guillaume Sam of Haiti was another president whose career was ended by violence with a vengeance when a mob even entered the French legation in 1915 to seize their quarry.

Breaking into the legation, they cornered the President in the bathroom where he had taken refuge, pulled him out, dragged him down the steps into the court-yard, and pulled him along the path leading to the locked gate. Throwing Sam's body over the gate, where it became impaled on the iron spikes, the mob dragged it to the ground and poured shot after shot into it.

Even this did not satisfy the passions of the mob. Machetes appeared out of nowhere and Sam's arms, legs, and head were hacked off, impaled on spikes and paraded through the streets, followed by his bloody torso dragged at the end of a rope. . . .[46]

SUCCESSION TO THE PRESIDENTIAL OFFICE WHEN VACANT

We in the United States attach much importance to the office of vice-president. As the number-two man in government, who has twice within the last two decades stepped into the breach to take over for a president who had fallen, he represents a shared political experience, continuity of policy, and orderly succession to the high office in time of national crisis.

In Latin America too, the vice-president performs some useful functions. He helps to balance the ticket, as important in Latin America as in the United States, thereby contributing to party and national unity. Thus in Bolivia, during the presidency of Victor Paz Estenssoro from 1952–56 and 1960–64, the vice-president during much of this time was Juan Lechín. President Paz is a middle of the roader whose policies and methods have decidedly moderated the social revolution which Bolivia has been undergoing since 1952. But Lechín is a far leftist, an admitted Communist who would have used far more drastic methods and policies to push the nation's social revolution more rapidly ahead. His selection as vice-president was to recognize the influential left-wing miners and other labor groups and to get their needed cooperation and support.

In Ecuador, the vice-president has helped to balance the ticket by

---

[46] James H. McCrocklin, *Garde D'Haiti, 1915–1934* (Annapolis, Md.: United States Naval Institute, 1956), pp. 15–16.

giving recognition to one of the two sensitive regions in the nation. Political parties have found it wise and expedient to have both the coast and the sierra represented in an administration; accordingly, the president customarily represents one of these regions and the vice-president the other.

Another important function of the vice-president is to preside impartially over the upper house, casting his vote on any issue when it is necessary to break a tie. His most important function of course is to take over the presidential office if for any reason the president is unable or unwilling to discharge his duties.

But in Latin America, the office of vice-president, a transplant from the United States, has never really taken root and flourished. In fact, only half of the 20 republics have a vice-president. These are: Argentina, Bolivia, Brazil, Chile, Costa Rica, Cuba, Ecuador, Honduras, El Salvador, and Panama. Two of these nations, Costa Rica and Panama, have two vice-presidents.

The general tendency of the other ten nations which have no vice-president, even sometimes of those who do, is to be very leery of the office. It has never acquired much stature in the region. The vice-president, usually representing a different faction or even party and frequently ambitious and chafing at being relegated to second place, has often forgotten his oath of office and sparked a revolt which managed to throw the president out.

Wary of such possible machinations by the vice-president, ten of the nations have made other arrangements regarding who should succeed to the presidential office in case it is vacant. In Colombia and Nicaragua, a *designado* appointed by the congress and having the same qualifications required of a presidential candidate would take over the office in an interim capacity. In Mexico a provisional president would be selected by the Congress. In other nations, the president of the supreme court, the president of the chamber of deputies, or a minister would temporarily take over the presidential duties.

EX-PRESIDENTS

The United States has not done a particularly commendable job of utilizing the interests, talents, and experience of its ex-presidents. In this respect, Latin America has been much more imaginative. In a number of the republics, including Nicaragua and Venezuela, a former president is honored by being made a member of the Senate for life. In Mexico, President Adolfo López Mateos did some thinking too regarding the nation's seven living ex-presidents; he offered every one of them a very responsible position in the government as project director or adviser to himself. Every one of the former presidents accepted the offer, including several who had previously been expending their energies in opposing the government.[47] President Mateos' course was a wise one for many reasons. It solved a long-standing problem as to how to recognize the honor and prestige of former presidents, and it also brought back into the government invaluable experience and expertise.

Perhaps most importantly of all, Mateos' recognition enabled restless ex-presidential political volcanoes to expend their energies usefully instead of spewing volcanic ashes of unrest, conspiracy, and revolution.

SUGGESTED READINGS

BLANKSTEN, GEORGE I. *Ecuador: Constitutions and Caudillos,* chap. v. Berkeley: University of California Press, 1951.

BUSEY, JAMES L. *Latin America: Political Institutions and Processes,* pp. 28–33; 57–60; 72–75; 110–12; 159–61. New York: Random House, Inc., 1964.

DAVIS, HAROLD EUGENE. *Government and Politics in Latin America,* chap. 10. New York: Ronald Press Co., 1958.

FITZGIBBON, RUSSELL H. " 'Continuismo' in Central America and the Caribbean," *The Inter-American Quarterly,* Vol. 2, No. 3 (July, 1940), pp. 56–74.

———. "Executive Power in Central America," *The Journal of Politics,* Vol. 3, No. 3 (August, 1941), pp. 297–307.

———. "Adoption of a Collegiate Executive in Uruguay," *Journal of Politics,* Vol. 14, No. 4 (November, 1952), pp. 616–42.

GÓMEZ, R. A. *Government and Politics in Latin America,* chap. 5 and pp. 27–28. Rev. ed.; New York: Random House, Inc., 1964.

———. "Latin American Executives: Essence and Variations," *Journal of Inter-American Studies,* Vol. 3, No. 1 (January, 1961), pp. 81–95.

———. "Intervention in Argentina, 1860–1930," *Inter-American Economic Affairs,* Vol. 1, No. 3 (December, 1947), pp. 55–73.

GOODSPEED, STEPHEN S. "The Development and Use of *Facultades Extraordinarias* in Mexico," *Southwestern Social Science Quarterly,* Vol. 34, No. 3 (December, 1953), pp. 17–33.

JORRÍN, MIGUEL. *Governments of Latin America,* chap. 4. New York: D. Van Nostrand Co., Inc., 1953.

LOTT, LEO B. "Executive Power in Venezuela," *American Political Science Review,* Vol. L, No. 2 (June, 1956), pp. 422–41.

MACDONALD, AUSTIN F. *Government of the Argentine Republic,* chaps. 8 and 10. New York: Thomas Y. Crowell Co., 1942.

NEEDLER, MARTIN. *Latin American Politics in Perspective,* pp. 135–52. Princeton, N.J.: D. Van Nostrand Co., Inc., 1963.

PIERSON, WILLIAM W., AND GIL, FEDERICO G. *Governments of Latin America,* chap. 8. New York: McGraw-Hill Book Co., Inc., 1957.

SCOTT, ROBERT E. *Mexican Government in Transition,* chap. 8. Urbana, Ill.: University of Illinois Press, 1959.

STOKES, WILLIAM S. *Honduras: An Area Study in Government,* chap. 7 and pp. 285–88. Madison, Wis.: University of Wisconsin Press, 1950.

---

[47] *New York Times,* March 18, 1962, p. 40, col. 1.

————. *Latin American Politics*, chap. 16. New York: Thomas Y. Crowell Co., 1959.

TUCKER, WILLIAM P. *The Mexican Government Today*, chap. 7 and pp. 81–82. Minneapolis: University of Minnesota Press, 1957.

VANGER, MILTON I. "Uruguay Introduces Government by Committee," *American Political Science Review*, Vol. 48, No. 2 (June, 1954), pp. 500–518.

CHAPTER 15

LEGISLATURES:
Echoes and Voices

LEGISLATIVE-EXECUTIVE RELATIONS

THE LEGISLATURE or congress in Latin America is theoretically an equal partner with the other two branches of government, the executive and the judiciary. However, this equality is usually more fiction than fact. In most of the nations the legislative body is greatly overshadowed by the president and does not even enjoy as much independence or influence as the judiciary.

"The unicameral legislature is almost always a rubber stamp of the president's wishes," write John and Mavis Biesanz, referring to Panama; "most of its members being concerned chiefly with seeing that they get their share of the government pork barrel."[1] This description of the legislature in Panama accurately characterizes the role of the body in most of the other nations too. The legislatures ordinarily kowtow to the president, cater to his slightest whims, and enjoy no more independence or popular respect than political sycophants could expect to.

There are many reasons for the predominance of the president and the minor supporting role played by most legislatures. In many of the nations the legislature is a hand-picked body, with the long influential hand of the president doing the picking. Often it is impossible to be elected without his personal approval.[2] Even when the president does not personally pass upon his party's candidates for the legislature, they may owe their election

---

[1] John and Mavis Biesanz, *The People of Panama* (New York: Columbia University Press, 1955), p. 141.

[2] For the influence which the president has exercised in Mexico, see Frank Tannenbaum, *Mexico: The Struggle for Peace and Bread* (New York: Alfred A. Knopf, Inc., 1954), pp. 89–90 and 96.

For presidential influence in Argentina, see Austin F. Macdonald, *Government of the Argentine Republic* (New York: Thomas Y. Crowell Co., 1942), p. 205.

entirely to riding into office on his coattails and be accordingly beholden to him.

Besides owing their election to the president, the legislators in most of the nations are well aware that in a power struggle he holds most of the trumps, especially the high ones such as the support of the armed forces and the national police. In a showdown of strength, he does not hesitate to play them either. In Haiti, dictator Duvalier had no compunction about ousting six members of the Senate on the trumped-up charges that they were betraying their national trust.[3] In Venezuela, President Betancourt, one of the most consistent liberals and supporters of constitutional government, reluctantly but forcefully "threw the book" at Communist members of the Congress who in his judgment were masterminding the sabotage and terrorism designed to paralyze the nation and prevent it from holding the elections scheduled for December, 1963. Despite their congressional immunities, President Betancourt had them put under house arrest and later put into prison.[4]

There are many other factors which help to explain the inconsequential role of the legislature in many of the nations. The prevailing illiteracy, poverty, and lack of political experience have had much to do with it. Denied the privilege of voting because of illiteracy, and hardly knowing what was going on even when given the suffrage, the great majority of citizens have never been really interested in the legislature's work, problems, or degree of independence. Conversely, the tradition of the strong leader who can capture the imagination of the mass has also served to relegate the representative body to a position of minor importance.

In most of the nations, as is illustrated in the case of Panama, the legislatures are merely rubber stamps. But this is certainly not true of some of the most important countries of the region, both large and small.

In Brazil the Congress is far from being a lackey. "Despite the Brazilian habit of strong presidential leadership," says James L. Busey, "the Congress is no pliant tool in the hands of the executive. . . . Though the President is strong, he cannot be sure that all his legislation will be approved, and provisions on the veto and means whereby it may be overridden, as well as on the various legislative powers of the Congress, are more than mere empty gestures to the forms of democratic government."[5]

The congress is even less a pliant tool in some of the other nations. In Chile at the opening session of May, 1961, members of the opposition rudely showed their lack of respect for the president by staging a slow march across the speaker's platform, interrupting the president's State of the Union Address.[6] While disagreement is usually not so crudely ex-

---

[3] *New York Times*, October 11, 1959.

[4] *Hispanic American Report*, Vol. XVI, No. 10 (December, 1963), pp. 978–79.

[5] James L. Busey, *Latin America: Political Institutions and Processes* (New York: Random House, Inc., 1964), p. 113.

[6] *Hispanic American Report*, Vol. XIV, No. 4 (July, 1961), p. 439.

pressed, Chilean legislators are traditionally quite independent in expressing their opinions, in supporting or opposing presidential programs, and most important of all, in casting their votes. This legislative independence is largely the result of the country's multiparty system.

In Costa Rica also, members of the legislature are not the least bit awed by the president. Only when his party has a large majority can he be assured that his program will be approved, and even then some members of his party may defect and oppose it. He cannot even be sure of the respectful attention of legislators during the reading of his annual message, which in most of the nations is a very ceremonious, pompous, and solemn event. His remarks may be greeted with derisive laughter, boos, hisses, and catcalls.[7]

In Uruguay too, the Congress insists on exercising the power and influence granted to it by the constitution. Although there, as in other nations, the role of the executive tends to be increasingly prominent,[8] the legislative branch has anomalously become more important too. "Its job is legislation, policy making if you will," writes Russell Fitzgibbon, "but more basically and more subtly it has the correspondingly greater responsibility of retaining fundamental control over the executive and the administrative machine. Uruguay's parliament well realizes and exercises that responsibility."[9]

Peru is another nation where the legislature is anything but a sycophant, lackey, or pliant presidential tool. In fact, it has been very obstructive to the program of President Belaunde. Although he easily won in the June, 1963, election, receiving almost 100,000 more votes than his closest challenger, the perennial APRA candidate Victor Haya de la Torre, nevertheless his party and coalition supporters were able to elect only 20 of the 45 members of the Senate, and only 52 of the 140 members in the Chamber of Deputies.

When Belaunde tried to bargain with the opposition, offering several ministerial posts in exchange for a commitment to pass a specified minimum of his planned legislation, also to give his party members several of the official positions in the Senate and Chamber of Deputies, APRA and UNO spurned the proposal. Instead of cooperating with Belaunde, they signed a pact giving their members all important posts in both houses of the legislature, including committee chairmanships. The alliance between the supposedly liberal APRA and the dyed-in-the-wool conservative UNO, consisting of supporters of Manuel A. Odria, dictator of the nation from 1948 to 1956, was one of the oddest coalitions in Peruvian legislative history. Earlier bitter enemies and not even on speaking terms, they were

---

[7] Busey, *op. cit.*, p. 74.

[8] This is of course a well-nigh universal trend. For a provocative discussion, "The Decline of Legislatures?" see K. C. Wheare, *Legislatures* (New York: Oxford University Press, 1963), chap. 9.

[9] Russell H. Fitzgibbon, *Uruguay: Portrait of a Democracy* (New Brunswick, N.J.: Rutgers University Press, 1954), pp. 155 and 161.

now kissing kin. Because of their control of the legislature, President Belaunde's program has been almost hamstrung.[10]

LEGISLATIVE EXPERIMENTATION

Whatever their legislative shortcomings, the nations have certainly shown a willingness to experiment with various forms and practices.

Seven of the countries—Costa Rica, El Salvador, Guatemala, Haiti, Honduras, Panama, and Paraguay—have unicameral legislatures. The decision to have only one house was usually made for cogent objective reasons. The nations are small and relatively homogeneous, have a unitary system of government, and prefer to economize by supporting just one house.[11]

However, the decision to adopt the unicameral system has not always been made on such an objective basis. In the spring of 1961, dictator-president Duvalier of Haiti in *caudillo* fashion arbitrarily reduced the bicameral legislature to a single-house body in preparation for the April 30 election. A single list of 58 candidates, all of them his personal supporters, was sponsored by the government and elected. By making the change, Duvalier eliminated the handful of followers of his opponent in exile, Louis Dejoie, who had held seats in the previous legislature.[12]

Another innovation, at least in the western hemisphere, is Ecuador's trial of functional representation since 1929. There are four national functional senators, representing public education, private education, journalism and the scientific and literary societies, and the armed forces. In addition there are eight regional functional senators apportioned equally between the sierra and the coast, representing for each region agriculture, commerce, industry, and labor. The 12 national and regional senators are elected every four years by electoral colleges so organized as best to reflect the interests of the particular group involved.[13]

Functional representation in the Ecuadorian Senate accomplishes two main purposes. It enables certain groups which are basic in the power

---

[10] *Hispanic American Report*, Vol. XVI, No. 6 (August, 1963), pp. 597–98 and Vol. XVI, No. 7 (September, 1963), pp. 705–6.

[11] For a concise analysis of the bicameral system in federal and nonfederal states and the unicameral system in nonfederal states, see Inter-Parliamentary Union, *Parliaments: A Comparative Study on the Structure and Functioning of Representative Institutions in Forty-One Countries* (New York: Frederick A. Praeger, Inc., 1961), pp. 4–13.

[12] Karl M. Schmitt and David D. Burks, *Evolution or Chaos: Dynamics of Latin American Government and Politics* (New York: Frederick A. Praeger, Inc., 1963), pp. 179–80.

[13] For the composition of each of the electoral colleges, see *Special Memorandum No. 21: Methods of Electing National Executives and National Legislatures in Latin American Countries* (Washington, D.C.: Institute for the Comparative Study of Political Systems), pp. 16–17.

structure to protect their interests better. It also tends to prevent any catastrophic disruption of the delicate balance of power between the sierra and the coast.[14]

Another bit of creative thinking on the legislative front led to the selection of *suplentes*, or alternate members, who take office if a regular member for any reason cannot perform his duties. The practice has many points in its favor. During a session, members often drop out for illness or other reasons. If this occurs, the *suplente* steps in to perform the duties. Elected in the same manner and required to have the qualifications of a member of the legislature, he is logically the best suited for taking over.[15]

Also an interesting device is the permanent committee, which is composed of members of both houses, and functions between sessions of the legislature. Acting as a sort of watchdog, it keeps a close eye on the activities of the president and executive departments, passes on the president's request for a state of siege, and calls the legislature back into session if the circumstances warrant.[16]

Still another experiment tried in some of the nations has been that of semiparliamentary government. Where this has been practiced, members of the cabinet may attend sessions of the legislature and participate in debate but not cast a vote. They may even be required to attend sessions and be subjected to grueling questioning. In Peru and Uruguay, if the legislature approves a motion of censure, the minister or ministers involved are removed.[17]

Many of the nations have also experimented with unusual means for the introduction of laws. State legislatures in Mexico are empowered by the constitution to propose laws to Congress. The Cuban people under the nation's 1940 constitution could initiate a law by having 10,000 voters sign a petition. Members of the judiciary and judicial officers in some of the nations prepare bills or assist in their preparation. In Honduras any bill which amends or repeals code law either must originate in the Supreme

---

[14] George I. Blanksten, *Ecuador: Constitutions and Caudillos* (Berkeley: University of California Press, 1951), pp. 106–7.

[15] This system is superior in many respects to that in the United States. If a congressional seat for any reason becomes vacant, the district is often without representation until the next election. If a senatorial seat is involved, the governor may arrange to appoint anyone he pleases, including himself, even though the appointee may belong to a different political party from that of the former holder, and for this or some other reason would hardly have been chosen by the electorate.

[16] In Mexico where the Permanent Committee has a considerable number of duties, constitutional authorities criticize it on the grounds that it has no fixed rules or minority members, and might possibly become dominant over the congress. However, there is apparently no strong move to abolish the committee. (William P. Tucker, *The Mexican Government Today* [Minneapolis: University of Minnesota Press, 1957], pp. 98–99.)

[17] For an extended discussion of this subject, see William S. Stokes, "Parliamentary Government in Latin America," *American Political Science Review* (June, 1945), pp. 522–36.

Court or its opinion must be heard by Congress before the bill is enacted into law.

The legislative commission established in Ecuador in 1944 represents one of the most novel experiments in the introduction of legislation. The commission, designed to prepare bills of major importance, is a very select, broadly representative body. The five-member group is composed of one senator, one deputy, one representative of the president, one representative of the judiciary, and the dean of the faculty of jurisprudence at the Central University at Quito. Bills formulated by the commission are presented directly to a joint session of Congress and are not considered by a standing committee of either chamber. A measure once passed by a two-thirds vote of the joint session is sent to the president for his signature and promulgation, with no choice of veto on his part.[18]

SELECTION OF MEMBERS

Qualifications

Citizenship is a requisite for legislators in every one of the nations. A majority of the countries, in fact, specify that legislators must be natural born citizens. In others, however, persons are eligible who have been citizens for a specified number of years or, in a few countries, from the moment they become citizens.

With regard to age, in countries which have the bicameral system, a member of the upper house in six of the nations must be at least 30 years old; in four, at least 35; and in one, at least 40. The Dominican Republic specifies 25, and Brazil, 21. One is eligible for the lower house at age 25 in eight nations; age 30 in one; and age 35 in one. Brazil and Venezuela specify 21; and Chile, only that one be eligible to vote. In the seven unicameral nations, 21 is the minimum age in two, 25 in four, and 30 in one, Haiti.

Residence within the nation for a minimum period preceding the election is sometimes required. In the Dominican Republic, if one is a naturalized citizen, two years' continuous residence immediately preceding the election is required. Some nations also specify that members must reside in the state, province, department, district, or other unit from which they are elected. In contrast to these, Brazil permits a candidate to run in any district he chooses, but he is not allowed to run in more than one. Uruguay does not have a residence requirement either; consequently, congressmen are often elected from departments other than the ones in which they reside.

Three of the nations have noteworthy additional requirements for

---

18 Blanksten, *op. cit.*, pp. 115–16.

members of the upper house. Argentina requires an annual income of 2,000 pesos, and Costa Rica, an income of 200 colones or property valued at 500 colones. Colombia emphasizes experience, specifying that, besides fulfilling the other requirements, a candidate for the Senate must have served as president of the republic, minister in the cabinet, chief of a diplomatic mission, governor of a department, or magistrate of a court, or have been a university professor for at least five years, or be a lawyer, doctor, or other professional person and have a university degree.

Besides establishing certain qualifications, the constitutions and laws also set up various disqualifications which can automatically bar election to the legislature. Those most usually disqualified are specified government officials, clergymen, members of the armed forces, persons having contracts with the government or in debt to the treasury, and close relatives of the president, vice-president, and cabinet members.

Apportionment

Members of the upper house are usually apportioned equally among certain specified electoral areas. This is true in both federal and unitary states. In Argentina two senators are allotted to each province and the federal capital, and in Bolivia, two to each department. Colombia follows a different principle, however, apportioning seats on the basis of population, one for every 190,000 inhabitants, with each department having a minimum of three senators. In Peru too, senators are apportioned on the basis of population.

Members of the lower house are usually chosen from the same electoral areas as senators, but on the basis of population. Paraguay with its unicameral legislature is an exception. The whole nation constitutes a single electoral district, and every member represents the nation as a whole.

The great increase in population has been accompanied by a corresponding increase in the size of the legislature. In Honduras many observers have been of the opinion that the population boom would soon result in a body of unwieldy proportions.[19] In Brazil the Chamber of Deputies is apparently already approaching the limit of manageable size. Although the population of the country is little more than a third that of the United States, the size of its lower house, 409 members, is almost that of the United States House of Representatives.

The massive trek to the city, especially to the national capital, is creating both a population and electoral imbalance. In Argentina the federal capital and province of Buenos Aires are allotted 85 out of the 192 deputies in the lower house—almost half of the total number. In Uruguay, Montevideo and adjacent Canelones department together have more than half—51 out of the 99 representatives in the lower house. As the migration to

---

[19] William S. Stokes, *Honduras: An Area Study in Government* (Madison, Wis.: University of Wisconsin Press, 1950), p. 269.

TABLE 15-1
Bicameral Legislatures
Senate

Country	No. of Members	Term—Years	Qualifications	Basis of Apportionment	Special Features
Argentina	46	9: ⅓ every 3 years	Age 30, citizen for 6 yrs., annual income of 2,000 pesos, 2 yrs. residence in province or born there	2 to each province and the Federal Capital	Indirect election: in provinces, by plurality vote of provincial legislatures; in Federal Capital, by electoral college
Bolivia	27	6: ⅓ every 2 years	Age 35; others as for deputies	3 to each department	
Brazil	66	8	Age 21; citizen by birth	3 to each state and the Federal District	⅓ or ⅔ of members elected every 4 years, respectively
Chile	45	8	Age 35; citizen, eligible to vote	5 to each provincial senatorial grouping or district	20 or 25 elected every 4 years, respectively
Colombia	98	4	Age 30, citizen by birth, have held high political, administrative, diplomatic, or judicial office or been professor or practiced profession, with degree	At least 3 to every department, 1 : 190,000	Membership equally divided under parity formula
Cuba	—	—	—	—	Last elections, Nov. 3, '58, annulled by revolutionary gov't in '59. None held since.

Country					
Dominican Republic	27	4	Age 30, citizen for 10 years with 2 years continuous residence preceding election	1 to each province and the National District	
Ecuador	51	4	Age 25, citizen by birth	2 to each province and 1 to Archipelago of Colon, directly; also 12 functional senators chosen by electoral colleges	
Mexico	60	6	Age 35, others as for deputies	2 to each state and the Federal District	Renewed in entirety
Nicaragua	19	4	Age 40, citizen, secular status	1 to every department	Presidential runner-up and popularly elected ex-presidents are members
Peru	53	6	Age 35, citizen by birth, eligible to vote	At least 1 to a department; for those over 400,000, up to a maximum of 9 for departments over 2,000,000	Renewed in entirety. Closed lists, PR
Uruguay	31	4	Age 30, citizen 7 years	All members elected from the whole republic regarded as a single electoral district	Closed lists, PR
Venezuela	50	6	Age 30, citizen by birth	2 to each state and the Federal District; also a number awarded by a national quotient	Past presidents also members

TABLE 15-2

BICAMERAL LEGISLATURES

CHAMBER OF DEPUTIES

Country	No. of Members	Term— Years	Qualifications	Basis of Apportionment	Special Features
Argentina	192	4: ½ every 2 years	Age 25, citizen 4 years, 2 years residence or born in province	At least 2 to a province and the Federal Capital, 1 : 85,000	Closed list, PR
Bolivia	72	4: ½ every 2 years	Age 25, citizen by birth, completion of military duties, inscription in the civic register	At least 4 to a department, 1 : 100,000	Open list, PR
Brazil	409	4	Age 21, citizen by birth	7 to 20 to a state, 1 : 150,000. Above 20, 1 : 250,000. Every territory a minimum of 1.	Renewed in entirety, open list, PR
Chile	147	4	Citizen, eligible to vote	1 : 30,000	Renewed in entirety, open list, PR
Colombia	181	2	Age 25, citizen with full rights	At least 3 to a department, 1 : 90,000	Membership equally divided under parity formula, closed list, PR

Country					
Dominican Republic	74	2	Age 30, citizen 8 years, 2 years continuous residence preceding election	To provinces and the National District, 1 : 50,000	A plurality when only 1 is elected, otherwise by PR
Ecuador	73	2	Age 25, citizen by birth enjoying rights of citizen	At least 2 to a province, 1 : 50,000	In all "pluripersonal" elections, a closed list, PR
Mexico	178	3	Age 25, citizen by birth, possessed of his rights, a native or resident of state for 6 months preceding election	At least 2 to a state, 1 : 200,000; 1 to a territory with less than 200,000	Renewed in entirety
Nicaragua	42	4	Age 25, citizen in the exercise of his rights, secular status	To departments, 1 : 30,000	Election according to PR
Peru	182	6	Age 25, citizen by birth, eligible to vote, a native of the dept. or 3 years continuous residence	2 to a department with population up to 100,000, to a maximum of 24 for departments over 2,000,000	Renewed in entirety
Uruguay	99	4	Age 25, citizen for 5 years in exercise of his rights	At least 2 to a department, figured on a "quotient of representation"	
Venezuela	50	6	Age 21, citizen by birth	At least 2 to a state and 1 to the Federal Territory, 1 : 50,000	Closed list, PR

TABLE 15-3

UNICAMERAL LEGISLATURES

Country	No. of Members	Term—Years	Qualifications	Basis of Apportionment	Special Features
Costa Rica	57	4	Age 21, literate, property valued at 500 colones or annual income of 200 colones, citizen, resident for 4 years after naturalization	To provinces, 1 : 30,000	No immediate reelection. PR
El Salvador	54	2	Age 25, citizen by birth, of known integrity and education, a native or resident of the district	To departments, 1 : 50,000	Renewed in entirety. Party with highest vote in department gets all the seats
Guatemala	66	4: ½ every 2 years	Age 21, citizen by birth, in the exercise of rights, secular status	At least 2 to an electoral district. In districts over 100,000, 1 additional for each 50,000	If three or more positions, a closed list, PR
Haiti	58	6	Age 30, citizen by birth, in enjoyment of civil and political rights, resident 2 years of department	1 to a district	
Honduras	58	6	Age 25, citizen by birth, in exercise of rights, native or resident of department	At least 1 to a department, 1 : 30,000	No immediate reelection
Panama	53	4	Age 25 and a citizen	At least 1 to a province, 1 : 25,-000	Renewed in entirety. Open list, PR
Paraguay	60	5	Age 25 and a citizen by birth	All members elected from the whole republic regarded as single electoral district, 1 : 25,000	

SOURCES, Tables 15–1, 15–2, 15–3: *Methods of Electing National Executive and National Legislatures in Latin American Countries*, Special Memorandum No. 21. Institute for the Comparative Study of Political Systems; and *Political Handbook and Atlas of the World*. Used by permission. Also constitutions of the several countries.

the city continues unabated, the lower house threatens in time to become in some nations mainly a national city council.

Method of Election

Members of the lower house are without exception elected by direct popular vote. In the upper house, members with two exceptions are elected in similar fashion. In Argentina the two senators from each province are chosen by the provincial legislature and the two from the federal capital by an electoral college. In Ecuador the 12 functional senators are also selected by electoral colleges.

ORGANIZATION OF THE LEGISLATURE

To discharge its functions effectively and expeditiously, the legislature as a first order of business proceeds to organize into a deliberative body. Most constitutions provide in detail for the internal organization which is adopted.

In a bicameral system, the vice-president is the presiding officer over the upper house, as in the United States. The lower house, in contrast, selects all of its officers, including the president and one or more vice-presidents and secretaries. Ordinarily they are chosen to serve for the entire session. In Mexico, however, they are elected for only a month at a time, which obviously lessens their influence over the body. As a rule the president of the nation has considerable influence with regard to the presiding officers who are selected; in those nations where he dominates the legislature, he practically dictates his choice.

As its presiding officer, the president of the body is in many countries virtually in a position to control its deliberations and determine what measures will be enacted into law. His power to recognize speakers on the floor is important; if he chooses, he may recognize only loyal party supporters, thereby denying the opposition an opportunity to be heard. Sitting in the prestigious speaker's chair, he also has the power to restrict debates, maintain order, and decide points of law. In addition he designates those who will serve on standing committees.

The selection, work, and importance of committees are quite different in some countries from others. In those where the president calls the tune, hardly challenged, the committees are puny; they seldom hold public hearings on proposed measures or permit witnesses from outside the executive branch to be heard. As a result most committee work is very superficial and does not constitute a serious review of the proposals submitted for examination. However, this is certainly not the case in those nations where the legislature really has powers and responsibilities. Especially in Chile, Costa Rica, and Uruguay, the committees are an important part of the legislative machinery and have a considerable influence upon the outcome of legislation.

THE LEGISLATIVE PROCESS

Most of the important bills considered by the legislature are formulated and presented by the executive. He alone is responsible to the whole nation for getting needed laws passed. Ordinarily he alone has the assistance of experts in drafting legislative proposals. Moreover, he is in a better position to be informed about the need for new legislation and what laws should be passed to cope with national problems. Accordingly, most constitutions recognize that the president has an important role in the legislative process. He is given exclusive authority to prepare and submit the national budget. Often the legislature is even specifically prohibited from increasing proposed expenditures unless it provides additional revenues to make up for the difference. In other fields too the president sometimes has the exclusive right of initiating legislation. In Paraguay, for example, only the executive council may initiate proposals regarding the public debt or increases in government personnel, salaries, retirement benefits, and pensions.

Private members are of course allowed to introduce bills, but they usually receive casual, if any, consideration. Consequently, to save face and preserve his *dignidad*, a member customarily does not propose a specific bill but instead merely presents his idea to the body. If it is favorably received, he may then embody it in a bill which he introduces. In contrast, bills originating with the executive enjoy a green light throughout the legislative process. Given preferential treatment, they are seldom subjected to close scrutiny either by the legislature as a whole or by a committee.

Normal procedure for the passage of a bill conforms to the general practice of democratic legislatures. A bill which is presented either by the executive branch or by a member of congress is assigned to a certain committee, which may consider the measure in private, hold a public hearing on it, or not consider it at all. Whichever course the committee follows, it must report a bill; it is not allowed, as in the United States, to pigeonhole a measure. In accordance with customary procedure, the measure is given three readings and usually debated only on the second and third. In the 13 nations which have a bicameral system, the approval of both houses is necessary before a measure is submitted to the president for his O.K. and promulgation.

Sometimes the two houses disagree in a bitter battle between themselves. A bill introduced into the Argentine Congress in 1958 to give private universities the right to award degrees and professional titles, thus ending the traditional system of state education at the university level, provoked just such a controversy. The Senate favored and approved the bill, but the Chamber of Deputies vigorously opposed it. The bill passed when the Chamber in a tumultuous night session failed to get the two-thirds majority necessary to override the Senate's approval.[20]

Such disagreement is quite the exception, however. Ordinarily, the order of business, who will do what, and even the outcome of the proceedings is a foregone conclusion. In fact, open debate in the legislature is mainly window dressing for the nation. Thus in Ecuador, any one "in the know" could reliably predict in advance such important matters as: who would make what motions, who would speak against them, how long the floor debate on a given issue would last, what aspects of the issue could not be debated because they were "delicate" or "inconvenient," and what the final vote on the issue would likely be.[21]

In discharging its constitutional duties as a nominally independent policy-making body, the legislature usually has many strikes against it. The selfish, narrow interests of its members often completely preclude their visualizing national interests and needs. Moreover, the president's enjoyment of the national spotlight enables him readily to mobilize public opinion on his side if he needs to. Easily one of the legislature's greatest drawbacks is a self-imposed one—the intransigent unwillingness of the dominant party in some of the nations to accord any rights or even respect to members of the opposition. Often they are given no recognition whatever—not recognized by the speaker and given the privilege of participating in debates on the floor or assigned to committees where they might present their views and convictions. The opposition under such circumstances has no status and is allowed to make no contribution whatever. As a result, all it can do is resort to obstructionist tactics, such as boycotting sessions, hoping thereby to prevent the legislature from having the quorum needed to transact business. In Honduras one frustrated member of the opposition resorted to the ultimate in obstructionist tactics—he set fire to the legislative palace with the intention of destroying it.

In view of the lack of respect, even vengefulness, shown members of the opposition, it is no wonder that members often challenge one another to duels and that violence sometimes occurs within the legislative chamber itself. On September 8, 1949, a dramatic and tragic gun battle erupted in the Colombian Congress, a microcosm of the nationwide interparty bitterness. Conservative members of the house opened fire on the liberals with pistols, killing in his tracks the one who held the floor and mortally wounding another. In all, more than 100 shots were fired.[22]

In October, 1961, the Ecuadorian Congress was also a scene of wild disorder. It apparently began when rocks and bottles were thrown from

[20] *New York Times,* September 21, 1958, p. 33, col. 4; September 25, 1958, p. 18, col. 6; and October 2, 1958, p. 10, col. 3.

[21] Blanksten, *op. cit.,* p. 117.

[22] Vernon Lee Fluharty, *Dance of the Millions: Military Rule and the Social Revolution in Colombia, 1930–1956* (Pittsburgh: University of Pittsburgh Press, 1957), pp. 112–13.

the gallery at antigovernment congressmen. The uproar ended in gunfire with the congressmen taking cover under their desks. In the ensuing volley, Vice-President Carlos Arosemena, who was presiding over the session, grabbed his chair as a shield, fired his revolver wildly at the ceiling, and fled.[23]

SESSIONS

The length of sessions ranges from two months or so in Costa Rica, the Dominican Republic, and Ecuador to five months in Argentina, eight in Brazil, and nine in Uruguay. Often a certain period will be specified by the constitution, with the proviso that the legislature may extend its sessions for another 30 days if the pressure of business warrants.

Members are usually paid on a per diem basis, which apparently has often tempted them to prolong sessions. Indeed one of the most common criticisms of the legislature is that it stays in session unnecessarily long[24]—a sort of legislative boondoggle. The stretch-out is well shown by the Mexican legislature, which in accordance with the constitution meets for up to four months a year. During most of that time, however, the body convenes for business only two or three days a week and for no more than an hour or two a day.

Attendance at meetings is notoriously poor. The constitutions have long taken cognizance of this and embody many provisions intended to remedy the situation, such as an absentee's losing his per diem or after so many absences being replaced by the *suplente*. The written penalties are almost never enforced, however, as a result of which legislatures are sometimes obviously handicapped. In Colombia sessions of the lower house often had to be adjourned during October, 1963, for lack of a quorum. The body's idleness, lack of responsibility, and apparent unconcern with the nation's serious problems were sharply criticized throughout the nation. To lessen absenteeism, the president of the house initiated a system of paying representatives' salaries on the basis of their attendance at the session.[25]

The short duration of sessions, even when unnecessarily prolonged, the skimpy hours of business and poor attendance all attest to the relative insignificance of the legislature and the predominance of the executive.

POWERS AND FUNCTIONS

The constitutions endow the legislatures with an impressive number of powers and functions, which cover the gamut of those usually given to

---

23 *Hispanic American Report*, Vol. XIV, No. 10 (December, 1961), p. 917.

24 Blanksten, *op. cit.*, p. 104–5; Stokes, *op. cit.*, p. 271; and Fitzgibbon, *op. cit.*, p. 171.

25 *Hispanic American Report*, Vol. XVI, No. 10 (December, 1963), p. 895.

policy-making bodies. Whether existing only on paper or being actually enjoyed, they may be broadly classified into four main groups: legislative, constitutive, electoral, and judicial.

Legislative Powers

The legislative power basically comprises the formulation of public policy and passage of laws for carrying it out. In the realm of finance, the legislature levies the taxes necessary to support the government and carry out its many activities. The legislature also approves loans obtained upon the credit of the nation, as well as the terms of their repayment. It provides too for the issuance or coinage of money and, theoretically at least, regulates its value.

The legislature's war powers too are quite significant and involve determining the size of the armed forces in time of peace and making appropriations for their support; authorizing the president to declare a state of war; and approving the use of national troops anywhere outside the republic and designating the time of their return.

The regulatory power extends to many aspects of national life. The legislature has control over the free navigation of interior rivers, also over land and maritime trade with foreign nations or between states or provinces. It creates or abolishes governmental departments and bureaus, and authorizes increases in governmental personnel, salary, or other benefits. It may even have to approve the president's leaving the country for a goodwill tour abroad or a visit to a foreign capital to promote the interests of the nation, such as arranging to borrow more money in the United States or to defer payment of obligations due.

The legislature also functions as a sort of custodian of the national territory, probably largely a holdover from earlier days when such *caudillos* as Melgarejo of Bolivia gave away huge chunks of the national domain. Legislative authorization is necessary for the entry of foreign troops into the country and determines the length of their stay. The legislature must also act to create new provinces or departments, determine their boundaries, and keep the principal ports in good condition. Argentina's borders for most of the past century have been quite secure, yet the constitution authorizes the Congress "to provide for the security of the frontiers, to maintain peaceful relations with the Indians, and promote their conversion to Catholicism."[26]

The legislative power, however, may be exercised negatively as well as positively; the policy-making body sometimes asserts its constitutional prerogatives by refusing to pass legislation which the president urgently requests. The Chilean Congress in 1952 turned thumbs down on President Carlos Ibáñez' request for dictatorial powers to deal with a nationwide strike but did give him special powers to combat inflation. The Ecuadorian Congress caused a national crisis by concluding its 1962 session on Novem-

---

[26] *Argentine Constitution* of 1853, Article 67, Paragraph 15.

ber 7 of that year without taking action on a request by the president for the promotion of 24 high ranking officers of the army, navy, and air force. The officers affected all turned in their resignations and requested to be retired, a move calculated to put pressure on the government. When the president's proposal to call a special session was vigorously opposed by the two largest labor unions, the disaffected members of the military backed down, stating that they would accept any decision taken by the Congress and would respect the Constitution.[27]

In exercising its legislative powers, a determined congress sometimes even overrides a presidential veto. In 1962 the Colombian Congress passed a bill to be effective in 1964 which would increase the salaries of the president, members of the cabinet, and congressmen. When President Valencia vetoed the measure, citing "the very difficult fiscal circumstances which the nation confronts," the congress overrode his veto and enacted the measure into law.[28]

Constitutive Powers

The legislature also plays a very significant role in the adoption of new constitutions or the amendment of existing ones. Since constitutions in some countries are changed so frequently and in others are amended so often, the power of congress to participate in the process is of no little importance.

If a new constitution is to be adopted, congress' role may be limited to calling a special constituent convention to formulate a new organic law. Six of the countries specify that this will be the procedure when a general revision is to be made.[29] In other nations, however, a new constitution may be formulated by congress itself, usually convened in special session, and also ratified by the congress, normally after a new election of members in order to give the electorate an opportunity to indicate its opinion. The 1961 constitution of Bolivia and 1964 constitution of Haiti are among those adopted under this procedure. Besides formulating and adopting new constitutions, the congress is frequently empowered by the constitution to propose and adopt amendments.

Another indication of the close tie between the legislative and the constitutive power is the frequency with which a constitutive convention, after having formulated a new constitution, becomes the nation's legislative body until new elections are held. In El Salvador, a constituent assembly, convoked by the civil-military directorate, formulated and adopted a new constitution which went into effect on January 25, 1962. Thereafter, the constituent assembly became the legislative assembly with its term ending May 31, 1964.

---

[27] *Hispanic American Report*, Vol. XV, No. 11 (January, 1963), p. 1035.
[28] *Ibid.*, Vol. XVI, No. 10 (December, 1963), p. 934.
[29] Argentina, Costa Rica, Cuba, El Salvador, Honduras, and Uruguay.

Electoral Powers

The legislature has a number of important responsibilities with regard to elections. Among these, it passes laws which govern the conduct of elections and may determine whether their procedure will be genuinely democratic or merely farcical.

In the election of the president especially, the legislature plays an important role. It canvasses the returns and officially proclaims who is the winner. Where elections are close and candidates contest or refuse to recogniz. the results, the duty is a delicate, unenviable one. In the multiparty nations, the legislature must sometimes even choose the president of the republic. In fact the multiparty system tends to put the selection in the lap of the legislature. Peru and Venezuela, which have the plurality rule, accept the results of the polls as final, even though it often means having presidents who received a decided minority of the total vote. Chile, on the other hand, requires that the winning candidate must receive a majority of the total votes cast. Since no candidate received such a majority in elections from 1942 to 1964, responsibility for making the choice fell to the lot of Congress, which in every case respected as much as possible the wishes of the electorate by selecting the candidate with the largest number of votes.

Judicial Powers

As a check upon the other two branches of government, the legislature may impeach and try the president, vice-president, officials in the executive departments, and judges. The lower house is charged with the duty of investigating the allegations made against them and drawing up a formal indictment if the evidence seems to warrant. The upper house then conducts a formal trial of the accused. In several of the nations which have unicameral legislatures, the trial is conducted by the supreme court. Although impeachment has often been threatened, only rarely have presidents been put on trial and removed from office. President Balmaceda of Chile was removed in 1891, Eloy Alfaro of Ecuador in 1933, and José Ramón Guizado of Panama in 1955.

LEGISLATIVE PRIVILEGES AND IMMUNITIES

In politically democratic nations members of the legislature enjoy certain unusual privileges and immunities. The free and untrammeled expression of their different points of view, though sometimes offensive, is absolutely necessary. In recognition of this fact, constitutions in Latin America accord to legislators a freedom of expression and action which ordinary citizens do not enjoy. They cannot be held responsible for statements made or acts committed in pursuance of their legislative duties.

us remarks made during the course of debate, however derogatory and vitriolic, are privileged and not subject to the laws of defamation or slander. In addition, legislators may not be arrested for ordinary offenses or subject to civil suit.

Some nations, such as Argentina, recognize immunity as extending over the legislator's entire term of office and protecting him against all but the most serious crimes. "No Senator or Deputy may be arrested," states Article 61 of Argentina's 1853 constitution, "from the day of his election until he ceases in office, except in case of being surprised *in flagrante delicto*, in the commission of a crime that deserves the penalty of death, or an infamous or other distressing one." In the Dominican Republic, on the other hand, immunity according to Article 28 of the constitution extends only to the duration of the legislative session. In practice, the constitutionally provided immunity is sometimes flagrantly violated, but it is usually respected and affords legislators the scope of freedom needed for performing their duties.

In retrospect, one may safely say that the legislature has not lived up to what has been expected of it and what it might have accomplished.

In short, as it now operates [in Mexico] the legislative branch of the national government is not really fulfilling its constitutional duties. . . . On the whole, it serves as little more than a convenient training ground for ambitious young politicians who wish to spend a few years in the national capital, as a kind of convenient patronage for certain political and functional interest association leaders, or as a quiet tapering-off appointment for older politicians who no longer are as efficient as they once were but are not quite ready to retire, or perhaps more nearly correctly, to remove their names from the public payroll.[30]

The legislature in Mexico, as well as in many of the other nations, does not measure up to what a policy-making body should be. Yet despite its imperfections, it is a main wheel in the governmental machinery. In fact its measure of effectiveness is probably the best single index of the true level of democracy.

SUGGESTED READINGS

BLANKSTEN, GEORGE I. *Ecuador: Constitutions and Caudillos*, chap. vi. Berkeley: University of California Press, 1951.

CHRISTENSEN, ASHER N. *The Evolution of Latin American Government: A Book of Readings*, No. 30. New York: Henry Holt & Co., 1951.

COX, ISAAC JOSLIN. "Chile: The Pseudo-Parliamentary Regime, 1891–1914," *Argentina, Brazil, and Chile Since Independence* (ed. A. CURTIS WILGUS), chap. 30. Washington, D.C.: George Washington University Press, 1935. Reissued in 1963 by Russell and Russell, New York.

---

[30] Robert E. Scott, *Mexican Government in Transition* (Urbana, Ill.: University of Illinois Press, 1959), p. 265.

JAMES, HERMAN G. *The Constitutional System of Brazil*, chap. iii. Washington, D.C.: Carnegie Institution of Washington, 1923.

JORRÍN, MIGUEL. *Governments of Latin America*, chap. 5. New York: D. Van Nostrand Co., Inc., 1953.

MACDONALD, AUSTIN F. *Government of the Argentine Republic*, chaps. 12 and 13. New York: Thomas Y. Crowell Co., 1942.

SCOTT, ROBERT E. "Legislatures," *Government and Politics in Latin America* (ed. HAROLD EUGENE DAVIS), chap. 11. New York: Ronald Press Co., 1958.

PIERSON, WILLIAM W., AND GIL FEDERICO G. *Governments of Latin America*, chap. 10. New York: McGraw-Hill Book Co., Inc., 1957.

STOKES, WILLIAM S. *Honduras: An Area Study in Government*, pp. 268–93. Madison, Wis.: University of Wisconsin Press, 1950.

———. *Latin American Politics*, chap. 17. New York: Thomas Y. Crowell Co., 1959.

———. "Parliamentary Government in Latin America," *American Political Science Review*, Vol. XXXIX, No. 3 (June, 1945), pp. 522–36.

———. "The Cuban Parliamentary System in Action, 1940–1947," *Journal of Politics*, Vol. 11, No. 2 (May, 1949), pp. 335–64.

TUCKER, WILLIAM P. *The Mexican Government Today*, chap. 6. Minneapolis: University of Minnesota Press, 1957.

CHAPTER 16

COURTS AND LAW:
The Last Word, Fact or Fiction

THE ADMINISTRATION of justice is one of the most important functions of government. The legal and equitable decision of controversies arising from conflicting rights of citizens or of citizens and the state is the weighty responsibility of the courts. The administration of justice in Latin America, as elsewhere, has never been easy. The Aztecs, who did not develop a systematic script forming an alphabet or syllabary, represented the purport of their laws and kept judicial records by means of painted pictures. The Incas devised a more ingenious system. The courts of justice kept records of their sentences by means of knots made on cords of various colors, the color signifying the kind of offense which had been punished. Small threads, also of various colors, attached to the cords indicated the punishment which had been meted out.[1]

The courts today do not have to draw pictures to portray concepts of justice or knot variegated cords to record judicial decisions, but the administration of justice is still a difficult as well as important responsibility.

PECULIAR ATTRIBUTES OF LATIN AMERICAN LAW

A Blend of Legal Systems

By far the major influence on the legal systems of the Latin American nations has been the Roman law, their common cultural heritage. The Roman or civil law had for many centuries provided the basis and much of the content of the law in both Spain and Portugal. "Remaining long under

---

[1] John H. Wigmore, *A Kaleidoscope of Justice* (Washington, D.C.: Washington Law Book Co., 1941), pp. 567 and 587–90.

Roman dominion," writes John Thomas Vance, "Spain's inhabitants became thoroughly Romanized. . . . Roman dominion introduced Roman
law into Spain on the basis of cultural influence."[2]

The civil law as recognized in Spain and Portugal was transplanted to
the New World by the conquistadors and settlers. It was as much a part
of the Iberian culture in the New World as was the use of the Spanish
and Portuguese languages. During the three centuries or more of colonial
rule, the colonies all had the legal systems which were in effect in the
mother countries. The civil law was as firmly rooted there by the time of
independence as was the English common law in the 13 colonies which
formed the United States.

Since independence, civil law transplanted from continental Europe
has continued to have a strong influence on the legal systems of Latin
America. A code of commerce promulgated in 1829 by Spain had a great
influence on the region's mercantile law, as did the renowned Code
Napoleon and 1864 civil code of Italy upon its civil and criminal law.

While the civil law has undoubtedly been the major influence, the legal
systems also strongly reflect the influence of the English common law.
Moreover, our doctrine of judicial supremacy has been gradually adopted,
sometimes with interesting modifications, as in Colombia and Panama,
with their Acción Popular, to provide an immediate test of the constitutionality of statutes and executive acts. Advisory opinions, following the
practice of a few of our state courts, have also been occasionally provided
for. Our writ of habeas corpus has also been adopted in most of the
countries, under that name in Cuba and some others. In Brazil it is known
as *mandado de seguranca,* and in Mexico and Central America, as the more
comprehensive *amparo.* Our homestead law, also common-law marriage
and legal grounds for divorce, are found too in the legislation of many of
the countries.[3]

The constitutional law and practice of the United States have also had
a considerable influence in Latin America, especially in the federal republic of Argentina and to a lesser extent in the federal republics of
Brazil, Mexico, and Venezuela. In Argentina, court decisions, lawyers'
briefs, and writings of commentators frequently contain citations of decisions rendered or works written in the United States.[4] In Colombia,
however, whose practice is much more typical of Latin America, judges
and scholars have not been interested in the judicial precedents of the

---

[2] John Thomas Vance, *The Background of Hispanic-American Law* (New York:
Central Book Co., 1943, pp. 30–32.

[3] Phanor James Eder, "The Impact of the Common Law on Latin America,"
Miami Law Quarterly, Vol. IV, No. 4 (June, 1950), pp. 436–38.

[4] Segundo V. Linares Quintana, "Comparison of the Constitutional Basis of the
United States and Argentine Political Systems," *University of Pennsylvania Law
Review,* Vol. 97, No. 5 (April, 1949), pp. 641–64.

United States. If a judge or scholar desires to study precedents elsewhere, he turns to French or other continental sources.[5]

Extensive Borrowings

Another characteristic of the Latin American legal systems is their propensity for borrowing or adopting from European nations, the United States, or one another. Bolivia in 1830 adopted verbatim the French civil code. Ecuador and Colombia, as well as several of the Central American republics, copied Chile's civil code of 1855. Paraguay in 1886 adopted the Argentine civil code of 1869. Our Uniform Negotiable Instruments Law was adopted practically word for word by Colombia and in slightly revised form by Chile.

But Latin America has by no means relied solely upon Europe or the United States in fashioning its legal systems. In fact, those laws which have been the most effective are the ones which were forged on the anvil of native experience, and were adapted to the conditions and requirements of the region. Just such laws were the mining legislation of Peru and Mexico, which were formulated to meet local needs and which form the basis of the mining codes of the nations today. These codes have also greatly influenced mining law in the United States and in many other nations throughout the world. Mexico's unique agrarian reform laws have also won international attention and have been adopted in at least a modified form by several nations.

Embodiment of the Law in Codes

Another basic characteristic of Latin American law is its embodiment in codes which are compact, precise, and systematic formulations of the law. Practically ignoring judicial precedent, also custom and usage, the codes adopted by the congress are a concise statement of the law of the land. And as the Latin American realizes, there are certainly some advantages in code law. Its very brevity is intriguing. The whole Codigo Civil, or Civil Code, of Venezuela, for example, can be printed in a 485-page pocket-size edition weighing about 10 to 12 ounces. In this code, as well as in the many others in Latin America, the law is succinctly laid down in unequivocal terms which anyone can read for himself. Moreover, "there is logic, composition, and symmetry which is impressive," concludes William S. Stokes. "The writing is usually lucid. The intent is to achieve certainty in the law. Everything is defined in detail. Standards are exact. Procedure is specific and definite."[6]

---

[5] J. A. C. Grant, " 'Contract Clause' Litigation in Colombia; A Comparative Study in Judicial Review," *American Political Science Review*, Vol. XLII, No. 6 (December, 1948), p. 1126.

[6] William S. Stokes, *Latin American Politics* (New York: Thomas Y. Crowell Co., 1959), p. 468. Another scholar, Phanor J. Eder, has expressed great respect for Latin American jurisprudence. "North Americans could learn much from Latin

These codes of Latin America are indeed a contrast to law as we know it in the United States. Based largely upon the English common law, our jurisprudence leans heavily upon the doctrine of *stare decisis* and judicial precedent, and recognizes custom and usuage as important sources of law. Thus, law in the United States consists not only of statutes passed by Congress and state legislatures but also of many judicial decisions, national and state, which interpret the law and refine its meaning. Consequently, while the federal government—and every one of the states too—has its own code of laws, these are bulky, detailed affairs which fill many large volumes and are replete with judicial decisions as well as laws enacted by the legislative bodies.

The common law, bulky though it is, has certain distinct advantages over the civil law. In applying the former, a judge has more discretion in interpreting the law in its application to many diverse circumstances. The common law has thus tended to be a dynamic, living body of law reflecting social customs and experience. In this respect it is decidedly superior to code law, whose rigid provisions as applied by judges exercising little discretion are sometimes ill-adapted to the peculiar circumstances of the case before the court.

In one respect, however, common and constitutional law as found in the United States operate under a decided disadvantage. Since they both consist largely of case law and judicial precedent, the study and practice of law become progressively unwieldy as a body of precedent grows. "Case law is gold in the mine—a few grains of precious metal to a ton of useless matter—while statute law is coin of the realm, ready for immediate use." In 1947, the student of common law faced the formidable problem of having to consider "325,000 pages of United States statute law and a yearly production of 500 volumes of court decisions."[7]

ORGANIZATION AND OPERATION OF THE COURTS

In most of the republics the constitutions give much less attention to the courts than to the executive and legislative branches of government. In fact, these two are usually authorized by the organic law to fill in the many necessary details regarding judicial structure, jurisdiction, and procedure. Mexico and Uruguay, however, unlike the other nations, have

---

American legislation. We need more scientific method of our law. We need to rid ourselves of our fear of the philosophy of law and of abstract reasoning. . . . As regards form, we could well imitate the clarity and simplicity of the Codes and learn to avoid the excessive verbosity and prolixity of many Anglo-American statutes. Every legislator ought to study the Code Napoleon." (Phanor James Eder, *Anglo-American and Latin-American Law* [New York: New York University Press, 1950], p. 142.)

[7] In Helen L. Clagett, "Law and Court Systems," *Government and Politics in Latin America* (ed. Harold Eugene Davis) (New York: Ronald Press Co., 1958), p. 334.

lengthy articles in their constitutions which provide in detail for the organization and operation of the courts.

The Supreme Court

The judicial system in each of the republics is headed by a supreme court, known by such various names as supreme court of justice, supreme tribunal, high federal court, or supreme federal tribunal.

Composition. The number of justices who compose the court varies sharply among the nations. Paraguay is very parsimonious; its court has only three members. Cuba despite its small size is quite lavish by comparison; its supreme tribunal of justice has 31 members, and is the largest of the bodies. In between these extremes, such courts in half of the nations number ten members or less, with the others having more than ten. According to the Constitution of Brazil, the composition of its federal supreme tribunal is notably flexible. It must have a minimum of 11 members, the constitution specifies, but the number can be increased upon the recommendation of the body itself.

Qualifications and Restrictions on Activities. The constitutions and laws establish specific and exacting qualifications for membership on the supreme court. Invariably, candidates must be native-born citizens, fully able to exercise a citizen's political and civil rights. To pin this down more specifically, Mexico adds a residence requirement, specifying that a prospective member of its supreme court of justice must have resided in the country during the preceding five years, except in case of absence in the service of the republic for a period of more than six months.

Age is another qualification. Many of the nations establish both a minimum age for appointment as well as a maximum age. To be eligible for the supreme court, one must be at least 30 years old in Argentina, the Dominican Republic, El Salvador, Haiti, Honduras, and Venezuela; and at least 40 in Cuba, Ecuador, Nicaragua, Peru, and Uruguay. The maximum age at which one may be appointed is 65 in Mexico, 70 in El Salvador, and 75 in Peru. Besides establishing maximum ages for appointment, some of the nations also specify that retirement is compulsory at a certain age; in Brazil, Mexico, and Uruguay it is age 70.

Exacting professional qualifications are also established for members of the high court. In a number of the nations, they must be qualified members of the bar and have practiced law for a minimum number of years. Colombia requires a minimum of 4 years legal practice; Mexico, 5; Haiti, 7; Chile, Ecuador, and Panama, 15; and Peru, 20. Other nations also require that members of the court must have had judicial experience as judges in the lower courts—thus coming up from the ranks so to speak. Several require competitive examinations.

Good conduct and reputation are still other qualifications established for members. Brazil's constitution lays down the line that candidates must be of "spotless reputation"; Nicaragua sets its sights high too by requiring "irreproachable conduct and good reputation." By comparison, Mexico is quite charitable and more willing to overlook human frailties. Its constitution states that candidates for the Supreme Court of Justice must enjoy a good reputation and not have been convicted of any crime punishable by imprisonment for more than one year in the penitentiary.

Still another requirement which is usually specified by law or the constitution is that a candidate possess good eyesight and hearing.

Sometimes, extraconstitutional requirements figure largely in the acceptability of a prospective member of the high court. In Ecuador, for example, the geographical division of the nation and prevailing political pattern practically requires that a careful balance be maintained in allocating the 15 judgeships between the jealous and highly competitive coast and sierra.[8]

There are also disqualifications which bar persons from being appointed to the court. Being a member of the priesthood automatically disqualifies an individual in most of the nations. Being related to either the president, who would normally make the nomination, or to a member of congress, who would confirm it, is another disqualification.

Once he becomes a member of the bench, there are many restrictions on a justice's activities. He cannot engage in the private practice of law, hold any other elective or appointive office, or participate in any sort of partisan political activity. In Ecuador he is not even permitted to vote. Peru, however, gives members of its supreme court of justice considerably more leeway than they are allowed in most other nations. According to Article 226 of the constitution, they may have a diplomatic assignment, teach at the university, aid codifying or amending commissions for the laws, represent the nation in international or scientific congresses and conferences, and act as arbiter or attorney in tribunals of international arbitration in which any Peruvian right may be disputed.

Selection of Judges. Although there are various differences in detail and refinements in practice, there are three main methods for selecting members of the supreme court.

1. The president may be empowered by the constitution to make the appointment. In Haiti he appoints solely on his own responsibility the judges of all judicial tribunals from the top to the bottom. In Chile the president appoints a member to the high court from a list of five individuals proposed by the court itself. The two ranking members in point of seniority on the court of appeals must be included in the list.

2. The president nominates members for the high court, with or without the advice or approval of some body as the council of state, and both houses of congress, maybe only one of them, confirms the appointment. In some instances the president does not recommend a specific individual but submits a list from which the congress may choose. This plan in its gen-

---

[8] George I. Blanksten, *Ecuador: Constitutions and Caudillos* (Berkeley: University of California Press, 1951), p. 121.

eral outline is the one which is followed by Argentina, Mexico, Panama, Paraguay, and Peru. In Brazil the federal supreme tribunal itself has a strong voice in the selection of its members; when a vacancy exists, the tribunal may nominate an individual, who is usually chosen by the joint action of the president and the senate. In Cuba nominations for the supreme tribunal of justice under the 1940 constitution were made by an electoral college of nine members, of whom four were proposed by the tribunal itself, three were designated by the president, and two were members of the faculty of law at the University of Havana.

3. The members of the court may be chosen by the congress, a procedure which is followed in Bolivia, Colombia, Guatemala, Honduras, Nicaragua, El Salvador, Uruguay, and Venezuela. Congressional action has many variations. In Bolivia the senate approves a list of nominees for the high office, and the chamber of deputies makes the final selection. In Colombia, the two houses of congress have a strictly equal voice in approving the membership of the court. Six members of the body are named by the senate, and six by the chamber of deputies.

The nations have experimented with many methods for appointing members to the supreme court and obviously have reached no conclusion as to which method is best. "If a generalization may be ventured," concludes Helen L. Clagett, "it is that the participation of both executive and legislative branches in judicial appointments has been found the most satisfactory method. The use of competitive examinations, the practice of appointing career judges, and the use of slates or panels prepared by other agencies, even by the judicial branch itself, have in some countries contributed to reducing political pressure in appointments."[9]

Tenure of Office. Permanence of tenure, subject only to the requirements of good behavior and proper discharge of duty, is essential for the independence of the courts. However, it has made slow progress in Latin America. Only six of the nations—Argentina, Brazil, Chile, Cuba, Mexico and Peru—provide that the judges of the supreme court will hold office during "good behavior," the legal term for permanent tenure.[10] Most of the republics prefer to establish specific terms of office. Four of the nations have relatively long terms; 10 years in Bolivia, Haiti, and Uruguay; and 18 years in Panama.

The other ten nations, however, keep a much closer checkrein on their justices. Costa Rica has a term of eight years; Ecuador, Honduras, and Nicaragua, six; and Colombia, the Dominican Republic, Paraguay, and Venezuela, five. In Guatemala the term of a justice is even less than that of the president, four years as against six. And El Salvador has the shortest

---

9 Clagett, *op. cit.*, p. 357.
10 In Argentina a judge can be removed only for failure to perform his duty, immoral conduct, or commission of a crime. Pablo A. Ramella, *Derecho Constitucional* (Buenos Aires; 1960), p. 643.

term of all, three years. A member of the Salvadorean high court has hardly taken the oath of office, gotten his bench warm, and acquired a judicial mien before he has to run for reelection.

The provisions for reelection too vary widely among the nations. Colombia permits a justice to be reelected indefinitely, but Uruguay stipulates that he cannot be reelected except after a lapse of five years. El Salvador and Guatemala, with their short terms of three and four years respectively, have added their own distinctive touches to permanence of tenure. If a member of the Supreme Court in El Salvador serves three consecutive elective terms of three years each, or in Guatemala, two such terms of four years each, he is regarded as having tenure for life until the compulsory retirement age.

Functioning of the Supreme Court. The supreme court is presided over by a *presidente* or chief justice. In some nations he is directly appointed to this position as in the United States; usually, however, he is selected by his colleagues. The basis of choice may be seniority, rotation in office, or vote of the members. The term which a member serves as chief justice may be one year, a number of years, or the entire duration of his service.[11]

In performing their judicial duties, the supreme courts of nine nations— Argentina, Brazil, the Dominican Republic, Haiti, Honduras, Nicaragua, Panama, Paraguay, and Uruguay—always function as a unit; members of the court sit in on all cases and have a voice in deciding them. In the other nations, however, the court instead of sitting as a single body divides its members into what was known as *salas* or *cámaras*. Each *sala* specializes in a certain type of judicial controversy. In Colombia, for example, the court is divided into four such groups to correspond to: cases under original jurisdiction, civil law appeals, criminal law appeals, and miscellaneous business.

The division into *salas* has its advantages; it enables members of the court to specialize in certain fields of law and consequently to weigh more expertly the many complex issues which come before them. Moreover, the division of labor helps to expedite the rendition of justice.

In Ecuador, as in the majority of the nations, the Supreme Court of 15 justices is divided into *salas*, three chambers of five judges each. But the rationale underlying the division is quite different from that of the other courts in Latin America. Each of the chambers handles all types of cases. The only principle in distribution of cases is that of chance, and this has been stressed in Ecuadorian law as an element of justice. Distribution on this basis has another advantage too. Under this system no one of the

---

[11] There are many variations in ground rules. In Peru where the president of the Supreme Court is elected for a term of one year, the custom has been established of reelecting a president who is approaching retirement. (José Pareja Paz-Soldan, *Derecho Constitucional Peruano* [Tercera edición; Lima, Perú: Ediciones de Sol, 1963], p. 306.)

chambers is overburdened with cases while the other two have relatively light dockets.[12]

The selection of *suplentes* and *fiscales* have also served to ease the burden of the courts. The *suplentes* are alternate or substitute judges who may be called on to serve whenever a regular member of the body is unable to. In some nations, a *suplente* is elected for each incumbent justice; in others, a panel of substitutes is named from which one is selected in the event of the death, serious illness, or resignation of a justice. The substitute justices, incidentally, must have the same qualifications as those established for regular members of the court.

The *fiscales*, or technical advisers, are also of great assistance to the court in the discharge of its responsibilities. They often make investigations for the justices, their findings and recommendations becoming part of the official record of the case.

Jurisdiction and Power to Punish Contempt. The supreme court, as its name implies, is the judicial body of last resort for the nation. To assure the uniform and equitable administration of justice, it is given a wide appellate jurisdiction over constitutional and legal questions.

The court also enjoys original jurisdiction over certain classes of cases which are of especial importance to the nation or have international implications. Original jurisdiction usually extends to all cases involving: proceedings against the president, members of the cabinet, national judges, diplomats, and other officials representing the central government; disputes between foreign countries and the nation; issues involving international law; and, in the case of federal states, conflicts between the union and the states or between states.

To discharge its responsibilities effectively, the court must have its own independent power to enforce respect for its operations. In Colombia, for example, contempt of court is a serious offense. The justices may order the arrest, limited to six days, or impose fines of from 5 to 50 pesos to compel parties to comply with court orders duly issued. In Panama too, justices can impose heavy penalties for contempt of court.[13]

Special Duties. The supreme court in the several nations has a number of special duties which are quite important. In Ecuador the president of the body attends the first meeting of the congress and personally reads his message regarding the administration of justice in the whole nation. On the basis of his information, observations, and recommendations, the congress will later pass legislation relating to the administration of justice.

In all of the nations the supreme court has extensive control over the lower courts in the land. It appoints or recommends for appointment the judges of these courts and closely supervises their work. Members of the high court are required by the constitutions or laws to visit the lower courts personally and observe at first-hand how they are conducted. These

---

12 Blanksten, *op. cit.*, pp. 121–22.
13 Eder, *Anglo-American and Latin-American Law, op. cit.*, p. 154.

visits are not announced in advance. Another aspect of the high court's supervisory control is its broad power to discipline judges of the lower courts and to correct any malfeasance or misfeasance in the exercise of judicial duty. In Honduras the supreme court has the right summarily to impose a fine as large as 30 *lempiras* on a member of the lower judiciary. In extreme cases where a judge's bad conduct is clearly proved after a hearing, the court may order his removal from office. But it can reward as well as penalize; it can recognize good service by granting vacations with or without pay and by recommending promotions.[14]

In addition to supervising the lower courts and being responsible for its own employees, budgetary needs, and other housekeeping duties, the court determines the caliber of lawyers who practice before it. Their preparation, ability, and performance have a direct influence on the effectiveness of the court and the quality of justice it dispenses. Recognizing this, the court under legal or constitutional authorization establishes standards and qualifications which lawyers who practice before it must meet, and disqualifies from appearing before it any attorneys who fail to meet these conditions.

Easily one of the more unusual extraneous duties of a supreme court is that imposed in Mexico by Article 97, of the 1917 constitution. Under this article, the court is "to investigate . . . any act or acts constituting a violation of any individual guarantee or abuse of the public vote, or any other offense punishable by the federal law." Under this sweeping grant of investigatory power, the court must conduct an investigation if one of the constitutional officers or agencies requests it, but it can use its own discretion as to whether or not to act if a nongovernmental or private group makes the request.

In practice the High Court never has attempted spontaneously to investigate a political dispute resulting from an election, and its record of acting on request points up clearly that political factors influence its decisions. A review of the cases in which the court did act demonstrates that requests from a national authority, and especially the executive, are likely to produce an investigation but that almost from the first years of the present constitutional era, starting in 1917, the court has preferred not to accede to petitions from state officials to review elections at that or the municipal level, on the grounds that such action would invade state sovereignty. This despite the clear mandate to do so in the constitution. Petitions from opposition political parties, which seem to come as a matter of course after every election now that the revolutionary party has become all-powerful, are even more apt to receive short shrift.[15]

The Lower Courts

The supreme court, whose organization and operation we have discussed at length, is of course only the superstructure of the judicial sys-

---

[14] William S. Stokes, *Honduras: An Area Study in Government* (Madison, Wis.: University of Wisconsin Press, 1950), p. 137.

[15] Robert E. Scott, *Mexican Government in Transition* (Urbana, Ill.: University of Illinois Press, 1959), pp. 270–71.

tem. By far the greater part of the judicial load in every nation is carried by the many lower courts which are on the front line so to speak, grappling with judicial controversies in the villages, towns, and cities.

In the unitary nations, which have a single hierarchy of courts, the understructure of the judicial system is very simple. At the bottom is the justice of the peace or a similar official who can try persons accused of less serious criminal offenses and adjudicate the less important run-of-the-mine civil controversies which arise between citizens. The quality of justice rendered by these judges varies considerably between the nations. In Uruguay, for example, to be eligible for appointment as a justice of the peace, one must have a law degree, which attests to his legal qualifications and assures a professional disposition of cases which come before the court.

In Honduras, however, where illiteracy is high, the J.P. courts have never been very satisfactory, mainly because of the difficulty of securing competent personnel. The quality of the justices who obtained office by popular election was so low that selection by appointment was adopted in 1924. The change, however, has not greatly improved the quality of justices of the peace. Moreover, raising the requirements for the position is hardly likely to provide the needed qualified justices. "It is not logical to criticize the low educational and professional requirements demanded for qualification for the office," says William S. Stokes, "because, if they were raised it is doubtful that all the positions could be filled."[16]

The district courts located in the larger towns have both original and appellate jurisdiction. Besides reviewing appeals from decisions of justices of the peace, they also try civil and criminal cases. Above the district courts in the judicial pyramid is the departmental court, located in the capital of the department and ranking next to the supreme court of the nation. Like the district court, it also has original and appellate jurisdiction. In several of the nations there is also a court of appeals with appellate jurisdiction only and ranking between the departmental and supreme courts.[17]

In the federal states, the administration of justice is more complicated. A dual system of courts, both federal and state or provincial, is charged with the responsibility of administering justice. The federal courts, established to maintain the supremacy of the union and to pass on national questions, enjoy the lion's share of the jurisdiction, commensurate with the activities and power of the national government. The state or provincial courts have a far more restricted jurisdiction; they often "twiddle their thumbs" for lack of judicial business while the federal courts are overburdened with work.

---

16 Stokes, *Honduras, op. cit.,* p. 128.

17 In Honduras, an appraisal of the intermediate courts shows that they have discharged their responsibilities quite competently. *Ibid.,* pp. 130–35.

The dual system of courts in the federal nations has not proved to be very successful. Venezuela experimented with both the unitary and federal judicial systems until 1945, when it merged the two sets of courts into one national system. Brazil too has long had misgivings about the wisdom of a dual system. In 1937 it acted to centralize the judicial power and eliminate duplication by merging federal and state courts at the intermediate levels, with the exception of a single federal court of appeals. In Mexico the dual system still exists, with the national and state governments both having their own courts.

Special Courts

There are many special courts and jurisdictions in Latin America today. They are by no means new to the region. During colonial days, special tribunals existed for such narrow ranges of offenses as cockfighting, crimes committed in uninhabited places, and crimes committed by doctors, pharmacists, or barbers.[18]

Special courts have long handled a wide range of specialized cases. Military courts, for example, have long functioned to try members of the armed forces who commit offenses against military, maybe even national law. Special courts exist too for juveniles and to handle disputes regarding taxes, accounts, and elections.

As the role of government has greatly expanded in recent decades, the number of special courts has greatly increased too. They deal with a wide range of modern social problems. The labor courts, for example, which are found in most of the nations, were established because the regular courts lacked the specialized knowledge and trained personnel for coping with complex labor-management problems. Moreover, such cases should have special consideration because of the need for a speedy solution of conflicts which might drag on interminably if processed through the regular courts of law, with great detriment to the employer, the employee, and the nation.

Although the special courts have many strong points in their favor, there are strong arguments against them too. "The principal objection [against them] . . .," says Helen L. Clagett, "is not so much that they are alien to the Judicial Power, but rather that they are exempt from its control. Another objection is that where executive and judicial functions are combined, the judge and one of the parties to the controversy became merged in a single person, which element fosters the danger of despotism."[19]

---

[18] Helen L. Clagett, *Administration of Justice in Latin America* (New York: Oceana Publications, Inc., 1952), p. 55.

[19] *Ibid.*, p. 57. In pp. 59–115, the author discusses at length the different kinds of special courts in Latin America and gives a country-by-country description of the courts found in each one.

INDEPENDENCE OF THE JUDICIARY

As one of the three coequal branches of government, the judiciary according to law and theory should enjoy an independence of authority and function within its constitutionally allotted sphere of operation. To bolster or further this independence, various measures have been adopted in the several republics.

Selection on the basis of professional qualifications rather than political partisanship is becoming increasingly accepted in the region. The voice which the supreme court often has in the selection of its own members and judges of the lower courts, also the requirement of competitive examinations in some nations, are commendable steps in the right direction. They aim to make judicial service a professional career rather than the bailiwick of political favorites or hacks.

Permanence of tenure is likewise of great importance to the independence of the judiciary. Although only six of the nations provide for it at present, several others, as we noted earlier, grant it to justices who have been reelected successively.

In some of the nations the courts have been able to achieve or approximate the independence of function which the constitution envisaged. In Brazil they have attained a "respected and generally independent position in the constellation of Brazilian governmental organs," according to James L. Busey. The respect which very strong presidents, including Vargas, have accorded them is unusual in the quasidictatorial republics of Latin America.[20]

In Costa Rica too the judiciary enjoys a degree of independence and respect seldom found in Latin America. "The Costa Rican Constitution uses all the ingenuity of human invention to guarantee the autonomy of the seventeen-member Supreme Court," says Busey. "There is no doubt that the Costa Rican judiciary is free of presidential control. . . . In Costa Rica, the judiciary functions as an independent branch, and can and does issue judgments which are contrary to presidential policy or design."[21]

But in most of the other nations, the judiciary is not nearly so fortunate. There, independence is a high-sounding phrase in the paper constitution and bears little resemblance to reality.

As a part of the tripartite division of government, the courts have many

---

[20] James L. Busey, *Latin America: Political Institutions and Processes* (New York: Random House, Inc., 1964), p. 114. In the opinion of Martin Needler, however, the fact that milder dictators such as Vargas permit the courts to continue to function as usual should not be regarded as an evidence of their strength but rather as an indication of their ultimate political weakness. (Martin C. Needler, *Latin American Politics in Perspective* [Princeton, N.J.: D. Van Nostrand Co., Inc., 1963], p. 155.)

[21] Busey, *op. cit.*, pp. 78–79.

highly significant relations with the other two branches of government. These relations afford the executive and the congress many opportunities to undermine the independence of the judiciary if they desire to.

In performing his constitutional duties, the president exercises many powers which have a direct and vital bearing on the independence and integrity of the courts. As we have seen, he appoints or nominates members of the supreme court, often judges of the lower courts as well, thus deciding or having a strong voice in who will sit on the bench. He also initiates legislation relating to the courts. His proposals may greatly help both the institutional and personal interests of the judges; they may also very adversely affect them. The executive also grants pardons and reprieves. He can exercise this power with restraint, as the constitution no doubt intends, or he can use it vindicatively, to free convicted offenders wholesale and to undermine the prestige and very *raison d'être* of the courts. The president has still another whip hand over the courts. Responsible for executing the laws of the nation and commanding its various enforcement agencies, he may respect the rulings of the courts and assiduously enforce them, or he may show his disdain by making no effort to carry them out.

With these strong controls over the courts, the president usually has decidedly the upper hand in his relations with the judiciary. In most of the nations, he can easily dominate the judicial branch if he so desires. He often does, too.

The complaints against undue presidential influence or even dictation are legion. In Peru criticism of the executive has been restrained and pitched to a relatively low key. To remedy his undue influence, a new law was being formulated.[22]

In most of the other nations, however, the president is often accused not just of influencing the courts but of actually controlling them. Panama well typifies the situation in these nations. "Even the Supreme Court appears to be putty in the president's hands," say John and Mavis Biesanz. "Although the five justices are appointed for ten-year terms, they rarely express a majority opinion contrary to that of the current president, for dissenters can be retired with pay. Only when he flagrantly violates the rules of the political game or arouses public opinion against him do the . . . justices venture to oppose him."[23]

The congress too has a number of controls over the judiciary. Sometimes these are exercised in subservience to the president; sometimes they represent quite independent expressions of congressional design. The congress may approve nominations for the court made by the president or

[22] R. J. Owens, *Peru* (Royal Institute of International Affairs) (New York: Oxford University Press, 1963), p. 69.

[23] John and Mavis Biesanz, *The People of Panama* (New York: Columbia University Press, 1955), p. 141.

may itself appoint the members. It also has the power to pass legislation regarding the organization and jurisdiction of the courts, thus being able to determine their structure, size, authorized agenda, and many other matters of fundamental importance. Control of the purse strings is significant too.

Congress' power of removal is in some nations a bludgeon for intimidating the judiciary. In Mexico, although the justices supposedly enjoy permanence of tenure, this is a blatant farce. For in accordance with Article 111 of the 1917 constitution, they may be removed at the drop of a hat, a presidential hat of course, and approval by an absolute majority of a rubber-stamp Congress.

Congress' power to amend the constitution, whether exercised independently or under presidential pressure, also has a critical bearing on the role and authority of the courts, as the experience of Guatemala shows.

The process of change is so simple in fact that a president in power who has complete control over his political party may change the Constitution almost at will. The role of the Supreme Court as interpreter of the Constitution has therefore been relatively unimportant. It may declare laws unconstitutional but in the past this has had little significance because any powers desired by the government could easily be obtained through amendment of the law.[24]

In most countries the judiciary even in normal times find it an uphill battle to maintain their supposed independence. In times of repressive dictatorship, their chances of independence are far less. Sooner or later they are almost certain to get the dictatorial axe, wielded either as a naked display of power or in compliance with at least the formalities of constitutionality. In Argentina, Lonardi's provisional government reconstituted the Supreme Court by executive fiat, dismissing four of the five Peronista judges and filling their places with his own appointees. He used the direct approach because he had no congress to assist him or to approve his actions against the justices. By contrast, when Perón purged the Supreme Court in 1946 to make way for his appointees, he used the slower process of impeachment as provided by the constitution, having Congress firmly under his control.

Dictatorship almost invariably plays havoc with judicial independence. Yet while many a Latin American matter-of-factly accepts its aberrations, he shrinks with dread from the very idea of social revolution, which he realizes will completely overturn the government as well as the rest of society. Paradoxically, the courts of Mexico and Bolivia have enjoyed more independence of action during the course of the social revolutions than many courts do under many a "normal" dictatorship in Latin America. In Mexico, even during the most hectic days of the revolutionary government's attempts to put into effect its land reform program by expropriating properties in accordance with law, the courts were not only

---

[24] Nathan L. Whetten, *Guatemala: The Land and the People* (Caribbean Series, 4) (New Haven, Conn.: Yale University Press, 1961), p. 326.

very much in business but even greatly obstructed the government's program of reform.[25]

In Bolivia too, the new revolutionary regime which came into power in 1952, bent on accomplishing a full-scale social revolution, respected the independence of the judiciary. The nation's crash program of land reform was, like Mexico's, greatly impeded by the revolutionary regime's respect for due process of law.

> One of the principal causes for the slowness of the execution of the agrarian reform decree was the fact that there were four stages at which the landowner could appeal the decision to expropriate his holding. . . . Most landholders took full advantage of this right to appeal. The result has been that many cases have lingered on for years.[26]

CIVIL AND CRIMINAL PROCEDURE

Judicial procedure in Latin America is very different from that which we are accustomed to in the United States. Since the procedure of Argentina in civil and criminal cases is very similar to that of the other nations, we will take a close look at it.

In accordance with Argentine practice,[27] the suitor has to rely almost entirely on written forms for presenting his case. After his attorney prepares the complaint and the necessary affidavits and presents them to the court, the trial in time takes place. It is a private hearing, closed to the public. A secretary presides over the proceedings and attempts to record verbatim everything that is said—sometimes in longhand, incidentally. Witnesses appear both for and against the suitor. Lawyers for both sides ask them as many questions as they desire and prepare rebuttals for each other's arguments. The lawyer's questions, rebuttals, and summaries often run to great length. The whole proceeding, or more exactly, as much as can be faithfully recorded in longhand, is transcribed on stamped paper which even in 1943 cost 25 cents a sheet.

The judge seldom bothers to put in an appearance; usually he does not come face to face with the participants in a case unless they happen to be friends or acquaintances. His august judicial judgment is based solely on the "book of evidence," the voluminous notes which the secretary has taken from the testimony of witnesses and the arguments, rebuttals, and summaries of opposing attorneys.

Justice rendered under such a procedure is perforce under a handicap.

---

[25] James G. Maddox, "Mexican Agrarian Reform," *American Universities Field Staff Reports Service* (Mexico, D.F., July 3, 1957), p. 22. Eyler Simpson terms the government's efforts to expropriate land "the battle of injunctions." (Eyler N. Simpson, *The Ejido: Mexico's Way Out* [Chapel Hill, N.C.: University of North Carolina Press, 1937], pp. 113–15.)

[26] Robert J. Alexander, *The Bolivian National Revolution* (New Brunswick, N.J.: Rutgers University Press, 1958), p. 69.

[27] This account is from Austin F. Macdonald, *Government of the Argentine Republic* (New York: Thomas Y. Crowell Co., 1942), pp. 270–73.

"If the secretary takes notes in longhand—which some of them do, and if in addition the handwriting is almost indecipherable—which sometimes it is, then the judge may be forced to guess the exact meaning of many sentences or paragraphs. There is no assurance, moreover, that the secretary's notes are accurate. Yet the judge has no other guide."[28]

In criminal cases, too, the procedure is very different from that of Great Britain or the United States. Anyone arrested and charged with a penal offense is taken before an "instruction judge" (*juez de instrucción*) who functions as a combination committing magistrate and grand jury. In a preliminary hearing, he decides whether or not the accused will be held for trial, and if so, whether he will be required to wait in jail until the trial begins or released on bail, personal recognizance, or the assurance of a responsible person that he will appear for trial. Meanwhile, the accused may be held incommunicado for days while the police attempt to obtain incriminating evidence, apparently sometimes by what are commonly regarded as third degree methods.

Eventually the trial takes place. As in the case of civil suits, it is conducted behind closed doors. Sometimes the trial judge may actually preside over a part of the proceedings, but he practically never presides over the entire trial. He bases his judgment almost entirely on the book of evidence which a secretary has prepared for him.

There are other notable variations too from Anglo-Saxon criminal procedure. The accused, if convicted, may appeal from the court's decision; but the public prosecutor may appeal the verdict too. Consequently, a person found innocent in the lower court may be adjudged guilty in the court of appeals or have his penalty increased.

Another significant variation is the lack of a jury for deciding upon the innocence or guilt of the accused. Juries are not used, although the constitution of 1853, in Article 24 and in Article 67, clause 11, clearly authorized the Congress to adopt the jury system.[29]

JUDICIAL REVIEW

Probably the single greatest influence which Anglo-American law has had upon Latin American law is judicial review. Borrowing the practice from the United States where it appeared to work so well, every one of the nations today has some form of review by the courts.

In Brazil, the constitution in Article 101 provides for review by the courts of acts of the other branches of government. In Argentina, judicial

---

28 *Ibid.*, p. 272.

29 In compliance with the constitutional provision, the Argentine Senate did pass a measure providing for the jury system, but the Chamber of Deputies sidetracked the measure by proposing that the president appoint a commission to study the question and make a report. The commission was appointed and the report made to congress in 1874. No further action, however, was taken on the matter. (*Ibid.*, p. 273.)

review is the result of decisions made by the court itself. Just as the Supreme Court of the United States in the landmark case of Marbury *vs.* Madison successfully staked out its claim for authority to review and invalidate government actions which were in violation of the Constitution, the Supreme Court of Argentina in two cases of 1875 and 1884 successfully asserted its own right of review, one considerably more limited than that of courts in the United States.[30]

Borrowing the doctrine of judicial review from the United States was a simple matter. All constitution makers had to do was add a relevant section, a paragraph, or even a sentence. But making it really effective has been quite a problem. Several basic questions have arisen.

1. Who should have the authority to review laws or acts of government officers when their constitutionality is challenged? About three-fourths of the nations confer a limited power of review on the courts. The others, however, have decided that the function should be shared jointly by congress and the courts or should be exclusively a responsibility of congress. Popularly elected, congress in the opinion of many best represents the national will; any law which it passes should therefore be nullified only by another act of congress itself.

2. If the courts are to exercise the power of review, what should be the scope of this review?

In Argentina, whose constitutional experience most nearly parallels that of the United States, judicial review has been interpreted to mean that the federal courts may declare unconstitutional an executive, legislative, or judicial act which is in violation of the constitution. Yet in practice the court does not challenge the executive on any important issue or declare unconstitutional a major law enacted by the congress.

In the other nations judicial review is limited only to a decision of the particular case before the court. The body has no authority whatever to declare that an act of either the president or the congress is unconstitutional.

A unique form of judicial review is Mexico's writ of *amparo*, provided by Article 103 of the 1917 constitution and expanded by the Law of *Amparo* enacted in 1936. Under this law, any citizen may apply to one of the federal courts for redress if a law or act of a government official or judge impairs any of his rights guaranteed to him by the first 29 articles of the constitution.[31] A decision made by the court applies only to a specific case and does not presume to declare unconstitutional, or even to question the constitutionality of, an act of congress or of the president.

"It is clear," concludes Busey, referring to court decisions involving *amparo*, "that the courts never take a position contrary to that of execu-

---

[30] *Fallos de la Corte Suprema de Justica Nacional*, Series II, Vol. 13 (1875), p. 458; and Series II, Vol. 3 (1884), p. 197.

[31] A detailed statement of these rights is given in Ignacio Burgoa, *Las Garantias Individuales* (México: Ediciones Botas, 1944).

ive policy. No writs of *amparo* are issued against actions by the President, by members of his official family, by leading members of the PRI, or against federal legislation which has been passed by the congress."[32]

The writ of *amparo* is a home-grown institution, as native to the region as maize. For almost three decades it has been Mexico's prized contribution to the protection of private rights.

"The practice of the amparo," justifiably boasts Felipe Tena Ramírez, associate justice of the Federal Supreme Court of Mexico, "has made that institution, not a defense of the paramount law, but a means of protecting the individual rights recognized by the Constitution; the comparative lack of effectiveness of the *amparo* as a direct and authentic defense of constitutionality has been compensated for by its extraordinary effectiveness as a safeguard of human rights."[33]

The writ of *amparo* has made quite an impression on other nations too. The Universal Declaration of Human Rights, proclaimed by the United Nations General Assembly on December 10, 1948, contained a modified version of *amparo* in Article 8. Moreover, both Costa Rica and Nicaragua in their constitutions of 1950 adopted *amparo* as a protection for the rights of citizens.

Yet while protecting the citizen in individual cases, *amparo* falls far short of being real judicial review. Hundreds, even thousands, of *amparo* cases may be the result of a single act of congress which, in the opinion of the justices, infringes upon private rights and should be amended or repealed. But all the justices can do is to give relief to each suppliant and hope that the president or congress will take cognizance of their findings and change the law.[34]

However, while the court is wishfully hoping for a change in the law, it is deluged with a flood of appeals for redress. By 1950, it was falling so far behind with its work that although it handled 33,957 matters of judicial business, it still had a backlog of 27,026 cases, almost all concerning writs of *amparo*. To ease the court's critical situation, an amendment in 1951 to the Organic Law of the Judicial Branch temporarily added a fifth *sala* to assist in cleaning up the backlog of cases. Even with this extra help, the number of *amparo* cases continued to increase so fast that in 1955 the Supreme Court found it necessary to establish stricter rules for obtaining the writ.[35]

The provision in the Law of Amparo whereby five uniform supreme court decisions create *jurisprudencia* or precedent has apparently been of limited aid to the court.

Accustomed as we are to a court's being able to declare a legislative or executive act unconstitutional, its having to try case after case after

---

[32] Busey, *op. cit.*, p. 39.

[33] Felipe Tena Ramírez, "The International Expansion of the Mexican Amparo," *Inter-American Law Review*, Vol. I, No. 1 (January–June, 1959), p. 163.

[34] Scott, *op. cit.*, p. 267.

[35] *Ibid.*, pp. 268–69.

case which involve a point of law or procedure that the court is convinced is unconstitutional seems a frustrating waste of time and talent. It is as though a rancher or cattle farmer spent his full time beside the watering trough, pumping fresh water every time a cow comes up for a drink. The rancher or farmer knows how to accomplish the same result with far less effort; he puts an automatic float on the trough, and goes about his other business.

In most of the other nations, judicial review does not afford an effective protection as in Mexico to private rights, and extends only to administration of the law, not to the law itself. In Ecuador, two types of unconstitutionality are recognized—procedural and substantive. The Supreme Court has the power to declare an action procedurally unconstitutional but does not have the authority to find a measure substantively unconstitutional.[36]

Restricting the courts to deciding specific cases and denying them the authority to rule on questions of law have largely been responsible for the slight attention given to precedent. Although supreme court cases are reported in every one of the nations, they are published in volume form in only a few of them, in Argentina, Brazil, Costa Rica, Uruguay, and Venezuela. Not a single one of the nations has a complete record since independence of decisions of their supreme courts. Decisions of lower courts are seldom reported. Even in Argentina, whose judicial records are probably the most complete of all the nations, court opinions until 1903 were so brief and sketchily written that it was almost impossible to tell how the judges arrived at their decision. In that year, however, Antonio Bermejo, a distinguished jurist, became a member of the court, serving for 25 years. Under his influence supreme court decisions became more complete and more lucid.[37]

The minor role which precedent plays in the decision of cases also explains why law students spend most of their time studying legal theory and philosophy. For a case, however interesting it may seem at the moment, is soon judicially forgotten, gone with the wind. But as the student knows, a thorough knowledge of the codes and skillful application of logic are always helpful in a case before the bench.

CRITICISMS OF THE COURTS

Various scholarly appraisals made of the courts of specific nations have in general been complimentary. In Honduras, the caliber of justices of the Supreme Court has been high; consequently, they have been honored and respected. The major weakness of the court has been its hesitancy to assert its leadership and supervise the administration of justice, a hesitancy that

---

[36] Blanksten, *op. cit.*, pp. 137–38.
[37] Macdonald, *op. cit.*, p. 279.

is being gradually overcome.[38] In Uruguay, the courts are "a good complement to her congress and to her executive branch."[39] In Ecuador, "of the three national functions, the judiciary has operated most effectively."[40]

However, there have been notable criticisms in many countries of judicial procedure and the administration of justice. The recording of legal testimony on stamped paper is quite expensive, greatly adding to the cost of a lawsuit. Lawyers with their volubility further aggravate the problem of court costs, since their fees are based on the volume of testimony recorded upon the expensive legal paper.

Another criticism often made of the courts refers to the cumbersome, antiquated judicial procedure. The judges' reliance on the book of evidence prepared by a secretary and often giving only longhand bits of the testimony is repugnant to more advanced concepts of justice. Certainly few judges would care to have their fate determined by the same consideration which they directly give to cases which they decide.

Probably the most trenchant criticism of all is the long delay in the rendition of justice, a situation which from reliable indications seems true in every one of the republics. In Colombia, the courts have a tremendous backlog of cases waiting to be tried, estimated unofficially to be 150,000. Some of these have been on the docket for as long as 22 years; as a result, there is little incentive for instituting legal actions today.[41]

In Peru also, the wheels of justice grind slowly in spite of the large number of practicing lawyers. In December, 1956, 9,558 prisoners were in Peruvian jails, 7,395 (77.5%) of whom were still awaiting trial. The time spent in jail just waiting to be tried is sometimes even longer than the sentence subsequently meted out. To make matters worse, "prison conditions are poor," says R. J. Owens. "As many as twelve men may now occupy one small room, sleeping on the floor, before even having their depositions before a judge."[42]

The Goddess of Justice is usually portrayed as blindfolded, supposedly symbolizing impartiality and fairness. One sometimes wonders, however, if the blindfold may not be intended to spare the Goddess the anguish of seeing the travesties committed in the name of justice.

SUGGESTED READINGS

BLANKSTEN, GEORGE I. *Ecuador: Constitutions and Caudillos*, chap. vii. Berkeley: University of California Press, 1951.

———. *Perón's Argentina*, pp. 122–32. Chicago: University of Chicago Press, 1953.

---

[38] Stokes, *Honduras, op. cit.*, p. 138–39.

[39] Russell H. Fitzgibbon, *Uruguay: Portrait of a Democracy* (New Brunswick, N.J.: Rutgers University Press, 1954), p. 164.

[40] Blanksten, *op. cit.*, p. 172.

[41] *Hispanic American Report*, Vol. XVI, No. 9 (November, 1963), pp. 887–88.

[42] Owens, *op. cit.*, p. 69.

CABRERA, LUCIO A. "History of the Mexican Judiciary," *Mexico: A Symposium on Law and Government*, pp. 23–31. University of Miami School of Law; Inter-American Legal Studies, No. 3. Coral Gables, Fla.: University of Miami Press, October, 1958.

CLAGETT, HELEN L. *Administration of Justice in Latin America*. New York: Oceana Publications, Inc., 1952.

——. "Law and Court Systems," *Government and Politics in Latin America* (ed. HAROLD E. DAVIS), chap. 12. New York: Ronald Press Co., 1958.

EDER, PHANOR J. *Anglo-American and Latin-American Law; A Comparative Study*. New York: New York University Press, 1950.

——. "The Impact of the Common Law on Latin America," *Miami Law Quarterly*, Vol. IV, No. 4 (June, 1950), pp. 435–40.

GRANT, J. A. C. " 'Contract Clause' Litigation in Colombia; A Comparative Study in Judicial Review," *American Political Science Review*, Vol. XLII, No. 6 (December, 1948), pp. 1103–26.

——. "Judicial Control of Legislation: A Comparative Study," *The American Journal of Comparative Law*, Vol. III (1954), pp. 186–98.

——. "Judicial Review by Executive Reference Prior to Promulgation: the Colombian Experience," *Southern California Law Review*, Vol. XXXI, No. 2 (February, 1948), pp. 154–71.

GRUENING, ERNEST. *Mexico and Its Heritage*, pp. 497–514. New York: D. Appleton-Century Co., Inc., 1934.

INTER-AMERICAN LEGAL STUDIES. *Mexico: A Symposium on Law and Government*. No. 3. Coral Gables, Fla.: University of Miami Press, 1958.

JAMES, HERMAN G. *The Constitutional System of Brazil*, chap. v. Washington, D.C.: Carnegie Institution of Washington, 1923.

JORRÍN, MIGUEL. *Governments of Latin America*, chap. 6. New York: D. Van Nostrand Co., Inc., 1953.

LINARES QUINTANA, SEGUNDA V. "Comparison of the Constitutional Bases of the United States and Argentine Political Systems," *University of Pennsylvania Law Review*, Vol. 97, No. 5 (April, 1949), pp. 641–64.

MACDONALD, AUSTIN F. *Government of the Argentine Republic*, chap. 14. New York: Thomas Y. Crowell Co., 1942.

PIERSON, WILLIAM W., AND GIL, FEDERICO G. *Governments of Latin America*, chap. 11. New York: McGraw-Hill Book Co., Inc., 1957.

STOKES, WILLIAM S. *Honduras: An Area Study in Government*, pp. 106–50. Madison, Wis.: University of Wisconsin Press, 1950.

——. *Latin American Politics*, pp. 465–83. New York: Thomas Y. Crowell Co., 1959.

TENA RAMÍREZ, FELIPE. "The International Expansion of the Mexican Amparo," *Inter-American Law Review*, Vol. 1, No. 1 (January–June, 1959), pp. 163–66.

TUCKER, WILLIAM P. *The Mexican Government Today*, chap. 8. Minneapolis: University of Minnesota Press, 1957.

VANCE, JOHN THOMAS. *The Background of Hispanic-American Law*. New York: Central Book Co., 1943.

WASHINGTON FOREIGN LAW SOCIETY. *A Symposium on the Law of Latin America*. Washington, D.C.: George Washington University Law School, 1959.

INDEXES

INDEX OF AUTHORS

A

Abelardo Ramos, Jorge, 357
Abraham, William I., 265
Adams, Richard N., 97, 119, 244
Alamán, Lucas, 55, 58
Alba, Victor, 75
Alberdi Bautista, Juan, 378
Aldor, 201
Alexander, Robert J., 82, 196, 203, 230, 286, 287, 288, 291, 292, 294, 297, 298, 300, 357, 465
Almond, Gabriel A., 337
Anderson, Charles W., 76
Arce, Lucio, 244
Arciniegas, German, 11, 266
Arévalo, Juan José, 356
Azevedo, Thales de, 172

B

Barnett, Clifford R., 169, 176, 283, 290, 293, 296
Beals, Carleton, 231
Beard, Charles, 254
Becket, James, 227
Belcher, Clifford, 323
Beltran, Fausto, 241
Benham, F., 20
Bereday, George Z. F., 130, 137
Berle, A. A., 324
Berry, Jim, 201
Besault, Lawrence de, 312
Betancourt, Angel C., 106
Betancur-Mejía, Gabriel, 120, 126, 133
Biesanz, John, and Biesanz, Mavis, 87, 91, 92, 95, 98, 104, 129, 169, 348, 429, 463
Blanksten, George I., 39, 158, 167, 298, 312, 313, 316, 328, 336, 337, 354, 381, 396, 401, 419, 433, 434, 443, 445, 455, 458, 468, 470
Bonilla, Frank, 142
Braden, Charles, 153
Brand, W., 287, 288
Brandenburg, Frank R., 341

Bresser Pereira, L. C., 71
Brown, E. H. Phelps, 283
Buitrón, Aníbal, 38
Bunkley, Allison Williams, 117
Burgin, Miron, 254
Burgoa, Ignacio, 467
Burks, David D., 342, 344, 348, 432
Burnett, Ben G., 279, 296, 298
Busey, James L., 398, 399, 430, 431, 462, 468

C

Cabot, John M., 69
Calderón, F. García, 3, 42, 116, 187, 312, 330
Calderón González, J. A., 406
Callcott, Wilfrid Hardy, 163, 172
Calvo, Nicolás A., 378
Carr, Donald L., 383
Carroll, Thomas F., 230, 249
Castaneda, Carlos E., 147
Castillo, Isidro, 124
Chapman, Charles E., 93, 306, 317
Chavarria Frias, Alfredo, 272
Cipnic, Dennis J., 261
Clagett, Helen L., 364, 453, 456, 461
Cline, Howard F., 295, 296, 298, 301
Collier, John Jr., 38
Cohen, Alvin, 274
Coleman, James S., 337
Considine, John J., 172, 175
Crawford, W. Rex, 317
Cumberland, Charles C., 119
Cutright, Paul Russell, 10

D

Davalos, Guillermo, 280
Davis, Harold Eugene, 328, 341, 453, 456
Debuyst, Federico, 282, 284
Diffie, Bailey W., 57, 58, 59, 60, 61, 62, 152
Dobyns, Henry F., 118, 123
Dubois, Jules, 358

475

E

Echaíz, René León, 340
Eder, Phanor James, 451, 452, 453, 458
Efron, David, 225, 228
Elliott, L. E., 36
Estrada, Adriana, 5, 26, 33, 34, 49, 79, 81, 112, 121, 170, 173
Estrada, José M., 415

F

Fals-Borda, Hans, 97, 98, 99, 103, 338
Faron, Louis C., 39
Febres Cordero, Facion, 138
Feldman, Arnold S., 287
Ferguson, J. Halcro, 45, 175
Fernandez, José, 241
Filho, M. B. Lourenço, 123
Finer, Herman, 274
Fitzgibbon, Russell, 94, 118, 169, 202, 271, 276, 317, 337, 361, 364, 377, 396, 404, 431, 470
Flores, Edmundo, 239
Fluharty, Vernon L., 14, 64, 66, 71, 73, 197, 199, 321, 443
Ford, Thomas R., 158, 222, 225, 305, 309, 373
Frazer, Sir James George, 103
Freyre, Gilberto, 42, 43, 44, 57, 62, 67, 75, 89, 96, 101, 168, 218
Furtado, Celso, 262, 269

G

Galíndez Suárez, Jesús, 157
Gallardo, Ricardo, 404
García, Aurelio, 373
Gil, Federico G., 351, 421
Gillin, John P., 76, 272
Gómez, R. A., 386, 396, 415
Goodspeed, Stephen S., 412
Graham, David L., 342
Grant, J. A. C., 452
Griffith, William, 128
Gruening, Ernest, 150, 153, 221, 286, 288, 289, 292
Gutierrez Ostria, Alberto, 240

H

Hall, Clarence W., 144
Hanke, Lewis, 11, 18, 37, 40, 67, 101, 117, 160, 271, 355
Hanson, Simon G., 27
Haring, Clarence H., 149
Harris, Marvin, 78, 85, 91, 101, 104
Havighurst, Robert J., 73, 105

Helguera, J. León, 202
Herrero, Vincente, 373
Herring, Hubert, 7, 13, 16, 56, 57, 60, 68, 117, 158, 206, 307, 308, 312, 339, 400
Hicks, Albert C., 321
Hirschman, Albert O., 75, 230
Holleran, Mary P., 155, 156, 157, 166
Holley, H.A., 20
Holmberg, Allan R., 119, 123
Hughlette, Lloyd, 258
Hutchinson, Harry W., 77

I

Interlandi, 200
Ireland, Gordon, 157
Isacovich, Marcelo, 19

J

Jaffe, A. J., 282
James, Preston E., 12, 15, 44
Johnson, John J., 75, 104, 105, 107, 163, 169, 188, 195, 196, 198, 275
Jorrín, Miguel, 396

K

Kantor, Harry, 351
Kautsky, John J., 257, 293
Kendall, Willmore, 340
Kennedy, John J., 86, 196
Kling, Merle, 343
Kneller, George F., 135
Koster, Henry, 110
Kybal, Elba, 270

L

Labelle, Yvan, 5, 26, 33, 49, 79, 112, 121, 170, 173
Lagardelle, Hubert, 280
Lannoy, Juan Luis de, 88
Lauwerys, Joseph A., 130, 137
Lavin, John, 308, 314, 315
Leonard, Olen E., 130
Leuschner, Bruno, 19
Lewis, Oscar, 39, 72, 237, 288
Lewis, Ross, 402
Lieuwen, Edwin, 187, 188, 192, 196, 197, 202, 204, 207, 208, 209, 210, 354
Lindberg, John, 238, 272
Long, Mott, 200
Longchamps, 311, 315
Lott, Leo B., 396
Lowenstein, Karl, 293, 319, 376, 383, 416
Luzardo, Rodolfo, 257

M

Macdonald, Austin, F., 379, 389, 411, 415, 416, 421, 424, 429, 465, 466, 468
MacGaffey, Wyatt, 169, 176, 283, 290, 293, 296
Maddox, James G., 234, 238, 465
Mañach, Jorge, 177
Mantovani, Juan, 137
Maranhão, Walmyr, 79
Martin, Edwin M., 356
Martz, John D., 167, 175, 348, 423
Matthews, Herbert L., 28, 39, 59, 227, 336
McBride, George McCutcheon, 66, 221
McCrocklin, James H., 425
McLaughlin, Kathleen, 28
Mecham, J. Lloyd, 147, 148, 150, 152, 157, 160, 174
Mejia Fernandez, Miguel, 281
Miranda, José, 402
Moody, Joseph N., 147
Moore, Wilbert E., 287, 292
Morse, Richard M., 69, 70, 87, 100, 107, 268
Morton, Ward M., 364, 374
Moses, Bernard, 35, 56, 153
Mosk, Sanford A., 254, 267, 275, 294, 317

N

Nanita, Abelardo R., 310
Needler, Martin C., 341, 419, 462
Nelson, Lowry, 71, 97, 102
Ness, Norman T., 225, 228
Normano, J. F., 257

O

Odell, Peter R., 17
Onís, Juan de, 188
Ostria Gutierrex, Alberto, 240
Owens, R. J., 463, 470
Ozaeta, Pablo, M., 130

P

Palacio, Vicente Riva, 57
Palomo, Eduardo, 239, 323
Pareja Diezcanseco, Alfredo, 309
Parkes, Henry Bamford, 191, 205, 221, 300
Patch, Richard M., 99, 101, 103, 108, 140, 141, 244, 343, 344
Paz-Soldan, José Pareja, 381, 406, 457
Pendle, George, 62, 190, 196, 338, 355
Pentony, De Vere E., 261
Pérez, Gustavo, 88
Pierson, Donald, 41, 43, 44, 61, 64, 65, 110, 149

Pierson, W. W., 317, 351, 421
Pike, Fredrick, 271, 352
Plazo, Galo, 125, 127, 270
Poblete-Troncoso, Moises, 279, 296, 298
Porter, Charles O., 82
Prewett, Virginia, 204

Q

Quezada, Abel, 326
Quijada, Ramón, 249
Quintana, Segundo V. Linares, 378, 451

R

Ramella, Pablo A., 417, 456
Ranney, J. Austin, 340
Ravines, Eudocio, 357
Reichard, Eugene C., 323
Reinsch, Paul S., 350
Reissig, Luis, 133
Rengger, J. R., 311, 315
Renne, Ronald R., 230
Rio, Angel del, 123, 177, 254
Rippy, J. Fred, 55, 151, 190, 305, 306, 309, 317, 320, 339, 373
Rivera, José Enstacio, 11
Romoli, Kathleen, 8, 15
Rosenblat, Angel, 49
Rourke, Thomas, 308, 314
Rubin, Vera, 100
Rycroft, W. Stanley, 38, 175

S

Sabogal Wiesse, José R., 176
Sáchica, Luis Carlos, 377
Sánchez, George I., 136, 142
Sánchez, Luis Alberto, 3, 137, 141
Santos, Eduardo, 198
Schaeffer, Wendell G., 56
Schmitt, Karl M., 342, 344, 348, 359, 432
Schneider, Ronald M., 357, 358
Schurz, William Lytle, 9, 15, 23, 57, 104, 120, 152, 172, 384
Scott, Robert, E., 209, 408, 409, 410, 416, 448, 459, 468
Senior, Clarence, 177, 232, 233, 234, 236, 250
Service, Elman R., and Service, Helen S., 87, 98, 99, 100, 101, 102
Shepherd, William Robert, 204
Siegel, Morris, 116
Silvert, K. H., 336
Simpson, Eyler N., 221, 235, 465
Smith, Raymond T., 100
Smith, T. Lynn, 47, 48, 97, 124, 176, 267
Soule, George, 225, 228
Spain, August O., 382

Staley, Eugene, 261
Stark, Harry, 253, 259, 292
Steinberg, S. H., 376
Sternberg, Hilgard O'Reilly, 107
Stevenson, W. B., 8
Steward, Julian H., 39
Stokes, William S., 108, 127, 142, 324, 381,
    402, 410, 412, 435, 452, 459, 460, 470
Street, John, 309
Szulc, Tad, 266, 307, 312

T

Tannenbaum, Frank, 18, 28, 39, 40, 48, 59,
    60, 61, 119, 123, 148, 149, 205, 206, 207,
    208, 227, 235, 249, 383, 429
Taylor, Phillip B., 364
Tucker, William P., 295, 433
Tumin, Melvin M., 89, 94

U

Uzcátegui, Emilio, 112, 113, 114, 116, 117,
    130

V

Vagts, Alfred, 191
Vance, John Thomas, 451
Vanger, Milton I., 396

Vega y Pagan, Ernesto, 311
Vernon, Raymond, 266, 343
Viamonte, 378
Villalpando, Abelardo R., 242
Vinacua, Rodolfo, 117

W

Wagley, Charles, 70, 74, 98
Wald, Haskell P., 225, 227
Warren, Harris Gaylord, 330, 331, 413
Washington, S. Walter, 141
Weil, Felix J., 218
Wheare, K. C., 431
Whetten, Nathan L., 86, 89, 104, 232, 233,
    361, 464
Whitaker, Arthur P., 317, 322, 354
Wigmore, John H., 450
Wilgus, A. Curtis, 152, 310, 313, 314, 315
Wise, George S., 318, 319, 364
Worcester, Donald R., 56
Wyckoff, Theodore, 199
Wythe, George, 262, 293

Y

Ydígoras Fuentes, Miguel, 358

INDEX OF SUBJECTS

A

Absenteeism, schools, 112
Acción Cultural Popular, 130
Acción Popular, 451
Aconcagua, 8
Adelberto Rivera, Julio, 397
Africa, effects on Latin America, 6
African pagan fetishistic cults, 176
Agrarian Code, Mexico, 233
Agrarian Reform law
  Bolivia, 238, 243
  Cuba, 245, 246
  Venezuela, 247
Agriculture
  concentration of land ownership, 215–18
  corporate mechanized farms, 218
  haciendas
    effects of, 222–26
    life at, 221–22
    origin of, 219–20
  latifundios, 217
  minifundios, 217
  peonage and exploitation of labor, 222–26
  percentage of population engaged in, 216
  productivity, 224
  types of large-scale enterprises, 218–27
Aguirre Cerda, Pedro, 67
Airplanes, 26–28
Airway systems, main lines and comparative distances, 26
Alamán, Lucas, 150
Alberdi, Juan Bautista, 377, 406
Aleijadinho (Antônio Francisco Lisboa), 43
Alessandri, Jorge, 297, 398, 410, 412, 420
Alessandri Palma, Arturo, 424
Alexander VI, Pope, 147
Alfaro, Eloy, 424, 447
Alliance for Progress, 69, 258, 266
Alpine Meadows, 12
Altiplano, 14, 118
Alto Beni, 243

Amadeo Cardoza, Carlos and Luis, 390
Amancebados, 88
Amancebamiento, 98
Amaro, Joaquín, 206, 207, 208
Amazon region, 14, 172, 219
Amazon River, 23, 27
America, 165
American School, Quito, 127
Américas, 46, 77, 115, 124, 131, 186, 217, 260, 263, 289, 290
Amnesty, 414
Amparo, 235, 398, 451, 467–68
Anchieta, José de, 62
Andes, 6, 8, 12
  comparison with Rockies, 7
Anticlericalism, 150–68
Antimony, 16
Apalabrados, 88
APRA (*Alianza Popular Revolucionaria Americana*), 140, 351–52
Aramayo interests, 19
Aramburu, Pedro Eugenio, 374
Arana, Barros, 155
Araucanians, 35
Arbenz, Jacobo, 82, 401
Arce, Lucio, 244
Area, 4
  comparison maps, 5
Argentina
  agriculture, per cent of population in, 216
  Catholics, per cent of population, 170
  coal, 19
  concentration of land ownership, 215, 217, 218
  constitutions, 371, 374, 376, 378, 379
  courts, 451, 454, 456, 457, 464, 465, 469
  executives, 397, 399, 401, 405, 406, 407, 410, 411, 414–15, 422
  intervention in provinces, 414–15
  federalism, 381
  immigrant influence, 37
  land problem, 220
  latifundios, 217
  legislature, 434, 435, 436, 438, 441, 442, 444, 445, 448

Argentina—*Cont.*
 minifundios, 217
 pampa, 11–12
 political asylum, 390
 population increase, 47–49
 production costs, 268
 railroads, renovation of, 22
 religious instruction in public schools,
  66, 157
 Sáenz Peña electoral reform, 364
 Sarmiento's influence, 117
 state-owned fleet, 24
 Teachers for the Americas plan, 124
 top-heavy government bureaucracy,
  271
 vice-president, 426
Argentine Association of English Culture, 217
Arguello, Leonardo, 182
Arica, 9
Armed Forces
 alternating trends of militarism, 185–89
 budgetary share of, 184, 185
 constitutional restrictions on, 193
 divided allegiance of officers, 201–2
 evaluation of as reformers, 197–99
 executive, selection or control of, 181
 influences lessening power, 192–95
 interest in social reform, 195–96
 interference in politics, 181–85
 interservice rivalries, 194
 middle class background, 195
 militarism
  and military interference, causes of,
   189–92
  effects of German, Italian and other
   missions, 191
 organized labor, relation to, 194
 political parties, relation to, 193–94
 public policy, control over, 183–84
 status of military, nations where
  dominating, 199–200
  nonpolitical, 202–4
  transitional, 200–202
Arosemena, Carlos Julio, 328
Arrivistas, 69
Arsenic, 16
Artigas, José Gervasio, 309
Arze, Guevara, 362
Assassinations, 424–25
Assimilation of Negroes, 41–42, 43, 44
Asunción, 22, 168
Atacama Desert, 15
Atlantico del Golfo, 245
Avellaneda, 300
Ave Maria, 176, 177
Avila Camacho, Maximino, 409
Aymara, 114
Aztecs, 450

B

Balmaceda, José Manuel, 447
Barrack boredom, 191
Barraganía, 152
Barrientos, René, 203, 397
Barros, Adhemar de, 70
Bates, Henry, 10
Batista, Fulgencio, 167, 312, 314, 321, 327,
  401, 423
Batlle y Ordóñez, José, 151, 169, 202, 275,
  328, 395
Beláunde Terry, Fernando, 397, 431
Bella Vista Barracks, 203
Betancourt, Rómulo, 182, 188, 353, 403,
  413, 430
Big House, 101, 168, 220
Bismuth, 16
Blancos, 345
Bleaching of race, 48
Bogotá, 265
Bolivia
 agriculture, per cent of population ac-
  tive in, 216
 ballot-stealing, 362
 colonization, 228, 243–44
 constitutions, 371, 374, 375, 376, 379
 courts, 452, 456, 464, 465
 executive, 397, 401, 405
 Indian's status, 39
 labor's support of government, 299,
  300
 land reform, 238–44
 legislature, 434, 435, 436, 438, 446
 military, subordination of, 203
 state of siege, 418
 tin, 16, 17, 18, 19
 vice-president, 425, 426
Book of evidence, 465
Boyer, Jean Pierre, 394
Bracero (wetback), 236
Branco Castello, Humberto, 397
Brasilia, 372
Brazil
 Big House of landed aristocracy, 28,
  67–68
 Brazilian Plateau, 9–10
 capital provided by exploitation of labor, 288
 celibacy, issue of, 152
 Church
  Church-state relations, 67
  receptivity to Protestantism, 172
  separation of Church and state, 159–
   60
 coal, 19
 constitutions, 373, 375, 376, 378
 courts, 451, 454, 456, 457, 462, 466, 469
 engineers, shortage of, 267
 executive, 393, 394, 395, 397, 400, 401,
  403, 413, 415, 416

Brazil—*Cont.*
 expression of political discontent, 363
 federalism, 382, 383, 384
 industrial development, 257
 intervention, executive, 416
 iron, 16
 land problem, 219
 legislature, 430, 434, 435, 436, 438, 444
 Negroes, acceptance of, 65
 vice-president, 426
 Volta Redonda Iron and Steel Co., 261
 water power, 20, 259
 workers
  benefits given, 293–94
  forbidden to strike, 288
  wage increases, illusory, 286
Brízola, Leonel, 384
Buenos Aires, 10, 166, 265, 300, 387, 390, 399
Bulnes, Francisco, 205
Busch, Germán, 198
Bustamente, José Luis, 184

C

Cabildos, 56
Cacareco, 363
Cadmium, 16
Café Filho, João, 400
Calles, Plutarco, 206, 207, 208
Cámaras, judicial, 457
Camayuras, 38
Campañia de Acero del Pacifico, 261
Campesinos, 87, 241, 242, 244
Cape Horn, 26
Captains-general, 55
Caracas, 9
 Archbishop of, 247
Cárdenas, Lázaro, 82, 206, 208, 209, 234, 235, 300, 388, 407
Carranza, Venustiano, 374, 424
Carrera, Rafael, 339
Casa chica, 90, 91
Case law, 453
Castillo Armas, Carlos, 424
Castro, Cipriano, 308
Castro Jijon, Ramón, 397
Castro Ruz, Fidel, 167, 397
Catholic League for the Protection of Religious Liberty, 161
Catholic Pontifical University, Chile, 176
Catholicism; *see* Church
Catholics, percentage of population, 170
Caudillos or dictators
 ability, 310
 absolute power, 312
 ambition, 309–10
 backgrounds, 306–11
 civilian or military status, 306
 concern for their safety, 315–16

Caudillos or dictators—*Cont.*
 contributions made, 319–20
 cuartelazos, 325–28
 differences between them, 306–9
 direct or indirect control, 312
 effects on society, 319–22
 election to office, 311–12
 family background, 307
 golpes de estado, 324–25
 harm done, 321–22
 henchmen, necessity of satisfying, 314
 legitimacy, preference for, 313
 mass, keeping in tow, 315
 opposition, keeping under control, 314
 origin and duration, 305–6
 personality, 308
 race, 307
 religion and morals, 308
 revolutions, kinds of, 322–33
  social, 331–33
 rise to power, means of, 311–12
 scope of authority, 307
 vanity, 310–11
 wars of independence, 322–24
 why they have continued to flourish, 316–19
Cedillo, Saturnino, 407
Center of Intercultural Formation (CIF Study No. 1), 5, 26, 33, 34, 49, 79, 81, 112, 121, 170, 173, 216, 224, 282, 284, 346, 347
Center of Latin American Studies, 346
Central America, area compared with Texas, 5
Central University, Quito, 434
Cerro de Pasco, 15
Chaco War, 182, 185, 203
Chaperé, 243–44
Chapetones, 56
Chase National Bank, 80, 285
Chávez, Ñuflo, 240
Chaviano del Rio, Alberto, 107
Chicha, 39
Child labor, 114, 284
Children, care and training of, 95–99
Chile
 cabinet, 420
 coal, 19
 constitutions, 371, 376
 copper, 16, 17
 courts, 452, 454, 455, 456
 earthquake damage, 9
 executive, 394, 397, 398, 401, 405, 407, 419, 420
 federalism, 381
 fomento, 273
 Huachipato steel plant, 261
 legislature, 410, 412, 430, 434, 436, 438, 441, 445, 447
 military, autonomy of, 202

Chile—*Cont.*
 multiparty system, 249–50
 nitrates, 16, 18
 production costs, 268
 registration of voters, 36
 speech and press, freedom of, 386, 387
 state of siege, 418
 vice-president, 426
 water power, 20
Chillán, 9, 273
Chinese immigrants, 36
Christian Action Party, 164, 165
Christian Democrats, 355
Christophe, Henri, 316, 393, 394
Church; *see also* Protestantism
 anticlericalism, 150–51
 banking, 158
 celibacy, 152
 cemeteries, 158
 Church-state relationships, classification of, 162
 colonial society
   crown control, 147, 148–49
   influence and activities, 148–49
 dictators, policy toward, 166–68
 education, 157–58
 expropriation of its wealth, 155–56
 financial straits, 171
 foreign clergy, 154
 Juan Perón, relation to, 166–67
 marriage and the family, 156–57
 patronage, 147
 politics, participation in, 162–68
 practicing Catholics, 163
 priesthood, reform of, 151–54
 Puerto Rican election of 1960, 163–65
 secular activities assumed by the state,
   156–59
 separation from state
   peaceable, 159–60
   violent, 160–62
 shortage of priests, 169–71
 social reform, challenge posed by, 176–
   78
 spirituality of priests, 153–54
 strength and influence, 170
 venality of priests, 152–53
 wars of independence
   hierarchy, role of, 149–50
   lower clergy, role of, 150
 welfare programs, 158
Cities, fast growth of, 45
Civil codes
 Argentina, 452
 France, 452
 Venezuela, 452
Civil constitution of the clergy, 152
Civil law, 450, 451
Cleveland, Grover, 36
Climate, temperature and rainfall, 13

Coal, 19
Cobalt, 16
Coca, 224
Cochabamba, 328
Codes, 452–53
Coeducation, 127
Colegiado, 395
Colegio Militar, Chapultepec, 207
Colombia
 Church
   relationship with state, 67, 157
   separation of Church and state, 158
 climate, 14
 constitutions, 371, 372, 376
 courts, 451, 452, 456, 457, 458, 470
 designado, 426
 executive, 397, 399, 401
 federalism, 381
 habeas corpus, 386
 impeachment, 423–24
 legislature, 434, 435, 436, 438, 443, 444,
   446, 447
 military, autonomy of, 202
 political asylum, 390
 railroads, renovation of, 22
 religion, freedom of, 388
 religious instruction in public school,
   66
 social classes today, 26–27
 speech and press, freedom of, 386
 state of siege, 417–18
 tax on farmland, 227–28
 topography, 8
 two-party system, 348
 University of, 134
Colonization, 228–29
Colorados, 345
Comadre, 103
Comisión de Reforma Agraria, Venezuela, 247, 248
Committee for Economic Development,
   139, 261
Common Education Law, 118
Common Market, 6
Communism and Communist Party, 256–
   59
Compadre, 45, 103
Compadrazgo, 103–4
CONCA, Bolivia, 242
Concepción, 9, 273
Confederate immigrants, 36
Consanguineous marriages, 101
Constitutions
 amendments, 379
 characteristics, 371–73
 foreign influences
   France, 377
   Mexico, 378
   Spain, 377
   United States, 377–78

Constitutions—*Cont.*
  formulation and adoption, 373–75
  large number, 375–76
  length, 371–72
  newness, 371
  "paper" versus "real," 372–73, 376
  table of, by countries, 376
Consul, life, 394
Contempt of court, 458
Continuismo, 404
Conviviente, 99
Cooperative for marketing rice, 242
COPEI, 355–56
Copello, Cardinal, 167
Cordoba, Catholic University of, 136, 137
Córdoba Concha, Luis, 175
Corporate mechanized farm, 77, 218
Costa Rica
  constitutions, 371, 376
  courts, 462, 468, 469
  executive, 397, 398, 399, 401, 406
  legislature, 431, 432, 434, 435, 441
  military, subordination of, 203
  Protection of Industries Law, 264
  state of siege, 418
  vice-president, 426
Courts and law
  attributes of Latin American law
    blend of systems, 450–52
    embodiment in codes, 452–53
    extensive borrowing, 452
  criticisms of courts, 469–70
  independence of judiciary, 462–65
  judicial review, 466–69
  lower courts, 459–61
  procedure, civil and criminal, 465–66
  special courts, 461
  supreme court
    composition, 454
    functioning, 457–58
    jurisdiction, 458
    power to punish contempt, 458
    qualifications of judges, 454–55
    restrictions on judges, 455
    selection of judges, 455–56
    special duties, 458–59
    tenure, 456–57
Creoles; see *Criollos*
Crias, 62
Criollos, 55, 56, 150, 154, 195
Cristero, 161
Cuba
  constitutions, 375, 376
  courts, 451, 454, 456
  executive, 397, 401, 405
  impeachment, 423
  inamoviladad, 290
  land reform program, 244–47
  legislature, 433, 434, 436
  military, family control of, 107

Cuba—*Cont.*
  vice-president, 426
  women, status of, 106
Cuban-American Sugar Company, 245
Cuzco, 9

D

Davila, Mario, 165
Davis, Archbishop, 164
Debt slavery, 59
Decision, 170
Decrees, 238, 411–12
Dejoie, Louis, 432
Delegated Committee, Venezuela, 408
Democratic Action, 182, 355, 397
Democratic Union Party, 166
Depression, the great, 187
Desacato, 386
Deserts, 15
Designado, 426
Díaz, Porfirio, 160, 206, 316
Díaz-potism, 206
Díaz Soto y Gama, Antonio, 235
Dictators and dictatorship; see *Caudillos*
Dignidad, 275, 442
Dominican Republic
  constitutions, 371, 373, 375, 376, 403
  courts, 454, 456, 457
  executive, 397, 401
  legislature, 434, 437, 439, 444, 448
  political asylum, 390
Dorticos Torrado, Oswaldo, 397
Douglas, William O., 374
Dress, 63
Dropouts, school, 112–13, 126
Dunphy, José María, 166–67
Dutch immigrants, 36
Duvalier, François, 166, 176, 316, 390, 394, 397, 401, 405, 430, 432

E

Earthquakes, 8, 9
Echandi, Mario, 204
Economic development; see Industry and industrial development
Ecuador
  constitutions, 375, 376, 379
  courts, 452, 454, 455, 457, 458, 470
  education
    compulsory, 111–12
    language requirements, 114–15
    literacy campaigns, 54, 129–30
    progress under García Moreno, 116–17
  executive, 396, 397, 401, 406
  federalism, 380
  legislature, 432, 434, 437, 439, 441, 443, 444, 445

Ecuador—*Cont.*
  private rights, 385
  religion, freedom of, 388
  vice-president, 425–26
Education
  adult education and literacy cam-
    paigns, 129–30
  constitutional and legal provisions re-
    garding, 110–12
  desire for an education, 118
  dropout, 112
  financial support, 120
  García Moreno, 116–17
  higher
    autonomous status, 136–37
    courses of study selected, 132–33
    curriculum, 132
    faculty, 135–36
    financial support, 134
    granting of degrees, 136
    methods of instruction, 134
    number of institutions and students,
      132
    physical facilities, 134–35
    politics, student, 139–41
      Reform Movement, Student,
        accomplishments, 137–38
        origin and objectives, 137
        shortcomings and abuses, 138–39
    violence, student, 141–43
  illiteracy, 113, 131
  importance recognized, 110
  Indians' resistance to, 115–16
  lack of incentive, 114
  language barrier, 114
  newspaper circulation, 115
  opposition of large landowners, 113
  overreliance upon legislation, 116
  poverty of the masses as a deterrent to,
    113–14
  primary and secondary
    absenteeism, 112
    centralized control, 128–29
    coeducation, 127
    compulsory attendance, 111–12
    curriculum, 125
    enrollment, 112, 125–26
    methods of instruction, 127–28
    schools, construction of, 114, 120–21
    segregation of sexes, 126–27
  teachers
    hardships, 123
    qualifications, 122
    responsibilities, 123–24
    salary, 122
    shortage, 122
  Vicos, an experimental program, 118–
    19, 123
Ejidatarios, 74, 232, 236
Ejidos, 231, 232, 234

El Dia, 169
Elections
  ballots, 362
  ballot stealing, 361–62
  campaign, 360–62
  corrupt practices, 363
  military supervision, 362
  opposition, restrictions on, 361
  protest, registration of, 363
  qualifications for voting, 359–60
  registration, 360
  suffrage, woman's, effects of, 360
  voter turnout, 362
El Pueblo, 166
El Salvador
  constitutions, 371, 373, 374, 375, 376
  courts, 454, 456, 457
  education, stress on, 111
  executive, 397, 399, 401, 405
  legislature, 432, 434, 441, 446
  National Autonomous University of,
    136
  steel mill, semi-integrated, 261
  vice-president, 426
El Teniente, 268
El Tiempo, 201
Emperors, 393–94
Encomienda, 58
English immigrants, 36
English common law, 451, 453
Enrollment, schools, 112
Esquire, 323
Estado de sitio, 416–18
Ethnic composition by countries, 34
Excommunication, 159, 167
Executive
  cabinet, 418–21
  caliber, 400
  committee or council, 395
  continuismo, 404
  dominant role, 396
  emperor, 393
  exposure to public, 424–25
  ex-presidents, 426–27
  life consul and life president, 394
  means of selection, 405
  methods of exercising control, 421–22
  monarch, 393
  powers
    administration, 408
    appointment and removal, 408–9
    armed forces, 406–8
    decree, 411–12
    finance, 412–13
    foreign relations, 413–14
    intervention, 414–16
    judicial, 414
    legislative, 409–11
    state of siege, 416–18

Executive—*Cont.*
 qualifications, 399–400
 reelection, eligibility for, 402–5
 responsibility, 422–24
 succession, 425–26
 term, 401–2
 transfer of office, 405–6
 types since independence, 393–96
Executives in office, February, 1965, 397
Export-Import Bank, 25, 273
Ex-presidents, utilization of, 426

F

Family; *see also* Church, marriage and
  the family
 children, care and training, 95–99
 compadre relationship, 103–4
 declining influence, 104–6
 extended, 100–104
 husband, authoritarian role, 89–90
  extramarital ventures, 90–92
 influence on society, 106–8
 lower class, 97–100
 machismo, 90, 91
 marriage, types of, 85–89
  civil, 85, 86
  consanguineous, 101
  consensual, 87–89
  religious, 86–87
 matrifocal or matrilineal family, 99–100
 middle and upper class family, 89–97
 wife, status and role of, 92–95, 97
Favelados, 78
Favelas, 78–79
Fazenda, 219
Fazendeiros, 110, 219
Federalism
 arguments for and against, 380–81
 background, 380
 operation, 381–84
Fiesta, 59
Figueres, José, 353, 413
Figueroa Alcorta, José, 422
Filippo, Virgilio, 166
Fiscales, 458
Flight of capital, 266
Flores, Edmundo, 240
Fomento, Chilean, 273–74
Foreign capital, 16
Fotrama, 178
Francía, José Gaspar Rodríquez de, 190,
  307, 311, 315, 316, 394
Franco, Rafael, 198
Frei, Eduardo, 350, 360, 397
French immigrants, 36
Frondizi, Arturo, 183, 184, 271, 401
Fueros, 55, 190, 191
Fundo Social Sindical, 297

G

Gachupines, 56, 150
Galindez, Jesús, 340
Gallegos, Rómulo, 184
Gamonalismo, 222
García Moreno, Gabriel, 116–17, 308, 388,
  424
García, Raul Alfonso, 241
Garrido, Tomás, 161
Gaucho, 11
Geographical aspects
 area, 3, 4, 5
 climate, 12–16
 earthquakes, 8–9, 273
  effects of, 4–6, 15, 28–30
 harbors, 24
 jungles or rain forests, 10–11
 location, 4–6
 mountains, 8–9
 pampas, 11–12
 plateaus, 9–10
 rainfall, 13, 15, 16
 rivers; *see specific name*
 topography, 6–12
German immigrants, 35
Gobernación, Ministry of, 419
Gold, 16
Gómez, Juan Vicente, 171, 308, 315, 316
Gómez, Máximo, 169
Goulart, João, 183, 395, 413
Grail, 171
Graphite, 16
Gross national product, 120, 257, 258, 263,
  328
Guaraní, 63, 375
Guatemala
 church, state of, 155–56
 communism, outlawing of, 361
 communist infiltration, 358
 constitutions, 376
 courts, 456, 457
 executive, 397, 401, 403
 expropriation of church properties, 65–
  66
 extramarital ventures, attempt to curb,
  90–91
 legislature, 432, 434, 441
Guayaquil, 328
Guia Didactica de Educación Rural No.
  2, 125
Guido, José María, 401
Guizado, José Ramón, 423, 447
Guzmán Blanco, Antonio, 319

H

Habeas corpus, 386, 451
Hacendados; see Social classes, upper;
  and Agriculture, haciendas

Hacienda, 218–27
Hacienda, ministry of, 419
Haiti
    constitutions, 371, 376
    courts, 454, 455, 456, 457
    executive, 393, 394, 397, 401, 405
    legislature, 430, 432, 434, 441, 446
    political asylum, 390
    population increase, 47
    state of siege, 416
Havana University, 136
Haya de la Torre, Victor, 352, 390, 431
Hernández Martínez, Maximiliano, 405
Hidalgo, Miguel, 150
Hijo de casa, 103
Hispanic American Report, 161, 162, 174,
    178, 268, 270, 288, 291, 346, 347, 349,
    375, 386, 387, 388, 390, 398, 408, 410,
    430, 432, 444, 446, 470
Hispaniola, 59
Hochschild interests, 19
Homestead Act of 1862, 220
Honduras
    constitutions, 375, 376, 379
    courts, 454, 456, 457, 459, 460, 469
    executive, 397, 401, 408, 410
    federalism, 381
    legislature, 410, 432, 433, 434, 435, 441,
        445
    military influence or control, 199
    vice-president, 426
Horizonte, 420
Huachipato, 19
Huancha, 114
Humboldt, Alexander von, 56

                          I

Ibáñez del Campo, Carlos, 198, 403, 420,
    445
Iberian peninsula, 36, 59
Illegitimacy, 87, 88, 107
Illia, Arturo Umberto, 288, 397
Illiteracy, 113, 116, 129, 130
Imbabura, 38
Immigration, 35–37
Impeachment, 422–23
Imposición, 341
Imposto Sindical, 297
Inamovilidad, 290
Incas, 223
Independence movements, 322–24
Indian; see People
Indian-ness, 37
Industry and industrial development
    background, 253
    capital, shortage of, 265–67
    cultural values and mores, effect of,
        271–72

Industry and industrial development
    —Cont.
    electrical energy output, 258–60
    engineers and skilled labor, shortage
        of, 267–68
    fomentos, 273–75
    GNP (gross national product), 258,
        262–64
    government's role, 272
    high cost of production, 268–71
    motivations to, 253–56
    obstacles to, 265–72
    opposition to, 256–57
    progress made, indexes of, 257–62
    protective tariffs, 262–64
    steel output, 261
    support of, 256
    tax incentives, 264
    traditional methods of promoting, 262–
        65
Inflation, 269–70, 287
Institute for the Comparative Study of
    Political Systems, 349, 350, 353, 360,
    432, 436–40
International Bank for Reconstruction
    and Development, 25, 227, 264, 274,
    275, 290
International Development Association
    (Honduras), 25
International Labour Office, 222, 225, 281,
    283
International Labour Review, 269, 284
Intervention, executive, 414–16
Iquique, 15
Iquitos, 23, 27
Irigoyen, Hipólito, 411, 415, 416
Irish immigrants, 36
Iron, 43
Isabella I, Spain, 152
Itabira iron deposit, 16
Italian immigrants, 35
Iturbide, Augustín de, 394

                          J

Jacques I, Haiti, 394
Japan Overseas Immigration Promotion
    Company, 228
Japanese immigrants, 36
Jefe politico, 205
Jesuits, 60
Jiménez, Pérez, 140, 167, 321, 359
John XXIII, Pope, 154, 171, 175, 178
Juárez, Benito, 151, 160
Juárez de Escobar, 153
Judicial review, 466–69
Juez de instrucción, 466
Julião, Francisco, 83
Julius II, Pope, 147

Jungle, 10–11
Jupía hydroelectric project, 258
Jurisprudencia, 469
Justices of the peace, 460
Justicialismo, 354
Justo, Agustín P., 411

K

Kennecott Copper Corporation, 268
Kennedy, John F., 384
Kubitschek, Juscelino, 373

L

Labor
  child labor, 284–85
  collective bargaining, 294–96
  dependence upon government, 296–97
  distribution of labor force, 282, 284
  forced labor, 57–59, 281
  general strike, 299–300
  goals and gains, 285–93
  involvement in politics, 296–301
  labor force, distinctive features of, 281–85
  labor-management relations, 293–94
  profit sharing, 291
  right to organize and strike, 285–86
  security of tenure, 290
  social security, 292
  supervision by government, 297–98
  trade unionism, origin and development, 279–80
  training in leadership, 293
  underemployment and unemployment, 281–83
  unscrupulous leaders, harm from, 292
  weapons used by, 299–301
  women, employment of, 283
La Laguna, 177, 233
Land reform
  colonization, 228–29
  concentration of land ownership, 215–18
  critical need for, 229, 267
  haciendas; *see* Agriculture
  land purchase programs, 228
  latifundios, 217
  minifundios, 217
  peaceful programs of reform
    Venezuela
      basis for expropriation, 247
      formulation, 247
      payment, 247–48
      redistribution, 248
      value as pilot project, 248–49
  piecemeal attempts at reform, 227–29

Land reform—*Cont.*
  revolutionary programs
    of reform—*Cont.*
    Bolivia
      administrative weaknesses, 240–41
      colonization
        Alto Beni, 243
        Chaparé, 243–44
      impact on production, 242
      inflation, 239
      moderation of program, 238–40
      payment, 239
      redistribution, 241
    Cuba
      administrative irregularities, 246
      distribution program, 245
      foreign ownership, 245
      payment, 246
    Guatemala, 244
    Mexico
      delay in execution, 234–35
      distribution of land, 234
      ejidos
        collective, 231–32
        individual, 232–33
      evaluation of, 235–38
      expropriation, 233
      payment, 233
    taxation, 227–28
Language, 63
La Paz, 265, 328
La Prensa, 45
Larrazábal, Carlos, 107
Larrazábal, Wolfgang, 107
Las Casas, 148
Las Siete Partidas, 60
Latin America, countries comprising, 3
Latifundios, 155, 178, 216–17, 220
Lavras, Minas Gerais, 174
Lebanese immigrants, 36
Lechín, Juan, 425
Legislature
  apportionment, 43
  approval of appointments, 409
  bicameral
    chamber of deputies, 438–39
    senate, 436–37
  decree laws, 412
  functional representation, 432–33
  intervention, 415
  lawmaking process, 442–44
  legislative-executive relations, 429–32
  legislative experimentation, 432–34
  method of election, 441
  ministerial responsibility, 433
  organization, 441
  permanent watchdog committee, 433
  powers and functions, 444–47
  privileges and immunities, 447–48
  qualifications of members, 434–40

Legislature—*Cont.*
  semiparliamentary government, 433
  sessions, 444
  size, 435–40
  state of siege, 417
  suplentes, 433
  term, 436–40
  unicameral, 432, 440
Lemus, José María, 136
Ley Mordaza, 387
Lima, 9, 27
Lisboa, Antônio Francisco (Aleijadinho),
  43
Lleras Camargo, Alberto, 327, 400
Location and its impact, 4–6
Lombardia, 231
Lombardo, Toledano, Vicente, 357
Lonardi, Eduardo, 464
López Arellano, Osvaldo, 397
López Hilario, José, 159
López Mateos, Adolfo, 162, 235, 388, 426
Los Angeles Times, 200

M

Macaqueiros, 77–78
Machado, Gerardo, 312
Machismo, 90, 91, 169
Mackenzie College, 173
Madero, Francisco I., 424
Madrina, 103
Magdalena River, 23, 24
Mandado de seguranca, 451
Manners, 63
Manumission, 41
Marbury vs. Madison, 167
Marriage; *see* Family
Martí, José, 169
Martín García, 300
Mata, Filomeno, 387
Matarazzo, Francisco, 69, 70, 87
Mater et Magistra, 178
Mato Grosso, 38
Maximilian I, Mexico, 394
Maya rebellion, 206
Medellín, 14
Meiggs, Henry, 21
Melgarejo, Mariano, 309, 314, 445
Mercury, 16
Mesabi Range, 16
Mestizo, 61–62, 307
Mexico
  cabinet, 419
  capital from exploitation of labor, 288
  church-state relations, 67, 160–62
  civil marriage, 86
  collective bargaining, 295
  Communist Party, 357
  constitutions, 371, 372, 373, 374, 376,
    378, 379

Mexico—*Cont.*
  courts, 451, 452, 453, 454, 455, 456, 459,
    464, 465, 467, 468
  education, literacy campaign, 129
  executive, 397, 398, 399, 400, 401, 407,
    408, 409, 411, 416
  federalism, 382, 383
  Indians' status, 39
  intervention, executive, 416
  labor-management relations, 294
  land problem, 220–21
  land reform, 233–38
  legislature, 409, 410, 411, 433, 434, 437,
    439, 448
  Mexican plateau, 9
  militarism, how curbed, 204–10
  National University of, 134
  profit sharing, 291
  qualifications for a political party, 337
  silver, 16
  speech and press, freedom of, 387
  supervision of labor unions, 298
Mexico City, 14
Militarism; *see* Armed Forces
Minas Gerais, 174, 400, 416
Minerals; *see* Natural resources
Minifundios, 175, 217, 225–26, 237, 246
Mining and minerals, 16–19
Minneapolis Tribune, 200
Miscegenation, 42
Mita, 58
Mitre, Bartolomé, 407
Mohammedanism, 146
Monarchs, 393
Monroe Doctrine, 5, 6
Monterrey, Mexico, 162
Montevideo, 45
Montufar y Coronado, Manuel, 156
Moors, 146
Morazán, Francisco, 339
Morelos y Pavón, José María, 150
Morones, Luis N., 292, 296
Mortmain, 155
Mountains; *see* Andes *and* Geographical
  aspects
Movimiento Nacionalista Revolucionario
  (MNR), 203, 238, 299, 343–45, 350
Mulattos, 61–62, 307
Muñoz Marín, Luis, 163, 164
Muñoz Reyes, Fadrique, 243

N

Nacistas, 424
Nardone, Benito, 396
National Agrarian Institute, 249
National Agrarian Reform Council, 241
National Conciliation Party (PCN), 396
National Institute for Agrarian Reform,
  246
National Liberation Party, 353, 397

National Pantheon of Heroes, 168
National Police Force, 203
National Service of Agrarian Reform, 238
Natural resources
  exportation, 18
  farmland, 20–21
  foreign ownership, 17–18
  minerals and petroleum, 16–19
  value to society, 17, 18, 19
  water power, 19–20
naturales, 62, 88
Negroes; *see* People
Newspaper Enterprise Association, 201
Newspapers, circulation in 1960, 115
Newsweek, 46, 90, 91
New York Advertiser, 315
New York Times, 48, 127, 129, 134, 136, 139, 154, 164, 165, 167, 168, 174, 175, 183, 236, 246, 248, 270, 287, 316, 361, 362, 363, 374, 384, 391, 396, 398, 413, 424, 427, 430, 443
Nicaragua
  constitutions, 376
  courts, 454, 456, 457, 468
  designado, 426
  executive, 397, 399, 401, 407, 411
  ex-presidents, utilization of, 426
  legislature, 434, 437, 439
  minifundios and *latifundios*, 217
  population active in agriculture, 216
Nitrates, 18
Nouveaux riches, 70
Nueva Italia, 231

O

OAS Special Committee, 133, 135
Oaxaca, Mexico, 163
Obregón, Alvaro, 207, 424
Occupation; *see also* Social classes
  distribution of labor force by major sectors, 282
Ocean liners, 24
Odría, Manuel, 68, 431
O'Higgins, Bernardo, 151, 171, 307, 320
Okinawans, colonization in Bolivia, 228
Ordaz, Díaz, 388, 397
Organization of American States (OAS), 135, 362
Oriente, 328
Orinoco River, 23, 24
Orlich, Francisco J., 397
Ortiz, Roberto M., 411
Otavlos, 38
Ovando, Nicolás de, 59

P

Pacem in Terris, 178
Padrinazgo, 103–4
Padrino, 103, 104

Pampas, 11–12
Panama
  consensual marriage, 89
  constitutions, 375, 376
  courts, 456, 457, 458, 463
  education, stress on, 111
  executive, 397, 401, 423
  impeachment, 423
  legislature, 429, 430, 432, 434, 441
  multiparty system, 349
  steel mill, semi-integrated, 261
Panama Canal, 27
Panama, University of, 134
Pan-American Highway, 25
Pan American Union; *see* Américas
Papal Volunteers for Latin America, 171
Paraguay
  colonization, 228
  constitutions, 375, 376
  courts, 452, 454, 456, 457
  executive, 394, 397, 399, 401, 403
  Guaraní, 63
  legislature, 432, 434, 435, 441
  political asylum, 390
Páramos, 12
Paraná River, 21, 23
Parliamentary government, 394–95, 433
Partido Liberal Nacionalista, 397
Partido Nacional Liberal, 397
Partido Revolucionario Institucional (PRI), 341–42, 419
Parties, political; *see specific party*
Patiño, Simón, 19
Patrão, 77
Patrón, 77, 218
Patronato, 147
Paulo Alfonso Falls, 20
Paz Estenssoro, Victor, 238, 362, 405, 425
Pedro I and II, Brazil, 393, 394, 413
Peña, Lázaro, 293
Peñaranda, Enrique, 400
Peninsulares, 55, 189
People
  Indians
    adaptation to high altitudes, 38–39
    Araucanians, 35
    assimilation, 35
    cacique aristocracy, 57
    Camayuras, 38
    controversy over their nature and effect, 40
    conversion to Catholicism, superficial, 75
    decreasing percentage of population, 49
    education, language problem, 114
      resistance to, 116
    encomienda, 58
    forced labor and mistreatment, 38, 57–59

People–*Cont.*
  Indians (*cont.*)
    mita, 58
    number, 37–38
    origin, 37
    Otavalos, 38
    reaction to Spanish culture and dom-
      ination, 38, 39
    repartimiento, 57
    sexual promiscuity, 61, 62
  Negroes
    acceptance and assimilation, 41, 42,
      43
    artistic and intellectual contributions,
      43
    manumission, 41, 60, 61
    miscegenation, 41–42, 62
    number, 40–41
    personality and temperament, 42
    physical courage and military prow-
      ess, 42–43
    rights under law, 60
    slave trade, 59, 60
    where found, 40
  racial composition, change in, 48
  spatial distribution of population, 33
  urban population
    growth faster than total, 80
    percentage of total, 79
    reason for increase, natural or migra-
      tion, 81
  Whites
    immigrants and their influence, 35–37
    where found, 33–35
Peralta Uzurdia, Enrique, 397
Pérez Jiménez, Marcos, 401
Perón, Juan, 82, 136, 140, 166, 167, 171,
  188, 196, 197, 217, 298, 299, 300, 312,
  321, 328, 354, 371, 417
Personalism, 335–36
Peru
  constitutions, 375, 376
  courts, 452, 454, 455, 456, 463, 470
  executive, 397, 399, 401, 405, 407, 419
  latifundios, 217
  Law of Yanaconaji, 227
  legislature, 431, 433, 434, 435, 437, 439,
    447
  minifundios, 217
  political asylum, 390
  population, percentage active in agri-
    culture, 216
Pesquera, José Felice, 165
Pierini, Archbishop, 174
Plateaus; *see* Geographical aspects
Plaza Lasso, Galo, 67, 125, 270
Polish immigrants, 36
Political Handbook of the World, 299,
  345

*Political Handbook and Atlas of the
  World*, 345, 436–40
Political parties
  characteristics of, 335–38
  identification of government with, 337
  instability, 336
  intolerance of opposition, 338
  leading parties and strength in recent
    elections, 346
  major parties, 350–59
  multiparty system, 349–50
  one-party system, 340–45
  personalism, 336
  second and third parties and strength
    in recent elections, 347
  traditional parties and issues, 345–48
Popular Democratic Party, 164, 165
Population
  age groups, Latin America, 284
  age groups, Latin America, United
    States, and Britain, 285
  density, 33
  distribution, 33
  growth rate, 46
  percentage Catholic, 170
  percentage Protestant, 173
  spatial distribution, 33
Portes Gil, Emilio, 382
Portuguese immigrants, 35
Potosí, 16
Poverty, 230
Practicing Catholics, 163
Prebisch, Raúl, 258, 270, 276, 322
Presbyterian Experiment Station and
  Agricultural Training School, 173–74
Presidents; *see* Executive
Press Control Law, Chile, 387
Private rights
  respect for, in general, 384–85
  specific rights
    physical liberty, 389
    political asylum, 389–90
    religion, 388
    speech and press, 385, 388
Privilegio de cuna, 72
Pronunciamentos, 199
Protection of Industries Law, 264
Protestantism, 171–77
Protestants
  challenge posed by, 175–76
  contributions of, 172–74
  percentage of population, 173
  persecution of, 174–75
  strength and influence, 173
Puerto Montt, 25
Puerto Rican election of 1960, 163–65
Pureza de sangre, 64

Q

Quadros, Jânio, 183, 395
Quebracho, 23
Quechua, 114
Querida, 90, 91, 93, 107
Quito, 12, 127, 172, 174, 328

R

Races; *see also* People *and* Social classes
  by countries, 34
Racial prejudice, 41–44
Radical Party, 415
Radish eaters, 74
Railroads, 21–22, 27
Rain forests; *see* Geographical aspects
Rebouças, André, 43
Recife, University of, 139
Reform Movement, Mexico, 160
Reichel, Gerardo, 64
Reid Cabral, Donald, 397
Religion; *see* Church
Religious instruction; *see* Education
Ramón, José Antonio, 423
Repartimiento, 57–58
Revolutions; *see* Caudillos
Rio Grande do Sul, 400
Rio de Janeiro, 10
Riondo, 245
Rio Turbio coal deposit, 19
Rivadavia, Bernardino, 152, 158, 171
Rivera, Cardinal Garibi, 174
River steamers, 23–24
Roads, 24–26
Robles, Marco Aurelio, 397
Roca, General Julio A., 35
Rodrígues Alves, Francisco de Paula, 403
Rojas Pinilla, Gustavo, 174, 175, 197, 423, 424
Rojas, Ricardo, 37
Rolon, Raimundo, 325
Roman Catholic Church; *see* Church
Roman law, 450, 451
Roosevelt, Franklin Delano, 167
Roosevelt, Theodore, 384
Rosas, Juan Manuel de, 220, 311, 320, 321, 338
Rosco, 19
Rurales, 221
Rural Life Conferences, 177

S

Sacred College of Cardinals, 175
Sáenz Peña, 364, 415
Salas, judicial, 457
Salcedo, José Joaquin, 130
Sam, Vilbrum Guillaume, 390, 425
San Carlos, University of, 134

Sánchez Cerro, Luis M., 424
Sanfuentes, Juan Luis, 68
San Juan de Ulloa, 286
San Marcos, University of, 135, 140, 141
San Martín, José de, 110
San Simón, Greater University of, 135
Santa Anna, Antonio López de, 308
Santa Cruz, 328
Santa Fe, 23
Santiago, Chile, 9
Santiago, Cuba, 107
Santos, 22
Santos, Eduardo, 198
São Francisco River, 20, 24
São Paulo, 20, 100, 173, 253, 260, 262, 267, 269, 363, 400
Sarmiento, Domingo Faustino, 117, 171, 407
Schick Gutierrez, René, 182, 397
Scotch immigrants, 36
Serra do Mar mountain, 20
Serrano, Francisco, 207
Servicio Nacional de Reforma Agraria, 240, 241
Servicio Social de Industria (SESI), 294
Seventh-day Adventists, 171, 172, 178
Sierra Maestra Mountains, 107
Siles Zuazo, Hernán, 238, 424
Silver, 16, 57
Sindicato de Campesinos de Durango, 177
Sindicato, Bolivia, 244
Siqueiros, David Alfaro, 387
Slavery, 60–61
Slave trade, 59–60
Social classes
  colonial society, 55–57
  conspicuous consumption, 56, 57
  criollos, 56
  determinants of social status, 63–65
  dress, 63
  effects of class structure, 82–83
  home, 63
  lower class
    power and influence, 79, 80
    rural, 77–78
    urban, 78–79
  manners, 63
  mestizos, 60, 78–79
  middle class
    ambition, 71
    characteristics, 71, 72
    composition, 72, 73, 74
    factors responsible for its rise, 73
    frustrations, 74, 75
    power and influence, 76
    program, 75–76
    size, 70–71
  miscegenation, 61, 62
  mulattos, 60

Social classes—*Cont.*
  occupation, 63–64
  peninsulares, 55, 56
  race, 64–65
  religion, 63
  upper class
    landed aristocracy, 65–69
    new moneyed elite, 69–70
  wealth, 64
  zambos, 60
Social Dissolution, Law of, Mexico, 387
Sociedad de Beneficencia, 158
Sociedad de Fomento, Chile, 293
Sociedad Nacional de Agricultura, 68
Sociedad Nacional de Industrias, 293
Somoza, Anastasio, 182, 424
Somoza, Anastasio, Jr., 182, 407
Somoza, Luis, 182, 407
Soroche, 15
Sourdis, Evaristo, 174
Spanish immigrants, 35
Stare decisis, 453
Statesman's Yearbook, 376
State of siege, 416–18
Steel production, 261
Stroessner, Alfredo, 397
Student Federation, University of
  Buenos Aires, 139
Succession, presidential, 425–26
Suplentes
  judicial, 458
  legislative, 433
Swiss immigration, 36
Syrians immigration, 36

T

Tabasco, state of, 161
Tabernilla, Carlos, 107
Tabernilla, Francisco, 107
Tabernilla, Francisco J., 107
Tabernilla, Marcelo, 107
Talavera, Ramón, 168
Taxation
  evasion of, 270
  regressive, 270
Tenentes, 196
Terra, Gabriel, 395
Terrazas, 225
Tierra caliente, 12, 14
Tierra del Fuego, 8
Tierra fría, 12
Tierra templada, 12
Tieté River, 20
Time, 143, 176, 177, 355, 400, 424
Tin, 19
Topography; *see* Geographical aspects
Tortorelli, Domingo, 360

Transportation and communication
  airplanes
    advantages, 26–27
    high freight rates, 27
    main airway systems, 26
  ocean liners, 24
  railroads
    different gauges, 22
    engineering problems in construc-
      tion, 21
    government control and ownership,
      22
    haphazard planning, 22
    high freight rates, 22
    mileage, 20–21
    renovation, 22
  river steamers, 23–24
  roads
    benefits of new ones, 71
    engineering problems and costs, 25
    Inca roads, 25
    mileage, 25
    Pan-American Highway, 25–26
Trujillo Molina, Rafael Leonidas, 167,
  185, 309, 310, 321, 372, 424
Tupinambás, 61

U

Ukrainian immigrants, 36
UN *Demographic Yearbook*, 285
UN Economic Commission for Latin
  America, 80, 228, 259, 260, 283
UN *Statistical Yearbook*, 261
UNESCO, 81, 111, 112, 113, 122, 124, 127,
  128, 228
Unicameral legislatures, 432
Uniform Negotiable Instruments Law,
  452
Unión Industrial Argentina, 293
Unitarios, 380
United Fruit Company, 245
United Industries, 70
Universal Declaration of Human Rights,
  468
Universities; *see* Education, higher
Uruguay
  anticlericalism, 169
  constitutions, 371, 375, 376
  Corte Electoral, 364
  courts, 353, 354, 356, 357, 460, 469, 470
  executive, 395, 397, 401
  legislature, 431, 433, 434, 437, 439, 441
  speech and press, freedom of, 386
  top-heavy government bureaucracy,
    271
  two-party system, 345, 348
Varella, José Pedro, 117–18
women, status of, 94

US News and World Report, 258, 270, 276

V

Valencia, Guillermo León, 397, 446
Valladores, Benedeto de, 416
Vanadium, 16
Varela, José Pedro, 117–18
Vargas, Getulio, 196, 298, 375, 403, 405, 416
Vasconcelos, José, 236
Vásquez, Horacio, 185, 312
Vatican, The, 154, 164, 166, 167
Vekemans, Roger E., 176, 177
Velasco Ibarra, José María, 324, 327, 336, 403
Velásquez, Severo, 167
Venezuela
  armed forces, family control of, 107
  constitutions, 371, 375, 376, 378, 379
  courts, 451, 452, 454, 456, 457, 469
  executive, 397, 401, 407, 408
  ex-presidents, utilization of, 426
  iron, 16
  land reform program, 247–49
    land distribution, 248
  legislature, 430, 434, 437, 439, 447
  petroleum, 16, 17
  registration of voters, 360
Vertical zones, 12
Veto, 410, 411
Viaticos, 241
Vice-president, 425–26

Vicos, 117–19, 123
Vieira, Pedro, 89
Villa, Pancho, 307, 316
Villarroel, Gualberto, 198, 424
Volta Redonda Iron and Steel Plant, 19, 261
Voz Andes, 174

W

War of the Reform, 160
War of the Triple Alliance, 43, 99
Wars of Independence, 149–50
Wetbacks, 236
Whites; *see* People
World Radio Missionary Fellowship, 174
World Today, The, 240, 243
World War I, 69, 195, 254, 255, 279, 296
World War II, 36, 37, 44, 188, 255, 280

Y

Yanacona, 227
Ydígoras Fuentes, Miguel, 90, 91, 171
Yucatán, 231
Yugoslav immigrants, 36

Z

Zambos, 61
Zapata, 250
Zapotec, 160
Zinc, 16

This book has been set in 10 point Janson, leaded 2 points, and 9 point Janson, leaded 1 point. Chapter numbers are in 10 and 30 point Bodoni Book; chapter titles are in 18 point Bodoni No. 375. The size of the type page is 27 by 47 picas.